# Lecture Notes in Computer Science     9739

Commenced Publication in 1973
Founding and Former Series Editors:
Gerhard Goos, Juris Hartmanis, and Jan van Leeuwen

More information about this series at http://www.springer.com/series/7409

Margherita Antona · Constantine Stephanidis (Eds.)

# Universal Access in Human-Computer Interaction

## Users and Context Diversity

10th International Conference, UAHCI 2016
Held as Part of HCI International 2016
Toronto, ON, Canada, July 17–22, 2016
Proceedings, Part III

 Springer

*Editors*

Margherita Antona
Foundation for Research & Technology –
  Hellas (FORTH)
Heraklion, Crete
Greece

Constantine Stephanidis
University of Crete / Foundation for
  Research & Technology – Hellas
  (FORTH)
Heraklion, Crete
Greece

ISSN 0302-9743            ISSN 1611-3349   (electronic)
Lecture Notes in Computer Science
ISBN 978-3-319-40237-6        ISBN 978-3-319-40238-3   (eBook)
DOI 10.1007/978-3-319-40238-3

Library of Congress Control Number: 2016940356

LNCS Sublibrary: SL3 – Information Systems and Applications, incl. Internet/Web, and HCI

Printed on acid-free paper

This Springer imprint is published by Springer Nature
The registered company is Springer International Publishing AG Switzerland

# Foreword

The 18th International Conference on Human-Computer Interaction, HCI International 2016, was held in Toronto, Canada, during July 17–22, 2016. The event incorporated the 15 conferences/thematic areas listed on the following page.

A total of 4,354 individuals from academia, research institutes, industry, and governmental agencies from 74 countries submitted contributions, and 1,287 papers and 186 posters have been included in the proceedings. These papers address the latest research and development efforts and highlight the human aspects of the design and use of computing systems. The papers thoroughly cover the entire field of human-computer interaction, addressing major advances in knowledge and effective use of computers in a variety of application areas. The volumes constituting the full 27-volume set of the conference proceedings are listed on pages IX and X.

I would like to thank the program board chairs and the members of the program boards of all thematic areas and affiliated conferences for their contribution to the highest scientific quality and the overall success of the HCI International 2016 conference.

This conference would not have been possible without the continuous and unwavering support and advice of the founder, Conference General Chair Emeritus and Conference Scientific Advisor Prof. Gavriel Salvendy. For his outstanding efforts, I would like to express my appreciation to the communications chair and editor of *HCI International News*, Dr. Abbas Moallem.

April 2016                                                                 Constantine Stephanidis

# HCI International 2016 Thematic Areas and Affiliated Conferences

Thematic areas:

- Human-Computer Interaction (HCI 2016)
- Human Interface and the Management of Information (HIMI 2016)

Affiliated conferences:

- 13th International Conference on Engineering Psychology and Cognitive Ergonomics (EPCE 2016)
- 10th International Conference on Universal Access in Human-Computer Interaction (UAHCI 2016)
- 8th International Conference on Virtual, Augmented and Mixed Reality (VAMR 2016)
- 8th International Conference on Cross-Cultural Design (CCD 2016)
- 8th International Conference on Social Computing and Social Media (SCSM 2016)
- 10th International Conference on Augmented Cognition (AC 2016)
- 7th International Conference on Digital Human Modeling and Applications in Health, Safety, Ergonomics and Risk Management (DHM 2016)
- 5th International Conference on Design, User Experience and Usability (DUXU 2016)
- 4th International Conference on Distributed, Ambient and Pervasive Interactions (DAPI 2016)
- 4th International Conference on Human Aspects of Information Security, Privacy and Trust (HAS 2016)
- Third International Conference on HCI in Business, Government, and Organizations (HCIBGO 2016)
- Third International Conference on Learning and Collaboration Technologies (LCT 2016)
- Second International Conference on Human Aspects of IT for the Aged Population (ITAP 2016)

# Conference Proceedings Volumes Full List

1. LNCS 9731, Human-Computer Interaction: Theory, Design, Development and Practice (Part I), edited by Masaaki Kurosu
2. LNCS 9732, Human-Computer Interaction: Interaction Platforms and Techniques (Part II), edited by Masaaki Kurosu
3. LNCS 9733, Human-Computer Interaction: Novel User Experiences (Part III), edited by Masaaki Kurosu
4. LNCS 9734, Human Interface and the Management of Information: Information, Design and Interaction (Part I), edited by Sakae Yamamoto
5. LNCS 9735, Human Interface and the Management of Information: Applications and Services (Part II), edited by Sakae Yamamoto
6. LNAI 9736, Engineering Psychology and Cognitive Ergonomics, edited by Don Harris
7. LNCS 9737, Universal Access in Human-Computer Interaction: Methods, Techniques, and Best Practices (Part I), edited by Margherita Antona and Constantine Stephanidis
8. LNCS 9738, Universal Access in Human-Computer Interaction: Interaction Techniques and Environments (Part II), edited by Margherita Antona and Constantine Stephanidis
9. LNCS 9739, Universal Access in Human-Computer Interaction: Users and Context Diversity (Part III), edited by Margherita Antona and Constantine Stephanidis
10. LNCS 9740, Virtual, Augmented and Mixed Reality, edited by Stephanie Lackey and Randall Shumaker
11. LNCS 9741, Cross-Cultural Design, edited by Pei-Luen Patrick Rau
12. LNCS 9742, Social Computing and Social Media, edited by Gabriele Meiselwitz
13. LNAI 9743, Foundations of Augmented Cognition: Neuroergonomics and Operational Neuroscience (Part I), edited by Dylan D. Schmorrow and Cali M. Fidopiastis
14. LNAI 9744, Foundations of Augmented Cognition: Neuroergonomics and Operational Neuroscience (Part II), edited by Dylan D. Schmorrow and Cali M. Fidopiastis
15. LNCS 9745, Digital Human Modeling and Applications in Health, Safety, Ergonomics and Risk Management, edited by Vincent G. Duffy
16. LNCS 9746, Design, User Experience, and Usability: Design Thinking and Methods (Part I), edited by Aaron Marcus
17. LNCS 9747, Design, User Experience, and Usability: Novel User Experiences (Part II), edited by Aaron Marcus
18. LNCS 9748, Design, User Experience, and Usability: Technological Contexts (Part III), edited by Aaron Marcus
19. LNCS 9749, Distributed, Ambient and Pervasive Interactions, edited by Norbert Streitz and Panos Markopoulos
20. LNCS 9750, Human Aspects of Information Security, Privacy and Trust, edited by Theo Tryfonas

## Universal Access in Human–Computer Interaction

**Program Board Chairs: Margherita Antona, Greece, and Constantine Stephanidis, Greece**

- Gisela Susanne Bahr, USA
- João Barroso, Portugal
- Jennifer Romano Bergstrom, USA
- Rodrigo Bonacin, Brazil
- Ingo K. Bosse, Germany
- Anthony Lewis Brooks, Denmark
- Christian Bühler, Germany
- Stefan Carmien, Spain
- Carlos Duarte, Portugal
- Pier Luigi Emiliani, Italy
- Qin Gao, P.R. China
- Andrina Granić, Croatia
- Josette F. Jones, USA
- Simeon Keates, UK
- Georgios Kouroupetroglou, Greece
- Patrick Langdon, UK
- Barbara Leporini, Italy
- Tania Lima, Brazil
- Alessandro Marcengo, Italy
- Troy McDaniel, USA
- Ana Isabel Paraguay, Brazil
- Michael Pieper, Germany
- Enrico Pontelli, USA
- Jon A. Sanford, USA
- Vagner Santana, Brazil
- Jaime Sánchez, Chile
- Anthony Savidis, Greece
- Kevin Tseng, Taiwan
- Gerhard Weber, Germany
- Fong-Gong Wu, Taiwan

The full list with the program board chairs and the members of the program boards of all thematic areas and affiliated conferences is available online at:

**http://www.hci.international/2016/**

# HCI International 2017

The 19th International Conference on Human-Computer Interaction, HCI International 2017, will be held jointly with the affiliated conferences in Vancouver, Canada, at the Vancouver Convention Centre, July 9–14, 2017. It will cover a broad spectrum of themes related to human-computer interaction, including theoretical issues, methods, tools, processes, and case studies in HCI design, as well as novel interaction techniques, interfaces, and applications. The proceedings will be published by Springer. More information will be available on the conference website: http://2017. hci.international/.

General Chair
Prof. Constantine Stephanidis
University of Crete and ICS-FORTH
Heraklion, Crete, Greece
E-mail: general_chair@hcii2017.org

**http://2017.hci.international/**

# Contents – Part III

**Technologies for ASD and Cognitive Disabilities**

## Universal Access to Media and Games

## Universal Access to Mobility and Automotive

# Universal Access to Education and Learning

# Encouraging the Learning of Written Language by Deaf Users: Web Recommendations and Practices

Marta Angélica Montiel Ferreira[1]([⊠]), Juliana Bueno[2], and Rodrigo Bonacin[1,3]

[1] FACCAMP, Rua Guatemala, 167,
Campo Limpo Paulista, SP 13231-230, Brazil
zmontefer@gmail.com, rodrigo.bonacin@cti.gov.br
[2] Department of Design, Federal University of Paraná,
Rua General Carneiro, 460, Curitiba, PR 80060-150, Brazil
juliana@inf.ufpr.br
[3] Center for Information Technology Renato Archer,
Rodovia Dom Pedro I, km 143, 6, Campinas, SP 13069-901, Brazil

**Abstract.** There are still various access barriers for deaf users on the Web. Previous studies and accessibility guidelines recommend that text should be written in a simple and clear mode. However, this recommendation is not always possible or applicable, and it does not include deaf users as content producers as well. Instead of trying to simplify or translate all the web content to sign language or simple text language, in this paper we explore how images, avatars and simple text explanations could be used to encourage the learning of written language. This article presents a set of recommendations, prototypes and practices with 15 deaf students and 2 teachers aiming to evaluate design alternatives related to deaf literacy using web resources. The objective is to include the deaf users as text producers and facilitate the communication between hearing and deaf users on synchronous and asynchronous artifacts. Results point out the potentiality, advantages and limitations of the proposed design alternatives and prototypes.

**Keywords:** Web accessibility · Deaf accessibility · Deaf literacy · Universal access

## 1 Introduction

Deaf users face many barriers related to written language on the Web. For example, the majority of deaf people have difficulties to reading long and complex text [6]. Many studies of deaf education consider sign language as the first and highest proficiency language, and a written language as a second language. Thus, many deaf people read word by word, trying to understand their meanings by associating each word with known signs. With respect to design, there are also several difficulties for designers in making the content accessible in all situations, such as to produce clear and simple texts, as suggested by W3C [11].

© Springer International Publishing Switzerland 2016
M. Antona and C. Stephanidis (Eds.): UAHCI 2016, Part III, LNCS 9739, pp. 3–15, 2016.
DOI: 10.1007/978-3-319-40238-3_1

Our previous studies investigated the Web accessibility requirements for people with hearing loss [3], as well as the use of computational resources on bilingual deaf literacy [2]. In this paper, we focus on design alternatives to encourage deaf users to learn written language while they use the Web. The article presents thirty-six recommendations to deal with the difficulties and requirements previously elicited. The recommendations were structured according to common usage situations in which the deaf users reported difficulties. These situations include specific barriers to the use of synchronous communication tools (e.g., to send a message in an instant message tool) and use of asynchronous communication (e.g., to post a message in a blog).

We performed a qualitative study with 15 deaf students and 2 teachers with the objective of analyzing these recommendations. The participants had various educational levels (from primary school to university graduate) and their ages ranged from 12 to 30 years old. All the students had high levels of hearing loss, were fluent in Libras (Brazilian Sign Language), and consider Portuguese (Brazilian official written language) as a second language. An interpreter and a teacher with many years of experience in teaching sign and written languages also participated in the study.

This paper presents and discusses recommendations, prototypes and results of the evaluation practices with the users. An analysis of the results points out limitations of the approach, as well as challenges from theoretical and technological perspectives. We intend to contribute with a better understanding of Web accessibility for deaf users and with design alternatives to stimulate written language learning.

The work is structured as follows: Sect. 2 presents the theoretical background and related work; Sect. 3 describes the recommendations, prototypes and practices with deaf users; Sect. 4 presents the interpretation of the results, discussions and limitations; and, Sect. 5 concludes the paper.

## 2   Theoretical Background and Related Work

This section begins by presenting concepts related to deaf culture and the importance of sign language as an support for written language learning (Sect. 2.1). It subsequently addresses Web accessibility and Web tools for deaf users (Sect. 2.2).

### 2.1   Deaf Culture and Bilingual Literacy

The literature reports many challenges related to the deaf social integration of the deaf, along with the full acceptance of their rights and duties to participate effectively in society, as well as fully exercise their citizenship. Even when immersed in a largely oral culture, deaf people have their own community, culture and language. Several studies (e.g., Chomsky [1]) point out that sign language has a crucial role in the intellectual development of the deaf.

Our study is aligned with the idea that a written language can be learned independently of the oral language that it represents [10]. Thus, when we introduce deaf learners to a written language, first it is necessary to situate the learners in a context making use of their first language, i.e., sign language [9]. In line with other studies (e.g., Sánchez [8]), we assume the necessity of bilingual contextualization and the promotion of written language literacy instrumented by sign language.

One of the challenges in deaf students' education is how to create opportunities that go beyond meaningful literacy experiences in the written language, by constituting a bilingual situation, in which the sign language is dominant in the situations of enunciation [4]. The written language, as a second language, supports the expansion of their social relations and appropriation of cultural elements of hearing people.

Nowadays, learning to read is vital for all individuals in society, and even more vital for the deaf [5]. However, there is still a lack of methods and pedagogical practices to teach written language in bilingual classes [13]. This limitation of bilingual educational practices is not restricted to the context of Brazil (or developing countries). The study of Marschark and Harris [7], for instance, highlights that deaf students of secondary schools in the United States were able to read, on average at the same level as 8 to 9 years old students. Despite advances in the field, other studies (e.g., Wauters et al. [12]) also point out challenges in deaf literacy education. In this context, the use of computational resources is a promising alternative for supporting and improving deaf literacy practices [3].

## 2.2   Technology and Web Accessibility for the Deaf

The use of techniques that explore virtual and Web environments may stimulate deaf students in bilingual literacy process. According to studies of Lorenzet [6], the use of interactive resources with Libras in virtual environments brings benefits for Portuguese language learning. These resources make the learning process pleasant and easier for the deaf learners. Her study also points out that the difficulties related to vocabulary and meanings can be minimized by including a sign language dictionary application. The association of written terms with sign language explanations made for the learning process more dynamic.

Various barriers that deaf users face when accessing the Web are related to the "Internet language". They include, for example, the use of foreign language terms, technical concepts, complex text and Internet slang [2]. A deaf user with low literacy typically reads one word at a time; she/he tries to understand the meaning by associating each word with a known sign. This results interferes with the comprehension of long and complex texts. The W3C standards for accessibility [11] emphasize this aspect by suggesting that text should be written in a simple and clear way. However, it is problematic to put this recommendation into practice.

Nowadays, there is a vast literature about web accessibility for the deaf. The literature includes the research of new technologies (e.g., tools for automatic translation from written language to sign language, and tools for text simplification), as well as design aspects of how to make use of the new technologies. The focus of our work is on how to use the Web as an instrument for written language learning. We aim to produce an inclusive process, which supports deaf users' interpretation of complex content and promotes their long term autonomy as web content consumers and producers.

## 3   Recommendations, Prototypes and Practices

This section starts with presenting 36 recommendations for inclusive design (Subsect.3.1). After that, Subsect.3.2 presents examples of interface prototypes constructed according to these recommendations, and Subsect.3.3 describes practices with deaf users that evaluated the proposed prototypes.

### 3.1   Web Design Recommendations for Encouraging the Learning of Written Language

The recommendations presented in this section were previously elicited with 29 deaf students [1]. The studies took place in the Deaf Service Center in the city of Macapá in Brazil - CAS (*Centro de Atendimento ao Surdo*), and the Deaf Mission (in Libras) of the Baptist Church of Macapá. The studies included interviews, semantic and norm analysis followed by participatory solutions proposals as presented in [1]. The studies resulted in 121 high level design recommendations, of which 36 concerns chat and blog writing activities, the focus in this paper. These recommendations were later discussed with a new group of deaf users in the context of this work.

According to the participants, the main difficulty concerning reading is the use/comprehension of long text with unusual terms. The users suggested including visual dictionary applications with avatars. By using these applications, deaf users can associate and learn new meanings by accessing explanations in sign language. In addition, examples of phrases in written language can also be proposed to contextualize the use of the difficult words.

Thus, we recommended the design of dictionary applications with explanations in sign language, visual resources, and examples in written language to explain and contextualize the use of the terms. The written problems should also be supported by explanations in sign language.

Table 1 describes recommendations and solutions for synchronous (e.g., online messages) and asynchronous (e.g., blogs) communication systems. A total of 36 recommendations were elicited with the users. The recommendations include the main grammatical rules and alternatives for supporting the learning of how to avoid written errors.

**Table 1.** Chat and blog design recommendations

| N° | Recommendations: Design alternatives to support deaf users to learn how not to violate written rules in chats and blogs |
|---|---|
| 01 | Include a warning when a grammar rule is violated (such as a spell and grammar checker) and to show the correct form, with examples contextualized using sign and written languages. |
| 02 | Include a warning every time that an article is not used before a proper name, with examples of how to use articles with images, text and sign language explanations. |

*(Continued)*

**Table 1.** (*Continued*)

| N° | Recommendations: Design alternatives to support deaf users to learn how not to violate written rules in chats and blogs |
|----|----|
| 03 | Include a warning every time that an article is not used before a substantive name, with examples of how to use articles with images, text and sign language explanations. |
| 04 | Include a warning every time that a possessive pronoun is not used before the subject, with examples of how to use possessive pronouns with images, text and sign language explanations. |
| 05 | Include a warning every time that a connective is not properly used, with examples of how to use connectives with images, text and sign language explanations. |
| 06 | Include a warning every time that a verb conjugation is not properly used, with examples of how to use verb conjugations with images, text and sign language explanations. |
| 07 | Include a warning every time that an adverb is not properly used, with examples of how to use adverbs with images, text and sign language explanations. |
| 08 | Include translation of foreign language words. To include examples using images, text and sign language explanations. |
| 09 | Include possible synonymous for the words and the use of polysemic words with examples of use through images, text and sign language explanations. |
| 10 | Include a warning with the correct personal pronoun of first person in the sentence, using images, text and sign language explanations. |
| 11 | Include a warning with the correct personal pronoun of second person in the sentence, using images, text and sign language explanations. |
| 12 | Include a warning with the correct personal pronoun of third person in the sentence, using images, text and sign language explanations. |
| 13 | Include a warning illustrating situations when the personal pronoun must be in plural, using images, text and sign language explanations. |
| 14 | Include a warning illustrating the combination of pronouns, using images, text and sign language explanations. |
| 15 | Include a warning illustrating situations when the personal pronoun is the subject, using images, text and sign language explanations. |
| 16 | Include a warning illustrating situations when the personal pronoun is the as verbal complement of the sentence, using images, text, and sign language explanations. |
| 17 | Include a warning illustrating situations when that personal pronoun is the as nominal complement of the sentence, using images, text and sign language explanations. |
| 18 | Include messages showing new vocabularies introduced by the technology, using images, text and sign language explanations. |
| 19 | Include a warning every time that there is a syntactic consistency error, using images, text and sign language explanations. |
| 20 | Include a warning every time that there is a semantic consistency error, using images, text and sign language explanations. |
| 21 | Include a warning every time that there is a logical consistency error, using images, text and sign language explanations. |
| 22 | Include messages showing which elements are part of a narrative text, using images, text and sign language explanations. |

(*Continued*)

**Table 1.** (*Continued*)

| N° | Recommendations: Design alternatives to support deaf users to learn how not to violate written rules in chats and blogs |
|----|---------------------------------------------------------------------------------------------------------------------------|
| 23 | Include messages showing which elements are part of a dissertative text, using images, text and sign language explanations. |
| 24 | Include messages showing which elements are part of an argumentative text, using images, text and sign language explanations. |
| 25 | Include messages showing intended meanings, using images, text and sign language explanations. |
| 26 | Include examples of texts showing how to use textual arguments. |
| 27 | Include examples of texts showing how to use subject elements. |
| 28 | Include examples of texts showing how to use verbal elements. |
| 29 | Include examples of texts showing how to use action elements. |
| 30 | Include a warning every time that the verb is misplaced in the phrase, using images, text and sign language explanations. |
| 31 | Include examples of how to use abbreviations. |
| 32 | Include a message explaining the structures consisting of subject, verbs and predicates |
| 33 | Include examples differentiating formal and informal texts. |
| 34 | Include examples showing how to use the rules of punctuation. |
| 35 | Include examples showing how to use accentuation. |
| 36 | Include examples showing how to use commas. |

### 3.2   Prototypes Designed According to the Recommendations

Figure 1 presents a low fidelity prototype that illustrates a solution to be used in synchronous communication artifacts. This solution proposes the inclusion of explanations about written errors. As in a grammar check tool, the explanations are linked to errors underlined in red. An important component is that the explanations use clear texts with terms that are well known by deaf users. In this prototype avatars and images are a second option, to be used when the user has difficulties understanding the explanation in written language. This prototype is in line with the recommendations in Table 1 (#1, #8, #10 and #17).

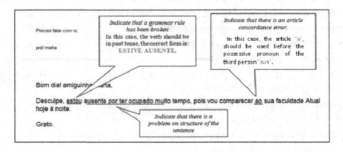

**Fig. 1.** Example of low fidelity prototype with links to explain grammar errors

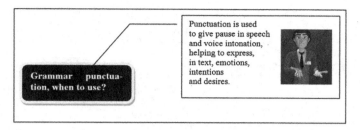

**Fig. 2.** Example of an avatar used to explain the use of grammar punctuation

Figure 2 presents a prototype with an avatar that gives explanations in sign language next to a textual description (recommendation 34 and 36). In this example, there is an explanation of how to use grammar punctuation rules.

Figure 3 presents a prototype with solutions to support deaf users to produce text in a blog. In this prototype, hints were included for supporting the designers in the modelling of functionalities to help deaf users compose blog posts. For example, the designer can include a dictionary option in the task bar (recommendation 18 and 33).

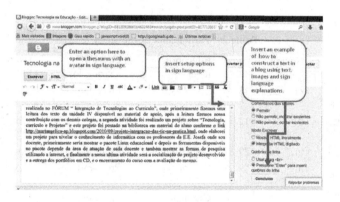

**Fig. 3.** Example of explanatory links to improve writing

Figure 4 presents an example of the prototype to deal with polysemic words, popular expressions and uncommon expressions. This prototype implements the recommendation to highlight and provide explanations about polysemic words (recommendation 9), popular expressions and uncommon expressions. In the example of Fig. 1, a blog' post makes use of the word "foot" (*pé* – in Portuguese) in different ways, for example: *pé da serra* (foot of the mountain- place), *pé de pato* (swimming fins – equipment) and *pé de moleque* (a kind of candy similar to peanut brittle). The words are highlighted by the prototype, and examples and explanations are provided using an avatar. The prototype provides explanations when the users read or produce texts, thereby, stimulating them to learn new ways of using the words and expressions.

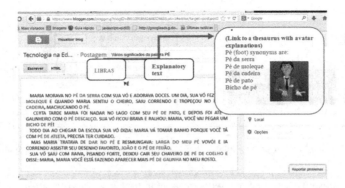

**Fig. 4.** Example of prototype with an avatar exemplifying polysemic words

## 3.3   Evaluating the Prototypes in Practices with Deaf Users

The studies took place in the Deaf Mission (in Libras) of the Baptist Church of Santana, Brazil. A teacher, an interpreter and 15 students participated in this study. Table 2 presents the basic profile of the participants in the study.

**Table 2.** Participants of the study

| n° | Name | Gender | Age | Education level | Level of hearing loss | Use libras | Lip reading |
|---|---|---|---|---|---|---|---|
| 01 | A. de J. S. B. | m | 29 | Secondary | Profound | Yes | Yes |
| 02 | A. V. C. da S. | f | 12 | Primary | Profound | Yes | Yes |
| 03 | A.O.B. | m | 29 | Undergraduate | Profound | Yes | Yes |
| 04 | A. dos S. N. | m | 29 | Secondary | Profound | Yes | No |
| 05 | C. da S. | f | 28 | Graduate | Profound | Yes | Yes |
| 06 | E. dos S. | m | 15 | Primary | Profound | Yes | No |
| 07 | J. C. da S. B. | f | 21 | Secondary | Profound | Yes | Yes |
| 08 | J. K. da S. O. | f | 15 | Secondary | Profound | Yes | No |
| 09 | J. L. C. O. | f | 19 | Secondary | Profound | Yes | Yes |
| 10 | M. M. da C. | f | 29 | Secondary | Profound | Yes | Yes |
| 11 | M. de P. R. | f | 13 | Primary | Profound | Yes | No |
| 12 | R. S. P. | f | 15 | Secondary | Profound | Yes | Yes |

*(Continued)*

**Table 2.** (*Continued*)

| n° | Name | Gender | Age | Education level | Level of hearing loss | Use libras | Lip reading |
|----|------|--------|-----|-----------------|----------------------|------------|-------------|
| 13 | R. A. S. | m | 16 | Primary | Profound | Yes | Yes |
| 14 | R. de S. C. | f | 30 | Undergraduate (teacher) | Listener | Yes | Yes |
| 15 | R.C. | m | 29 | Undergraduate (interpreter) | Listener | Yes | Yes |
| 16 | R. da S. O. | m | 14 | Secondary | Profound | Yes | Yes |
| 17 | T. E.da S. P. | m | 27 | Secondary | Profound | Yes | No |

**Practice 1** (recommendations 9, 18 a 33)

*Objective:* This practice aimed to explore the meanings of the word foot (pé). The practice also included the following themes: figure of speech, informal language and text structure. The text reading activities were performed using the Blog editor of Fig. 4.

*Procedure:* The practice was performed in four steps as follows. In the first step, we presented a text without support of images and sign language interpreters. The objective was to verify how the users make sense of a text with various meanings of the word foot (pé). Table 3 summarizes central aspects of the first step of practice 1, including the goal, number of participants, number of sessions, number of students who performed the task correctly, and remarks about the students' performance.

**Table 3.** Summary of the first step of the first practice

| First step – practice 1 (text reading) | Learning the various meanings of the word "foot" (Recommendation 9) |
|-----------------------------------------|---------------------------------------------------------------------|
| Goal | Read a text without the support of an interpreter and images |
| Number of participants | 15 students and 2 interpret/teachers |
| Number of sessions | 1 |
| Number of students who understood the text | 3 |
| Number of students who did not understand the text | 10 |

REMARKS: The majority of participants were not able to properly interpret the text. Ten students were only able to read isolated words without make sense of the multiple meanings of the word, the students also had difficulties in understanding figures of speech or popular phrases.

During the second step, we presented a text with images and an avatar that explained the various meaning of the word foot (pé). The overall performance of the students on text comprehension was better as compared with the first step, however, some students also demanded support of the interpreters. Table 4 summarizes central aspects of the second step of practice 1, including the goal, number of participants, number of sessions, number of students who performed the task correctly, and remarks about the students' performance.

**Table 4.** Summary of the second step of the first practice

| Second step – practice 1 (text interpretation) | Learning the various meanings of the word "foot" (Recommendation 9) |
|---|---|
| Goal | Read a text with the support of an interpreter and images |
| Number of participants | 15 students and 2 interpret/teacher |
| Number of sessions | 2 |
| Number of students who understood the text | 11 |
| Number of students who did not understand the text | 2 |
| REMARKS: Most of students understood the meanings of words; however they also demanded intervention of interpreters (in addition to images and avatars). | |

The third step of practice 1 included the application of an individual questionnaire with open questions: "Did you understand the text?", "Did you know these meanings previously?" and "Did you like this practice?". In addition, we asked them to give suggestions of how to improve the prototype.

During the fourth step, each individual evaluation was analyzed and discussed in group; each participant presented his/her suggestions, problems and possible solutions to improve the prototype.

**Practice 2** (recommendations 1, 8, 10 and 17)

*Objective:* This practice aimed to investigate alternatives of how to perform a synchronous communications between deaf-deaf and deaf-hearer using instant message tools. This practice was performed in pairs, with the objective of making an appointment, including the day, hour and place, as well as to plan an agenda for this appointment.

*Procedure:* The practice was performed in three steps as follows. In the first step, the teacher and interpreter presented the objectives of the practice and the instant message tool. They also performed an example of how to execute the task (i.e., make an appointment using an instant message tool). Immediately after, they asked the deaf students to perform the task in pairs. The majority of the participants were able to establish a successful communication and make an appointment as requested. Few students had problems related to the technology (i.e., in the use an instant message tool) (Table 5).

**Table 5.** Summary of the second step of the first practice

| First step – practice 2 (synchronous communication) | Make an appointment using an instant message tool (Recommendations 1, 8, 10 and 17) |
|---|---|
| Goal | Deaf to deaf conversation using an instant message tool |
| Number of participants | 14 students and 2 interpret/teachers |
| Number of sessions | 2 |
| Number of pairs who successfully preformed the task | 5 pairs |
| Number of pairs who did not preformed the task | 2 pairs |

REMARKS: The majority of students performed the task without problems. Two pairs, who failed, had difficulties in using the instant message tools.

In the second step, we asked to the students to make an appointment with a hearing colleague. As in the step one, this task included to determine the place, date, and agenda (Table 6).

**Table 6.** Summary of the second step of the second practice.

| Second step – practice 2 (synchronous communication) | Make an appointment using an instant message tool (Recommendation 1, 8, 10 and 17) |
|---|---|
| Goal | Deaf to hearing conversation using an instant message tool |
| Number of participants | 15 students, 15 hearing colleagues e 2 interpret/teacher |
| Number of sessions | 2 |
| Number of pairs who successfully preformed the task | 2 pairs |
| Number of pairs who did not preformed the task | 5 pairs |

REMARKS: The majority of pairs had difficulties in this step. During the practices the hearing colleagues understood the individual words written by the deaf colleagues; however they had difficulties to understand the entire sentences and goals.

In the third step of practice 2, we asked each student to evaluate the prototype individually, indicating problems and giving suggestions of what could be improved in the prototype.

## 4  Interpretation of the Results, Discussion and Limitations

The results confirmed previous studies about the difficulties of deaf users to interpret, to produce, and to communicate on the Web. The results indicate that the proposed recommendation can improve the accessibility of Web applications; however, they also highlight some limitations of the proposed recommendations and prototypes.

In general, we highlight the following results from these practices:

1. Deaf students had difficulties to interpret and use figure of speech, even with the use of exemplifying images. In some cases, they needed the support of a interpreter to complete the task;
2. In some cases, the explanations using written language were not sufficient. During the discussions some students emphasized the limitations of these explanations for the comprehension of complex texts. The students also acknowledged that written explanations are less efficient than explanations using sign language, yet written explanation potentially stimulate the learning of written language;
3. They considered the Portuguese grammar rules too complex to be explained using short warnings. Longer explanations in sign language with examples in written language are needed in some cases;
4. According to the participants, design solutions for deaf accessibility can include various images to support a better understanding of the textual content, nevertheless additional explanation in sign language is necessary for a better understanding of the complex terms;
5. The participants suggested that instant message applications could include "animated emoticons" in order to support the direct correspondence of sign language with the most commonly used words. According to the participants, this feature may improve the communication between deaf users, as well as help hearing people to learn basic signs.

The practices with the students highlighted that, in some cases, the explanations in written language and sign language (using avatars) are not sufficient to learn new concepts. In such cases, interpreters and teachers have to provide additional explanations according to the individual difficulties and the students' previous knowledge. This confirms the central role of educators in deaf literacy and the role of the technology as supporting artifacts. The results also point out possibilities of future research on generation of dynamic explanation based on the students' difficulties.

This study is limited in number of participants; consequently, the results are not statistically conclusive. Particularly, the communication between deaf students and researchers is limited by the proficiency of the researchers in sign language or the number of interpreters. Consequently, studies with a lager numbers of students demand undue resources. Despite of the size limitations, this study contributed with preliminary evidence for the value of the use of visual resources (images and avatars) in design solutions for encouraging the learning of written language by deaf students.

## 5 Conclusion and Future Work

The written language is one of the most difficult barriers to Web accessibility for deaf users. Despite of the advances in the field, deaf literacy is still an educational research challenger. In this paper, we presented a set of web recommendations, prototypes and practices with users aiming to investigate design alternatives to improve Web accessibility. The objective was to use Web resources to stimulate deaf literacy and autonomy on the web.

Results from practices with deaf students pointed out the potential of associating images and avatars in synchronous and asynchronous communication artifacts, while it also identified difficulties and the central role of the teachers on the process. In addition, the results highlighted design implications and future research activities. As the next steps of this research, we propose to improve the prototypes, use them in longer studies (e.g., an entire semester), and evaluate their use in daily activities. The future work also includes research for the automatic generation of personalized explanations according to the individual needs and context.

# References

1. Chomsky, N.: Language and Problems of Knowledge: The Managua Lectures. The MIT Press, Cambridge (1998)
2. Ferreira, M.A.M., Bonacin, R.: Eliciting accessibility requirements for people with hearing loss: a semantic and norm analysis. In: Kurosu, M. (ed.) HCI 2014, Part III. LNCS, vol. 8512, pp. 277–288. Springer, Heidelberg (2014)
3. Ferreira, M.A.M., Bueno, J., Bonacin, R.: Using computational resources on bilingual deaf literacy: an analysis of benefits, perspectives and challenges. In: Antona, M., Stephanidis, C. (eds.) UAHCI 2015. LNCS, vol. 9176, pp. 362–372. Springer, Heidelberg (2015)
4. Fernandes, S.F.: Educação de Surdos, 2nd edn. IBPEX, Curitiba (2011)
5. Hermans, D., et al.: The relationship between the reading and signing skills of deaf children. J. Deaf Stud. Deaf Educ. 13(4), 518–530 (2008)
6. Lorenzet, E.C.: Processo de ensino/aprendizagem de leitura para surdos mediado por computador. Dissertação de mestrado, Programa de Pós-Graduação em Letras, Universidade católica de Pelotas – RS (2005)
7. Marschark, M., Harris, M.: Success and failure in learning to read: the special case (?) of deaf children. In: Cornoldi, C., Oakhill, J. (eds.) Reading Comprehension Disabilities: Processes and Intervention, pp. 279–300. LEA, Hillsdale (1996)
8. Sánchez, C.L.: Educación de los sordos em um modelo bilíngue. Diakonia, Mérida (1991)
9. Salles, H.M.M., et al.: Ensino de língua portuguesa para surdos: caminho para as práticas pedagógicas. SEESP, MEC, Brasília, vol. 1, no. 2 (2007)
10. Vygotsky, L.S.: Mind in Society. The Development of Higher Psychological Processes. Edited by Cole, M., John-Steiner, V., Scribner, S., Souberman, E., Cambridge, Massachusetts, Harvard University Press (1978)
11. W3C - World Wide Web Consortium. Web Content Accessibility Guidelines (WCAG) 2.0. (2008). http://www.w3.org/TR/WCAG20/. Accessed October 2015
12. Wauters, L.N., Vanbon, W.H.J., Tellings, A.E.J.M.: Reading comprehension of Dutch deaf children. J. Read. Writ. Interdisc. J. 19, 46–76 (2006)
13. Witkoski, S.A.: Educação de surdos e preconceito: bilinguismo na vitrine e bimodalismo precário no estoque. Tese de Doutorado em Educação, Setor de Educação, da Universidade Federal do Paraná, Curitiba (2001)

# Design Engineering for Universal Access: Software and Cognitive Challenges in Computer Based Problem-Solving

Gisela Susanne Bahr$^{(\boxtimes)}$, Stephen Wood, and John William Blood

Florida Institute of Technology, 150 W. University Blvd, Melbourne, FL 32901, USA
{gbahr,swood}@fit.edu, jblood2012@gmail.com

**Abstract.** Computer-supported problem solving has become ubiquitous in work and home environments. Within an educational context, specifically design engineering, this paper investigates a framework that integrates two aspects of these interactions that influence the outcome of computer based problem solving: software and mind-set involved in the interaction. The review indicates a number of research opportunities for interaction science to enhance problems-solving and is focused primarily on software tools and solutions that enhance cognitive performance for specialized user populations.

**Keywords:** Access to education and learning · Adaptive and augmented interaction · Design for all education and training · Interaction science for universal access

## 1 Introduction

Computer-supported problem solving, frequently online, has become an everyday task. This phenomenon is the result of increasingly migrating everyday problem solving tasks involving interactions with people and real-life materials [1] to computer supported contexts. This trend has been observable in Western society among many domains, including education, and particularly in *design engineering*. The challenges that have arisen for this specialized user population in computer supported problem solving, are relevant for universal access as the scope of computer use related to problem solving increases.

The practitioners and students in the discipline of design engineering are considered highly creative individuals who invent novel solution to ill-defined, non-routine problems [2, 3]. The problems they solve are unstructured and ill-defined and require the use of inferences, coordination of information, with leaps of intuition and creativity. The primary tool in this field is the use of computer aided design (CAD) software. This paper reviews and describes cognitive and creative interaction challenges associated with CAD supported problems solving and identifies opportunities for interaction science to enhance cognitive performance of specialized user populations. These interaction challenges are related to universal access issues with focus on open-ended problem solving. This paper reviews research on CAD and problem

© Springer International Publishing Switzerland 2016
M. Antona and C. Stephanidis (Eds.): UAHCI 2016, Part III, LNCS 9739, pp. 16–25, 2016.
DOI: 10.1007/978-3-319-40238-3_2

solving, the effect of software properties on creativity in problem solving, relevant prior research in cognitive psychology, and the implications and challenges for interaction design to support non-routine problem solving.

## 2    CAD and Problem Solving

CAD software was initially developed for the drafts(wo)man to convert the hand drawings of the design engineer into digital drawings that could be saved on the computer. The software was later adapted so that the design engineer could enter his or her drawings directly into the computer without waiting for the drafts(wo)man to do so. In the process more capabilities were added to CAD software to aid the designer. The evolution of CAD began with 2D, then 3D, computerized drawing tools that led to parametric CAD solutions. Parametric approaches change parameters and automatically update corresponding elements.

Over the years, design engineers have come to rely on CAD software for the entire design cycle from conceptual development to layout design to final concept design, and production. However, CAD was initially not intended for the "creative" phases of product design, nor to support divergent thinking during concept development.

The notion of treating product development and innovation as a non-routine and creative problem solving task is well established in research and practice [4]. As a result, software supported problem solving has been investigated in the areas of engineering and architectural computing [5]. In this context, computing supports the entire process from idea generation to transferable solution. During this process, it appears that creativity is instrumental during the early stages of design [6], which include concept development and the investigation of the problem space.

Problem solving using CAD in engineering contexts provides opportunities as well as challenges. For example, [7] suggest that the use of CAD tools promise more rapid and inexpensive problem-solving because of the use of simulation and that this practice is likely to create possibilities for learning and design innovation. Similarly, [8] support the idea that virtualization of knowledge-based processes is likely to result in new solutions.

An empirical study how CAD applications affect the problem solving process is Fixson and Marion [9] 2012 investigation of CAD use in product development. The study evaluated the whether the advantages attributed to the use of parametric CAD software are grounded in fact. For example, CAD use supports design iteration, testing and faster transmission of the design, compared to previous practices during product development. Moreover, it is generally accepted that CAD enhances product development through wider exploration of the solution space and by requiring faster and less development resources. The cost savings are accomplished through the use of computer-based simulation, early in the design process (front-loading). This practice is expected to reduce the need for prototyping, which tends to be costly and occurs during the later stages of product development.

The investigation confirmed that the availability of CAD systems tends to reduce prototyping costs but it also revealed that CAD availability does not accelerate product development but reduces concept development by facilitating detail design too early in the process. Moreover, the ease of making changes has the potential to erode process discipline and can lead to last minute changes. They refer to these CAD effects on problem solving as back-loading, in contrast to the front-loading, i.e. simulation early in the development.

The authors conclude that *"[The] side effects of digital design come from its major strength, the ability to iterate detailed models. This study illustrates that the different thinking modes that underlie divergent and convergent phases in product development as well as process discipline effects need to be considered when applying the idea of front-loading via extensive use of digital design tools such as CAD...In short, front-loading the downstream process should not result in a quasi back-loading of concept development work into the detailed design phase; the different thinking modes that are appropriate for each phase make this merger counterproductive. Nor should a quasi back-loading occur due to pushing detailed design issues into the tooling phase just because it is possible."* [p.154].

In summary, the nature of interaction support in online problem solving, here during CAD interactions, is a driver of problem solving cognition and leads to changes in the process as well as outcomes. It appears that the medium or tools used during the design are capable to fundamentally guide and shape the underlying cognition. CAD in particular was not originally designed to support concept development and the divergent thinking phases of design. Moreover it appears that one of the key properties that enables the front-loading and back-loading phenomena is parametric design, the ability to make changes relatively easily that automatically propagate and update the design.

## 3   CAD Software Properties and Their Effects on Creativity in Problem Solving

Parametric approaches change parameters and automatically update corresponding elements. Hence designs can be adjusted and tweaked easily and likewise new solutions can be derived from prior solutions with relative ease. As such the capabilities of the interfaces not only influence the interaction, but may also influence the generation and type of problem solutions.

Research on engineering design creativity has explored the relationships of cognitive styles, creative quality and quantity of solutions. For example, [10] investigated the relationship between cognitive styles and problem solution quality and quantity. The measurements and comparisons of the participants based on their cognitive style using the Kirton Adaption-Innovation Inventory (KAI) were nonsignificant. The KAI is a psychometric instrument intended to measure cognitive style along a continuum, from adaptive to innovative. This measure was not correlated to the generation of derivative versus novel solutions when comparing engineers to a control group.

However, the researchers observed that problem solvers who base their design on previous solutions generate more solutions than problem solver who invent and create novel, non-derivative approaches. They base this observation on paper design and prototypes build from a fixed set of material (each set included 1 plastic bag, 8 rubber bands, 8 pipe cleaners, 8 Popsicle sticks, a $4'' \times 8''$ piece of foam core, a $4'' \times 12''$ flat foam sheet, and $12''$ of tape). (For a review of alternative creativity measures see [11].

One might argue that using an initial design as a basis for additional deigns is systematic as well as the result of the limitations of the medium. The question arises whether the addition of drafting technology capabilities facilitates creativity and innovation?

Chang [12] investigated student cognitive abilities and problem solution performance on design engineering tasks using 3-D CAD compared to a control group. They found that measures of spatial ability were moderately correlated with creative performance, i.e., spatial ability accounted for 6–12 % of the variance. In addition, results indicate a difference between students in the CAD user group and the drafting control group, suggesting enhanced creative performance primarily relating to aesthetics, in the CAD condition. While these finds are encouraging, it is noteworthy that the apparent effects of 3D-CAD use are confounded with the instruction technique used for the 3D-CAD user group and the traditional design group.

For example, the traditional design group received (1) General introduction to graphic design and graphic recognition (2) Types of graphics (3) Introduction to common graphics tools (4) Presentation of object shapes: isometric plan, oblique drawing, perspective drawing and orthographic view. On the other hand, the 3D-CAD user group was instructed in (1) Purpose and types of 3D-CAD software (2) Thinking corresponding to the visual basis and digital operation (3) Reverse thinking pattern for modeling (4) CAD basic exercises and comprehensive application: basic geometric style, basic geometric style change, construction of concave surface of contour lines and comprehensive application of commands. Given the difference in the instruction, it is not clear whether the observed differences are the result of different conditions (drafting tool), or the instruction, or both.

To examine the potential impact of CAD tools on creative problem solving, [13] conducted an on-line survey with 212 experienced users on the ways that CAD use may influence their ability to design creatively. Results suggest that for immature designs (concept development), CAD use was not preferred and that experienced designers preferred free hand sketching, drawing boards and verbal discussions. Some survey respondent pointed out that they over-used CAD and that this appeared to restrict their spontaneous thought and expression. Another possible influence of CAD use is related to circumscribed thinking. Ideally a design engineer is motivated to find a solution based on the requirements given. Circumscribed thinking occurs when the capabilities of the tool or the designer's proficiency of the tool use affect the solution. The results indicate that circumscribed thinking that shapes the solution (instead of or in addition to the requirements), is a wide spread issue. Respondents attributed negative as well as positive outcomes to the phenomenon. Another aspect investigated was the phenomenon of premature fixation. Self-reports indicate that full use of CAD early in the design is more likely to be associated with premature fixation. It appears that designers deliberately downgrade CAD capabilities and use CAD as a simple drafting tool for computer based sketching and that they thereby avoid CAD's parametric and 3D capabilities.

It appears that CAD is less useful during concept development, leads to solution fixation if used during concept development and facilitates circumscribed thinking.

In light of these findings, the conclusions put forth by the investigators are (1) the use of smart interfaces that actively support creative thinking and practices of the user and (2) the control of feature creep, which is the distraction of the user from the core tasks by elaborate new features and busy interfaces. Clearly, problem-solving enhanced CAD environments must strike a balance not to disrupt and yet facilitate the creative process of the design engineer. The next section highlights relevant research in cognitive psychology that is related to building CAD environments that support non-routine problem solving.

## 4    Related Prior Research in Cognitive Psychology

In 1972 in their seminal book on the theory of human problem solving, Newel & Simon's laid the foundation for conceptualization human problem solving as the search of the problem space [14]. Because problem spaces of non-routine problems can be quite large, corresponding searches are guided by heuristics or rules of thumb in order to select from a large number of options without conducting exhaustive and time consuming comparisons. The use of heuristics or some form of prior knowledge and preferences during non-routine problem solving tasks, does not address unpredictable "leaps of intuition" and insights that occur during solution search. The seminal work in the domain of insight in problem solving was conducted by Koehler in 1910s who investigated apes who apparently demonstrated insight in problem solving situations [15]. One of the primary observations of this and later studies with humans was that while thinking about a problem, problem solvers can "restructure" their representations of the problem. This change in the representation can lead to a flash of insight that enables problem solvers to invent a novel solution.

Kaplan and Simon [16] investigated insight in the mutilated chessboard problem and found that different visualization of the problem representation had an effect on the occurrence on insight. (See for [17, 18] an overview of the mutilated chessboard problem.) The mutilated chessboard is a tiling problem, where two diagonally opposite tiles have been removed from the board and the task is to cover the remaining 62 tiles or squares with 31 dominos that cover 2 squares at a time. The task is impossible. Kaplan and Simon's investigation suggests that problem solvers who attempted to search the problem space by simulating the solution had difficulty remembering and keeping track of their solutions. On the other hand, problem solvers who recognized that each domino must cover two differently colored squares realized that it would be impossible to cover the board because two squares with the same color had been removed. This insight to the impossibility was greater when the two colors the chessboard squares were labeled bread and butter, respectively.

The approach of restructuring a solution to inspire insight is related to the notion of mind-set and functional fixedness. An example how mindset or frame of mind can prevent reaching a simple, uncomplicated solution is this riddle: A man visited the pyramids in 1993. The trip moved him deeply and he promised himself that if he ever had children to bring them to see the pyramids. Finally, in 1978 he took his very own son to see the sights. How was this possible? (The answer is provided at the end of this paper.)

The riddle may seem unrelated to problem solving in engineering at first but it illustrates the influence of mindset and assumptions (Einstellung) on problem solving. A recent example are the terrorist attacks that occurred on September 11, 2001 in metropolitan areas of the USA [19, 20]. Four planes (commercial jets, which are generally considered means of transport for goods and people) were used as weapons and killed thousands of people. The realization is that the function of a plane is not limited to preconceived notions, such transportation, but that the possible uses of an object depend on the characteristics of the object. While unintuitive, it was obvious to the terrorists that planes could serve as airborne, target finding bombs. Appearances, whether they take the form of a problem context or the current usage of an object, lead problem solvers to adopt a particular mindset (Einstellung) [21]. This finding is not surprising except that the consequences extend beyond the laboratory, as seen in the 9–11 example. Moreover, functional fixedness and Einstellung are considerable obstacles to seeing alternative solutions. Based on prior research it appears that restructuring of a problem representation can alleviate these phenomena and lead to insights that reveal a solution. The implications of this work in context with CAD are the topic of the next and last section.

## 5    Challenges for Interaction Design to Support Non-routine Problem Solving

Despite the belief that sophisticated CAD solutions support creative processes, there appears to be some evidence from surveys with experienced engineers as well as from studies with junior/novice engineers that this idea requires investigation. Several challenges for using CAD as a non-routine problem solving environment have emerged during this review.

- CAD was not designed for divergent thinking but detail design.
- CAD use during product development undermines concept development.
- CAD use early in the design process is associated with premature solution fixation, circumscribed thinking and feeling cognitively restricted.

Given the limitation and impact of CAD when used early in the design cycle or product development, it appears that a framework is required that integrates the demands on cognitive processing with the workflow and the capabilities of the interaction tool. Hence, a solution implies the flow of continuous interfaces with different capabilities that appropriately support the underlying thought processes such as divergent and convergent thinking. Rather than relying on one CAD environment to support a multiplicity of tasks and encumbering the user with inappropriate features, a cognitively friendly CAD environment that support problem solving consists of a suite of continuous interfaces that easily transition between the support for idea generation, concept development to layout design and details design. In particular during the creative phases, such as idea generation and concept development, alternative interfaces should supply tools for hand drawing, peer communications and easy idea sharing. Such interfaces would be void of the sophisticated drafting tools because at this state in the development they are irrelevant and potentially commit the user prematurely to a solution.

The availability of creative CAD support tools does not guarantee their use. In particular, under time pressure any workable solution is deemed acceptable, whether innovative or not. The reality of time as a limited resources, adds a considerable constraint to design engineering that can impact and abbreviate concept development regardless of the tools used. It remains to be shown how the concept development can be accelerated with cognitive support tools that alleviate possible negative impacts of time pressure and alleviate solution faction and derivative design. For example, when time is of the essence, solution fixation is likely to arise to step up progress on the project. However, it is important to consider alternative solution to prevent expensive backtracking or back-loading resulting from solution fixation. A smart CAD support tool may supply alternative solutions when designer fail to adopt divergent thinking styles. Hence divergent thinking or exploration of the solution space can be actively prompted by the interface.

Related existing CAD solutions are "design advisors," that serve an error checking function by searching for design violations [22, 23]. For example, a sheet-metal design advisor will prompt the CAD user if a hole is too close to an edge, which is a point of failure, i.e., a weak or breaking point. Similarly, a plastic injection molding design advisor may alert the user to choose correct angular settings so that the mold will be able to release the plastic part. [24] More sophisticated types of advisors could involve restructuring of problem representations by suggesting alternative solution components.

An example is the design of the bottom of a wave tank (see Fig. 1). A wave tank contains thousands of gallons of water and is used to simulate ocean waves and to measure the effects of objects in the wave flow. The shape of the bottom of tank (bottom bathymetry) is critical to the realistic simulation of the ocean floor. An open-ended design problem is how to create an adjustable system to shape the tank bottom as needed with specific parameters. A number of ways are possible. For instance, one might empty the tank and cover the bottom with a new, specifically molded surface each time changes in the simulation environment are necessary. Similarly, one might conceive of a scuba diver to reshape the bottom by adding, removing or adjusting devices. On the other hand, a design engineer may be tasked to design an automated solution to make tank bottom bathymetry adjustable. Typical approaches to such a system could utilize a flexible bottom that is raised by electric pistons or hydraulic cylinders. Another functionally related, albeit less obvious solution is the use of a cam system. Camshafts are generally found in automobile engines (see Fig. 2). A camshaft consists of a series of cams attached to a shaft. Using an individual cam is equivalent to using an individual piston or hydraulic cylinder, where each has a specific location under the wave tank bottom and can raise or lower to contour the bottom. During the concept development of such a system the functional equivalence can be presented by the CAD system in order to expand the solution space with concepts from automotive engineering. Presenting multiple possibilities to the designer during concept development has the potential to alleviate solution ⁻ fixation by changing mind-set and the mental model of the problem representation, and by creating association to other domains. The effect is likely to occur regardless of time pressure because it relieves the cognitive workload associated with idea generation and compensates for a lack of knowledge and stimulates divergent thinking.

**Fig. 1.** Ohmsett Wave Tank in Leonardo, New Jersey, USA. [25]

**Fig. 2.** Image of automobile camshaft. (Camshaft rotates to actuate pistons, not depicted.) [26].

It is easy to see that enhanced CAD interfaces that support problem solving must strike a balance not to disrupt and yet facilitate the creative process of the design engineer. This implies the use of multiple interfaces that are designed to support different cognitive processes as well as advisors that suggest functionally related solution to prevent solution fixation under time pressure or because of conventional CAD overuse. Likewise problem solving in universal access requires awareness of the underlying cognitive demands on the user and appropriate interface design. The notion of one size fits all, i.e., one interface fits all cognitive processes underlying problem solving, has been questioned in CAD research and has implications for problem solving support beyond design engineering communities. Future research is likely to illuminate the complexity involving computer supported problem solving in everyday life, such as planning your vacation on a budget or organizing a funeral in a short amount of time. The universal accessibility to computers for problem solving creates challenges not only as the result of disabilities but also because of the cognitive needs and demands of the task to be accomplished. Hence the notion of universal access is inclusive not only of enabling access to information technology, but also of finding ways to cognitively assist the users of information to solve problems in a meaningful and productive way with computer support.

## 6 Riddle Solution

The man made his trip in 1993 *BC* and took his son 15 year later on his second trip in 1978 *BC*.

## References

1. Diehl, M., Willis, S.L., Schaie, K.W.: Everyday problem solving in older adults: observational assessment and cognitive correlates. Psychol. Aging **10**(3), 478–491 (1995)
2. Wood, S., Bahr, G.S., Ritter, M.: Cognitive tools for design engineers: a framework for the development of intelligent CAD systems. I-COM J. Interact. Coop. Media **14**(2), 138–146 (2015)
3. Bahr, G.S., Wood, S.L., Escandon, A.: Design engineering and human computer interaction: function oriented problem solving in CAD applications. In: Antona, M., Stephanidis, C. (eds.) Universal Access in Human-Computer Interaction. Access to Today's Technologies. LNCS, vol. 9175, pp. 13–24. Springer, Heidelberg (2015)
4. Jerrard, B., Newport, R.: Managing New Product Innovation. CRC Press, Boca Raton (2003)
5. Gero, J.S.: Design Computing and Cognition '06. Springer, Dordrecht (2006)
6. Shai, O., Reich, Y., Rubin, D.: Creative conceptual design: extending the scope by infused design. Comput. Aided Des. **41**(3), 117–135 (2009)
7. Thomke, S.H., Fujimoto, T.: The effect of "Front-loading" problem-solving on product development performance. J. Prod. Innov. Manag. **17**, 128–142 (2000)
8. Becker, M.C., Salvatore, P., Zirpoli, F.: The impact of virtual simulation tools on problem-solving and new product development organization. Res. Policy **34**, 1305–1321 (2005)
9. Fixson, S.K., Marion, T.J.: Back-loading: a potential side effect of employing digital design tools in new product development. J. Prod. Innov. Manag. **29**(S1), 140–156 (2012)
10. Jablokow, K.: Exploring the impact of cognitive style and academic discipline on design prototype variability. In: 121st ASEE Annual Conference & Exposition, pp. 1–12 (2014)
11. Charyton, C., Jagacinski, R.J., Merrill, J.A., Clifton, W., Dedios, S.: Assessing creativity specific to engineering with the revised creative engineering design assessment. J. Eng. Educ. **100**(4), 778–799 (2011)
12. Chang, Y.: 3D-CAD effects on creative design performance of different spatial abilities students. J. Comput. Assist. Learn. **30**(5), 397–407 (2014)
13. Robertson, B., Radcliffe, D.: Impact of CAD tools on creative problem solving in engineering design. Comput. Aided Des. **41**(3), 136–146 (2009)
14. Newell, A., Simon, H.A.: Human Problem Solving. Prentice-Hall, Englewood Cliffs (1972)
15. Köhler, W.: The Mentality of Apes Harcourt. Brace & Company Inc, New York (1926)
16. Kaplan, C.A., Simon, H.A.: In search of insight. Cogn. Psychol. **22**, 374–419 (1990)

17. Black, M.: Critical Thinking: An Introduction to Logic and the Scientific Method, 1st edn. Prentice Hall, New York (1946)
18. Knuth, D.E.: The Art of Computer Programming, Volume 4A: Combinatorial Algorithms (Part 1). Addison Wesley, Boston (2011)
19. Schmemann, S.: Hijacked Jets Destroy Twin Towers and Hit Pentagon, sect. A, pp. 1–14. New York Times, 12 September 2001
20. Grunwald, M.: Washington Post, Terrorists Hijack 4 Airliners, 12 September 2001
21. Luchins, A.S.: Mechanization in Problem Solving, vol. 54. Psychological Monographs, Washington, DC, Whole no. 248 (1942)
22. Creo Plastic Advisor: Introduction to Pro/ENGINEER Plastic Advisor - PTC, Boundary Systems, Inc., Cleveland, Ohio (2014). Accessed http://www.boundarysys.com/services/4-products/ptc/212-plastic-advisor
23. Yeh, S., Kamran, M., Terry, J.M.E., Nnaji, B.O.: A design advisor for sheet metal fabrication. IIE Transactions 28(1) (1996). Accessed http://www.tandfonline.com/doi/abs/10.1080/07408179608966247?journalCode=uiie20
24. C3P Software: "Form-Advisor for Creo, new generation sheet metal forming solution". C3P Engineering Software International Co., LTD, 30 Jan 2013 (2013). Accessed https://www.youtube.com/watch?v=X7I8d6E48AU
25. Ohmsett Wave Tank: "Sound Waves May Help Clean oil Spills," Virginia Institute of Marine Science, 18 April 2012 (2012). Accessed http://www.laboratoryequipment.com/news/2012/04/sound-waves-may-help-clean-oil-spills
26. Pkwteile, "Nockenwelle & Ein und Auslassventil Steuerung," Nockenwelle & Ein und Auslassventil Steuerung Online Shop (2016). Accessed http://www.pkwteile.de/ersatzteil/nockenwelleEe

# Visual Debuggers and Deaf Programmers

Marcos Devaner do Nascimento[1]([✉]),
Francisco Carlos de Mattos Brito Oliveira[2],
Adriano Tavares de Freitas[3], and Lidiane Castro Silva[1]

[1] Computer Science Department, Ceará State University,
Itaperi Campus, Fortaleza, Brazil
marcos@projetolead.com.br, lidcastro@gmail.com
[2] Computer Science Department, University of Fortaleza, Fortaleza, Brazil
fran.oliveira@unifor.br
[3] Computing Department, Federal Institute of Ceará, Maracanaú Campus,
Maracanaú, Brazil
adriano.freitas@ifce.edu.br

**Abstract.** We investigated how visual debuggers impact the performance of a Java programmer who is deaf or hearing impaired (DHI).
In previous work, we had shown that despite having attended accessible
java course, deaf programmers still perform poorer than their hearing
counterparts in tasks like debugging. In this text, we show that visual
debuggers present a hope of bridging the gap between the two populations. Typical debugging tasks were assigned to both groups who used
industry standard IDE (Eclipse) and a Visual Debugger (JGrasp). Qualitative and quantitative analysis show advantages for the former.

**Keywords:** Debugger · Accessibility · Usability · Performance

## 1 Introduction

To secure a position in the workplace for deaf or hearing impaired (DHI) programmers, studies must show that they have performance similar to their hearing
counterparts. The *Laboratory of Distance Education for People with Disabilities*
creates and offers seven courses in information technology (IT) through our
accessible learning management system (LMS), among them a basic Java course
using the industry-standard Eclipse programming environment. Although our
LMS is equipped for the DHI and those with missing limbs, the focus of this
text is on the DHI java graduate.

We are interested in empowering the DHI programmer in the daily tasks of
a regular software engineer, such as software evolution, debugging. Some lessons
on our Java course are reinforced by programming exercises (or programming
workshops). Java workshops are implemented on LMS, which allows online collaboration between a tutor, a translator and the DHI [25]. Such collaboration is
part of our strategy to create and promote a collaborative environment between
a DHI programmer and a hearing coworker (tutor is not versed in sign language).

M. Antona and C. Stephanidis (Eds.): UAHCI 2016, Part III, LNCS 9739, pp. 26–37, 2016.
DOI: 10.1007/978-3-319-40238-3_3

We know that DHI graduates from our courses has inferior performance in debugging tasks when compared to their hearing counterparts who took the very same courses [11]. We expect visual debuggers and direct manipulation might improve the performance of the DHI programmer. We compare how a visual debugger (JGrasp) affects the activities of a DHI programmer in this paper. Ten participants from our basic Java course were recruited to debug code in JGrasp and Eclipse, in a between-subjects experiment. We emphasize that all subjects have already had contact with the Eclipse tool for debugging activities in our course.

Performance was measured by: (a) Time to complete the task (TCT); (b) Number of times the subject asked for external help assistance (HA) and (c) Number of tasks completed successfully (TCS). These metrics were submitted to the *Mann-Whitney U-Test*, the results were not statistically significant at $p \leq 0.05$. But, although the Eclipse tool may have be benefited due to the background of the participants, the TCT, HA and TCS variables show a similar performance between the two tools, with JGrasp showing some advantage. We can conclude that the JGrasp makes use of elements that allow a better familiarization of the features available.

A questionnaire based on the System Usability Scale (SUS) [5] was also applied. The average SUS score for JGrasp was 72 and 50 for Eclipse. The answers submitted to the *Mann-Whitney U-Test* give us a *p-value* of 0.01, a statistically significant result, thus we can conclude that JGrasp was better evaluated, usability-wise.

A simular study is presented in [11]. However, in this paper, we show some aspects of the teaching of DHI. In this way, we can justify more appropriately the use of visual tools in the deaf learning. Besides, the analysis of the results is more robust and consistent: the statistical test in the previous work was not very suitable for the experimental design and sample size; furthermore, we show, in this article, a qualitative analysis of the studied tools which allows us to understand what the DHI feel and think on the use of visual tools.

The structure of this paper is as follows: we show some aspects of deaf learning in Sect. 2. We, then present the theoretical background in Sect. 3, which deals with direct manipulation and development environments. In Sect. 4, we present related work concerning visual debuggers. Section 5 shows our study design and subject profile; and in Sect. 6 we present and discuss the results. Finally we present our proposal to build an integrated development environment (IDE) that should keep the gains of an accessible java learning environment, as reported in [25] and add a direct-manipulation inspired visual debugger.

## 2   Deaf Learning

Research shows that students with profound deafness degree have lower academic achievement compared with their hearing counterparts in all educational environments [14, 18, 27].

Bull and colleagues [6] show that deaf students have more difficulty in absorbing mathematical concepts when compared to listeners during their learning process.

But hearing loss can not be the cause of the problem. Nunes and Moreno [19] argue that poor mathematical performance comes from a risk factor related to time, type of education and learning opportunities for deaf students. To support this thought, Zarfaty and colleagues [29] showed that 3–4 year-old deaf children have spatial and time skills comparable to his hearing colleagues with the same age and they also have better spatial numerical skills.

Barbosa [1] argues that deaf children and listeners seem to have similar performance in cognitive functions less dependent on linguistic stimuli. For Boroditsky [4], bilingual people show divergence on the same subject when they have to approach it in both languages. This change in language also has an impact on memory. Finally, the author posits that language shapes even the most basic dimensions of human experience: space, time, causality and relationships with others.

Most of the educational materials were designed for listeners. For Perlin [21], the "listener culture" is essentially made up of auditory signals that deaf people do not use. On the other hand, the deaf use visual signals to understand the world around them. Furthermore, It is not just the lack of appropriate teaching materials, the Brazilian Sign Language (Libras) is relatively young and has a poor vocabulary, compared to Portuguese and lacks many technical terms in many areas. Online forums can be used for creating these terms. Oliveira and colleagues [20] present a comparative study on the acceptance of signs created in person and remotely. They show that acceptable and legitimate signs can also be produced using web discussions and the users can not distinguish from which method they come from.

Blatto-Vallee and colleagues [3] show that the use of visual-spatial schematic representations is a strong positive predictor of mathematical problem solving performance for deaf students. For Pinto [22], visuality seems to represent, for the deaf, the main channel for thinking and processing schemes which naturally allows the acquisition, construction and expression of knowledge, values and experiences that, otherwise, would be unreachable. The visual channel allows the reading of the deaf world and it is the support of their mental processing. The authors report the improvement self-esteem, interest and engagement among the deaf, when drawings, images and visual manipulations were used in science education, geography, art and history.

Although there are various visual Java debuggers, to our knowledge, none had been tested with the deaf. Before proceeding with the discussion of visual Java debuggers available, we must warn that users who use sign language hold less information in their short-term memory when compared to non-DHI [2]. This may be partly due to the nature of the visual-spatial information necessary for the DHI [28].

In a recent research, Sorva and colleagues [26] point out that in the last three decades, dozens of software systems have been developed in order to illustrate the runtime behavior of software for novice programmers. However, a desirable visual debugger for the deaf student should: (1) not overload the visual mode; (2) offer the programmer portability and flexibility to be used in different workplace settings; (3) have intuitive interface with accessibility features.

# 3   Direct Manipulation and IDE's

For Hutchins [15], direct manipulations are visual interfaces in which users operate on a representation of objects of interest. Rose [23] argues that visibility of objects and actions on these objects produce a significant difference in productivity. In some studies cited by the author, these features allow a better domain of the interface; more competence in performing tasks; ease of learning both basic and advanced functions; confidence that the user will continue to dominate the interface even if she stops using it for a while; satisfaction in using the system; increases the will of teaching others; and the desire to explore more advanced aspects of the system [23].

Some integrated development environments (IDEs) have applied not only the concept of direct manipulation as well as the concept of visualization, to making complex tasks like debugging a code simpler and more intuitive. Moreno [17] argues that say that because of the ease of using these instruments, which are intended for the early stages of a programmed learning process, the strategy is to make the objects and values visible and manipulated graphically.

Cypher and collegues [10] show that the concepts of direct manipulation applied to development environments can generate greater productivity for developers. It is a concept that helps in the development of logic, since materializes abstract concepts, allowing less cognitive demand for the interpretation of mathematical logic and also allowing the implementation of computational logic in the development of algorithms.

DHI are strongly rely on visual input [12] and it is reasonable to assume that they will benefit from an IDE with these characteristics.

# 4   Related Work

Visual debuggers implement, by its conception, direct manipulation strategies. In this section, we show some visual debuggers, briefly discuss how they implement such strategies. We also choose one of them to use in the study reported in this text and justify our choice.

## 4.1   Visualizing Programs with Jeliot 3

*Jeliot 3* [17] is a tool designed for pupils to learn procedural or object-oriented programming. Its main feature is the total or partial view of source codes and control flows. Using this tool, students can develop and, at the same time, see the visual representation of a running code. During this process students acquire a mental model of computing that helps to better understand the construction of the program.

The system is easy to use, has consistent, complete and continuous view and supports viewing a large subset of programs written in Java. The layout of this tool is divided into four parts: methods, constants, area for expression evaluation and instance area as we can see in Fig. 1.

This program seeks to be as consistent as possible in order to reduce the cognitive load of students during learning. Despite its many qualities, we evaluated that the tool has too many visual information presented at once and that

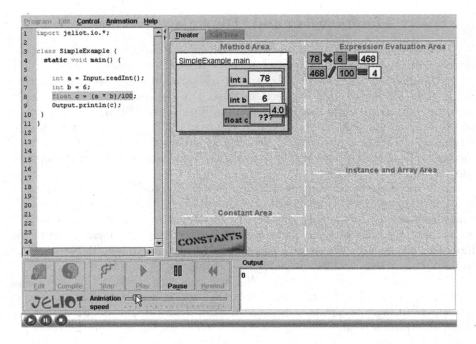

**Fig. 1.** Jeliot Interface

might confuse the deaf student. Complex diagrams easily become confused and difficult to read. Studies show that graphical approaches are more efficient when the task requires pattern recognition, but not when the visual field is too full of objects and the task requires detailed information [13].

### 4.2 Java Interactive Visualization Environment (Jive)

*Jive* [7] is an interactive execution tool developed by the Department of Science and Computer Engineering from the University of Buffalo. This system is used for: (a) debugging Java programs with rich views of object structure and interactions between methods; (b) facilitating maintenance software; providing insight into the dynamic behavior of programs and (c) teaching and learning Java.

It was originally designed as a stand-alone Java application. Later it was redesigned to the Eclipse platform and consists of a set of plug-ins and features. Its distribution takes place using the Eclipse update manager. It provides two main views to display the running Java programs: the object diagram view and the sequence diagram view.

This tool uses the object diagram that demand prior knowledge of this type of diagram, which can generate DHI greater cognitive effort by removing the focus of logic to the concepts linked to the diagram. Therefore, we judged that it is not appropriate for the studied scenario.

### 4.3  JGrasp

*JGrasp* [8] is an IDE developed to provide dynamic and illustrative views of Java data structures. These views are generated automatically and synchronized with the data structures in the source code. The user can step through the code in debug mode or workbench. This integration allows a single environment for learning data structures. The use of this tool in classroom has been an important aide for teaching students who deal with such structures, the authors claim.

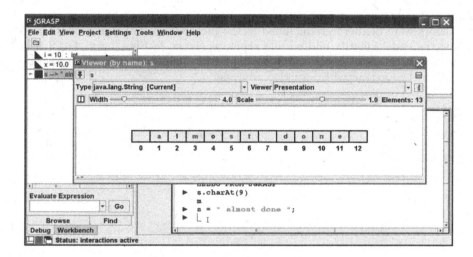

**Fig. 2.** JGrasp Interface

Studies conducted with students indicate that the tool can have a positive and significant impact on student achievement [9]. Pupils were more productive and more capable of detect and fix logic errors using *JGrasp* [16].

*JGrasp* runs mainly in Java Swing and its components implement parts of the Java Accessibility API. This allows some elements to be available for assistive technologies. The elements include: text of the source code, text of other UI components and an alternative text to graphics components. It also produces source code and views at runtime [8]. Among other visual debuggers surveyed we can identify that this tool uses the technique of direct manipulation of objects which made it stood out from the others. In this tool, students can drag a variable, drop it into the canvas window and a Presentation viewer opens to scan it, as shown in Fig. 2.

## 5  The Study

We were poised to investigate the effects of a visual code debugger, which uses the *direct manipulation technique* in the performance of DHI programmers. We compare the DHI performance in tasks using *JGrasp* and Eclipse.

### 5.1   Participants and Methodology

We recruited ten deaf participants, all male, aged between 25–36 of age, all graduates from the basic Java course offered by our laboratory. In a between-subject design, the participants were ramdomly assigned to either one of two groups: the first group performed the tasks using the JGrasp tool and the second group using Eclipse.

The participants received a Java algorithm that simulates bank transactions: *withdraw* (Subtract any value of the remaining balance) and *deposit* (Add some value to the balance exists).

Errors were deliberately included in the methods so that participants could debug the code, identify and correct them, as shown in Figs. 3 and 4. All trials were videotaped and partcipants interviewed for qualitative analysis. Quantitative data were extracted from video analysis.

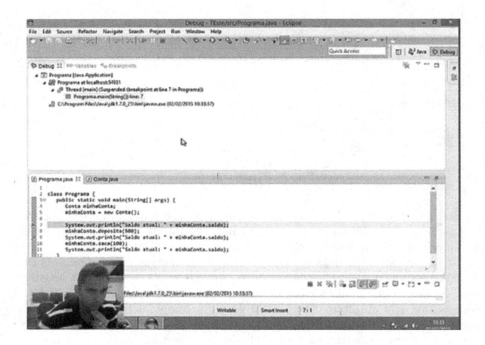

**Fig. 3.** Subject using Eclipse IDE

A script with four tasks was given to participants to assist them in the process: (a) Adding a breakpoint in the *Withdraw()* and *Deposit()* methods; (b) Debugging to check if the return values are consistent with the objective of the method; (c) Fixing any problems found; (d) Debugging again to verify if the calculations are correct.

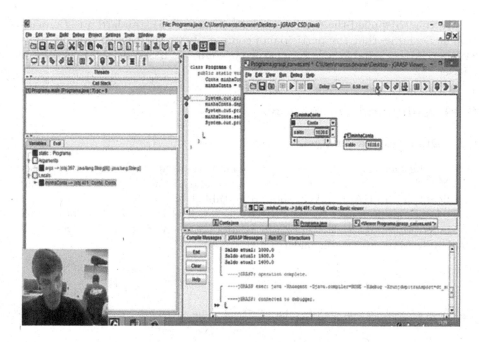

**Fig. 4.** Subject using Jgrasp IDE

**Table 1.** Results by Task - Situated Analysis

| Tasks | TCS | | HA | | Average TCT | |
|---|---|---|---|---|---|---|
| | JGrasp | Eclipse | JGrasp | Eclipse | JGrasp | Eclipse |
| Adding a breakpoint in the Withdraw() and Deposit() methods | 4 | 5 | 1 | 2 | 00:26 s | 01:02 s |
| Debugging to check if the return values are consistent with the objective of the method | 4 | 2 | 5 | 4 | 02:06 s | 02:51 s |
| Fixing any problems found | 5 | 4 | 3 | 4 | 01:39 s | 02:08 s |
| Debugging again to verify if the calculations are correct | 4 | 2 | 4 | 4 | 01:46 s | 02:45 s |

Methods, analysis and evaluation were applied to both experimental conditions. We use the situated testing technique to measure participants' performance when debugging task. For this analysis we observe the following variables: (a) time to complete the task (TCT); (b) number of times the subject asked for external help (HA) and; (c) number of tasks completed successfully (TCS).

We've also applied the System Usability Scale (SUS) standard questionnaire (Likert Scale) so that the participants could evaluate the usability of the tools. SUS provides a reliable way to measure usability, is based on the heuristics of Nielsen [5].

# 6    Results and Discussions

## 6.1    Quantitative Analysis

Despite the fact that subjects were familiar with Eclipse (it was the tool used in their 120 h Java course), the numbers favor JGrasp, although not statistically significant. TCT, HA and TCS showed in Table 1 indicate that.

For each participant, we submitted the TCS, HA and TCT values to the two-tailed *Mann-Whitney U-Test*, the results obtained are shown in Table 2. All the results were not significant at $p \leq 0.05$.

**Table 2.** Two-tailed *Mann-Whitney U-Test* results

|      | U-value | Critical value | p-value |
|------|---------|----------------|---------|
| TCS  | 6       | 2 at $p \leq 0.05$ | 0.2113  |
| HA   | 6.5     | 2 at $p \leq 0.05$ | 0.25014 |
| TCT  | 7       | 2 at $p \leq 0.05$ | 0.29834 |

The average SUS score for JGrasp was 72 and 50 for Eclipse. Researches indicate that a SUS score above 68 [24] is considered above average. The results indicate that JGrasp tool has better usability, according to participants evaluation.

We also applied the SUS scores to the two-tailed *Mann-Whitney U-Test*. The *U-value* obtained was 1 and the *p-value* was 0.02144. The result is therefore significant at $p \leq 0.05$. In other words, there is a significant difference in the usability of the two tools.

## 6.2    Qualitative Analysis

When asked if they would like to use this system frequently, three of five participants who used JGrasp strongly agree that they would like to use the system more often. They commented that the use of the debugger increases the knowledge through practice. This is possible due to the well location of information on the screen which facilitates the use of the tool. On the other had, from the five participants who tested Eclipse, two strongly liked. From their comments, some participants had forgotten some functions and they also said that they need more practice to be able to use all features of the systems.

When questioned about complexity of the system, all participants disagreed that JGrasp is complex. Eclipse was described as complex for 40 % of its users.

In the comments, they reported lack of knowledge or difficulty in finding icons in toolbars.

We also asked if the system is easy to use. All five JGrasp users reported no difficulty. Eclipse users, on the other hand, reported that although the tabs are well positioned, the windows are not easy to interpret. They said it is due to visual appeal and one reported that the system needs to be more visually organized because this is an important issue for a deaf user.

The need of assistance to use the system was another question to the participants. Two JGrasp users agreed that they do not need help to use the system. Only one Eclipse user strongly disagrees with the need of assistance. The lack of knowledge of the system was the cause that justify the need of help to answer the tasks.

The subjects were asked whether the various system functions were well integrated. All JGrasp users reported that it is well organized and easy to use and three of them answered that the system is not complicated because it offers best practices for working with the programmer. Eclipse users commented it contains not grouped windows and features; and the icons are not interactive, therefore hindering the understanding of the tool. Three of the users said reported that the functions are far from one another.

When asked if most people would learn to use the system quickly, all users commented that it depends on development experience and training, and the learning would be fast both in JGrasp as in Eclipse. Confidence when using the system was well evaluated in both tools. They say that the more knowledgeable you are in programming, the more confident you get using the tools.

Finally we asked whether it is needed to learn many things before using the system. All users reported that they need to learn and practice before the use of the systems. Two JGrasp users strongly agree with the question, while four Eclipse users strongly agree.

The use of JGrasp platform among deaf users was more acceptable for presenting visual appeal and better distribution of functionality to the developer. Although the activities to be developed for both two groups needed the assistance for completion, we must emphasize that some users who were in the Eclipse group already knew the tool. Thus it is justified the use of JGrasp as a good debug tool for deaf.

## 7   Conclusion

Providing adequate learning materials, environment and tutoring is not enough to bridge performance gap between deaf or hearing impaired programmer and their hearing confederates in real world tasks. Debugging is just part of the many activities a software developer is involved in. In this paper, we discuss various concepts and research to improve the performance of DHI programmers in tasks related to debugging. We found that systems with a visual approach combined with direct manipulation of objects are preferred by the DHI community.

The findings reported here just encourage further investigation. There is lot to be done. One thing is sure: We have to intervene in the workspace to improve productivity of the DHI programmer. How far should we use vision is a tricky question. Vision has greater importance the DHI and we should avoid overloading it. We will carefully design a visual debugger for the DHI, having that in mind. We should also integrate this visual debugger with our learning object *JLoad* [25]. In this way we will have an interactive development environment and Java code debugging, which followed the standards of accessibility and will allow students to create their codes in an interactive web environment, eliminating the installation and configuration of an IDE on your machine, bringing mobility for students.

We are currently investigating how several information visualization techniques can be used (alone or in a combined way) to cement that improvement and embed it in our LMS. No visual debugger was conceived with the DHI programmer in mind.

# References

1. Barbosa, H.H.: Initial mathematical skills in listeners and deaf children. Cad. Cedes **91**, 333–347. Title in Portuguese: Habilidades Matemáticas Iniciais em Crianças Surdas e Ouvintes
2. Bavelier, D., Dye, M.W., Hauser, P.C.: Do deaf individuals see better? Trends Cogn. Sci. **10**(11), 512–518 (2006)
3. Blatto-Vallee, G., Kelly, R.R., Gaustad, M.G., Porter, J., Fonzi, J.: Visual-spatial representation in mathematical problem solving by deaf and hearing students. J. Deaf Stud. Deaf Educ. **12**(4), 432–448 (2007)
4. Boroditsky, L.: How language shapes thought. Sci. Am. **304**(2), 62–65 (2011)
5. Brooke, J.: Sus - a quick and dirty usability scale. Usability Eval. Ind. **189**(194), 4–7 (1996)
6. Bull, R., Blatto-Vallee, G., Fabich, M.: Subitizing, magnitude representation, and magnitude retrieval in deaf and hearing adults. J. Deaf Stud. Deaf Educ **11**(3), 289–302 (2006)
7. Cattaneo, G., Faruolo, P., Petrillo, U.F., Italiano, G.F.: Jive: java interactive software visualization environment. In: 2004 IEEE Symposium on Visual Languages and Human Centric Computing, pp. 41–43. IEEE (2004)
8. Cross, J.H., Hendrix, D., Umphress, D.A.: JGRASP: an integrated development environment with visualizations for teaching java in CS1, CS2, and beyond. In: 34th Annual Frontiers in Education, FIE 2004, pp. 1466–1467. IEEE (2004)
9. Cross, J.H., Hendrix, T.D., Jain, J., Barowski, L.: A: dynamic object viewers for data structures. ACM SIGCSE Bull. **39**(1), 4–8 (2007)
10. Cypher, A., Halbert, D.C.: Watch What I do: Programming by Demonstration. MIT press, Cambridge (1993)
11. do Nascimento, M.D., de Mattos Brito Oliveira, F.C., de Freitas, A.T: How do deaf or hearing impaired programmers perform in debugging java code? In: Anais do Simpósio Brasileiro de Informática na Educação, vol. 25, pp. 593–601 (2014)
12. Gesueli, Z.M., de Moura, L.: Literacy and deafness: the words display. ETD: Educação Temática Digital **7**(2), 110–122 (2006). Title in Portuguese: Letramento e surdez: a visualização das palavras
13. Graciano, A.B.V.: Object tracking based on pattern structural recognition: Ph.D. thesis, São Paulo University (2007). Title in Portuguese: Rastreamento de objetos baseado em reconhecimento estrutural de padrões

14. Gregory, S.: Mathematics and deaf children. Issues Deaf Educ. 119–126 (1998)
15. Hutchins, E.L., Hollan, J.D., Norman, D.A.: Direct manipulation interfaces. Hum. Comput. Interact. **1**(4), 311–338 (1985)
16. de Aquino Leal, A.V.: Teaching programming in high school: An approach using standards and games with concrete materials. Master's thesis (2014). Title in Portuguese: Ensino de Programação no Ensino Médio Integrado: Uma Abordagem Utilizando Padrões e Jogos com Materiais Concretos. http://repositorio.bc.ufg.br/tede/handle/tede/3613
17. Moreno, A., Joy, M.S.: Jeliot 3 in a demanding educational setting. Electron. Notes Theor. Comput. Sci. **178**, 51–59 (2007)
18. Nogueira, C.M.I., Zanquetta, M.E.M.: Deafness, bilingualism and traditional teaching of mathematics. Zetetiké: Revista de Educação Matemática **16**(30), 219–237 (2009). Title in Portuguese: Surdez, bilingüismo e o ensino tradicional de Matemática: uma avaliação piagetiana
19. Nunes, T., Moreno, C.: Is hearing impairment a cause of difficulties in learning mathematics. Dev. Math. Skills, 227–254 (1998)
20. de Oliveira, F.C., Gomes, G.N., de Freitas, A.T., de Oliveira, A.C., Silva, L.C., Queiroz, B: A comparative study of the acceptability of signs for the brazilian sign language created in person and remotely. In: Proceedings of the 46th ACM Technical Symposium on Computer Science Education, pp. 207–211. ACM (2015)
21. Perlin, G.: The place of deaf culture. A invenção da surdez: cultura, alteridade, identidade e diferença no campo da educação, pp. 73–82 (2004). Title in Portuguese: O lugar da cultura surda
22. de Souza Pinto, M.A., dos Santos Gomes, A.M., Nicot, Y.E.: The visual experience as a facilitator in science education for deaf students. Revista Areté: Revista Amazônica de Ensino de Ciências **5**(09) (2014). Title in Portuguese: A experiência visual como elemento facilitador na educação em ciências para alunos surdos
23. Rose, A., Plaisant, C., Shneiderman, B.: Using ethnographic methods in user interface re-engineering. In: Proceedings of the DIS 1995: Symposium on Designing Interactive Systems, pp. 115–122 (1995)
24. Sauro, J., Lewis, J.R.: Quantifying the User Experience: Practical Statistics for User Research. Elsevier (2012)
25. Silva, L.C., de Oliveira, F.C., de Oliveira, A.C., de Freitas, A.T.: Introducing the jLoad: a java learning object to assist the deaf. In: 2014 IEEE 14th International Conference on Advanced Learning Technologies (ICALT), pp. 579–583. IEEE (2014)
26. Sorva, J., Karavirta, V., Malmi, L.: A review of generic program visualization systems for introductory programming education. ACM Trans. Comput. Educ. (TOCE) **13**(4), 15 (2013)
27. Traxler, C.B.: The stanford achievement test: national norming and performance standards for deaf and hard-of-hearing students. J. Deaf Stud. Deaf Educ. **5**(4), 337–348 (2000)
28. Wilson, M., Emmorey, K.: Comparing sign language and speech reveals a universal limit on short-term memory capacity. Psychol. Sci. **17**(8), 682–683 (2006)
29. Zarfaty, Y., Nunes, T., Bryant, P.: The performance of young deaf children in spatial and temporal number tasks. J. Deaf Stud. Deaf Educ. **9**(3), 315–326 (2004)

# Learning Object Design for Teaching Descriptive Geometry: A Study from the Perspective of Gamification and Accessibility

Guilherme P.G. Ferreira, Rafael Andrade, Sabrina T. Oliveira[(✉)], and Vânia R. Ulbricht

Universidade Federal do Paraná, Curitiba, Brazil
guilhermepgf@gmail.com, rafael@tabadesign.com.br,
binah.oliveira@gmail.com, vrulbricht@gmail.com

**Abstract.** Technology has enabled significant advances in the distribution of information for education. With the Internet the information was available to the global context immediately through computer networks. To treat the contents and structure the information for education groups of researchers and developers worked to create groups of information entitled Learning Objects. This paper demonstrates the re-design of a learning object, in order to adjust it to criteria of gamification and accessibility. The methodological process consisted of: defining the project requirements and the structuring of a storyboard for the collaborative development of learning objects (Braga 2015b; Kethure 2010). Thus, the proposed interface incorporates playful elements for presentation of immersive and interactive content, so as to encourage learning also to people with disabilities, related to low vision, blind and deaf. In this sense, the objective of this paper is to present the process of developing a new interface for content learning about "Triangles and its characteristics" content, this treaty in Descriptive Geometry Course in the Graduate Graphic Design and Product. At the end of this document, we present the resulting learning object of this process, designed from gamification elements and affordability. The methodological procedure used as a base, collaboration in the development of learning objects, and includes: Concept Map, Navigational maps and Storyboard. Besides this, a Storyboard created to meet the needs of this collaborative development is presented. The paper presents a case study focusing on the use of Learning Objects to the teaching content of triangles in the university. The collaborative development process to redesign this platform featured a master's degree and two doctoral students of the Graduate Program in Design at the Federal University of Parana, and the project was prepared during the course of accessibility and gamification.

**Keywords:** Digital design · Gamified · Accessible learning

## 1 Introduction

Technology has enabled significant advances in the distribution of information for education. With the Internet, the information became available to the global context and accessed immediately through computer networks. In this context, new fields started to

© Springer International Publishing Switzerland 2016
M. Antona and C. Stephanidis (Eds.): UAHCI 2016, Part III, LNCS 9739, pp. 38–48, 2016.
DOI: 10.1007/978-3-319-40238-3_4

be explored allowed by the maturation in research and development of learning objects and improvement of information sharing, like the gamification.

In learning objects the gamification explores the use of techniques, practices and tools that can promote information and immersion of the users. This approach may be useful to approximate the learning content of technological and digital world in which the students are insert.

This paper aims to present the process of remodeling a learning object and its contents, about the topic "Triangles and its Characteristics" subject of a lesson included in the Geometry discipline. The following sections of this document will explore the theme: Accessible and Gamified Development Process of a Learning Object (LO) for teaching geometric content. The LO was developed aiming it use by people interested in better understanding the triangles; such as regular education students and the general public; also considering, for its accessibility features, people with low vision, blind and deaf. Following is shown the LO result of this process.

The document closes, bringing considerations about the process of developing a Gamified Learning Object (GLO) proposal for learning triangles, and argues against literature review the role of LOs in the educational context and possible future developments such as the migration of these contents for mobile environments, such as phones and tablets.

Should be elucidate that will be considered in this document the learning objects only when belonging to the digital context. That statement must be clear because some authors and educational consortiums believe that learning objects can be observed both in the digital context as well in the physical, to endorse practices and teaching tools that enable reuse for educational purposes. Our focus in LO mainly comprises the digital environment with the objective to promote a better adaptation of the content for the needs of diverse users.

## 2   Methodology for Gamified LO Development

In the literature there is not a specific methodological approach to gamification in LO. Meanwhile, it is up to developers the best use of various tools for the design of educational elements that aims to implement aspects of games. The work of Manrique (2015), promote an overview of aspects of gamification that could be applied in the design of learning objects or other kinds of contents (Table 1).

In this document, the development of the gamified LO used as base, the INTERA Methodology presented in Braga (2015b), that integrates features of ADDIE (ADDIE - Analyze, Design, Develop, Implement), and also the set of project management knowledge (PMBOK). According to the authors, the INTERA Methodology (Intelligence, Educational Technologies and Accessible Resources) is iterative and considers the LOs development process as a project, and thus, contemplates the project life cycle.

The INTERA Methodology considered the following project components: *phases, roles, steps and artifacts*. In this document, we highlight the component steps of the methodology that are:

**Table 1.** Extracted from Manrique (2015)

| |
|---|
| **Quest**; mission with concrete objectives that leads to some kind of reward. |
| **Experience Points**; points that increase the player´s level |
| **Virtual Goods**; any kind of virtual item that can be bought in the game |
| **Special Events**; time-limited events that only take place once in a while |
| **Social Area**; areas that allow further social interaction |
| **Epic Challenge**; special challenge that is only up for pro players |
| **Tutorial**; learning process that develops the player´s initial skills |
| **Progress HUDS**; any type of HUD that shows the player´s progress |
| **Customization**; allows players to customize their virtual appearance |
| **Access Item**; special item that unlocks new content |
| **Trading System**; mechanic that enables an in game market structure |
| **Vanity Item**; rare items that represent skill / status |
| **Levels**; Mechanic that displays the player´s overall and current state |
| **Badge**; Achievement to be unlocked by special conditions |
| **Equipment**; Any items our characters have |
| **Gifting**; Collaborative mechanic that increases P2P |
| **Social Ranking**; Relative ranking focused on the player´s social graph |
| **Chat Systems**; Communication channels that allow social interaction World; where it all takes place within a gamified system |
| **Absolute Ranking**; standing that shows the top players of the system |
| **Skills / Traits**; mechanics that modify the player´s characteristics |
| **Random Rewards**; rewards that are randomly given a drop rate |
| **Free Lunch**; rewards achieved with other´s actions |
| **Ambassador**; game experts that act as mentor, developers or viralizers. |
| **Avatar**; a virtual representation of the player |
| **Fixed / Variable Reward**; rewards given by any kind of fixed or variable condition |
| **Power-up**; positive but limited effect on the player´s action |
| **Easter Eggs**; special secrets that are yet to be discovered |
| **Party / Team**; the more, the merrier. |
| **Player vs Player**; mechanic that allows direct competition between players |
| **Lifejackets**; give players some rest after difficult game levels |
| **Relative Leaderboard**; it show the player´s position relative to others of a similar rank |
| **In-Game Currency**; virtual or real currency that server as in-game money |
| **Game Constraints**; rules that keep the system stable |
| **Guilds**; Association of players for common purposes |

- contextualization, which presents the theoretical base to be addressed
- requirements, demonstrates the accessibility requirements
- architecture, define the general layout of the LO
- development, are presented, the navigation maps and the screens and functions tests and quality, activities of verification and adjustments in the prototype
- availability, development of delivery document for programming the LO
- evaluation, later stage programming for final alignment of LO

To promote the accessibility we observed the guidelines presented in the thesis of Macedo (2010), the author introduces elements of accessibility related in documents of various entities that discuss the web accessibility. As the author points out, the guidelines *"observe international standards for the creation of learning objects of IMS and SCORM, associated with the standards of accessibility of IMS, the W3C WCAG 1.0 and*

*WCAG 2.0, with the principles of universal design applicable to the development of digitized content*". Briefly the guidelines proposed can be observed in the following Table 2:

**Table 2.** Acessibility guidelines - extracted from Macedo (2010), translated and adapted by the authors.

| |
|---|
| **TEXT** |
| - Solid color background. |
| - Colors changeable, noticeable without color. |
| - Transformation in textual pages. |
| - Structure and formatting. |
| - Graphics or sound to text equivalents. |
| **TABLE** |
| - Check that the reading will be done linearly through auditory means. Screen readers read line to line, continuously or in selected sections. |
| - Give clear identification of the table headings, headers, rows and columns. |
| - Introduce summary tables. |
| - If you have complex tables look divide them into simple tables. |
| - Do not use tables as formatting, content distribution or screen layout. |
| **GRAPHIC** |
| - Bar graphs, line graphs, pie charts can be converted into simple table. |
| **STATIC IMAGE** |
| - Media alternatives to the whole image. |
| - High contrast. |
| - Scalable. |
| **MOVING IMAGE** |
| - Alternative media, at least one option. |
| - Alternative text and / or equivalent text for any video or at least for the most relevant parts. |
| - Title or description of the image subject. |
| - Possibility of monochrome display. |
| - Sound and image synchronized when. |
| - Audio, when, without background sound. |
| **AUDIO** |
| - Legend, caption or complete description. |
| - Translation in sign language. |
| - Visual alternative text. |
| - Volume control, pause, on / off all the relatives. |

In this LO was not included accessibility for blind users, this restriction was due to the project scope and digital media in which this content would be displayed.

# 3   Contextualization

The context is the issue to be addressed in the LO project. This document has been selected a layer of content that deals with understanding of the triangles and their characteristics. This project used as a base reference for design and content a PUCPR (Pontifical Catholic University of Paraná) LO that was no longer in operation by changes in web browsers support of operating applets (Fig. 1).

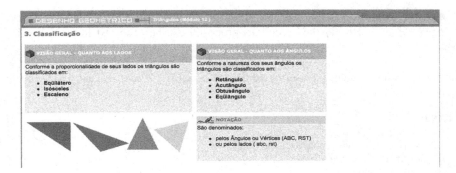

**Fig. 1.** Base LO – screenshot from the PUCPR repository

Through this referential base, the redesign objectives to update the contents, but also implement gamification features and accessibility to extend the range of LO. The subjects of this layer are (Fig. 2):

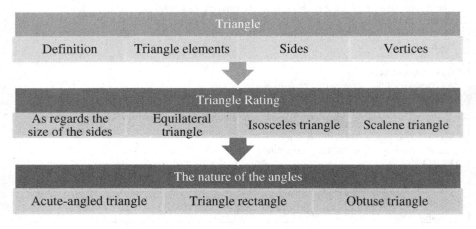

**Fig. 2.** The subjects of the LO – authors

## 4  Requirements

As general requirements for this project were defined:

– Use gamification elements to enhance learning and immersion in the content
– Use, whenever possible, accessible solutions.
– Redesign and upgrade the reference LO to make it appropriate to the context of use.

# 5    Architecture

According the process suggested in Kethure (2010) was developed a Concept Map and the gamified LO (GLO) Storyboard, respectively (Fig. 3).

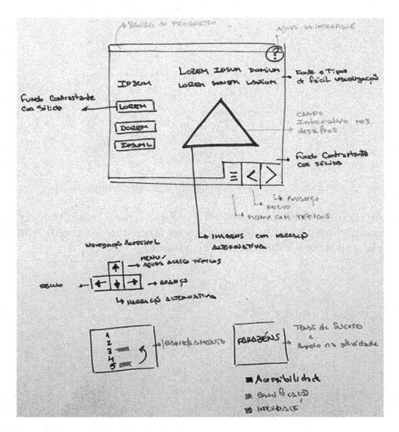

**Fig. 3.**  Concept map - authors

From the user name insertion, encoding occur, resulting in a fictitious name, some sort of triangle (equilateral, for example), this name would be as the user in the context of navigation. The adoption of this code would serve as the first user immersion element in the context of the GLO. In sequence, some elements of gamification received a first draft on the project (Fig. 4).

This scheme, structured the information area and user interaction; it shows the progress bar that provides real-time feedback on user interface about their situation. Has been added a help button on all splints, which when activated displays the navigation keys that help the user to understand the working mechanics of the GLO, determining the user how you can interact with the platform.

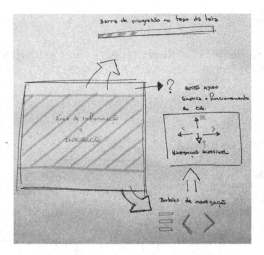

**Fig. 4.** Information architecture sketch - authors

The storyboard included the organization of GLO screens, prioritizing an accessibility screen that would be an introductory screen, where the user could control if you would like to activate or not the accessibility mode (Fig. 5).

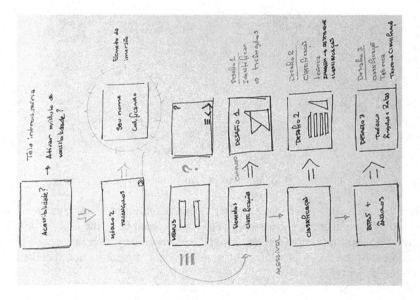

**Fig. 5.** Storyboard – authors

In a second stage were idealized the menus, the presentation of content and the content of fixation exercises, presented to the user in the form of challenges along their learning. The exercises would be applied at the end of each content block and served to better learning and memory, and were classified in: Challenge 1 - Identification of different types of triangles; Challenge 2 - Classification of triangles; Challenge 3 - Straight and angles.

Subsequently, was studied the module to display and insertion of the user's name. From the user name insertion, encoding occur, resulting in a fictitious name, some sort of triangle (equilateral, for example), this name would be as the user in the context of navigation. The adoption of this code would serve as the first user immersion element in the context of the GLO, extracted precept of gamification.

# 6   Development

Were developed two navigation maps for this application. The first includes a handy navigation for users with low vision or blind, and does not address fixing activities whose user interaction request the viewing screen elements. This mode presents the information through voice over and may include additional information through simplified access the directional keys on the keyboard (Fig. 6).

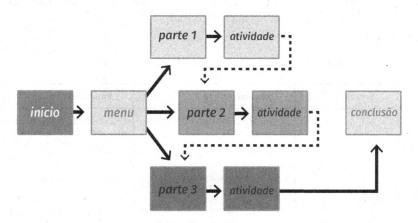

**Fig. 6.**  The GLO paths - authors

Access for users with visual impairment does not include the first two activities that have focused on visual user interaction with the LO through the mouse. These activities are represented with dotted lines and are only in the complete GLO. The full mode, displays the information and interactive activities through the human computer interface using as main peripheral access the mouse or touchscreen. This mode also provides information through voice over and may contemplate additional information help through simplified access by LO navigation interface. A map screen-to-screen was then developed contemplating the entire route that the user can access on the LO. An excerpt of this map can be see illustrated in the following (Fig. 7).

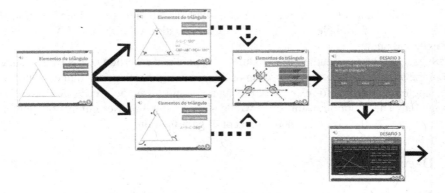

**Fig. 7.**  Excerpt map screen-to-screen - authors

As an additional tool to the navigation map, a table explain every screen and functions to be developed by programmers. Table 3 depicts the screen, the description of the screen and account items, as well as physical and virtual function buttons. Such data include the description of each of the screens, stories suggested for the comprehensive and affordable navigation, functions applied to each of the available buttons and operation information, screens and challenge.

**Table 3.**  Excerpt descriptions and functions – authors

| Screen | Description | Functions |
|---|---|---|
| Screen 4 - triangles and its elements | It presents the theme: Triangles and its elements.<br><br>Voice Over 1: Triangles and its elements. Triangle is all regular or irregular polygon containing three sides and three angles.<br><br>VO 2 through the lower directional: (repeats screen audio description: VO 1)<br><br>Adds: Polygons are closed figures formed by line segments, being characterized by the following elements: angles, corners, diagonal and sides. According to the number of sides in the figure is named. | Directional physical buttons: right (advances to Regular Polygon screen), left (returns the previously accessed screen), higher (access menu), lower (repeat description screen audio).<br><br>Navigation buttons per click: advance (advances to next screen), decrease (returns the previously accessed screen) menu (LO access the menu).<br><br>Regular Polygon button - Opens explanation<br><br>Irregular Polygon button - Opens explanation |

Many of the features are included in the developed prototype and can be experienced by programmers for better understanding.

# 7   Availability

Developed documents, as well as figures, text and slide presentations, will be available in conjunction with this document to dealings by pedagogues and LO programmers. The prototype can be accessed by the link: https://goo.gl/2iKeAQ.

Developed in public and federal level, the Learning Object is licensed under a Creative Commons License - Attribution 4.0 International.

# 8   Evaluation

Throughout the development of the previously demonstrated screens the project team made several checks on the functionality and quality of available information. Thus, it should be noted that the screens and logistical shown here are the result of work cycles to better match the GLO, and occurred throughout the project. In this project by limiting its scope, and development time were not understanding of tests with users focus gamified LO. These tests should be conducted to analyze the collection of information for general users, visually impaired and blind. The data should be used to increase and improve the proposal.

# 9   Final Considerations

This paper aimed to present the process of instructional GLO re-design for teaching content of triangles based on LO descriptive geometry course at the Catholic University of Paraná. For this purpose, the presented process of digital design, taking into account the establishment of design requirements set to the accessibility of gamification.

The platform digital design left the following guiding questions of project: How to structure the development of GLO? How to promote the memorization, learning, content retrieval and enable accessibility in the digital environment?

Given these problems, it was established that would also be used gamification concepts on the platform, to establish interaction, involvement and immersion of the user in the content presented. In addition to these criteria, also was used the gamification when the progress bar for the user to know in real time on your navigation and on its degree of interaction and apprehension of the content in the virtual environment was planned. For people with special needs can enable the accessibility mode that allows continuous audio description of all content presented to blind people, as well as expansion of characters or images to people with low vision. For blind people, it is possible to print the exercises in Braille and embossed figures and illustrations. Still, with a focus on meeting also subjects with hearing impairment, all presented content is explained in detail on the screen to facilitate learning.

The collaborative approach to development of GLO allowed respectively development: Requirements, Conceptual Design (Concept Map and Storyboard) and Digital Modeling.

It was found that the accessibility and gamification must be project prerogatives that must be established when the genesis of the project and not later, when implemented, only aiming at their adaptation to these contexts. The developed GLO is concerned from accessibility criteria to allow teaching and instructional content can reach a greater number of subjects with and without hearing or impaired vision (blind and people with residual vision - low vision).

Thus, it is important to understand that in the absence of a single definition, theories of learning objects can be seen as complementary, and develop LOs is an important step to understanding these objects as well as for the promotion of education.

# References

Afonso, M.C.L.: Banco Internacional de Objetos Educacionais (BIOE): normas para a definição dos metadados/ Maria da Conceição Lima Afonso. – Brasília: CESPE/UnB (MEC 2010) (2015). http://objetoseducacionais2.mec.gov.br/retrievefile/normas

Braga, J., (Org.) Objetos de Aprendizagem Volume 1: introdução e fundamentos. Santo André: UFABC, p. 157 (2015a). http://pesquisa.ufabc.edu.br/intera/wp-content/uploads/2015/11/ObjetosDeAprendizagemVol1_Braga.pdf

Braga, J., (Org.) Objetos de Aprendizagem Volume 2: metodologia de desenvolvimento. Santo André: UFABC (2015b). pesquisa.ufabc.edu.br/intera/?page_id=370

Bratina, et al.: Preparing teachers to use learning objects the technology source 2002 (2015). http://ts.mivu.org/default.asp?show=article&id=1034

IEEE 1484.12.1-2002- Draft standard for learning object metadata, ieee learning technology standards committee (LTSC 2002) (2015). http://ltsc.ieee.org/wg12/files/LOM_1484_12_1_v1_Final_Draft.pdf

Levi, J.: developing learning objects within dokeos 2.0. faculty of social and economic sciences. University of Geneva 2009 (2015). https://plone.unige.ch/ntice/documentation-ntice/MasterThesisJoelleLevi.pdf/view

Kethure, A.O.: Uma experiência para definição de storyboard em metodologia de desenvolvimento colaborativo de objetos de aprendizagem. Brazil. Ciências & Cognição (2010)

Macedo, C.M.S.: Diretrizes para criação de objetos de aprendizagem acessíveis. Universidade Federal de Santa Catarina (2010)

Manrique, V.: 35 Gamification Toolkit. (2015). http://www.epicwinblog.net/2013/10/the-35-gamification-mechanics-toolkit.html

Mcgreal, R.: Learning Objects: A practical definition. Int. J. Instruct. Technol. Dist. Learn. Setembro 2004 (2015). http://itdl.org/index.htm

Vicari, R.M., Bez, M., Silva, J.M.C., Ribeiro, A.M., Gluz, J.C., Passerino, L.M., Santos, É.R., Primo, T., Rossi, L., Behar, P., Filho, R., Roesler, V.:. Proposta Brasileira de Metadados para Objetos de Aprendizagem Baseados em Agentes (OBAA). RENOTE. Revista Novas Tecnologias na Educação, vol. 8, pp. 1–10, 2010 (2015). https://www.lume.ufrgs.br/bitstream/handle/10183/29300/000758918.pdf?sequence=1

Wiley, D.A.: Connecting learning objects to instructional design theory: a definition, a metaphor, and a taxonomy. In Wiley, D.A., (ed.) The Instructional Use of Learning Objects, pp. 1–35. Setembro 2002 (2015). http://www.reusability.org/read/chapters/wiley.doc

# The Development of an eBook for Teaching and Learning Mathematics

Mauro Figueiredo[1(✉)], José Bidarra[2], and Rune Bostad[3]

[1] University of Algarve, ISE, CIMA, CIAC, Faro, Portugal
mfiguei@ualg.pt
[2] Open University (UAb), CIAC, Lisbon, Portugal
[3] Nord University, Bodø, Norway

**Abstract.** Mobile devices, smartphones, phablets and tablets, are widely available. This is a generation of digital natives. We cannot ignore that they are no longer the same students for which the education system was designed traditionally. Studying math is many times a cumbersome task. But this can be changed if the teacher takes advantage of the technology that is currently available. We are working in the use of different tools to extend the classroom in a blended learning model. In this paper, it is presented the development of an eBook for teaching mathematics to secondary students. It is developed with the free and open standard EPUB 3 that is available for Android and iOS platforms. This specification supports video embedded in the eBook. In this paper it is shown how to take advantage of this feature, making videos available about lectures and problems resolutions, which is especially interesting for learning mathematics.

**Keywords:** eBooks · Mathematics · m-learning · EPUB

## 1 Introduction

As we look toward the future of education in the 21st century, the prominence of a robust STEM (Science, Technology, Engineering, and Mathematics) curriculum is unquestioned. However, low achievement in mathematics education has been an increasing problem in the recent years in Portugal. In 2014, the average classification in the 12th grade exam, from 0–20, was of 7.8. Mathematics exams in the 1st cycle, 2nd cycle and 3rd cycle had an excessive percentage of negatives (levels 1 or 2), 36 %, 54 % and 47 %, respectively.

Moreover, according to a recent study on the changing pedagogical landscape [1] the importance of lectures in higher education usually precludes other teaching and learning techniques, such as projects, laboratories, seminars and tutorials. But there are signs that this situation is changing to varying degrees, with the introduction of new pedagogies harvesting the affordances offered by new technologies. Another EU study by the High Level Group on the Modernisation of Higher Education in 2014 [2], indicates that MOOCs and other recent innovations are only one part of a wave of change in higher education, recognizing that blended learning or other forms of on- and off-campus learning are now widespread. However, the lack of clear assistance as to how

© Springer International Publishing Switzerland 2016
M. Antona and C. Stephanidis (Eds.): UAHCI 2016, Part III, LNCS 9739, pp. 49–56, 2016.
DOI: 10.1007/978-3-319-40238-3_5

the higher education system would need to change, in order to accommodate students needs, results in most universities being unwilling to follow high risk strategies, either alone or together.

It is also important to note that these students are the generation of digital games and social networks. We cannot ignore that they are no longer the same for which the education system was designed a few decades ago. See, for example, the prospect of Heide and Stilborne [3], for whom "the technological revolution has produced a generation of students who grew up with multidimensional and interactive media sources. A generation whose expectations and world views are different from those that preceded it" (p. 27). Online interaction has become a way of life for students wherever they are: at home, on the move, or in schools. For the institutions this is good news, as for the first time in history we have educational technologies that cost (almost) nothing to governments and schools: smart mobile phones (most students have one), networking software (freely available, e.g. Hangouts, Messenger, Skype), learning applications (freely and increasingly available, e.g. Apple Store, Google Play) and open educational resources (in growing supply, e.g. MOOCs, iTunes U, Khan Academy). There are other free tools available for learning organizations, such as collaborative tools (e.g., blogs, wikis, knowledge-building software), immersive environments (e.g. virtual worlds), media production and distribution tools, and many more.

Online activities may be accomplished, for example, through the use of mobile communication and wireless technologies, allowing for experimentation, augmented reality, image collection, map sharing, and communication with other students, anytime and anywhere. In this context it is wise to consider the integration of digital media and mobile devices (iPad, iPod, tablets, smartphones), allowing students to set personal goals, to manage educational content and to communicate with others in the right context. In the near future, eventually everyone will have a smartphone or a tablet. This will make it possible for a teacher to develop educational activities that can take advantage of mobile technologies for improving learning activities.

In this paper, we present the design and development of an eBook for STEM teaching and learning of mathematics. Students can use this eBook in the classroom or outside the classroom in a blended learning model to solve problems. When students have difficulties in solving a problem they can watch the resolution of it. In this way, we want to provide the same opportunities to low-achieving students that may struggle to learn the materials covered in class. Students have also access to complex problems that may provide additional stimulation for top performers students. In this way, we can provide a platform that is student-centered and teacher-friendly.

## 2 Motivation

Results from the 2012 Program for International Student Assessment (PISA), show that Norway, Portugal, Spain and Turkey are below the OECD average in mathematics, with a mean performance of 489, 487, 484 and 448 score points.

The countries that show significant improvement in PISA performance – Brazil, Germany, Greece, Italy, Mexico, Tunisia and Turkey – are those that manage to reduce the proportion of low-achieving students. In Norway, Portugal and Spain about one out of four students, in Turkey about one out of two students, still do not attain the baseline proficiency Level 2 in mathematics. It means that in the best of the cases, low achievers students can extract relevant information from a single source and can use basic algorithms, formulae or procedures to solve problems involving whole numbers.

Regardless the controversy over PISA tests results, this situation calls for actions aiming at improving instruction strategies for teaching and learning mathematics.

In this paper we present an eBook that is set for improving mathematical performance and achievements for all students, including also low achievers and the top performers. The development plans for this eBook aim to extend the traditional learning environment to a virtual classroom setting that will keep students connected and effectively learning mathematics through the exploration of math tools that will enable students to practice more. This eBook enables the exploration of video lectures in smartphones, phablets or tablets.

This eBook will contribute for the implementation of a blended model for teaching and learning mathematics that will accommodate problems of different complexity and resolution with different detail. It has three different levels of problems complexity: beginners, intermediate and advanced. On the other hand each problem has two levels of explanations/resolutions: detailed and concise.

In this way, all students are accommodated in a learning environment centered in the student. The low-achieving students that may struggle to learn the materials covered in class, can study and repeat the materials as many times as they want. Students will have access to complex problems and activities that may provide additional stimulation for top performer students. Teachers will also be more confident to give homework activities to their students, to help struggling or underachieving students to learn the material covered in class, ensuring that the material is stored in students' long-term memory, or providing additional stimulation to high performers. But homework can be particularly burdensome for disadvantaged students. Their parents' may not have the skills to help them, and they may not have the resources to support them on private lessons. We aim at providing the same support for all the students so that we can contribute to improve the relationship between students' socio-economic background and mathematics performance.

## 3   eBook Authoring Tools

There are several ecosystems and tools that can be used to create ebooks and distribute them for personal computers and mobile devices. The simplest way to create digital books, for multiple mobile platforms, is to start with PDF or RTF files and use applications, like Calibre, that converts PDF files in multiple formats such as EPUB, or MOBI for the Kindle, among others. Calibre is a free application that runs on Windows, Mac OS X and Linux.

There are other free or open applications that support the creation of electronic books. For example, the application eCub allows the creation of simple books in EPUB or MobiPocket, from text files or XHTML. However, eCub is very limited, with no

WYSIWYG capabilities. It is suitable for the production of simple ebooks with front and back pages with an image, index, a title page and it can convert content to a sound file (WAV or MP3). The eCub is free and is available for Windows, Mac OS X, Linux, FreeBSD and Solaris.

Booktype is an open platform, available since 2012, which allows editing and writing of ebooks for different platforms by exporting in PDF, EPUB, MOBI, ODT and HTML. This application also exports the ebook directly to Amazon, Barnes & Noble and iBook-store online stores, as well as to online printing sites. Digital books written with this application are immediately available in any of these platforms. When writing the ebook, the author does not need to worry about formatting, since it will automatically be formatted to work in these different platforms. Booktype also provides a set of collaborative tools for reviewers, editors, translators, designers, and authors, enabling the different participants to work collaborative in the production of an ebook. Some of the features offered by this platform include: intuitive drag-and-drop tools, chat, messages, adding images and text formatting. Booktype also maintains a history of all changes, which allows the author to compare different editions and return to a previous edition. It is even possible to use snippets (pieces of computer code). One of the disadvantages of this platform is the need for installing on a server and accessing via web browser, which requires some additional expertise.

The Firedocs eLML editor can also be used to create ebooks [4]. The eLML framework (eLesson Markup Language) is an XML platform for creating online classes using XML. It exports produced materials in SCORM, HTML, PDF and EPUB format. The main objective is to ensure that classes are modeled according to the ECLASS reference, which defines five distinct sections: Entry, Clarify, Look, Act, Self-assess, Summary. Current implementation only supports JPG, PNG, GIF and SVG images. It does not allow Java scripts and forms, so some of the functionalities as the glossary, references to labels and self-assessment tests are not available in the EPUB format.

Sigil is an open WYSIWYG editor used by Google to create ebooks following the EPUB3 specification for Windows, OS X and Linux. This application imports, creates and edits XHTML documents and exports them into EPUB3 documents. Ebooks created with Sigil may contain text, pictures and links, video or sound. It also provides multiple views of the work: book, code and a split mode. In the book view, it allows content edition in WYSIWYG mode.

Finally, we should mention the electronic books created in the iBook format from Apple. These ebooks are created with a free application - the iBooks Author tool. The format is proprietary, although based on the EPUB standard specification, with some differences in the CSS3 tags. This tool makes the process of creating ebooks very easy, by presenting a very complete set of integrated features, including: sound, image, video, dictionary, text underline, annotations, text-to-speech conversion, navigation and many widgets to enhance the interactive experience. The introduction of widgets in the iBook is an enriching experience for readers of an electronic book. iBook Author offers seven types of pre-defined widgets: (1) photo gallery, (2) video or audio media file, (3) review questions, (4) slide show; (5) interactive tagged images, to give detailed information on specific parts of an image or graph, (6) 3D models, and (7) objects created in HTML. The ease of creating widgets allows users to add any object to an interactive iBook, and there are many possibilities, from calculators, puzzles, maps, YouTube videos, among many others.

## 4   Design and Development of an eBook for Math Teaching

This section presents an eBook that students can use to study in or outside the classroom with the produced materials in an accessible and organized way.

In this way, teachers can extend the class into a virtual class in a form of blended learning in which students can solve and visualize video lectures and home works outside the classroom. This is especially interesting for learning mathematics. If students can learn at home from watching video lectures and solving problems, time in-class can be dedicated to explore more motivating problem solving. Math teachers have a difficult situation. Studying math is many times a cumbersome task. But this can be changed if the teacher takes advantage of the technology that is currently available. Students are surrounded by multiple devices, such as smartphones and tablets, which give them access to multiple media that is easily available. This is an opportunity for the teacher. The technology related to teaching/learning will have a vital role in the coming years in the education field.

We decided to use the EPUB3 format and the SIGIL platform.

EPUB is a format based on open specifications, primarily written in XML and XHTML. The EPUB format is supported by a wide range of devices and platforms, including Android devices, Nook, iPhone, iPad, iPod, MobiPocket, Adobe Digital Editions, FBReader, Stanza, Sony Reader, and many other readers and applications. The newest specification EPUB3 allows the creation of ebooks with sound, images and video. This specification introduces innovative features to address structure limitations, such as: precise layouts specialized for comic books, support for MathML, support for multimedia, and introduction of notes. In this way, the EPUB3 has the advantage that runs in both iOS and Android platforms and it is possible to make appealing layouts like those of the iBooks, which runs only in the iOS.

We choose Sigil because it runs in both Mac and Windows platforms, it is free and it has an intuitive interface, making it easy for teachers to create the eBooks for the students with the problems and video resolutions.

Figure 1 shows the layout of the cover and the index, which is generated automatically from the eBook content. This design while simple is effective since it is very easy to navigate in the eBook. The student can look form problems of a given chapter or look in the solution section for the video resolutions of those problems.

Figure 2 shows mathematic problems that the teacher prepared for students. These exercises are organized according to the math curriculum, in this case for the 10th grade, in chapters and sections.

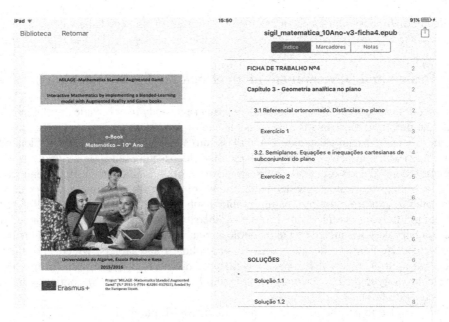

**Fig. 1.** eBook front page and index for the learning of mathematics

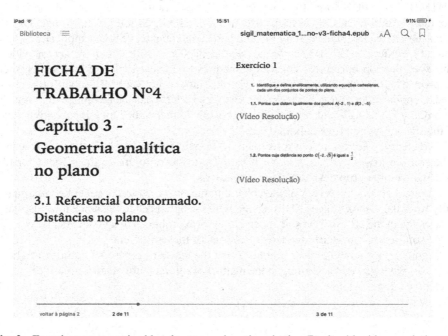

**Fig. 2.** Exercises are organized by chapters and sections in the eBook with video resolution of the mathematical problem

The use of videos for teaching and learning is effective for both visual and auditory learners as there is video and narration that is less complicated than written explanations [5]. Video recording is well suited for demonstrating basic concepts and problem solving. It allows students to learn at their own pace and in their own learning style. Video lectures are well adapted for classes with students who have different levels of knowledge of the subject. There are students that can view the materials once and have a good understanding of the subject. Other students can view the videos several times to better understand the subject. This is an advantage over the traditional classroom where many times the students do not understand and do not ask to repeat the subject until they are able to understand.

With the number of students increasing in the class this is an important tool to enable students to work at home and leave classroom time to implement problem based learning methodologies together with virtual learning classrooms.

Figure 3 shows the integration of the video resolutions of problems in the eBook. Students can see the videos after solving one problem using the link that is available together with the problem (Fig. 2) or going directly to the Solutions section from the Index (Fig. 1).

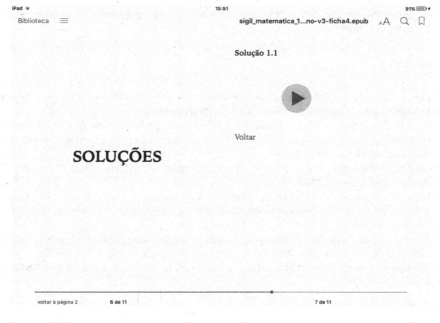

**Fig. 3.** Video resolutions of problems are available in the section *Solutions* of the eBook

In this way, students can easily navigate in the eBook and teachers can put together all the problems that they prepare for them.

# 5 Conclusions

In this paper we present the development of an interactive eBook to make available mathematic problems and the videos of their resolution, enabling the expansion of the classroom into a virtual space where students can have more time for practicing problem solving. This is possible because most students have a smartphone or a tablet and teachers should take advantage of these resources in the teaching and learning.

By using today's flexible, interactive and mobile technologies with the appropriate pedagogies, we believe it is possible to have students more motivated in maths, and expect a more creative response to the world problems that surround them. Moreover, information technology today has intuitive interfaces, is simple to use and is effective in the results. This is also an opportunity for teachers to produce content that is personalized and has high motivational impact on students. Producing an eBook with materials used and prepared by the teacher is one such opportunity. We also believe that technology is accessible and easy to use by math teachers and students, and much more can be improved with further work done in the field.

**Acknowledgments.** We would like to thank the support from Project "MILAGE -MathematIcs bLended Augmented GamE" (Ref. 2015-1-PT01-KA201-012921), Erasmus + program, funded by the European Union.

# References

1. European Commission. The changing pedagogical landscape (2015). http://bookshop.europa.eu/en/the-changing-pedagogical-landscape-pbNC0415435/ (Retrieved)
2. European Commission. Report to the European Commission on New modes of learning and teaching in higher education (2014). http://ec.europa.eu/education/library/reports/modernisation_en.pdf (Retrieved)
3. Heide, A., Stilborne, L.: Guia do Professor para a Internet - Completo e fácil. Porto Alegre – Brasil, Artmed Editora (2000)
4. Weibel, R., Bleisch, S., Nebiker, S., Fisler, J., Grossmann, T., Niederhuber, M., Collet, C., Hurni, L.: Achieving more sustainable elearning programs for GIScience. Geomatica **63**, 109–118 (2009)
5. Spilka, R., Manenova, M.: Screencasts as web-based learning method for math students on upper primary school. In: WSEAS Conference Proceedings, 4th European Conference of Computer Science, World Scientific and Engineering Academy and Society (WSEAS), pp. 246–250 (2013)

# Learning Programming and Electronics
# with Augmented Reality

Mauro Figueiredo[1](✉), Maria-Ángeles Cifredo-Chacón[2],
and Vítor Gonçalves[3]

[1] Algarve University, ISE, CIMA, CIAC, Faro, Portugal
mfiguei@ualg.pt
[2] Cádiz University, Cádiz, Spain
mangeles.cifredo@uca.es
[3] S. Brás Secondary School, São Brás de Alportel, Portugal
vitor.goncalves@aejbv.pt

**Abstract.** Digital native generations have been technology consumers all their life. Our children should be educated to be capable to contribute, as active producers, to the digital framework with a maturity and critical attitude. To do that children should learn to program from very early stage at school and combine this with electronics can be the right way to motivate them to develop skills such as reasoning, problems resolution, logic, creativity, perseverance and team work. This paper describes the development of an augmented reality book that can be used by children to learn programming and electronics. Students alone, in groups, at home or in the classroom can use mobile devices (smartphones or tablets) and augmented reality to help them in the electronics assembly. We believe that the use of augmented reality will change significantly the teaching activities by enabling the addition of supplementary information that is seen on a mobile device.

**Keywords:** Learning programming · Learning electronics · m-learning · Augmented reality · Mobile devices

## 1 Introduction

It is expected by 2020 about 1 million more jobs requiring coding knowledge, however only 5 %−10 % of schools in the United States offer Computer Science programs [1].

In 2013 Hadi Partovi founded the education non-profit Code.org to bring awareness of the value of including computer science in the core curriculum in every school, as other science, technology, engineering, and mathematics (STEM) courses, such as biology, physics, chemistry and algebra [2].

In 2013, Code.org organized the Computer Science Education Week and the first "Hour of Code" reached over 15 million students and over 35,000 events across 167 countries. In January of 2016, the Hour of Code reached 200 million students making it the largest education campaign ever [3].

Code.org foundation made a great contribution for a revolution in which coding is no longer for the anti-social nerds but for the cool kids.

M. Antona and C. Stephanidis (Eds.): UAHCI 2016, Part III, LNCS 9739, pp. 57–64, 2016.
DOI: 10.1007/978-3-319-40238-3_6

We believe that this is an opportunity to go further to teach programming and electronics together to students. Programming and electronics is the right combination where they can develop programming skills and at the same time they can apply to life applications. We think that we should go beyond developing programming skills. Students should also learn electronics. A review into the labor market shows that most jobs offered are related to technology, and there is a business boom with electronics in general. Electronics applies to every sector of our daily lives. However, electronics is also often ignored in the school's curriculum.

One of the cheapest solutions to teach electronics is the Arduino open-hardware. However, mostly teachers with an electronic background dare to make use of the Arduino. The main reason is because programming a microcontroller, for some, is a difficult task [4].

This paper presents the design and implementation of a novel augmented reality book that can be used in the classroom or at home by students to learn programming and electronics. This book combines the description of activities for Arduino and its programming with videos shown with an augmented reality application to help students in the assembly of electronic circuits and its programming. In this way, with this augmented reality books can learn programming and electronics effectively and autonosmously.

## 2   Learning Electronics

Today we live in an amazingly high-tech world, surrounded by electronic gadgets that everyone – engineers, educators, entrepreneurs, students, and artists alike – can benefit from learning more about them. Building circuits and making programs for them can be fun and a way to promote computational thinking and strengthen physics, math or technology subjects.

Today's circuits are built around an electronic component called microprocessor, which is complex and very powerful. The microprocessor controls all the remaining parts and decides different actions based in the information gathered around. To achieve this behavioral, one needs to follow instructions that are programmed into it. The electronic circuit can receive input from the world by connecting to electronic devices called sensors. Electronic circuits can also control different actions such as movement, turn on light, and many other by the use of electronic parts called actuators.

We are designing a book with introductory lessons, that we consider suitable for middle-school students. The lessons explain basics of electricity, electronic devices and circuits, by means of hand-on activities. The computational thinking is reinforced with an introduction to computer programming by interacting between the electronic devices and the processor.

The equipment needed to do the proposed activities is cheap: batteries of different voltage, different value resistors, LEDs, potentiometers, a breadboard and a low-cost microcontroller-based board called Arduino UNO. The software used to program the microcontroller are Arduino IDE and Scratch for Arduino [5], which are free to download.

In our opinion, there are several unavoidable ideas about Electronics to learn. This book focuses on basic principles of Electricity and Electronics and it explains the following ideas:

- Voltage: what it is and its units, volts.
- Current: what it is and its units, amperes and its submultiples, miliamperes, etc.
- Resistance: what it is and its units, ohms.
- The relationship between the previous magnitudes, Ohm's law.
- The first approach is to the introduction of several electronic components:
- The battery, the electric power to feed the circuit
- A first actuator, the electronic component named LED (Light-emitting diode)
- A first sensor, the potentiometer as a position sensor.

We would like to emphasize that these concepts are found out by students when they assembly the proposed circuits. Each student or pair of students should have a kit of components. The students are suggested to assembly the same circuit with different value parts in order to watch how the circuit works in a different way. For instance, in a circuit with a battery, a resistor and a LED, the last one, shines more or less depending on the current through it. Moreover, that current can be modified changing the resistor in the circuit. They will find out too that, by changing the batteries, the same effect, by the Ohm's Law, can be observed.

## 3 Learning Programming

A common myth is that kids are not capable of learning how to code. We believe that students can learn programming by the assembly of electronic circuits.

The Arduino microprocessor is capable of processing the information gathered by sensors and give orders to actuators. These actions have to be programmed by means of a programming language. Therefore, by programming a microprocessor like Arduino enables students to develop computer-programming skills.

In the past, teaching computer programming was a very hard task. Making syntax errors was easy regarding text-oriented programming languages and this can be discouraging, particularly when you are a middle-school student. Another drawback of computer programming learning is to understand the control structures.

In the eighties, there was an initiative to make children acquire programming skills. It was the Logo language [6]. A small turtle could be moved with very simple instructions in Logo language.

Mitchel Resnick, founder of Scratch, showed that computer programming can be optimized for children [1]. Scratch is one of many programs enabling kids to code through a simpler and more child-friendly experience. Scratch replaces complex coding syntax with simple coding building blocks, making it easy for kids to learn through playing and building games. The true value in teaching kids to code is not in the syntax but in the way it teaches kids to think using a step-by-step logical flow to solve problems and build projects.

Nowadays, there is a boom of graphical-oriented programming language, but most of them are based in Scratch. These languages facilitate teaching of computer programing and foster the computational thinking among the children.

By using Scratch for Arduino, which is a visual language, teachers can take advantage of this trend to motivate middle-school students on how to make and program electronic circuits in an easy way. We explore this language to solve the hands-on activities in the book. The microcontroller in Arduino reads the sensors and writes the actuators with the code created by the students with S4A. Nevertheless, taking in account, that more powerful performance, can be accomplished with a text-oriented programming language, the book proposes to do the hands-on activities with S4A and later compares it with a solution in text-oriented programming language, the Arduino language, which is similar to the C language.

We are convinced that middle-school students will better understand the programming control structures by means of graphical environments. Later, it will be easier to explain the syntax in other textual languages. When the students program the microcontroller they come to realize how the electronic circuit should act and how simple and well defined the instructions should be. In that way, programing Arduino will be promoting computational thinking.

## 4 Augmented Reality

Augmented Reality (AR) applications combine virtual objects with a 3-D real environment in real time [7, 8]. Virtual and real objects appear together in a real time system in a way that the user sees the real world and the virtual objects superimposed with the real objects. The user's perception of the real world is enhanced and the user interacts in a more natural way. Virtual objects can be used to display additional information about the real world that is not directly perceived.

In general, augmented reality applications fall in two categories: geo-base and computer vision based.

Geo-based applications use the mobile's GPS, accelerometer, gyroscope, and other technology to determine the location, heading, and direction of the mobile device. The user can see 3D objects that are superimposed to the world in the direction he is looking at. However, this technology has some problems. The major problem is imprecise location, which makes difficult for example the creation of photo overlays.

Computer vision based applications use image recognition capabilities to recognize images and overlay information on top of this image. These can be based on markers, such as QR (Quick Response), Microsoft tags or LLA (latitude/longitude/altitude), or marker less that recognize an image that triggers the overlay data.

There are currently many augmented reality applications and development systems for Android and iOS (iPhone Operating System) smartphones and tablets.

The most popular ones are: Wikitude [9], Layar [10], Metaio [11], Aurasma [12] and Augment [13].

Wikitude delivers the Wikitude World Browser for free, which is an augmented reality web browser application, and the Wikitude SDK (software development kit) for developers, which is free for educational projects and the educational version of the wikitude SDK always displays a splash screen and the wikitude logo. The wikitude browser presents users with data about their points of interest, which can be the surroundings, nearby landmarks or target images, and overlays information on the real-time camera view of a mobile device. Augmented reality learning activities can be realized with the wikitude SDK. The wikitude SDK can be used to display a simple radar that shows radar-points related to the location based objects. It is also possible to recognize target images and superimpose 2D or 3D information on top of them. The developer can also combines image recognition and geo-base augmented reality. However, the building of these capabilities using the wikitude SDK requires programming knowledge.

Layar has the Layar App, an augmented reality web browser, and the Layar Creator, which is a tool for creating interactive printing documents. With the Layar Creator it is very easy to make an interactive document for a teaching activity. There is no need to do any programming and, in this way, it does not require any developers with programming skills. The teacher can easily upload the trigger page to which he wants to associate augmented information. Marker less image recognition techniques are used and with the Layar Creator interface, the teacher can easily associate a video, for example. Later, with the Layar App, the student can view, on the display of his mobile device, the overlaid information associated to the page. These applications are both free. However, every trigger image published within the Layar's publishing environment is paid. For this reason, it is not affordable for developing interactive printing documents for teaching. Geo-location based augmented reality information is free of charge.

Metaio delivers the junaio, metaio Creator and a development SDK. Junaio is the metaio's free augmented reality browser and is free. The metaio Creator is an augmented reality tool to create and publish augmented reality scenarios and experiences within minutes. With the metaio Creator the teacher can connect 3-D content, videos, audio, and webpages to any form of printed medium or 3D map (object-based or environment-based). Nonetheless, this tool is paid. If a user wants to develop augmented reality applications for iOS or Android, the developer can use the metaio SDK. However, this development SDK is also paid.

Aurasma delivers the Aurasma App and the Aurasma Studio. The Aurasma App is available for Android and iOS and uses advanced image recognition techniques to augment the real world with interactive content such as videos, 3D objects or animations associated to trigger images or geo-based information. The Aurasma Studio is an online platform that lets the teachers create and publish their own augmented reality information in an intuitive and user-friendly environment. It is not required any programming knowledge and very teacher can upload trigger images that can be associated to videos, images, 3D objects or other information.

Augment is another application for Android and iOS that uses augmented reality to visualize 3D models triggered by QR codes. After registering at the augment website, the teacher can upload a 3D model that is triggered by a QR code.

## 5  Augmented Reality Book for Teaching Programming and Electronics

With a greater number of students in the classroom, reaching many times thirty students, it is a difficult task for the teacher to guide many students in the classroom to assembly the circuits in a right way. The suggested activities are not risky or life threatening. The maximum voltage used is 9 V. However, students can damage the microprocessor or components. To avoid damages, each student will be guided individually throughout the activities using an Augmented Reality application running in a mobile device, like a smartphone or a tablet. Students can work autonomously in the classroom and the teacher does not need to, continuously, check every circuit while they are assembling it. Students follow directions presented by augmented reality and teachers check and solve some minor problems that might happen.

Time in class is also reducing in schools and teachers lack time to dedicate to teach technology subjects. Using augmented reality and videos explaining the assembly procedure is time effectively so that the time needed to learn the introductory ideas about Electronics and Programming Computers is reduced, and more time can be dedicated into building circuits and programming them.

Students are guided throughout the hand-on activities by means of the augmented reality book and the teacher will be available to solve questions. He does not spend time explaining one-by-one on how to assembly each circuit. The student will learn the basics of electronics and computer programming by doing and will have time to assembly circuits and learn to do it autonomously. The availability of this augmented reality book gives students the possibility to assembly circuits and program them outside the classroom.

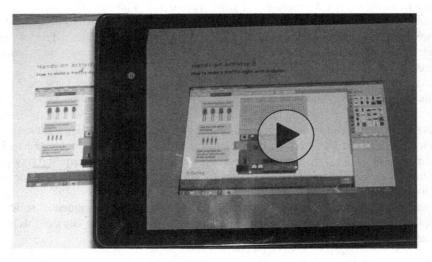

**Fig. 1.** The video is triggered and displays in the mobile device (smartphone or tablet) the circuit assembly with the augmented reality app.

Teaching electronics and programming with the help of an augmented reality book has several advantages. Each student is guided individually to assembly and program electronic circuits. The teacher can dedicate more time to solve questions.

As described in the previous section, there are currently many augmented reality applications and development systems for Android and iOS (iPhone Operating System) smartphones and tablets. However, we decided to build an augmented reality application because (i) we want to integrate gamification concepts in the process of learning and (ii) we want students to use the application independently of the Internet. Applications commonly available require access to the Internet. Figure 1 presents the use of the developed augmented reality application to show the video that helps students in the assembly of a circuit.

Figure 1 shows the image that will be found by the students in the "Hands-on" activities. With their smartphones or tablets, students point the smartphone or tablet to the augmented reality book page to play a video about how to assembly the circuit and how to program it.

## 6 Conclusions and Future Work

This paper presents an augmented reality book that middle school students can use to learn programming and electronic skills.

We believe that electronics and programming can be learned together and students will benefit. In present time and in the future, most jobs will require these abilities.

We think that using Arduino open hardware platform is accessible and, combined with a visual programming tool like Scratch for Arduino, is also motivating for students.

It is shown in this paper one way to teach these subjects by means of hands-on activities guided by an augmented reality book. The help offered by AR allows students to assembly a large number of electronic circuits and programming the Arduino platform. This is the perfect combination for students to learn electronics and programming.

## References

1. Los Angeles Times, Want to prepare kids for the future? Teach them to code (2014). http://articles.latimes.com/2014/apr/07/news/la-ol-teach-students-code-computer-science-20140406. Accessed 25 Jan 2016
2. CSEd Week: About (2016). https://csedweek.org/about. Accessed 25 Jan 2016
3. Code.org. https://code.org
4. Gupta, N., Tejovanth N., Murthy, P.: Learning by creating: interative programming for indian high schools. In: IEEE International Conference on Technology Enhanced Education (ICTEE), pp. 1–3 (2012)
5. Scratch for Arduino. http://s4a.cat
6. Logo language (2016). https://en.wikipedia.org/wiki/Logo_(programming_language)

7. Milgram, P., Kishino, F.: A taxonomy of mixed reality visual displays. IEICE Trans. Inf. Syst. **E77-D**(12), 1321–1329 (1994)
8. Azuma, R.T.: A survey of augmented reality. Presence: Teleoperators Virtual Environ. **6**(4), 355–385 (1997)
9. Wikitude. http://www.wikitude.com/
10. Layar. https://www.layar.com/
11. Metaio. https://www.metaio.com/
12. Aurasma. https://www.aurasma.com/
13. Augment. http://www.augment.com/

# Voice Recognition System to Support Learning Platforms Oriented to People with Visual Disabilities

Ruben Gonzalez[✉], Johnnathan Muñoz, Julián Salazar, and Néstor Duque

Universidad Nacional de Colombia, Manizales, Colombia
{rdgonzalezb,johmunozmor,jnsalazarv,ndduqueme}@unal.edu.co

**Abstract.** The use of a speech recognition system allows access to an simple and efficient interaction, among others, for people with disabilities. In this article, an automatic speech recognition system is presented. It was developed as a system that allows an easy adaptation to different platforms. The model is described with clarity and detail looking for reproducibility by researchers who wish to resume and advance in this field. The model is divided into four stages: acquisition of the data, preprocessing, feature extraction and pattern recognition. Information concerning the functionality of the system is presented in the section named experiments and results. Finally, conclusions are set and a future work is proposed, in order to improve the efficiency and quality of the system.

**Keywords:** Voice command recognition · Mel Frequency Cepstral Coefficients · Assistive technology · Universal access to education

## 1 Introduction

As one of the most natural and comfortable modes of human interaction, speech could be considered an ideal medium for human computer interaction. A simple solution of this problem would be possible if machine could mimic the human production and understand of speech. One of the most promising applications of speech technology is spoken dialogue system, which offers the interface for simple, direct and hand free access to information [1]. This issue is particularly important if the user has a disability that prevents the standard interaction with the system.

However, Automatic Speech Recognition (ASR) is not a trivial problem [2]. The differences between speaker's speech, noise levels, variations in the speed of pronunciation and mood of the user, generate errors that affect the recognition task and produce very low success rates. In that sense, most of the current systems are restricted to controlled environments, uses limited to a small group of people or special requirements related to the microphone's positioning, resulting in unnatural interfaces [3].

Several methods for ASR have been proposed [3–5]. The most robust are based on Hidden Markov Models (HMM) [6]. Although currently these systems have achieved a high level of accuracy, many of them have still not succeeded in solving the problem of high computational cost. Moreover, most of them are presented as commercial software with high prices that prevent access to these solutions. Also, due to copyright, it

© Springer International Publishing Switzerland 2016
M. Antona and C. Stephanidis (Eds.): UAHCI 2016, Part III, LNCS 9739, pp. 65–72, 2016.
DOI: 10.1007/978-3-319-40238-3_7

is not possible to access to the source code, even if the objective is purely scientific, e.g., to implement improvements or couple such systems with new platforms.

There is thus a need to design an ASR system as own development, oriented to eliminate the limitations presented above, i.e., a simple system (low computational cost), accessible, reliable and suited to the requirements of any platform.

## 2   State of the Art

A systematic review of the state of the art for ASR systems was performed, using a tool named Tree of Science (TOS)[1], developed at the Universidad Nacional de Colombia. In this way, it was possible to take a look at the articles that have most influenced the progresses made by the scientific community in order to achieve improvements in terms of accessibility, accuracy and efficiency of ASR systems. In the first speech processing researches, it was used the Short Term Spectral Amplitude (STSA), using the minimum mean square error estimator (MMSE) [7]. By then, this algorithm was quite complex but offered greater accuracy compared to others. Later, the use of more robust methods based on Hidden Markov Models (HMM) began to grow. This technique uses the Mel-frequency Cepstral Coefficients (MFCC) during the stage of feature extraction [6]. Until today the HMM remain as an important approach for continuous speech recognition systems with large vocabulary, due to the good results that it produces. Moreover, other articles mentions a method known as PARADE (Periodic Component to Aperiodic Component Ratio-based Activity Detection), accompanied by a method of feature extraction called SPADE (Subband based Periodicity and aperiodicity Decomposition), which achieves significantly greater accuracy with regard to the final choice of the words [8]. In [9] it is used the Dynamic Time Warping algorithm (DTW), which is currently one of the most extensively used algorithms for not very complex systems because of the advantages that it offers in terms of the computational cost. However, the disadvantage of this method is that it is restricted to small vocabularies. Current research is focus on achieving the correct recognition of speech and also seeks to create and implement tools able to segment words, that is, identify the beginning and end of each word to reduce the complexity of processing required with continuous speech recognition [10].

## 3   Proposed Model

A system that allows identifying a given number of voice commands and which can be coupled, among many systems, with virtual learning tools is proposed. The possibility to interact with applications via voice can become a tool for inclusion, especially if that possibility has certain features such as ease of access and interaction by the end user and developers.

The proposed model can be extended for interaction with many applications, but it was conceived with the interest of providing the possibilities to interact with digital

---

[1]  http://tos.manizales.unal.edu.co/.

learning resources to people with physical and sensory disabilities. Even though it already exist several tools like JAWS[2], the group decided to design an experimental tool that could be more easily coupled to other developments for diverse needs. In particular, it was incorporated to a framework named GAIATools, which is oriented to the construction of Accessible Learning Objects for inclusion of people with visual disabilities. The authoring tools that comprise GAIATools in its initial version are: dictionary, text editor and reader, game for learning and assessment through questionnaires. In addition, it guides the designer to develop learning objects and the visually impaired users to interact with them effectively in the context of educational activities [11].

Considering the context of developing countries, where socio-economic limitations are more evident, tools such as the proposed here are of particular importance. The motivation to target the audio recognition system primarily as a complement to educational tools born of the certainty that education is a fundamental way to overcome the above mentioned socio-economic problems.

Currently, the system is able to recognize ten isolated words in low noise environments. However, it is possible to increase the database by a simple process. The intention with this is that the system becomes adjustable to the particular needs of each user, who previously must record every new word. It is important to note that in its original design, the system recognizes words in Spanish, but there is no impediment if someone requires to enter a new command in another language to the database.

The proposed system is divided into four stages, as shown in Fig. 1. The first stage consists of the acquisition of the audio signal that contains the information that should be recognized. Subsequently, a preprocessing stage is executed, where the signal is filtered to eliminate noise and its unwanted segments, such as the silence at the beginning and end of the recording. Follows the stage of features extraction, where a matrix that contains the Mel Frequency Cepstral Coefficients (MFCC) is calculated. Finally, the system executes an algorithm to calculate a Euclidean distance that compares the features matrix entered related to the corresponding patterns stored in the database, this way making a decision that completes the process of recognition.

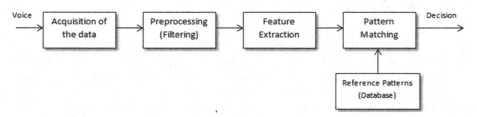

**Fig. 1.** Architecture of the proposed model

---

[2] http://www.freedomscientific.com/Products/Blindness/JAWS.

## 3.1 Audio Acquisition

During this stage, the user pronounces the word that is expected to be recognized. The system records a vector of t *Fs audio samples, where t is the time of recording and Fs is the sampling **frequency**; for this case 2 s and 44100 Hz, respectively. The sound is mono, i.e., only one audio channel is recorded.

## 3.2 Preprocessing

The preprocessing stage is divided, in turn, in three steps: filtering, normalization and silence suppression.

The implemented filter is the result of performing a process of spectral analysis on several audio recordings, where common noise frequencies in various environments (office, outdoor, home, etc.) were identified. Subsequently, a general frequency range where is expected to find useful information was established. Thus, the filter that provided the best results was a Hamming windowing FIR filter, band pass type, with sampling frequency of 44100 Hz and cutoff frequencies of 200 Hz and 8000 Hz.

Once the signal was filtered, it was normalized in order to limit it to standard values (between 0 and one) and thereby facilitate the development of the following steps. Normalization is especially important considering that the intention is to compare several audio samples that could possibly have different amplitude ranges, due to variables which control is difficult, such as the intensity of the speaker's voice or noise levels.

Finally, for silence detection and suppression, the signal is segmented and the energy of each segment is calculated. The value obtained must exceed a threshold to be considered as useful information, otherwise it will be deleted. The energy threshold was defined by comparing the noise energy values with the values obtained from randomly pronounced words. This is done in order to reduce the computational cost of the algorithm, which otherwise would have to consider signal segments that do not provide relevant information and instead may hinder the process of recognition.

## 3.3 Feature Extraction

The features used to represent each of the commands are the MFCC. According to the review of the state of the art, using these coefficients in an ASR system, it is possible to achieve an appropriate level of accuracy with low computational cost. The MFCC are a set of decorrelated parameters of the discrete cosine transform which are computed through a transformation of the logarithmically compressed filter-output energies, derived through a perceptually spaced triangular filter bank that processes the Discrete Fourier Transformed of the audio signal [12].

The MFCC were calculated as follows: the audio signal was segmented into intervals of 1024 samples length. The increase for segmentation is of 410 samples, which means that there is an overlap between the segments in order to avoid information lost when performing a windowing (through window Hamming in the time domain), considering that with this process the beginning and end of each segment will be attenuated. For each one of the segments 14 MFCC coefficients were calculated (excluding the 0th coefficient). To perform this procedure 30 filters were used in the filter bank, with 0 as the low end of the lowest filter and 0.1815 as the high end of the highest filter. Once the MFCC are calculated, matrix of size NXC is stored, where N is the number of segments in which the audio signal was divided and C is the number of MFCC calculated, which are 14 for this case, as already mentioned. The number of rows of the matrices of features is not a constant because after performing the silence suppression in the recorded signals, the length of these may be different from the others. The parameters used for calculating the MFCC coefficients were selected according to the results obtained through several test, as the one described in the next section.

For each command that the system is able to recognize, it is necessary to calculate a matrix of features that will be stored as a "pattern matrix", and that represent the class of the command. Additionally, each time that a new recording is entered in order to execute the recognition; the system calculates a new matrix of features that will be known as "new matrix".

### 3.4 Decision Stage

The aim at this stage is to assign the entered matrix within a specific, in order to identify to which command corresponds the recording. This is accomplished by comparing the new matrix with the pattern matrices, looking for the best match among them.

To make the comparison between matrices, we must remember that each row represents a segment of the audio signal in terms of the MFCC coefficients. Therefore, to compare each row of the new matrix with the rows of the pattern matrix will be the same as comparing each segment of the new recording with the segments of the pattern recordings. However, there is no guarantee that the two recordings will match in terms of time of pronunciation, leading to compare different audible segments of the same word. In order to solve this problem, an individual error is calculated, represented by a Euclidean distance, between one row of the new matrix and each one of the rows of the pattern matrix. Later the least of these individual errors is taken and this value is assigned as the contribution of the row being analyzed to the total error. This process is repeated for each of the rows of the new matrix. At the end, there will be as many total errors as classes are taken and by identifying the least of them, it will be possible to know which command was pronounced in the entered recording. Although this process may seem complex, the operations are performed through algebraic arrangements rather than iterations, which reduce greatly the computational cost.

Finally, it has been established that the selected value as the minimum of the total error must be under a certain threshold; otherwise the user is requested to repeat the command more clearly in order to have an adequate level of reliability.

## 4 Experiments and Results

In order to test the performance of the implemented model, a test, which counted with the participation of 30 users, was designed. Since it was desired that the voices considered during the test were as dissimilar as possible, the participants were men and women of various ages. The experiment, which was developed within moderate noise environments (study rooms, bedrooms, etc.), was divided into two parts: the first was the creation of a database with the voice of the participants and the second was the validation of the system.

The database was created trying that the recorded word was spoken out clearly and naturally. After performing this process, the participants were asked to repeat four times each of the following words in Spanish: open, back, enter, right, left, save, home, help, view, and internet; that is, for this stage 40 recordings were obtained for each user. In each attempt it was checked if the system was able to recognize the word or not. The detailed results of these tests can be seen in Table 1.

**Table 1.** Results of the test

| User | Number of hits | Percentage |
|------|----------------|------------|
| 1 | 36 | 90 % |
| 2 | 39 | 97.5 % |
| 3 | 34 | 85 % |
| 4 | 36 | 90 % |
| 5 | 34 | 85 % |
| 6 | 36 | 90 % |
| 7 | 36 | 90 % |
| 8 | 40 | 100 % |
| 9 | 34 | 85 % |
| 10 | 32 | 80 % |
| 11 | 32 | 80 % |
| 12 | 34 | 85 % |
| 13 | 39 | 97.5 % |
| 14 | 39 | 97.5 % |
| 15 | 34 | 85 % |
| 16 | 39 | 97.5 % |
| 17 | 38 | 95 % |
| 18 | 32 | 80 % |
| 19 | 32 | 80 % |
| 20 | 32 | 80 % |
| 21 | 27 | 67.5 % |
| 22 | 26 | 65 % |
| 23 | 36 | 90 % |
| 24 | 28 | 70 % |
| 25 | 36 | 90 % |
| 26 | 34 | 85 % |
| 27 | 39 | 97.5 % |
| 28 | 34 | 85 % |
| 29 | 33 | 82.5 % |
| 30 | 38 | 95 % |

# 5    Conclusions

An ASR system has been proposed as a tool to complement the development of educational platforms, in order to make these affordable, among others, for people with visual disabilities. Although levels of recognition accuracy achieved are promising, the system does not reach levels as high as other commercial systems. However, the proposed model has a low computational cost, can be easily coupled with other platforms, allows the developer to make changes through a simple process and can be adapted to the particular needs of any user, allows for including new words in its database with a single recording.

As future work, the authors plan to consider other characterization methods such as autoregressive coefficients or strategies of classification as the Hidden Markov Models (HMM), in order to achieve continuous speech recognition, making even easier the interaction with applications. In addition, it is desirable to improve the preprocessing stage through the implementation of more efficient filters, this way achieving greater robustness in the system, eliminating the problems caused by differences in tone, pronunciation or noise. Finally, it is important to achieve the generalization of the system, in a way that it can be able to recognize any user without the need for prior registration of his voice.

**Acknowledgments.** The research presented in this paper was partially funded by the COLCIENCIAS project entitled: "RAIM: Implementación de un framework apoyado en tecnologías móviles y de realidad aumentada para entornos educativos ubicuos, adaptativos, accesibles e interactivos para todos (Implementation of a framework supported by mobile technologies and augmented reality for ubiquitous, adaptive, accessible and interactive learning environments for all)" of the Universidad Nacional de Colombia, with code 1119-569-34172.

# References

1. Aggarwal, R.K., Dave, M.: Recent trends in speech recognition systems. In: Tiwary, U., Siddiqui, T. (eds.) Speech, Image, and Language Processing for Human Computer Interaction: Multi-modal Advancements, pp. 101–127 (2012)
2. Rosdi, F., Ainon, R.N.: Isolated Malay speech recognition using Hidden Markov Models. In: International Conference on Computer and Communication Engineering, 2008. ICCCE 2008, pp.721–725, 13–15 May 2008
3. Bedoya, W.A., Munoz, L.D.: Methodology for voice commands recognition using stochastic classifiers. In: 2012 XVII Symposium of Image, Signal Processing, and Artificial Vision (STSIVA), pp. 66–71, 12–14 Sept. 2012
4. Ibarra, J.P., Guerrero, H.B.: Identificación de comandos de voz utilizando LPC y algoritmos genéticos en Matlab. Rev. CINTEX **15**, 36–48 (2014)
5. Abushariah, A.A.M.; Gunawan, T.S.; Khalifa, O.O., Abushariah, M.A.M.: English digits speech recognition system based on Hidden Markov Models. In: 2010 International Conference on Computer and Communication Engineering (ICCCE), pp. 1–5, 11–12 May 2010
6. Gales, M., Young, S.: The application of hidden Markov models in speech recognition. Found. Trends Signal Process. **1**(3), 195–304 (2008)

7. Ephraim, Y., Malah, D.: Speech enhancement using a minimum-mean square error short-time spectral amplitude estimator. IEEE Trans. Acoust. Speech Signal Process. **32**(6), 1109–1121 (1984)
8. Ishizuka, K., Nakatani, T., Fujimoto, M., Miyazaki, N.: Noise robust voice activity detection based on periodic to aperiodic component ratio. Speech Commun. **52**(1), 41–60 (2010)
9. Zhang, X., Sun, J., Luo, Z.: One-against-all weighted dynamic time warping for language-independent and speaker-dependent speech recognition in adverse conditions. PLoS ONE **9**(2), e85458 (2014). doi:10.1371/journal.pone.0085458
10. Komatani, K., Hotta, N., SATO, S., Nakano, M.: Posteriori restoration of turn-taking and ASR results for incorrectly segmented utterances. IEICE Trans. Inf. Syst. **E98.D**(11), 1923–1931 (2015)
11. Duque, N., Giraldo, M., Jaramillo, I.D., Salazar A.F.: GAIATools: Framework para la creación de objetos de aprendizaje accesibles. In: CAVA - VII Congreso Internacional de Ambientes Virtuales de Aprendizaje Adaptativos y Accesibles. Brasil (2015)
12. Hossan, M.A.; Memon, S.; Gregory, M.A.: A novel approach for MFCC feature extraction. In: 2010 4th International Conference on Signal Processing and Communication Systems (ICSPCS), pp. 1–5, 13–15 Dec. 2010

# Lesson Learnt from an EEG-Based Experiment with ADHD Children in Malaysia

Syariffanor Hisham[1(✉)] and Abdul Wahab Abdul Rahman[2]

[1] Faculty of Information and Communication Technology,
Universiti Teknikal Malaysia Melaka, 76100 Durian Tunggal, Melaka, Malaysia
syariffanor@utem.edu.my
[2] Kulliyah of Information and Communication Technology,
International Islamic University Malaysia,
P.O. Box 10, 50728 Kuala Lumpur, Malaysia
abdulwahab@iium.edu.my

**Abstract.** There are growing interests among researchers worldwide pertaining to efficacy of electroencephalography (EEG) as diagnostic tools and noninvasive treatment for children with special needs. However, there are very limited studies discuss the efficacy of EEG-based experiment protocols among young children with ADHD particularly from the perspective of human-computer interaction methodologies. Thus, this paper provides some background on related studies in EEG for children with attention-deficit/hyperactive disorder (ADHD) and some insights on Malaysia experience with regards to ADHD detection and intervention programs. The lesson learnt presented in this paper highlights the factors that affect young children participation in EEG-based experiments that is relevant and beneficial for researchers who are working with children with special needs.

**Keywords:** ADHD · Electroencephalography · EEG · Neurofeedback

## 1 Introduction

Attention-deficit/hyperactive disorder (ADHD) is one of the most prevalent disorders among children worldwide. American Psychiatric Association (2013) classifies ADHD as psychiatric disorders in the Diagnostic and Statistical Manual of Mental Disorders (DSM-V) [1]. ADHD symptoms are associated with a person inability to concentrate and impulsivity which often misunderstood as misbehavior or disobedient especially among young children [2]. Despite its various epistemology, ADHD symptoms also co-morbid with other learning difficulties and behavioral disorders such as dyslexia, autism and tic disorder [3].

The use of electroencephalography (EEG) to examine human brain cortical activities including in children with behavioral problem was first explored in mid 70 s [4]. The later study in 1991, Lubar proposed the Theta/Beta EEG ratio as a measure that could indicate ADHD symptoms among children [5]. After two decades of clinical and scientific debates on the efficacy of EEG as diagnostic tools for ADHD, the United State Food and Drug Administration (US FDA) has approved Neuropsychiatric EEG-Based Assessment Aid (NEBA) system for ADHD in 2013.

© Springer International Publishing Switzerland 2016
M. Antona and C. Stephanidis (Eds.): UAHCI 2016, Part III, LNCS 9739, pp. 73–81, 2016.
DOI: 10.1007/978-3-319-40238-3_8

EEG is also used as a noninvasive treatment for ADHD known as neurofeedback (NF). It is a real-time approach that helps a person to control specific aspect of his/her brain activities. NF therapy aims to improve a person cognitive abilities based on immediate feedback of his/her brain activities during therapy session [6–8].

Literature study on NF and ADHD are well established for the past ten years and continue to gain interests among researchers across disciplines such as medical, neuroscience, engineering, and computer science [9–11]. However, there are some inconsistencies were reported across studies due to methodological shortcomings such as sampling size, bias controlled condition, instrumentation and analysis methods. It is also difficult to compare across datasets that were collected with different EEG devices and software [12].

In addition to the above issues, there are limited literatures discussed on EEG-based experiment protocols. Lesson learnt from earlier studies will be useful for other researchers in devising their experiment protocols particularly for studies that involved children with special needs. Building on the current related studies, this paper discusses the lesson learnt from a preliminary study of EEG-based experiment conducted with dyslexia children who have symptoms of ADHD and a control group children in Malaysia.

Findings from this preliminary study provide useful insights on participants' selection method, experiment protocols, suitability and limitations of the wireless EEG device as well as other factors that affect children participation in the EEG-based experiment. Therefore, more rigorous protocols can be devised for future experiments that will be conducted as part of this on-going research.

## 2   ADHD

The prevalence of ADHD worldwide was reported between 5.9 % to 7 % [11, 13]. In most cases, the symptoms of ADHD only become apparent during pre-schools when the children started to socialize with other children of similar age group. Children with ADHD are often described as lack of discipline, easily distracted, disorganized and impulsive. Although all these behaviors are common symptoms of ADHD, it can be classified into two types – inattention and hyperactive.

The hyperactive group is more common among boys whilst there is no significant difference between genders in inattentive cases [2]. However, age and gender were not included in a multivariate model of a comprehensive meta-analytic review of ADHD prevalence that involved 103 studies in 2007 [11]. Many studies on EEG in ADHD do not classify ADHD symptoms into two types described earlier with the main reference is DSM-V by the American Psychiatric Association. Therefore, ADHD discussion presented in this paper is referring to both inattention and hyperactive cases.

### 2.1   ADHD in Malaysia

Report by National Health and Morbidity Survey 2015 revealed that the prevalence of ADHD among children aged 5 to 15 years old in Malaysia was 4.6 % [14]. Like many other countries worldwide, the number was also higher among boys than girls with more cases were reported in urban areas. According to UNICEF Malaysia report, ADHD is categorized under learning difficulties together with conditions such as autism and dyslexia [15]. Early detection and intervention of children with learning difficulties are administered and monitored by both the Ministry of Health (MOH) and Ministry of Education (MOE).

Despite various initiatives by MOH and MOE in improving the quality of life of children with learning difficulties in Malaysia, there are two main problems highlighted by UNICEF Malaysia pertaining to the current implementation of early detection system as follow [15]:

- lack of validated and recognized screening tools including lack of comprehensive identification procedure,
- limited number of doctors, educational psychologists, pediatricians and trained specialists to conduct assessment.

These two problems may contribute to inaccurate diagnoses of ADHD cases particularly in co-morbidity cases. This will later affect the effectiveness of intervention programs and treatment prescribed for the children. Currently, ADHD intervention programs among children in Malaysia are carried out at public and private schools, private institutions as well as non-government organizations (NGOs) such as Dyslexia Association Malaysia.

## 3 EEG in ADHD

Due to co-morbidity conditions discussed earlier, there is possible confusion in diagnosing a person with ADHD. For example, a child with inattention type of ADHD could be misdiagnosed for dyslexia or other related learning difficulties due to the fact that both disorders are sharing similar genes, symptoms and characteristics. Therefore, the child could not benefit from appropriate intervention programs to overcome his/her difficulties.

However in 2013, EEG-based assessment aid (NEBA) was finally accepted by US FDA as a commercial tool in diagnosing children with ADHD and it is only available in the US. Although its approval received mixed reactions but results from a clinical investigation by a multidisciplinary team of NEBA concluded that integration of EEG-based assessment with clinician's evaluation may help improve the accuracy of ADHD diagnosis [16].

Many children and young adults with ADHD rely on medications that resulted in short-term and long-term side effects. However over the last decade, there are growing numbers of study that look into alternative treatments for ADHD including the use of EEG known as NF therapy [17, 18]. This noninvasive treatment operates at different brainwave frequencies as described in Table 1 [6].

During NF therapy, one or more electrodes will be placed on the scalp to capture and measure the EEG brainwave patterns before it will be recorded in a computer. Visual and auditory feedbacks will be provided to the person under treatment – thus, he/she can retrain their brainwaves to achieve the desired frequencies [19].

**Table 1.** EEG bands

| Band | Frequency | Brain state |
|------|-----------|-------------|
| Gamma | Above 30 Hz | Associates with peak performance that refers to highly concentration brain activity |
| Beta | Above 13–30 Hz | Alertness and intellectual activity |
| Alpha | 8–12 Hz | Relaxation |
| Theta | 4–8 Hz | Deep relaxation |
| Delta | 0.5–3.5 Hz | Sleep |

It is important to highlight that each children undergo NF therapy requires tailored protocol because each ADHD case may have different combination of symptoms and conditions. Therefore, correct assessment is crucial before personalized NF treatment is prescribed for a child. With the advancement of brain-computer interface technology, more studies are conducted to improve NF therapy by introducing computer games. Studies show that computer games can potentially increase participation and eliminate boredom among children who undergo NF therapy [17, 20].

Despite the promising potential of NF games, the biggest challenge is to turn the off-the-shelf games into NF games. The problems with the current NF games do not only require intelligent and simultaneous feedback but it also involves other aspect of game design that currently receives little attention by NF clinicians.

## 4   EEG-Based Experiment

The study presented in this paper is part of a preliminary work on multimedia intervention for children with ADHD in Malaysia. The main objective of this preliminary study is to test the EEG-based experiment protocols with ADHD children and a control group. This experiment also help the researchers to have better understanding on ADHD assessment and intervention programs in Malaysia including other factors that may affect children participation in EEG-based experiment.

### 4.1   Participants

There were seven children took part in the study with four of them are dyslexia children with ADHD symptoms and three children without any learning difficulty as a control group. All the dyslexia children were diagnosed with dyslexia by a special education specialist but never been diagnosed with ADHD despite of having the symptoms as observed by their parents and teachers at intervention center running by Dyslexia Association Malaysia (PDM). All of these potentially ADHD children were selected by their teachers who were trained as a special education teachers at the PDM's center and have more than five years working with children with learning difficulties.

As for the control group, the children were recruited through their parents who voluntarily nominated their children for the study. These three children attended the

**Table 2.** Demographic details

| Participant | Gender | Age (years old) | Ethnicity |
|---|---|---|---|
| P1 | Boy | 6 | Malays |
| P2 | Boy | 5 | Malays |
| P3 | Boy | 5 | Malays |
| P4 | Girl | 6 | Malays |
| C1 | Boy | 6 | Other |
| C2 | Boy | 6 | Malays |
| C3 | Girl | 6 | Malays |

*P – Children with ADHD Symptoms.*
*C – Control group.*

same classes in a private kindergarten. Demographic details of the children participated in the study are shown in Table 2.

## 4.2  Experiment Setting

The experiment at PDM center was held in a computer room that was noise-free and suitable for conducting experiment. However, experiment with a control group was conducted at the research lab that was less convenient for experiment. Therefore, the children from a control group were prone to distraction due to setting of the room.

A wireless EEG headset with 14-channels was used for the experiments with two units of laptops. One unit laptop was connected to a flat screen monitor to display clips and interfaces of multimedia application. Another unit of laptop was used to record EEG readings during the experiment. A computer mouse was available for the children to use while performing specified tasks during experiment. An external speaker was placed next to the monitor for audio experiment.

Teachers or parents of the children were asked to fill up a consent form and a questionnaire comprises standard questions on their children behaviors and characteristics at home and school. At PDM center, the children were waited in their classroom while waiting for their turns. They were called one by one and ushered to the experiment room by a researcher. Although there was a waiting area for the control group at the research lab, the children was actually in the same room with the experiment area. The children were free to come in and out from the room although they were accompanied by their parents.

## 4.3  Experiment Protocols

Prior to the experiment, a wireless EEG device was placed on the child's head and short testing was conducted to test the quality of signals on all electrodes. The EEG device recorded the brain signals while the children performing tasks as specified in Table 3. A video camera was assembled to monitor the children's responses throughout the experiment.

**Table 3.** Experiment protocols

| Protocol | | Duration (minute/s) |
|---|---|---|
| Baseline recording | Eyes opened | 1 |
| | Eyes closed | 1 |
| Emotions database | Happy | 1 |
| | Sad | 1 |
| | Fear | 1 |
| | Calm | 1 |
| Audio database | Angry | 1 |
| | Happy | 1 |
| | Neutral | 1 |
| | Sad | 1 |
| Interactive courseware | MyLexics | 5–10 |
| NF game | Cube | 4 |
| Total estimated time | | 19–24 min |

*P – Children with ADHD Symptoms.*
*C – Control group.*

The first protocol is baseline recording which is a standard protocol for EEG-based experiment consists of eyes opened and eyes closed. During eyes opened, the children were asked to look on a white screen for 1 min followed by another 1 min with their eyes closed. The children were also asked to sit still and minimize their movements during recording.

The second protocol is emotion database. This task requires the children to watch clips of children facial expressions of emotions – happy, sad, fear and calm for the total duration of 4 min. The emotional faces displayed on the screen help the child to change his/her emotion.

Similar with the second protocol, the third task needs the children to listen to four different audios – angry, happy, sad and neutral. The intonation of the audios triggers the child to change their emotion during this audio protocol. Each of the audios was played for 1 min on the external speakers.

The forth protocol involves a self-paced learning on an interactive courseware named MyLexics. The courseware has four learning modules and three activities on basic reading and spelling in Malay language. The children were allowed to explore the courseware for 5 to 10 min on their own.

The final protocol is NF game. The children were given 4 min to play a simple cube game. During the session, they must retain their concentration in response to visual feedback from the game. This game comes together in a package with the wireless EEG device.

## 5   Lesson Learnt

Table 4 shows the experiment completion status, setup time and total experiment time by each children involved in the study. Four out of seven children managed to complete all the five experiment protocols and total time taken (excluding setup time) by them

Table 4. Findings summary

| Participant | Experiment completion status | Setup time (min) | Total experiment time (min) |
|---|---|---|---|
| P1 | Completed | 8 | 25 |
| P2 | Incomplete | 23 | 18 |
| P3 | Completed | 15 | 20 |
| P4 | Completed | 8 | 20 |
| C1 | Completed | 8 | 23 |
| C2 | Incomplete | 17 | 10 |
| C3 | Incomplete | 10 | 15 |

*P – Children with ADHD Symptoms.*
*C – Control group.*

are ranging between 20–25 min. One potentially ADHD children (P2) withdraw from the study during the audio protocol although he had completed all other protocols. He also took the longest setup time which is 23 min.

Despite a less suitable setting for the control group, one of the children successfully completed all the experiment protocols in 23 min while his other two friends were distracted throughout the experiment. These two children only completed the baseline recordings but failed to finish other protocols. The researcher decided not to try the audio protocols with the two children (C2 and C3) because they were struggle to sit still and focus on the tasks. These inputs were derived from video recording during the experiments.

Time factor is crucial in EEG-based experiment with children, 20 min experiment excluding setup up time is daunting for many children. This might resulted in lack of engagement and withdrawal from the experiment. Random sequence of tasks was implemented to maintain their interest but baseline recording remains as the first task of the protocols for all children. Therefore, it is suggested that EEG-based experiment for children should not exceed 15 min excluding setup time. P2 took the longest setup time because of the poor brain signals from the wireless device. He also looked frustrated during the setup time because the device was taken a few times on and off from his scalp. He was cooperative and settled down as the experiment started but asked to stop the audio protocol immediately by taking off the device from his head and refused to continue.

Although wireless EEG device is cheaper and easier to setup compared to other EEG machine, the placement of electrodes are not firm and it can be easily dislocated even with a slightest movement especially among young children. Therefore, this might affect the quality of the signals captured during EEG recordings. However this might not be the case with older children and adults who have more controls over their movements during the experiment. The quality of signals captured also affected by the setup layout and distance of the Bluetooth dongle and its wireless EEG headset.

All children enjoyed the interactive courseware task and able to use the courseware independently with minimum assistance. Majority of the children easily adapted to the NF game except C2. He was annoyed every time he failed to retain his concentration during the task. Almost all children found that audio protocol was difficult to engage with and they become anxious when the audio played through the external speakers.

Other external factor that should be taken into consideration in conducting EEG-based experiments with children is the researchers ability to interact with the children. Although researchers have to minimize their communication with the children but the researchers ability to friendly interact with the children does affect their participation in the experiment. The children were a lot calmer during the experiment with a presence of someone they are familiar or comfortable with. It is advisable to have at least three researchers involved during the experiment, one person in charge on the EEG recording and setup, one person at the waiting room/area to prepare the children before the experiment and another person to facilitate the children during the experiment.

## 6   Conclusion

While EEG-based experiments are getting more attention these days and cheaper EEG device to capture the signals are available in the market, there is lack of study reported on the devising protocols for the EEG-based experiment involving young children. Through the preliminary study presented in this paper, the researchers found that time factor including setup time and experiment duration, suitability of the device as well as human factors play significant role in young children participation throughout the experiment for both potentially ADHD children and control group. Thus, it is hoped that the lesson learnt highlighted in through paper will provide some insights to other researchers who are interested in conducting EEG-based experiment with young children with special needs.

**Acknowledgement.** This work was supported by a grant from Ministry of Education Malaysia (FRGS14-130-0371). The authors would like to thank teachers, parents and children at Dyslexia Association Malaysia and International Islamic University Educare for their cooperation and participation in the study.

## References

1. American Psychiatric Association: Diagnostic and Statistical Manual of Mental Disorders, 5th edn. Washington, DC (2013)
2. Selikowitz, M.: ADHD: The Facts, 2nd edn. Oxford University Press Inc., New York (2009)
3. Russell-Chapin, L., Kemmerly, T., Liu, W.-C., Zagardo, M.T., Chapin, T., Dailey, D., Dinh, D.: The effects of neurofeedback in the default mode network: pilot study results of medicated children with ADHD. J. Neurother. **17**, 35–42 (2013)
4. Lubar, J.F., Shouse, M.N.: EEG and behavioral changes in hyperkinetic child concurrent with training of the Sensorimotor Rhythm (SMR). J. Biofeedback Self-Regul. **1**, 293–306 (1976)
5. Lubar, J.F.: Discourse on the development of EEG diagnostics and biofeedback for attention deficit/hyperactivity disorders. J. Biofeedback Self-Regul. **16**, 201–225 (1991)

6. Hammond, D.C.: What is neurofeedback: an update. J. Neurother. **15**, 305–336 (2011)
7. Ghassemi, F., Hassan Moradi, M., Tehrani-Doost, M., Abootalebi, V.: Using non-linear features of EEG for ADHD/normal participants' classification. In: Procedia - Social and Behavioral Sciences, pp. 148–152 (2012)
8. Niv, S.: Clinical efficacy and potential mechanisms of neurofeedback. J. Personal. Individ. Differ. **54**, 676–686 (2013)
9. Willis, W.G., Weyandt, L.L., Lubiner, A.G., Schubart, C.D.: Neurofeedback as a treatment for attention-deficit/hyperactivity disorder: a systematic review of evidence for practice. J. Appl. Sch. Psychol. **27**(3), 201–227 (2011)
10. Halperin, J.M., Bédard, A.-C.V., Curchack-Lichtin, J.T.: Preventive interventions for ADHD: a neurodevelopmental perspective. J. Neurother. **9**, 531–541 (2012)
11. Willcutt, E.G.: The prevalence of DSM-IV attention-deficit/hyperactivity disorder: a meta-analytic review. J. Neurother. **9**, 490–499 (2012)
12. Loo, S., Makeig, S.: Clinical utility of EEG in attentiondeficit/hyperactivity disorder: a research update. J. Neurother. **9**, 469–587 (2012)
13. Schweitzer, J.B., McBurnett, K.: New directions for therapeutics in ADHD. J. Neurother. **9**, 487–489 (2012)
14. Institute for Public Health. National Health & Morbidity Survey, vol. II (2015). http://www. iku.gov.my/images/IKU/Document/nhmsreport2015vol2.pdf
15. UNICEF Malaysia. Children with disabilities in malaysia: mapping the policies, programmes, interventions and stakeholders. http://www.unicef.org/malaysia/UNICEF-Children_with_Disability_in_Malaysia_2014_lowres.pdf
16. Snyder, S.M., Rugino, T.A., Hornig, M., Stein, M.A.: Integration of an EEG biomarker with a clinician's ADHD evaluation. J. Brain Behav. **5**, e00330 (2015)
17. Ninaus, M., Witte, M., Kober, S.E., Friedrich, E. V.C., Kurzmann, J., Hartsuiker, E., Neuper, C., Wood, G.: Neurofeedback and Serious Games. In: Connolly, T.M., Hainey, T., Boyle, E., Baxter, G., Moreno-Ger, P. (eds.), pp. 82–110. IGI Global (2014)
18. Liu, T., Wang, J., Chen, T., Wang, R., Song, M.: Neurofeedback treatment experimental study for ADHD by using the brain-computer interface neurofeedback system, pp. 1537–1540 (2013)
19. Cmiel, V., Janousek, O., Kolarova, J.: EEG biofeedback. In: 4th International Symposium on Applied Sciences in Biomedical and Communication Technologies. ACM Press, New York (2011)
20. Mandryk, R. L., Dielschneider, S., Kalyn, M. R., Bertram, C. P., Doucette, A., Taylor, B. A., Keiver, K.: Games as neurofeedback training for kids with FASD. In: Interaction Design and Children 2013. ACM Press, New York (2013)

# Increasing Educational Opportunities Through Digital Participation

Anna-Maria Kamin[✉] and Dorothee M. Meister

Media Pedagogy and Empirical Media Studies, Universität Paderborn, Paderborn, Germany
{anna-maria.kamin,dm}@uni-paderborn.de

**Abstract.** The article introduces and discusses the background, concept, evaluation results as well as educational sociological perspectives of an interview-based research project on the digital participation of socially disadvantaged children and adolescents. The main thesis is that adolescents can be supported in their participation in society through access to computers and the acquisition of comprehensive media competencies in the form of pedagogical media training. The evaluative results of the project indicate that these flanking measures are especially helpful for primary education families looking to improve their social standing. A milieu of little cognitive stimulation and limited cultural capital within the family lead to a rash dissipation of the effects achieved through media training therefore making it clear that further support is necessary.

**Keywords:** Social disadvantage · Media literacy facilitation · Media competence · Open-source software · Recycling PC · Cultural capital

## 1 Introduction

A multi-perspective understanding of inclusion as outlined by the World Health Organization sees disability not as a singular phenomenon that is constructed through one criterion but rather as a condition that develops from the combination of different factors such as bodily functions and structures, activities and contextual components [18]. The term inclusion, therefore, refers not only to including people with disabilities but also encompasses migrants as well as socially disadvantaged groups of people [9]. Traditionally, adolescents are especially in the focus of the debate over inclusion. The goal here is to make their transition from school to their work lives easier while also ensuring the possibility for participation in society. Digital media can play a key role here, a fact required by a perspective of technology for inclusion and participation from a media pedagogical view.

## 2 Background: Digital Media for the Advancement of Inclusion

Digital media offer a multitudinous potential for social, individual, communal and political participation. Digital media competencies - as seen in the German and European understanding [1] - are however, necessary in order to be able to participate socially in

© Springer International Publishing Switzerland 2016
M. Antona and C. Stephanidis (Eds.): UAHCI 2016, Part III, LNCS 9739, pp. 82–92, 2016.
DOI: 10.1007/978-3-319-40238-3_9

a knowledge and information-based society. It is especially important during job training, at university and during one's work life to understand, use and communicate information transmitted by media. If children and adolescents only have limited possibilities to develop their media competence at an early stage, then one can assume that they will find it difficult to initiate in social participation and take advantage of educational opportunities later in life. Against this backdrop media competence must be seen as the fourth cultural technique alongside reading, writing and arithmetic [10]. The opportunities for extensive participation in media competence are, however, unequally distributed among the populace. In Germany, correlations between people's attainment of media literacy and the education level of their parents and therefore in many cases also the socioeconomic status of the family itself, have been established empirically. The higher the formal education level of the family, the faster and more flexible skills and competencies in dealing with analog and digital media are developed and therefore also the greater the tendential extent of media literacy [16]. Existing disadvantages can therefore be amplified through digital information and communication technologies. Despite educational political activity and advancement, these results are largely constant [5, 11] thus threatening permanent exclusion of socially disadvantaged children and adolescents. The socio-economic surroundings – i.e. family, school, free time activities – of the people affected therefore must be surveyed. When referring to family surroundings, parents with low socio-economic status naturally should not be subjected to normative condemnation – and therefore the assumption of a lack of engagement and interest in reference to media literacy promotion. It appears much more rather to be the difficult daily parameters of these families, such as unemployment, migration or being single parents, that hamper media education and media competence development. [14, 17] According to the findings of representative studies on media in the daily lives of children and adolescents, there is no longer a difference between families of differing education levels in regards to the presence of digital information and communication technologies. Virtually 100 percent of all households possess a laptop/computer. [13] Only one fifth of all 6–13 year olds, however, have their own computer or laptop [13]. Additionally, many parents are uncertain when it comes to media education especially in relation to the use of digital media [12, 17]. Up to now it has remained unclear as to how media competencies and thus also possibilities for social participation can be systematically advanced, especially in reference to socially disadvantaged families.

## 3    Intervention: Media Literacy Training

The Paderborn recycling PC project (the pb.re.pc Project) tackles this problematic situation at a regional level and contributes to inclusion and also to decreasing a growing digital divide. Its goal is to support children and adolescents from deprived families to participate in digitally supported learning opportunities not only in reference to technological access (media ownership) but also in reference to the establishment of educational opportunities (acquisition of media competencies).

The project is conducted on a volunteer basis through the club MTKJ (*Medien und Technik für Kinder und Jugendliche* (Media and Technology for Children and

Adolescents)) e.V. as well as other clubs and welfare institutions and in cooperation with the instructors from the Media Pedagogy and Empirical Media Studies work group at the University of Paderborn. Members of MTKJ collect unwanted computers from companies, institutions and private households, service and repair the computers and outfit them with open-source software (Linux, Firefox, etc.). The volunteers are then joined by students from the University of Paderborn's Bachelor of Education program who help conduct a five-day media pedagogy training session during their vocational internship. Instructors from the University of Paderborn provide the corresponding pedagogical and academic supervision. After they have successfully completed the training, the participating children and adolescents receive a recycled computer free of charge. Further continued training sessions are conducted one to two times per year during the following two years. These sessions expand on and deepen the participants' previous knowledge and skills. Since 2011, over 100 children and adolescents between the ages of 8 and 19 years from all types of schools - including children with learning disabilities and cognitive limitations - have been trained and provided with a computer (see Fig. 1).

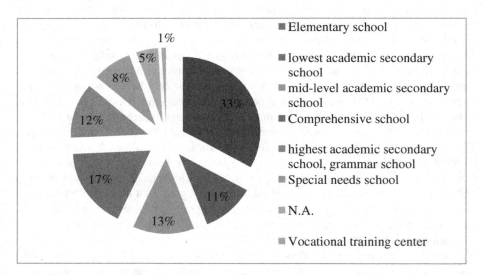

**Fig. 1.** Division of participants in the training program based on their school type (N = 109) (Color figure online)

### 3.1 Project Concept and Training Session Content

The concept of the training sessions contains a project and product centered approach that is preferred when dealing with media work with socially disadvantaged adolescents [10]. In contrast to media consumption, this type of media work entails the "processing and development of subject areas within social reality with the help of media such as printing, photography, sound, video, computer, multimedia and the Internet. The media are 'enlisted' by their users, i.e. wielded automatically and used as a means of communication" [15]. The reasoning behind this approach is that the media work with disadvantaged children and adolescents is therefore not interpreted as deficient and/or problematic but rather the participants' potential plays a more central role. The Bielefeld Media Competence Model, an approach that has been empirically confirmed on multiple occasions, forms the theoretical basis for the training concept [2]. Following the ideas of Dieter Baacke, media competence is differentiated into the four dimensions of media criticism, media knowledge, media usage and media design. Of central importance in this model is the concept that media competence extends beyond a purely "instrumental-qualificational" (the extrapolated ability to use new devices) usage competency.

Exclusively Linux Distribution Edubuntu is used as the operating system for the training sessions and for the recycled computers. Within its standard components, Edubuntu contains a wide array of preinstalled programs that support learning. Additionally, using Edubuntu is intuitive and offers a plethora of applications, some of which are even accessible to people with disabilities. For example, drawing programs, graphic applications and photo editing programs are preinstalled in addition to the usual office applications. Furthermore, the distribution offers an entire series of educational software covering topics such as language, music, geography or mathematics. Therefore it is not necessary to purchase commercial software in order to create a joy for learning and to transmit knowledge playfully. The training sessions aim to support the participants, train their ability to use media, develop participants' research strategies as well as their strategic ability to use media purposefully.

### 3.2 Project Experiences and Reflection

In the past four years the project has run extremely successfully.[1] The initial concerns expressed by the project team that the weekend training sessions would not be accepted by the children and adolescents have since been proven to be unfounded. In their feedback the participants have told the project team that they greatly enjoy coming to the training sessions; in fact, they usually regret it when the sessions come to an end. Additionally, the children and adolescents as well as their parents have shown an immense commitment to the project. Only individual children have so far abandoned the project or have had unexcused absences during the training sessions. Our experience has been that the children and adolescents see it as a privilege to participate in an extracurricular education program offered by the university. This is true despite some initial concerns expressed by some of the students. For example, one 11 year old comprehensive school student, who, in a report about the first day of the training session created for the training session itself, wrote: *"I didn't really want to go to the university because I thought it would be strict"*. After a short time, however, the sessions' positive aspects frequently

---

[1] The project was received with positive recognition and appreciation both at the regional and national level. In 2012, it received the Dieter Baacke Prize for exemplary media pedagogic projects. It also received a further laurel in 2013 from the community energy service provider *Westfalen Weser Energie* when it was named an exceptional "lighthouse project" for citizen community dedication and action. Additionally, in January of this year, the pb.re.pc Project was crowned as an exceptional education idea of 2013/14 during the competition *"Ideen für die Bildungsrepublik"* (Ideas for the Education Republic).

prevail as can be seen in how one girl ended her report: *"[...] unfortunately we had to end and I had to wait such a long time until we had a training session again. [...] Time moved slowly. [...] But I realized that I love the university. [...] Thank God I'm here."*

Similarly, we experienced a high level of commitment and acceptance from the parents' side. This acceptance was present throughout the program from the registration to the accompaniment of the training session to the stipulated collection of the computer. Many parents are very grateful that their children had the possibility to participate in the project. In one such instance, the team received a note from the mother of a 10 year old student, who would later attend a *Gymnasium* (grammar school). In the note the mother wrote: *"I really hope that my daughter has the chance to take part in your training sessions and hope she receives a PC. [...] I don't have the means to purchase a computer for her myself [...] since I am living off of unemployment support level ALG II[2]. [...] Most children already had a computer in elementary school [...]. The grammar school will probably just require a PC"*. This demonstrates that parents from socially disadvantaged groups are also very dedicated to improving the educational opportunities of their children.

Working with the students also proved to be especially enriching. We quickly realized that the student interns served as role models for an academic educational path for the participants. This was especially true if the student interns and the participating children and adolescents came from the same or similar cultural backgrounds.

### 3.3   Accompanying Academic Research

It is important to take different research perspectives into account in order to verify the project's success and indentify further needed intervention. A systematic accompanying research study of the project has taken place since 2014. On the one hand, it is interesting to note which effects a media pedagogic intervention in the form of training sessions and providing a computer have on social participation. This means that it has to be determined how children and adolescents who have participated in the program use their computer in their daily lives, how they apply the knowledge they have gleaned from the training sessions and where possible continuing support is needed. For this reason standardized surveys, which take place before and after the first training session as well as during the following session, are part of the project evaluation. These surveys are especially intended to examine changes in the children's and adolescents' media literacy. The surveys therefore offer information about how well and for how long the training sessions impact the participants. Furthermore, we expect to see indicators about possible curricular development of the training sessions' content in order better to tailor the sessions to the heterogeneous needs of the participants and to be able to identify necessary intervention points after the training sessions have ended.

On the other hand, the surveys are intended to produce richer findings relating to the practical application of media education in socially disadvantaged families. In order to realize this goal, we conduct ethnographic studies [8] in some of the families that have

---

[2] Unemployment level ALG II is a level of state welfare offering basic minimum unemployment benefits for able-bodied job seekers.

participated in the project. The ethnographic studies consist of qualitative interviews with the children and adolescents who took part in the project as well as with their parents. Additionally, we conduct an ancillary analysis of the families' surroundings (living conditions, media resources) consisting of a combination of an observation questionnaire and documentary photography. Furthermore, the children and adolescents complete qualitative questionnaires at the end of the first round of training sessions and during the debrief session.

***Selected Evaluation Results.*** The empirical accompanying research makes clear that an extracurricular education program is both motivating and exciting for socially disadvantaged children and adolescents. The evaluation results demonstrate that in the aftermath of a media pedagogic training program, instrumental-qualificational abilities, meaning the abilities to use new media devices, increase and media use becomes more varied. This is especially true for the (professional) expertise imparted during the training sessions. The participants more frequently report carrying out activities such as "writing texts", "creating presentations" and playing "educational games" "sometimes" or "often" after the training sessions than was the case before the sessions had begun (see Fig. 2).

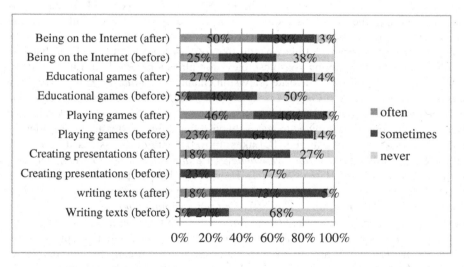

**Fig. 2.** Evaluation results: "What do I use my computer/laptop/tablet-PC for?" before and after the training sessions (N = 22) (Color figure online)

The results of the questionnaires demonstrate that not all children profit from the training equally and that the effects can even be very different over the course of time. Moreover, the cognitive and motivational atmosphere in the families has demonstrated itself to be of central significance. This problem is made clear by the case studies of

Lukas[3] and Yasin, two elementary school students who took part in the pb.re.pc Project and the corresponding accompanying research.

Lukas, who is nine years old, has a 15 year old brother and six year old sister. His German parents have been living together as life partners in a large city in Westphalia for 12 years. His father, however, has intermittently lived separately from the family and does not care for his family. His mother is unemployed and has not completed any job training. The family lives in a five-room apartment with a balcony in an apartment house. Their apartment and their furniture are in very poor shape. The rooms are cluttered and untidy. Their neighborhood can be classified as a socially troubled hotspot.

The computer provided by the pb.re.pc Project is in Lukas's room. It is used only sparingly due to a lacking Internet connection. Additionally, the family has a diverse array of other media such as three televisions, a stereo system, a broken laptop and six gaming consoles in total. The gaming consoles are made up of a Wii, a PlayStation 3, 2 and 1 and two children's consoles. During his free time, Lukas enjoys painting and playing with the neighborhood children or friends outside. During the interview it becomes clear that the electronic media primarily serve to entertain Lukas. The Wii is especially interesting for its sports programs: *"On the Wii I play //uhm//darts or bow-eling [sic] //uhm//baseball //well//tennis" (Lines 187–188)*[4]. He prefers playing the action adventure game *Wheelman* on the PlayStation. The 9-year old currently only infrequently uses the PC in his room since it, according to his statements, often has technical difficulties and because it is not connected to the Internet. As soon as the computer has been repaired, Lukas would like to play more games on it and listen to music. Alongside the gaming consoles, television plays a large role in Lukas's media usage. He has the following favorite television channels: *"Actually I mostly watch the Disney Channel or (.) KiKA or for example (.) Super RTL //uhm//no, not that good and Nickelodeon. Those are the only children's channels" (Lines 230–232)*. Lukas has set times for how long he is allowed to watch television at a time. After about one hour the television is supposed to be turned off. Lukas enjoyed the training sessions at the university. He especially enjoyed *"that we whenever we ate brakfast [sic] //well//that there were such tasty things" (Lines 303–304)*. He was less happy about the times when he was unable to activate online games during the training session: *"and for me I couldn't, uh, get into the Internet there or whatever on my computer there or for example not play = play games //uhm//on it. //Uhm//that don't [sic] work on it then" (Lines 289–291)*. Despite Lukas's prevalent interest for entertainment orientated computer usage, it is clear that Lukas was able to improve his media literacy greatly through his participation in the training sessions. In the interview he described how he was able to restore a computer game that his teacher had deleted: *"But I when I was then in the computer class (.) now I know how to re-sore [sic] Pushy Pushy" (Lines 262–263)*

Yasin, who is also nine years old and was born in Syria, fled to Germany with his parents and his two younger siblings (three and five years old) 18 months ago. The family

---

[3] All names have been changed to preserve the participants' anonymity.

[4] The interviews were transcribed in German following Bohnsack's suggestions for the transcription of interviews. The English translation has attempted to preserve the speech patterns of the participants as accurately as possible [3].

lives in a four-room apartment on the outskirts of a city. Both of his parents worked as instructors in Syria. His father has already found a job as an English teacher at an industrial company in Paderborn. Yasin enjoys playing soccer in the local neighborhood soccer club. The family has various electronic media. There are two televisions, one in the living room and one in Yasin's room. Both parents and Yasin each have a smart phone. Additionally, the family has a tablet PC and two computers. There is one PC that is used by all of the family members. The recycling computer provided to Yasin is in his room. The nine-year old has in total the following media: one television, his own cell phone with Internet access and the recycled computer. From the start, Yasin contributed to the training sessions with great interest. He was extremely receptive to the teachers and pedagogical leaders of the sessions and demonstrated a strong desire to learn. After the family had picked up the recycled computer after the last session, Yasin used it primarily for playing and learning: *"So, after two days we hooked the computer up and put the things in it, mouse and controller. (2) Then I got on it and we played with it a little 'nd [sic] I learned a little" (Interview 2, lines 15–17).* He is primarily using educational games to expand his knowledge of German and mathematics. Furthermore, he enjoys watching videos on YouTube or communicating with friends with the email account he set up during the training sessions. He prefers listening to music on the computer less. On average he spends half an hour on his computer per day.

The nine-year old mainly receives support in using his computer competently from his father: *"He shows something and then I get on it and go to it" (Interview 2, line 141).* His father provides him, for example, with assistance using the educational programs. According to Yasin, his mother is less versed in using the computer.

Additionally, his father provides Yasin with clear rules for using the PC. Yasin describes his father's rules in the interview: *"You are only allowed to go on it for twenty minutes, don't play too many games. You also have to learn" (Interview 2, lines 230– 231).*

All in all, Yasin enjoyed the training sessions. He enjoyed that he could use many different entertainment offerings on the computer and could learn new things simultaneously: *"So I enjoyed that we played and that we learned" (Interview 1, line 3).* He especially enjoyed putting the computer together during the hardware training session. One educational experience Yasin took with him from the training session was how to create texts in a document and how to write with a keyboard: *"So for example (3) making a colon and (3) capitalizing words" (Interview 2, lines 126–127).* He demonstrated a great thirst for knowledge and was also interested in computers as a medium outside of the training session: *"I want to know what the first computer in the world was. Invent computers and stuff" (Interview 2, lines 260–261).* Furthermore, he would like to know more about downloading programs himself and the fees associated with purchasing programs. Likewise, he would like to expand his knowledge about writing emails in future training sessions and learn more about restrictions for children in the Internet and what children are allowed to do and not do in the Internet.

These examples show that both children profited from the media pedagogic training sessions and expanded their knowledge. The interviews, however, also reinforce how great of an influence the parents and their educational motivation have on their children. While Lukas barely receives motivation and support in how he can use his computer productively to meet his needs, Yasin receives educational impulses from his father's guidance. This demonstrates that in daily familial media education, attitudes and stances are handed down. The educational orientation in Yasin's family is decisive for the sustainability of the project's success. In comparison to Lukas's media usage options and interests, Yasin's go beyond purely entertainment and most likely are continually expanding. Lukas is able to apply the knowledge he gained only sparingly and he is barely able to expand this knowledge at all. Therefore his previous desire merely to play games will continue to dominate his media usage in the future.

*Interpreting the Results.* Pierre Bourdieu's [6] habitus approach provides one of the most elaborate models for explaining and interpreting differences in recipients' media usage as well as the ramifications of different media preferences. Bourdieu's habitus theory postulates that the allocation of an individual to a social class as well as the appraisal of that individual's social influence in modern society is not only dependent upon the distribution of economic capital (material ownership) but also social (relatives, relationships), cultural (education, titles) and symbolic capital (clothing, body language, conduct). Bourdieu [7] sees "capital" as also being able to consist of accumulated work that is present either in the form of material or in an internalized "embodied" form. According to Bourdieu, the individual strives to obtain and accumulate these types of capital. The extent of the types of capital over which one has ownership centrally deter-mines the acquisition and exercise of competencies; this is also the case for the devel-opment of media literacy. Cultural capital has exceptional influence here. It exists in embodied (taste, conduct, knowledge), objectified (books, paintings or also digital media) and institutionalized (educational degrees, academic titles) form. The availability of cultural capital is determined by different forms of acquisition of (and interest for) cultural offerings, including preferences for media usage, as is made clear in the different interests present in Lukas's and Yasin's families. While objectified cultural capital is transferable – in this case providing a person with a computer –embodied cultural capital is tied to thought processes, processes of action, value orientation and behavioral char-acteristics. It is also "physically bound" and requires internalization. This form of capital can thus not be passed along to third parties – through training sessions for example. It is acquired – as is shown by the interviews – in the primary socialization of the family and transformed in educational institutions (school, job, etc.). As a result, social differ-ences are constantly reinforced. Hence the danger exists that the resulting habitus inter-pretive models and behavioral patterns permanently influence a person's motivation and thereby his/her willingness to learn. Therefore, future participation in society is unequally more difficult for children like Lukas than is the case for children who grow up in families with a distinct orientation toward education.

## 4   Outlook

The project and the accompanying research show that continual and long-term support measures are needed in order to assist children and adolescents in safe-guarding their educational opportunities. Therefore it is necessary to research the reasons for educa-tional disadvantages more deeply. Additionally, the social starting point for children, their family surroundings, the processes of change initiated by the project as well as possible relevant areas of need must be worked out [4]. Further research in the form of long-term studies is necessary in order to accomplish these goals. In the long run, we need to establish indicators as to whether the training session participants' chances for a better school degree and thus corresponding career desires and job prospects have improved.

An empirically founded institutionalization of the project as a media school run in cooperation with the pb.re.pc Project would be desirable. In addition to the training currently offered, this would also allow media usage counseling to be created for the parents of a particular target group. It is also conceivable that adolescents who have already completed the program could be trained as mentors and therefore offer peer-to-peer training sessions themselves. An integration of the program with school education could be possible with job training sessions specifically designed for teachers and pedagogical aides. This concept would contain within it the chance to make digital media bear fruit for the social development of inclusion with the goal of ensuring "[. . .] all people the same full right for individual development and social participation regardless of their personal needs for support" [9].·Thus the goal is to make digital media fruitful for inclusion and therefore to contribute to the reform of habitus situations.

# References

1. Aufenanger, S.: Media approachs in Germany. discourses of media competence in Germany and Europe. http://www.academia.edu/4433352/Aufenanger_media_competence_Germany_Europe (w.J.)
2. Baacke, D.: Medienkompetenz - Begrifflichkeit und sozialer Wandel. In: von Rein, A. (ed.) Medienkompetenz als Schlüsselbegriff (Theorie und Praxis der Erwachsenenbildung), pp. 112–124. Klinkhardt Verlag, Bad Heilbrunn (1996)
3. Bohnsack, R.: Rekonstruktive Sozialforschung. Einführung in qualitative Methoden. 5. Barbara Budrich Verlag, Aufl. Opladen (2003)
4. Bronfenbrenner, U.: Ökologische Sozialisationsforschung. Klett-Cotta, Stuttgart (1976)
5. Bos, W., Eickelmann, B., Gerick, J., Goldhammer, F., Schaumburg, H., Schwippert, K., et al. (eds.): ICILS 2013. Computer- und informationsbezogene Kompetenzen von Schülerinnen und Schülern in der 8. Jahrgangsstufe im internationalen Vergleich. Waxmann, Münster, Westf (2014)
6. Bourdieu, P.: Die feinen Unterschiede. Kritik der gesellschaftlichen Urteilskraft. Suhrkamp, Frankfurt am Main (1982)
7. Bourdieu, P.: Ökonomisches Kapital, kulturelles Kapital, soziales Kapital. In: Kreckel, R. (ed.) Soziale Ungleichheiten. Schwartz, Göttingen (1983)
8. Friebertshäuser, B., Panagiotopoulou, A.: Ethnographische Feldforschung. In: Friebertshäuser, B., Prrengerl, A., Langer, A. (eds.) Handbuch qualitative Forschungsmethoden in der Erziehungswissenschaft. 3. vollständig überarbeitete Neuausgabe, pp. 301–322 (2010)
9. Hinz, A.: Integration. In: Antor, G., Bleidick, U. (eds.) Handlexikon der Behindertenpädagogik, pp. 97–99. Kohlhammer, Stuttgart (2006)

10. Kutscher, N., Klein, A., Lojewski, J., Schäfer, M.: Medienkompetenzförderung für Kinder und Jugendliche in benachteiligten Lebenslagen. Konzept zur inhaltlichen, didaktischen und strukturellen Ausrichtung der medienpädagogischen Praxis in der Kinder und Jugendarbeit. Landesanstalt für Medien Nordrhein-Westfalen (LFM). Düsseldorf (2009)

11. Livingstone, S., Haddon, L., Görzig, A., Ólafsson, K.: Risks and Safety on the Internet: The Perspective of European Children. Full Findings. EU Kids Online, LSE, London (2011)

12. MPFS: FIM-Studie 2011 Familie, Interaktion & Medien. Untersuchung zur Kommunikation und Mediennutzung in Familien (2011). http://www.mpfs.de/fileadmin/FIM/FIM2011.pdf

13. MPFS: KIM-Studie 2014 Kinder + Medien, Computer + Internet. Basisstudie zum Medienumgang 6- bis 13-Jähriger (2014). http://www.mpfs.de/fileadmin/KIM-pdf14/KIM14.pdf

14. Paus-Hasebrink, I., Kulterer, J.: Praxeologische Mediensozialisationsforschung. Langzeitstudie zu sozial benachteiligten Heranwachsenden. 1. Nomos, Aufl. Baden-Baden (2014)

15. Schell, F.: Aktive Medienarbeit. In: Hühter, J., Schorb, B. (eds.) Grundbegriffe Medienpädagogik. kopaed, München (2005)

16. Treumann, K.P., Meister, D.M., Sander, U., Burkatzki, E., Hagedorn, J., Kämmerer, M., et al.: Medienhandeln Jugendlicher. Mediennutzung und Medienkompetenz. VS Verlag für Sozialwissenschaften, Bielefelder Medienkompetenzmodell (2007)

17. Wagner, U., Gebel, C., Lampert C. (eds.): Zwischen Anspruch und Alltagsbewältigung. Medienerziehung in der Familie. Vistas, Berlin (2013)

18. WHO (World Health Organization): ICF. International classification of functioning, disability and health. World Health Organization, Geneva (2001)

# Multimodal Accessibility for Deaf Students Using Interactive Video, Digital Repository and Hybrid Books

Vassilis Kourbetis[✉], Konstantinos Boukouras, and Maria Gelastopoulou

Institute of Educational Policy, Athens, Greece
{vk,kboukouras,gelm}@iep.edu.gr

**Abstract.** Modern inclusive educational approaches try to eliminate educational inequalities and barriers in the learning and teaching process. For this reason, and by using Information and Communication Technologies (ICT), it is necessary to differentiate educational material and tools in order to allow all students, including those with disabilities, to access education. The objective of this paper is to present the innovative interactive applications for the education of Deaf and Hard of Hearing (D/HH) students. The content of the educational documents is rendered in Greek Sign Language (GSL). The multimedia electronic form of the Hybrid books combines the presentation of the original printed book in GSL, the text in subtitles underneath the GSL video, videos with text navigation as well as the audio recording of the text by a native speaker. The applications are free and accessible to all via the web, offer various benefits to students, teachers, parents and others involved in the education of D/HH students.

**Keywords:** Interactive technology · Hybrid books · Inclusive education · Accessibility · Deaf education

## 1 Introduction

Modern educational approaches are based on the principles of inclusive education that promote equal learning and participation opportunities for all students including students with disabilities [1–3]. In this context educational systems design and develop policies and practices, educational environments and means accessible to all students following the principles of Universal Design for Learning (UDL) and differentiated teaching. All the above enable students to use their own learning paths, ways and strategies for the acquisition of knowledge [4, 5]. This requires adaptations and variations according to the educational needs and the learning profile of each student. The dynamic relationship between UDL and ICT is a powerful tool towards differentiated teaching and inclusive education, as technology supports accessibility and differentiation of the content, material and the educational learning environments [3, 6].

The rapid development of ICT increases students participation and autonomy, triggers their interest, supports the understanding of teaching content and promotes accessibility. For D/HH students technological solutions are effective for enhancing the learning process in all subject areas, for developing their academic and world knowledge, and for expressing their needs, opinions and beliefs [7–10].

© Springer International Publishing Switzerland 2016
M. Antona and C. Stephanidis (Eds.): UAHCI 2016, Part III, LNCS 9739, pp. 93–102, 2016.
DOI: 10.1007/978-3-319-40238-3_10

For D/HH students in particular, whose basic learning channel is visual, the results from the use of interactive applications that include signed language are impressive since they can minimize the loss of incoming information. Besides, as it is supported by the international scientific community, the most effective approach of D/HH students is the bilingual educational model, with the use of signed language as a first language [11–14]. An alternative interactive application to support the acquisition and process of information of D/HH students are visual displays with transcripts that can be read along with their translation into the national signed language [3, 9]. The D/HH realize the world through vision and operate in all areas and aspects of their lives by mainly using the sense of sight. Moreover, as they structure their thinking and language through vision they do not view their hearing particularity as problematic. The ability of D/HH people to exploit their sense of sight is their main common characteristic. This fact necessitates the strengthening of visual stimuli and the development of material that take into account their ability to see [14].

Recently and within the context of technological evolution and its use in education, various interactive tools and applications that expand the students' access to knowledge and the learning process have been designed [9]. The present work aims to present supportive interactive applications for signed language navigation and text presentation as well as proposals for their use in the learning and teaching process of D/HH students. The project, the methodology and the applications will be presented below.

## 2   The Project

The Institute of Educational Policy (IEP) aims to implement in the Greek educational system the decisions taken at the UN International Convention on the Rights of Persons with Disabilities [15] related to the development of inclusive policies and practices using ICT and specifically interactive applications. In this context, IEP has implemented the project "Design and development of accessible educational material and software for students with disabilities" and has developed supportive interactive open source applications adapted to the needs of D/HH students. It includes the development of video applications with interactive subtitles and the design of textbooks that provide a simultaneous use of Greek Sign Language. All applications include a comprehensive user's guide and a teacher's manual in accessible formats.

These applications were necessary in order to support the educational use of the developed material. Particularly, the applications were needed for the most efficient use of the adapted textbooks of the two first grades of primary school for D/HH students. For the implementation of this task the following questions were addressed:

1. What is the most appropriate interactive application for the most efficient support of D/HH students?
2. What are the criteria, characteristics and procedures for the development of the application?
3. How can the application be used by everyone involved in the learning or studying of signed languages?

# 3    Methodology

This project follows the principles of a qualitative methodological approach and thematic and content analysis of texts, multimedia applications and research data. The analyzed texts were institutional, scientific, European, international and research data related to inclusive education, disability and deafness. In particular, the project focuses on the contribution and use of ICT in the learning process and modern teaching methodologies related to the pedagogical and scientific documentation of criteria and development standards of interactive applications for D/HH students [16]. At the same time, it refers and draws on emancipatory methodological approaches since Deaf native signers have been fully involved during the implementation of the project [17].

Moreover, special experts have developed the needed standards and criteria for the project while they sought for corresponding on-line software. Some of the mandatory criteria were the following: the application had to be licensed as open source software, it had to offer quick and easy navigation and also to be editable and adaptable to the needs of the D/HH. Specifically, it had to provide all available teaching material with Greek Sign Language (GSL), and so a corpus of more than twenty-two thousand sign videos was built, using interactive subtitles and natural voice recordings, presenting as such all information multimodally. Multimodality allows D/HH children to have a better understanding of the text [18]. Other standards followed was full screen video, all known functions of playing video (i.e. custom regulated speed and text navigation) and screen captures for individual sign printing, a useful tool in the hands of D/HH teachers.

The most appropriate application for the interactive digital library that was chosen from the search results and met the necessary criteria was pan.do/ra (http://pan.do/ra#about). Pandora is a free, open-source platform of digital files that allows the management of large video collections, the collaborative creation of metadata and time based annotations. Finally, it offers the option to view files as a network application on any computer.

The platform is based on a java digital library (OxJS) (https://oxjs.org/#about). Initially this application was translated into Greek and then adapted to the needs of the D/HH students and GSL. It was updated with the use of GSL in films of educational context, natural voice (in Greek), and finally transcripts were added on the entire content of the material which was further divided into subject areas. This is a procedure that many renowned researchers and developers have followed [16, 18–21].

# 4    Interactive Digital Library

The development of this application for the education of D/HH students was created to cover the need for designing and developing differentiated and accessible educational resources and materials drawing from the principles of Universal Design for Learning (UDL) [22, 23]. The application is free and accessible to everyone interested or involved in the teaching and learning process of D/HH and hearing students. Access to the platform is available in the project website www.prosvasimo.gr. The application allows users to browse the filmed content through the use of time defined transcripts, set next to the video in the form of selectable menus that link to the respective time point in the video. The educational content is rendered both in natural voice, in GSL and includes video transcripts that can be read by the users. This multisensory approach and use of a bilingual educational environment motivates students, increases their participation, allows access to information and enhances understanding of the teaching material. In addition, this specific application supports GSL teaching and learning of GSL [16, 24, 25]. This interactive application involves (a) the use of interactive smart subtitles, and (b) the creation and enrichment of a digital library-repository.

**Fig. 1.** Playback of educational material with interactive video subtitles (A. Browse video using subtitles, B. Search for subtitles in the video being played, C. Search for subtitles in all the videos of the platform.) (Color figure online)

The filmed educational material for D/HH students that is uploaded on the platform, such as tales, stories, textbooks and presentations, is presented with interactive subtitles. The user can browse the video by selecting subtitles (Fig. 1A) and also search for words and phrases included in the subtitles (Fig. 1B) with a simultaneous playback of the video in the specific-selected point. The total number of search results can also be displayed and users can navigate among them. It is also possible for users to search subtitle content among all videos (Fig. 1C) of the platform. The application supports the introduction of new subtitles and their processing, the presentation of the video in time series (time - line) in four different forms (Anti-Alias, Slit-Scan, Keyframes, Waveform), and gives users the option to select and play back certain segments of the filmed material. Furthermore, the users can add new material or combine information that has already been collected in the platform. During video playback there is an option to repeat the current scene of the video, the possibility to upload videos in mpeg and mp4 formats and to optimize the playback quality (playback videos in high definition (1080p). All users can download in a WebM format the presented videos using direct download or torrent software. Another feature is the possibility to save the URL address of the video as it is being played, at a specific time, and then use this address for the video playback, starting from the time when the URL address was saved. The video is stored and played from a local server, without the use of a central video service like YouTube. The entire application with its material can be installed either in schools or locations which do not have internet access but have computing units (with good processing power and storage options), or in schools whose computers are interconnected in a local area network.

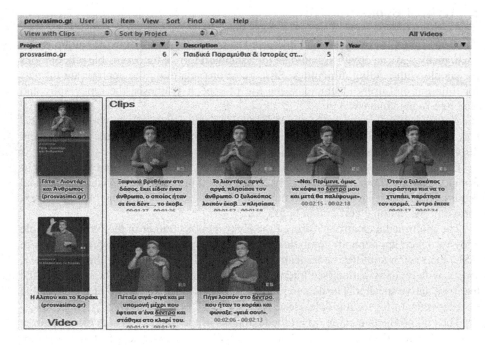

**Fig. 2.** Search Example. Displays the videos on the left and the corresponding clips containing the word "tree" on the right. (Color figure online)

Except for the possibility to use interactive video subtitles, this platform is actually a digital database, a repository that apart from audiovisual material can also accept documents (PDF, Word) which can be then either combined with or linked to specific videos. In this way an integrated content base is created.

All materials along with the subtitled text are quickly and easily available through the use of advanced search options where the user can search for specific words and phrases among the subtitles. Search results can be limited to either a video or contain elements from all the material of the platform. Search can display the videos or clips which include the word or phrase that has been searched, classify them by using various filters (e.g. duration, title, resolution etc.) and also play each clip or video separately. In every search the detected words or phrases are highlighted in yellow.

The material of the interactive application is characterized by ergonomy and visually appealing graphics. The interactive application operating as a digital library offers the alternative to archive and search through the uploaded material (Fig. 2) within the framework of several criteria: thematic, calendrical and geographical. Users can also view the history of the uploaded files. These features support both educational and administrative work. The application can be used to archive student data as well as to evaluate them [26]. In addition, all the material (documents and visual components) can be printed and are automatically distributed during upload into separate folders.

## 5   Hybrid Books

A recent study [24] of dyslexic children in Denmark suggests that hybrid audio books are in many ways an obvious candidate for a standard format for accessible schoolbooks for people with reading difficulties. Still, questions regarding the appropriate formats for different end users or contexts, the use of speech synthesis, the typography and structure remain unanswered.

A similar technology used by the Masaryk University known as "Hybrid Book" [27] was used as a model for the creation of study materials aimed at users with different disabilities such as visual, hearing, motor, mental and others.

Our initial focus group consists of D/HH students attending the first two grades of primary school. The format that has been developed in order to cover the educational needs of this age group and to avoid further differentiation, is following the original text format of the national curriculum books.

The multimedia electronic form of the Hybrid books (either in the form of a single copy or a web application) combines the presentation of the original printed book in GSL, the text in subtitles underneath the videotaped presentation of the GSL video, videos with text navigation (see Interactive digital library) as well as the voicing of the text by a native speaker. The data in multimedia PDF, video and audio files is available in independent files for multiple uses.

The end products include (a) all the textbooks of the first two grades of elementary school, developed by using written and spoken Greek and Greek Sign Language (see sample screen shot in Fig. 3) (b) the development of special education material for language readiness (Kindergarten) and the learning of Greek Sign Language (GSL) as a first language in the first two elementary grades.

Major attention was given to the relationship between the spoken and the sign language text, so that end-products will be used effectively in bilingual educational practices. The signed text is in accordance with the Greek text at a word, phrase or period level. The quality of the text in GSL is the most important aspect of accessibility and has also played a key role in the evaluation of the end-product. The translation of a text in GSL is either very close to the original context or it is more flexible and closer to an adaptation. Using the same textbooks, the authors sometimes either seek for content comprehension or place emphasis on learning vocabulary, Modern Greek grammar or the acquisition of phonological awareness. If the objective is to understand the text, then the signers - interpreters have followed an approach that tolerates distance from the text

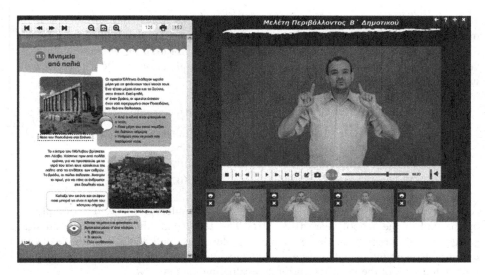

**Fig. 3.** Screen from a Hybrid book whose accessible interface presents the text with the use of Greek Sign Language for the deaf and hard of hearing students.

and focuses on the gist. If the objective is grammatical, syntactic or phonological aware-ness, then interpretation mostly follows the original source.

It is made evident from all the previous productions that signing Greek texts is an extremely demanding and difficult task [9]. The signing of the texts is done, on the one hand, in cooperation with experienced native signers, deaf tutors or consultants (all fluent in Greek) and on the other, with professional interpreters of GSL. These two categories of professionals have worked collaboratively forming a team of bilingual translators. Their subject knowledge, the knowledge of the target group and their expe-rience in educational interpreting are also important factors that have been taken into account.

It is emphasized that, during the conversion of textbooks to accessible educational materials, much significance has been given to signed text because the efficient use of GSL constitutes the core of the project.

Finally, all material developed aim to fulfil the requirements of Design-for- All and are compatible with international practices such as the DAISY Web Player [28].

## 6    Results

The deliverables of the Project have been evaluated by a group of experts, teachers and pre-service teachers of Deaf children.

The evaluation of the sample and the final material was based on the evaluation criteria developed by the expert committee and resulted in the above mean values results. The evaluation scale was developed to either decline the deliverables if they were rated below 80, accept them if they were rated from 80 to 100 and strongly accept them when the deliverables where rated from 100 to 110. All the accepted samples were rated from

107 (Interactive digital library) to 109,4 (Hybrid books for D/HH) and all the final material was rated between 107 (Interactive digital library) and 110 (Teaching Greek Sign Language as a first language), (Table 1). This high rating of the final material is very encouraging for any further developments and applications while it is consistent with the overall evaluation.

**Table 1.** Evaluation of both the sample and the final material

| Subjects | GSL (2 subjects) | Hybrid books (4 subjects) | Interactive digital library |
|---|---|---|---|
| Sample | 109 | 109,4 | 107 |
| Final | 110 | 109,5 | 107 |

Evaluation of the pilot implementation is currently underway and will be completed by the end of the school year 2015–2016. The accessible educational material was presented in four regions of Greece (Ioannina, Alexandroupoli, Volos and Rhodes) with impressive quantitative and qualitative initial results. More than 200 in-service and pre-service teachers of the Deaf are currently evaluating the material.

A formative assessment of the overall project was carried out to ensure its quality and effectiveness when put into broader practice. The project and its deliverables were evaluated by the European Union (European Social Fund – ESF 2007-2013). As a result of this evaluation the project was rated as one of the 11 best of the Ministry of Education and one of the 30 best in Greece. These results are very encouraging, particularly for continuing the development of accessible educational material for students with disabilities and special educational needs.

## 7    Conclusions

The benefits of the application are multiple and affect students, teachers, parents and everyone involved in the educational process. D/HH students can thus acquire access to knowledge and information, the national curriculum and the learning of GSL. Hence, their involvement in the learning process is increased and their capability to understand and handle the incoming information is enhanced [5, 6, 10, 21, 29]. Moreover, teachers can use the application in the design and implementation of educational programs, in the evaluation process and in many other aspects of their work. Parents can use it not only to support their children, but also to learn GSL by themselves. Finally, any other professional interested in expanding their skills and understanding the problems of special education may optionally use this application.

The development of this application promotes accessibility to education and thus minimizes barriers to learning, particularly among D/HH students, at the same time, it also creates the right environment for the implementation of inclusive practices. This application apart from supporting the education and learning process of D/HH students and their learning of GSL, can be also used by all students. Such broader usage and practice can make it more viable, further developed and adapted to various environment. The innovative use and development of interactive subtitles makes it the appropriate tool, accessible to all, freeware, and adapted to the needs of D/HH students. It is an application that could be also used as a repository for the collection and processing of new material like videos and documents.

**Acknowledgments.** This research has been co-financed by the European Union (European Social Fund – ESF) and the Greek national funds through the Operational Program "Education and Lifelong Learning" of the National Strategic Reference Framework (NSRF) under the project: "Design and Development of Accessible Educational & Instructional Material for Students with Disabilities".

# References

1. Armstrong, F.: Difference, discourse and democracy: the making and breaking of policy in the market place. Int. J. Incl. Educ. **7**(3), 241–257 (2003)
2. Booth, T., Ainscow, M.: Index for Inclusion: Developing Learning and Participation in Schools, 3rd edn. Centre for Studies on Inclusive Education (CSIE), London (2011)
3. UNESCO: ICTs in Education for People with Special Needs. Review of Innovative Practice. UNESCO, Institute for Information Technologies, New York (2011)
4. Fox, J., Hoffman, W.: The Differentiated Instruction, Book of lists. Jossey-Bass, San Francisco (2011)
5. Tomlinson, C.A.: How to Differentiate Instruction in Mixed-Ability Class-Rooms, 2nd edn. ASCD, Alexandria (2001)
6. Smith, G., Throne, S.: Differentiating instruction with technology in K-5 classrooms. International Society for Technology in Education, Belmont (2007).
7. Burnett, C.: Technology and literacy in early childhood educational settings: a review of research. J. Early Child. Lit. **10**(3), 247–270 (2010)
8. Gentry, M., Chinn, K., Moulton, R.: Effectiveness of multimedia reading materials when used with children who are deaf. Am. Ann. Deaf **149**(5), 394–403 (2005)
9. Kourbetis, V.: Design and development of accessible educational and teaching material for deaf students in Greece. In: Antona, M., Stephanidis, C. (eds.) UAHCI 2013, Part III. LNCS, vol. 8011, pp. 172–178. Springer, Heidelberg (2013)
10. Mich, O., Pianta, E., Mana, N.: Interactive stories and exercises with dynamic feedback for improving reading comprehension skills in deaf children. Comput. Educ. **65**, 34–44 (2013)
11. Debevc, M., Peljhan, Ž.: The role of video technology in on-line lectures for the deaf. Disabil. Rehabil. **26**(17), 1048–1059 (2004)
12. Hilzensauer, M., Dotter, F.: Sign On, a model for teaching written language to deaf people. In: 2011 IST-Africa Conference Proceedings (2011)
13. Hoffmeister, R.: Language and the deaf world: difference not disability, language. culture, and community in teacher education, pp. 71–98 (2013)
14. Kourbetis, V., Hatzopoulou, M.: I Can with my Eyes: Educational Approaches and Practices for Deaf Students. Kastaniotis, Athens (2010). (in Greek)
15. UNESCO: Convention on the rights of persons with disabilities (2007). https://www.un.org/development/desa/disabilities/convention-on-the-rights-of-persons-with-disabilities.html. Accessed 11 May 2015
16. Mason, J.: Qualitative Researching. Sage, London (2002)
17. Barton, L.: Emancipatory research and disabled people: some observations and questions. Educ. Rev. **57**(3), 317–327 (2005)

18. Rosas, R., Véliz, S., Arroyo, R., Sánchez, M.I., Pizarro, M., Aparicio, A.D.: PAPELUCHO: a model for developing inclusive digital books for deaf children. In: Proceedings of 22nd International Congress on the Education of the Deaf, p. 161 (2015)

19. Barman, C.R., Stockton, J.D.: An evaluation of the SOAR-High Project: a webbased science program for deaf students. Am. Ann. Deaf **147**(3), 5–10 (2002)

20. Easterbrooks, S., Stephenson, B.: An examination of twenty literacy, science, and mathematics practices used to educate students who are deaf or hard of hearing. Am. Ann. Deaf **151**(4), 385–397 (2006)

21. Fajardo, I., Parra, E., Cañas, J.: Do sign language videos improve web navigation for deaf signer users? J. Deaf Stud. Deaf Educ. **15**(3), 242–262 (2010)

22. Blamires, M.: Universal design for learning: re-establishing differentiations as part of the inclusion agenda? Support Learn. **14**(4), 158–163 (1999)

23. CAST: Universal Design for Learning Guidelines (version 2.0). Author, Wakefield (2011)

24. Kourbetis, V.: Design and development of accessible educational and teaching material for deaf students in Greece. In: Stephanidis, C., Antona, M. (eds.) UAHCI 2013, Part III. LNCS, vol. 8011, pp. 172–178. Springer, Heidelberg (2013)

25. Tuomi, I.: Open educational resources and the transformation of education. European Journal of Education **48**(1), 58–78 (2013)

26. UNESCO: ICTs in education for people with special needs. UNESCO Institute for Information Technologies in Education, New York (2006)

27. Hladík, P., Gůra, T.: The hybrid book - one document for all in the latest development. In: Miesenberger, K., Karshmer, A., Penaz, P., Zagler, W. (eds.) Computers Helping People with Special Needs. LNCS, pp. 18–24. Springer, Heidelberg (2012)

28. Eberius, W., Haffner, A.: Multimodal enhancements and distribution of DAISY-Books. In: Proceedings DAISY 2009 (2010)

29. Hockings, C., Brett, P., Terentjevs, M.: Making a difference-inclusive learning and teaching in higher education through open educational resources. Distance Educ. **33**(2), 237–252 (2012)

# The Effect of Literacy Learning via Mobile Augmented Reality for the Students with ADHD and Reading Disabilities

Chien-Yu Lin[1(✉)], Wen-Jeng Yu[2], Wei-Jie Chen[1], Chun-Wei Huang[1], and Chien-Chi Lin[3]

[1] Department of Special Education, National University of Tainan, Tainan 70005, Taiwan
linchienyu@mail.nutn.edu.tw
[2] National University of Tainan Affiliated Primary School, Tainan 70005, Taiwan
[3] Department of Tourism, Food and Beverage Management, Chang Jung Christian University, Tainan 711, Taiwan

**Abstract.** This study focuses on the effects of mobile augmented reality (MAR) on word recognition learning. The study developed an interactive effect and corresponding video on word learning in MAR. MAR uses the camera of the mobile phone. It is installed in to interpose virtual objects on the real life view through the camera. The study participants were two fifth-grade elementary school children with Attention Deficit Hyperactivity Disorder (ADHD) and reading disabilities. The study followed a single-case design using ABA' models in which A indicated the baseline, B indicated the intervention and A' indicated the maintenance phrase. The experiment period was almost 3 months. The independent variable was word recognition teaching with MAR on Chinese literacy ability of 'read the words' and 'select the correct the word to blank line'. The experimental results demonstrated that the scores for 2 children with ADHD and reading disabilities increased considerably during the intervention and maintenance phrases. The developmental applications of these results are also discussed.

**Keywords:** Performance of word recognition · ADHD · Reading disability · Mobile augmented reality

## 1 Introduction

Recently, multimedia in the interactive learning environment included words, pictures, animation and other innovative digital teaching aids in learning and instruction [1]. Teachers could transfer complete knowledge from multimedia teaching materials for vocabulary practice with struggling students [2]. The integration of real-time interactive multimedia as a support represents a significant improvement in traditional teaching strategies [3]. Augmented reality (AR), as an emerging interactive technology, has been applied to various fields [4]. AR technology enables the merging of virtual with real objects, resulting in AR environments [5] and can be used for a live direct or indirect view of a physical, real-world environment, the elements of which are augmented by computer-generated sensory inputs, such as animation [6]. The design of a mobile

© Springer International Publishing Switzerland 2016
M. Antona and C. Stephanidis (Eds.): UAHCI 2016, Part III, LNCS 9739, pp. 103–111, 2016.
DOI: 10.1007/978-3-319-40238-3_11

augmented reality (MAR) system that using recognized from a large database to track the corresponding content [7]. AR-guide for exhibitions supported between the virtual space and the physical scenes; that is, enhance the interaction between the additional, virtual information and the real exhibits [8].

MAR environments support virtual object overlay of real objects to change users' view of their environment [9]. The main advantages of MAR applications used across different fields have been widely discussed, such as exploring cities [10], education [11], language services [12], language learning [13], management system [14], awareness services [15], textiles, surgical interventions [16], games [17], home-training system, teaching [18] and learning disabilities [19]. MAR can enhance students' learning motivation.

ADHD can be considered a generalized impulsivity disorder and is one of the most prevalent mental health disorders in childhood [20]. Children with ADHD find it difficult to receive visual information and have an attention deficit; their learning abilities are hampered because in the process of receiving information, they are unable to grasp the correct information or receive too much information, which could disrupt their judgment. Studies of the academic achievements of children with ADHD imply that they are more likely to obtain lower grades in standard measures than control children of equivalent intelligence [21]. Students with ADHD experience problems with learning in an academic setting, often encountering difficulties with reading, spelling and writing [22]. Furthermore, they are rated below their peers on behaviours that enable academic success, such as motivation, engagement and study skills [23]. The development of children with attention and learning problems is discussed in both Bach and Pacton [24, 25]. Attention skills improved during action multimedia game training [26], using cognitive assistive technology in settings, indicate a higher frequency of participating in work for ADHD [27]. Assistive Technology is proving to be a critical in ensuring the success of students with learning [28].

Therefore, the MAR design could stimulate children's motivation for the learning process. It has advantages for teaching materials design, because through the free software and open source platform with contents that can be easily duplicated and combined, MAR could be a flexible interface for designing teaching materials for children with reading disabilities. As the platform is free, teachers and parents need not worry about the high price like assistive technology.

## 2      Materials and Methods

### 2.1      Participants

There were two participants in this study: twins with ADHD who were compared with regards to reading disabilities. Formal consent was obtained from their parents prior to the commencement of study. This study designed individual vocabulary learning for the special needs of the participants to enhance their learning motivation. We obtained formal consent from their parents for this study designed to enhance the learning motivation and effectiveness.

Participant A, an 11-year 1-month-old male. Wechsler Intelligence Scale for Children-Third Edition (WISC-III), full scale: 93; verbal scale: 99; performance scale: 88; verbal comprehension index (VCI): 101; perceptual organization index (POI): 85; freedom from distractibility index (FDI): 79; processing speed index (PSI): 106.

Participant B, an 11-year 1-month-old male. Wechsler Intelligence Scale for Children-Third Edition (WISC-III), full scale: 100; verbal scale: 102; performance scale: 98; verbal comprehension index (VCI): 105; perceptual organization index (POI): 104; freedom from distractibility index (FDI): 79; processing speed index (PSI): 103.

The twin brothers, in addition to their diagnoses of ADHD and reading disabilities, lagged behind their peers in class in terms of academic performance; literacy words amount is poor; difficulty in recognizing and reading words; inability to write the words that were taught and using more or fewer strokes in words' structure. Overall, their short-term memory was good, but their long-term memory not as well as short-term memory.

## 2.2  Apparatus, Material and Setting

Teaching content included six units, a total of 60 target words via mobile phone with AR as the teaching process. According to the results of the evaluation assessment from the two participants, the level of basic literacy was 1300–1400, and this study used 60 target words from the sequence 1401–1500 of the 'Elementary School Children Common Words Report'. These 60 words could nor adopted in the textbooks, via the amount of the word's strokes, and Average distribution in different unit, also excluded the words appear in the textbook, the word stokes, as Table 1, and design the digital content via MAR.

The three subtests in the Mandarin Literacy Assessment included 'read the words', 'write the words' and 'fill the selected word in the sentence'. Each subtest selected three words from ten target words, randomly selected from six teaching units, for a total of 18 questions. In total, Mandarin Literacy Assessment includes 54 questions, establishing equivalence copies to avoid repeating the practice effect. Two special education teachers, with 12 and 15 years of experience, reviewed and revised each assessment.

The free Aurasma© application is available on both iOS and Android. Once installed, any user with a 3G or WiFi connection can use the app via a smart phone or tablet for free. Two teachers and two assistants conducted this study; they designed the word flash cards and arranged the corresponding Aurasma video, via the platform function, to combine flash card and corresponding film. The participant could then use a mobile phone to scan the image and create videos, animations or data.

The study contents include teaching literacy programs and teaching assistive technology. The participant used the Aurasma application on a mobile phone to scan the flash card, then will show the relative film, the screen show process as Fig. 1, in the teaching process, the teacher also offer paper work for real write the word to increase the memory the words. The concept of the study is shown in Fig. 1.

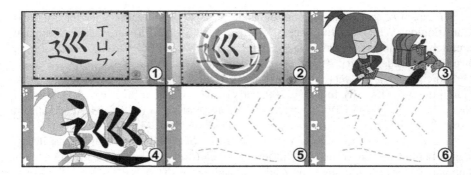

**Fig. 1.** The MAR concept of the study

## 2.3   General Procedure

The Aurasma© application is available on both iOS and Android. The user environment should provide 3G or WiFi connection via a smart phone, following the free channel with the content designed by the teachers' team. The study used Android and WiFi. Before the experiment, the teacher should explain how to participate in the process and demonstrate the same for the participants. Figure 2. shows the experimental setup.

**Fig. 2.** The experimental device and setup

To control the participants' mood in different situations, this study selected a resource classroom used for normal activities. Teaching experimental period: baseline phrase during 6−24 October 2014; intervention phrase during 27 October−5 December 2014; maintenance phrase 15 December 2014−2 January 2015. To avoid potential interference from other students and ensure the study produces the appropriate effects, this study was separately handled. The teaching process was adopted in one-on-one session to control other factors.

The experimental design adopted an ABA for single-case research as the assessment method, in which A (baseline phase) was followed by B (intervention phase), and then followed the maintenance phase. The A represented baseline phases while the B represented intervention phases with the MAR system. Single-case design is a research method involving deliberate assignment of different conditions to the same individual and measurement of one or more outcomes over time (Hedges). Cohen offered an effect size for predictive regression equations that could indicate the actual effect including a large (> 0.35), medium (0.15–0.35) or small effect size (0.02–0.15).

The data was collected over 3 months. In the first phase, Baseline 1 (baseline phase) —Conduct 'Mandarin Literacy Assessment' Quiz—we collected three data points. The second phase, Intervention (B1), used a mobile phone, the augmented system and the relative teaching materials, for a six-week teaching intervention. There were a total of six teaching units, three lessons a week—a total of 120 min in each week. After the end of each unit, a Mandarin Literacy Assessment was conducted as an immediate assessment of the effectiveness of data collection, from which we collected six data points. We waited for one week and then, executed the maintenance phase, from which we collected three data points; this phrase used similar teaching materials, and a Mandarin Literacy Assessment was conducted.

# 3   Results

The results of this study included both a descriptive and qualitative analysis of the data. The data collected from all three phases were presented on graphs, in which the x-axis indicated the three phases of the study, and the y-axis showed the scores that the participant received for each task. This study investigated the effect of literacy learning via MAR for ADHD compare attention deficit, divided into three parts.

## 3.1   The Effectiveness of the Subtest of "Read the Words"

Figure 3 shows the effectiveness of the subtest of 'read the words'. Participant A is denoted with a square and participant B is denoted with a circle.

At baseline, participant A's mean score is 1.67, with a range of 1–2; participant B's mean score is 2.33, with a range of 2–3. The results of baseline indicated that participant A lacked the effectiveness of the subtest of 'read the words'. When the experiment proceeded to intervention stage, participant A's mean score was 10.67, with a range of 6–16; participant B's mean score was 8.83, with a range of 5–14—a completely different phrase. In maintenance stage, the intervention was withdrawn; participant A's mean score was 14.67, with a range of 14–15; participant B's mean score was 12.67, with a range of 12–13. From this single-subject research using an ABA structure, the effect analysis of participant A in baseline and intervention was xt's $p = .008 < .05$, with a slope *change* effect size of 3.5897. The effect analysis of participant B in baseline and intervention was xt's $p = .008 < .05$, with a slope *change* effect size of 2.6211. For baseline and maintenance phases of participant A, the xt's $p = .520 > .05$ and an intercept *change* effect size = 47.4923. For baseline and maintenance phases of participant B, the xt's $p = .520 > .05$ and an intercept *change* effect size = 38.8769. The maintenance phase showed a significantly increased effect compared with the baseline phase. A large effect can be seen between the maintenance and baseline phases. The maintenance phase showed a significantly increased effect compared with the baseline phase. From the data

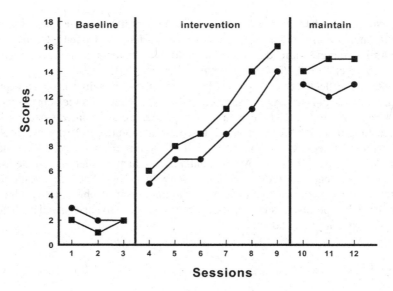

**Fig. 3.** The effectiveness of the subtest of 'read the words'

analysis, it was demonstrated that the intervention and maintenance phrases had a positive effect on participant A and participant B. We also used the Kolmogorov–Smirnov
statistical test, the results of which also highlighted the significant improvement between
the baseline and intervention phases ($p = .00 < .05$); the results indicated that the
improvement between the baseline and intervention was significant.

### 3.2 The Effectiveness of the Subtest of 'Select the Correct the Word to Blank Line'

Figure 4 shows the effectiveness of the subtest of 'select the correct the word to blank
line'. Participant A is depicted with a square and participant B is depicted with a circle.

At baseline, participant A's mean score is 1.67, with a range of 1–2; participant B's
mean score is 2.33, with a range of 2–3. The results of baseline indicated that participant
A lacked the effectiveness of the subtest of 'select the correct the word to blank line'.
When the experiment proceeded to intervention stage, participant A's mean score was
7.83, with a range of 4–10; participant B's mean score was 8.17, with a range of 4–11
—a completely different phrase. In maintenance stage, the intervention was withdrawn;
participant A's mean score was 7.67, with a range of 7–8; participant B's mean score
was 8, with a range of 8–8. From this single-subject research using an ABA structure,
the effect analysis of participant A in baseline and intervention was xt's $p = .045 < 0.05$,
with a slope change effect size of 1.4058. The effect analysis of participant B in baseline
and intervention was xt's $p = .018 < 0.05$, with a slope change effect size of 2.3998. For
baseline and maintenance phases of participant A, the xt's $p = .520 > 0.05$ and an
intercept effect size $= 14.4198$. For baseline and maintenance phases of participant B,
the xt's $p = .225 > .05$ and an intercept effect size $= 33.8800$. The maintenance phase
showed a significantly increased effect compared with the baseline phase. A large effect

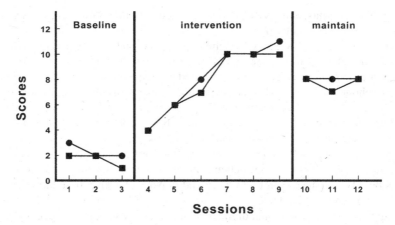

**Fig. 4.** The effectiveness of the subtest of 'select the correct the word to blank line'

can be seen between the maintenance and baseline phases. The maintenance phase showed a significantly increased effect compared with the baseline phase. From the data analysis, it was demonstrated that the intervention and maintenance phrases had a positive effect on participant A and participant B. We also used the Kolmogorov–Smirnov statistical test, the results of which also highlighted the significant improvement between the baseline and intervention phases ($p = 0.00 < 0.05$); the results indicated that the improvement between the baseline and intervention was significant.

## 4   Discussion

The two study participants had ADHD compare with reading disabilities. In the study, via MAR teaching materials and mobile phone, there are significant effects observed in the intervention and maintenance phases.

The study by MAR builds a multi-sensory learning environment, via an interactive man–machine, increases the opportunities for participants to operate MAR; attracts their interest and attention and, through visual and auditory feedback, enables participants via different sensory stimulation activities to enhance students' effective absorption of knowledge.

Via MAR and the free applications, this study amounts to an assistive tool that saves time, money, effort and is suitable to promote learning motivation. The target words used in this study are often used in real-life situations; the instructional videos captured daily life combined with the actual situation; it is possible to match the participants' learning level and life experiences; the tool improves understanding of abstract words and then guides participants to apply these words in real environments to maximize the effectiveness of how to teach Chinese words.

In interviews with the participants' tutors, tutor A had 11 years of teaching experience (participant A's tutor), and tutor B had 11 years of teaching experience (participant

B's tutor). Their enthusiasm for teaching indicated that they could clearly grasp the learning situation of the participants.

Tutors A and B, though the MAR teaching materials and teaching process, enhanced the rate of correct responses in read and write words and improved the progress in selecting words in sentences. Tutor A represented participants A's very skilled operation of a mobile phone, and the MAR teaching materials were easy to use, and it enhanced the learning motivation for participant A. Tutor B found participant B lively and happy to participate in a dynamic curriculum. MAR may allow students to have direct operation and thus, increase their motivation of learning process.

Overall, participants who can take visual and auditory cues from colour pictures and dynamic videos, with easy to comprehend literacy content, not only acquire learning outcomes but also enhance their confidence and in particular, use these target words in real-life circumstance. ADHD compare reading disabilities could use multimedia for this learning process, and abundant digital teaching materials could enhance their attention and thereby promote their learning efficiency.

**Acknowledgement.** This work was financially supported by the National Science Council, Taiwan, under the Grant 100-2410-H-024-028-MY2.

# References

1. Mayer, R.E.: Incorporating motivation into multimedia learning. Learn. Instr. **29**, 171–173 (2014)
2. Ely, E., Kennedy, M.J., Pullen, P.C., Williams, M.C., Hirsch, S.E.: Improving instruction of future teachers: a multimedia approach that supports implementation of evidence-based vocabulary practices. Teach. Teacher Educ. **44**, 35–43 (2014)
3. Poyade, M., Clunie, L., McGeough, B., Lysakowski, A., Rea, P., Anderson, P.: Toward the development of an accurate 3D human body model implemented in a real-time, interactive application to enhance anatomy teaching. FASEB J. **29**(1 Supplement), 692–713 (2015)
4. Gandy, M., Julier, S., Kiyokawa, K.: Guest editor's introduction to the special section on the international symposium on mixed and augmented reality 2013. IEEE Trans. Visual. Comput. Graph. **5**, 555–556 (2015)
5. Ke, F., Hsu, Y.C.: Mobile augmented-reality artifact creation as a component of mobile computer-supported collaborative learning. Internet High. Educ. **26**, 33–41 (2015)
6. Yilmaz, R.M.: Educational magic toys developed with augmented reality technology for early childhood education. Comput. Hum. Behav. **54**, 240–248 (2016)
7. Yang, X., Cheng, K.T.: Learning optimized local difference binaries for scalable augmented reality on mobile devices. IEEE Trans. Visual. Comput. Graph. **20**(6), 852–865 (2014)
8. Chang, K.E., Chang, C.T., Hou, H.T., Sung, Y.T., Chao, H.L., Lee, C.M.: Development and behavioral pattern analysis of a mobile guide system with augmented reality for painting appreciation instruction in an art museum. Comput. Educ. **71**, 185–197 (2014)
9. Jung, T., Chung, N., Leue, M.C.: The determinants of recommendations to use augmented reality technologies: the case of a Korean theme park. Tour. Manag. **49**, 75–86 (2015)
10. Di, G.B., Raquel, C.: Augmented reality by mobile devices: proposed application to explore the city through music, history and interactivity. Blucher Des. Proc. **1**(2), 1043–1055 (2014)

11. Reinders, H., Lakarnchua, O., Pegrum, M.: A trade-off in learning: mobile augmented reality for language learning. In: Contemporary Task-Based Language Teaching in Asia, p. 244 (2015)
12. Lin, H.F., Chen, C.H.: Design and application of augmented reality query-answering system in mobile phone information navigation. Expert Syst. Appl. **42**(2), 810–820 (2015)
13. Perry, B.: Gamifying French language learning: a case study examining a quest-based, augmented reality mobile learning-tool. Procedia-Soc. Behav. Sci. **174**, 2308–2315 (2015)
14. Shatte, A., Holdsworth, J., Lee, I.: Mobile augmented reality based context-aware library management system. Expert Syst. Appl. **41**(5), 2174–2185 (2014)
15. Lin, P.-J., Chen, S.-C., Li, Y.-H., Wu, M.-S., Chen, S.-Y.: An implementation of augmented reality and location awareness services in mobile devices. In: Park, J.J.H., Adeli, H., Park, N., Woungang, I. (eds.) Mobile, Ubiquitous, and Intelligent Computing. LNEE, vol. 274, pp. 509–514. Springer, Heidelberg (2014)
16. Lapeer, R.J., Jeffrey, S.J., Dao, J.T., García, G.G., Chen, M., Shickell, S.M., Philpott, C.M.: Using a passive coordinate measurement arm for motion tracking of a rigid endoscope for augmented-reality image-guided surgery. Int. J. Med. Robot. Comput. Assist. Surg. **10**(1), 65–77 (2014)
17. Lu, S.J., Liu, Y.C.: Integrating augmented reality technology to enhance children's learning in marine education. Environ. Educ. Res. **21**(4), 525–541 (2015)
18. Crandall, P.G., Engler, R.K., Beck, D.E., Killian, S.A., O'Bryan, C.A., Jarvis, N., Clausen, E.: Development of an augmented reality game to teach abstract concepts in food chemistry. J. Food Sci. Educ. **14**(1), 18–23 (2015)
19. McMahon, D., Cihak, D.F., Wright, R.: Augmented reality as a navigation tool to employment opportunities for postsecondary education students with intellectual disabilities and autism. J. Res. Technol. Educ. **47**(3), 157–172 (2015)
20. Lawton, K.E., Gerdes, A.C., Haack, L.M., Schneider, B.: Acculturation, cultural values, and Latino parental beliefs about the etiology of ADHD. Adm. Policy Ment. Health Ment. Health Serv. Res. **41**(2), 189–204 (2014)
21. Donnadieu, S., Berger, C., Lallier, M., Marendaz, C., Laurent, A.: Is the impairment in temporal allocation of visual attention in children with ADHD related to a developmental delay or a structural cognitive deficit? Res. Dev. Disabil. **36**, 384–395 (2015)
22. Luman, M., Goos, V., Oosterlaan, J.: Instrumental learning in ADHD in a context of reward: intact learning curves and performance improvement with methylphenidate. J. Abnorm. Child Psychol. **43**, 1–11 (2014)
23. Rogers, M., Boggia, J., Ogg, J., Volpe, R.: The ecology of ADHD in the schools. Curr. Dev. Disord. Rep. **2**(1), 23–29 (2015)
24. Bach, S., Richardson, U., Brandeis, D., Martin, E., Brem, S.: Print-specific multimodal brain activation in kindergarten improves prediction of reading skills in second grade. Neuroimage **82**, 605–615 (2013)
25. Pacton, S., Foulin, J.N., Casalis, S., Treiman, R.: Children benefit from morphological relatedness when they learn to spell new words. Front. Psychol. **4**, 696 (2013)
26. Franceschini, S., Gori, S., Ruffino, M., Viola, S., Molteni, M., Facoetti, A.: Action video games make dyslexic children read better. Curr. Biol. **23**(6), 462–466 (2013)
27. Lindstedt, H., Umb-Carlsson, Ō.: Cognitive assistive technology and professional support in everyday life for adults with ADHD. Disabil. Rehabil. Assistive Technol. **8**(5), 402–408 (2013)
28. Coleman, M.B., Cramer, E.S., Park, Y., Bell, S.M.: Art educators' use of adaptations, assistive technology, and special education supports for students with physical, visual, severe and multiple disabilities. J. Dev. Phys. Disabil. **27**(5), 637–660 (2015)

# Exploring the Relationship Between Implicit Scaffolding and Inclusive Design in Interactive Science Simulations

Emily B. Moore[1(✉)], Taliesin L. Smith[2], and Emily Randall[1]

[1] University of Colorado Boulder, Boulder, USA
{emily.moore,emily.randall}@colorado.edu
[2] OCAD University, Toronto, Canada
talilief@gmail.com

**Abstract.** Interactive science simulations are commonly used educational tools. PhET Interactive Simulations are a popular suite of free science simulations used by teachers and students worldwide. These simulations are designed using implicit scaffolding, a design framework developed by the PhET project. Implicit scaffolding supports student learning without the use of instructions or other explicit guidance within the simulations. Recently, the PhET project has begun expanding the inclusive features in the simulations and aims to broaden implicit scaffolding beyond the visual. In this work, we present results from an analysis of user interviews exploring the relationship between auditory description design and implicit scaffolding. Findings indicate that our approaches to auditory descriptions can result in productive user interactions, similar to those found in prior work on implicit scaffolding with visual designs, demonstrating that implicit scaffolding approaches can include non-visual design.

**Keywords:** Web accessibility · Usability · Inclusive design · Non-visual user interface · Text description · Interactive science simulation

## 1 Introduction

Educational interactive simulations can be powerful tools to support student engagement and achievement in science disciplines [1, 2]. Interactive science simulations contain an underlying model based on scientific phenomena (e.g., current and voltage in a circuit simulation). By allowing students to change model parameters and experience the outcome of these changes, interactive simulations can be particularly useful for supporting students' engagement in authentic science practices in the classroom and enjoyment of the process [3–5].

PhET simulations (sims) are a popular suite of interactive simulations developed by the PhET Interactive Simulations project [6] at the University of Colorado Boulder. The PhET project impacts classrooms around the world through over 130 interactive science and mathematics sims and associated teacher resources. The sims are run over 75 million times per year, across K-16 levels, and have been translated into 75 languages. Despite the potential of PhET sims to foster engagement and participation in science education,

© Springer International Publishing Switzerland 2016
M. Antona and C. Stephanidis (Eds.): UAHCI 2016, Part III, LNCS 9739, pp. 112–123, 2016.
DOI: 10.1007/978-3-319-40238-3_12

they are currently inaccessible for many students with disabilities – due in part to their reliance on visual representations.

In 2014 PhET began to design new inclusive features to enhance the accessibility of the sims [6]. In collaboration with the Inclusive Design Research Centre, we began developing prototypes of inclusive features [7], prioritizing initial efforts on keyboard navigation and auditory descriptions (to be read by screen readers). Our long-term goals are to transform our growing suite of PhET sims into the most inclusive learning tools possible, and to develop and share research and design guidelines for the inclusive design of other interactive educational resources.

## 2    Implicit Scaffolding and Science Learning

A hallmark of PhET sims is their design through the implicit scaffolding design framework, an approach developed by the PhET project for the design of interactive science sims [8–10]. Implicit scaffolding includes the use of affordances and constraints to cue and guide students to engage in pedagogically productive interactions, while maintaining students' agency and choice during the learning process. The end result is that students can be (implicitly) guided along beneficial and efficient learning paths without the sim being directive or inhibiting active engagement or the students' feeling of control – key components of successful science learning [11]. In other words, PhET's sim designs guide students to engage in productive interactions without students feeling guided. To date, PhET's work on the implicit scaffolding design framework has centered on visual cues and choice of interactions compatible with mouse or touch-interfaces.

As we began the design of inclusive features for PhET sims, we wanted to ensure that the outcomes of implicit scaffolding – e.g., productive learning interactions, active engagement, and agency in the learning process – extended to inclusive features, and ultimately could be experienced by all students. Foundational components of implicit scaffolding [8] include: (1) sequence and interactions, (2) framing engagement, (3) enabling sense making, and (4) continued engagement. To ensure that students engaging with PhET sims experience equivalently engaging and effective learning experiences regardless of what inclusive features they may utilize, we want to understand the relationships between implicit scaffolding and inclusive design. In this work, we analyze how users with visual impairments interact with a prototype PhET sim utilizing a screen reader and compare this with our prior work on how users engage with PhET sims visually, to broaden our original implicit scaffolding design framework to include non-visual design.

## 3    Design of *Capacitor Lab: Basics* Simulation

For this work we focused on design and user testing of the HTML5 prototype sim *Capacitor Lab: Basics* [12]. The design of this sim reflects a specific sequence (ordering of screens, representations, and interactions), and set of interactions (the choice of what representations are interactive, and the specifics of that interactivity) to address the selected learning goals of the sim. In this section, we introduce the learning goals, and associated sequence and interactions of the *Capacitor Lab: Basics* sim, to provide a concrete example of PhET's implicit scaffolding approach.

### 3.1    Setting Scope of the Sim: Learning Goals

The *Capacitor Lab: Basics* sim focuses on the physics of capacitors at the advanced high school (16–18 year olds) and introductory college levels. The sim was designed to support students to be able to: (1) Predict how capacitance changes with changes in voltage, capacitor plate area or separation; (2) Explain the relationships between voltage, charge, stored energy, and capacitance, and (3) Describe how a capacitor can be used to light a light bulb.

### 3.2    Sequence and Interactions

To achieve these learning goals, *Capacitor Lab: Basics* contains two screens for users to explore, the Capacitance screen and the Light Bulb screen (Fig. 1). For the purpose of this paper, we will focus on the Capacitance screen only. In the Capacitance screen, there is a capacitor (two parallel metal plates) connected to a battery; a bar graph that displays the value of the capacitance (a measure of the stored electrical charge); a voltmeter that allows the user to measure voltage at various points on the circuit and across the capacitor plates; and a control panel with checkboxes to add or remove the bar graph, and the plate charge, electric field, or current representations.

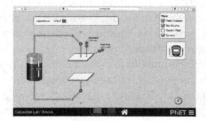 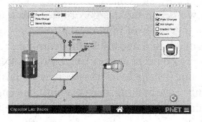

**Fig. 1.** Capacitor *Lab: Basics Simulation*. Capacitance screen (left), Light Bulb screen (right). Images reproduced with permission from PhET Interactive Simulations.

The user can change the voltage on the battery, the capacitor plate separation and plate area, and learn how these changes affect capacitance. Visual representations of plate charge and electric field are overlaid on the capacitor and change dynamically as the user interacts with elements in the circuit. Plate charges are represented by "positive" and "negative" symbols evenly distributed across the plates that change in number as voltage, plate area, and plate distance are changed. Electric field is represented by vector arrows that change in length, number, and direction as the voltage, plate area, and plate distance are changed.

## 3.3   Inclusive Feature – Auditory Descriptions

For the *Capacitor Lab: Basics* sim, we focused on the design of the user experience for those accessing the sim with a screen reader – specifically, navigating the screen with a keyboard and utilizing screen reader shortcut keys to access auditory descriptions and interact with the sim. For technical details regarding the implementation of these inclusive features, please see [7].

**Scene Description.** When a user first opens the sim, using a screen reader, they can navigate through a Scene Description. The Scene Description describes the layout and interactive features of the sim, and is structured hierarchically through the use of headings, paragraphs, etc. This description starts with a general overview of what is available on the screen (labeled as a Heading 1: "The Scene for the Capacitance Screen"), followed by section headings that describe each area of the sim screen (each area labeled as Heading 2: "Play Area", "Graph Panel", and "Control Panel"). After each heading are subheadings that list the interactive elements found in that area, the current state of these elements, and – in cases where the interaction may not follow standard conventions – a description of how to interact with that element. In Table 1 we present an example of the first three subheadings and descriptions found after "Play Area".

**Table 1.**  "Play Area" section of scene description

| Structure | Text description for "play area" and its subheadings |
|---|---|
| **Heading 2** | **Play Area** |
| Paragraph | A place to play with a capacitor in a circuit with a battery. |
| **Heading 3** | **Circuit** |
| Paragraph | The circuit contains a capacitor and a battery. The capacitor is currently connected to the battery. |
| **Heading 4** | **Battery** |
| Paragraph | The battery has a slider on it that controls voltage. The current voltage is 0 volts. Use the arrow keys to change the voltage of the battery. |
| **Heading 4** | **Capacitor** |
| Paragraph | The capacitor is represented by two rectangular plates, one on top of the other, separated by a small space. It has a slider above it that controls the separation of the plates, and a slider next to it that controls the area of the plates. There are no charges visible on the plates. |

*Note: The "Play Area" description continues on to include "Switches" (H4), "Toolbox" (H3), and "Voltmeter" (H4).

**Interactive Elements.** Users can also navigate to each interactive element in the sim and hear a description of that element. As the user makes changes in the sim with the interactive elements, they hear live updates of changes to that element and to all other impacted sim features. For example, the battery in the circuit can be navigated to by pressing the "Tab" key to navigate to the circuit group, and then pressing the "Enter" key to enter the circuit group. The battery is the first interactive element in the circuit group. The battery consists of a slider, allowing control of the voltage available to the circuit. As the user changes the battery voltage (using the arrow keys to change the voltage slider) the user is updated on the current voltage value, and any other changes in the sim that may occur as a result of this voltage change (e.g., the flow of current).

## 4   Methods

As part of the iterative design process, we conducted user interviews to explore and refine design ideas. Each interview was structured into three sections. First, users were asked three conceptual questions to help assess their knowledge of the sim topic, capacitance. Next, users were provided with a computer, equipped with the screen reader NVDA [13] with the sim open and ready for use, and were asked to "Explore the simulation, and try to think out loud as you explore." The sim use portion of the interview was conducted in a think aloud format, where users were asked to think aloud as they explored the sim, with little to no interruption from the researcher. After exploring the sim, users were again asked three conceptual questions to help assess any knowledge they may have gained through using the sim, as well as general questions about usability and sim design.

During the interview, we collected audio recordings of users' verbalizations, and video recordings of the computer screen and of users' keyboard interactions and gestures. We analyzed these data sources for evidence of the sim's non-visual scaffolding in supporting or inhibiting the users from productive interactions.

### 4.1   Participants

A total of three interviews have been conducted with *Capacitor Lab: Basics* prototypes, with the inclusive features of keyboard navigation and auditory descriptions. The first interview was conducted with an early prototype, and the user encountered significant technical barriers to sim use. In this work, we present results from the remaining two user interviews with the sim, both conducted with the same prototype of *Capacitor Lab: Basics*. We will identify users by the pseudonyms Amy and Leela. Amy was a recent college graduate, and Leela was a college senior. Neither had, nor were pursuing, degrees in a physical science. Both users identified as being blind, and used a screen reader on a daily basis. Each user was interviewed individually, for about one hour. In this work, we focus on the sim exploration section of the interview. Amy used the sim for a total of 21 min, and Leela used the sim for a total of 29 min. Both users had used the screen reader NVDA prior to being interviewed.

## 5   Results and Discussion

We start by summarizing the user interviews with the *Capacitor Lab: Basics* prototype. We then go through components of the implicit scaffolding design framework and present examples of user interactions that highlight ways the design of the prototype sim with inclusive features supported the screen reader users (or not) to engage in productive interactions.

## 5.1   User Interview Overview

Though Amy and Leela each chose a unique sequence of interactions there were numerous similarities in the two user interviews. Both users started their interaction by navigating sequentially through the Scene Description (described in Sect. 3.3), and listening to all (Amy) or most (Leela) of the descriptions. While listening to the descriptions, each decided on a specific element they wanted to interact with first. They then started interacting with elements in the circuit group, the battery voltage and the capacitor plates. After interacting with all of the sim's interactive elements (in Amy's interview, all except for the voltmeter), both users chose a specific conceptual goal to pursue. Amy wanted to determine how all of the interactive elements in the circuit group (battery voltage, capacitor plate area and separation) impacted the capacitance (as indicated by the capacitance graph readout). Leela chose to use the voltmeter tool to try to determine what interactive elements in the circuit group impacted the voltage of the circuit.

At this point, the two interviews began to differ significantly. Amy encountered no usability challenges while determining the relationships between the circuit elements and capacitance, while Leela had significant usability challenges with the voltmeter. The result is that Amy was able to focus on learning from the relationships represented in the sim, and Leela spent a significant amount of time trying to make productive use of the voltmeter. As Amy was able to explore the concepts presented in the Capacitance screen more deeply, there was not enough interview time for her to explore the Light Bulb screen. In Leela's interview, she spent the majority of her Capacitance screen time focused on determining if changing the circuit features (battery voltage or capacitor area or distance) impacted the circuit voltage (hindered by usability issues with the voltmeter), and was then prompted by the interviewer to try exploring the second screen of the sim, the Light Bulb screen. On this screen, she set a goal to light the light bulb. To light the light bulb she needed to increase the battery voltage to charge the capacitor, and then connect the capacitor circuit to the light bulb. She was able to successfully light the light bulb in under three minutes after starting on the Light Bulb screen, and was pleased to accomplish this task.

Ultimately, both users were able to access the Scene Description and the interactive elements of the sim. They were able to fluidly navigate to all sim elements, and aside from the voltmeter, make productive use of these elements. Even though neither user was given a specific goal (other than to explore the sim), both were able to meet some of the learning goals (see Sect. 3.1) intended by the designers. Amy was successfully able to meet all of the learning goals of the Capacitance screen. Leela struggled with usability issues in the Capacitance screen, but was able to rapidly accomplish a main goal of the Light Bulb screen.

## 5.2   Scaffolding Insights from User Interviews

Here, we go through two components of the implicit scaffolding design framework – framing engagement and enabling sense making – and highlight specific interview segments that provide insights into the relationship between implicit scaffolding and inclusive features. To present the interview data, we show interview segments with time points in the min:sec format (starting from first auditory description read aloud by the screen reader), followed by a brief summary of the user's interactions and verbalizations in that time segment. When brief, full quotes and interaction patterns are provided. Lengthy quotes or interaction patterns are abbreviated or summarized.

**Framing Engagement.** *Framing* can be thought of as the way in which a user determines an answer to the question "what sort of activity is this?" [14]. For PhET sims, a goal of the design is for students to interpret use of the sim as an opportunity to actively explore and make sense of the representations and the relationships found in the sim. In this section, we look at how two users of the sim prototype, utilizing screen readers, interpreted the activity of sim use and how they framed their engagement.

*Initial Listening.* Amy and Leela each started their sim use by using the keyboard to navigate through, and listen to, the Scene Description for the Capacitance screen. Here are the users first few minutes with the sim, starting with Amy, when primarily focused on listening to the Scene Description and spatially orienting themselves to the representations on the screen.

0:00    Amy hears first readout from Capacitance Screen, begins navigating and listening to rest of Scene Description, listening to some descriptions multiple times.
1:10    Begins using left hand to gesture, indicating locations of objects being described, continues gesturing until has listened to all descriptions.
4:16    Screen reader stops. Amy says *"Okay. I think I more or less know the parts."*

In total, Amy spent just over four minutes listening to the descriptions. As she listened, she paid particular attention to the spatial cues provided, as indicated by the corresponding hand gestures she made as she heard each spatial description. Here are Leela's first few minutes with the sim.

0:00    Leela hears first readout from Capacitance Screen, begins navigating and listening to rest of Scene Description, skimming some quickly (without waiting for full description) and listening to some descriptions twice. Quietly repeats portions of descriptions to herself.
0:48    Repeats out loud from the description "There's a capacitor to the left."
2:14    Screen reader stops reading. Leela changes screen reader from "browse" mode to "forms" mode and begins interacting with the battery's voltage slider.

Consistent with prior research on the use of screen readers [15], both users engaged in an initial listening phase following a remarkably similar pattern. Interestingly, both users indicated a focus on spatial aspects of the descriptions, though each indicated this in different ways – Amy gestured and Leela verbalized. Later in the interview, both users verbalized some of the information provided in the Scene Description to help them with sim use, and each navigated back to the Scene Description later to look for specific information.

*Transition to Interaction.* After listening to the Scene Description, Amy and Leela differed in how seamlessly they transitioned to interacting with the sim's features. Amy did not realize that the screen reader needed to be switched from the "browse" mode it was currently in, to "forms" mode to allow her to interact with sim elements.

4:36  Amy says *"It's not clear..."* and goes on to describe how she is confused by the descriptions that say "press enter" to interact, but she does not know where keyboard focus should be when pressing enter. She navigates screen reader focus to different headings and tries various keyboard keys, all unsuccessful.

6:00  Interviewer suggests switching screen reader to "forms" mode. Amy makes this change, and begins navigating around the sim's elements, passing the circuit group, but not entering the circuit group.

6:52  Amy indicates she is unclear how to navigate to the interactive capacitor plates by saying she is looking for the *"left right slide and the up down slide to kind of change how far apart the capacitance were and how large they were. So I'm looking for that right now, because I figured that's the first thing I would start playing with."* She continues navigating around the sim, searching for the capacitor plate sliders.

7:59  Interviewer suggests pressing the "Enter" key when on the circuit group. Amy does this and navigates to the plate separation slider and begins changing the plate separation. She does not require any further prompts from the interviewer through the rest of her sim use.

In contrast, Leela recognized independently that the screen reader needed to change into "forms" mode, and did this without prompting once she was done listening to the Scene Description, as indicated in the description of Leela's initial listening.

A note regarding screen reader modes – the sim is compatible with different screen readers, each with different modes and unique methods for changing modes. An unmet challenge we face is the design of appropriate descriptions to cue users that they may need to switch screen reader modes when transitioning from listening to the Scene Description to interacting with the sim's elements. This sim prototype did not contain any descriptions regarding changing modes, and from these interviews it seems that some users may infer that a change of mode is needed, while others will need some description to support them in making this transition.

Aside from the challenges Amy faced transitioning to using the sim's interactive elements, both users seemed to take similar approaches to sim use and framed the activity of sim use in similar ways. Both listened to the Scene Description, and from this, selected a specific interactive feature they wanted to explore. They then navigated to that feature to begin exploring. For comparison, students utilizing the visual design of the sim (not using a screen reader), typically begin using the sim by first taking a few seconds to visually scan the sim and then begin interacting with sim elements [3, 8, 16]. For *Capacitor Lab: Basics*, initial interactions are typically with the elements in the circuit group. These particular elements are highlighted visually through their central location, large size, and brightly colored touch or mouse target areas (blue slider knob for the voltage slider and green arrows for capacitor plates).

Amy and Leela utilized a different approach with the use of the screen reader, though obtained a similar outcome. Their initial choice of interactions (Amy choosing the capacitor plate separation, and Leela choosing the battery) is consistent with those of users exploring the sim visually, indicating our auditory descriptions may appropriately cue users to explore, starting with features in the circuit group.

**Enabling Sense Making.** We designed the sim's representations and interactive elements to support students in making sense of the underlying scientific or mathematical relationships. This requires that the users interact with the sim (nothing occurs in PhET sims prior to user interaction), receive feedback from the sim based on their interaction (e.g., the form of changes in the representations) and appropriately interpret this feedback to form their conception of the underlying relationships. In this section, we look to the interviews to understand how the feedback provided was working to support understanding of the underlying relationships.

In Amy's interview, she articulates the goal of sense making in an interesting way. As described previously, she begins interacting with the sim by changing the capacitor plate separation (7:59). Next, she articulates a need for a larger purpose, and uses the sim to seek one out.

8:24    Changes capacitor plate separation, plate area, battery voltage, and navigates through all of sim's interactive elements.
11:05    Changes from "forms" mode to "browse" mode, and begins listening to the Scene Description.
11:39    Says *"…I'm looking for where it would tell me… so if I can control voltage, I can control size and I can control distance…so that all goes together to… so what's the output?"* Continues listening through description.
13:20    Listens to description of graph, which reads "Capacitance Graph, measures the capacitance of the capacitor". Amy says *"I guess I'm looking for capacitance."*

In this segment, Amy has explored multiple sim elements that she can change, and recognizes that there must be some larger purpose to changing these elements. She then actively searches out what this could be, and determines that the larger purpose could be related to capacitance.

As designed, the capacitance value changes when the capacitor plate separation or area is changed and the screen reader provides live updates to the user of the new capacitance value. Unfortunately, the screen reader was not providing live updates of the capacitance value as it changed (a technical issue that appeared during the interview), so Amy was only aware of the capacitance from the Scene Description and from navigating by the capacitance graph in her exploration. If this issue had not come up, Amy would likely have recognized sooner that changing the circuit group elements impacted capacitance. Once Amy indicates an interest in capacitance, the interviewer lets Amy know the technical issue with the capacitance readout, and that Amy can access the capacitance information by asking the interviewer as needed. Amy goes on to engage in experimentation with the circuit group elements with her newfound focus on capacitance.

13:27  The interviewer tells Amy that the capacitance value should be read out by the screen reader each time her actions result in a change in capacitance, but that this is not occurring due to a technical issue with the sim. Any time Amy would like to know the capacitance value, the interviewer can read it aloud to her – the current value of the capacitance was 0.11 pF (where pF is picofarads, a unit of capacitance). Amy indicates she understands, pauses to think about what capacitance is, and decides to experiment and find out. She switches from "browse" mode to "forms" mode.

14:25  Amy makes an initial prediction before interacting *"I assume that if I push the voltage up, the capacitance is also going to go up, but it might stay the same because it might not be dependent on – I don't know, so I'm going to check."* She navigates to the battery's voltage slider, increase the voltage and asks *"How many picofarads?"*. Capacitance was 0.11 pF. Amy says *"Okay, so it's the same. So voltage does not impact – okay."*

15:29  Amy navigates to plate area slider, currently with a value of 121 mm$^2$ (millimeters squared, a unit of area). *"Okay, so I had it at 121."* She increases area to 144 mm$^2$. *"Okay, so if I go up, then what is it?"* Capacitance was 0.13 pF. She increases area to 169 mm$^2$. *"Okay, what is it there?"* Capacitance was 0.15 pF. *"Okay, the size of the capacitor is increasing, umm, I don't know if exponentially is the right word."* She goes on to describe to the interviewer, using hand gestures and capacitance values, her ideas about the mathematical relationship between the plate size and capacitance.

18:01  *"I'm going to take the size back down to where the default was."* She decreases the plate area back to 121 mm$^2$, and navigates to the plate separation slider. She decreases plate separation, and then increases it back to maximum (10 mm). *"Okay, so it's back to 0.11 there, right?"* Interviewer agrees. Amy decreases the plate separation from its maximum (10 mm) to its minimum (5 mm), asking for the capacitance readout with each change. She then describes to the interviewer, using hand gestures and capacitance values, her ideas about the mathematical relationships between the plate separation and the capacitance.

While each PhET sim provides multiple representations and interactive elements to explore, it is ultimately the goal for students to explore these features and attend to specific relationships between them rather than attend only to each in isolation. Amy's interview provides an example of a user recognizing that there must be more to the sim than simply interacting with the individual elements. It was unfortunate that the capacitance readout was not updating as intended, but it was illuminating to see her process of seeking – and finding – relationships to engage in sense making with.

Student exploration of PhET sims using the visual design typically includes use of all or most of the sim's interactive elements before selection of specific relationships for deeper sense making. Amy and Leela's use followed this pattern of exploration before deeper sense making behavior, though required more time. In the example above, Amy spent three minutes exploring the sim's features before seeking an underlying relationship to explore. In contrast, prior analysis of 22 student groups freely exploring a PhET sim during a college chemistry class showed that students explored 18 out of the 23 interactive elements available across the sim's three screens – and each screen's interactive elements were typically explored in less than a minute [3].

# 6    Future Work

While successful in many ways, this work also encountered multiple challenges to be addressed in the future. Some of these challenges include:

- **Technical Implementation Challenges.** Amy and Leela differed significantly in their overall learning experience with the sim – in large part due to technical difficulties inhibiting Leela from making productive use of the voltmeter.
- **Inclusive Design Challenges.** Some representations were not used consistently for sense making (e.g., Amy not using voltmeter, Leela not making use of the capacitance readout). Additionally, not all representations were described (i.e., electric field, charges), or were not described usefully (e.g., current).
- **Designing for Efficiency Challenges.** Some aspects of sim exploration took longer in the user interviews than is typical for those visually exploring the sim. Some of this additional time seemed intrinsic to the screen reader users' approach (e.g., listening before interacting) while others (e.g., the amount of time required to explore all interactive elements) indicate that the efficiency of the interactions could be improved.

# 7    Conclusions

Results of our analysis indicate that the underlying premise of implicit scaffolding is indeed multi-dimensional, and prior work in implicit scaffolding for visual interfaces can be applied to non-visual interfaces. To do this, some components need to be broadened and expanded, and initial assumptions need to be replaced with more inclusive perspectives. For example, in prior work [8] we specify that implicit scaffolding is "neither written nor verbal" to highlight that implicit scaffolding provides guidance without explicitly providing a series of actions for the user to enact. In this work, we show that providing verbal scaffolding can be done implicitly, resulting in productive user actions and learning. This result provides a direct relationship between the implicit scaffolding design framework and inclusive design, connecting science education research and inclusive design through the use of an interactive science simulation.

**Acknowledgments.**   We would like to thank Jesse Greenberg for his implementation support. This work was supported by the: National Science Foundation (DRL #1503439), William and Flora Hewlett Foundation, and the University of Colorado. Any opinions, findings, and conclusions or recommendations expressed in this material are those of the authors and do not necessarily reflect the views of the National Science Foundation.

# References

1. Scalise, K., Timms, M., Moorjani, A., Clark, L., Holtermann, K., Irvin, P.S.: Student learning in science simulations: design features that promote learning gains. J. Res. Sci. Teach. **48**, 1050–1078 (2011)
2. D'Angelo, C., Rutstein, D., Harrison, S., Bernard, R., Borokhovski, E., Haertel, G.: Simulations for STEM Learning: Systematic Review and Meta-Analysis. Technical Report, SRI International (2014)
3. Moore, E.B., Herzog, T.A., Perkins, K.K.: Interactive simulations as implicit support for guided-inquiry. Chem. Educ. Res. Pract. **14**, 257–268 (2013)
4. Perkins, K.K., Loeblein, P.J., Dessau, K.L.: Sims for science: powerful tools to support inquiry-based teaching. Sci. Teach. **77**, 46–51 (2010)
5. Podolefsky, N.S., Perkins, K.K., Adams, W.K.: Factors promoting engaged exploration with computer simulations. PRST-PER. **6**, 020117 (2010)
6. PhET Interactive Simulations. http://phet.colorado.edu
7. PhET Interactive Simulations: Accessibility. http://phet.colorado.edu/en/about/accessibility
8. Podolefsky, N.S., Moore, E.B., Perkins, K.K.: Implicit scaffolding in interactive simulations: design strategies to support multiple educational goals. http://arxiv.org/abs/1306.6544
9. Paul, A., Podolefsky, N.S., Perkins, K.K.: Guiding without feeling guided: implicit scaffolding through interactive simulation design. In: Proceedings of the 2012 PER Research Conference, vol. 1513, pp. 302–305 (2012)
10. Renken, M., Peffer, M., Otrel-Cass, K., Girault, I., Chiocarriello, A.: Simulations as Scaffolds in Science Education. Springer, Heidelberg (2015)
11. Bransford, J., Brown, A., Cocking, R.: How People Learn: Body, Mind, Experience and School. National Academy Press, Washington (2000)
12. Capacitor Lab: Basics – PhET Prototype Simulation. http://www.colorado.edu/physics/phet/dev/html/capacitor-lab-basics/1.0.0-dev.14/capacitor-lab-basics_en.html?accessibility
13. NVDA. http://www.nvaccess.org
14. Hammer, D., Elby, A., Scherr, R.E., Redish, E.F.: Resources, framing, and transfer. In: Mestre, J.P. (ed.) Transfer of Learning from a Modern Multidisciplinary Perspective, pp. 89–120. IAP, Greenwich (2005)
15. Fakrudeen, M., Ali, M., Yousef, S., Hussein, A.H.: Analysing the mental modal of blind users in mobile touch screen devices for usability. In: Ao, S.I., Gelmen, L., Hukins, D.W.L., Hunter, A., Korsunsky, A.M. (eds) Proceedings of the World Congress on Engineering (vol. II), pp. 837–842. Newswood Limited, London (2013)
16. Chamberlain, J.M., Lancaster, K., Parson, R., Perkins, K.K.: How guidance affects student engagement with an interactive simulation. Chem. Educ. Res. Pract. **15**, 628–638 (2014)

# The Accessibility of MOOC Platforms from Instructors' Perspective

Norun C. Sanderson[(✉)], Weiqin Chen,
Way Kiat Bong, and Siri Kessel

Oslo and Akershus University College of Applied Sciences,
Post box 4 St. Olavs Plass, 0130 Oslo, Norway
{nsand, weichin.chen, way.bong, siri.kessel}@hioa.no

**Abstract.** MOOC (Massive Open Online Course) provides remarkable learning opportunities for a great diversity of people. MOOCs have been studied from several perspectives, including accessibility. However, little attention has so far been paid to investigating whether MOOC platforms themselves are accessible for instructors who are the authors of MOOCs. To ensure universal and equal access to the MOOC platforms, a systematic study of the accessibility of the MOOC platforms from instructors' perspective is essential. This paper presents results from a heuristic evaluation of the Canvas platform, focusing on its accessibility to instructors creating course contents in MOOCs. We have based the evaluation on Part A of the Authoring Tool Accessibility Guidelines (ATAG) 2.0 by W3C Web Accessibility Initiative (WAI). The preliminary results show that although Canvas provides much support for instructors to create accessible MOOCs, it does not comply fully with ATAG 2.0.

**Keywords:** Universal design · Accessibility · MOOC platforms · Canvas · Instructors · Heuristic evaluation

## 1 Introduction

MOOC (Massive Open Online Course), as a type of E-learning and distance education, provides unique learning opportunities for underprivileged people, including people with disabilities, elderly and people who live in countries with low infrastructure. Different MOOC platforms such as Coursera, edX, Desire2Learn, Canvas, and FutureLearn host hundreds of courses with millions of participants. For example, by August 2015, Coursera offered more than 1100 courses from 121 partner universities and 15 million users [13].

In Norway, MOOC has drawn much attention in both research and education recently. MOOC.no[1] is a Norwegian MOOC platform built upon Canvas that hosts courses offered by Norwegian educational institutions. This platform is provided by BIBSYS[2], an agency under the Norwegian Ministry of Education and Research. Most recently, our college together with seven other European universities received funding

---

[1] http://www.mooc.no/.
[2] http://www.bibsys.no/en/.

© Springer International Publishing Switzerland 2016
M. Antona and C. Stephanidis (Eds.): UAHCI 2016, Part III, LNCS 9739, pp. 124–134, 2016.
DOI: 10.1007/978-3-319-40238-3_13

from the EU Erasmus + programme for the MOOCAP project (MOOC Accessibility Partnership) in order to develop a series of MOOCs in accessibility and universal design of ICT. The Norwegian government has appointed a MOOC-committee to investigate how the Norwegian educational authorities and institutions should meet the challenges posed by the rapid growth of higher education delivered over the Internet. In their report [6], the committee stated, "MOOCs have the potential to strengthen both the access to and quality of higher education for persons with reduced functional ability, thus making it possible for them to choose higher education". According to the committee, high-quality technology and contents, and adherence to the principles of universal design are a prerequisite for the ability of MOOCs to make education more accessible to everybody.

Literature has shown that although MOOC courses have been studied from data analysis, student activities, pedagogy, and accessibility perspectives [4, 7, 10], very little attention has been paid to the accessibility of the platforms from instructors' perspectives [2, 8, 9]. Although some platforms provide accessibility guidelines to enable instructors to create accessible course contents, it is also important that the MOOC platforms themselves are accessible for instructors. By instructors, we mean the people that use MOOC platforms to create courses, including people with disabilities. We argue that a systematic study focusing on the accessibility of the MOOC platforms from instructors' perspective is necessary to ensure universal and equal access to the MOOC platforms.

In this paper, we present results from a heuristic evaluation of Canvas conducted as part of an ongoing project where we examine the accessibility of a carefully selected group of MOOC platforms and their support to instructors in order to create accessible course contents. The goal of this project is to investigate the accessibility of MOOC platforms from instructors' perspective, identify accessibility problems, and propose recommendations for addressing the problems. Our overall aim is to contribute to the global efforts in ensuring universal design of MOOCs and equal access to education.

## 2   Background and Related Work

With the increasing popularity of MOOCs, research communities on accessibility have started to pay attention to the accessibility of MOOC platforms and courses. Such research is still in its early stage. In this section, we will present the current research on MOOC and accessibility.

The majority of research published so far focus on the accessibility of courses. For example, Al-Mouh et al. [1] tested the accessibility of Coursera courses from users and experts perspectives. For users, they tested a set of essential tasks using screen readers. For experts, heuristic evaluations were conducted with 10 courses. They found that the courses failed to comply with WCAG 2.0 guidelines. Sanchez-Gordon and Luján-Mora [8] selected five Coursera courses and conducted heuristic testing to identify the potential accessibility problems for elderly students. They found that all the courses have accessibility issues. Calle-Jimenez et al. [3] used three automated tools to evaluate a Geo-MOOC course. They found that although one of the tools reported more accessibility problems that the others, there are still issues that none of the tools could detect. They further argued that user testing should be conducted in order to complement results from expert testing and testing with automated tools.

Another category of research focuses on the platforms and providers. For example, Bohnsack and Puhl [2] evaluated MOOC platforms including Udacity, Coursera, edX, OpenCourseWorld and Iversity. They used protocol observation when conducting user testing with blind users, rather than W3C guidelines. edX was found to be the only platform that is accessible with their test configurations for blind users. Iniesto et al. [5] analysed the degree of accessibility of two MOOC providers (UNED COMA and UAb iMOOC). Their findings showed that none of the platforms have achieved a level that could indicate that they are accessible and understandable to the users.

## 3   Evaluating Canvas

### 3.1   Canvas

We have chosen Canvas[3] as our case for the evaluations. Canvas is an open source Learning Management System (LMS) from Instructure[4] used as a MOOC platform, e.g., in the Canvas Network[5].

LMS platforms aim to serve educational institutions having a managed number of users (administrative staff, teachers, and students), making scalability predictable, and offering a relatively advanced portfolio of services for course creation, course and class management and administration, as well as tools for creating and editing learning materials. MOOC platforms aim to offer a number of courses to a less predictable number of users, thus entailing much higher requirements for scalability. MOOC platforms usually offer only a subset of the tools that an LMS offer.

Canvas, from the instructor's perspective, is organised as a dashboard for navigation, courses, grades area, and a calendar. It contains a number of tools for planning and managing course content, learning materials, and students. The Dashboard is the page displayed after login. It presents the user with a list of recent activities, a list of upcoming tasks, and link to a calendar view. Through the Dashboard, users navigate between activities, tasks and the calendar. In addition, instructors can add a new course here, if s/he has permission to add courses. The Modules area is used for organising a course, and displays as the course home page to students. The course home page is the first page students see when they open a course. In Modules, the instructors can create and edit modules in a course, manage the content elements in a course module, and reorder modules and elements to organise the course flow. Functionality offered for managing course modules and content elements include add, edit, delete, move, and rename. In addition, the modules and content elements in a module can be individually published or unpublished.

There are several kinds of content elements that can be added to a module; pages, files, discussions, assignments, quizzes, announcements, and other learning materials.

---

[3] https://www.canvaslms.com/.

[4] https://www.instructure.com/.

[5] https://www.canvas.net/.

Each offers necessary functionality to add/edit content and to set element specific options. *Pages* is for adding content and learning materials to a course or a class wiki in the form of text, images, video, as well as links to other pages and files/resources. Specific user access can be set for each page. The page history is available to the instructor. *Files* allows the instructor upload learning materials and other resources such as documents, images, and media in different formats. Resources may be course specific. Discussions is for graded or non-graded class discussions of course related topics. *Assignments* provides opportunities for assessing students. It may include quizzes and discussions that may be graded. *Quizzes* allows creating and administering online quizzes and surveys, and can be used to conduct exams and assessments. *Announcements* offers functionality for communicating with students and post course-related topics. In addition, Canvas offers a number of other tools, including tools to manage grades, syllabi, evaluate course components and student performance, as well as to conduct real-time lectures or conferences.

The text editor is utilised in most of these content elements. The WYSIWYG text editor in Canvas is from TinyMCE[6], which is a text editor available in several similar platforms, for example as a plug-in for Moodle. TinyMCE offers both an html editor and a rich content editor and supports embedding video content, math formulas, and other rich media. Instructors can use both editors when adding content to courses.

## 3.2   Methods

We have evaluated the accessibility of the Canvas platform from instructors' perspective through heuristic evaluation based on the Authoring Tool Accessibility Guidelines (ATAG) 2.0 by W3C Web Accessibility Initiative. Three researchers performed the evaluation, two of the researchers have several years of teaching experience in higher education and uses LMS tools on a daily basis. All three researchers have a background in computer science; two have many years' experience with research in the area of digital accessibility.

ATAG 2.0 is a set of principles organised into guidelines and criteria for accessible authoring tools. It is divided into two parts, one targeting the accessibility of the authoring tool interface for authors/users (Part A), and the other how these tools support the creation of accessible content (Part B). ATAG 2.0 shares the conformance model in Web Content Accessibility Guidelines (WCAG) 2.0 and has three levels of conformance: A (lowest), AA (middle), and AAA (highest). Each higher level builds on and incorporates the lower level(s), thus conformance to level AAA implies conformance to levels AA and A, and conformance to level AA implies conformance to level A. It is necessary to conform to all success criteria on a certain level to be regarded compliant with ATAG 2.0 on that level. Our aim is to investigate the accessibility of the platform as experienced by instructors creating and managing MOOC courses, therefore we have used ATAG 2.0 Part A in our heuristic evaluations. Based on an examination of the principles and success criteria in ATAG 2.0 Part A, we selected 28 success criteria relevant for our evaluation.

---

[6] https://www.tinymce.com/.

The open source version (not production version) of Canvas used for the evaluation was installed on a server running Ubuntu 14.04 in early December 2015. The main bulk of evaluations took place in December 2015 and January 2016, and were conducted on laptops with operating systems Ubuntu 14.04, Windows 7 Enterprise, Mac OS X El Capitan v.10.11.3, and browsers Firefox 39.0 and 44.0, Chrome 47.0.2526.111 m, and Safari v. 9.0.3. Assistive technology used in the evaluations include screen readers NVDA v. 2015.3 and VoiceOver v. 7.0, in addition to built-in magnifiers for Windows and Mac OS X (no magnifiers were used with Ubuntu).

As we are looking into accessibility from instructors' perspective, we first identified the main tasks instructors may have to handle in relation to creating, running, and maintaining a MOOC course. These tasks were grouped into three categories; (1) Course access management; (2) Creating and organizing course content; and (3) Grading and feedback.

**Course access management** involves tasks such as enrolling students and allowing or removing access to the course for course instructors and others. As administrative staff commonly handles these tasks, we have concentrated our evaluation on the two other categories that contain tasks typically handled by course instructors.

**Creating and organizing course content** covers the main tasks that a course instructor will perform as part of preparing and running a MOOC. These include creating and editing a course page and a course plan, modules, syllabus list, assignments, announcements, and quizzes. In addition, this task includes preparing and/or uploading learning materials such as lectures and relevant resources.

**Grading and feedback** includes grading assignments and giving feedback to students. As participating in discussions with other students is an important part of a MOOC for many students, we have included creating and editing discussions as one of the tasks in this category.

To evaluate the accessibility of Canvas for instructors, we selected a set of Canvas elements relevant for a chosen set of the above tasks. The Canvas elements used in the evaluation includes Dashboard, Modules, Files, Pages, Quizzes, Assignments, Announcements, and Discussions. The researchers first conducted individual evaluations. After that, the individual results were collected and discussed together by all the researchers.

## 4   Evaluation Results

The results from our evaluation show that Canvas does not fully comply with ATAG 2.0, Part A. From the 28 criteria used in the evaluation, we found that Canvas complies fully with 11 criteria, complies partially with eight, and does not comply with one criterion. Eight criteria were not applicable or not available. An overview of our evaluation results can be seen in Table 1. Please note that partial compliance in some cases indicate variations in results among the browsers included in the evaluation. In other words, if Canvas complies to one criterion in one browser, but not in another, it is considered as partial compliance.

Looking at levels of conformance (A, A, AAA), we can see that from the 14 evaluated level A criteria, Canvas was found to comply fully with 6, partially with 5,

**Table 1.** Overview of Canvas compliance with ATAG 2.0. C = compliant, not ,C = not compliant, partial = partially compliant, n/a = not applicable or not available.

| Principles | Guideline | Success criteria | Level | Conformance |
|---|---|---|---|---|
| A.2 | A.2.1 | A.2.1.1 Text Alternatives for Rendered Non-Text Content | A | partial |
| | | A.2.1.2 Alternatives for Rendered Time-Based Media | A | n/a |
| | A.2.2 | A.2.2.1 Editing-View Status Indicators | A | partial |
| | | A.2.2.2 Access to Rendered Text Properties | AA | C |
| A.3 | A.3.1 | A.3.1.1 Keyboard Access (Minimum) | A | partial |
| | | A.3.1.2 No Keyboard Traps | A | partial |
| | | A.3.1.3 Efficient Keyboard Access | AA | partial |
| | | A.3.1.4 Keyboard Access (Enhanced) | AAA | C |
| | | A.3.1.5 Customize Keyboard Access | AAA | not C |
| | | A.3.1.6 Present Keyboard Commands | AAA | C |
| | A.3.2 | A.3.2.1 Auto-Save (Minimum) | A | C |
| | | A.3.2.2 Timing Adjustable | A | C |
| | | A.3.2.3 Static Input Components | A | C |
| | | A.3.2.4 Content Edits Saved (Extended) | AAA | n/a |
| | A.3.3 | A.3.3.1 Static View Option | A | partial |
| | A.3.4 | A.3.4.1 Navigate By Structure | AA | n/a |
| | | A.3.4.2 Navigate by Programmatic Relationships | AAA | n/a |
| | A.3.5 | A.3.5.1 Text Search | AA | partial |
| | A.3.6 | A.3.6.1 Independence of Display | A | n/a |
| | | A.3.6.2 Save Settings | AA | n/a |
| | | A.3.6.3 Apply Platform Settings | AA | C |
| | A.3.7 | A.3.7.1 Preview (Minimum) | A | C |
| | | A.3.7.2 Preview (Enhanced) | AAA | n/a |
| A.4 | A.4.1 | A.4.1.1 Content Changes Reversible (Minimum) | A | partial |
| | | A.4.1.2 Settings Change Confirmation | A | n/a |
| | | A.4.1.3 Content Changes Reversible (Enhanced) | AAA | C |
| | A.4.2 | A.4.2.1 Describe Accessibility Features | A | C |
| | | A.4.2.2 Document All Features | AA | C |

none were not compliant, and 3 were not applicable or not available. For the 7 level AA criteria, Canvas complies fully with 3, partially with 2, none were found not compliant, and 2 were not applicable or not available. For the 7 level AAA criteria, Canvas fully

**Table 2.** Overview according to level of compliance (A, AA, AAA)

|     | Total | C | Partial | Not C | N/A |
|-----|-------|---|---------|-------|-----|
| A   | 14    | 5 | 6       | 0     | 3   |
| AA  | 7     | 3 | 2       | 0     | 2   |
| AAA | 7     | 3 | 0       | 1     | 3   |

complies with 3, none partially, 1 not compliant, and 3 not applicable or not available. An overview of Canvas according to level of compliance is shown in Table 2.

During the evaluation, we identified the following accessibility issues for the partial and not compliant cases. The relevant guideline(s) are shown in parenthesis:

- Not all non-text icons show text alternatives when mouse-over. (2.1)
- Spelling errors are not always indicated visually or read by screen readers. (2.2)
- The screen reader does not read alternative text for all buttons in the text editor toolbar in all browsers. (2.1, 2.2, 3.1)
- No customization for keyboard shortcuts. (3.1)
- No keyboard shortcut to save editing contents. (3.1)
- Animated gifs cannot be stopped. (3.3)
- Search results do not include alternative text for embedded images in the editing view. (3.5)
- Number of matches after text search is not indicated by the screen reader when using some screen readers and browsers. (3.5)
- Only option for Undo/Redo in editing view is by using keyboard shortcuts. (4.1)
- No undo/redo option or confirmation when uploading files. (4.1)

Please note that all the accessibility issues involving the editing view do not belong to the Canvas platform itself, but is related to the fact that there is no search tool in the text editor plug-in used in the version of Canvas that we evaluated. Consequently, the searches in this evaluation were performed using the search functionality available in the browsers.

In the following, we present some examples of the above accessibility issues. In the Modules tool, some non-text icons do not show text alternatives while mouse over, but the screen reader reads the alternative text (2.1.1). Misspellings are indicated visually (red underline) in the text editor, but there is no indication of spelling errors when adding title to a course element, such as an announcement, discussion, page etc., with the exception of Safari with VoiceOver. Screen readers indicate spelling errors when using Safari and Firefox, but not in Chrome. In IE, the NVDA screen reader reads "button" for most buttons in the text editor toolbar, except a few (font colour, background colour, paragraph, font size) (2.2.1).

Although navigation by keyboard works relatively well in the evaluated tools, the keyboard focus often ends up in the address field (URL-field) of the browser after closing a dialog box, which may be experienced as troublesome by the user, adding a number of unnecessary keystrokes trying to find back to where s/he was on the page (3.1.3).

Search results in the editing view are only visually indicated, the screen reader does not indicate if there are any matches, with the exception of Safari with VoiceOver. Search results do not include matches in alternative text for embedded image (3.5.1).

, In *Files*, there is no Undo/Redo option, but there are Cancel & Open buttons. Once the user has chosen the Open button, the file upload starts without any further confirmation from the user to proceed. This may present a problem in cases where the user accidentally clicked the button, or the file is very large (4.1.1).

Other accessibility issues that instructors may find challenging include the screen reader not reading all pop-up messages, for example in the *Files*, where the warning informing users how to improve accessibility when moving files is not read by the screen reader, and the poor contrast of non-visited elements in the left hand side menu, as shown in Fig. 1.

**Fig. 1.** Poor contrast in left hand side menu

Canvas provides hints to users about how they can improve accessibility by giving context-relevant warnings in some tools, which is a very useful feature. For example in Modules, where a warning message pops up when the user hits the module reordering button by mouse-over or by keyboard navigation. Another similar example is the Calendar, where users are advised to use the Agenda view for improved accessibility. However, for users not able to perceive the screen visually, navigate by keyboard and use assistive technology, some of these messages are difficult to find unless already known, and may therefore be missed by the very users they are intended for. Figure 2 shows a warning message for improved accessibility in Modules.

**Fig. 2.** Warning message hint for improved accessibility in Modules

## 5   Discussion and Recommendations

The role of the instructor varies among different MOOC platforms. In some platforms, instructors do not have direct access to the platform; they instead hand their course material over to someone who will take care of uploading the course material and manage the platform. After uploading, the instructor can view the course material, but has no direct access for making amendments. Consequently, instructors do not have any relations at all with the MOOC platform itself in these cases. In Canvas, the instructor has direct access to the platform for managing course modules and editing course contents, which from an instructor's point of view may be an advantage. However, this also poses a greater challenge regarding the accessibility of the platform with a potentially greater diversity of people accessing it.

The evaluation results for Canvas accessibility are relatively positive in comparison with findings in our previous research where we evaluated LMS platforms [11, 12], including Moodle, which is another LMS commonly used for MOOCs. There are, however, other issues relating to the Canvas platform that may present additional obstacles for instructors. In the following, we explore some of these potential challenges.

Users are informed through the online documentation[7] that Canvas supports the two latest versions of any browser, and recommend users to update to the newest browser and most up-to-date Flash plug-in available. In addition, Canvas presents the user with a list of supported browser versions. There is however no information about backward compatibility to earlier versions of the listed browsers. Assistive technology, such as screen readers, rarely manage to keep up with the rapid update of versions that is common in software such as browsers. In addition, many users use older equipment, computers, operating systems and other software due to a variety of reasons, including their familiarity, availability, and infrastructure, as well as economic or other reasons. This makes backward compatibility with older versions an important issue to ensure equal access for a diversity of instructors using a wide range of equipment.

In the online documentation, Canvas also informs users which screen readers are supported for certain browsers. For example, for PCs, JAWS is supported for Internet explorer versions 10 and 11, and NVDA for the latest version of Firefox. Users are also informed that there is no screen reader support for Canvas in Chrome.[8] This places limitations on what browsers users of assistive technology can use with Canvas, and considering that Chrome, according to the browser statistics in 2015[9,10] is by far the most used browser worldwide, this may affect many instructors that are screen reader users.

In a previous project [11, 12], we have investigated three LMSs from teachers' perspective: Moodle, Fronter, and SAKAI. The results from the Canvas evaluation shows fewer accessibility issues than we found in our investigation of Moodle and the other two LMSs, but there were some common issues in all platforms. In the following,

---

[7] Canvas guides, https://guides.instructure.com/.

[8] https://guides.instructure.com/m/4152/l/82542?data-resolve-url=true&data-manual-id=4152.

[9] W3Schools browser statistics, http://www.w3schools.com/browsers/browsers_stats.asp.

[10] StatCounter GlobalStats, http://gs.statcounter.com/.

we compare the results from the Canvas evaluation with results from our previous research [11, 12], specifically the evaluation of Moodle.

Both platforms have only static input components (3.2.3), and previews show the course content as it will be presented to students (3.7.1). Neither of the two platforms provide options for customising keyboard shortcuts (3.1.5). Canvas complies fully with more criteria than Moodle; there are nine criteria only Canvas complies fully with (2.2.2, 3.1.4, 3.1.6, 3.2.1, 3.2.2, 3.6.3, 4.1.3, 4.2.1, 4.2.2), while Moodle complies fully with one criteria that Canvas complies with only partially (3.3.1). Both platforms partially comply with five criteria (2.1.1, 2.2.1, 3.3.1, 3.5.1, 4.1.1).

Considering possible reasons for these differences, particularly as Moodle and Canvas both use the same text editor plug-in, one reason may be the time span of almost three years between the evaluations of Moodle and Canvas and the focus on accessibility has increased the past few years. We hope that this is an indication of improved accessibility in general in these and similar platforms.

Based on the evaluation of the selected Canvas course elements according to ATAG 2.0 criteria, we recommend the following for increasing accessibility in Canvas.

**Improve Support for Efficient Keyboard Navigation.** Ensure keyboard focus comes back to the place it was before opening a dialog box. Add keyboard shortcut to save editing contents (in text editor).

**Improve Support for Screen Readers.** Ensure that screen readers always indicate spelling errors and the number of matches in search results. Ensure screen reader support for all commonly used browsers, e.g., Chrome, and in particular free screen readers such as NVDA.

**Improve Options for Avoiding or Correcting Mistakes.** Ensure confirmation from user before starting upload of large files. Provide Undo/Redo options, including keyboard shortcuts, when setting properties for elements, e.g., when creating a quiz. Provide Undo/Redo options as visible choices in the text editor, for example as buttons, to avoid that this feature is available only as shortcuts.

Other recommendations include adding options for stopping or not automatically starting animated gifs (in text editor), include alternative text in search results, and ensure backward compatibility with older browsers.

# 6    Conclusion and Future Work

Focusing on Canvas' accessibility for instructors creating course contents in MOOCs, we have presented our findings from a heuristic evaluation of the Canvas platform based on a selected set of 28 success criteria from ATAG 2.0, Part A. We have also compared the results with results from our previous evaluation of Moodle. Our results show that Canvas complies better with the selected criteria when compared with Moodle. Our research shows that Canvas provides much support for instructors to create accessible MOOCs, but it does not comply fully with ATAG 2.0.

We have not included ATAG 2.0 part B in our evaluations so far. To investigate how well Canvas supports instructors in creating accessible course content, we will need to conduct heuristic evaluations of ATAG 2.0 part B. In addition, user testing on Canvas with a diverse group of participants will be necessary to discover further possible challenges that cannot be revealed by heuristic evaluations alone.

To continue our systematic investigation of accessibility of MOOC platforms from instructors' perspective, we are planning evaluation of other MOOC platforms. Future work includes user testing on the evaluated platforms with instructors in order to validate the results from the heuristic evaluations and identify any further accessibility problems not revealed in the heuristic evaluations.

# References

1. Al-Mouh, N.A., Al-Khalifa, A.S., Al-Khalifa, H.S.: A first look into MOOCs accessibility. In: Computers Helping People with Special Needs, pp. 145–152. Springer (2014)
2. Bohnsack, M., Puhl, S.: Accessibility of MOOCs. In: Miesenberger, K., Fels, D., Archambault, D., Peňáz, P., Zagler, W. (eds.) ICCHP 2014, Part I. LNCS, vol. 8547, pp. 141–144. Springer, Heidelberg (2014)
3. Calle-Jimenez, T., Sanchez-Gordon, S., Luján-Mora, S.: Web accessibility evaluation of massive open online courses on Geographical Information Systems. In: Global Engineering Education Conference (EDUCON). IEEE (2014)
4. Draffan, E.A., Wald, M., Dickens, K., et al.: Stepwise approach to accessible MOOC development. In: Assistive Technology, pp. 227–234 (2015)
5. Iniesto, F., Rodrigo, C., Moreira Teixeira, A.: Accessibility analysis in MOOC platforms. A case study: UNED COMA and UAb iMOOC. In: Libro de Actas del V Congreso Internacional sobre Calidad y Accesibilidad de la Formación Virtual CAFVIR (2014)
6. NOU 2014:5. MOOCs for Norway: New digital learning methods in higher education. Ministry of Education and Research Norway, Oslo (2014)
7. Reich, J.: Rebooting MOOC research. Science 347(6217), 34–35 (2015)
8. Sanchez-Gordon, S., Lujan-Mora, S.: Web accessibility of MOOCs for elderly students. In: Proceedings of International Conference on Information Technology Based Higher Education and Training (ITHET 2013), pp. 1–6. IEEE (2013)
9. Sanchez-Gordon, S., Lujan-Mora, S.: Adaptive content presentation extension for open edX. Enhancing MOOCs accessibility for users with disabilities. In: Proceedings of International Conference on Advances in Computer-Human Interactions (ACHI 2015), pp. 181–183 (2015)
10. Sarasa-Cabezuelo, A., Sierra-Rodríguez, J.-L.: Development of a MOOC management system. In: Proceedings of the Second International Conference on Technological Ecosystems for Enhancing Multiculturality (TEEM 2014), pp. 155–162. ACM (2014)
11. Chen, W., Sanderson, N.C., Kessel, S., Królak, A.: Heuristic evaluations of the accessibility of learning management systems (LMSs) as authoring tools for teachers. First Monday, [S. l.], September 2015. http://firstmonday.org/ojs/index.php/fm/article/view/5430. ISSN: 13960466
12. Chen, W., Sanderson, N.C., Kessel, S.: The accessibility of learning management systems from teachers' perspective. In: Proceedings of the 21st International Conference on Computers in Education, pp. 437–442 (2013)
13. Wang, T.: Coursera Charts Course for International Expansion With $49.5 M in Series C Funding (2015). https://www.edsurge.com/news/2015-08-25-coursera-charts-course-for-international-expansion-with-49-5m-in-series-c-funding

# A Tangible Interaction Platform as Concrete Support for Blind Children Literacy in Braille

Laura Sánchez García[1(✉)], João Hilton Sayeg de Siqueira[2], Juliana Bueno[1], and Patric Galera Forcelini[1]

[1] Federal University of Paraná, Curitiba, PR, Brazil
{laura,juliana,pgforcelini}@inf.ufpr.br
[2] PUC-SP, São Paulo, SP, Brazil
joahilton@uol.com.br

**Abstract.** The supposition that the Literacy through the Direct Way Methodology (LDWM) will also fit the blind children's context led us to take advantage of a PhD thesis that built a set of requirements for an application to help teachers and deaf students in this method's activities. Our main objective was to investigate how a tangible interaction for blind children's literacy should be. This goal was pursued mapping the set of requirements elicited for deaf children to the context of blind ones, through conceptual readings, a working process continuously close to a blind teacher - also a national reference in Braille literacy, and the searching for proper interface elements and interaction techniques for blind students placed in the reading and writing acquisition process. This paper describes the research path and the results achieved up to date.

**Keywords:** User experience · Blind children · Literacy · Braille · Tangible interaction

## 1 Introduction

Part of Computer Science (CS) social responsibility is placed on the appropriation of its innovative potentiality to support Education, especially on the effort in Literacy. The need for social inclusion of disabled communities gives CS – more exactly, Human Computer Interaction - a complementary role. We have occupied this space based on three principles: an inter and transdisciplinary approach, participatory design and Action-Research (AR) practices. A PhD theses built within our research group and published in 2014 [1] identified, based on the Literacy through the Direct Way Methodology (LDWM) [2–5] and by means of AR, a set of a computer application requirements to support the teaching-learning processes of Portuguese written language reading and writing to/by deaf children. The LDWM is based firstly on the appropriation of children's Literature – followed by several genders, on the need for critical reading, collaborative classroom activities and, mainly, text treatment as sequences of concrete significant pieces of objects. While traditional oral literacy aims at the acquisition of coding and decoding abilities, is dependent on the oral capacity and does not grant effective critical reading of the written language, this approach defines Literacy as an

© Springer International Publishing Switzerland 2016
M. Antona and C. Stephanidis (Eds.): UAHCI 2016, Part III, LNCS 9739, pp. 135–146, 2016.
DOI: 10.1007/978-3-319-40238-3_14

individual state in which the person manages to make plain usage of reading and writing in social context. For its authors, to be a reader implies having high degrees of autonomy and criticism over a text. This methodology, built and widely used during more than two decades by a civil French organization (www.lecture.org), has proved to be effective virtually in all cases: for either a first or a second language, for children, teenagers and adults and for learners with no literacy success by Orality, of which deaf children are an special case. An interview of a blind teacher – a reference from Instituto Benjamin Constant (IBC), the pioneer Latin America Institution for Education of visually impaired people [6] called us to the urgency of supporting the rescue of literacy practices of the Portuguese Language teaching and learning through the Braille system. She referred to the "desbraillização" ("dis-braille-zation") process, hypothetically caused by the accom-modation of blind people to the screen-readers. The cause-effect subject is polemic, but the fact, reported before in the USA [7], is that a regression of Braille literacy practice is in course, in spite of blind children literacy experts having proved the sine-qua-non characteristic of the Braille System as the passport to the plain social inclusion of the blind [8].

All this took us naturally to the research question: "Is it possible – and, in this case, which would be the associated activities and tools – to map the set of requirements elicited for deaf children literacy to the context of blind children?". The main objective became, then, to investigate how a tangible interaction for blind children's literacy should be. This goal was pursued mapping the set of requirements elicited for deaf children to the context of blind ones, through conceptual readings, a working process continuously close to a blind teacher - also a national reference in Braille literacy, having, then dual role in the process - and the searching for proper interface elements and inter-action techniques for blind students placed in the reading and writing acquisition process.

Among the challenged faced, we select the need to attend to literacy practices with congenital visual impaired children [21] and to identify concrete representations of Braille that could allow for language manipulation both individually and collaboratively in classroom situations. The knowledge of real literacy practices together with these concrete representations for texts in Braille would bring us the blind children's corre-spondent requirements for the specific ones identified by Bueno [1] for deaf children literacy. We also looked for ways of registering the children's productions and associate to them different oral representations (the children's himself, the teacher's and the screenreader's), in order to make the comparison (a metalinguistic one), together with several additional classroom activities possible, but the latter are not covered by the present paper, since our main focuses here are the tangible aspects of the interface and of the associated interaction.

## 2   Related Work

We visited related work, comprehending latest results focused firstly on input/output devices and interfaces for visually disabled people [9–11].

We also revised applications that were meant to support Braille "literacy" - limited to the motor coordination abilities and the code learning [12–14]. An interesting work developed at Carnegie Mellon University consisted on the participatory and iterative design process of an intelligent tutor of Braille [14]. The main challenges of the authors included the avoidance of the right-to-left writing obligation – due to the inaccessibility of the Braille typewriters (Perkins machines) for developing countries, together with the production of feedback for each symbol typing in satisfactory time intervals (neither available in the traditional writing nor in the addressed one within the populations in context, which are limited to the puncher). Equally motivated by the need to support blind children literacy with low cost solutions, researchers from the University of Madison Wisconsin and from the Birla Institute of Technological Sciences developed a robotic device called "Write Tutor" [12]. These authors state that the Write Tutor can teach children and people of any age group the art of writing. Including, within its architecture, a speech recognition system, the tutor guides the user to write what he/she says, holding his wrist by the robotic arm. Their system has got built-in modules that "allow for teaching reading and writing simultaneously" [12]. Another related work available, published in 2015, is Mudra [13], a multimodal interface integrated with an speech recognizing module implemented in Android for Braille teaching. The authors state that their work shows the way in which multimodal interfaces could be used "to teach Braille in a quicker and more efficient way", as well as "without effort" [13]. The paper does not present evidences of those statements. Never-the-less, even in the supposition of their existence, it is still possible to claim that the concern of these authors was, once more, limited to the capabilities of encoding-decoding, and did not refer to the binomial teaching-learning of the critical reading and writing as it does in our approach.

Last but not least, few works shared our approach of plain literacy concept [15–18]. The research reported in [15] refers to the need for "nurturing" Braille. These authors' investigation looked forward maximizing the access and the motivational aspect for Braille learning and use. The paper presents the results of five interviews with blind persons, composed by teachers and students. The authors created scenarios and projected software and hardware solutions in order to motivate for the discovery and the strengthening of the resilience of Braille literacy [15]. We have verified that both the principles and the objectives are aligned with ourselves', and we registered some issues that could be of potential contribution to our solution. The authors reinforce the special advantages of Braille over other writing systems for the blind populations, specially its huge flexibility to represent different knowledge areas writing systems, from which we can quote Math and Music, and the reduced number of significant elements to define a cell, that makes a seven-key keyboard possible and eliminates the need for larger areas.

A one-day workshop at CHI 2014, in Toronto [16], brought together designers, researchers and general HCI practitioners to analyze the opportunities and directions to take in designing more natural interactions based on spoken language and to look at the ways in which recent advances in speech processing could reinforce the acceptance of speech and natural language interaction. The Workshop abstract states that humans' most natural forms of communication, speech and language, are also the most difficult modalities for machines, as they suppose, by the width of their channels. From the participant of this workshop view, the effort to improve machines' ability to understand speech and natural language has been neglected as interaction modalities, mainly because of the challenges imposed by its high error rates and computational complexity. Among the issues stated at this workshop, we can bring the fact of the wide range of tasks in which speech can be useful, clearly not limited to direct interactions [16]. One example of a huge potentiality of speech refers to the area of access to multimedia repositories. As these people state, the rate in which video resources, for instance, are uploaded at YouTube (72 h by min) [16, 24], makes it increasingly difficult to search for information and to navigate through large and usually multilingual collections. This problem is being faced by our research, which had identified the vantages of using noises, sounds, music and songs bases to take advantage of the direct and fastest communication channels for blind people, together with their associated background.

We were also curious, by what else could be extracted from speech, beside speech-segments (phonemes and longer ones). Additionally, the authors of [16] questioned themselves – as we do ourselves) about how speech could be combined with other modalities to better interfaces' usability and soundness. Another idea related and complementary to this one is what else could be added to speech to make it more expressive and natural. This is also our concern and will be the object of future research.

A work-in-progress paper presented at CHI 2014 [17] dealt with our principal interest: supporting teaching and learning processes of blind children literacy, under-stood in its whole multi-dimensional complexity. The authors were developing tech-nologies to support teachers and parents in creating replicable tactile graphics. They refer to "emergent literacy" [17, 25] as the process by which a child can construct concepts about the functions of symbols and print, being based on experiences and meaningful language facilitated by interaction with adults. Co-reading experiences between parents and child can lead to emotional bonds, join one-another into discovering surrounding environments, objects and relationships, as well as extend creativity and vocabulary acquisition, together with continuous semiosis [17].

The authors of [17] also claim that tactile picture books aid in the development of the child's tactile acuity and mobility, as well as in their sense of feeling of their envi-ronment, apart from the confidence to explore and construct new associations through touch. They claim, also, that available tools for creating tactile books are difficult to learn and require significant time to use and to adapt, since they usually have confusing guidelines or focus on scientific graphics. These authors [17] refer to a technical report [26] to state the difficulty in publishing creditable literacy research results in the space of visual impairment due, from their research experience, to the "low incidence nature of visual disability" which limits both the methods and the conclusions that can be drawn. Based on that premise, the authors of [17] looked for getting to know about this popu-lation and taking advantage of as many different ways as possible, having visited sites, attended to workshops, and distributed questionnaires. We suppose we are protected in this aspect, not only by the theoretical studies – which proved, once again, not to be enough for making neither conclusions nor working hypotheses, but by our permanent contact with Maria da Gloria Almeida, as well whose life-long experience – along the overlapping roles of a blind child that learned to read and write in Braille and of a Braille literacy expert, has continuously limited our confidence and taken us back to the chal-lenge of creating proper and potentially useful solutions. Among the initial findings of the authors of [17], we were interested specially by the emerging insight that shows the agencies, even those who are really committed to create affordable product to be socially used by the intended users, struggling to make product that meet all the specific requirements, in spite of the fact that teachers of visual impaired children and other related professionals being eager to testing primitive products. This finding is coherent with our premise of the higher relevance of the solutions' context-adherence over high-technologies creation and use, especially where the latters would not be financially accessible, even if developed in time. The authors of [17] state that there are efforts to make 3D printing and easy and efficient way for creating matrixes for tactile graphics. Since this facility was not available, we designed the open solution based on LEGO® 3D illustrations, which was deconstructed at the very first test by our genuine representative of the final users' profile. As research opportunities, the authors of [17] include the need to explore methods to exchange information regarding child's learning experiences at home and while at school, as well as to find techniques for transcribing images in the way experienced artists do, together with the application of established guidelines practiced and refined by teachers of visually impaired children. These ideas appeared natural for our research and are part of our future work too, since we had experienced difficulties to find related literature and we had reached, even by a different path, awareness about the need for further exploring of image description within our working space.

A visionary work was presented in [18]. Its authors claim that the tangible reading experience of interactive books for children in general is inaccessible for blind children. Their paper presents an innovative set of 3D-printable models designed as building blocks for creating movable tactile pictures that can be touched, moved and understood by children with visual impairments. Models examples of what they proposed are canvases, connectors, hinger, spinners, sliders, lifts, walls and cuttouts. They map a range of spatial concepts such us input/output, up/down, and high/low. They based their proposed models on a three-step methodology including a survey of popular interactive books, two workshops on the processes of creating movable pictures by hand (physically, using LEGO® and Play-Doh) and the creation wood-based prototypes and informal testing with sighted preschoolers. Their System creates a 3D-printable model from a given specification. Supported by [28], these authors state that books that include tangible interaction encourage children interests into the content, stimulating their perceptual motor skills that evolve to linguistic ones [18]. They also claim, now based on [29], that holding children's attention was proved to be the key to develop emergent literacy in association with books [18]. This statement is completely aligned with the principles of the LDWM [2–5] and our PhD thesis of hypotheses [1]. These authors' methodology, in the step of physical constructions of 3D-scenarios by children, shares our observation of children's building actions from LEGO® an LEGO®'s Story-Starter, a commercially available set that includes Playmobil-like objects like socially common characters' (such us a policeman, a – stereotyped - girl, a boy, …) and building elements that help to build other roles, as a pointed hat and a broom, to compose a witch. The design requirements stated by these authors were: (i) Easy to move and touch. (ii) Easy to print. (iii) Easy to assemble. (iv) Easy to customize. (v) Easy to reuse. (vi) Hard to break. Except from the facility to print, inherent to their technological innovation, we shared all their requirements. These authors inform that many premade, ready-to-print objects are now available on sharing sites as Thingiverse. These tools are candidates to be included in our future visionary architecture to support the DWML for blind children that we intend to build after having arrived to a rather comprehensive list of requirements and, mainly, after having conducted tests with real end users, what can only be done during lessons time, which in Brazil starts effectively on March. The authors of [18] refer to the importance of physical analogies to the real world in toys such as cars and trains for visually impaired children. These analogies are in consonance with [19, 20] since they keep the significant features that characterizes the object concept, which is the case in cars and trains, regarded the teacher's explanation associated to the difference in size, which happens to be one of the features that cannot be reproduced at classroom environments [19, 20].

Our further research on material for blind children's requirements took us also to [30]. Among the justifications for the special relevance that courseware assumes in visually impaired people, there is the difficult of blind persons to be in contact with the physical environment, the risk of the child be conducted to "verbalism" - expression that denotes the mere verbal repetition of enunciations with no significance, the dependency that the concept construction has to the child's contact with the real world objects. In this, the authors are aligned with [19, 20]. In [30] the authors remark the relevance of courseware building from simple and easily available materials, as matches, string and cardboard. They claim that this practice enhances the reproduction of the courseware by the totality of the intended users. They also remark other requirements: (i) abundance. They must be attend simultaneously to several children; (ii) variability. To instigate the child's interest and his/her experimentation; (iii) significance. In the sense of its potentiality of being perceived by the tactile sense (as also stated in [19, 20]); (iv) size. They explain that very small elements do not allow for detail identification (requirement stated in [19, 20] too) and, also, that very big objects do not allow for the totality apprehension. This was also remarked by [19, 20], together with the explanation of the need for telling the children, verbally, any feature of the real object that could not be correctly represented. In [30], the authors refer to the need for the appropriation of contrasts, such as smooth/rough and thin/thick in order to facilitate distinctions in value. They claim, further, that the material cannot cause any kind of irritation, nor unpleasant feeling at handling. The faithfulness of the representations to the real objects, also claimed by these authors, reinforces what was said [19, 20]. The authors of [30] also refer to the facility to manipulate and to the need for robustness, two features already placed in our conceptual working space.

The need for tangible interfaces carried us naturally to the LEGO® concept. Looking after combining LEGO® to Braille including pictures, took us to think about a solution where the Braille cells would be represented by LEGO®'s 3 × 2 blocks, added by a 3D pictures representation, which seemed natural for blind children, whose main communication sense is tactile. This took us easily to the commercially available LEGO Educational Story Starter®, which offers the possibility of building stories scenarios with LEGO® blocks in sequential panel bases and its photographic recording and correspondent snapshots input into texts. By the capabilities perceived and as far as the documentation is concerned, this application does not consider blind children. This, together with the ideas found at the related reviewed papers, motivated our first solution attempt.

The option for LEGO® building bases was justified by what we think to be the main capability of this solution, namely the possibility of integrating, within the same production space, the proper text with alternative representations, among which we underline the 3D scenarios. This was supposed to work as a metaphor with "ink texts" illustrations, which was supposed to allow for the child to perceive, recognize and understand the role of texts illustrations, while it would additionally act stimulating creativity in texts production (feature inherent to Story-Starter® product as written in its official description) and making the concrete building of non-textual representations, specially the stories illustrations, possible for the blind child. It is worth reinforcing that the sighted child also needs physical experimentation [23].

The appropriation of the LEGO® blocks for representing the Braille cells was adopted form the analogy with the need, determined by the Literacy Direct Way Method of the availability and the treatment to/by the child of different graphic letters representations, including their form - handwriting in the general case - and diverse fonts and sizes, among others. Our solution intends to help blind children in current literacy processes in the language acquisition by means of the representation of possible variants of letters references. We expect that from the cell's concrete representation – in the form of LEGO® blocks or in any other one that conserves its main characteristics, the blind child will be aided to grasp the significant, determinant features of the Braille system. In the context of the Portuguese Language teaching and acquisition (as occurs in natural languages in general), this need is associated to the concept of "neutralizing", process by which the child establishes commutative pairs, makes the comparison and the substitution, with the intention of identifying the language signs. Our expectation is that the blind child will associate the Braille cells representations to Braille real cells in a similar way to that used by the seeing child to identify the available variants of words oral referents as its phonetic matrix [22].

An academic poster published at SUI'14 [27] described a research process then searching for ways of sighted children modeling tactile books by LEGO® pieces and those pieces being converted to digital models and that could be printed. These authors focused image recognition, mainly of 3D pictures. Their methodological steps were: (i) Putting sighted children to choose a book to model; (ii) using LEGO® pieces to construct physical 3D interpretation of the book's contents; (iii) scanning the models by a 3D-scanner, in 3 views: top, front and side; (iv) extracting key features through the projections; (v) matching these features to retrieve visually similar 3D models from large repositories [27]. Though interesting for our own purposes, the solution described in [27] can be though to work in a future visionary architecture mainly because it seems to be rather content-dependent, together with the interaction elements proposed by the innovative work in [18].

## 3   A Concrete Attempt for an Artifact to Support Braille Literacy Teaching and Learning by the Direct Way Literacy Methodology

As a first solution, we created a Tangible User Interface (TUI) made of LEGO® blocks, together with LEGO® blocks adapted for the Braille alphabet, which could be easily connected to a computer by inner components. Our first attempt was justified by the discovery of the sharing of elements and principles with Maria da Gloria Almeida's thesis that proved the special relevance of good children's literature for blind children literacy, and by her assertion about the need for concrete scenarios manipulation for this same audience. The proposal had as one of its innovative characteristics, the integration of text in Braille (by means of LEGO® blocks adapted) with 3D illustrations, made possible by the LEGO's Story Starter®, which allows for some well-known social characters creation (like a policeman, a fireman, a boy, a witch, between others). A hypothetical scenario of this proposal usage is shown in Fig. 1. The scene consisted of a Braille text-like area - respecting what could be words and spaces between them, and a 3D illustration composed by a witch carrying a broom pursuing a running boy carrying a cat, presumably the witch's one.

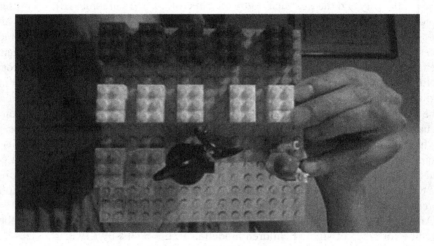

**Fig. 1.** The first TUI proposal built, tested and rejected by the blind teacher

This solution proposal was presented to the blind teacher as a test for the intended audience (blind children at the beginning of the literacy process, 6 to 7-year-old) during a working meeting at her office. We gave her the built scenario (Fig. 1) and asked her to manipulate it and say what she could perceive of it as a Braille text representation for blind children at the ages of hypothesis.

After having manipulated the platform and broken the "human" characters, she made determinant remarks that showed the inappropriateness of our proposal. First of all, she pointed to the necessities of the objects to be manipulated being tough, even more thinking on their intended audience. Also, the distance between different scene object must be enough to allow for the object manipulation from every side of them. These observations caused the immediate failure of the 3D illustration proposal. Additionally, she pointed out that the LEGO® blocks could not be easily manipulated by the target children, since they were excessively tied to the base. It is worth noting that the intended LEGO®'s tool for blocks removal demands manual and motor abilities those children do not usually have because of the lack of previous needed opportunities of manipulating concrete objects [19]. This report buried totally the tested proposal.

## 4   Towards an Adequate Solution

From the review of related literature, added to our background in the Direct Way Literacy Method, we composed a set of guidelines. It is worth remarking that some of the guides are known ones at Human-Computer Interaction community, but we decided to include them because we though they were relevant enough in its specific (context-dependent) form.

The design process and the tangible interface solution that can be able to support blind children to take advantage of the LDWM in the context of Braille must attend to the following four maxims:

1. Research methodology – The joint work of designers and real blind children teachers is a proved sound research methodology;
2. Literacy activities planning – The activities to be planned must be meaningful for the blind children and include opportunities for cooperative, collaborative and interactive work;
3. The proper tangible interface – The device to provide the computer-human interaction must be as natural as possible, including the attendance to the requirements related to the blind children's motor and cognitive real situation that can grant accessibility, and, also, mobile linguistic components;
4. The interaction – The interaction process must take advantage of multimodal and multimedia resources, in order to enhance communication, language acquisition and text production.

Based on these maxims, we developed a second solution based on well-known and widely used materials, a "bags" and "pockets" system and contact fixation of the three level of elements (character symbols, words and text lines) on the working space. The scheme for a text row representation can be seen in Fig. 2.

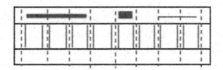

**Fig. 2.**   A row of the second solution

The solution includes:

1. A white rectangular cotton fabric, with lateral borders in the length direction folded up in order to allow for the placement (easy and precise) of the Braille cells made from a thin rubber sheet;
2. Tough vertical fixation seams to prevent from the cells horizontal slipping after insertion;

3. A contact fixation strip on the top margin allows for the placing of three tactile (for the children perception) and visual (for the system recognition) different marking ribbons corresponding to different linguistic aspects currently focused in the real classroom activity (that could be, for instance, names, adjectives and verbs).
4. The same fixation system behind the word structure allows for the fixation of the words on the text row structure, which is, in turn, also mobile.
5. Braille cells made of a thin rubber sheet with the dots marked precisely with black plastic paste, with top and bottom edges to be inserted in the cells boxes, together with an arrow on the top edge to indicate the up-direction for reading purposes.
6. A panel to accommodate the whole text built by a child or by a group in a collaborative activity, with trails marked by contact pasting material to guide the construction of the text lines, to be fixed on the "blackboard" or tied on a table or even fixed somehow on the floor.

The fabric, the line and the sewing must be strong enough for the blind children to manipulate at least during a reading project period (about two months).

The physical solution to be used for the input of the children's productions was taken from the idea proposed in a work on free playing with music elements [31], a TUI based on computer vision that can be downloaded, printed and used by any user with a personal computer and a webcam. Using cheap common materials, the solution can be adapted to our work's domain since the camera can stay behind the panel, while the children can be informed of its presence and concentrate on the text reading and production. The software solution to be adopted is a program written in Python language using the computer vision library OpenCV [32] for processing the visual rules of our TUI. On the other side, the solution will also include a set of physical rules to satisfy the blind children needs.

## 5 Conclusions and Future Work

The solution was built with the continuous support of the teacher from IBC, eliminating, by construction, the possibility of factoring elegant technological solutions with no use in real blind children classrooms. After the discovery of the shared concept of literacy with our consultant teacher, our first proposal integrated a few features collected from literature into a physical platform. When she rejected that solution, we managed to propose the main elements for a tangible interaction platform made from known, cheap and easily available materials that can act as a concrete support for blind children literacy in Braille and can be used both in the stand-alone way and as the concrete part of the TUI.

The concrete concepts translation is done at Brazilian public school of little resources by educational toys build from Ethylene Vinyl Acetate (EVA), as in maps or simple classical games. In this context, we can state that the solution built and presented here has as one of its characteristics its potential use within inclusive educational environments. This feature is socially relevant, and, form a technological point of view, its defines one more axes for innovation in our solution for blind children literacy in Braille, since it can be appropriated both by special literacy time-periods activities (which, for us, must complement the genuine inclusive education because of the need for different conditions to grant equal opportunities) and in the context of inclusive education classrooms.

The solution under construction will allow recording, maintaining and recovering different versions of the children's textual productions. The physical part of the solution is currently being tested with blind children in the addressed scenarios with beginning indicators of success. Our future work will concentrate on integrating all the interface elements presented here with real interaction in order to get a self-contained, working tool.

# References

1. Bueno, J.: Pesquisa-Ação na Construção de Insumos Conceituais para um Ambiente Computacional de Apoio ao Letramento Bilíngue de Crianças Surdas, Tese de Doutorado - Universidade Federal do Paraná (2014)
2. AFL: École d'etê. Aurillac, France (2013)
3. Foucambert, J.: A Leitura Em Questão. Artes Médicas, Porto Alegre (1994)
4. Foucambert, J.: Modos de ser leitor: Aprendizagem e ensino da leitura no ensino fundamental. UFPR, Curitiba (2008)
5. Razet, C.: De la lecture d'une histoire à la lecture d'une écriture. Synergies Brésil. **10**, 59–74 (2012)
6. Melare, J.: Novas tecnologias facilitam a leitura e o letramento de deficientes visuais. ComCiência. 154 (2013)
7. National Federation of the Blind, Jernigan Institute: The Braille Literacy Crisis in America: Facing the Truth, Reversing the Trend, Empowering the Blind (2009)
8. Riles, R.: Braille as a predictor of success. In: Dixon, J. (ed.) Braille into the Next Millennium, pp. 463–491. Library of Congress's National Library Service for the Blind and Physically Handicapped, Washington, DC (2000)
9. Grossner, C., Radhakrishnan, T., Pospiech, A.: An integrated workstation for the visually handicapped. IEEE Micro **3**, 8–16 (1983)
10. Presscher, D., Weber, G., Spindler, M.: A tactile windowing system for blind users. In: ASSETS 2010, pp. 91–98. ACM, New York (2010)
11. Russomanno, A., O'Modhrain, S., Gillespie, R., Rodger, M.: Refreshing refreshable braille displays. IEEE Trans. Haptics **8**, 287–297 (2015)
12. Parthiban, C., Parthiban, R.: Write tutor. In: IEEE International Conference on Technology for Education, pp. 279–282. IEEE, New York (2011)
13. Srivastava, A., Dawle, S.: Mudra: a multimodal interface for braille teaching. In: AH 2015 The 6th Augmented Human International Conference, pp. 169–170. ACM, New York (2015)
14. Kalra, N., Lauwers, T., Dewey, D., Stepleton, T., Dias, M.: Iterative design of a Braille writing tutor to combat illiteracy. In: ICTD 2007. pp. 1–9. IEEE, New York (2007)
15. Guerreiro, J., Gonçalves, D., Marques, D., Guerreiro, T., Nicolau, H., Montague, K.: The today and tomorrow of Braille learning. In: ASSETS 2013. Article 71. ACM, New York (2013)
16. Munteanu, C., Jones, M., Whittaker, S., Oviatt, S., Aylett, M., Penn, G., Brewster, S., d'Alessandro, N.: Designing speech and language interactions. In: CHI 2014 Extended Abstracts on Human Factors in Computing Systems, pp. 75–78. ACM, New York (2014)

17. Stangl, A., Kim, J., Yeh, T.: Technology to support emergent literacy skills in young children with visual impairments. In: CHI 2014 Extended Abstracts on Human Factors in Computing Systems, pp. 1249–1254. ACM, New York (2014)

18. Kim, J., Yeh, T.: Toward 3D-printed movable tactile pictures for children with visual impairments. In: CHI 2015, pp. 2815–2824. ACM, New York (2015)

19. Almeida, M.: Physical meeting. Rio de Janeiro, 14–15 October, 2015

20. Almeida, M.: Telephone meetings. July–November 2015, February 2016

21. Nunes, S.: Desenvolvimento de conceitos em cegos congênitos: caminhos de aquisição do conhecimento, Dissertação de Mestrado – Universidade de São Paulo (2004)

22. Saussure, F.: Curso de linguística geral. Cultrix, São Paulo (1971)

23. Piaget, J.: L'epistémologie génétique. Presses Universitaire de France, Paris (1970)

24. Youtube Upload statistics (2012). http://www.youtube.com/t/press_statistics

25. Stratton, J.: Emergent literacy: a new perspective. J. Vis. Impairment Blindness **90**, 177–183 (1996)

26. Ferrell, K., Mason, L., Young, J., Cooney, J.: Forty Years of Literacy Research in Blindness and Visual Impairment. National Center on Low-Incidence Disabilities (2016)

27. Kim, J., Stangl, A., Yeh, T.: Using LEGO to model 3D tactile picture books by sighted children for blind children. In: 2nd ACM Symposium on Spatial User Interaction, SUI 2014, p. 146. ACM, New York (2014)

28. Hengeveld, B., Hummels, C., Overbeeke, K., Voort, R., van Balkom, H., Moor, J.: Tangibles for toddlers learning language. In: 3rd International Conference on Tangible and Embedded Interaction, TEI 2009, pp. 161–168. ACM, New York (2009)

29. Bus, A.: Joint caregiver-child storybook reading: A route to literacy development. In: Neuman, S., Dickinson, D. (eds.) Handbook of Early Literacy Research, pp. 179–191. The Guilford Press, New York (2003)

30. Cerqueira, J., Ferreira, E.: Recursos didáticos na educação especial. Revista Benjamin Constant **5**, 24–29 (1996)

31. Costanza, E., Giaccone, M., Kueng, O., Shelley, S., Huang, J.: Tangible interfaces for download: initial observations from users' everyday environments. In: CHI 2010 Extended Abstracts on Human Factors in Computing Systems, pp. 2765–2774. ACM, New York (2010)

32. OpenCV. http://opencv.org

# A Balloon, a Sweater, and a Wall: Developing Design Strategies for Accessible User Experiences with a Science Simulation

Taliesin L. Smith[1], Clayton Lewis[2], and Emily B. Moore[2(✉)]

[1] OCAD University, Toronto, Canada
talilief@gmail.com
[2] University Colorado Boulder, Boulder, USA
{clayton.lewis,emily.moore}@colorado.edu

**Abstract.** Interactive computer simulations are effective learning tools commonly used in science education; however, they are inaccessible to many students with disabilities. In this paper, we present initial findings from the design and implementation of accessibility features for the PhET Interactive Simulation, *Balloons and Static Electricity*. Our focus: access for screen reader users. We designed an interaction flow that connected keyboard interactions with reactions in dynamic content. Then using a *Parallel Document Object Model (PDOM)*, we created access to simulation content and interactive sim objects. We conducted interviews with screen reader users to evaluate our progress, and to understand better how they engage with interactive simulations. We share findings about our successes and challenges in the design and delivery of dynamic verbal text description, of efficient keyboard navigation, and the challenges we faced in making a keyboard accessible drag and release mechanism for a highly interactive simulation object, a Balloon.

**Keywords:** Web accessibility · Usability · Blind users · Inclusive design · Non-visual user interface · Parallel document object model · Keyboard interaction · Text description · Educational simulation · Interactive science simulation

## 1 Introduction

Interactive computer simulations are commonly used science education resources shown to be effective in supporting student learning [1, 2]. Interactive simulations allow students to investigate scientific phenomena across a range of size and time scales, and allow for experimentation when physical equipment is either not available or not accessible to the student. While the use of simulations has been shown to benefit student learning, they are often inaccessible to students with disabilities. Interactive simulations are generally highly visual and designed for mouse- or touch-driven interactions–making them particularly inaccessible to students with vision loss.

The PhET Interactive Simulations project [3] has created a popular suite of over 130 interactive science and mathematics simulations. These highly interactive simulations (or "sims") are run over 75 million times a year by teachers and students around the

© Springer International Publishing Switzerland 2016
M. Antona and C. Stephanidis (Eds.): UAHCI 2016, Part III, LNCS 9739, pp. 147–158, 2016.
DOI: 10.1007/978-3-319-40238-3_15

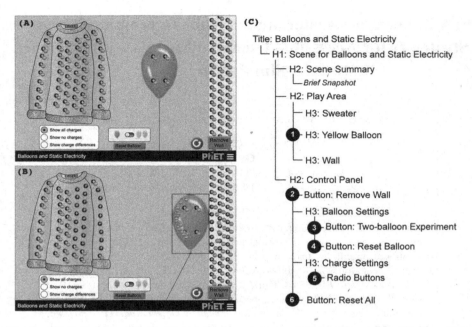

**Fig. 1.** (A) *Balloons and Static Electricity* sim on page load, before interaction. (B) Sim while Balloon has keyboard focus (pink box), released and attracted to Wall. (C) Simplified *Parallel DOM* shows heading hierarchy (H1 to H3) and tab order (circled numbers). Images reproduced with permission from PhET Interactive Simulations. (Color figure online)

world, and are pushing the capabilities of web technologies and standards to their limits. In this paper, we present findings from the design and implementation of accessibility features for the PhET sim *Balloons and Static Electricity* [4]. Our goal was to make this sim accessible and usable by screen reader users. In the process, we addressed challenges in the delivery of dynamic content and interactions, design of efficient keyboard navigation and operation, and user interaction with complex sim features. We conducted interviews with screen reader users to evaluate our progress, and to understand better how screen reader users engage with interactive simulations. We found that when access is successful, user engagement and learning can take place.

## 2    PhET Sim: *Balloons and Static Electricity*

The *Balloons and Static Electricity* sim (Fig. 1A, B) can be used to support student learning of topics related to static electricity, including transfer of charge, induction, attraction, repulsion, and grounding. This sim is used in classrooms from middle grades up to introductory college level, with students from age 10 to adult. Upon startup, the user encounters the sim's Play Area, containing a Sweater on the left side, a centrally located Balloon, and a Wall on the right side. Representations of positive and negative charges are shown overlaying all of these objects. At the bottom of the screen is the Control Panel area, including: a set of three radio buttons that control what charge representations are shown (all charges, no charges, or charge difference), a toggle switch that allows the user to change between experimenting with one Balloon or two, a Reset All button that resets the screen to its initial state, and a Remove Wall button that adds or removes the Wall.

The Balloon can be moved and rubbed against the Sweater (resulting in a transfer of negative charges from the Sweater to the Balloon) and the Wall (resulting in no transfer of charges). Releasing the Balloon results in the Balloon being attracted to the Sweater or Wall, depending on the total amount of charge present on the Balloon and its proximity to either the Sweater, or the Wall. For example, rubbing the Balloon on the Sweater results in a transfer of negative charges from the Sweater to the Balloon, and the now negatively charged Balloon, upon release from the middle of the Play Area, is attracted to (moves toward and "sticks" to) the now positively charged Sweater. Releasing the Balloon near the Wall may result in the Balloon attracting to the neutral Wall (Fig. 1B) or attracting back to the Sweater.

In the original sim all interactions, including moving the Balloon and activating buttons and radio buttons, were mouse or touch events. No verbal description of visual representations or dynamic changes were provided.

## 3    Accessible Design Features

To provide access for screen reader users, we implemented the following enhancements.

### 3.1    Access to Sim Content and Interactions

To make the content and interactions of the sim accessible to assistive technologies (AT), we designed a semantically rich HTML-based hierarchical representation of the sim that describes all objects and interactions. We refer to this accessible feature as the *Parallel Document Object Model* (or "PDOM"). The reasoning for the PDOM approach has been addressed previously [5]. In this work, we enhanced the PDOM with the rich semantics available in HTML. Through native semantics, the use of headings, and the linear order of elements, we created a hierarchy that conveys the spatial layout of the sim and the relationships among the sim objects. This structure makes it possible for screen reader users to perceive these relationships as they explore the sim, gaining an understanding of how the relationships relate to the interactions in the sim. For example, the Play Area contains three objects: the Balloon, the Sweater, and the Wall. We communicate that the objects have an important relationship through their heading structure. Each object's label (or name) is marked up as an H3 heading. The heading for the Play Area is an H2, conveying that it is the parent of these sibling objects. Details about each object are contained in a paragraph under each of the respective objects' headings. Design features that provide visual users with clues, within the design itself, on how to interact with the sim are referred to as "implicit scaffolding" [6]; providing hierarchical structure and a *Tab order* (Fig. 1C, circled numbers) that is based on pedagogical importance is an attempt to provide implicit scaffolds for screen reader users.

### 3.2 Keyboard Navigation and Operation

The PDOM described in the previous section provides meaning through heading hierarchy. It also provides a mechanism for efficient keyboard navigation and operation via navigable elements such as landmarks and regions. With screen reader commands, users can efficiently navigate by landmarks, regions, or headings. In *Balloons and Static Electricity*, the Scene Summary, Play Area, and Control Panel were coded as navigable regions (HTML section element) that each start with an H2 heading. With this structure, a screen reader user can navigate to the Play Area either with the region command or via the heading, thus providing efficient navigation from anywhere in the sim. We employed native HTML form controls and standard interaction design patterns [7], in order to create interactive sim objects that were findable and operable by users. For example, all interactive sim buttons are real HTML buttons and recognized by screen readers as such. They are reachable via the keyboard with the *Tab key* and can be operated upon (activated) by pressing either the *Spacebar* or the *Enter key*.

### 3.3 Timely Description that Connects Interactions with Dynamic Content

Descriptions of changing information such as Balloon charge, Balloon position and Balloon behavior (direction and velocity during attraction and repulsion) must be delivered in a timely fashion while minimizing disruption. Our approach involved announcing dynamically changing charge information using ARIA live regions [8]. Live regions provide a way for screen readers to present new information that occurs away from where the user is currently reading (or has *focus*). For example, when a user rubs the Balloon on the Sweater, a transfer of charge occurs causing changes in the descriptive content associated with both the Balloon *and* the Sweater. Through the use of live regions the user is made aware of changes in charge levels for both objects, even though the user technically is only "reading" the Balloon. In designing our descriptive text strings, we aimed for brevity, consistency and clarity [9].

### 3.4 Keyboard Interaction and Engagement with Balloon

In order to explore the sim with a screen reader, the learner needs to be able to grab the Balloon, drag it to different locations, rub it on the Sweater (or Wall), and release it (to see how it attracts and repels) using keyboard interactions. To achieve this, we created the following mechanisms:

1. **Grab, Drag & Rub Interaction.** These interactions are integrated into one (similar to the mouse-driven grab, drag, and rub interaction). To grab, drag, and rub the Balloon, the user navigates keyboard focus to the Balloon and then presses one of a set of four directional movement keys, the *W, A, S,* or *D keys*. These keys correspond to up, left, down, and right movements of the balloon, respectively. These keys were selected as they are commonly used for directional movement in the computer gaming community. The sim includes a description of the interaction so it can be used (learned) without prior gaming experience. Note, our initial design utilized

*Arrow keys* for directional movement, but unfortunately, the A*rrow keys* already have assigned meaning (as *cursor keys*) essential to screen reader control.

2. **Release mechanism.** We provided three ways to release the Balloon: *Spacebar*, *Control + Enter* and *Tab*. The *Spacebar* was chosen for its alignment with the established interaction of submitting a form. Pressing *Control + Enter* is another standard way to submit a form, so for consistency this key press combination was implemented as a release for the Balloon. Pressing the *Tab key* moves focus away from the Balloon, and as a result (intentional or unintentional) must release the Balloon so that the non-visual interactions (and representations) remain in sync with the visual representations.

3. **Balloon interaction keyboard shortcuts.** We implemented the *Shift key* as a semi-modal acceleration key so that the user can make the Balloon move in larger increments (in the chosen direction). We also designed four, letter-based (non-case-sensitive), hotkey combinations to *jump* the Balloon to pedagogically strategic locations in the Play Area: *JW* (to W̲all), *JS* (to edge of S̲weater), *JN* (to N̲ear Wall) and *JM* (to M̲iddle of Play Area). By using pairs of keys for the hotkeys, we avoided conflicts with browser hotkey functionality [9]. To address other potential conflicts with screen reader functionality, we used the ARIA role *application* on the Balloon. The *application* role informs the screen reader to pass key presses to the web application (the sim) for an alternate purpose. Note, this approach does not work for the *Arrow keys*, but does work for letter keys – many of which are used as hotkeys for screen reader navigation.

## 4    Iterative Usability Evaluation

In order to test and refine our designs, we conducted a series of interviews with blind users. We asked users to explore the sim and, while interacting, to "think aloud" [10, 11]. Between interviews we made modifications to the software in response to user experiences.

### 4.1    Methods

**Participants.** We recruited 12 screen reader users to participate in interviews – and conducted 11 in-person interviews and 1 remote interview. The users, 5 women and 7 men, spanned a diverse age range (19 years to 61 years). Users demonstrated a diverse level of expertise with their screen reader: one user used both a refreshable Braille display and a screen reader. All users had at least some post-secondary education, the youngest being in their first year of college.

**Apparatus.** We gave the 12 users the option to use their own computer or one that we provided. Overall, the hardware and software setups were varied:

- **Hardware:** desktop PCs (2), Mac Air (2), Surface Pro 3 Tablet (1), Lenovo E541 (1), Lenovo T520 (6)

- **Browsers & Screen readers:** Chrome & JAWS 17 professional (1), IE11 & JAWS 17 Home (1), Firefox & JAWS 17 Home (1), Firefox & JAWS 17 demo (5), Firefox & JAWS 15 (1), Safari & VoiceOver (2) and Firefox & NVDA 2015 (1)

Each interview was video recorded, with the camera positioned to capture the participant's screen and keyboard.

**Procedure.** Most interviews took approximately 1 h. Each interview proceeded as follows:

1. **Describe the process** and outline the order and components of the interview.
2. **Ask background questions** regarding interests in science, demographics, educational background, system specifications, habits on daily computer use, use of AT, level of expertise with AT, and online education.
3. **Explain the state of the prototype** that we would be using. For example, it was necessary to explain that the prototype was fully keyboard accessible, but that some parts of the verbal descriptions were not yet implemented. Thus, information about the sim would be coming from both the screen reader and the interviewer, who would be playing the part of the screen reader for yet-to-be-implemented descriptions. This aspect was inspired by the Wizard of Oz method [12]. While speaking out the live description, the "wizard" followed a planned description script (where possible), but improvisation was required at times.
4. **Describe the Think Aloud Protocol(TAP) and conduct a TAP warm-up exercise.**
5. **Introduce use of the sim as a learning activity** by asking users to imagine they were in middle school science class starting a unit on static electricity and that their teacher had given them this sim to explore.
6. **Provide access to the sim prototype** via a link or a downloaded file.
7. **Ask the user to freely explore** for 20–40 min and to think aloud while doing so. As the user explores, the interviewer/wizard provides live descriptions of unimplemented dynamic content, and occasionally reminds user to think aloud.
8. **Ask follow-up questions to gain an understanding of their perspective** and thoughts on the experience and suggestions for how to improve the design.

## 5    Discussion & Results

Analysis of user interviews provided significant insight into effective (and ineffective) design approaches for making the interactive sim, *Balloons and Static Electricity,* accessible to visually impaired users. We describe here, for each inclusive design feature described in Sect. 3, what worked well and what challenges were found.

### 5.1    Access to Sim Content and Interactions

We found the *Parallel Dom* (PDOM) to be an effective approach for providing access to sim content and interactive (i.e. controllable) sim objects.

**What Worked Well.**

- Some sim content is static, meaning it does not change or changes very little, and some content is dynamic and changes a lot (see Sect. 5.3). Users were able to easily access, review and locate all static content and some dynamic content in the sim. All users accessed content successfully with the *Arrow keys* line by line. Most used a combination of strategies in addition to the *Arrow keys*. Access to this content is a significant achievement that allowed most users to explore, ask their own questions, and experiment to answer their own questions.
- When first encountering the sim, most users employed a strategy that consisted of first listening and then interacting. This behavior of listening before interacting is consistent with prior research with blind users [13, 14]. Some users listened just to the brief Scene Summary that introduces the sim and then took the suggested navigation cue (*Press Tab for first object*) at the end of the Scene Summary. Some listened to everything in the sim at least once before interacting with the *Tab key* or activating one of the buttons in the Control Panel. Both strategies were effective.

**Challenges.**

- Some users encountered challenges that they were not easily able to overcome. For example, one user's navigational approach involved listening to descriptions (sometimes listening to descriptions in full, other times listening to descriptions minimally), then using the *Tab key* to navigate quickly around the sim, and then listening again – without seeming to set any specific goals for exploration. In this case it seemed the descriptions were not supporting the user to find a productive path of exploration so her navigation seemed aimless.
- Browser implementation inconsistencies led to some confusion about interactions. For example, with Safari, VoiceOver reads out the Balloon as, "Application 3 items. Yellow Balloon". Upon hearing a number of items, one user tried, unsuccessfully, to interact with the Balloon as if it were a list.
- We learned how to optimize *label* and *description* text as we understood more fully how the interactive objects were read out by screen readers. *Label* text is the essential information for the control and is always read. *Description (or help)* text is additional information that can help the user understand what to do with the interactive object. Descriptions can be read out by default along with the label text or not. Changes to *label* and *description* text were made throughout the project and these changes improved the auditory experience in two ways: reduced screen reader verbosity and improved clarity. We found it useful to optimize *label* text to reduce the use of *help* text.

## 5.2 Keyboard Navigation and Operation

In this category, we also found the PDOM approach to provide affordances that supported effective keyboard navigation and operation.

**What Worked Well.**

- The PDOM approach allowed users to employ strategies developed from past experience to explore and interact with the sim. With the content structured and accessible in familiar ways, users were provided full agency to independently solve problems that arose – including science learning and technical challenges. For example, one user utilized the *Tab key* to navigate through the sim twice, while listening minimally to descriptions. Without the descriptions, she did not have enough information to successfully explore, and eventually changed her strategy. Her second strategy involved using a screen reader command to bring up a list of all headings. From there, she chose to navigate to the Scene Summary and began listening, ultimately resulting in her proceeding along a more productive path. In an example of a strategy change in response to a technical issue, one user encountered a technical issue where using *Tab* or *Shift-Tab* did not appropriately navigate away from the Reset All button. In one case the user made use of the *Arrow keys* to navigate away from the button, while in another case they used a screen reader navigation command (the *B key* in the JAWS screen reader) to navigate to the next button.
- In general, users found navigation and operation of common controls (e.g., buttons and dialog box) to be straightforward. If the label text was clear and read out correctly by the screen reader, the users seemed to know how to interact based on prior web experience.

**Challenges.**

- Navigation cues (telling the user explicitly what to do) were sometimes helpful, but significantly increased screen reader verbosity. Some users missed navigation cues by not listening long enough. Providing cues on demand may be a better approach.
- Some navigational cues were poorly placed which led to unsuccessful interaction attempts. We found that navigational cues need to be operable at precisely the same time that they are delivered.

### 5.3   Timely Description that Connects Interactions with Dynamic Content

We found that connecting interactions with changing content helped to create a successful interaction flow.

**What Worked Well.**

- All users understood that *something* changed when they rubbed the balloon on the sweater. Most perceived and understood that the overall charge had changed from neutral to positive (Sweater) or negative (Balloon). Only some noticed the charge description update, "a few more", "several more" and "many more". We chose this three-point relative scale to convey charge levels because it is the relative amount of charge, not the total number of each charge type, that is foundational to the underlying concepts. One user commented that a relative scale was useful, but another participant commented that the difference between "several more" and "many more" was too subtle. At least two users said that a numerical value for the level of charge would be more useful.

- Live description, though difficult to execute, worked well to test out a complex description plan for comprehensibility, usability and effectiveness before implementation. As part of the live description, some sound effects were produced by rubbing an actual balloon to indicate Balloon on Sweater and hitting the balloon to indicate reaching the Wall. These sounds received positive reactions from some users. However, live sounds were difficult to execute, and were not presented consistently. Further research will explore the use of sounds to augment verbal descriptions.
- Announcing changes to the Play Area when a user activated a button (e.g. "Wall removed from Play Area") was clearer to users than listening only to the changed button text.

**Challenges.**

- We found certain descriptions were particularly challenging for some users, and need to be refined. The description including "no more negative charges than positive ones" was interpreted by one user as no charge at all, rather than a net zero, or neutral charge. Not describing positive charges caused some users to think that the balloons had no positive charges at all, rather than the intended goal of cueing users that the negative charges were more relevant than the positive charges for exploration. The description of induced charge in the wall was misunderstood by a few users. These users thought that the Wall was actually repelling the Balloon when they heard "[…] negative charges in the wall are repelling away" from the negative charges in the Balloon.
- There were some implementation issues that need to be addressed. For example, one user was confused when they came across the Wall via the *Arrow keys* directly after intentionally removing it. Details in the Scene Summary sometimes led to confusion as they were not implemented to update dynamically. If users re-read the brief Scene Summary after interacting, the information was no longer aligned with the current sim state.
- Some descriptions needed to be more succinct and new or changed information needed to come first. Details about charges were missed if a user did not listen to the full update. One user said, "There is a lot of talking going on. I have to be honest, I tend to tune it out." This user repeatedly stopped dynamic updates prematurely, and as a result sometimes missed important details.
- We found capturing certain object behavior in strings of text to be particularly challenging. For example, a Balloon with a small net negative charge will attract to the Sweater slowly at first, speeding up as it gets closer. This behavior involves continuous change over distance and time, while text is better for describing change occurring in discrete units.

## 5.4  Keyboard Interaction and Engagement with Balloon

The Balloon object presented an interesting interaction design challenge. Ultimately, we want users to easily understand how to grab, drag, rub and release it with as little explanation as possible. The challenge is that there is no single HTML form control (or ARIA role) that provides a way to increment and decrement two separate values (Balloon position $x$ and $y$) by simply operating the *Arrow keys*. In other words, it is difficult to represent the Balloon in code in a way that users will intuitively understand how to interact with it. We tried different types of HTML input controls, all in combination with the ARIA role application, to achieve the required keyboard interactions. All users were eventually successful in grabbing, dragging, rubbing, and releasing the balloon – though several needed guidance from the interviewer. An analysis of how to optimize implementation of the Balloon and how to best describe the interactions is ongoing.

**What Worked Well.**

- We found the directional movement keys (*W*, *A*, *S*, and *D*) to be an understandable alternative to the *Arrow keys*. Three users needed no additional explanation; some users were curious about our choice of these keys, but nevertheless easily used them. One user exclaimed, "Oh, they are just like the *Arrow keys*!" commenting on the layout of the keys on the keyboard. Only the first user trying these keys had significant trouble mastering their use. An improvement to the description of the interaction seemed to improve understanding for subsequent users.
- The *Spacebar* and *Tab key*, as release mechanisms, were quickly learned and used repeatedly by all users. Other than some surprise with the *Tab key*, e.g., "I keep forgetting that when I tab away, I release the balloon," the interaction was understandable. There were no issues with the *Spacebar*. One user mentioned that *Spacebar* is used in some computer games to pick up and drop objects, confirming our choice for the *Spacebar* as a useful release mechanism for the Balloon.
- The jump hotkey combinations, (e.g. *JS*, *JW*) appear to be quite understandable and memorable. One user commented "It's like using *J* like a *Shiftkey*. Those commands make sense." This user did not actually employ the hotkeys; regardless, during the wrap-up questions, they were able to correctly recall three out of four of the hotkeys. Another user made extensive use of the jump hotkeys.
- The Balloon acceleration operation (*Shift key* plus a direction key) showed promise as a useful way to move the Balloon more efficiently; however, its initial effect was found to be negligible. We have since increased the amount of acceleration the *Shift key* provides.

**Challenges.**

- The pronunciation of "*W*, *A*, *S*, and *D keys*" in the interaction cue was not clear with a high screen reader speed. "*D*" sounded like "*T*".
- Instructions for the jump hotkeys and the accelerator key were not easy to find. They were only available at the bottom of the Keyboard Commands help dialog. Moving the information to the top of the dialog will likely improve discoverability.
- Screen readers announce aspects of the Balloon that are not directly meaningful to users. For example, "Application. Yellow Balloon. Three items", or "Application. Yellow Balloon. Draggable. Read-only." Some users were more tolerant of this

verbosity than others. Decreasing this verbosity by improving the Balloon's representation in code is currently in progress.

## 6 Conclusions

We faced a number of challenges in the design of a screen reader accessible interactive science simulation, *Balloons and Static Electricity*. The main challenges, determined by a study of 12 blind users, related to the delivery of complex descriptions in dynamic situations, and the lack of a native role for the main interactive sim object, the Balloon. In spite of the challenges reported here, all the users were excited about the research and their participation in the research.

The web standards (HTML and WAI-ARIA) that pertain to making highly interactive web applications accessible are complex and evolving. These standards are implemented inconsistently by browsers and screen readers, complicating our implementation approaches. Cases where native elements and roles could be directly applied to interactive sim objects seemed to be the easiest for users to discover and utilize.

The outcome of our efforts, thus far, is an interactive simulation prototype that is entirely operable by keyboard. Visual users who use alternative input devices such as a switch or joystick to browse the web can now access, operate, and learn with our prototype. Many sim features are now technically and functionally accessible for visually impaired users. Future work will focus on sonification (the use of non-speech sound to convey information), complementing ongoing work on a more complete description strategy.

**Acknowledgements.** We would like to thank Jesse Greenberg (PhET software developer) for his significant implementation efforts and design insights. We would also like to thank Shannon Fraser and Sambhavi Chandrashekar for support during the interviews. Equipment and space for interviews was provided by DELTS Media Services (thanks to Darcy Andrews and Mark Shallow) at Memorial University and by the Inclusive Design Research Centre (thanks to Vera Roberts and Bert Shire). Funding for this work was provided by the National Science Foundation (DRL # 1503439), the University of Colorado Boulder, and the William and Flora Hewlett Foundation. Any opinions, findings, and conclusions or recommendations expressed in this material are those of the authors and do not necessarily reflect the views of the National Science Foundation.

## References

1. Rutten, N., van Joolingen, W.R., van der Veen, J.T.: The learning effects of computer simulations in science education. Comput. Educ. **58**, 136–153 (2012)
2. D'Angelo, C., Rutstein, D., Harrison, S., Bernard, R., Borokhovski, E., Haertel, G.: Simulations for STEM Learning: Systematic Review and Meta-Analysis. Technical report, SRI International (2014)
3. PhET Interactive Simulations. http://phet.colorado.edu/
4. Balloons and Static Electricity – PhET Prototype Simulation. http://www.colorado.edu/physics/phet/dev/html/balloons-and-static-electricity/1.2.0-accessible-instance.11/balloons-and-static-electricity_en.html?accessibility

5. PhET Interactive Simulations: Accessibility. http://phet.colorado.edu/en/about/accessibility
6. Podolefsky, N.S., Moore, E.B., Perkins, K.K.: Implicit scaffolding in interactive simulations: design strategies to support multiple educational goals. Cornell University Library. [physics.ed-ph] (2013). arXiv:1306.6544
7. Scheuhammer, J., Cooper, M., Pappas, L., Schwerdtfeger, R.: WAI-ARIA 1.0 Authoring Practices, March 2013. http://www.w3.org/TR/wai-aria-practices/
8. Craig, J., Cooper, M.: Accessible Rich Internet Applications (WAI-ARIA) 1.0, March 2014. https://www.w3.org/TR/wai-aria/
9. Keane, K., Laverent, C.: Interactive Scientific Graphics Recommended Practices for Verbal Description. Research, Wolfram Research Inc., Champaign, IL (2014). http://dgramcenter.org/accessible-dynamic-scientific-graphics.html
10. Maximova, S.: J, K, or How to Choose Keyboard Shortcuts for Web Applications, November 2013. https://medium.com/@sashika/j-k-or-how-to-choose-keyboard-shortcuts-for-web-applications-a7c3b7b408ee#1.mrzwq3n1q
11. Chandrashekar, S., Stockman, T., Fels, D., Benedyk, R.: Using think aloud protocol with blind users: a case for inclusive usability evaluation methods. In: Proceedings of 8th International ACM SIGACCESS Conference Computers and Accessibility, pp. 251–252. ACM Press, Portland, Oregon (2006). http://portal.acm.org/citation.cfm?doid=1168987.1169040
12. Lewis, C., Rieman, J.: Task-centered user interface design: a practical introduction. Copyright Lewis, C. and Reiman, J. Boulder, Colorado (1993). http://hcibib.org/tcuid/
13. Green, P.: The Wizard of Oz: A Tool for Rapid Development of User Interfaces. Final report (1985)
14. Fakrudeen, M., Ali, M., Yousef, S., Hussein, A.H.: Analeysing the mental modal of blind users in mobile touch screen devices for usability. In: Proceedings of World Congress on Engineering vol. II, WCE 2013, London, U.K., July 2013
15. Kurniawan, S.H., Sutcliffe, A.G., Blenkhorn, P.L., Shin, J.E.: Investigating the usability of a screen reader and mental models of blind users in the Windows environment. Int. J. Rehabil. Res. **26**, 145–147 (2003)

# GyGSLA: A Portable Glove System for Learning Sign Language Alphabet

Luís Sousa[1], João M.F. Rodrigues[1(✉)], Jânio Monteiro[2],
Pedro J.S. Cardoso[1], and Roberto Lam[1]

[1] LARSyS and ISE, University of the Algarve, 8005-139 Faro, Portugal
luiscarlosrsousa@outlook.com, {jrodrig,pcardoso,rlam}@ualg.pt
[2] INEC-ID (Lisbon) and ISE,
University of the Algarve, 8005-139 Faro, Portugal
jmmontei@ualg.pt

**Abstract.** The communication between people with normal hearing with those having hearing or speech impairment is difficult. Learning a new alphabet is not always easy, especially when it is a sign language alphabet, which requires both hand skills and practice. This paper presents the GyGSLA system, standing as a completely portable setup created to help inexperienced people in the process of learning a new sign language alphabet. To achieve it, a computer/mobile game-interface and an hardware device, a wearable glove, were developed. When interacting with the computer or mobile device, using the wearable glove, the user is asked to represent alphabet letters and digits, by replicating the hand and fingers positions shown in a screen. The glove then sends the hand and fingers positions to the computer/mobile device using a wireless interface, which interprets the letter or digit that is being done by the user, and gives it a corresponding score. The system was tested with three completely inexperience sign language subjects, achieving a 76 % average recognition ratio for the Portuguese sign language alphabet.

**Keywords:** HCI · Gesture recognition · Sign Language · Assistive technologies

## 1 Introduction

Sign Language (SL) is a communication medium for the deaf and mute people, and Natural User Interface (NUI) is a term used for Human-Computer Interaction (HCI) where the interface is invisible or becomes invisible after successive user-immersion levels. Typically relies in nature or human natural elements.

Sign language uses manual communication and body language to convey meaning, which can involve simultaneously combining hand shapes, orientation and movement of the hands, arms or body, and facial expressions to fluidly express a speaker's thoughts.

In terms of NUI, currently there are several sensors with the ability of tracking and recognize body gestures, such as Kinect [6], Leap Motion [8] and Structure Sensor [11]. All these sensors have a great importance to the industry of

© Springer International Publishing Switzerland 2016
M. Antona and C. Stephanidis (Eds.): UAHCI 2016, Part III, LNCS 9739, pp. 159–170, 2016.
DOI: 10.1007/978-3-319-40238-3_16

gaming and user-machine interaction tools. These sensors, when supplemented with the appropriate software, have the ability to detect the body structure and/or the user's hand, and accurately replicate that structure on a 3D mesh, allowing gestures detection. Nevertheless, all these sensors are based on color cameras (RGB) and/or depth (infrared) and therefore have problems of space limitations, e.g., the user has to be located near the device and in the area where these cameras are pointing, otherwise, they will not work properly. In addition to spatial limitations, in most cases, these devices do not work well when they are near an infrared source (e.g., on sunlight) or in a room with fluorescent lamps.

In a system where the major interest is to develop a NUI to teach sign language alphabet to inexperienced persons, it is important that those persons can move openly in any environment with a system which should be free from "environmental" errors. A good solution to this problem is to develop a wearable glove, where the users can freely practice the signs, integrated with an application that can work in a standard personal computer or in any mobile device.

Wearable gloves are not a novelty, as examples from big commercial companies exist, see e.g., [3]. In 2012, Benbasat and Paradiso [1] described an inertial gesture recognition framework composed of three parts. The first, is a compact, wireless 6-axis inertial measurement unit to fully capture three-dimensional (3D) motion. The second part comprises a gesture recognition algorithm, that analyzes the data and categorizes it on an axis-by-axis basis, as simple motions with magnitude and duration. The third part allows an application designer to combine recognized gestures, both concurrently and consecutively, to create specific composite gestures that can then be set to trigger output routines. Mehdi and Khan [7], also in 2012, presented a sensor glove to capture signs of American Sign Language performed by a user and translates them into sentences of the English language. In that work, artificial Neural Networks (NN) are used to recognize the sensor values coming from the sensor glove. See [9] for another example of the use of NN to recognize American Sign Language words. In 2014, Praveen et al. presented an approach for interpreting the sign language using a portable smart glove [10]. Kim et al. [5], in 2015, presented a sign language recognition system using a data glove composed of 3-axis accelerometers, magnetometers, and gyroscopes. The information obtained by the data glove is transmitted to an host application, implemented on a MS Window program, running on a personal computer (PC). Next, the data is converted into angle data, and the angle information is displayed on the host application and verified by outputting 3D models to the display.

In this paper a completely portable glove system is presented, to teach a sign language alphabet. The main contribution of the paper stands in the developed NUI: a portable system integrating a wearable glove with a game application (used to learn the alphabet). The system can be used anywhere with a mobile device, or in standard personal computers.

## 2    Sign Language Alphabet Learning System

This section describes the implementation of the GyGSLA system, created to help people in the process of learning a sign language alphabet. To do it, (a) a computer game-interface and (b) a hardware device (wearable glove), called GyroGlove (GyG), were implemented. When interacting with the computer or mobile device interface, the user is asked to represent alphabet letters by replicating the hand and fingers positions, which are obtained using the GyroGlove module. Then, the GyroGlove uses a wireless interface to send the acquired information to the computational device, which interprets the gesture that is being done by the user and gives it a corresponding score. In the following, we start by describing the implementation of the GyroGlove, followed by the game interface.

### 2.1    GyroGlove

The GyroGlove is based on Inertial Measurement Units (IMU) sensors (see e.g. [1,4]) to detect the user's 3D rotation of the hand and fingers positions. An IMU sensor is an electronic device capable of measuring various types of inertial forces. Depending on the composition of the device, it can be formed by several independent sensors such as gyroscopes, accelerometers, magnetometers and, less commonly, altitude sensors (atmospheric pressure). Each IMU present in the GyroGlove contains an accelerometer and a gyroscope, each one of three axis, thus becoming an IMU sensor with 6 degrees of freedom (DoF).

Accelerometers can measure acceleration (in $g$-force) from one to three axes. Those that support three axes are the ones that have more functionality. Although accelerometers are fairly accurate when acquiring data from devices stable during long periods of time, they are unstable in short time data acquisitions. In other words, when an accelerometer is placed in a device that moves or shakes significantly, it is very difficult to accurately measure all the acceleration data. The gyroscope is a sensor capable of measuring the angular velocity (measured in degrees per second, °/s), being used to obtain the moving direction of an object. The data acquisition range of the gyroscope can be selected taking into consideration that there is a trade-off between range and accuracy. If a low range is chosen, the device can be quite accurate, but cannot exceed its maximum angular velocity. On the other hand, if the maximum value is too high, the accuracy is reduced. Thus, those values must be adjusted according with the desired application. There are also gyroscopes able to measure the angular velocity, from one to three axes. While the gyroscopes are very accurate in measuring angular velocity, they suffer from drift problems measuring low constant angular velocities, even when immobilized. Unlike the accelerometer, the gyroscopes are very accurate in short periods of time, and inaccurate otherwise. In such a way, accelerometer and gyroscopes should and can be combined.

The GyroGlove has several IMU MPU-6000 sensors (Magnetic Pickup Unit) [4] and a central controller module whose function is to program and configure all the IMU sensors and to serve as interface between the glove and the computational device. Each sensor has an accelerometer and a gyroscope, both

3-axis, with configurable ranges varying from $\pm2g$ up to $\pm16g$ and $\pm250°/$s up to $\pm2000°/$s, respectively. As the sensors are placed in the user's hand, high values of $g$-forces or high angular velocities are not expected. Thus to keep the values as much accurate as possible, it was decided to use a range of $\pm2g$ for the accelerometers and $\pm500°/$s for the gyroscopes.

To minimize the number of sensors without constraining the capability of capturing the rotations of the whole hand, so as to be able to extract the 3D rotation of each finger and also the hand itself, the sensors are strategically placed on the glove. The hand/finger bones that were considered more important for the gesture representation were the distal, intermediate and proximal phalanges (see Fig. 1 left). In this sense, the use of 11 sensors on the locations presented in Fig. 1 right was decided, enabling the extraction, without limitation, of all the rotational data of the fingers and hand. Because the distal bones are very short, it is very uncommon to fold this finger part without moving his adjacent one. The exception is the thumb, which is the only finger that does not have this characteristic. Thus, in the thumb it was decided to put two sensors, one in the distal phalange and another in the proximal phalange. All other fingers have also two sensors, in the intermediate and proximal phalanges. The last sensor (sensor 11) is placed on top of the hand, next to the main module, and is used to extract the overall orientation of the hand. This latter sensor is the basis for the correlation of all other sensors, as explained next.

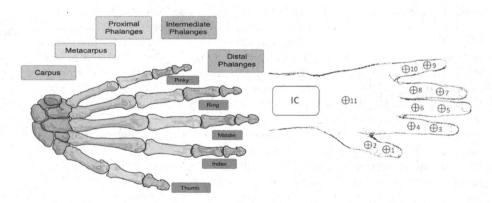

**Fig. 1.** On the left, hand bones anatomic names (adapted from https://en.wikipedia.org/wiki/Hand). Location and number identification of the sensors $(1, 2, \ldots, 11)$ and main module (IC) on the right .

In summary, the hardware system consists of 3 major modules: (a) a main controller, (b) a receiver connected to the PC or mobile device, and (c) eleven MPU-6000 sensors. Each IMU sensor has a size of $17 \times 23$ mm (millimeters).

The main controller, (a), acts as the intermediary interface between the sensors and the application on the computer, being responsible for programming/configuring all sensors and for sending the data via Bluetooth to the receiver on the computational device. The main controller consists of: (i) a microcontroller ATMega Atmel 328p with a 8 MHz oscillator; (ii) a USB-UART converter (FT232RL) that converts the Micro USB port data to the microcontroller and vice versa; (iii) a LiPo battery charger (MCP73831); (iv) a voltage supervisor circuit (BD523G); (v) a LED emitting a warning to the user if the battery is low; (vi) a voltage regulator (TPS13733), that regulates 5 V from the USB or battery voltage to the main 3.3 V of the circuit; (vii) a charge distributor (LTC4413) that provides an automatic way of selecting the power source; and (viii) a Bluetooth module (HC-06). The battery is used in the circuit when it is the single power source. The USB becomes the main power source when connected, regardless of how many sources are available (USB and/or battery).

The receiver, (b), is a Bluetooth module similar to that used in the controller, but with the ability to be used as a master device, i.e., it has the initiative to bind to other Bluetooth modules. Similar to the controller circuit, the circuit of the receiver has: (i) a USB-UART converter (FT232RL), converting the USB micro port data to the Bluetooth, and a (ii) Bluetooth module. Mobile devices (tablets or smartphones) only need to be equipped with a standard Bluetooth for the system to work.

Figure 2 top shows: on the left the prototypes of the printed circuit boards (PCBs), and on the right the prototype of the GyG module assembled on the glove. To achieve the required performance, the transmission of data to the computational devices has to be done as fast as possible. For this reason, as represented in Fig. 2 bottom, the microcontroller and Bluetooth modules are programmed to use a 115200 bps (bits per second) transmission rate, which is the maximum possible rate allowed by the devices. The rate limitation results from the fact that the 8 MHz oscillator on the micro-controller does not allow higher speeds. For the same reason, the interface between the microcontroller and the sensors communicates at a top speed of 2 MHz SPI (Serial Peripheral Interface). The maximum frequency of the ATMega328P on the SPI interface is 1/4 of the oscillator frequency. These transmission speeds allow the system to update all data on the computer at a frequency of 33.3 Hz (validated by practical speed tests).

Finally, (c), each of the 11 MPU sensors placed in the glove (see Fig. 1 right), integrates a DMP (Digital Motion Processor) [4] that is used to process complex algorithms of 6-axis motion fusion. These algorithms are proprietary, registered by InvenSense [4], and the mode of operation is not of public knowledge. One solution to eliminate or reduce the problems of inaccuracies of the sensors is to use a filter to join the data from the accelerometer and gyroscope (existing in the same silicon die). This filter combines in a single expression, a low pass filter for gyroscope and a high pass filter for the accelerometer. But, by doing this, the angle around the $z$-axis of the accelerometer cannot be calculated as was done with the $y$- and $x$-axis, because accelerometer computations rely on gravity pointing in the $z$-axis (this is a phenomenon known as Gimbal Lock, which is a problem/limitation that occurs when working with Euler angles).

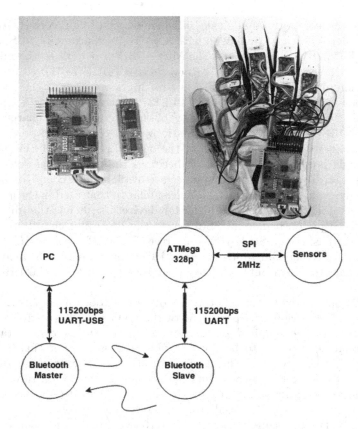

**Fig. 2.** On the top, the PCB prototype on the left, and the assembled glove on the right. On the bottom, the communications scheme between the GyG and the PC.

This implies that the angle with the $z$-axis can only be calculated using the gyroscope, therefore, this angle will suffer from a small drift along time.

As a result, the DMP system has the highest importance. This proprietary system uses quaternions, that do not suffer from the Gimbal Lock limitation. The quaternion is an alternative way to represent an angle on a 3D space: $Q = q_w + q_x x + q_y y + q_z z$, where $q_x$, $q_y$ and $q_z$ are the values of the position direction vector and $q_w$ is the rotation about this axis, formed by the direction vector. These are necessary for the calibration and communication with the application, as shown next.

## 2.2  Application

The application has two main modules: (a) calibration and (b) game-learning application for the sign language alphabet.

For calibrating purposes, (a), an application was made using the Unity 3D [12] software, being its development out of the scope of this paper. One of the main reasons to use Unity is the easy deployment to different mobile platforms (e.g., Android and iOS). The application replicates the user's hand position, using a 3D model of a human hand, as shown on Fig. 3 top row, where two different situations are shown: hand with index finger pointing and a with tilted position.

| 1 Byte | 1 Byte | 1 Byte | 1 Byte | 1 Byte | 1 Byte | 1 Byte | 1 Byte | 1 Byte | 1 Byte | 1 Byte | 1 Byte |
|---|---|---|---|---|---|---|---|---|---|---|---|
| $ | $X_m$ | $X_l$ | $Y_m$ | $Y_l$ | $Z_m$ | $Z_l$ | $W_m$ | $W_l$ | $i$ | $CR$ | $LF$ |
| | $X$ | | $Y$ | | $Z$ | | $W$ | | | | |

**Fig. 3.** Top row shows examples of the user's hand and the replication on a human hand 3D model. In the bottom, the structure of the transmitted packet between the GyroGlove and the computational device.

For the calibration, and the transmission of the angles between the GyG and the PC/mobile, the DMP system can itself calculate the exact rotation of each sensor but needs an initial set up configuration, for which there is no control. This auto-configuration aims to reduce and possibly eliminate the drift problem caused by the gyroscope, as explained earlier. After the system starts, all the sensors enter into an auto-configuration procedure which lasts between 10 and 20 seconds. When the procedure finishes, all sensors will be stable. During this time the extracted rotational data is not usable, suffering from extreme drift. To correct the offset problem it is necessary to know, a priori, the state of the rotation of all sensors, i.e., to position all sensors in a known orientation.

Being $Q$ a quaternion with an unknown direction, setting $K = Q^{-1} \times Q$ gives a quaternion with no rotation, stabilized. In the application running on the computer/mobile device, objects that replicate the users' hand orientation require initialization. In a process guided by the calibration application, the user has to place his hand with a certain orientation, before powering up the system. Being $i$ the sensor number and $t_1$ the time at which the initial configuration is finished, all rotations of the sensors in time $t_1$ are stored in the quaternion $U_{it_1}$. Now, if $K_{it} = U_{it_1}^{-1} \times S_{it}$, being $S_{it}$ the data from the sensors after the initial setup configuration (i.e., after $t_1$), then $K_{it}$ contains the final rotations which is equal to the user's hand rotations. If the user's hand is not placed with all the sensors stabilized, then $K_{it}$ must be obtained from $K_{it} = (U_{it_1}^{-1} \times D_i)^{-1} \times S_{it}$, where $D_i$ is the quaternion with the offset rotation of each sensor, available before powering up the system.

To initialize the system, the user must keep his hand as straight as possible on a table or horizontal plane during the setup. Then, $K_{it} = U_{it_1}^{-1} \times S_{it}$ is applied, avoiding the offset rotations of the sensors, with the exception of the ones positioned on the thumb. In fact, as can be easily seen from Fig. 2 top right, when the hand is positioned horizontally on a table, all sensors are straight (without rotation), with the exception of the two sensors in the thumb. In this particular case, the estimation of the associated rotation of the two thumb sensors is necessary and applied to each of them, $K_{it} = \left(U_{it_1}^{-1} \times D_i\right)^{-1} \times S_{it}$. We opted to apply an initial rotation of $-45°$ (obtained empirically) to both $x$- and $y$-axis.

Having now a way to compute the angles, the communication between the glove and the computer/mobile device is made using a character oriented packet with the format shown in Fig. 3 bottom row. Each sensor transmits a packet with their associated quaternion data. The packet starts with a $ character, followed by the quaternion data, $X$, $Y$, $Z$ and $W$, formed by 16-bit sets, i.e., two sets of 8 bits $(X_m, X_l)$, where $m$ and $l$ represent the most and less significant elements, respectively, followed by the index number of the respective sensor $i$, (as identified in Fig. 1 right). The end of the packet is done by $CR$ (Carriage Return) and $LF$ (Line Feed) characters.

After developing the GyroGlove and implementing the transmission data between GyG and the computer/mobile device, the game-application, (b), was implemented (again using the Unity 3D) to help the learning of a sign language with GyG.

As the GyroGlove only allows (for now) the detection of a "static" position of the rotation of all fingers and hand, there is no way to learn sign language words, phrases or sentences. On other words, the system only accepts sign language alphabet, where each letter and digit possesses a direct relationship with the hand position and fingers. Since the GyGSLA system was developed in Portugal, the alphabet and digit used in the initial testing (see Fig. 4 top row) was the Portuguese Sign Language (PSL)[2]. Other alphabets can easily be integrated in future developments.

To recognize each of the hand's positions shown in Fig. 4, it is necessary to compare all the rotations of the sensors with all the rotations associated with a particular letter of the alphabet. Several classification methods could be used (e.g., NN as in [7]). However, since the goal was to be able to run the application in any mobile device, a "simpler" and less CPU/GPU demanding method was chosen.

Instead of comparing the quaternion of each sensor, a comparison was made between the quaternion of a pre-defined set of adjacent sensors, as well as the relation between the quaternion of the hand sensor (number 11 on the glove) and the vertical axis. This last one is used to determine the overall direction of the hand (face up, down, left etc.). There are 11 distinct relations $(R_j)$. To obtain

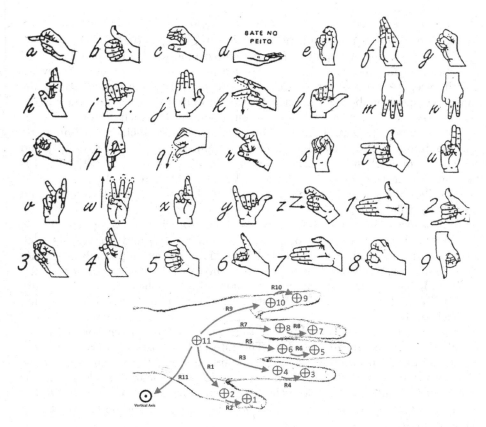

**Fig. 4.** On the top, the Portuguese sign language alphabet (adapted from [2]). On the bottom, the association ($R_k$) between adjacent sensors and between sensor 11 and the vertical axis.

these relations, the angle of each rotation is calculated between all sets of related sensors. As illustrated by Fig. 4 bottom, each sensor is associated with one or more sensors. For example, sensor number 8 (ring proximal finger) is related to sensor 7 and 11, identified as relation $R_8$ and $R_7$, respectively.

As a quaternion defines a rotation and not a vector in space, the rotation of each quaternion to a known vector must be applied, in our case, $\vec{V}_f = (0, 0, 1)$. From $\vec{V}_i = K_i \times \vec{V}_f$ results a vector with the rotation of $K_i$ (raw quaternion data obtained from the sensors).

After obtaining the orientation of each sensor in the 3D space, $\vec{V}_i$, the absolute angle between the orientation vectors is calculated. These angles are computed between each related sensors pair (shown in Fig. 4 bottom), applying formula: $A_j = \left| (180/\pi) \times \arccos\left( \vec{V}_n \cdot \vec{V}_m \right) / \left( \left\| \vec{V}_n \right\| \left\| \vec{V}_m \right\| \right) \right|$. Angles $A_j$ range from 0° to 180° and represent the angle formed between each set of related sensors ($n$ and $m$, with $n, m \in \{1, 2, \ldots, 11\}$) and also between the main hand sensor (sensor number 11) and the vertical vector, $\overrightarrow{V}_{up} = (0, 1, 0)$.

Before deploying the application, the reference positions for each letter/digit are obtained and recorded. These reference positions are later used to evaluate the user's hand position when he tries to perform some letter/digit of the sign language alphabet. As previously, this is done by calculating the angles, $A_j$, between each sensor and its reference sensor, for each letter and digit of the alphabet, $\{a, \ldots, z, 1, \ldots, 9\}$. The reference values include the minimum and maximum angles, such that: $Smin_{j,l} = \min \{A_j[m] : t - \Delta_s \leq m \leq t\}$ and $Smax_{j,l} = \max \{A_j[m] : t - \Delta_s \leq m \leq t\}$, where $l \in \{a, \ldots, z, 1, \ldots, 9\}$, $A_j[m]$ is the angle at instant $m$ and $\Delta_s$ comes from the fact that the hand's position needs to hold for a certain time ($\Delta_s$ seconds) to be associated with a letter, and posteriorly validated.

Whenever a new hand data is available, the application computes the $A_j$ angles and checks if they are comprised between $Smin_{j,l}$ and $Smax_{j,l}$ for each letter and during a minimum period of time, $\Delta_s = 1s$ (set empirically). In other words, if during $\Delta_s$ seconds the inequalities $Smin_{j,l} - \Delta_m \leq A_j \leq Smax_{j,l} + \Delta_m$ - where $\Delta_m$ is a margin value in order to allow adjusting the detection sensitivity (set to 20) - and $l \in \{a, \ldots, z, 1, \ldots, 9\}$, are verified then a positive gesture detection is considered.

Figure 5 shows some examples of the game-application developed for the learning of sign language alphabet. The interface consists of 4 parts: (1) the letter and hand's position of the corresponding image, (2) a visual input of the hand position replicated in a 3D human model, (3) a scoring system, and (4) a level bar to indicate how close the user is standing next to the goal. On the left it shows the system working in a portable computer, and on the right on a Android mobile device.

## 3   Tests and Results

When the users interact with the application, random letters are shown. The user then has to replicate the image shown in the right side of the screen (PC case). When he/she is well succeeded, the system scores the associated result, according with the time spent to do the associated letter and the correctness of the hand's position, as well as the application game-level.

The implemented application was tested by three inexperience sign language evaluators. During these tests, the following parameters were quantified for each alphabet letter: (i) the success ratio, or percentage of letters that were correctly recognized; (ii) the failure ratio; and (iii) the average time in seconds taken by the evaluators to replicate the letter that was shown. Each evaluator was identified by T1, T2 and T3 and each one of them respectively tested all letters for 5, 8 and 10 repetitions.

The results of the system regarding all the letters and digits, achieved an average success ratio of 76 %, with an average time to detect each letter/digit of approximately 3.6 s. Although this does not seem very generous, 35 % of the

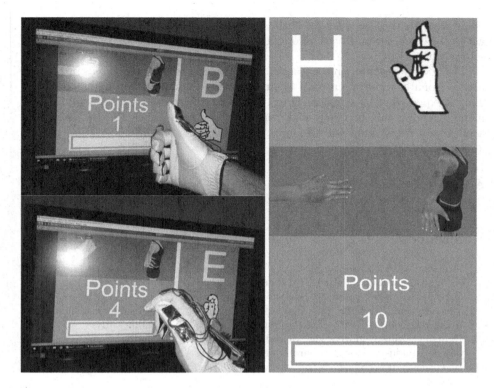

**Fig. 5.** Application for learning stimulation of alphabet sign language. The user is encouraged to replicate the hand position. Left, the system working in a portable computer, on the right in á Android mobile device.

letters/digits had a success ratio over 90 % (many of those achieved 100 %), and only 19 % had a success rate below 70 %. The tests indicated that some letters are particularly difficult to be detected by the system, such as the R, Q, U and V (with a resulting average of success ratio around 46 % and a detection time of approximately 6 s). As a note, most of the failure ratio was due to a system inaccuracy created by the estimation of the initial rotation of the two sensors placed on the thumb.

## 4 Conclusions

In this paper, a portable NUI system that supports the learning of a sign language alphabet was presented. The system combines a computer/mobile device interface-game and an hardware device - wearable glove. When interacting with the computer or mobile device, the user is asked to represent sign language alphabet letters by replicating the hand and fingers' positions, which are obtained using the wearable glove. The glove then sends that information to the computer/mobile device using a wireless interface, which interprets the letter that is being done by the user and gives it a correspondent score. The glove uses IMUs with accelerometer and a gyroscope, each one of 3 axis, thus becoming an IMU sensor with 6 DoF.

For now, the system presents satisfactory success results, and it was presented in a personal computer, currently being converted and tested in mobile devices. This is expected to be a smooth transition, since the software was already implemented having this in mind. In terms of future work, both the NUI and the accuracy of the system will be improved, expanding the system to also detect and train words.

**Acknowledgements.** This work was partially supported by the Portuguese Foundation for Science and Technology (FCT) project PEst-OE/EEI/LA0009/2013.

# References

1. Benbasat, A.Y., Paradiso, J.A.: An inertial measurement framework for gesture recognition and applications. In: Wachsmuth, I., Sowa, T. (eds.) GW 2001. LNCS (LNAI), vol. 2298, pp. 9–20. Springer, Heidelberg (2002)
2. Vivendo em Silencio: Dactiologia portuguesa. https://vivendoemsilencio.files.wordpress.com/2010/07/dactl-lgp.jpg (2015). Accessed 15 June 2015
3. Fujitsu: Fujitsu glove-style wearable device. http://vandrico.com/wearables/device/fujitsu-glove-style-wearable-device (2015). Accessed 14 Dez 2015
4. Invensense: InvenSense. http://www.invensense.com/ (2015). Accessed 15 June 2015
5. Kim, K.-W., Lee, M.-S., Soon, B.-R., Ryu, M.-H., Kim, J.-N.: Recognition of sign language with an inertial sensor-based data glove. Technol. Health Care **24**(s1), S223–S230 (2015)
6. Kinect.: Kinect for Windows. http://goo.gl/fGZT8X (2014). Accessed 10 Nov 2014
7. Mehdi, S.A., Khan, Y.N.: Sign language recognition using sensor gloves. In: Proceedings of the 9th International Conference on Neural Information Processing, vol. 5, pp. 2204–2206. IEEE (2002)
8. Motion, L.: Leap motion. https://www.leapmotion.com/ (2014). Accessed 10 Nov 2014
9. Oz, C., Leu, M.C.: American sign language word recognition with a sensory glove using artificial neural networks. Eng. Appl. Artif. Intell. **24**(7), 1204–1213 (2011)
10. Praveen, N., Naveen Karanth, M.S., Megha.: Sign language interpreter using a smart glove. In: International Conference on Advances in Electronics, Computers and Communications, pp. 1–5. IEEE (2014)
11. Structure: Structure sensor. http://structure.io/ (2014). Accessed 10 Nov 2014
12. Unity: Unity 3D. https://unity3d.com/pt (2014). Accessed 10 Nov 2014

# ChartMaster: A Tool for Promoting Financial Inclusion of Novice Investors

Hong Zou[1(✉)] and Sambhavi Chandrashekar[2]

[1] CIBC Investor Services Inc., Toronto, ON, Canada
birdswimming@gmail.com
[2] OCAD University, Toronto, ON, Canada
schandrashekar@faculty.ocadu.ca

**Abstract.** ChartMaster is a digital tool developed by Hong Zou in 2015, through co-design with visually impaired screen reader users, to improve the accessibility and usability of interactive stock market charts. The first ChartMaster usability study, conducted with screen reader users, demonstrated that the tool not only helped them access data points quicker and easier, but also proved to be "educational." The next usability study, conducted with sighted novice investors to examine ChartMaster's educational value, is described in this paper. Novice investors found it easier to discover features, learn action possibilities and locate specific data through ChartMaster than through direct interaction with stock market charts. Several of their experiences, such as finding the summary feature helpful in understanding the chart, were similar to those reported previously by visually impaired screen reader users, suggesting comparable cognitive and emotional barriers to financial literacy for both groups. Improvements to Chart-Master were also suggested.

**Keywords:** Interactive stock market charts · Visually impaired · Screen reader users · Accessibility · Usability · Novice investors · ChartMaster · Educational tool · Inclusive design

## 1 Introduction

The stock market has grown dramatically in the last few decades. Capitalization of the world stock markets has more than doubled between 2008 and 2015, and the volume of share trading increased from US$88 trillion to US$114 trillion, during the same period [1]. Along with the growth of the stock market, the number of shareholders is rapidly increasing. Globally, the number of direct shareholders was approximately 382 million in 2009, and this number is steadily increasing [2]. Within this data set, there are an increasing number of self-directed investors who rely on their own research and judgment to make financial decisions without the involvement of a financial advisor. The majority of stock market investors, however, are novice investors who lack sufficient knowledge and skills, and might not be familiar with essential research tools, such as stock market charts [3].

© Springer International Publishing Switzerland 2016
M. Antona and C. Stephanidis (Eds.): UAHCI 2016, Part III, LNCS 9739, pp. 171–180, 2016.
DOI: 10.1007/978-3-319-40238-3_17

On the other hand, continuous evolution and innovation of investment products has made the stock market and its research tools increasingly complex [4]. Online static charts have been replaced with interactive charts that enable investors to perceive, compare and analyze data points with merely a few clicks [5]. However, there is very little research published about the accessibility of these interactive charts to individuals with visual, cognitive or dexterity constraints or to those who lack adequate technological and financial knowledge and skill. Such individuals could well be missing critical financial information needed to make informed investment decisions confidently, and, as a consequence, be excluded from full participation in financial markets [6]. Failing to improve financial literacy, especially for socioeconomically disadvantaged subgroups, will not only have negative impacts in personal financial wellbeing, but also initiate a vicious cycle of poverty and economic inequality, both in wealth and in earnings [7]. Therefore, improving the accessibility and usability of financial research tools is essential to improve the financial outcomes for all those who choose to participate in financial investments.

During 2014–15, Hong Zou conducted a preliminary expert usability evaluation study of ten major financial news and research websites such as Google Finance and Bloomberg, which revealed significant access barriers for visually impaired users. Following this, she developed a digital tool called ChartMaster using Inclusive Design[1] principles through iterative co-design with visually impaired screen reader users to facilitate their effective use interactive online stock market charts. Results of a usability study showed that this tool not only helped screen reader users access data points quicker and easier, but also assisted them in looking for information that they might have overlooked due to lack of investment knowledge, thus proving to be an educational tool [8].

To examine the scope of the educational benefits of ChartMaster, a second study was conducted, this time with sighted novice investors, to assess its usability in promoting self-learning for interacting with and making sense of stock market charts. This paper presents details about the second study—providing a description of interactive stock market charts and the ChartMaster tool, outlining the methodology adopted for the study, presenting the results, and discussing the implications of significant findings, including a comparison with findings from the earlier study involving visually impaired screen reader users. Contributions and future work are indicated at the end.

## 2    Interactive Stock Market Charts

Developments in information technology, such as HTML5, scripting languages and the capability of pulling live market data, have caused a major shift in investor research behaviour. Technical analysis, or charting, has gained momentum since early 2000 and has become more popular today than ever [9]. Online interactive stock market charts present statistics generated by market activity, such as past prices and volume, and

---

[1] Inclusive Design is designing for the full range of human diversity with respect to ability, language, culture, gender, age and other forms of human difference (www.idrc.ocadu.ca).

enable investors to observe the historical performance of a security and predict future price movements.

Generally, a stock market chart has the following five components:

1. A line graph on the top of the chart presenting the change in share prices
2. A bar graph at the bottom presenting the changes in the volume of shares traded
3. Options to define the time frame through which the chart will be rendered
4. Identifiers for events such as dividend, split, or quarterly financial report release
5. Functions to enable a comparison with other stocks or indices.

A typical stock market chart is presented in Fig. 1.

**Fig. 1.** A typical stock market chart (Resource: Google Finance)

Data visualizations, such as stock market charts and graphs, are ubiquitous sources of financial and investment information. In fact, technical analysis, one of the two major methods investors use to predict the future trend of a given stock, is primarily based on the study of stock market charts. Because stock market charts are so important when making investment decisions, this research focuses on developing ChartMaster as a tool to improve the accessibility of these infographics not only for screen-reader users but also for individuals with less comfort and skill in understanding how to use and analyze stock market charts.

## 2.1  ChartMaster

ChartMaster is a digital tool initially developed to make online interactive stock market chats more accessible and usable to visually impaired screen reader users. It employs a series of dropdown menus to enable users to obtain key data points from a stock market chart, such as price, volume and events (dividend payout or split) for one or multiple stocks. It was developed using HTML to generate the front-end interface and JavaScript to control the back-end data retrieval and calculation. ChartMaster works with the same data set used to generate the graph by storing it in a Java ArrayList.

By default, ChartMaster is displayed as a link, grouped with other commonly used stock chart tools and placed at the top of a stock market chart (See Fig. 2). Once activated, the tool is then expanded, pushing the chart down onto the page and enabling the user to obtain information by interacting with a series of dropdown menus. The dropdown menus are grouped into three categories: (1) information type; (2) time frame; and (3) specific data set. Once the user makes the required menu choices and activates the "Ask ChartMaster" button, the answer is displayed as a textual summary at the bottom of the dropdown menus. This text is also accessible to screen reader software for reading out aloud.

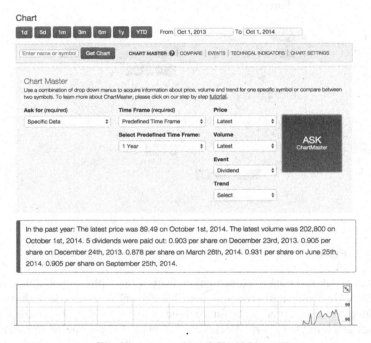

**Fig. 2.** A screenshot of ChartMaster

The answers are composed of three key components: (1) the data input by the user through the dropdown menus and associated text input fields, such as "6 months" and "average price," (2) the data pulled or generated by the system according to the data input by the user, and (3) a template (including the wording and punctuation marks) which arranges and presents all the data mentioned above in a meaningful and grammatically-correct way to the user.

The next section outlines the methodology adopted to test the usability of this tool for sighted novice users.

# 3   Methodology

Nine English-speaking adults familiar with the use of computer and the Internet, who were self-declared novice investors, not knowledgeable in the use of online financial charts, participated in the study. Within a broad framework of Human-Computer Interaction, this study involved usability testing sessions of direct interactions with stock market charts as well as interaction using the ChartMaster tool by the participants. Each session lasted one hour. Participants were paid $20 each as compensation. The sessions consisted of the following steps:

- Answering a short questionnaire about overall experience with charts, to establish a baseline.
- Interacting with three to four stock market charts from popular investment research sites—Yahoo finance, Google finance, Wall Street Journal and Bloomberg.
- Performing tasks with a stock market chart using the ChartMaster to assess discoverability, learnability and usability. The tasks involved finding answers to questions such as "what was the highest volume in the past month?" and "what is the return of the stock you bought on January 14, 2013?"
- Answering a quiz examining the connection between the investment knowledge of the participants and key metrics based on their task performance and questionnaire responses

Transcripts of session recordings and observational notes were analyzed using content analysis employing the framework of discoverability, learnability and usability, while being open to other useful insights and surprises.

# 4   Findings

## 4.1   Direct Interaction with Stock Market Charts

The study showed the participants facing significant barriers while interacting with stock market charts due to problems in discoverability, learnability, and usability. These barriers were due to design defects in the charts in the areas of *interactive design, visual design*, and *information design*. Unfamiliar terminologies and uncommon abbreviations on the charts, coupled with their lack of adequate investment knowledge, hampered discoverability, learnability and usability, leaving them overwhelmed. Overall, the experience with stock market charts was more negative than positive. The problems are described below.

**Discoverability.** Key information such as legends not being incorporated in the chart, made users struggle to discover the chart's intended meaning(s), evoking remarks like, "I don't know what this whole chart is trying to tell me." Further, because relevant information was not grouped together, such as, for example "hover over" text was not physically placed near the mouse cursor, this defect made it more difficult for the participants to make a connection between the part of the chart that the mouse hovered over and the extra information about it provided elsewhere. System feedback was inappropriate or absent. When participants hovered over an individual volume bar, the system provided no feedback to let participants know if that bar was in focus. In several other cases, the feedback was provided on the price chart instead of on the volume bar where participants' cursor was focused. Such a mismatch between the chart design and participants' mental model confused them when they were attempting to interpret the chart.

**Learnability.** The absence of contextual help and tutorials made it difficult for novice investors to learn more about using the charts, which discouraged them from exploring further. One participant said, "I can't figure out how this works. I don't know what they mean right away. It seems they are trying to attract people who are already in the market; someone that has experience."

**Effectiveness and Efficiency.** Although participants could understand that interactive stock market charts are designed to help them quickly grasp the overall trend through data visualization and acquire specific data points through interaction with the chart, they struggled to interpret it or interact with it. Tiny font size, fine chart graphics, and subtle contrast used in the charts resulted in most participants, regardless of their age, leaning close to the screen in order to be able to read the content on the page or place their mouse cursor at a particular point on the chart. Further, imprecise labels and unconventional formatting of information such as uncommon abbreviations and ambiguous date formats proved to be obstacles for novice investors to comprehend stock market charts.

**Suggestions for Improvement.** Participants made the following suggestions with respect to design of interactive charts:

- Add legend and axis labels
- Provide various level of help information to facilitate users' interaction and interpretation of the charts
- Use bigger graphs, which would be easy to target, and offer appropriate contextual feedback;
- Employ larger font size;
- Avoid using abbreviations.

## 4.2   Interaction Through ChartMaster

During their interactions with ChartMaster, participants expressed several positive feelings and remarks as well as provided suggestions for improvement. The same framework was used to examine data from these tasks.

**Discoverability.** It was easy for participants to locate important information and discover the key features of ChartMaster. All participants noticed and read the introduction paragraph first as it was placed on the very top of the tool. All drop down menus were also easily accessed as they were organized into columns according to their functionality. By clicking on each drop down menu, participants quickly discovered what

ChartMaster could do. "The drop down menus seem to be 'parameters' to find specific data," P5 remarked. Similarly, P3 remarked, "If I want to know the dividend, I just select Dividend." In addition, all participants discovered the call-to-action button, "Ask Chart-Master" and the textual summary generated once the button is clicked. "It looks like I can go straight and find the data instead of hovering over the chart. I don't need to even look at the chart. The information shows up right here," P1 said.

**Learnability.** It was apparent that the learning curve for ChartMaster was very smooth. Most of the participants immediately started to interact with it without seeking any assistance from the facilitator. To illustrate, one participant remarked, "Oh, this is... instead of having to hover, you just enter exactly what you want ... the exact information you want."

**Effectiveness and Efficiency.** Participants found ChartMaster to be "useful" in terms of assisting them with acquiring specific data points relatively fast, such as finding the price and volume on a particular day; figuring out the return of the stock; and analyzing the chart by presenting a summary of the trend within a given time period. In addition, participants appreciated how efficient ChartMaster was in helping them complete these tasks. P6 said, "It is so much easier! Everything is accessible and detailed. Instead of looking at those tiny bars, you just select ... here."

**Suggestions for Improvement.** Participants also gave some suggestions for improving the ChartMaster:

- Add connectivity between the textual summary and the chart; for example, highlighting the sentence describing an uptrend in the textual summary while, at the same time, highlighting the segment of the chart that was referred to.
- Associate acceptable data format for input field directly with the labels (i.e., specific day).
- Provide error messages and/or error identification on the input boxes themselves when user fails to select required fields such as 'Ask for', or 'Time Frame'.
- "Flatten" the design by showing the two options for "Ask for" drop down menu upfront rather than burying them inside the menu.
- Provide customization and self-configuration options for the overall trend by providing only a high-level summary as a default and enabling user to see more detailed descriptions through further choices.
- Group the option "Return" under "Price" drop down menu instead of placing it under "Trend" so it aligns with novice users' mental model.
- Make labels more precise, intuitive, and easier to understand such that even novice investors might comprehend; for example, "stocks" instead of "symbols"
- Consider changing the name ChartMaster because it doesn't communicate the exact features the tool can provide to assist users to interact with stock market charts.

# 5  Discussion

One of the most surprising findings was that participants found the Trend Summary (the textual summary describing the trend of the chart) generated by ChartMaster to be "extremely useful". "The summary gives me an idea of how to understand the chart," P3 pointed out. This disproved wrong the researchers' initial expectation that sighted users might not be interested in the summary because they might get the information just by looking at the chart. While novice users were able to perceive the trend visually, they had difficulty interpreting it due to their low investment knowledge. As one partic-ipant pointed out, "Visually I can see that it is going up, but I don't know what that means." With the Trend Summary feature, novice users felt greater trust for ChartMaster as they did not need to analyze the chart "(because) the computer does that" for them and consequently they experienced less cognitive load. In addition, participants pointed out that even after they acquire the knowledge to interpret the trend, having a textual summary could still be beneficial as they "might be too tired to analyze it sometimes".

Participants also appreciated ChartMaster as a useful "add-on" tool to find specific data. In fact, in many cases, participants mentioned that they actually preferred to use ChartMaster to perform such tasks. Since a majority of the participants had mentioned in the pre-session questionnaire that they were "comfortable" dealing with charts in general, the researchers expected them to interact easily with stock market charts. Surprisingly, however, the study revealed that due to unfamiliarity with design conventions of stock market charts (i.e. hovering over to display additional information and press-and-drag to scroll through the chart), it became quite challenging for novice investors to complete tasks that seem very easy from the perspective of advanced online investors. This is because they do not possess sufficient knowledge to interact with the chart using various methods. In addition, some of the visual and interactive design defects, such as the use of small font and missing feedback also contribute to this pref-erence. Furthermore, participants also realized that because "not everybody has the patience and time to go through the chart," the capability of providing specific data points through a series of drop down menu would likely reduce their stress level when inter-acting with the chart.

This study strengthened the hypothesis that ChartMaster is a useful "educational" resource for novice investors. Much like the visually impaired participants in the first study, the sighted participants in this study also thought that ChartMaster could be a handy tool to guide novice investors through its drop down menus in obtaining key information that investors need to acquire from charts. While both groups liked the textual summary, visually impaired users considered it merely "informative" as it communicated the data visualization using text format, while novice investors consider it an useful feature to learn how to interpret the chart. In short, novice investors recog-nized that visual representation is critical but the summary puts their mind in ease when they attempted to make sense of the chart.

In addition, the findings from the study point toward the likelihood that improving participants' investment knowledge by providing educational material might enhance their experience as well as improve their understanding, comfort and confidence while interacting with stock market chart. For example, the study showed that the two participants who scored the highest in the post-session quiz (both of them got 88 % while the average is 68 %), were much less stressed when initially introduced to the stock market chart. They were able to explain the chart and find information quicker and easier than those who did poorly in the quiz. Most of the users exhibited awareness of the impact of this knowledge gap, and suggested that the next version of the ChartMaster should provide educational material to help users understand key investment terminology as well as methods of interpreting chart data. It is worth noting that both visually impaired participants as well as novice investor participants expressed this idea. Three levels of educational materials, as shown in Table 1, are planned for addition to ChartMaster's next version to provide contextual or just-in-time help to satisfy the needs of users with different knowledge levels and appetites for learning. These design enhancements echo the inclusive design implication that a variety of options need to be offered to cater to the self-knowledge and self-determination of a diversity of users [10].

**Table 1.** Three levels of educational materials that could be added to **ChartMaster**

|  | Tool tips | Glossary | Education Centre |
|---|---|---|---|
| Placement | Beside dropdown menu headers | A separate page | An section of a site |
| Access | Immediate access to information | Quick links or main navigation menu | Through main navigation menu |
| Scope | One definition | Multiple glossaries | Multiple topics |
| Features | Brief explanation | Short explanation | Detailed explanation |
|  |  | Sorted categories | Organized categories |
|  |  | Keyword search | Keyword search |
| Level | Novice | Intermediate | Advanced |

# 6  Conclusion

Over the decades, worldwide interest in financial literacy and investor education has intensified. In response, this study examined whether ChartMaster, a tool originally developed for making stock market charts accessible to visually impaired screen reader users, could serve as an educational tool for novice investors.

From a human-computer interaction perspective, findings from this study expose the cognitive and emotional barriers that novice investors face while interacting with stock market charts. The study illustrates how novice investors, who lack investment knowledge and are unfamiliar with the stock market chart design conventions, are able to analyze the chart and acquire specific data with the assistance of ChartMaster. The study identified the usability gaps that can potentially be closed or reduced by offering users various educational components, both for ChartMaster and for current stock market charts. In addition, the study highlighted the importance of offering novice users preference to access information according to personal interests and needs; much the same as was discovered in the earlier study with visually impaired users. Through these findings, some components of the next inclusive design iteration of ChartMaster have been derived to make it better fit the needs of a greater diversity of users. This will serve to expand the application of the tool to a much broader audience.

This study did not attempt to improvise on the information architecture of the earlier version of ChartMaster, such as the categorization of the different drop down menus and the data points included in each drop down menu. Further work is planned for investigating the adequacy of the current question set and modifying it if found necessary. Another area of future work would be to developing a mechanism to enable ChartMaster "pull" real-time live market data instead of just using historical data. It is also on the researchers' agenda to allow the system to automatically generate an accurate chart trend summary according to the nature of the stock.

The "curb cut" phenomenon in Inclusive Design holds that designing to address challenges faced by people in the margins spurs innovation, and Inclusive Design ultimately benefits everyone [11]. This idea will continue to inspire ChartMaster and related studies.

**Acknowledgment.**    Our special thanks are due to David Lawson for his editorial assistance.

# References

1. MarketWatch    Report.    http://www.marketwatch.com/story/global-stock-market-cap-has-doubled-since-qes-start-2015-02-12
2. Camargo, A., Fonseca, I.: The race for self-directed investors - developments in online trading among brokers and banks (2013). http://info.scivantage.com/INV_Whitepaper.Celent_Self-Directed.Mar2013.html?mktNetwork=plusone
3. Cogent: Uncovering Opportunities in the Self-Directed Marketplace (2014). http://landing.marketstrategies.com/the-self-directed-investor
4. OECD/INFE: OECD/INFE High-Level Principles on National Strategies for Financial Education (2012). http://www.oecd.org/daf/fin/financial-education/OECD-INFE-Principles-National-Strategies-Financial-Education.pdf
5. Bebee, G.: Is self-directed investing right for you? The Globe And Mail, 11 September 2014. http://www.theglobeandmail.com/globe-investor/is-self-directed-investing-right-for-you/article20555144/
6. Zou, H.: Making Stock Market Charts Accessible through Provision of Textual Information in a Common Interface. Master's Degree in Inclusive Design, Ontario College of Art and Design, Canada (2015). http://openresearch.ocadu.ca/306
7. Kimball, M., Shumway, T.: Investor sophistication, and the participation, home bias, diversification, and employer stock puzzles. Unpublished Manuscript, University of Michigan (2006)
8. Zou, H., Treviranus, J.: ChartMaster: a tool for interacting with stock market charts using a screen reader. In: Proceedings of the 17th International ACM SIGACCESS Conference on Computers & Accessibility (2015)
9. Murphy, J.: Charting Made Easy. Wiley, Hoboken (2012)
10. Inclusive Design Research Centre (IDRC). http://idrc.ocad.ca/index.php/about-the-idrc/49-resources/online-resources/articles-and-papers/443-whatisinclusivedesign
11. Treviranus, J.: Leveraging the web as a platform for economic inclusion. Behav. Sci. Law **32**(1), 94–103 (2014)

# Technologies for ASD and Cognitive Disabilities

# Designing Therapeutic Activities
# Based on Tangible Interaction
# for Children with Developmental Delay

Clara Bonillo$^{(\boxtimes)}$, Eva Cerezo, Javier Marco, and Sandra Baldassarri

GIGA Affective Lab, Universidad de Zaragoza, Zaragoza, Spain
{clarabf, ecerezo, javi.marco, sandra}@unizar.es

**Abstract.** This paper presents a set of activities specially designed for children with developmental delay to be run on vision-based tangible tabletops. This way, the benefits that the combination of tabletop devices and Tangible Interaction offers to the treatment of cognitive problems can reach the children, which is the final aim of the work presented here. Two evaluations with children have been carried out as the result of a collaboration with an occupational therapy center, which has allowed us to detect some usability problems in the developed activities and to extract some conclusions that are also presented in this work.

**Keywords:** Tabletop · Developmental delay · Children with special needs · Activities · Tangible Interaction · Therapy

## 1 Introduction

Developmental disabilities are a group of related chronic disorders of early onset estimated to affect 5 % to 10 % of children [6]. The developmental delay is a subset of developmental disabilities defined as a significant delay in two or more of the most common developmental domains (gross/fine motor, speech/language, cognition, social/personal, activities of daily living) whose main problem is that there is not a specific method to cure it, so any treatment plan will have to take every child's uniqueness into account and it will be designed to focus on the child's individual needs.

Regarding this matter, our group (the AffectiveLab at the University of Zaragoza, Spain) has developed NIKVision, a vision-based tangible tabletop device designed for very young children and children with special needs [1] in which the interaction is carried out by positioning objects on the tabletop surface (Tangible Interaction), allowing children to play with the computer manipulating conventional toys. NIKVision has been tested in nurseries, schools and special education schools, proving its usefulness when working with this kind of children [5].

Based on our experience over the past years when working with children with special needs, the objective of the work presented here has been to develop tangible tabletop activities for the NIKVision tabletop specially designed for children with developmental problems.

M. Antona and C. Stephanidis (Eds.): UAHCI 2016, Part III, LNCS 9739, pp. 183–192, 2016.
DOI: 10.1007/978-3-319-40238-3_18

This paper is organized as follows. Section 2 describes the state of the art. Section 3 presents the methodology used to develop the activities. In Sect. 4 the evaluation of the activities is presented. Finally, Sect. 5 is given to the conclusions and future work.

## 2 State of the Art: Tangible Interfaces and Tabletops for Children with Developmental Delay

In this section several examples of the use of tangible interfaces and tabletops to work with children with developmental delays are analyzed, in order to determine how our work can contribute to this field.

On the one hand, regarding some works that make use of tangible interfaces, LinguaBytes [3] is a research programme which aims to develop an interactive and adaptive educational environment that stimulates the language and communicative skills of multiple handicapped children aged 1–4 years. Two tools have been developed during that project: E-scope and KLEED.

E-scope is a tangible device aimed to children with language and communication developmental problems. The prototype consists of a wooden ring-shaped toy with sensors and actuators, a computer with a wireless station and a screen. Using E-scope the children can listen to stories or play educational games by rolling the E-scope over different pictures that trigger different stories.

KLEED is a modular system consisting of exercise mats that can be connected to a central console. In this case, the child interacts with the device by placing physical tagged objects over the mats in order to listen to interactive stories or to realize exercises.

Also, Hunter et al. [4] have developed activities to teach children aged 4–7 yearsspatial concepts and sentence construction by using Siftables, hybrid tangible-graphical user interface devices that allow wireless communication and that can detect other devices of the same kind. Two main activities can be done with these devices: 'Make a Riddle' and 'TeleStory'.

In 'Make a Ridle' the child has to use three Siftables to create a sentence that will update an image in a fourth Siftable. Not all the combinations have an associated image. That way, the child will feel more motivated to create different combinations in order to obtain an image.

In 'TeleStory' the child can influence the story of a cat and a dog that are traveling. In this case the child uses the Siftables to change the elements of the story: for example, if the child uses a Siftable that is displaying a sun, the scene of the story will become daytime.

Finally, the Interactive Fruit Panel [2] is a tangible interface designed to help children with communication problems connect real objects (in this case fruits) with their graphical representation. In addition to their communication skills, the activity also makes the children work out their concentration and memory.

On the other hand, the only work that uses a tabletop to work developmental problems is [8], where the authors use Reactable, a tangible tabletop that allows the creation of music pieces, to work with autistic children, in order to offer them an alternative means of communication. The interaction with Reactable is usually carried out by using special objects but it also allows a direct interaction.

Analyzing the examples above it can be concluded that although there are several works that use tangible interfaces to work with children with developmental problems, the use of tabletops in this field is not very widespread. Besides, the works that make use of tangible tabletops usually focus on working just a definite developmental delay, without offering the possibility of working with children with different problems.

Therefore, the objective of this work was to create a set of tangible tabletop activities that could be useful for children who suffer from a varied range of developmental problems.

# 3 Developing Tangible Therapeutic Activities

The process had two differentiated parts: the establishment of the therapeutic goals that our activities had to fulfill in order to be useful for different children (analytic stage) and the creation of the activities (executive stage).

## 3.1 Establishing the Goals

We made contact with the center ENMOvimientTO, an Occupational Therapy Center (OTC) specialized in the early identification of delays and disorders in children aged 0–16 years.

The main objective of this OTC is to help these children carry out their daily activities, and since NIKVision had previously proven to be useful with children with special needs [5] the therapists of the center were interested in seeing whether it could help this kind of children as well.

Thanks to the documentation and advice of the OTC therapists, we were able to establish some therapeutic goals that had to be achieved by the activities that we were going to design. In order to decide on these goals, we took into account the possibilities offered by the combination of the NIKVision tabletop and the Tangible Interaction. Furthermore, from the great variety of disabilities of the children visiting the OTC, we had to choose the most common ones, since our objective was to develop activities that could help most of the children.

## 3.2 Development of Activities

The executive stage comprises two stages as well.

In the first instance, once we chose the therapeutic aspects to work with we started designing the activities. Then, we created simple concepts of the new activities and asked the OTs for their opinion. Finally, once we were sure that the activities fulfilled the necessary requirements for the children visiting the OTC, we implemented them.

The activities that were developed as a result of this interchange were:

- Bees: this activity helps to exercise visual attention.
- Fishing: this activity helps to practise coordination and fine motor skills.

- Twister: this activity helps to make use of bilateral coordination. In order to realize this activity, the children have to be able to tell apart their left hand from their right hand.

In the second place, a fourth activity had to be developed after the first evaluation session since we discovered that the 'Twister' activity was too complicated for most of the children, as it will be explained in the Sect. 4:

- Plumber: this activity helps to practise bilateral coordination but in this case the children do not need to tell apart their right hand from their left hand.

Following all the activities are explained in detail.

**Bees.** In this activity, the tabletop surface shows an animation of a tree full of hives with several bees flying around. The animation also shows a beekeeper standing under the tree. After some seconds, the bees stop flying and each one of them disappears into a different hive. Among the bees, there is only one that carries honey (see Fig. 1 Left).

**Fig. 1.** Bees activity. Left: Background-animation shown on the tabletop surface. Right: Physical honey pot toy to interact with the tabletop.

The activity is completed when the child places a honey pot toy (see Fig. 1 Right) under the hive where the bee with honey disappeared.

In order to give feedback to the child, we use the beekeeper character and different sounds:

- If the child places the honey pot toy under a wrong hive, the beekeeper will show a sad expression and a sound saying that there is no honey in the hive will be reproduced.
- If the child places the honey pot toy under the correct hive, an animation of honey falling out of the hive will appear, the beekeeper will begin to jump for joy and a sound saying that the honey has been collected will play.

**Fishing.** In this activity, the tabletop surface shows an animation of a pond with a pier where a cat is standing. Also, next to the cat there are shapes of the fishes that the cat likes (see Fig. 2 Left).

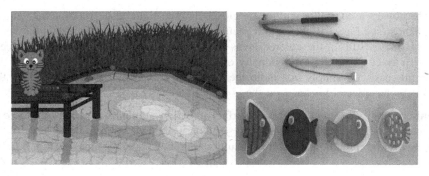

**Fig. 2.** Fishing activity. Left: Background-animation shown on the tabletop surface. Top-Bottom Right: Physical rod and fish toys to interact with the tabletop.

In this case, two different sets of objects are used: fishing rods of different length (see Fig. 2 Top-Right) and fish toys of different shapes and colors that are placed on the tabletop surface (see Fig. 2 Bottom-Right). To complete the activity, the child has to use one of the rods to catch the fish that have the same shape and color as the ones next to the cat and place them on the pier.

In order to give feedback to the child, we use the cat character and different sounds:

- If the child places the wrong fish on the pier, the cat will show a sad expression and a sound saying that the cat does not like that fish will be heard.
- If the child places the correct fish on the pier, the cat will start to applaud and a sound saying that the cat likes that fish will play.

**Twister.** This activity is a tabletop version of the original Twister game. The surface of the tabletop shows a twister roulette and four rectangular areas of different colors where the child has to place his hands (see Fig. 3 Left).

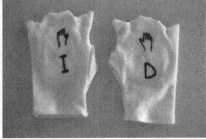

**Fig. 3.** Twister activity (multiplayer). Left: Background-animation shown on the tabletop surface. Right: Physical gloves to interact with the tabletop.

The objects used in this activity are gloves that the child has to wear on his left and right hands (see Fig. 3 Right), and a peculiarity of this activity is that the child has to keep his hands still on the colored areas until new instructions appear on the screen. The activity can be played individually or cooperatively.

In this case, we simply use audio feedback instead of using a character to tell the child if he has placed his hand on the correct area or not.

**Plumber.** In this activity, the tabletop surface shows an animation of a pipe composed of segments of different colors. Some of those colored segments present water leaks of the same color. The animation also shows a plumber standing under the pipe (see Fig. 4 Left).

**Fig. 4.** Plumber activity (multiplayer). Left: Background-animation shown on the tabletop surface. Right: Physical gloves to interact with the tabletop. (Color figure online)

The objects used in this activity are gloves of different colors that the child has to wear on his left and right hands (see Fig. 4 Right). The variety of the colors of the pipe segments, water and gloves depends on the number of children playing:

- If just one child is playing, the pipe will only have blue and red segments and just the blue and red gloves will be used.
- If two children are playing, the pipe will have blue, red, yellow and green segments and every child will wear different gloves: one child will wear the blue and red gloves and the other child will wear the yellow and green gloves.

To complete the activity, the child has to place his gloved hands over the segments of the pipe that have water leaks.

In order to give feedback to the children, we use the plumber character and different sounds:

- If a child places his hand over a segment whose color is not the same as the color of the glove, the plumber will show a sad expression and a sound saying that the color is not the same will be played.
- If the child places his hand over a segment whose color is the same as the color of the glove, the plumber will dance with happiness and a sound saying that the water leak is fixed will be reproduced.

## 4   Evaluation

When a first prototype of the first three activities was implemented, a NIKVision tabletop was installed in the OTC and an evaluation with the children was planned in order to detect usability problems in the developed activities.

### 4.1   Methodology

The evaluation was carried out for a week with the participation of a total of ten children who had several developmental issues like visual attention, coordination, fine motor skills and bilateral coordination.

During the evaluation, the children tested all the activities mentioned in the previous section except the 'Plumber' activity (which was developed as a result of the first evaluation as it will be commented further on) allowing us to detect some aspects of the activities that had to be corrected.

In order to locate usability problems we used a video analysis usability method consisting of a simplification of DEVAN [7], so that all the sessions with the children were video recorded for that purpose.

After the evaluation, a usability expert reviewed the videos and labeled them using five categories of usability events (see Fig. 5.). If an event happened in more than 50 % of the cases, it was considered a "critical point", meaning that a correction in the game had to be made in order to prevent that event from appearing again. Otherwise, the event could be considered an "isolated case" and be ignored.

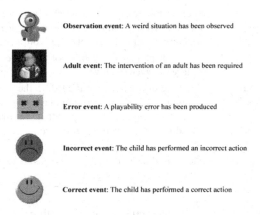

**Fig. 5.**  Events we take into account while the children play

In the Fig. 6 an example of labeling is shown.

Since some usability errors were found in the developed activities, we carried out a second evaluation session for another week with the same ten children when a second version of the activities was available.

**Fig. 6.** Example of labeling a video. Left: the child uses his two hands to grab the rod instead of using just one hand (error event). Right: The child is able to complete the task (correct event).

## 4.2    First Session

Regarding the first evaluation session, Table 1 shows the critical points that were found when the children tested the developed activities.

**Table 1.** Critical points of the actitivites

| Activity | Times | Event | Explanation |
|----------|-------|-------|-------------|
| Bees | 7 | Error | While the bee is still flying, the child begins to move the honey pot toy over all the hives, so that he is able to complete the activity without paying attention to the bee |
| | 6 | Error | After an incorrect action, the child chooses the correct hive but the wrong sound that was reproduced with the first incorrect action keeps playing, confusing the child |
| | 5 | Adult | Instead of putting the honey pot toy under the hive, the child places it over the hive |
| Fishing | 7 | Error | The child does not return the fish to the water once the task is completed, so when the next task begins there are already some fish placed on the pier that can make the audio feedback play even when the child has not done anything yet |
| Twister | 8 | Error | The child does not know that he has to keep his hands still on the tabletop during all the activity |

As shown in the table, in the "Bees" activity there were three critical points that had to be fixed:

The first critical point was resolved by deactivating all the areas in which the child can place the honey pot while the animation of the flying bees is being reproduced. That way, even if the child tries to guess the correct hive by probing all of them he does not get any kind of response and consequently he is forced to pay attention to the bee in order to see what hive is the correct one.

In order to solve the second critical point, it was decided to give priority to the correct feedback. That way, the moment the child performs a correct action the other sounds that could still be playing stop and just the correct sound remains, eliminating the possibility of confusing the child with contradictory feedback.

Lastly, regarding the third critical point we considered to modify the game so that the child could place the honey pot over the hive instead of under it. However, during the evaluation we also observed that some children immediately realized what they had done wrong when seeing the animation of the honey falling from the hive, so in the end it was decided not to change the game.

Also, the evaluation showed that most of the children could complete the activity without problems. Therefore, we decided to increase its level of difficulty for the next evaluation by adding more distractors to the animation (more bees that carry no honey) and by increasing the speed of the bees.

The 'Fishing' activity had just one critical point that could be easily fixed by adding an intermediate task in which the child has to return the fish to the water. That way, the possibility of a task being affected by the fish that the child has placed in the previous task disappeared.

Finally, the 'Twister' activity had just a critical point but in this case it was rather difficult to fix it because even when children were told to keep their hands still, they usually forgot to do so and removed them from the tabletop. Also, most of the children found difficult to tell apart their left and right hands even when the gloves that they were wearing had the indication on them. After studying the problem we concluded that to fix those problems would imply to change the 'Twister' activity completely, so it was decided to design another activity that could supply the 'Twister' problems. As a result, the 'Plumber' activity appeared, as it was mentioned in the Sect. 3.2.

### 4.3 Second Session

Once the critical points mentioned in the Table 1 were fixed and the new 'Plumber' activity was created, we carried out the second evaluation session for another week.

We tested again all the previous activities and the 'Plumber' activity with the same ten children who had participated in the first evaluation.

This time, no critical points were found in any activity so it was concluded that the second version of the activities was definitive.

## 5  Conclusions and Future Work

After analyzing several examples that make use of tangible interfaces and tabletops to work with children with developmental delay, we have created a set of four tangible activities that can help children with different developmental issues.

Thanks to the collaboration with the Center ENMOvimienTO we have been able to test the developed activities with a total of ten children. Also, the first evaluation session that was carried out allowed us to detect some usability problems in the first version of the activities that could be fixed for the second session.

After that second evaluation, the therapists of the center confirmed the utility of the activities, since the children had felt very motivated to use them.

In the very next future, we intend to keep working on the developed activities and to create new ones that cover a wider range of developmental issues so they could be useful for more children.

**Acknowledgements.** We want to thank Javier Llorente, María Llorente and all the staff of the Center ENMOvimienTO for their advice and complete support when we were developing the activities, and for allowing us to carry out the evaluation sessions with their children. Also, we want to thank the parents and children who participated.

# References

1. Cerezo, E., Marco, J., Baldassarri, S.: Hybrid games: designing tangible interfaces for very young children and children with special needs. In: Nijholt, A. (ed.) More Playful User Interfaces, pp. 17–48. Springer, Singapore (2015)
2. Durango, I., Carrascosa, A., Gallud, J.A., Penichet, V.M.R.: Tangible serious games with real objects to support therapies for children with special needs. In: Proceedings of the XVI International Conference on Human Computer Interaction, pp. 353–352 (2015)
3. Hengeveld, B., Voort, R., Hummels, C., de Moor, J., van Balkom, H., Overbeeke, K., van der Helm, A.: The development of LinguaBytes: an interactive tangible play and learning system to stimulate the language development of toddlers with multiple disabilites. Adv. Hum. Comput. Interact. **2008**, Article ID 381086, 13 (2008)
4. Hunter, S., Kalanithi, J., Merrill, D.: Make a riddle and TeleStory: designing children's applications for the siftables platform. In: Proceedings of the Ninth International Conference on Interaction Design and Children (IDC 2010), pp. 206–209. ACM Press (2010)
5. Marco, J., Cerezo, E., Baldassarri, S.: Bringing tabletop technology to all: evaluating a tangible farm game with kindergarten and special needs children. Pers. Ubiquit. Comput. **17** (8), 1577–1591 (2013). ISSN: 1617-4909
6. Shevell, M., Ashwal, S., Donley, D., et al.: Practice parameter: evaluation of the child with global developmental delay: re-port of the Quality Standards Subcommittee of the American Academy of Neurology and the Practice Committee of the Child Neurology Society. Neurology **60**, 367–380 (2003)
7. Vermeeren, A.P.O.S., den Bouwmeester, K., Aasman, J., de Ridder, H.: DEVAN: a detailed video analysis of user test data. Behav. Inf. Technol. **21**, 403–423 (2002)
8. Villafuerte, L., Jordá, S., Markova, M.S.: Acquisition of social abilities through musical tangible user interface: children with autism spectrum condition and the reactable. In: Proceedings of the ACM Conference on Human Factors in Computing Systems (CHI 2012), pp. 745–760 (2012)

# Socialization of People
# with Autism Through Social Networks

Thais Castro[1(✉)] and Ulrike Lucke[2]

[1] Institute of Informatics, Federal University of Amazonas, Manaus, AM, Brazil
thais@icomp.ufam.edu.br
[2] Department of Computer Science, University of Potsdam, Potsdam, Germany
ulrike.lucke@uni-potsdam.de

**Abstract.** People with autism spectrum disorder have different levels of impairment regarding to communication, interaction, and imagination - three social skills necessary to engage in face-to-face interaction. One way to possibly overcome these inabilities is to seek for online communities where they can express themselves freely without being judged for their appearance or difficulty of eye gazing and talking conventionally. Although there are other implications to consider, as the ones related to online security or bullying, there are social skills which could be better learnt through these communities. In this paper we review this relatively new way of social organization and we discuss the current gains and possible prospects.

**Keywords:** Autism and social abilities · ASD and social networks · Online communities and autism

## 1 Introduction

Online communities have been created in online social networks for different purposes. A basic search about autism on the most used open access online social networks, such as facebook, tumblr and blogger, will show that there are many existing communities for parents, therapists and people with autism spectrum disorder (ASD). ASD [1, 2] is a condition that affects people's abilities to communicate, interact and imaginate, three social abilities necessary to engage in face-to-face interaction. Whoever lives or works with a person with this condition continuously seeks for information and support, and that could be partially supplied by these communities, as this review is going to show.

Prior to the beginning of this review, on a random free exploration of some evidence of online communities created specifically for autistic persons, we found a few that have been created within specific contexts, as it is the case described in the ethnographical study about Autcraft (a community for Minecraft for autistic adolescents) in [3] and the ones dedicated for adults as described in [4]. These communities have been very successful in providing a space for people on the autism spectrum to talk about their feelings and thoughts. What is interesting about these communities is that they were created for a very specific purpose and turned out to be helpful in building ties of friendship among their participants. In a way of speaking, they changed their main reason of being a community of practice to be a group therapy space.

© Springer International Publishing Switzerland 2016
M. Antona and C. Stephanidis (Eds.): UAHCI 2016, Part III, LNCS 9739, pp. 193–202, 2016.
DOI: 10.1007/978-3-319-40238-3_19

Autistic persons, regarding their level of difficulties with social abilities, have a unique way of thinking and learning. The best description is in Temple Grandin's report [5] where she explains her own process of thinking as a collection of instant photo frames. If one is missing, the thinking process is not complete. Usually, an autistic person is a visual thinking, what make sense when one considers how many autistic persons have mastered the use of electronic visual devices as computers and smartphones. In that case, for parents and therapists to think about improving their social abilities using a virtual space as a simulation for the "real world" is worth a try. Nevertheless, the topic demands a thorough review and discussion about the risks underlying it.

Given the context for this review, before even start to brainstorm for keywords, we have defined target categories of online networks based on [6]. Calvão defines social networks depending on the level and intention of message exchange among participants. In this work, we use the term *communities of practice* (*i*) for those social networks restricted to subscribed participants directed to a specific topic. We call a *complete social network* (*ii*) like Facebook, an environment containing micro blog, chat, email, forum, and news feed. Finally we call a *video driven social network* (*iii*) when subscribers usually are consumers of contents, and comments are only occasionally made by other users who watch those videos [7], that is the case of YouTube.

In this article we evaluate how people in the autism spectrum and/or their relatives have been using each of these categories of social network, and discuss specific issues like the technical needs of interface adaptation especially of types (*i*) and (*ii*) of social networks, as well as broader aspects like online inclusion of autistic people and possible impacts on their social behaviour.

## 2  Method

The systematic review used in this work is based on [8]. This method suggests the addition of more studies to complement the automatic literature review. We also intended to include some online communities in this review, but since there are so many online communities on Facebook only, we would not have enough time to do a proper filtering and compare results we decided to postpone that analysis.

The nature of this review is to carry out comparative studies on ways autistic people to engage in a virtual social network. For this reason, aiming at clarifying our research questions and finding out the keywords for search the electronic library collections, we did a mind map, showed on Fig. 1.

In Fig. 1 there is a connection between persons with and without ASD. Their connection is represented with a dotted line because that bridge has not been completely built yet, i.e. both groups lack clues for more successful interaction. Social Networks are at the centre of the research. Results depend on efforts for achieving a better use of these networks in communities, complete social networks or video social networks. At last, we also were searching for reports about the use of socialization techniques in or for social networks.

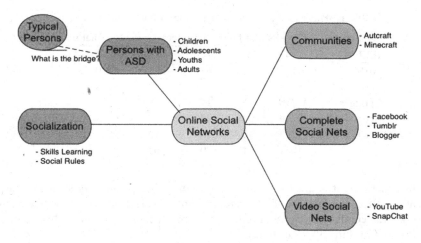

**Fig. 1.** Mind Map for defining questions and search terms

## 2.1 Review Details

Based on our mind map and first exploratory analysis, we raised three questions: (Q1) Did individuals with active participation in any social network show improved face-to-face social abilities after starting to use the network? (Q2) What are the benefits of using social networks? (Q3) Are there risks especially for people with ASD in using social networks? If so, what are they? We will show on the results section which questions were addressed by each set of papers.

From the questions above, this review objective is to compare case studies, software proposals, technology-mediated approaches and reports on the usage of online social networks by persons with ASD and their relatives in order to draw a prospective view about of the connection between autism and social networks.

The inclusion criteria are: (C1) paper's main argument is about autistic people's social abilities within an online community; (C2) research techniques used are still recent; (C3) preferably about the use of social networks (private or open) by autistic adolescents. Exclusion Criteria: (E1) publication is before 2011. To include a publication before 2011, it is only the case if the title matches exactly all the search keywords (results list and title exam); (E2) Books, indexes and editorials (results list exam); (E3) Keywords do not sufficiently match the topic (title exam).

## 2.2 Libraries Datasets and Extraction

The first author defined the keywords: autism, "social network", "virtual community", socialization, "face-to-face interaction" and depending on the library, changed to its other appearances as communit*, network* or alternating with "interaction". The libraries searched were: IEEE, ACM, PubMed, Springer, Scopus, and Science Direct.

Keywords and the first search strings candidates were defined in November, 2015. Each library has specific rules to search the dataset, and we intended to make our string

**Table 1.** Paper extraction and application of filters within criteria

| Dataset | Results | 1st filter | 2nd filter | Abstracts | Total read |
|---|---|---|---|---|---|
| IEEE | 40 | 22 | 17 | 13 | 4 |
| ACM | 123 | 96 | 51 | 21 | 10 |
| PubMed | 4 | 2 | 2 | 2 | 0 |
| Springer | 778 | 11 | 11 | 9 | 6 |
| Scopus | 19 | 4 | 2 | 2 | 2 |
| Science Direct | 103 | 16 | 16 | 16 | 3 |
| | 1067 | 151 | 99 | **63** | **25** |

as more general as it could be so we could refine other parameters such as year of publication after yielding the first search results. Table 1 shows how our search extraction was conducted considering the criterion for inclusion and exclusion in our first, second and third filter (abstract).

One paper from IEEE library was outside of C1 for being from 2010, but the keywords matched completely. Consequently, it made part of the review. On ACM the same happened with two papers. On PubMed two passed the first and second filter but the abstracts were out of context. Springer and Science Direct were completed exclusively on the web. Two filters were applied in parallel, remaining only the selected abstract to be read. As the first author does not have access to Springer, she contacted the nine authors responsible for the selected papers. Six of them provided their proof copy. Finally, two of the pre-selected papers from Scopus were already on ACM.

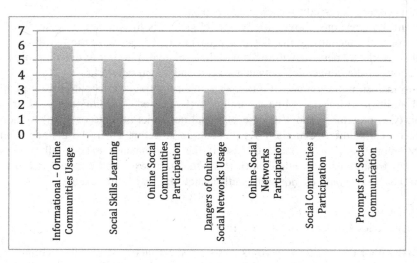

**Fig. 2.** Amount of publication per category

# 3   Results

Although the extracted publications had very diverse categories of study (7 defined as shown in Fig. 2) the data for the studies concentrates mostly on the United States, followed by Australia, New Zealand and UK, with only two papers using data from worldwide, as shown in Fig. 3.

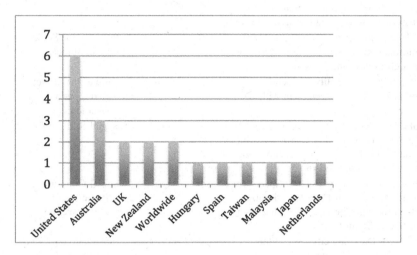

**Fig. 3.**  Countries where population samples used in the publication are from

Regarding publication categories, the most frequent was "Informational – Online Communities Usage". In this category, there are papers that present arguments for the use of online social networks but do not have any case or empirical study about its use by ASD persons. This category is followed closely by "Social Skills Learning" and "Online Social Communities Participation". Papers in the "Social Skills Learning" group present computational tools for autistic children, adolescents or youth to learn specific social skills while practicing them with their peers during practice sessions. In the "Online Social Communities Participation" group, there are papers on the usage of online communities by persons with autism or their relatives. It is worth to mention that we are using the classification presented on the introductory session for these categories. The communities mentioned in these papers are communities of practice as in definition *(i)*. Some of them work on a bigger social network but are members-only.

Regarding the remaining four categories, papers in the "Dangers of Online Social Networks" point out the intrinsic risks that more vulnerable users, as persons with autism, may find when sharing their information with all kinds of people. Among these are: bullying increasing risks, turning into cyberbullying, asking and receiving advice from malicious people, etc. "Online Social Networks Participation" contains papers about the current usage of complete social networks *(ii)* mainly by relatives of persons with autism who use them as supporting groups. A couple of papers are about how

**Table 2.** Classification for the extracted papers

| Title | TP | Q | Category |
|---|---|---|---|
| Accessing Peer Social Interaction: Using Authorable Virtual Peer Technology as a Component of a Group Social Skills Intervention Program | JP | Q3 | Social Skills Learning |
| VR4VR: Vocational Rehabilitation of Individuals with Disabilities in Immersive Virtual Reality Environments | CN | Q3 | Social Skills Learning |
| MyCalendar: Fostering Communication for Children with Autism Spectrum Disorder Through Photos and Videos | CP | Q1 | Prompts for Social Communication |
| Investigating the usability of social networking sites for teenagers with autism | CN | Q1 | Online Social Networks Participation (Adolescents) |
| SocialMirror: Motivating Young Adults with Autism to Practice Life Skills in a Social World Collaborative Technologies for Children with Autism | EA | Q2 | Social Skills Learning |
| Imagine That: Creating a 'Third Space' for Young People with High Functioning Autism through the Use of Technology in a Social Setting | CN | Q2 | Social Communities Participation (Adolescents) |
| Overcoming Data Scarcity of Twitter: Using Tweets as Bootstrap with Application to Autism-Related Topic Content Analysis | CP | Q2 | Informational – Online Communities Usage |
| Making "Safe": Community-Centered Practices in a Virtual World Dedicated to Children with Autism | CP | Q2 | Online Social Communities Participation (Adolescents) |
| Investigating the Use of Circles in Social Networks to Support Independence of Individuals with Autism | CP | Q1 | Online Social Communities Participation (Youth) |
| Collaborative Technologies for Children with Autism | CDP | Q2 | Social Skills Learning |
| Specializing Social Networking Services for Young Adults with Autism | EA | Q2 | Informational – Online Communities Usage |
| Social Playware: Device-Mediated Social Interaction for Therapeutic Activities | CP | Q2 | Social Skills Learning |
| Prospects for the Use of Multiplayer Online Games in Psychological Rehabilitation | CP | Q2 | Informational – Online Communities Usage |
| Research into the Treatment of Autism Using Virtual Communities | CP | Q2 | Informational – Online Communities Usage |
| Are Our Online "Friends" Really Friends? | MP | Q2, Q3 | Informational – Online Communities Usage |

*(Continued)*

**Table 2.** (*Continued*)

| Title | TP | Q | Category |
|---|---|---|---|
| Online social networks and mental functioning: a case study | C P | Q2, Q3 | Dangers of Online Social Networks Usage |
| Online social networks as a tool to support people with special needs | J P | Q1, Q2 | Online Social Communities Participation |
| Cyberbullying among male adolescents with attention-deficit/hyperactivity disorder: Prevalence, correlates, and association with poor mental health status | J P | Q1, Q2, Q3 | Dangers of Online Social Networks Usage |
| Seeking social support on Facebook for children with Autism Spectrum Disorders (ASDs) | JP | Q1, Q2 | Online Social Communities Participation (Parents) |
| Interactive Digital Storytelling and HCI Techniques Applied for Edutainment in Interactive Health Projects: Analysis of Two USC's Labyrinth Projects | CP | Q2 | Informational – Online Communities Usage |
| Do Social Networks Differ? Comparison of the Social Networks of People with Intellectual Disabilities, People with Autism Spectrum Disorders and Other People Living in the Community | JP | Q2 | Social Communities Participation (Adults) |
| Flourishing on Facebook: virtue friendship & new social media | J P | Q2, Q3 | Dangers of Online Social Networks Usage |
| Affective, Linguistic and Topic Patterns in Online Autism Communities | C P | Q1, Q2 | Online Social Communities Participation (Adult + Parents) |
| Facebook Use by Persons with Disabilities | J P | Q1, Q2 | Online Social Networks Participation (18+) |

adults with autism cope with face-to-face communities and be active on them; this group is called "Social Communities Participation". In the last category there is only one paper because it could not fit adequately in any other category. It is "Prompts for Social Interaction" where a computational tool is presented as an information manager for parents and the children with autism themselves to upload photos and videos within their daily agenda. It is used during classes for socialization.

Analysing the extracted publications and keeping track of the categories where case studies have been conducted, this review may not be globally representative for the whole population of autistic people. South America for instance, is not represented, as shown on Fig. 3.

Table 2 shows all the extracted papers, with its type, category and underlying question addressed for this review. JP stands for journal paper, CN for conference note,

CP for conference paper, EA for extended abstract, CDP for conference demo paper and MP for magazine paper.

# 4   Discussion

Regarding the extracted papers, space constraints lead us to illustrate typical issues through discussion on two exemplary categories: (a) "Informational – Online Communities Usage" and (b) "Online Social Communities Participation".

From category (a) they all answer research question (Q2) about the benefits of using online social networks, and one of them also answers question (Q1) about the existence of any improvement on face-to-face interaction. Below there is an overview of papers from this category: In "Overcoming Data Scarcity of Twitter: Using Tweets as Bootstrap with Application to Autism-Related Topic Content Analysis" authors find trend topics related to autism on twitter. There is no distinction between provenances of posts. Parents usually post the most, and there are posts by adults with ASD, or by kids with ASD; and other may post some by any other people. - On other direction, "Specializing Social Networking Services for Young Adults with Autism" is a PhD research proposal. The author proposes a tool for question and answer (Q&A) as a result of his investigation in an online community with Asperger. His objective is to amplify autistics communication networks that pass through changes from adolescence to adulthood trying to have their needs attended. - In a more optimistic direction is the work "Prospects for the Use of Multiplayer Online Games in Psychological Rehabilitation" which proposes possible clinical applications of MOGs like Second Life to help on specific therapies and socialization. It could be used for autism, but the paper only gives suggestions and no experimental evidence. - Moving towards autism treatment, the paper "Research into the Treatment of Autism Using Virtual Communities" proposes the use of virtual communities as a space for treating autism. They used a realistic clinic model. That proposal has not been put to practice yet. First arguments seem right, but the idea of "treatment" with doctors and psychologists don't seem to be practical or effective. - Continuing on the topic of using social networks extensively as a way to attenuate some of the difficulties of autism but already alerting for some dangers is the work "Are Our Online 'Friends' Really Friends?". In this magazine article authors comment about the usage of Facebook by youths and adults with ASD as being beneficial because it empowers them with abilities for some social interaction they cannot keep in real world, and things happen there because they are able to respond to messages at their own pace and for whomever they deem to. On the other hand, this kind of interaction is dangerous, as they do not have enough experience to know who is trustworthy. They are much more vulnerable than their neuro-typical peers. The research suggests Facebook to incorporate some reputation mechanism.

Regarding category (b), the questions they address depend on the paper. It is a category with many different viewpoints. On "Making 'Safe': Community-Centered Practices in a Virtual World Dedicated to Children with Autism" the authors describe an immersive virtual community for adolescents with ASD and their parents called Autcraft. It has many explicit rules, with some administrative levels, involving parents and kids (10–17y). The aim is to be a safe social environment. This is the reason why there are so many rules like "don't talk about dating", "treat everyone respectfully", "no swearing", etc. The claim is that with this sort of safe and artificial environment, kids will learn how to protect themselves in the real world. - The paper "Investigating the Use of Circles in Social Networks to Support Independence of Individuals with Autism" describes communities developed specifically for this case study, which was an experiment with three youth Aspergers to stimulate their independence through the use of a social network service, in private mode, with the app GroupMe. In this network, people create their circles, contacting people according to common topics. In the case of these youths, they created only one circle with their relatives and their main caretaker, in many cases, their mum. The experiment worked in a way to prove that it is possible to share their overdependence related to their primary caretaker among other people who can also help giving opinion about many daily topics. And they also learn to socialize in this safe environment. - More on Online Communities, "Online Social Networks as a Tool to Support People with Special Needs" is about the whole process of developing and using a social community from scratch. They conducted a pilot study for a year with patients and their contact networks in this devised online social community. Data points out that all contact networks have been strengthened among participants and they felt confident enough to share information on this space. - Further, the paper "Seeking Social Support on Facebook for Children with Autism Spectrum Disorders (ASDs)" again brings the subjects of communities for supporting parents of children with ASD. Their findings were very meaningful: Authors categorized the messages and realized the most common ones were for seeking and giving advice, what benefits directly parents who just received diagnosis for their child. - Lastly, the paper "Affective, Linguistic and Topic Patterns in Online Autism Communities" mines autistic online communities, including parents and Asperger's communities. They found the most common words that appear in messages and categorize them according to feeling scales.

# 5  Conclusion

In this work we presented a systematic review on literature about autism and use of online social networks. We grouped the extracted papers on seven categories based on our mind map of the topic and questions to be addressed. Among these categories, the four concentrating most of the papers (79 %) were: Informational – Online Communities Usage; Social Skills Learning; Online Social Communities Participation; and Dangers of Online Social Networks Usage. The first two were detailed on the Sect. 4. On all categories, most of the works describe a specific requirement scenario for using (i) communities of practice or (ii) complete social networks.

It has been evidenced by this review that there are several online communities, with open and closed access. Both types have the potential to support persons with ASD to improve their social skills, but there are several other aspects raised that represent risks for autistic people. For instance, inherent dangers of using online social networks are specially alarming for young people on the spectrum because of their lack of experience in recognizing malicious intentions allied to their natural will of involvement on networks. As suggested by Shyong in [9], social networks such as Facebook should have a reputation mechanism to reduce that risk.

Finally, there are some prospective issues to consider for immediate following work. While analyzing our data we realized that as confirmed by some of the extracted papers [9, 10], people with ASD who are "more functional" and have job placements, have reservations about exposing themselves in an autism community by fear of being discriminated, this aspect might have impacted on the amount of reports. Even when these people participate on online communities they do not want to be recognized. In that case, we intend to do a field study with some closed communities of Aspergers and Autistics in other regions and compare the data gathered from this review to check whether it was representative enough for those places as well.

# References

1. American Psychiatric Association: Cautionary statement for forensic use of *DSM-5*. In: Diagnostic and Statistical Manual of Mental Disorders, 5th edn. (2013). doi:10.1176/appi. books.9780890425596.744053
2. Wing, L.: The autistic spectrum. Lancet **350**(9093), 1761–1766 (1997)
3. Ringland, K.E., Wolf, C.T., Dombrowski, L., Hayes, G.R.: Making "Safe": community-centered practices in a virtual world dedicated to children with Autism. In: Proceedings of the 18th ACM Conference on Computer Supported Cooperative Work & Social Computing (CSCW 2015), pp. 1788–1800. ACM, New York (2015). doi:http://dx.doi.org/10.1145/2675133.2675216
4. Davidson, J.: Autistic culture online: virtual communication and cultural expression on the spectrum. Soc. Cult. Geogr. **9**(7), 791–806 (2008)
5. Grandin, T.: Thinking in pictures: and other reports from my life with autism (1995)
6. Calvão, L.D., Pimentel, M., Fuks, H.: Do email ao Facebook: uma Perspectiva Evolucionista sobre os meios de Conversação da Internet. Translation: "From email to Facebook: an Evolutionary Perspective about Internet Conversational Media". UNIRIO. Rio de Janeiro (2014). E-BOOK. ISBN: 978-85-61066-50-5
7. Wattenhofer, M., Wattenhofer, R., Zhu, Z.: The YouTube social network. In: ICWSM (2012)
8. Petticrew, M., Roberts, H.: Systematic Review Sintheses on Social Sciences: A Practical Guide. Blackwell Publishing, Malden (2006)
9. Shyong, T.K., Lam, J.R.: Are our online "friends" really friends? Computer **45**(1), 91–93 (2012). doi:10.1109/MC.2012.5
10. Shpigelman, C.-N., Gill, C.J.: Facebook use by persons with disabilities. J. Comput. Mediated Commun. **19**, 610–624 (2014). doi:10.1111/jcc4.12059

# Smart Objects for Autism: A Proposal of Classification of the Objects Based on the Autism Symptoms

Roberta Grimaldi[1,2(✉)], Mauro Palatucci[2],
and Carlo Maria Medaglia[1]

[1] Link Campus University, Rome, Italy
{r.grimaldi,c.medaglia}@unilink.it
[2] ISIA Roma Design, Rome, Italy
mauro.palatucci@gmail.com

**Abstract.** The Technology could have a greater impact on the life of people, especially for disabled people. In this paper we focus on smart objects designed for the autistic people. In fact the IoT technologies are proving their suitability for these users. So we made a review and a qualitative analysis of the actual offer of these objects, adding also items for disabled people and not specifically designed for autistic people. Its general aim is try to understand if the smart objects could be useful for the autistic people and how they do this. As result, we present a proposal of classification of the smart objects for the autistic people, based on the symptoms of the Autism on which the object could have an effect.

**Keywords:** Smart object · Autism · Assistive technology · IoT · Interaction design · Tangible interaction

## 1 Introduction

Technology allows us to do things until now unimaginable and sometimes *magic*. But the technology with the greater impact on our life are the technologies with a real and concrete impact, which improve our daily activity. Every improvement achieved in the life of able people assumes a greater value in the life of people with any type of disability. In this paper we focus on technologies designed for the autistic people. Children with Autism have been noted to be skilled at using computers [1]. In this field, many project of innovative technologies have been carried out. On the base of the actor which the technology is made for, we can organize them on three different levels. For the autism researcher, technologies application can allow to collect large scale data for the deepest study and earlier diagnostic of this little-know disease. For the operators, psychologists and families, the potentialities are the monitoring of the users for a more personalized treatment [2]. For the end users, the technologies can be a support for the therapies, a tool for trainings of some skills, an appliance to communicate. Among others, some research of the Assistive Technology field have focused on the technologies designed for the autistic people, such as the development of a type of Ambient Assisted Living based on the Internet of Things infrastructure and device [3]. Just the

M. Antona and C. Stephanidis (Eds.): UAHCI 2016, Part III, LNCS 9739, pp. 203–212, 2016.
DOI: 10.1007/978-3-319-40238-3_20

IoT devices, based on Ubiquitous Computing paradigm [4], are proving their suitability for these users, in a way that their characteristics of pervasiveness and ubiquity, invisibility and integration in the every-day object, network connection make them versatile across the various fronts of the complex world of the Autism. This type of devices is called 'Smart Object' and consist of physical object in which is integrated: computational power, sensors, actuators, and possibly memory and connectivity [5, 6]. Our focus on the use of the smart objects for the autistic people is made also in a viewpoint of the potentialities of tangible interaction. In this paper we made a review and a qualitative analysis of the smart objects designed and objects for the autistic and disabled people. Its general aim is try to understand if the smart objects could be useful for the autistic people and how they do this. As result, we present a proposal of classification of the smart objects for the autistic people, based on the symptoms on which the object could have an effect. Its aim is to give a general direction to the future design of these devices, through some recurring design characteristics, and to be a tool for the designer to better understand this world of devices.

In the following section we describe the Autistic Spectrum Disorder. Then we make an overview of the several application of the technology for this disorder. The fourth section illustrate, firstly, the method of the smart object review. In the second part of this section a table with the characterization results is provided, and some qualitative analysis are reported. In the fifth section we describe the proposal of classification of the smart object for the autistic people and we identify some recurring design elements for each group of objects. In the last section we illustrate the conclusion.

## 2   The Autism Disorder

Autism (from the greekαὐτός [aw'tos], it means *self*: himself, herself, itself) is a neurodevelopmental disorder that affects the way a person experiences and interacts with the world. It was identified by psychiatrist Leo Kanner and, more than 60 years after its definition, its classification is still uncertain as well as its causes. In the fifth edition of the Diagnostic and Statistical Manual of Mental Disorders (DSM-V), Autism was defined as a spectrum of conditions, also more different between them, which regards the right development of social, cognitive, emotional, communicational skills. Indeed it was included in the Autistic Spectrum Disorder (ASD) with Asperger's disorder and childhood disintegrative disorder and pervasive developmental disorder not otherwise specified (PDD-NOS).

The Autism disorder symptoms and their severity level vary widely depending on the level of development of the disorder and chronological age of the subject. But all autistic people are characterized by a so-called autistic triad: impaired social interaction, delay and disorder in the communication and restricted interest and repetitive behavior. The social interaction impairments regard deficits in understanding how to behave and interact with other people: lack or absence of social interaction initiative; difficulty understanding and using nonverbal behavior (e.g. eye contact, facial expression); unaware of the different ways to interact with the others (e.g. difficulty in adapting behaviors according to social contexts; difficulty understanding other people's points of view or feelings). Impairments in the communication concern deficits in ability to communicate effectively with other people as: unusual or repetitive language; absence of desire to communicate; total lack of language or delayed or impoverished language development; talking about own interests regardless of the listener's response; comments inappropriate to the context. The impairments in the activities and interests consist in deficits in flexible thinking regarding interests, routines as: incapacity of generalize information; fixation in some interests; stereotypic patterns of behavior (unusual or repetitive gestures or actions); rigid routines and resistance to the change; fascination with object parts.

Autism has been documented in all the world's peoples, of every race or social environment. Its estimated prevalence, considering the Autism Spectrum Disorders, it's 1 in 68[1]. About the causes of autism, as said previously, there are no certainties. More and more scientific evidence points to genetics, though scientists note that it's likely there is no single cause. Among the other popular theories, in the public mindset, there are factors such as parental age, poisoning from heavy metals, vaccines and so on. The scientific evidence continues to refute these hypotheses, and also to suggest that different combinations of factors can be linked to different manifestations of Autism spectrum disorders. For our competence, whatever are the causes, it is vital to focus on issues of pressing concern to actual autistic persons and their families today, such as serene growth, enhancement of their ability, housing, employment and long-term supports.

## 3   An Overview of the Innovative Technology for Autistic People

Goodwin [7] provide a complete overview of the innovative technology developed for the Autism disorder: from the use of Internet as a support for the long-distance clinical health care and communications; to the use of Virtual Reality technology to practice rule learning in social skills or as teaching aid; to the wearable sensors to record physiological reaction, helping the autistics, and the people who interact with, to understand their physical state, so their emotions. The latter application was a part of the Affective Computing field, which focus on the potentials of the physiological communication and social-emotional skill development technologies. Autistic people, especially nonverbal, have trouble to communicate their emotions and to communicate on the outside what they experience on the inside (e.g. pain for headache). This gap can be fill up tracking of the physiological state (e.g. electrodermal activity) through the wearable device, as a small wristband. This type of device can have several aims: to make adjustments to the treatment plan; to identify the elements that enable a better focusing on some tasks or cause "meltdowns"; to collect long-term data for the research community to produce new insights for the Autism disorder; and to bring to the Autism people tools to recognize their emotions, self-regulate and calm themselves [2, 8]. For the education and

---

[1] Data referred to the prevalence of Autism in the United States released by the Centers for Disease Control and Prevention (CDC). In Europe many countries - including Denmark, Sweden, Portugal and the United Kingdom - lack of updated data on the prevalence of these disorders.

the therapy application, among others, an interesting and innovative trend explores the use of different kinds of robots with the aim to develop social and behavioral skills in a safe and controlled environment. Robota, a humanoid robotic doll, engages child with autism, through a bodily interaction, in an imitative interaction games [9]. ShyBot is a personal mobile robot designed to embody shyness behaviors, and through a Replay technique, to elicit reflection in the child on this type of behaviors via associating their outward observations with their inward feelings [10].

Nowadays, thanks to the IoT developments more researchers and developers are focused on developing various smart devices that can support autistic users in their daily routine, improving their quality of life. The smart objects, with their capability of identifying, locating, sensing and connecting, lead to new forms of communication between people and things and things themselves. Furthermore, they enable a tangible interaction that may be well suited for the autistic people providing a tangible focus for activities and taking advantages from an active learning, experienced through body and sensory awareness [11]. In addition, the interaction enabled through these objects puts the child in control, under possible guidance of and feedback from the teacher, but with the child learning at his/her own peace [9]. This advantage, although valid for the technology in general, is especially true in the case of the smart objects, that are based on a much focused and closer end-user interaction.

## 4    Smart Object Review

### 4.1    The Review Method

Until now, more attention is given on the objects itself without a general thinking system and trans-disciplinary approach. Stated this, we made a review and a qualitative analysis of this type of smart objects which general aim is try to understand if the smart objects could be useful for the autistic people and how they do this, through the various interaction ways and patterns. This type of objects can be applied in three scenarios, which illustrate the use of smart devices on different scales: small, medium and large scale [12]. For our aim, the impact on autistic people and their life, we focus on the smart objects of the small scale operating within buildings. Furthermore, we clarify that our focus were physical objects that enable a kind of purely physical and sensorial interaction. Therefore, we have excluded the numerous projects consisting of apps and platforms. We have decided also to rule out the humanoid robots that currently represent a growing trend in the treatment of the Autism. In this case, we consider they refer to a different field of study.

For the review, we have conducted an Internet search and the results have showed there are many projects of smart objects designed for the people with Autism. Many of them were proof of concepts, others were the results of research application for the Academy and many others were real products on the market. So we have decided to include objects at any state of the development of the product. Then, to have the most complete overview of the field, we have included the smart objects designed for other types of disabilities, which functionalities could be useful for the autistic person. The selection has then been extended to those smart objects whose design and functionalities are strongly related to the key concepts of Autism: from development of the social interaction skills, to expression of the emotions. In fact, this type of smart objects, although they are not specifically created for these users, is made for the development of some necessary abilities and skills, lacking in the autistic people. We have decided, lastly, to include also the *traditional* objects for people with special needs, that is objects without the 'augmented' part (e.g. computational power). In fact, it is important not to underestimate the world of knowledge grown before the development of the technologies, in a way that their interaction patterns can be still valid and applicable to the smart object field.

First of all, we have characterized the objects through a series of comparable and general elements referred to the Technological Features, the Objects Behavior and the Interaction Modes. The three macro aspect have been detailed in some elements that usually characterize a smart object. The Technological Features regard the hardware and software characteristics and the related functionalities. So we have examined if the object: (a) is equipped with an app, (b) connects and interacts with his peer, (c) conducts a monitoring activities via sensors, (d) and tracks the activities. The Object Behavior is referred to the behavior model of the object toward the user, to be understood as increasing in terms of responsiveness to the user. The behavior of the object could be (a) Passive, in a way that only reveal something (e.g. quality of the air). The following model (b) is based on a simply Input/Output relations, so the smart object that is manipulated through certain inputs produces certain outputs. The Proactive behavior (c) is characterized by a more advanced responsiveness for which the object is resourceful and solicits the user. The last pattern is the User Adaptive model (d) for which the objet uses every information learned in the interaction with the user to adapt dynamically its behavior. The Interaction Modes regard the interaction way through the object communicates and engages the users. The interaction could be mediated through (a) hands, through (b) the body (full body movements), through (c) senses (e.g. use of lights or scents), and through (d) body and senses.

After this first characterization, we have analyzed each object through a qualitative analysis of the interaction. The general aim of the qualitative analysis is to examine in depth every object, each one with own several features and interaction mode, to learn useful consideration for the design. The qualitative analysis of the interaction is based on the three implicated perspectives: the product design field, the interaction design field and the medicine field (neuropsychiatry). For the product design analysis level, we have identified the physical and digital aspects of the object: dimensions, shapes, colors, materials and characteristics, product type and any technological features. This physical characteristics, that give a certain affordances [13], are fundamental in a way that affecting how people use the object, what people think about it, how they hold it, and how they handle it. For the interaction design level of analysis, we have identified the interaction frameworks and patterns between the child and the object (e.g. the use of light or movements for feedback), and the use of certain organizational and interaction metaphors [14]. The metaphors form the conceptual infrastructure for the Ubiquitous Computing project, especially for the smart objects. For the neuropsychiatric analysis level, we have deduced a link between the symptoms disorder and the object features and its interaction. This last level of analysis allow us to suppose how these objects could intervene, in a positive way, in the course of the disease. The analysis is to be intended in this order. So only after a clear understanding of the physical characteristics and the features of the object, that create and enable the interaction with the users, we can deduce the impact on the symptoms of the autism.

## 4.2 Results of the Review

We have selected and analyzed 19 objects: 5 are smart objects designed specifically for autistic and ASD people, 2 is a smart object for disabled people, 8 are smart objects related to the key concepts of Autism, and 4 are traditional objects. This list is certainly nor exhaustive nor complete of the existing offer of this type of objects, probably we have not identified many projects and many other projects are launched while we are finalizing this paper. However, this activity of selection and review of these objects is to be intended as in progress. Following, we provide the table of the results of the characterization of the objects (Table 1).

**Table 1.** Results of the characterization of the objects analyzed

| | Features | | | | Object behavior | | | | Interaction modes | | | |
|---|---|---|---|---|---|---|---|---|---|---|---|---|
| | (a) | (b) | (c) | (d) | (a) | (b) | (c) | (d) | (a) | (b) | (c) | (d) |
| The Boezels | | | | | • | | | | | | | • |
| Repeat | | | • | | • | | | | • | | • | |
| T3 Objects | | • | • | • | • | | | | | | • | |
| Cradle | | | | | • | | | | | • | | |
| Snug Vest | | | | | • | | | | | • | | |
| Squeeze Chairs | | | | | • | | | | | • | | |
| Auti | | | | | | • | | • | | | | • |
| Ubooly | • | | • | • | | | • | • | • | | | |
| Cubemate | | | | | • | | | | | | • | |
| I Mirabilia | | • | • | | | | • | | | | | • |
| Sleep sheep | | • | | | • | | | | | | | • |
| Topobo | | | | | • | | | | • | | | |
| Paro | | | | | | | • | | | | | • |
| Soma mat | | | | | • | | | | | | | • |
| Rolling pins | | • | | | • | | | | • | | • | |
| Moti | • | | • | | | | • | | | | • | |
| Edwin the duck | • | | | | • | | | | • | | • | |
| Keepon pro | | • | • | | | | | • | | • | | |
| + Me | • | | | | | | • | • | | | | • |

As regards the qualitative analysis of the interaction, we provide a recap of two of the carried out analysis: Auti and Soma Mat.

Auti is an interactive toy designed for individuals with ASD, which aims to encourage positive social skills. These subjects have difficulties in acquiring useful skills to interact with other children. Their 'extreme' behavior, in the sense they do not always control their voice and body, or the behavior not appropriate to the context tend to scare other children. Auti takes a series of a typical aspects of social interactions and puts them in a safe environment, in which the child can experience them through play, without social risk. Auti is a spherical toy, whose body is made of soft fur of opossum and has 4 legs. It is equipped with a series of sensors, servo motor and accelerometer, which allow it to move, to detect sounds, talking, and, in general, to interact with the child. Its operation mode is based on positive and negative reinforcement that work to change challenging behavior. So when the child proves negative behaviors (e.g. yelling), Auti will pulls in and shut down. On the other hand, every time the child will behave in a socially positive way, stroking, or talking with a moderate tone of voice, Auti will respond with engaging behaviors, as various dances. The interaction metaphor used is the Animism, so the devices become our pets or peer and we are led to interact with them as if we were really interact with our friends and pets [14]. Furthermore, the interaction metaphor used lead child to grow fond of Auti. Its design and its affordances allow an interaction with close contacts, since its shape and its size allow child to pick it up easily. The Auti purpose to encourage the positive social behavior makes it a useful tool for the impairments related to the sphere of social interaction, considering that they could appear just as difficulties in the development and maintenance of social rapport and difficulties to accord behavior to social contexts.

Soma Mat [15] is a mat designed as a tool for the own body awareness exercises, according to the Somaesthetic philosophy. Somaesthetics is an interdisciplinary field which asserts the importance of the body and our body movements as part of our ways of being and thinking. Therefore, increasing the awareness of our body, engaging in various forms of training, we can become more perceptive and aware in the physical world in which we live and act. Soma Mat uses heat feedback in different parts of the mat corresponding to different part of the body to support the ability to direct user attention to that particular part of the body while he/she performs the exercises of the training lesson. The experience becomes both intensely pleasurable and help to follow directions and instructions for the exercises. Soma mat consists of a series of layers of foam in which are integrated a set of heat pads controlled by an Arduino micro controller, programmed to follow the audio script of the lesson. The interaction metaphor used is which ones of the Enchanted Objects. This metaphor implies adding something 'magical' to an existing object and it implies that the object is mostly like its earthly counterpart, but with significant behavioral differences given to it by the technology [14]. The use of the heat, helping to focus attention on the parts of the body in correspondence, makes the interaction with soma mat very intimate, infusing the subject with a sense of calm, relax and focus on him/herself. In fact, these mode of interaction enables in the subject a more general process of meditative bodily introspection through a full and total awareness of own body. So Soma Mat could be useful to the symptoms related to the stereotypic behaviors and movements and restricted interests. These symptoms, especially the meltdowns and the stereotypic movements, often occur in situations of high stress and anxiety.

## 5  Proposal of Classification

The qualitative analysis of the interaction of the objects reveals a classification applicable to the objects and smart objects for people with Autism and based on the triad of symptoms of the disorder. From each qualitative analysis, we have observed how each object could match with only one of these symptoms. Furthermore, we have identified some recurring design elements in the objects belonging to the same group. The proposal of classification provides three type of objects: Enablers of Social Interaction, Supports for Learning and Inhibitors of Behavior.

The Enablers of Social Interaction are the objects designed for the issues related to the Social field, that regard social and emotional development, reciprocity, and interaction. These objects are characterized by features that, through their digital and physical design, enable, stimulate, and solicit in the children the relationship skills and their development. Included in this group are 9 objects: The Boezels, Auti, CubeMate, I Mirabilia, Topobo, Paro, Rolling Pins, Keepon Pro, and +Me. This type of objects often have in common a series of design elements: the product type, i.e. the toys; the interaction metaphors used, i.e. the Animism; and the Interaction Multimodal Mode based on sensory and bodily stimuli and feedback. With this type of objects the children can explore and discover the interaction skills rather than being taught explicitly, through objects designed as toys. Furthermore, the use of the metaphor of animism lead child to grow fond of the object, enabling the type of unconstrained and unstructured interaction, characterized by a multimodal interaction, that engage the attention of autistic children.

The second type of objects aims to be a tool for the issues of the Communication field, precisely for the symptoms of cognitive and communication impairments. These objects are the supports for the cognitive training and the language learning. Included in this group are 5 objects: Repeat, T3 objects and T3 board, Ubooly, Moti, and Edwin the Duck. This type of objects often have in common some technological features, that are the tracking functionalities and the app. For the interaction modes these objects are characterized by a hands-on or a multisensory interaction. Through these design elements this type of objects are a real learning tools that goes beyond the object itself and consist of a complete learning and training system that, through the app, provides the training exercises for the users and, through the tracking features, gives to the teachers or the parents (or to the users too) the possibility to collect and view the data. Furthermore we have noticed that the interaction enabled through these objects is more 'formal', as based on hands-on interaction and sensorial reinforcements. To reinforce this last consideration there is another recurring element in the design of these objects: the use of plastic materials, which perception to the tactile contact is much colder and pretended.

The Behavior Inhibitors pose themselves as a 'remedy' to the occurrences of symptoms of repetitive and stereotypic behaviors and movements. Indeed, these objects are characterized by features that allow children to calm, engaging their attention in other activity, or allow them to relax. Included in this group are 5 objects: Cradle, Snug Vest, Squeeze Chairs, Sleep Sheep, and Soma Mat. These objects have in common the product types, as furniture or wearable, and interaction modes focused on body or multimodal stimuli and feedback. Furthermore, these objects often are not a smart object or they have very basic technological features, so their behavior are based on input/output relations and they are more focused on the physical and sensorial interaction through primordial stimuli (e.g. heat in Soma Mat or white noise in Sleep Sheep).

This proposal of classification aims to inform and give a general direction to the future design of these devices, not only through the identified recurring design characteristics but also providing a tool to better explore and understand the actual offer of these objects, facilitating the conceptualization of new smart objects for the Autism disorder.

## 6 Conclusion

In this paper, starting from an overview of the potentialities of the technologies for the Autism disorder, we focus on the smart object that, given their versatility and the technical features, are among the most important innovations for people with special needs, as the autistic people. To better understand this trend, we have explored and characterized the actual offer of these objects, adding also items for disabled people and not specifically designed for autistic people in a viewpoint of theoretical debate and pure inspiration. For each object we made also a qualitative analysis of the interaction on the base of the three implicated perspectives: the product design, the interaction design and the medicine field. Thanks to this qualitative analysis we could deduce the correlation between the smart object features and design characteristics and Autism symptoms. So we present a proposal of classification of the smart object for the autistic people, based on the symptoms on which the object could have an effect. The proposal of classification provides three type of objects: Enablers of Social Interaction, Supports for Learning and Inhibitors of Behavior. Its aim is to give a general direction to the future design of these devices, through some recurring design characteristics, and to be a tool for the designer to better understand these world of devices.

Currently, we are just at the beginning of the development of the smart objects for the Autism but, from this study and the resulting classification, we can understand as all the implicated fields in the design of a smart object for the autistic people are fundamental in its final effectiveness. So, we aim to underline the necessity of a shared and trans-disciplinary approach of the design. Stated this, the classification here proposed is not to be understood as definitive, because on one hand the review will continue to include new objects and on the other hand the classification will be refined together with specialists, such as therapists, as well as together with autistic children's parents. Furthermore, given the complexity of this disorder and as in the development of all UbiComp devices [6], we believe it is necessary to find the ways to get involved the end users, and their care-givers, at different stages of the process (e.g. through test users with real prototypes).To conclude, the key result of this paper is there are not best solutions for each symptom of the Autism, but rather it is necessary to develop an ecosystem of devices, flexible and adaptable to match the unique needs of this kind of users and their personal severity level of the disorder symptoms.

# References

1. Murray, D., Lesser, M.: Autism and computing. In: For Autism 1999 Online Conference Organised by the NAS with the Shirley Foundation (1999)
2. Picard, R.W., Goodwin, M.: Innovative technology. The future of personalized autism research and treatment. Autism Advocate **50**(1), 32–39 (2008)
3. Sula, A., Spaho, E., Matsuo, K., Barolli, L., Xhafa, F., Miho, R.: A new system for supporting children with autism spectrum disorder based on IoT and P2P technology. Int. J. Space-Based Situated Comput. **4**(1), 55–64 (2014)
4. Weiser, M.: The computer for the 21st century. Sci. Am. **265**(3), 94–104 (1991)
5. Kranz, M., Schmidt, A.: Prototyping smart objects for ubiquitous computing. In: Proceedings of the International Workshop on Smart Object Systems in Conjunction with the 7th International Conference on Ubiquitous Computing (Ubicomp) (2005)
6. Papetti, A., Iualé, M., Ceccacci, S., Bevilacqua, R., Germani, M., Mengoni, M.: Smart objects: an evaluation of the present state based on user needs. In: Streitz, N., Markopoulos, P. (eds.) DAPI 2014. LNCS, vol. 8530, pp. 359–368. Springer, Heidelberg (2014)
7. Goodwin, M.S.: Enhancing and accelerating the pace of autism research and treatment: the promise of developing innovative technology. Focus Autism other Dev. Disabil. **23**(2), 125–128 (2008)
8. Picard, R.W.: Future affective technology for autism and emotion communication. Philos. Trans. R. Soc. Lond. B Biol. Sci. **364**(1535), 3575–3584 (2009)
9. Dautenhahn, K., Billard, A.: Games children with autism can play with Robota, a humanoid robotic doll. In: Universal Access and Assistive Technology: Proceedings of the Cambridge Workshop on UA and AT 2002, pp. 179–190. Springer, London (2002)
10. Lee, C.H.J., Kim, K., Breazeal, C., Picard, R.: Shybot: friend-stranger interaction for children living with autism. In: CHI 2008 Extended Abstracts on Human Factors in Computing Systems, pp. 3375–3380. ACM (2008)
11. Farr, W., Yuill, N., Raffle, H.: Collaborative benefits of a tangible interface for autistic children. In: Proceedings of the Workshop on Tangibles for Children, CHI 2009, pp. 1–4. ACM (2009)
12. EURESCOM: Smart Devices 'When Things Start to Think?' Strategic Study - Project P946-GI (2000)
13. Gibson, J.: The theory of affordances. In: Shaw, R., Bransford, J. (eds.) Perceiving, Acting, and Knowing. Lawrence Erlbaum Associates, Hillsdale (1977)
14. Kuniavsky, M.: Smart Things: Ubiquitous Computing User Experience Design. Morgan Kaufmann, San Francisco (2010)
15. Höök, K., Ståhl, A., Jonsson, M., Mercurio, J., Karlsson, A., Banka Johnson, E.C.: COVER STORY: Somaesthetic design. Interactions **22**(4), 26–33 (2015)

# On the Creation of a Persona to Support the Development of Technologies for Children with Autism Spectrum Disorder

Ana Leal[1], António Teixeira[2,3], and Samuel Silva[2,3(✉)]

[1] University of Aveiro, Aveiro, Portugal
travessaleal@ua.pt
[2] DETI – Department of Electronics, Telecommunications and Informatics, University of Aveiro,
Aveiro, Portugal
{ajst,sss}@ua.pt
[3] IEETA – Institute of Electronics and Informatics Engineering of Aveiro, University of Aveiro,
Aveiro, Portugal

**Abstract.** When developing technologies for persons with autism spectrum disorder (ASD) there are multiple aspects posing challenges to the community. First of all, there are several viewpoints at stake, from the targeted person to family and caretakers, needing careful consideration and yielding conflicting interests and motivations that need to be considered. Second, design and development teams often include people with a very diverse background, from psychologists to software engineers, who need to be able to fully communicate their knowledge and ideas regarding the users, and understand the different team viewpoints towards the best possible outcome. In this context, we argue that Personas (and in particular, families of Personas) can be a powerful tool to tackle these challenges. As a first stage of our work, we present the methods considered for the creation of a Persona for a 10 years old kid with ASD along with its full description. At this stage, the Persona has been evaluated by a panel of experts and was considered in the design of a first application prototype for children with ASD.

**Keywords:** Persona · User-centered design · Autism spectrum disorder · Children

## 1 Introduction

When developing technologies for persons with autism spectrum disorder (ASD) there are multiple aspects posing challenges to the community. First of all, there are several viewpoints at stake, from the targeted person to family and caretakers, needing careful consideration. Therefore, conflicting interests and motivations among those who will use (or supervise the use of) the proposed system need to be carefully tackled and articulated (Hendriks et al. 2015).

A second challenge concerns the multidisciplinary nature of the required intervention, gathering knowledge and views from psychology, education, therapy, signal processing and human-computer interaction (Odom et al. 2014; Porayska-Pomsta et al. 2012). This requires that different experts are able to communicate and discuss their

M. Antona and C. Stephanidis (Eds.): UAHCI 2016, Part III, LNCS 9739, pp. 213–223, 2016.
DOI: 10.1007/978-3-319-40238-3_21

ideas using a shared language, fostering a better understanding of what is at stake. For example, technology developers often have a limited knowledge regarding the target impairment and, therefore, have trouble deciding how to balance the different interests and where to focus their approach. In this case, the knowledge and views of different stakeholders regarding the focused condition, contexts, intervention approaches, and technical aspects need to be discussed and put to practice in a tight collaboration effort.

Considering these challenges, we argue that Personas, especially considering approaches in line with those presented, e.g., in Queirós et al. (2013), can be very useful in tackling both a common language among elements of a multidisciplinary team, promoting a greater understanding of the targeted individuals and condition, and articulating the different motivations of stakeholders.

Despite that Personas are widely considered in the literature, in several domains, to the best of our knowledge no substantial use of this tool has been described in the context of technology development for people with ASD. Therefore, our main goal is to propose a family of Personas (Matthews et al. 2011), i.e., a group of Personas encompassing the various stakeholders (e.g., family, teachers), based on data gathered from the different stakeholders (e.g., parents, therapists, and children) and from studies regarding autistic children communication, aiming to be a complete and well supported base to develop technology for children with ASD. In this context, we argue that a simple list of user characteristics is not enough. An empathy needs to be created with the Persona to enable a greater understanding of what is at stake.

In the scope of Marie Curie IAPP project IRIS (Freitas et al. 2014), one of the main goals is enhancing communication among individuals, particularly targeting those with speech limitations. In this context, the targeted users include children with autism spectrum disorder (ASD), providing us the application scenario for our Persona proposal.

As a first step of our work, this article presents the methods and outcomes for the creation of the Persona of a 10 years old kid with ASD. Section 2 details the method for creation of the Persona and Sect. 3 presents the first version of the Persona and its evaluation by a panel of experts. Section 4 presents a brief example regarding how, starting from the proposed Persona, we can engage in design and development of a novel application. Finally, Sect. 5 presents some conclusions and ideas for future work.

## 2  Building the Persona

Personas are considered a powerful communication tool for how the potential users behave, think and want to accomplish. Despite being fictitious persons, they are defined through research and observation of characteristics, needs, behaviors, motivations and expectations of real people (Queirós et al. 2013).

Personas provide a common language, which facilitates the interdisciplinary dialogue, necessary to the development of applications for groups with specific characteristics, and help to determine the features that the product should include and how it should operate. Furthermore, it is a reality check tool, which allows the multiple intervenients to test and elect, during the development process, the best design options. This also makes it possible to achieve more viable results at the time of testing with real users (Ferreira et al. 2013).

### 2.1 Method for Persona Creation

The proposed method was based on the methodology described by (Cooper et al. 2007) and (Queirós et al. 2013). First, to systematize the characteristics of children with ASD at a social interaction level, receptive-expression language, communication and adaptive behavior, several online searches were conducted using search engines, such as *Scopus*, *Web of Science*, *PubMed*, *Google*, and ASHA. Additionally, the research also included scientific books about ASD and specific studies on the communication skills of children with ASD in Portugal, resulting from previous work at our institution (Araújo 2009; Batista 2011; Pedro 2011; Reis and Teixeira 2012).

Secondly, in order to complement the retrieved information and obtain additional details regarding the daily routine of these children, we sought the opinion of experts in the field. Thereby, caretakers and professionals, whose work is mainly with ASD children, were contacted by *e-mail* and telephone.

Based on the collected information, a set of characteristics and the most important objectives to be included in the description of the Persona were defined and expressed in a small narrative about the Persona and his lifestyle.

## 3  Results – Persona and Its Evaluation

The main results of the work presented in this article are the full description of the Persona for a 10 years old kid with ASD and its evaluation by a panel of experts. Both outcomes are described in what follows.

### 3.1 Persona of Nuno Rocha

The following text includes the description of our first version of the Persona of Nuno Rocha, a 10 years old child with ASD. For the sake of simplicity and compactness, it already includes, underlined, information added as a result of the evaluation conducted with field experts (as described in Sect. 3.2).

*Nuno Rocha, born on February 20th, 2005 in Moita, Anadia county, Aveiro district, Portugal, lives with his father, mother and a 13 year old sister. At the age of 2 he went to a development appointment in the district hospital, because his parents suspected that something was wrong with his development, where we was, posteriorly, sent to an autism exam to the Pediatric Hospital of Coimbra. At the age of 3, he was diagnosed with Autism Specter Disturbance (level 2 in the scale of severity), with associated cognitive deficits.*

*He currently attends the 4ᵗʰ grade in Anadia's Basic School, were he benefits from a UEE support that delivers him a structured learning model (TEACCH) and the application of interdisciplinary intervention methodologies. It is in the school context that he also benefits from Speech Therapy sessions.*

*Nuno is a student with a specific individual curriculum (that consists of changes to the normal curriculum, mostly consisting on the introduction, substitution and/or elimination of goals and contents). On a daily basis, for 2 h, he attends the regular class, and the goal is to work in the social sense, whereas functional classes (like functional Portuguese, world knowledge, functional math and every day activities) are learned at the unit.*

*At home, he prefers to watch TV and play computer games, so when he is asked about the professional preferences, he mentions he would like to stay at home with his mother and watch TV or play computer games.*

*He appears to dominate the basic functions of a computer; however, he only uses his ability to play computer games. He is not able to research information on any search engine, nor does he use the social networks for communication.*

*He appears to understand simple oral material, specifically words or sentences related with his social and familiar day-to-day. On the other hand, difficulties are observed on the comprehension of longer sentences that lack visual support or that are out of the context.*

*The elected mean of communication is speech. [He is mostly capable of using short and simple sentences (subject ± verb ± object). As far as it concerns reading, he recognizes all the letters from the alphabet, but he seems to struggle on the reading process, mostly syllabic, associated to a loss of purpose and hesitations]. He writes with orthographic correction but he needs support on the structuring of small texts and in answering questions. He also presents difficulties using markers and morphosyntatic constituents by omitting link words, such as prepositions, along with difficulties in number/gender agreement for definite articles. He also has trouble in matching the verbal form with the personal pronoun (e.g., "I does"). He makes requests in his areas of interest, and when questioned he has difficulties in answering, sharing daily experiences, and beginning and keeping a conversation. He shows difficulties in keeping eye contact, respecting interaction shifts and adjusting to the context and to the interlocutor. In some situations, he verbalises incoherent phrases and out of context (delayed echolalia).*

*In the school context, when he does not recognize his surroundings, he walks front and forward, not addressing the employees for help. [He gets anxious every time his routine is changed or when he's thwarted, presenting inappropriate and sometimes aggressive behaviors, as yelling, pinching, and biting whoever is around].*

*He shows attention/concentration deficit, namely failing to pay attention in the classroom, which leads him to easily demotivate if the proposed activity is not of his interest.*

*Regarding the daily routine activities (such as dressing and personal hygiene), usually he is able to conclude them with autonomy, requiring, from time to time, supervision to accomplish their sequence.*

**Motivation:** *Nuno would like to be more autonomous using social networks to communicate. Plus, we would like to be able to share with his parents the activities that he does in school through the day.*

The motivation is also an important part of the Persona as it sets what are the main long term goals at stake, providing guidelines to the Persona's expectations that would potentially have a greater impact and receptivity, if attended.

## 3.2   Persona Assessment by Field Experts

According to Cooper et al. (2007), the data that is included in the Personas' description should mainly be collected through the observation of the potential users in real context and by conducting interviews based in ethnographic techniques. However, in this first stage of our study, due to time constraints, and agenda of the intervenients, the information used in the creation of the Persona was based in the information available in the literature and in the experts' opinion. This way, in order to assess the adequacy of the statements included in the description, as well as the necessity to include or remove some data, a validation questionnaire was considered, and presented to a panel of experts.

### 3.2.1 Persona Assessment by Field Experts

The validation questionnaire was divided into two parts. In the first, we gathered data to characterize the selected experts regarding age, gender, profession, academic status, number of years as a professional, school/institution where they develop their activities, research topics of interest, and number of scientific publications in the area. The second part was designed to collect information concerning the experts' overall opinion about the whole Persona and regarding each of the statements included in its description, concerning their plausibility, representativeness, and adequacy to real life situations. The overall opinion about the Persona could be expressed, by the experts, using a five level Likert scale (very good, good, reasonable, bad, and very bad). For the detailed assessment of each of the statements included in the Persona, 11 questions were formulated, and the answers to those questions were obtained considering a three level Likert Scale (I disagree, I do not agree or disagree, I agree). The study's objective and contextual information were provided on the first page of the questionnaire. The anonymity and confidentiality of the data were guaranteed.

Concerning the selection of the experts' sample, a non-probabilistic sample method was used, by convenience/accident (Fortin 1999). Therefore, five experts were contacted, three Special Education Teachers and two Speech Therapists who were working at a structured teaching unit for ASD students. The average age was 37 years and the average practice was about 12 years. None of the experts had research or publications on the subject. At this stage of the investigation, these professionals were considered the most suited to provide a first validation regarding the issues under study due to their close relationship with these children.

Qualitative data, provided by the experts, were analyzed and allowed to make minor adjustments to the contents of the described Persona.

### 3.2.2 Evaluation Results

By analysing the experts' answers, it was observed that, overall, the description of the Persona was evaluated as "Very Good" by 40 % of the experts, "Good" by 20 % and "Reasonable" by 40 % (see Fig. 1). It was also observed that in 70 % of the situations the experts agreed with the included statements and they maintained a neutral opinion in 23.3 % of the situations, only disagreeing with 6.7 % of the cases (Fig. 2).

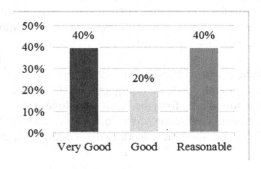

**Fig. 1.** Experts' opinion on the statements included in the Persona Description.

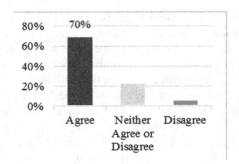

**Fig. 2.** Global evaluation of the proposed Persona.

In the disagreeing situations, participants did not always provide a suggestion on how to improve. In fact, only one expert from the panel suggested that a more detailed characterization of the children's speech should be provided, more specifically concerning the type and structure of the sentences they use, and showing examples of the types of behavior they have. The changes resulting from expert suggestions are underlined in the Persona description for Nuno Rocha.

As can be observed from the presented results, the experts expressed a positive opinion regarding the overall contents of the Persona description and mostly agreed with the particular characteristics described for Nuno. Including the improvements suggested by the experts, the Persona was considered for the design and development of a first prototype of an application for children with ASD, as described in the following section.

## 4   Application Example

The advances in technology and informatics opened a new world filled with communicative possibilities and information access, potentially yielding a helpful tool to all children with special educative needs. The information and communication technologies increasingly allow these children in schools, making the whole educational process easier, and the goal being the integral education (Liu et al. 2007; Williams et al. 2006). Sometimes the solution for the barriers that the ASD children find is an accessible educative resource. Therefore, given their unique characteristics and their functional limitations to the conventional means, the development of applications based on tools that ease the specifications of their characteristics, necessities, and interests is fundamental.

To illustrate how the proposed Persona can serve as grounds for technology development targeting children with ASD, we briefly present the steps that need be taken to develop a novel application starting from the Persona of Nuno. This example is extracted from our ongoing work considering the scope and goals of project IRIS (Freitas et al. 2014) and supported initial development work as described in (Vieira 2015).

### 4.1 Context Scenario

The context scenarios describe how an application may be used in a certain context and for a certain period of time (Queirós et al. 2013). In this specific context scenario a story is described in which Nuno's Persona is able to recreate his day-to-day routine at school and improve his communicating and learning capabilities, by using a special application previously installed in a tablet. The scenario also provides a description of the surrounding environment that needs to be explored, the information requirements that need to be incorporated in the application, and the functional and interaction requirements.

*Nuno just finished an activity he was performing during speech therapy and he would like to take a picture to keep it and share the moment. To do so, he only needs to access the system and touch the icon corresponding to the camera, available on the main menu. The system takes the picture and saves it automatically.*

*Then, the system exhibits the editing menu, where Nuno has the chance of associating an emotion to the picture, add a little informative text about what he has been doing in the speech therapy class, and share the picture in his diary. The diary shows the information by its occurring order, as well as the day and hour of the entry. Using a mobile gadget and accessing their Facebook accounts, **Nuno's parents and friends may view the shared pictures**, therefore knowing all the activities Nuno is doing through the school day, as well as the interdisciplinary team elements that intervene.*

*Shortly after, Nuno heads to the Special Teaching Unit and when he consults his schedule he realizes that his next activity consists in solving math exercises. Knowing that this is an activity that Nuno does not like, the teacher recurs to a quiz game, available on the main menu, which is meant to make this activity more likeable and obtain a bigger motivation and participation from Nuno in the execution of the proposed tasks. Using another device, the **teacher defines the questions and the answering options and sends them to Nuno's tablet**. He chooses the option and the system informs if the option is correct or incorrect.*

*When he finishes his math exercises, Nuno decides to consult his diary. The picture he shared concerning the speech therapy class has a comment from his mother, in which she congratulates him for his work. Nuno reacted with happiness and asked the teacher for help so he could reply to his mother comment.*

The context scenario contains a set of elements that are worth of note. First, it contains a set of actions (a selected set is underlined in the text) that are very important for identifying the functional requirements for the envisaged application. Second, it identifies activity from other important actors (e.g., the teacher, as depicted in bold face) making it clear that the application will also serve third parties for particular actions. These other actors will have their profile and motivations that need to be considered and their identification further emphasizes the importance of our long term goal of proposing a family of Personas for developing technology for children with ASD. In the particular case of this context scenario, having a Persona for the teacher (and parents) would be one important asset and is part of our ongoing work.

### 4.2 Main Requirements

In line with the context scenario, the application was projected to minimize the difficulties that ASD children present in describing whatever concerns their daily activities, to promote their reading and writing skills, to develop their ability to handle different emotions, to simplify their access to social networks, and facilitate information sharing between care-takers and the professionals from the interdisciplinary team.

The list of requirements to incorporate in the application's prototype was based on the characterization of the potential users and on the context scenario description. Thus, the system must allow: (1) picture taking; (2) automatically saving the pictures; (3) eliminating pictures; (4) picture editing; (5) picture sharing, on a diary; (6) showing the information by order of entry; (7) registering others' information; and (8) accessing all the information shared on his diary with others. The system must also: (9) avoid information overload by presenting only a few possibilities to choose from, at each time; (10) be user-friendly; (11) use simple, everyday words; (12) use easily recognizable icons; and (13) allow customization.

## 4.3   Conceptualization Using Application Mockups

The conceptualization and specification process of the application was structured based on the requirements, in order to be able to respond to the target audience specificities and necessities. Figure 3 shows some examples of the proposed interface mockups that were initially presented to the various team elements for discussion. During the discussions concerning the definition of requirements and the design of the application all intervenients were asked to continuously consider the Persona of Nuno Rocha.

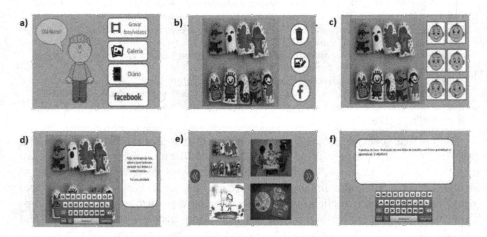

**Fig. 3.** Examples of user interface mockups for the application: (a) main menu; (b) editing menu; (c) "assign an emotion" section; (d) "add a description" section; (e) "my pictures" section; and (f) "notepad" section.

At this moment, the first version of the applications prototype is under development. Figure 4 depicts two of the interfaces already developed, enabling the user to login into the application prototype.

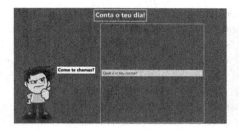

**Fig. 4.** Screen capture for two login alternatives available in the application prototype: left, insert name; and right, choose the correct fruit.

One of the login screens presented in Fig. 4, asking the user to select a fruit, is actually the support to one of the aspects we wish to explore in the future. As described in the Persona, Nuno has difficulties in keeping eye contact. Since eye tracking is becoming an affordable technology to use in everyday interaction (Vieira et al. 2015), we wish to explore how this new technology can be harnessed to help children with ASD, not only for interaction, but also potentially contributing to the development of a more social behavior. In the particular case of the login screen presenting the fruits, the child can answer by simply looking to the correct fruit. Based on the assessment of the usage results we acquire from this feature, which will enable us to evaluate the receptivity and utility of eye tracking in this context, we will then move to more advanced uses of the technology inside the application. This also serves to highlight how the Persona can provide a clear and powerful insight into user characteristics with an impact on design and development.

## 5   Conclusions

In this article we argue that in the scope of technology development for children with ASD, families of Personas can play an important role in fostering the dialog among multidisciplinary team members and in balancing the motivations of different stakeholders. As a first step of our work, we present a first version of a Persona for, Nuno Rocha, a 10 years old kid with ASD. From the analysis of experts' responses to the validation questionnaire, we found that the description of the Persona was not challenged, overall, and improved in a few details. Although there were some disagreements concerning some aspects, the experts did not offer any suggestion for its improvement. In future evaluations, as we keep evolving the proposed Persona, it may be interesting to further explore the reasons for these disagreements, maybe by conducting the questionnaire in a conversation, leading to a more detailed discussion.

In line with our initial idea that Personas would be a valuable communication instrument among the different stakeholders, we observed that to be true, since it already fostered the communication, validation, and understanding of the characteristics of Nuno, the proposed Persona, involving teachers, speech therapists, and software engineers.

Considering that the long term goal of our work is the creation of a "family of Personas", as suggested in the methodology proposed by Matthews et al. (2011), six other people were identified (mother, father, sister, special education teacher, speech therapist, and regular teaching teacher), representative of the individuals who establish a direct connection with Nuno's Persona, and playing an important role in the interactions with the application. For each of these, a Persona will be researched and built, using a similar methodology as the one considered for the Persona presented in this article. This will enable the definition of their different characteristics and motivations, and will be a first step towards their balancing when developing technologies for children with ASD.

**Acknowledgements.** The work presented in this chapter has been partially funded by IEETA Research Unit funding (Incentivo/EEI/UI0127/2014) and Marie Curie IAPP project IRIS (ref. 610986, FP7-PEOPLE-2013-IAPP).

# References

Araújo, J.: As Perturbaçõeses do Espectro do Autismo na Região Autónoma da Madeira. Master Speech and Hearing Sciences, DETI/DLC/SACS, Universidade de Aveiro (2009)

Batista, J.: O Perfil do Terapeuta da Fala em Portugal. Master Speech and Hearing Sciences, DETI/DLC/SACS, Universidade de Aveiro (2011)

Cooper, A., Reinmann, R., Cronin, D.: About Face 3: The Essentials of Interaction Design. Information Visualization, vol. 3. Wiley Publishing, Inc, Indianapolis (2007). doi:10.1057/palgrave.ivs.9500066

Ferreira, F., Almeida, N., Rosa, A.F., Oliveira, A., Casimiro, J., Silva, S., Teixeira, A.: Elderly centered design for interaction – the case of the S4S medication assistant. In: 5th International Conference on Software Development and Technologies for Enhancing Accessibility and Fighting Info-exclusion, DSAI (2013)

Fortin, M.-F.: O Processo de Investigação: Da concepção à realização. Lusociência, Loures (1999)

Freitas, J., Candeias, S., Dias, M.S., Lleida, E., Ortega, A., Teixeira, A., Orvalho, V.: The IRIS project: a Liaison between industry and academia towards natural multimodal communication. In: Proceeding Iberspeech, pp. 338–347. Las Palmas de Gran Canaria, Spain (2014)

Hendriks, N., Slegers, K., Duysburgh, P.: Codesign with people living with cognitive or sensory impairments: a case for method stories and uniqueness. CoDesign **11**(1), 70–82 (2015). doi: 10.1080/15710882.2015.1020316

Liu, Y., Cornish, A., Clegg, J.: ICT and special educational needs: using meta-synthesis for bridging the multifaceted divide. In: Shi, Y., van Albada, G.D., Dongarra, J., Sloot, P.M. (eds.) ICCS 2007, Part IV. LNCS, vol. 4490, pp. 18–25. Springer, Heidelberg (2007)

Matthews, T., Whittaker, S., Moran, T., Yuen, S.: Collaboration personas: a new approach to designing workplace collaboration tools. In: SIGCHI Conference on Human Factors in Computing Systems, pp. 2247–2256 (2011). doi:10.1145/1978942.1979272

Odom, S., Thompson, J., Hedges, S., Boyd, B., Dykstra, J., Duda, M., Bord, A.: Technology-aided interventions and instruction for adolescents with autism spectrum disorder. J. Autism Dev. Disord. **1**, 1–15 (2014). doi:10.1007/s10803-014-2320-6

Pedro, M.J.N.: O Terapeuta da Fala e o Autismo. Master Speech and Hearing Sciences, DETI/DLC/SACS, Universidade de Aveiro (2011)

Porayska-Pomsta, K., Frauenberger, C., Pain, H., Rajendran, G., Smith, T., Menzies, R., Lemon, O.: Developing technology for Autism: an interdisciplinary approach. Pers. Ubiquit. Comput. **16**(2), 117–127 (2012). doi:10.1007/s00779-011-0384-2

Queirós, A., Cerqueira, M., Martins, A.I., Silva, A.G., Alvarelhão, J., Teixeira, A., Rocha, N.P.: ICF inspired personas to improve development for usability and accessibility in Ambient Assisted Living. Procedia Comput. Sci. **27**, 409–418 (2013). doi:10.1016/j.procs.2014.02.045

Reis, R., Teixeira, A.: Morphosyntactic analysis of language in children with autism spectrum disorder. In: Caseli, H., Villavicencio, A., Teixeira, A., Perdigão, F. (eds.) PROPOR 2012. LNCS, vol. 7243, pp. 35–45. Springer, Heidelberg (2012)

Vieira, D.: Enhanced multimodal interaction framework and applications. Dep. of Electronics, Telecommunications and Informatics, MSc thesis, Univesity of Aveiro (2015)

Vieira, D., Freitas, J.D., Acartürk, C., Teixeira, A., Sousa, L., Silva, S., Dias, M.S.: Read That Article: Exploring Synergies between Gaze and Speech Interaction, pp. 341–342 (2015). doi: 10.1145/2700648.2811369

Williams, P., Jamali, H.R., Nicholas, D.: Using ICT with people with special education needs: what the literature tells us. Aslib Proceeding (2006). doi:http://dx.doi.org/10.1108/00012530610687704

# Investigating the Use of Social Media Technologies by Adults with Autism Spectrum Disorder in Saudi Arabia

Alaa Mashat[✉], Mike Wald, and Sarah Parsons

University of Southampton, Southampton, UK
{a.mashat,mw,s.j.parsons}@soton.ac.uk

**Abstract.** People diagnosed with Autism spectrum disorder (ASD) face difficulties in everyday life with their communication and interaction skills. Previous studies have shown that the use of social networks could be used by people with ASD to help them build connections and overcome their difficulties with social skills. However, most autism intervention research has involved young children in Western cultures. In Arab countries, adults on the autism spectrum experience the same difficulties in addition to dealing with other issues, such as stigma within society, a lack of services, cultural rules and the inability to sufficiently benefit from existing technologies designed according to the culture and language of Western countries. This study focuses on exploring and observing the use of social media by people with ASD (high-functioning autism and Asperger syndrome) in Saudi Arabia. The aim of this research is to understand the role that technology plays in the lives of adults with ASD in Saudi Arabia, in order to make recommendations for research and practice. This research could also help future researchers to understand the needs and behaviours of Arab individuals with ASD towards social technologies, and it could be a leading research for the autism community in Arab countries.

**Keywords:** Social media · Technology · Accessibility · Usability · Communication · Social skills · Culture · Arabs · Adults · Autism

## 1   Introduction

Autism spectrum disorder (ASD) is a lifelong developmental disability. People with ASD face difficulties with social communication and interaction and restricted repetitive patterns of behaviour, interests or activities [1]. A high number of adults with ASD experience difficulties with face-to-face communication and may try to avoid social interaction and group activities [2]. By working on finding ways to support communication in more comfortable and less threatening ways, people with ASD may have a better chance to be employed, be in a relationship, have friends, increase independence, have a better life and be part of the community [3].

---

The original version of this chapter was revised: In Table 1 on page 229 of the original version of the paper the last 5 rows were missing. The erratum to this chapter is available at 10.1007/978-3-319-40238-3_62

© Springer International Publishing Switzerland 2016
M. Antona and C. Stephanidis (Eds.): UAHCI 2016, Part III, LNCS 9739, pp. 224–236, 2016.
DOI: 10.1007/978-3-319-40238-3_22

It has been claimed that computer-mediated communication (CMC), such as emails, blogs, online social networks and text messaging, for social support are ideal methods for individuals with ASD because they provide the user with some control over the conversation as well as more processing time [3, 4]. However, adults on the autism spectrum receive much less research attention compared to children, and most autism intervention research has involved young children mostly in Western cultures [5, 6]. Consequently, there is very little research regarding the experiences and preferences of adults with ASD regarding technology use, and almost no research about this topic in non-Western countries.

In addition, people with ASD have difficulties understanding unwritten social rules and cues in their daily lives [2, 7]. Several studies have shown a positive impact of social technologies on individuals with ASD within the Western culture [8], however, Arabic cultures have a different set of beliefs and social, religious, moral and political rules and restrictions that are carried from the lives of people offline to the online world and could affect the behaviour of such users when using an online system [9, 10]. In Arab countries, less research generally has been carried out regarding ASD [11], and research focusing on the use of social networks by people with ASD who are Arabs and who live within the Arabic culture has not been investigated before. These issues demonstrate the importance of implementing a study considering investigating the role of technology in the lives of people with ASD in Arab countries. This study will discuss the use of social media by the participants, how and why they are using different social networks, what challenges they are facing in regards to their culture or their social skills, and what benefits they feel the social networking sites bring to them.

## 2   Related Work

**Social Media for ASD.** Social networking sites (SNS) have been very popular in the past few years, and a large number of people are connecting via these networks, with around 29 % active users of the world's population in 2015 [12]. These communication technologies can have a potential impact on people's communication, socialising and learning [13]; it is a type of human-human interaction rather than just a computer-human interaction [14]. Social networks provide users with the ability to connect and socialise without the pressure of time and immediacy that they face in real-life social situations. It has also been reported by [15] that adults and adolescents who are not confident socially prefer to communicate online because they feel more comfortable and less shy than when communicating face-to-face, as stated in [8]. Also, according to several studies, communicating via online social media has been beneficial for socially anxious individuals, providing the ability to increase the quality of friendships, enhance engagement and decrease loneliness, which raised the issue that social media could be relevant and well-suited for adults with ASD as well [8].

Recognising these potential benefits, some social networks have been designed for people with ASD and their caregivers for sharing information, improving their awareness and capacity to communicate in a safe space, such as MyAutismTeam by [16] and Squag by Sara Winter [17]. However, these social networks are specially designed for children and do not focus on improving their ability to connect, socialise and be independent. Supportive Eyes, or Miradas de Apoyo is a social network that enables users to organise groups to provide support for any individual who needs it, such as someone with ASD [18]. In 2014, a social network "Connect" was created by Autism West Midlands. The social network is a supportive network, which was designed to help people with autism in the UK and their families to meet new people and find friends [19].

Other studies have used social networks to help individuals with ASD build independence. A study by [20] considered the use of a supportive social network aiming to provide young adults and adolescents with Asperger syndrome with the opportunity to gain support from a group of family and friends instead of over-relying on one caregiver. The idea was to use circles (a feature in social networks that brings together a group of people interested in a particular topic or people with a common social connection) to seek information and advice and to build independence [20]. In addition, another study integrated a supportive social network into a mirror implemented by the Graphics, Visualization & Usability Centre in Georgia. The design is called the SocialMirror; the aim was to help adults with ASD to be more independent by providing them on-demand support and to learn daily life skills, based on an idea similar to prompting systems [21]. These two projects used private social networks and involved family and friends to provide support for the individuals with ASD. Parental communication and their involvement in online activities of persons with ASD showed that it could reduce the effect of cyber victimisation and provide higher levels of self-esteem [22, 23].

Independence and autonomy are important for an individual with a disability, but the concept differs between cultures [24]. In most Arab countries, the culture prevents single individuals from moving out of their family homes unless there are specific reasons, so the chance of moving out is less than in other countries, especially for women [25]. Although this is a dated reference now, this situation still remains the case in Saudi Arabia. Therefore, technologies that seek to promote autonomy and independence developed in Western countries may be of much less relevance to people with ASD in Arab countries.

People with ASD tend to have less understanding of sexual behaviours, lack judgment, are socially naive and have difficulties with social awareness [26]. In addition, it was found that people with intellectual disabilities could be more vulnerable socially then others [27]. For example, in Arab countries some female users are strict about using their real names, adding their photos or adding videos of themselves in general online social networks [28]. They could use nicknames or drop their last name, and add comic or other type of images as their profile photo on Facebook to cope with the restrictions they could face [29]. This could increase the chance of being tricked by people with fake identities. For Arab users with ASD, conservatism and privacy could be one of the factors that affect the use of social networking technologies. It could cause ambiguity in online dating, chats or any other type of online social networks.

In addition, in regards to communicating and building friendships, in some Arab countries, the situation is more difficult with more cultural communication restrictions, as communicating with the opposite gender is already an issue with many people [30]. Also, awareness of ASD in these countries is limited [31], and families are more likely to hide their diagnosed children to prevent themselves from feeling shame and to protect themselves from harsh societal judgments, which could increase the social isolation of people with ASD [32]. However, the use of such social networks by adults with ASD may have a different implication as they are less aware of the social restriction and social cues [7], and yet this has not previously been explored in research. Therefore, this current research focuses on finding out what technology devices adult Arabs with ASD are using, how they are using social networks and for what, nature of their online relationships and communication, and the effect of online social networks on their lives.

**Technologies for ASD in Arab Countries.** In regards to Arab adults with ASD and the use of social networks, no Arabic social networks specifically designed for people with ASD exist, nor do any support the Arabic language. Although adults with ASD can use the more popular social networks, such as Facebook, Twitter and MySpace, the use of social networks has not been studied for Arabs with ASD.

Only a few studies regarding the use of technology among people with ASD in Arab countries were found in a literature search. A study [33] was conducted a study on the development of a multimedia environment for teaching vocalisation to children with autism. The goal of the project was to help the children with their communication skills [33]. However, it has been reported that the development of the system is still in process and has not been completed. In [34] a portable and configurable augmentative and alternative communication (AAC) tool for Arabic-speaking users called "Touch-to-Speak", which was aimed to support people with speech and language impairments in carrying out their daily conversations was introduced. It works by translating a series of pictures into well-structured Arabic sentences; it supports Modern Standard Arabic (MSA), in addition to various local Arabic dialects. However, the target users of the tool are children with ASD and elderly people following a stroke, so it may not be very useful for adults with high-functioning autism or Asperger syndrome. In addition, a study of an Arabic app called "Talk the Talk", designed by Fatani and Mashat for teaching conversational skills to children with ASD, was reported in the Al-Watan online newspaper as the first Arabic app in this field [35]. The implementation of the app has not been yet completed; therefore it is not evaluated or reported in a peer-reviewed literature.

However, other AAC applications such as "Tap to Talk" and "LetMeTalk" are available in Arabic language, but are mainly designed for children [36, 37]. Consequently, there remains a substantial gap in knowledge with regard to whether and how adult Arabs with ASD are using online social networks in their daily lives.

## 3    Research Method

People with ASD are not all the same, and there is limited information about the people with ASD in Saudi Arabia. In order to seek in depth information about the participants, face-to-face interviews were implemented.

Reaching individuals with ASD and recruiting them for the study was extremely challenging. This could be because in Arab countries individuals with ASD might be hidden, not diagnosed or do not admit the disability [32]. Nevertheless, participants were eventually reached via 'snowballing' or 'chain sampling' techniques [38], in addition to an online recruitment survey addressed to the caregivers. In total, 13 adults/adolescents with ASD in Saudi Arabia have been interviewed.

The interview was focused on investigating the use of social networks by adults with ASD and exploring the impact of cultural factors, on their usability and sociability of social media. These factors were identified previously as a "Framework for Autistic Arab's Social Communication and Interaction Technology" FAASCIT) [39], suggesting that these factors might have an influence on Arab users when it comes to using social media technologies. Some of the factors are cultural or tradition factors, related to the people themselves or to the social rules in Arab countries, and other factors could be considered as technical such as language, Internet access, gender differences, photographs, communication with the opposite gender, privacy, conservatism, autonomy, relationships and music.

The structure of the interview was designed in different sections, and the questions were semi-structured. For example, participants were asked some personal questions such as their age, occupation, what devices they own and what social media applications they use. They were also asked to connect to the Internet and to open a social network they are using, in order to observe their ability of accessing their own social networks' accounts. In addition, questions were asked about the language they prefer using, the information they display online, the number of friends they follow or have, their communication with family and friends and the main things they do on social networks. Also, participants were asked to read some sentences in English and also sentences written in Arabizi, which is Arabic language written with Latin letters [40]. The questions were in general directed for the participants, but the caregivers could be involved during the interview also.

Ten of the participants were males and three were female, all from Saudi Arabia: two from Al-Hasa, three from Makkah and eight from Jeddah, all of whom are known to be diagnosed with ASD. One participant from Riyadh initially agreed to take part but withdrew before the interview. The participants are coded with (P1, P2...Pb13), where P1, P2, P3 and P4 are the eligible participants who were reached from the online survey, and Pbn, n(5-13) are the participants who were reached during the interview stage by personal contacts. The interviews were audio recorded and were all conducted in Arabic apart from the interview with Pb10, which was conducted in English. Information collected from the participants are saved securely and all data are anonymised.

## 4   Findings

The study initially aimed to include participants with high-functioning autism or Asperger syndrome, however, due to the recruitment difficulties not all participants were high functioning. Due to the differences in the level of functioning, only seven of the participants (P1, P2, P3, P4, Pb5, Pb10 and Pb13) were able to contribute during the interview, one of whom was female, see Table 1. The other participants had less advanced verbal abilities, and the caregivers were interviewed instead. However, P2, P3, P4, Pb5, Pb10 and Pb13 were the participants who were using social media. Currently, P1, P3 and Pb5 are working, P2 is going to college, and P4, Pb10 and Pb13 are attending mainstream schools. Pb7, Pb9 and Pb12 still go to autism centres, whereas Pb6, Pb8 and Pb11 had to stop attending the centre at a certain age and now are staying at home.

**Table 1.** Participants' uses of social media

| Participant | Gender | Age | Devices | Used SN | Created SN for the study |
|---|---|---|---|---|---|
| P1 | Male | 30 | Ipad (shared with his sister) | None | Instagram |
| P2 | Male | 23 | Smartphone ipad PC Laptop | WhatsApp, (Facebook and Twitter, could not access it) | Instagram |
| P3 | Male | 22 | Smartphone Galaxy 5S laptop (broken) | WhatsApp, Snapchat | Instagram |
| P4 | Male | 19 | iphone 5S | WhatsApp, Snapchat, Instagram Facebook, Twitter, Keek, Path, BB messenger | None |
| Pb5 | Male | 23 | ipad 2 | WhatsApp | None |
| Pb6 | Male | 16 | ipod | None | None |
| Pb7 | Male | 25 | Galaxy smartphone and uses his sister's iphone 6 | None | None |
| Pb8 | Female | 19 | ipad 2 | None | None |
| Pb9 | Female | 15 | Does not have her own device | None | None |
| Pb10 | Female | 15 | xbox, playstation3, playstation4, ipod, iphone, wii, wii U, PC, laptop, Graphic drawing tablet | YouTube, Tumbler | None |
| Pb11 | Male | 28 | Samsung Galaxy smartphone, Toshiba Laptop | None | Instagram |
| Pb12 | Male | 15 | Does not have his own device | None | None |
| Pb13 | Male | 18 | Lenovo Smartphone, Tablet (being repaired) | WhatsApp, (Instagram and Facebook, could not access it) | None |

**The Use of Social Media.** In regards to the six participants who used social media (P2, P3, P4, Pb5, Pb10 and Pb13), P2 said he has a Facebook account, but he prefers using Twitter. He could not access Facebook as he could not remember his username and password. His mother did not know about the Facebook account and she said he might have created an account lately. He opened his Twitter account, but then it appeared that the Twitter account was not his account, but rather his sister's account, which was opened on his ipad. He uses WhatsApp for chatting (with his family and uncles), and has a family group of 5 people who are his close family. He chats with his friends with direct messages on WhatsApp for college work. His mother said only the people who might have a good influence on him or add some useful knowledge to him are the people who are allowed to chat with him. She does not want him to waste time with people on WhatsApp or chat with people who might tease him or make jokes out of his mistakes. She was asked to create an Instagram account for him in order to be able to watch his activities and interactions. She created the account for him but he has not been using it.

P3 is using WhatsApp and Snapchat. After having Instagram and Facebook explained to him, he was asked if he would like to create a Facebook account but he said "no". He agreed to create an Instagram account. After he had created it, he got excited and asked to create a Facebook account. The Internet connection was not good enough and he had to go upstairs every time he needed to download something. He could not download Facebook and he became disappointed and did not want to do it. He was happy to use the Instagram account, but has only used it on the day of the interview when he created it and a few times afterwards with limited activities.

P4 uses Facebook, Instagram, Snapchat, Keek, Blackberry messenger, Twitter and Path. He uses Instagram, Snapchat and Path the most. He is active and has lots of online friends. He uses Snapchat to post comedy snaps for entertaining people.

Pb5 was interviewed with his teacher at the centre. He uses WhatsApp daily and chats with his family and friends. With regard to creating an Instagram account for him, he had to ask his parents before setting up an account, and he does not yet have an email address. He was asked to get permission from his mother, but he did not ask and the teacher has not responded in this regard. He has been active on WhatsApp and is sending photos, mainly photos of money notes.

Pb10 has a channel on YouTube and she posts videos about her awkward life, as she says, and she is a new user on Tumblr. Watching the number of people who have viewed her videos or subscribed to her YouTube channel makes her excited. She likes drawing comics, and she started posting them on her blog. When she was asked about Facebook she said, "No, I don't like Facebook. I am more like a video fun person, Tumblr person". When she was asked about Instagram she said "I am not a cliché of the generation". Then she said she does not like Facebook because her spelling is not good and she is kind of dyslexic.

Pb13 has both Facebook and Instagram accounts. He only uses his smartphone at weekends. He could not remember the usernames for his accounts. On Facebook his account could not be found even with the given name and profile picture, and with the help of his caregivers, which could be a result of the privacy settings. The Instagram account was found once, after a while the account was not there anymore.

On the other hand, P1 has good verbal abilities, but he needs to be directed and taught how to use social networks. P11 has less verbal abilities, but his mother tried to help him and created an Instagram account for him. Instagram was chosen as it appeared to be preferred over Facebook, and it requires less information and steps for setting up an account and less functionality.

The other participants who are lower-functioning Pb6, Pb7, Pb8, Pb9 and Pb12 mainly watch YouTube cartoon songs, and tended to use fewer educational apps. This could also be due to the lack of Arabic applications and programs for people with ASD, but even the available Arabic apps such as "Talk to Talk" and "Touch to Speak" are not being used by these participants.

**Friendship and Family Relations.** Participants were asked about their friendships and relationships with others, in order to have an overview of how they communicate with their friends, and whether or not they have friends offline, and if they have any online contact with family and friends. In regards to P1, he does not use any online social networks, so he did not have any online communication, however, during the interview he was searching on Google and said he is looking for a girl to play with. He said, "I want a girl".

P2 has friends on Facebook, he mentioned only male names. He said he has three friends on Facebook who are his friends from college. However, his mother and siblings are not friends with him on Facebook, as he mentioned. WhatsApp is used by the family more than other social media application, he have a family group on WhatsApp consisting of five members who are his parents and siblings, he also have contact with his uncles and his friends from college on WhatsApp in a private chat, but no contact with his cousins online.

P3 uses Snapchat to contact people by sending photos to them; he has about 50 contacts on Snapchat mainly his relatives, and he does not have any concerns about contacting his female relatives. He has only two of his friends on Snapchat, and he said he speaks with his friends when he meets them in person and not via Snapchat. On WhatsApp he also contact his family and relatives, he has WhatsApp chatting groups with his aunts from both of his parents sides.

P4 has 160 friends on Facebook, which he said they are relatives and friends, and on Instagram he has 1380 followers and is following 2301 people. He also has friends at school, but he said he only has one friend out of school. However, he might not know the people in the entire list in person, but he is communicating with his friends via social networks, mainly Instagram and Snapchat.

Participant Pb5 is working at the centre, which he used to go to. He still has his friends there and also he is still in contact with his old friends. He chats on WhatsApp with his cousins, and also with his friend P3, who was at the same centre he attended.

Pb10 is in a mainstream school, and she only has one friend at school, she talks with her in English. If she wants to speak with her out of school she just makes a normal phone call. She does not use any chatting social networks.

Pb13 is also at a mainstream school but he is in the class with only five other students. His stepbrother is also his friend and is always helping him at home. In the interview, he said he would like to have Skype to call his friend, who was his previous bus driver.

The participants who used social media were asked to be added by the researcher for online communication. None of the participants rejected, but only P3, P4, Pb5 have been staying in contact, and P3 with only limited communication. P1 has been followed on his new created Instagram account, but he does not know how to access it. P2 used a Twitter account to be in contact, which is his sister's account. He also created an

Instagram account, which he never used. Participant Pb10 has been contacted via Tumbler, but she does not reply as she has started using it recently and might not be accessing it regularly. Whereas, Facebook and Instagram accounts for Pb13 were provided by the caregivers after the interview, but neither could be reached or found.

**Cultural Differences in Technology Use.** Cultural differences could appear in some particular situations, and also it could be different for different users. One of the main cultural aspects is language, limited English abilities had appeared for example, when asking P2 to sign in to his Facebook account, he entered "hotmel" instead of "hotmail", this could prevent him from accessing his account, however, he had problems remembering his password and also accessing his email. Another example is with one of the caregivers, she is making her daughter learn from an app, which is in Spanish, when asking her "It is in Spanish, she said not its English". However, the app has Portuguese, Spanish and English versions, but she was not using the English one.

In regards to the difficulties in understanding a different culture, one situation appeared when using an application game about the UK political system by participant Pb10, she could not understand the meaning of several words and when she was trying to play the game, she was asking about everything. She is more fluent in English than in Arabic, but she still could not understand the system. She also said that her mother does not know English well enough to help her understand the difficult words.

Another aspect is the conservatism of presenting personal photos of female online, which appeared not to be an issue for the female participant Pb10, as she was posting videos of herself on YouTube and talking about her life. In addition, the caregiver of Pb8 suggested taking a picture of her daughter if it was needed. On the other hand, P1 was more conservative and he does not post any photos of himself online. However, more cultural exploration and mapping the collected data from the interviews to the factors identified in FAASCIT [39] will be discussed in a future paper to examine these cultural factors in more detail.

## 5 Discussion

From the interviewed participants, it has been shown that the use of social networks differs from one participant to the other, and generalization of experiences would be difficult to make. Each participant has his/her own way of using social networks, and also they all had different educational opportunities, and experienced different situations in their lives. While such variability may be expected, and typical, these insights into individual lives, and uses of technologies, by adult Arabs with ASD are very rare in the literature and thus contribute new knowledge about this largely invisible group in Saudi Arabia.

As mentioned earlier, building independence for adults with ASD is important. However, the participants in our study still required support, P2, Pb13 had difficulties connecting to the Internet and accessing their online accounts, P3 and Pb10 keep their account details saved, but they also needed assistance when they forgot their account log in details. Pb5 needs to get permission from his mother for creating an account online. In addition, some caregivers watch the online activities and use of social media by the participants, such as the mother of P2 which checks what YouTube videos her son watches, and also makes control of the people her son can chat with on WhatsApp. However, P2 had a Facebook account created by the help of one of his siblings, which his mother did not know about before the interview. This could be argued that the mother is trying to protect her son, and making sure he is in a safe space to prevent him from any vulnerability, but not over controlling him. Additionally, P1 does not has his own device, sharing his sister's device or using his teacher's device might always restrict his independency and also restricts him from using social networks.

P4 and Pb10 were the most active users on social networks. P4 uses Snapchat for posting comedy videos, and uses Instagram to post photos of himself and his drawings. Pb10 uses Tumbler to post her comics, and YouTube for uploading videos of herself talking about her life. They both have a target, which could be a reason for why they are more interested in the use of social networks. In this study, Pb10 usage of social media showed that gender differences was not a factor for her in relation to her use of social media, though this is an aspect that requires further investigation with more participants.

Pb10 was asked about her time spent on the Internet, she replied: "daily, I don't have anything else better to do". However, Pb10 do not have online connections with her friends, she feels lonely but also does not like using Facebook or chatting with people online, because she is not comfortable with her spelling. Pb10's case does not support the claim that adults and adolescents could be more comfortable with online commu-nications as they have less pressure than face-to-face communication [8]. However, Pb5 uses WhatsApp to stay in touch with his old friends, teachers and family members, so the quality of friendship is enhanced by his use of social media. Building friendships and communicating with new people could also be possible as P4 has around 1380 followers on Instagram and is following 2301 other accounts.

The mother of P2 was the one who is more conservative about proving his full name on the written forms and online, and only wrote his first and middle names. This was more of a result of being conservative about the family name and reputation. However, all of the caregivers of the interviewed participants were relaxed and talked openly regarding the diagnosis of autism. Though, the caregiver of Pb11 said that sometimes people in public do not respect a person with a disability, and that she had some bad experiences with people offending her son, which made her decide to isolate herself and her son from many people.

In addition, having proper support from the family, and better educational experi-ences could have an impact on their social skills and digital literacy and correspondingly in their abilities of using social media. For example, P4, Pb10 and Pb13 are all attending mainstream schools, however, Pb13 is not receiving proper education as claimed by his caregivers, instead of integrating him with the typical developing students who are at the same age and level, they isolated all students with different special needs in one class. The caregivers were not happy with the quality of education provided, as their son is not learning from school. This resulted in his limited language abilities, but there are not many options in their city.

However, some limitations of this study is that the findings were according to what has appeared during the interviews, or what have been told by the participants or their caregivers. There could be more situations facing the participants, which will require more time spent with the participants and more family support, to be investigated. In addition, the findings were regarding the participants who could be reached and who their family agreed to participate.

## 6 Conclusion

Previous studies showed that the majority of social skills technologies for people with ASD have been developed for children and mainly in Western countries, and limited research is implemented regarding ASD in Arab countries. From detailed interviews and observations with six high-functioning participants with ASD, this research has documented much individual variability in skills, awareness and autonomy with regard to social media use. Results showed that different high-functioning participants use social networks for different reasons, such as chatting, posting videos and photographs or for educational reasons. For some participants, the use of social media showed the ability to enhance friendship relations and communication with people. However, there was some evidence that conservatism in using social networks by the participants was related to the caregiver's beliefs and restrictions, highlighting the relative interdependency between individual use and wider family context. How such rules and beliefs operate within families, and influence social media use, remains an important and interesting focus for future study.

## References

1. American Psychiatric Association. The Diagnostic and Statistical Manual of Mental Disorders: DSM 5: bookpointUS (2013)
2. Burke, M., Kraut, R., Williams, D.: social use of computer-mediated communication by adults on the Autism spectrum. In: ACM Conference on Computer Supported Cooperative Work (2010)
3. Grandin, T., Attwood, T.: Different not less: inspiring stories of achievement and successful employment from adults with Autism, Asperger's, and ADHD. Future Horizons Incorporated (2012)
4. Brosnan, M., Gavin, J.: How technology is used by people with Autism Spectrum Disorder (ASD). How those with ASD thrive in online cultures but suffer in offline cultures. In: Rosen, L. (ed.) The Handbook of Psychology, Technology and Society. Wiley Blackwell, Hoboken (2015)
5. Edwards, T.L., Watkins, E.E., Lotfizadeh, A.D., Poling, A.: Intervention research to benefit people with Autism: how old are the participants? Res. Autism Spectrum Disord. 6(3), 996–999 (2012)
6. Parsons, S., Guldberg, K., MacLeod, A., Jones, G., Prunty, A., Balfe, T.: International review of the literature of evidence of best practice provision in the education of persons with autistic spectrum disorders (2009). Research Reports No 2
7. Bishop, J.: The internet for educating individuals with social impairments. J. Comput. Assist. Learn. 19(4), 546–556 (2003). doi:10.1046/j.0266-4909.2003.00057.x
8. Mazurek, M.O.: Social media use among adults with autism spectrum disorders. Comput. Hum. Behav. 29(4), 1709–1714 (2013)

9. Askool, S.S.: The use of social media in Arab Countries: a case of Saudi Arabia. In: Cordeiro, J., Krempels, K.-H. (eds.) WEBIST 2012. LNBIP, vol. 140, pp. 201–219. Springer, Heidelberg (2013)
10. Omoush, A., Saleh, K., Yaseen, S.G., Alma'aitah, M.A.: The impact of Arab cultural values on online social networking. the case of facebook. Comput. Hum. Behav. **28**(6), 2387–2399 (2012)
11. Amr, M., Raddad, D., El-Mehesh, F., Mahmoud, E.-H., El-Gilany, A.-H.: Sex differences in Arab children with Autism spectrum disorders. Res. Autism Spectrum Disord. **5**(4), 1343–1350 (2011). doi:10.1016/j.rasd.2011.01.015
12. Kemp, S.: Digital, Social & Mobile Worldwide in 2015. We Are Social (2015). http://wearesocial.com/uk/special-reports/digital-social-mobile-worldwide-2015. (Accessed on 22 Jan 2016)
13. Veltri, N.F., Elgarah, W.: The role of national cultural differences in user adoption of social networking. Paper presented at the Southern Association for Information Systems Conference, Charleston (2009)
14. Spolsky, J.: It's Not Just Usability. Joel on Software (2004). http://www.joelonsoftware.com/articles/NotJustUsability.html. (Accessed on 10 Feb 2016)
15. Goby, V.P.: Personality and online/offline choices: MBTI profiles and favored communication modes in a Singapore study. CyberPsychol. Behav. **9**(1), 5–13 (2006)
16. Rochman, B.: MyAutismTeam: a new site for families with Autism. TIME.com (2011). http://healthland.time.com/2011/12/08/myautismteam-for-parents-of-kids-with-autism-new-site-offers-advice-and-emotional-support/. (Accessed on 10 Feb 2016)
17. Winter, S.: The story of Squag. MaRS (2012). http://www.marsdd.com/2012/08/02/the-story-of-squag/. (Accessed on 10 Feb 2016)
18. Supportive Eyes. https://www.miradasdeapoyo.org/acierta/ChangeLocale.do?language=en&country=US&page=/loggined.do. (Accessed on 10 Feb 2016)
19. Francis, S., Begley, J.: Connect: creative social networking for the UK Autism community. Paper presented at the 2nd international conference on Innovative Technologies (IT) for Autism (ASD), Paris (2014)
20. Hong, H., Yarosh, S., Kim, J.G., Abowd, G.D., Arriaga, R.I.: Investigating the use of circles in social networks to support independence of individuals with autism. Paper presented at the Proceedings of the SIGCHI Conference on Human Factors in Computing Systems (2013)
21. Hong, H., Kim, J.G., Abowd, G.D., Arriaga, R.I.: Designing a social network to support the independence of young adults with Autism. Paper presented at the Proceedings of the ACM 2012 conference on Computer Supported Cooperative Work (2012)
22. Kowalski, R.M., Morgan, C.A., Drake-Lavelle, K., Allison, B.: Cyberbullying among college students with disabilities. Comput. Hum. Behav. **57**, 416–427 (2016)
23. Özdemir, Y.: Cyber victimization and adolescent self-esteem: The role of communication with parents. Asian J. Soc. Psychol. **17**(4), 255–263 (2014)
24. Robertson, C.: Autonomy and identity: the need for new dialogues in education and welfare. Support Learn. **16**(3), 122–127 (2003)
25. Boyd, M.: Ethnic variations in young adults living at home. Canadian studies in Population **27**(1), 135–158 (1944)
26. Mehzabin, P., Stokes, M.A.: Self-assessed sexuality in young adults with high-functioning Autism. Res. Autism Spectrum Disord. **5**(1), 614–621 (2011). doi:10.1016/j.rasd.2010.07.006
27. Lough, E., Flynn, E., Riby, D.M.: Mapping real-world to online vulnerability in young people with developmental disorders: illustrations from Autism and Williams Syndrome. Rev. J. Autism Dev. Disord. **2**(1), 1–7 (2014)
28. Al-Jarf, R.S.: Connecting students across universities in Saudi Arabia (2005)

29. Al-Awsat, A.: 68 percent of saudi girls drop last name on facebook (2010). http://english.aawsat.com/2010/01/article55252114/68-percent-of-saudi-girls-drop-last-name-on-facebook. (Accessed on 11 Feb 2016)
30. Alsheikh, T., Lindley, S.E., Rode, J.A.: Understanding Online Communication through Arab Eyes. Paper presented at the CHI 2010, 10–15 April 2010, Atlanta (2010)
31. Essa, M.M., Guillemin, G.J., Waly, M.I., Al-Sharbati, M.M., Al-Farsi, Y.M., Hakkim, F.L., Ali, A., Al-Shafaee, M.S.: Increased markers of oxidative stress in autistic children of the Sultanate of Oman. Biol. Trace Elem. Res. 147(1–3), 25–27 (2012). doi:10.1007/s12011-011-9280-x
32. Nasr, O.: Autism in the Middle East. Anderson Cooper 360°, CNN. http://ac360.blogs.cnn.com/2008/04/02/autism-in-the-middle-east/. (Accessed on 11 Feb 2016)
33. Al-Wabil, A., Al-Shabanat, H., Al-Sarrani, R., Al-Khonin, M.: Developing a multimedia environment to aid in vocalization for people on the autism spectrum: a user-centered design approach. ICCHP 2010. LNCS, pp. 33–36. Springer, Heidelberg (2010)
34. Al-Arifi, B., Al-Rubaian, A., Al-Ofisan, G., Al-Romi, N., Al-Wabil, A.: Towards an arabic language augmentative and alternative communication application for autism. In: Marcus, A. (ed.) DUXU 2013. LNCS, vol. 8013, pp. 333–341. Springer, Heidelberg (2013)
35. Al-Ghamdi, F.: Two Students Design the First Rehabilitation Application for Autistic Children. Al-Watan (2014). http://www.alwatan.com.sa/nation/News_Detail.aspx?ArticleID=174185&CategoryID=3. (Accessed on 11 Feb 2016)
36. Al-Wakeel, L., Al-Ghanim, A., Al-Zeer, S., Al-Nafjan, K.: A usability evaluation of Arabic mobile applications designed for children with special needs—Autism. Lecture Notes Soft. Eng. 3(3), 203 (2015)
37. Let Me Talk. http://www.letmetalk.info/ar. (Accessed on 11 Feb 2016)
38. Patton, M.Q.: Qualitative Evaluation and Research Methods. SAGE Publications Inc., Beverly Hills (1990)
39. Mashat, A., Wald, M., Parsons, S.: The role of photos in social media interactions of adult Arabs with Autism spectrum disorder. In: 9th International Technology, Education and Development Conference, Madrid, 2–4 March 2015
40. Darwish, K.: Arabizi detection and conversion to Arabic (2013). arXiv preprint arXiv:1306.6755

# Development of Assessment Tool Judging Autism by Ocular Movement Measurement

Ippei Torii$^{(\boxtimes)}$, Kaoruko Ohtani, Takahito Niwa, and Naohiro Ishii

Department of Information Science, Aichi Institute of Technology, Aichi, Japan
{mac,b15724bb,ishii}@aitech.ac.jp, ruko2011@gmail.com

**Abstract.** In this study, the development of the objectivity index for the diagnosis of the children who has Kanner syndrome with a lack of the communication ability and an evaluation of the curative effect using the ocular movement measurement is discussed. In past study, we developed communication applications "Eye Talk" and "Eye Tell" for people who have difficulty in conversation and writing such as children with physical disability, ALS patients or elderlies using the blink determination system. The team of Dr. Kitazawa in Graduate School of Frontier Biosciences in Osaka University performed the clinical application to distinguish Kanner syndrome group by measuring "where and when" he/she looks at using Tobii eye tracker. Our study is a judgment by the ocular movement measurement. We developed the image processing technique by afterimage used in the blink determination. First the eye area is captured by a front camera of laptop PC. Second, we extracted the pixels of pupils with 30–40 fps of accuracy and digitized eyeball movements. We converted the difference in eyeball movements between the right and left eyes into a graph and define it in multidimensional measure. We measured the amount of the degree that the eyes of the subject run off the track based on the afterimage, then added up the amount of change of right and left eyes and showed the total. After we corrected data, we set the identification border with density function of the distribution, cumulative frequency function, and ROC curve. With this, we established an objective index to determine Kanner syndrome, normal, false positive, and false negative. Furthermore, after analyzing the data in a two-dimensional coordinate, difference between autistic group and typical developmental group became clear. There were few differences in children who are on the border line between autistic and non-autistic comparing with typical developmental children when we validated with the fixation. However, the identification border could be detected definitely in pursuit.

It was revealed that this inspection technique to capture eyeball movements by afterimage could detect disorders of sociability clearly and easily. In many educational institutions, this method can be used to evaluate learning and curative effects in future.

**Keywords:** Oculomotor · Autism · Kanner syndrome · ROC curve · Afterimage

© Springer International Publishing Switzerland 2016
M. Antona and C. Stephanidis (Eds.): UAHCI 2016, Part III, LNCS 9739, pp. 237–248, 2016.
DOI: 10.1007/978-3-319-40238-3_23

# 1 Introduction

This paper shows the development an assessment tool to diagnose Kanner syndrome by the measurement of eyeball movements.

Kanner syndrome is a developmental disability of communication and the social nature. The number of patients have been increasing, but the basic mechanism of the onset is not yet elucidated and effective cures or precautionary measures are not established [1–4]. In Japan, it is reported that approximately 10 % of boys and 4–5 % of girls in primary schools are considered to have some developmental disabilities. Act on Support for Persons with Developmental Disabilities is passed in 2003, and the special support education to children with disabilities is started in 2006. [5, 6] Also, the body of laws and administrative frameworks are maintained. Based on such background, an assessment tool to evaluate not only intellectual abilities and the individual developmental characteristic but also the adaptive behavior or the ability that is necessary to live in society are demanded with medical and welfare institutions to adopt to a real daily life. In addition, it is necessary to support children with developmental disabilities on a long-term basis from infants to adults. To detect and respond to disabilities in early stage, the assessment tool which everyone can give diagnoses is needed.

# 2 Purpose of the Study

In past study, we developed communication applications "Eye Talk" and "Eye Tell" for people who have difficulty in conversation and writing such as children with physical disability, ALS patients or elderlies using the blink determination system. These applications receive strong supports from not only special support schools in Japan but also some researchers in foreign countries [7–9].

Then we developed the image processing technique by afterimage used in the blink determination. First the eye area is captured by a front camera of laptop PC.

Even when a person gazes at one point and his/her eyeballs always stay fixed at that point, their eyes perform subtle fixating movements (i.e. tremors, drifting, microsaccades) to keep the retinal image clear. Particularly, the microsaccades link with nerves and reflect the mechanism that process sight in a brain. We converted the differences between these movements into numbers.

The process of the conversion is as followed:

(1) Select the pixel indicating the subject's pupil from images of captured frames.
(2) Set up a reference image, known as an afterimage, from the pixel indicating the subject's pupil.
(3) Divide the pupil of the subject into four from the center in the acquired frame image.
(4) Select the pixel in each divided part and count the number of the pixels of the overlapping part with the present pixel based on the afterimage.
(5) Process the images with precision in 30–40 fps from a camera and convert the amount of change in the pixels of the movements of the right and left eyeballs in to numbers.

Then the pixels of pupils were extracted with 30–40 fps of accuracy and eyeball movements were digitized.

We converted the sequence of eyeball movements into a graph and define it in multidimensional measure. Then we set the identification border with density function of the distribution, cumulative frequency function, and ROC curve. With this, we established the objective index to determine Kanner syndrome, normal, false positive, and false negative. With this method, we developed the objective evaluation indicator to judge non-autistic and autistic people more clearly in early stage.

By this new assessment, the degree of disabilities and the needed supports become clear. In addition, more accurate and suitable supports can be offered to each children who has Kanner syndrome by considering the intelligence level or the degree of development. The additional evaluations including the possibility to jobs are enabled by grasping a merger of the mental disabilities and the psychoneurotic merger (Fig. 1).

**Fig. 1.** Acquisition of the blurring of gaze of the eyes of children who has Kanner syndrome

## 3   Structure of the System

### 3.1   Definition of Afterimage and Digitizing Oculomotor Change

The difference in the area of the amount of change occurs by measuring the difference between the afterimage in consecutive frames and the present frame. We set the amount of change to the quantity of the eyeball movements. This method made it possible to detect a change of the eyeball movements in numerical value. We compared the difference in these movements between non-autistc and autistic people and analyzed the result.

The definition of the afterimage and the detection process are as follows.

When the area (C, Fig. 2) that is overlapping part of the afterimage of iris (A, Fig. 2) and the current iris situation (B, Fig. 2) is diminishing rapidly comparing from a few frames before, we determine it as closing of the eyes. It is possible to exclude a slow change and capture a rapid change. By using the afterimage, the number of past frames to compare increases and we can capture changes with high accuracy. As a result, we can quantify the changes of series of movements "eye-opening → eye-closing → eye-opening". And it is possible to determine the blinks as short blinks, long blinks, or closing the eyes continuously, except the malfunction due to fine movement of eyes. Figure 2 shows determination by afterimages visually. A is the afterimage to be compared, B is the iris in current frame, and C is the overlapped area of the afterimage and current frame.

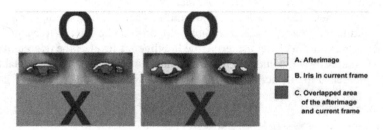

**Fig. 2.** Detection of Unconcious Blink by Afterimages, Visually

Figure 3 is an illustration indicating the states to judge opening and closing of eyes. Since it is difficult for a subject with weak muscular strength to close his/her eyes perfectly, it may be with a halfshut blink even if it were to be a conscious blink, as shown in the middle and lower section of Fig. 3.

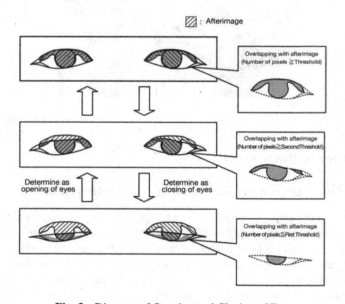

**Fig. 3.** Diagram of Opening and Closing of Eye

Figure 4 is the illustration indicating of the relations with the number of frames and the blink judgment. Even if a subject has weak muscle strength, an unconscious blink (a blink carried out naturally) is faster than a conscious blink.

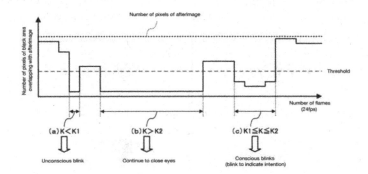

**Fig. 4.** Relationship Between Number of Frames and Blink Determination

The number of the first frames K1 is set from a few frames to more than 10 and less than 20 frames to remove such a fast unconsciousness blink. In this way, we can remove the unconsciousness blink from the closing and opening of eyes that continued in a few frames (Fig. 4(a)). On the other hand, the number of the second frames K2 is set from in dozens of frame degree (ex; 50 frames) to remove the blink that is slower than a normal, consciousness blink. It makes it possible to cover a case where a subject with weak muscle strength continues closing his/her eyes because he/she becomes tired to watch a screen from conscious blinking (Fig. 4(b)). In this way, we remove an unconsciousness blink and the case that a subject continues closing his/her eyes and determine it as a conscious blink when K (the number of the frame acquisition) is in the range between K1 (the number of the first frame) and K2 (the number of the second frame) to judge a conscious blink appropriately. In addition, if the sensitivity in blink judgment sensitivity setting part 44 becomes higher (if it gets closer to value 100), K1 is set in a small value and K2 is set in a big value, and the appointed number range will increase. Then, the fast blink that is almost an unconsciousness blink is judged as a consciousness blink. For this issue, we can remove an unconsciousness blink and the continued closing of eyes properly by adjusting it to an appropriate set point.

The application "Eye Talk" which the selected letters are pronounced with is developed by using this highly precise blink judgment. We focused on making it possible to choose a letter less.

The definitions of the afterimage generation are as followed: After judging white or black, the part that is being recognized as black is determined to be an afterimage.

When it continues being recognized, it means that it is judged as black more than about 13f in the case of 24 fps and it is determined to be an afterimage.

Images are always judged consecutively. All pixels have Persistence Value and subtract 1 frame from every value.

In addition, Persistence Value does not become less than 0 and is always an integer. When it is determined that a pixel is black, 5 values are added.

We define the black part as an afterimage based on value of image persistences. The value becomes - 1 + 5 when the value of image persistences is judged to be black, and we make the program considering it as an afterimage when the value is over 50. Over 50 means the part which is judged as a black part during approximately 0.45 s is determined as an afterimage because 24–30 frames are processed per a second (Fig. 5).

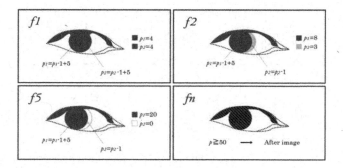

**Fig. 5.** The Change of Persistance Value

In the eye movement measurement with a tablet, the position sensing of the eyes part using the OpenCV HAAR-like assorter burdened the image processing (Fig. 6).

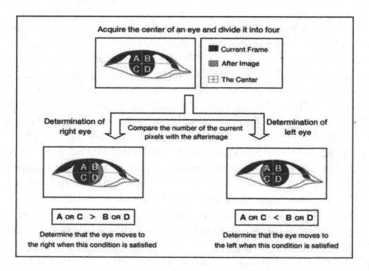

**Fig. 6.** Gaze Direction Detecting

Therefore we decided to use the image from the front camera of the laptop PC this time instead of a tablet. With parallel computation by PC multitasking, we can always demand ocular centers. We divided the iris of the eye into 4 parts from the center point and set the image persistence value. When the value is beyond "50 level", it assumes as an afterimage. We compare the number of the current pixels with the afterimage and determine it as eye movement in right and left when each condition is met. Figure 12 shows the condition of each judgment.

This blink determination and gaze detraction detecting make it possible to choose letters remarkably fast (Fig. 7).

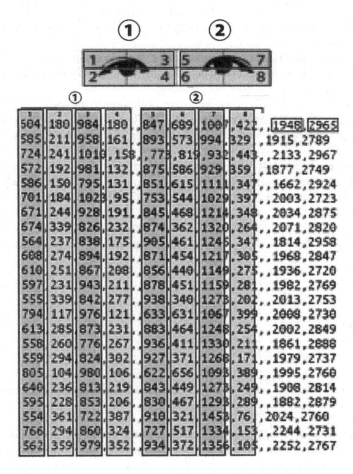

**Fig. 7.** Number of the pixels of afterimage divided into four parts

We measured the amount of change of the eyeball movements of right and left eyes with precision of 14 fps–18 fps by the comparison with the afterimage. The right part [Fig. 7] summarized the number of the pixels of right and left eyes divided in 4 in every 1 flame. We divide the right eye into number 1 to 4, and the left eye into number 5 to 8 and digitize the number of each pixel.

## 4    Clinical Application of Using the Blurring Gaze of Eyes Judgement for Handicapped Children

The team of Osaka University discovered abnormality of the gaze activity of children with Attention Deficit Hyperactivity Disorder (ADHD) by measuring fast oculomotor movement (saccade ocular movement) using eye-tracking (Tobii) in "Research trends in eye-hand coordination of mentally retarded persons" [10–13].

Diagnosis are made based on a comparison of "how long we look into the subject's eyes", that is the time of gazing an object in the conventional autistic study [14–16], but the results do not match.

In this study, the subjects of experiments are 54 children in the special support school who had diagnosed as Kanner syndrome. We showed them the animation combined factor of the fixation and pursuit which a ball moves and stops for 15 s and measured the blurring of gaze of the eyes.

We measured the amount of the degree that the eyes of the subject run off the track based on the afterimage, then added up the amount of change of right and left eyes and showed the total. Figure 8 is the distribution map which showed the oculomotor dispersion of each group.

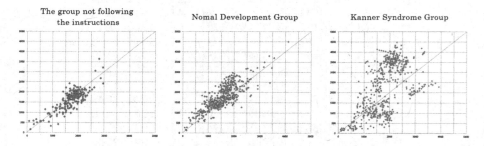

**Fig. 8.**    Difference of eyes dispersion between normal development group and Kanner syndrome group

While the dots were concentrated in the center line in the normal development group, they were scattered around the area in the Kanner syndrome group. It indicate that subjects in the normal development group can follow pursuit the moving target with eyes, but gaze of subjects in the Kanner syndrome group run off the track easily. By comparing the distance from the center line of this distribution in each group, it is proved that the distance of the Kanner syndrome group is significantly farther than the normal development group in both children and adults.

We compare the data of 30 normal developing people with the data which we acquired by this experiment in density function and calculate each identification border.

Figure 9 shows the relations of the normal development group and the Kanner syndrome group by the function of density of probability.

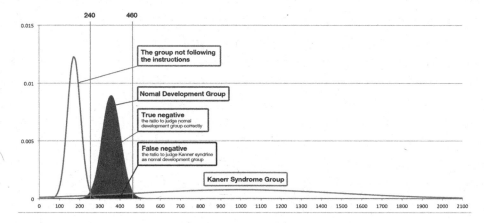

**Fig. 9.** Relations of normal development group and the Kanner syndrome group with the density of probability

We also compare the group that cannot to follow the instructions, the autistic group and normal developing group in density function and calculate each identification border.

The red line is the group not following the instructions, the blue line is normal developing coup and the green line is the Kanner syndrome group (Fig. 9).

From the results, the identification border between the group not following the instructions and the normal developing group is 240. The border between the Kanner syndrome group and normal developing group is 460.

The true negative rate that could judge the normal development group is 99 % and the false positive rate is 1 % (Table 1).

**Table 1.** Boolean table indication whether positive or negative

|  | FALSE | TRUE |
|---|---|---|
| Negative (240 <) | False negative rate 0.04 | True negative rate 0.99 |
| Positive (≤240) | False negative rate 0.01 | True negative rate 0.96 |

The truth positive rate to judge the Kanner syndrome group is 96 % and the false negative rate that judges an Kanner syndrome person as normal (Table 1).

Then we measure the reliability of the results using ROC curve [17, 18]. The reliability that could distinguish a normal developing person to an autistic one is 98.77 % (Fig. 10). On ROC, the shape shifts to the top left when there is little heap of two density functions, and shows that the performance of the decision surface line is high. AUC(Area under the curve) surrounded by the ROC curves is AUC = 0.9877. Since the area is big, it is considered that the reliability of this method is high.

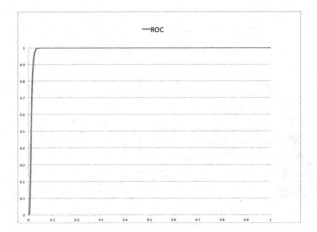

**Fig. 10.** The reliability measurement using ROC curve

From this result, the identification method of this study considered quite useful for the judgment of people who has Kanner syndrome.

## 5    Conclusion

In this study, it was intended to establish the objective index using the blurring of gaze of the eyes to be used for the diagnosis of children who has Kanner syndrome based on our past researches. We succeeded to develop the method of the gaze of the eyes measurement with highly precise. By using the front camera of the popular laptop PC, we established the objective index to judge the Kanner syndrome group, the normal development group, the truth negative and the false negative without using an expensive devise.

Children who has Kanner syndrome tend not to make eye contacts. In the study of Osaka University, they used Tobii and showed that their gaze moves and are not fix. From this, it is considered that this measurement is the technique that is epoch making as a diagnosis of the Kanner syndrome by the eyes detection. Even if the final diagnosis is entrusted to a child psychiatrist, utility value and the versatility of this measurement as a supporting assessment are relatively high. Particularly, it is thought that it has a huge meaning just to understand possibility of the Kanner syndrome for the parent of the child in the gray zone. This measurement is stress free because it does not require to restrict a subject and takes only 15 s. The measurement is also unique in the point of showing the possibility of ASD without doing action observation.

Children who has disabilities change their behaviors through trainings or experiences and get used to the society. Special support schools aim to independency in both daily and social lives and occupational self reliance. Self reliance means they can get some supports depending on their needs.

This method can carry out important tasks as the supporting assessment tool of the judgements of psychiatrists to discover disabilities in children and consider appropriate correspondence. In addition, as well as a judgment, it is considered that this method leads to evaluations of education and curative effects in educational fields.

# References

1. Kitazawa, S. Where tactile stimuli are ordered in time. "Probabilistic mechanisms of learning and development in sensorimotor systems" ESF-EMBO symposia on "Three-Dimensional Sensory and Motor Space", San Feliu de Guixols, Spain, October 2005
2. Kitazawa, S.: Reversal of subjective temporal order due to sensory and motor integrations. In: Attention and Performance XXII. Sensorimotor foundations of higher cognition, Chateau de Pizay, France 2–8 July 2006
3. Kitazawa, S.: Reversal of subjective temporal order due to eye and hand movements. In: ESF-EMBO symposia on "Three-Dimensional Sensory and Motor Space", SantFeliu de Guixols, Spain 10 October 2007
4. Kitazawa S. Nishida S.: Adaptive anomalies in conscious time perception. In: Tutorial workshop in the 12th Annual Meeting of the Association for the Scientific Study of Consciousness, Taipei (2008)
5. Ministry of Health, Labour and Welfare: Guidelines about person of development child with a disability support and the assessment (2013)
6. Guidelines about person of development child with a disability support and the assessment (2012)
7. Torii, I., Ohtani, K., Niwa, T., Ishii, N.: Detecting eye-direction using afterimage and ocular movement. in: ACIS 2nd International Symposium on Computational Science & Intelligence (CSI 2015), pp.149–154 (2015)
8. Torii, I., Ohtani, K., Niwa, T., Ishii, N.: System and method for detecting gaze direction. In: The 6th International Conference on Information, Intelligence, System and Applications (IISA2015) (2015)
9. Torii, I., Ohtani, K., Niwa, T., Ishii, N.: Verbal communication aid application with eye-blink. In: WCCAIS' International Conference on Computer Information Systems (ICCIS 2015), pp. 296–302 (2015)
10. Nakano, T., Tanaka, K., Endo, Y., Yamane, Y., Yamamoto, T., Nakano, Y., et al.: Atypical gaze patterns in children and adults with autism spectrum disorders dissociated from developmental changes in gaze behaviour. Proc. R. Soc. B $277$(1696), 2935–2943 (2010)
11. Kitazawa, S.: Eye Tracking Research. http://www.tobii.com/Global/Analysis/Marketing/JapaneseMarketingMaterial/CustomerCases_JP/Tobii_CustomerCase_Clinical_application_and_eye_tracking_gaze_tracking_in_autism.pdf
12. Nakano, T., Ota, H., Kato, N., Kitazawa, S.: Deficit in visual temporal integration in autism spectrum disorders. Proc R Soc B. $277$(1684), 1027–1030 (2010)
13. Kitazawa, S.: Towards the understanding and treatment of Autism. In: Ota, J., Aonuma, H. (eds.) Social Adjustment Expression Mechanism and Dysfunction. Mobiligence, vol. 4, pp. 213–254. Ohmsha, Ltd, Tokyo (2010)
14. Y. Kimura, H. Kobayashi: Clinical Study on movement education application of autistic children - approach to enhance the Motor Imitation. In: The 25th Japan Special Education Society Papers, pp. 446–447
15. Iwanaga, R., Kawasaki, C.: For sensorimotor disorder of high- functioning autism children, Children Spirit Nerve $36$(4), 27–332

16. Fukuda, S., Okamoto, M., Kato, K., Murata, E., Yamamoto, T., Mohri, I., Taniike, M.: A perception of the others' gaze for children with Pervasive Developmental Disorders. Hum. Dev. Res. **25**, 135–148 (2011)
17. Kawashima, H., Hayashi, N., Ohno, N., Matsuura, Y., Sanada, S.: Comparative study of patient identifications for conventional and portable chest radiographs utilizing ROC analysis. Japan. Soc. Radiol. Technol. **71**(8), 663–669 (2015)
18. Kitashoji, E., Koizumi, N., Lea, T.L.V., Usuda, D., Edith, T.S., Winston, G.S., Kojiro, M., Christopher, M., Efren, D.M., Jose, V.B., Ohnishi, M., Suzuki, M., Ariyoshi, K.: Diagnostic accuracy of recombinant immunoglobulin-like protein A-based IgM ELISA for the early diagnosis of Leptospirosis in the Philippines, public library of science. PLOS Neglected Trop. Dis. **9**(6), e0003879 (2015)

# M-Health Solutions to Support the National Health Service in the Diagnosis and Monitoring of Autism Spectrum Disorders in Young Children

Catherine Tryfona[(✉)], Giles Oatley, Ana Calderon, and Simon Thorne

Cardiff Metropolitan University, Cardiff, UK
{ctryfona,goatley,acalderon,sthorne}@cardiffmet.ac.uk

**Abstract.** With estimates of prevalence between 1 in 68 and 1 in 88 children [11], accurate and early identification of autism spectrum disorders (ASDs) in young children remains a pressing public health issue. In the absence of a single biomarker for ASD, however, a diagnosis is currently reached on the basis of a portfolio of evidence assembled by various health care professionals, parents and educational specialists. Studies have shown that early diagnosis and subsequent intervention are key to a favourable prognosis for children with autism. Many families, however, experience long periods of time between appointments with health care professionals, thus delaying the diagnosis and subsequent access to support and interventions. In this paper, we consider the potential role of m-health software solutions in supporting the diagnosis and ongoing monitoring of ASDs in young children. We consider their application particularly within the context of the UK's National Health Service. This paper also presents a review of some of the current literature on user-behaviour analysis software on mobile computing devices such as tablet computers and smartphones, along with some of the emerging m-health solutions for supporting the diagnosis of ASD in children.

**Keywords:** Autism spectrum disorder · M-Health · User behaviour analysis

## 1 Autism Spectrum Disorders and the Challenges Associated with Diagnosis in Young Children

According to the National Autistic Society [1] it is thought around 700,000 people in the UK are living with autism, with many remaining undiagnosed. Autism and autism spectrum disorders (ASDs) are lifelong developmental disabilities [2]. Autism is considered a spectrum condition, meaning that those at the lower-functioning end may require lifelong specialist support, whilst those at the high-functioning end may lead relatively independent lives [8].

A diagnosis of autism has been traditionally reached in the UK on the basis of the so-called triad of impairments: social impairments, communication difficulties and rigid and repetitive interests and activities [3]. More recently, however, the Diagnostic and Statistical Manual of Mental Disorders–Fifth Edition (DSM-5) of the American Psychiatric Association (APA) has redefined ASD based on a dyad of impairments in social-communication and inflexible behavioural traits [4]. It should be noted, however, that,

M. Antona and C. Stephanidis (Eds.): UAHCI 2016, Part III, LNCS 9739, pp. 249–256, 2016.
DOI: 10.1007/978-3-319-40238-3_24

although much of the research literature refers to the US DSM-4 and DSM-5 manuals, the UK's National Health Service use the World Health Organisation's International Classification of Diseases (ICD) [5]. In spite of this, it could be argued that the publication of the DSM-5 has had some cultural impact in the UK and within the National Health Service (NHS) more specifically, given the controversy over the need for a separate diagnosis for Asperger Syndrome.

Despite progression in understanding of the nature of ASD and possible etiological factors, there is no single biological marker for ASD at this time and so diagnosis is based on a portfolio of evidence collected from clinical observations and parental reports, which tend to reveal different information [6–8]. The accuracy and stability of a diagnosis is dependent, then, on reliable and comprehensive information being obtained from multiple sources [8]. In the absence of definitive tests, there remains the potential for bias in reporting and Taylor et al. [6] assert that the MCHAT-type (Modified Checklist for Autism in Toddlers) questionnaire, typically completed by caregivers, has the potential to result in over and under identification of ASD in young children in the absence of supporting evidence.

Whilst the average age of diagnosis of autism has reduced [9], early diagnosis remains key to improving the prognosis. Studies have shown that the impairments associated with ASDs can be ameliorated when interventions and support are accessed early on [10].

Within the NHS, cases of suspected ASD in young children are typically discussed at cross-disciplinary meetings, during which, a number of health care professionals such as speech and language therapists (SALTs), pediatricians and psychologists will present their findings based on their interactions with and observations of the child. These discussions may also be supported by parental reports or evidence supplied by educational professionals. This process, however, relies on snap-shot observations and accurate reporting in order to reach an accurate diagnosis of autism and this can result in the process taking several months or even years. In turn, this can result in families and schools experiencing delays in accessing support services and funding which are unlocked only once a formal diagnosis has been reached.

With estimates of prevalence being between 1 in 68 [11] and 1 in 88 children, accurate and effective identification of ASD in young children remains a pressing public health issue [6]. With continued financial pressures on the National Health Service there is perhaps a need to find cost-effective, efficient and reliable ways to of collecting evidence of behaviours indicative of the presence of an autism times in order to support and expedite the diagnosis process.

In this paper, we consider the potential for user-behaviour analysis software on tablet computers or smart phones, along with other m-health solutions, to provide a cost-effective opportunity for the NHS to support the diagnostic process and to assist in the ongoing monitoring and development of children with ASD.

## 2 M-Health Solutions to Support the Diagnosis Process

Digital Health is the umbrella term referring to the interventional and diagnostic technologies that depend on the use of ICT (Information Communication Technology) [12]. According to Thummler [12] the growth of the digital health industry has been rapid in recent years, facilitated by a move towards *distributed patient-centered care* (Fig. 1), where the need for physical contact between patients and professionals is reduced. The EU Horizon 2020 Research and Innovation programme calls for research into improving ability to "monitor health and to prevent, detect, treat and manage disease" (European Commission, 2015) and spending on ICT in healthcare is expected to grow to €18 billion globally by 2017 [12].

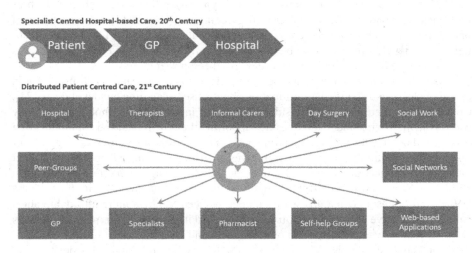

**Fig. 1.** Distributed Patient Centred Care in the 21st Century (Source: Thummler, 2015) [12]

M-health (Mobile Health) refers more specifically to mobile computing, medical sensor and communication technologies for health [13]. According to Istepanian (2010) [14], m-health was first introduced in 2003 and has since been of increasing importance in key areas of healthcare, including wellbeing, disease management and diagnostics.

Mobile technology, particularly over the past ten years, has become commonplace in the everyday lives of the general populous with 93 % of UK adults owning a mobile phone, around 7 out of 10 of which are smartphones [15, 16]. Similarly, the average price of tablet computing device has dropped from £400 in 2011 to £179 in 2014 resulting in an increase in the UK households owning a tablet from 22 % in 2012 to 55 % in July 2014 [16].

Given the popular nature of mobile technology, there is growing interest in the role of mobile devices in healthcare initiatives [17, 18]. Tablet computers and mobile phones present a potentially affordable technological solution to epidemiological and health-based challenges, particularly in the context of a global move towards distributed patient-centred healthcare models [12, 19]. As part of a broader initiative to improve digital health provision, m-health can play a role in bridging a health workforce gap where resources are stretched [20] such as the United Kingdom's NHS and, with the proliferation of mobile technology in developing countries, improve access to healthcare globally [20, 21].

Whilst many children enjoy interacting with technology, children on the autism spectrum often feel a strong affinity for computing technology, as it is seen as a safe environment to learn and practice skills that may be difficult in everyday life [22]. Children with ASD may experience difficulty with cooperative play with other children and often prefer their own repetitive activities [23], e.g. playing with specific games or apps for extended periods or in a repetitive manner. User-behaviour analysis software on mobile computing devices, therefore, represent an interesting opportunity to collect rich data that can be analysed in order to look for signs of possible ASD.

Whilst laptop or desktop computers have typically relied on peripherals such as traditional keyboards, mice or click-pads for user interaction, tablet computers and smart phones typically rely on touch-screen technology. With the advent of touch-screen technology, young children are now able to independently interact with computing devices from a younger age than might have previously been possible.

Each user's interaction with a touchscreen device is unique and touch-usage based profiling can reveal significant information about a user, including gender and age [24]. Consequently, there has been considerable interest in the role that mobile technology can play in improving understanding and supporting the educational and communication needs of those on the autism spectrum [25–28]. There is also an emerging area of research and a number of recent initiatives in using mobile technology to collect evidence to support the diagnostic process and the ongoing observation of autism in children, with a view to identifying support strategies and managing their effectiveness [19, 29, 30]. Sensors contained within mobile devices can be a more affordable alternative to expensive eye-tracking software often used in assessing communication skills of those with or who are suspected of having autism [19, 31].

Tablet computers and mobile phones not only serve as communication devices, but also recreation devices and are packed with embedded sensors such as gyroscopes, GPS, accelerometers and touch-screens [32]. In combination with access to user's calendars, contacts and other personal information, mobile computing devices can infer where their users are and what they are doing, potentially providing rich contextual information for the purposes of user-behaviour analysis.

Such m-health solutions provide the advantage of being able to collect evidence of behaviours suggesting the presence of an autism spectrum disorder at home and within the child's natural environment [33]. Tablet computers are also increasingly used within primary school education settings, widening the scope to collect data outside of the clinician's office. Data could then be uploaded to the clinical teams via a secure, bidirectional wireless communication link (Fig. 2). The ability to access such data in advance of appointment times could facilitate the clinician in planning the agenda for an appointment and planned observations.

User-behaviour analysis software can be acquired as off-the-shelf or bespoke software packages or could be created using open-source software such as Funf [34].

The Funf framework consists of a number of basic data collection objects that collect data on user interaction with a smartphone or tablet computer, including GPS, location,

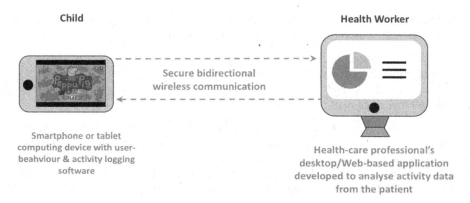

**Fig. 2.** Example of child to healthcare worker software

accelerometer, browser history, running apps and screen on/off sate. The modular architecture of Funf also enables the addition of new 'probes' by 3$^{rd}$ party app developers [34]. Such software could be used as a platform on which to develop user-behaviour analysis software relatively quickly. It would require, however, some level of technical expertise, which may be lacking or expensive to obtain for health care providers.

One notable example of off-the-shelf user-behaviour analysis software is the Play.Care Apple iPad application developed by Harimata [35] in conjunction with researchers at various academic institutions across Europe. According to Harimata [35] the child begins the assessment by playing a set of two educational games which have been designed to "encourage motor, social, and cognitive behaviours". During the session, the software gathers data in relation to the user's behaviour using the device's touch-screen and motion sensors, including the accelerometer and gyroscope. Through the application of machine learning algorithms, a risk assessment of autism is conducted based on comparisons with children in which the condition has already been identified. Harimata claim that the algorithms underpinning their tablet-based software, which principally aims to identify the possible risk of autism through movement pattern analysis, achieved 90 % accuracy in differentiating behavioural patterns related to autism from those in typically developing children [35]. Potential risks associated with this approach, however, might include a lack of engagement with the specific games the user is required to play, particularly given the restrictive and repetitive nature of play behaviours that children on the autism spectrum might display. Nevertheless, the Play.Care application represents an interesting and novel application of machine learning techniques in supporting the diagnosis process.

M-health solutions can also guide the user through the process of collecting evidence of behaviours using a smartphone video camera. NODA smartCapture [33] is a mobile phone-based application that enables parents to record clinically relevant prescribed video evidence of their child's behavior. This approach guides the parent through the process based on the clinical needs of the healthcare professional. According to Nazneed et al. [33], it supports the recording and uploading of four, up to 10-min long naturalistic observation diagnostic assessment (NODA) scenarios, that were chosen based on pilot research on video-based diagnosis of autism. These scenarios include:

1. the child playing alone,
2. the child playing with a sibling or peer,
3. a family mealtime, and
4. any behavior that is of concern to the parent.

Working alongside NODA smartCapture, the NODA Connect web portal has been developed to allow healthcare professionals to access the child's developmental history. This functionality facilitates remote diagnostic assessments by liking evidence of behaviours tagged in the videos to DSM criteria. This method still calls on the clinical judgment of the healthcare professionals. As already noted in this paper, however, the NHS in the UK relies on the World Health Organisation's International Classification of Diseases (ICD) [5].

## 3    Conclusions

Identifying signs of autism spectrum disorders in young children is key to securing an early diagnosis and the accessing the subsequent support and interventions necessary to ensuring the best possible prognosis. In the absence of a single biomarker for autism, the diagnosis of ASD in a young child is still heavily reliant on a portfolio of evidence based on clinical observations made by healthcare professionals, parental reporting and the feedback of educational professionals. This process can be difficult where there is a risk of parental bias in terms of reporting and observations and where there are lengthy gaps between appointment times with health care professionals, particularly within a stretched health service. Within the NHS, the various teams involved in the care and monitoring of a child suspected of having an ASD may be working to different agendas and experiencing unique pressures making it difficult to harmonize the process across different departments.

Whilst there are m-health solutions emerging to assist in the diagnosis and ongoing monitoring of autism in young children, there are also limitations associated with these approaches. In order for these software products to support the NHS, it is vital that the user-requirements elicitation and modelling processes effectively capture the unique and evolving needs of the various professionals working within a dynamic organization such as the NHS. This will also ensure that software can evolve to reflect changes in our understanding of ASDs. M-health solutions, however, do present an interesting opportunity for health care professionals to make observations of children between appointment times and within their home environment or familiar education setting, thus potentially speeding up the diagnosis process.

## References

1. National Autistic Society (2015) http://www.autism.org.uk/about.aspx. (Accessed 28 February 2016)

2. Matson, J.L., Goldin, R.L.: Diagnosing young children with autism. Int. J. Develop. Neuroscience **39**, 44–48 (2014). http://doi.org/10.1016/j.ijdevneu.2014.02.003
3. Happé, F., Ronald, A.: The "fractionable autism triad": a review of evidence from behavioural, genetic, cognitive and neural research. Neuropsychol. Rev. **18**, 287–304 (2008). http://doi.org/10.1007/s11065-008-9076-8
4. Williams, D.M., Bowler, D.M.: Autism spectrum disorder: fractionable or coherent? Autism **18**(1), 2–5 (2014). http://doi.org/10.1177/1362361313513523
5. National Health Service. Asperger's not in DSM-5 mental health manual (2012). http://www.nhs.uk/news/2012/12December/Pages/Aspergers-dropped-from-mental-health-manual-DSM-5.aspx. (Accessed 25 April 2015)
6. Taylor, C.M., Vehorn, A., Noble, H., Weitlauf, A.S., Warren, Z.E.: Brief report: can metrics of reporting bias enhance early autism screening measures? J. Autism Dev. Disord. **44**(9), 2375–2380 (2014). http://doi.org/10.1007/s10803-014-2099-5
7. Ousley, O., Cermak, T.: Autism spectrum disorder: defining dimensions and subgroups. Current Dev. Disord. Rep. **1**, 20–28 (2013). http://doi.org/10.1007/s40474-013-0003-1
8. Bishop, S., Luyster, R., Richler, J., Lord, C.: Diagnostic assessments. In: Chawarska, K., Klin, A., Volkmar, F. (eds.) Autism Spectrum Disorders in Infants and Toddlers, pp. 23–43, New York (2008)
9. Corsello, C.: Diagnositic instruments in autistic spectrum disorders. Encycl. Autism Spectrum Disord. 919–926 (2013)
10. Valicenti-McDermott, M., Hottinger, K., Seijo, R., Shulman, L.: Age at diagnosis of autism spectrum disorders. J. Pediatrics **161**(3), 554–556 (2012). http://doi.org/10.1016/j.jpeds. 2012.05.012
11. Centers for Disease Control and Pre. Autism Spectrum Disorder (ASD) (2015). http://www.cdc.gov/ncbddd/autism/facts.html. (Accessed on 25 April 2015)
12. Thummler, C.: Digital health. In: Fricker, S., Thummler, C., Gavras, A. (eds.) Requirements Engineering for Digital Health, 1st edn, pp. 1–22. (2015)
13. Alepis, E., Lambrinidis, C.: M-Health: supporting automated diagnosis and electonic health records. SpringerPlus **2**(1), 103–111 (2013)
14. Istepanian, R.S.H.: M-Health: a decade of evolution and impact on services and global health (2010)
15. OFCOM. Media Facts and Figures (2015). http://media.ofcom.org.uk/facts/. (Accessed on 22 April 2015)
16. Mintel. Tablet Computers UK Executive Summary - November 2014 (2015)
17. Begale, M., Duffecy, J., Kane, J.M., Mohr, D.C.: Strategies for mHealth research: lessons from 3 Mobile intervention studies, pp. 157–167 (2015). http://doi.org/10.1007/s10488-014-0556-2
18. Norris, A.C., Stockdale, R.S., Sharma, S.: A strategic approach to m-health. Health Inform. J. **15**(3), 244–253 (2009). http://doi.org/10.1177/1460458209337445
19. Anzulewicz, A.: HARIMATA-Embracing mobile devices for early diagnosis of autism spectrum disorders. In: ITASD 2014 Paris Conference, France (2014). http://www.dailymotion.com/video/x27j03l_harimata-embracing-mobile-devices-for-early-diagnosis-of-autism-spectrum-disorders_webcam
20. Bollinger, R., Chang, L., Jafari, R., O'Callaghan, T., Ngatia, P., Settle, D., Al Shorbaji, N.: Leveraging information technology to bridge the health workforce gap. Bull. World Health Organ. **91**, 890–892 (2013). http://doi.org/10.2471/BLT.13.118737
21. Chib, A.: The promise and peril of mHealth in developing countries. Mobile Media Commun. **1**, 69–75 (2013). http://doi.org/10.1177/2050157912459502

22. Benton, L., Johnson, H., Ashwin, E., Brosnan, M., Grawemeyer, B. Developing IDEAS: supporting children with autism within a participatory design team. In: CHI 2012, pp. 2599–2608, Austin (2012). http://doi.org/10.1145/2207676.2208650
23. Boucenna, S., Narzisi, A., Tilmont, E., Muratori, F., Pioggia, G., Cohen, D., Chetouani, M.: Interactive technologies for autistic children: a review. Cogn. Comput. **6**(4), 722–740 (2014)
24. Antal, M., Bokor, Z., Szabó, L.Z.: Information revealed from scrolling interactions on mobile devices. Pattern Recogn. Lett. **56**, 7–13 (2015). http://doi.org/10.1016/j.patrec.2015.01.011
25. Aziz, M.Z.A., Abdullah, S.A.C., Adnan, S.F.S., Mazalan, L.: Educational app for children with autism spectrum disorders (ASDs). Procedia Comput. Sci. **42**(c), 70–77 (2014). http://doi.org/10.1016/j.procs.2014.11.035
26. Bertou, E., Tilburg, A.B.: Low-fidelity prototyping tablet applications for children, pp. 257–260 (2014). http://doi.org/10.1145/2593968.2610466
27. Chien, C.F., Lin, K.Y., Yu, A.P.I.: User-experience of tablet operating system: an experimental investigation of Windows 8, iOS 6 and Android 4.2. Comput. Ind. Eng. **73**, 75–84 (2014). http://doi.org/10.1016/j.cie.2014.04.015
28. Zapata, B.C., Fernández-alemán, J.L., Idri, A., Toval, A.: Empirical studies on usability of mHealth Apps: a systematic literature review (2015). http://doi.org/10.1007/s10916-014-0182-2
29. Abowd, G.: Pilot evaluation of a novel telemedicine platform to support diagnostic assessment for autism spectrum disorder. In: ITASD 2014 Paris Conference, Paris (2014)
30. Billeci, L.: Eye-tracking technology to assess joint attention deficit in children with Autism spectrum disorders. In: ITASD 2014 Paris Conference, France (2014). http://www.dailymotion.com/video/x27izmy_eye-tracking-technology-to-assess-joint-attention-deficit-in-children-with-autism-spectrum-disorders_webcam
31. Brady, N.C., Anderson, C.J., Hahn, L.J., Obermeier, S.M., Kapa, L.L.: Eye tracking as a measure of receptive vocabulary in children with autism spectrum disorders. Augmentative Altern. Commun. **30**, 147–159 (2014). http://doi.org/10.3109/07434618.2014.904923
32. Stanford University. Cell Phones, Sensors and You (2012). http://web.stanford.edu/class/cs75n/. (Accessed on 25 April 2015)
33. Nazneen, N., Rozga, A., Smith, C., Oberleitner, R., Abowd, G., Arriaga, R.: A novel system for supporting autism diagnosis using home videos: iterative development and evaluation of system design, 3(2) (2015)
34. FUNF Open Sensing Framework (2015). http://funf.org/about.html. (Accessed on 1 January 2016)
35. HARIMATA play care technology (2015). http://harimata.co/. (Accessed on 1 April 2015)

# "Look to Remove":
# A Virtual Reality Application on Word
# Learning for Chinese Children with Autism

Pinata Winoto[✉], Clerk Nuo Xu, and Adam An Zhu

Media Lab, Department of Computer Science,
Wenzhou Kean University, Wenzhou, China
{pwinoto,xunu,zhua}@kean.edu

**Abstract.** Till now, very few works have studied Virtual-Reality (VR) based intervention on Chinese children with Autism Spectrum Disorder (ASD), which motivates our study here. In particular, we designed a VR room where players learn new words through the 'look' of its visual form on one of the walls of the room. The integration of audio and visual modalities in the VR environment further promotes children's word-recognition skills. This study offers early insights into the acceptability of such intervention technique among Chinese parents and their children with ASD. Moreover, the study also attempts to examine how children explore and scan their field of view, and how these eye-gaze patterns relate to their word-learning skill.

**Keywords:** Virtual reality · Word learning · Chinese · ASD

## 1 Introduction

Virtual reality (VR) is a computer based simulation where real-life elements are projected as virtual visual elements to enable users to manipulate and interact. Various intervention techniques using VR have been applied to help both children and adults with Autism Spectrum Disorder (ASD) (Herrera et al. 2008; Kandalaft et al. 2013).

Till now, to the best of our knowledge, no published works have examined VR intervention on Chinese children with ASD. Based on current research and interviews with children and parents at two autism centers, the majority of them still rely on the traditional teacher-children and teacher-parent-children interactions in the classroom, while technology-based intervention (TI) at home is rare (Tang et al. 2015). Therefore, it is unclear how existing TI techniques used in the developed countries can be directly applied in China, because some cultural, developmental and environmental settings unique to this population may alter the effectiveness of these interventions (Lu et al. 2015). The first contribution of this study is to provide early insights into the acceptability of such intervention technique among Chinese parents and their children with ASD. The second contribution is to examine how children explore and scan their field of view, and how these eye-gaze patterns relate to their word-recognition skill.

To this end, we designed a VR environment where some typical daily items are put on the walls in a simulated room where a player wearing a VR headset will be

M. Antona and C. Stephanidis (Eds.): UAHCI 2016, Part III, LNCS 9739, pp. 257–264, 2016.
DOI: 10.1007/978-3-319-40238-3_25

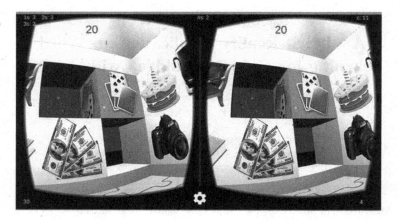

**Fig. 1.** The game as viewed from wearing the eye-glass

immersed (Fig. 1). The goal of such an environment is to train children's word identification skill (a key process in making sense of text) which is a cognitive skill that is
commonly delayed in children with ASD (Randi et al. 2011).

## 2   Related Work

### 2.1   VR in ASD Research

The effectiveness of VR as an intervention tool has been examined and demonstrated in
prior works to help both children and adults overcome fear, anxiety, and stress (Riva
2005), including adolescents and adults with ASD (Strickland et al. 1996; Herrera et al.
2008; Kandalaft et al. 2013). One notable advantage with its extensively use in
healthcare is that it offers a natural and safe environment under a controlled and
consistent protocol (Bellani et al. 2011; Aresti-Bartolome and Garcia-Zapirain 2014).

Earlier works examined the degree of acceptability and usability of the VR and virtual
environments for individuals with ASD (Parsons et al. 2004; Strickland et al. 1996;
Strickland 1997), which had laid the ground for later studies aim at applying various
intervention techniques (Kandalaft et al. 2013; Parsons et al. 2005; Cheng and Ye 2010).

Two types of VR equipment are commonly used in ASD research: highly
immersive (e.g. VR headset with 3D glasses) and less immersive ones (e.g. desktop
PC). Many studies have shown that using highly immersive VR equipment can cause
symptoms of motion sickness (LaViola 2000). Hence, many prior works adopt the less
immersive ones. However, with the massive availability of VR headsets in recent years,
our work aims to study the acceptance and feasibility of the highly immersive VR
headsets among parents and children.

## 2.2 Multisensory Information Binding Skills, Word Recognition Skills and Speech Comprehension for Individuals with ASD

Individuals with ASD are known to lack of a strong ability to combine information pieces from various sources into a unified perceptual whole, a prominent theory describing autism known as the weak central coherence (Happé and Frith 2006). Previous research has indicated that such failure to bind discrete information from multiple sensory modalities could impair the individuals' abilities to identify a single object or event which typically requires both the visual and auditory modalities. Such impaired processing of complex stimuli might in turn offer solid interpretations in their deficit in speech perception and comprehension (Iarocci and McDonald 2006). In particular, for example, (Woynaroski et al. 2013) found that children with ASD exhibited reduced speech perception for matched audiovisual stimuli; while (Stevenson et al. 2014) were able to demonstrate a strong link between multisensory temporal function and speech perception abilities among individuals with ASDs: the larger the gap between an individual's temporal acuity across auditory and visual processing (a so-called large temporal binding window), the poorer their overall perceptual binding abilities, which could in turn greatly affect their speech comprehension.

Although in our current research we do not intend to evaluate autistic children's abilities in recognizing matched or unmatched audiovisual stimuli, our future experiments intend to train children with ASD to improve their overall perceptual binding abilities, which might offer an early and yet additional observations along this research avenue. For examples, by putting associative images together (e.g. poker cards and money, or camera and birthday cake) may help children to build association among various words.

## 3 The Virtual Reality Game

### 3.1 The Design Rationale

Unfortunately, little previous empirical evidence can directly inform us of the design for such a VR-enabled environment specifically for Chinese children with ASD. However, due to our on-going experiences with these children, we will offer our design rationale in this section.

We have been working with one of the children's autism educational development center for almost a year and have observed the various culturally-specific factors that have been inspiring our design:

- TI at school is rare;
- systematic TI at home has not been applied;
- TI at both home and school is welcome by special education teachers;
- TI at both home and school is deemed suspicious by parents/grandparents; and
- VR based intervention is rare at home and school.

During one of our testing sessions, we were invited to participate in a 45 min Lovass session in which the children learn to pair words with visual objects and are rewarded with toys when they successfully match a word with an object (Lovaas 1987).

The only technology used during the entire session is a desktop computer. The situation at government-funded special education center is relatively better; however, the number of children who can be admitted to these centers is extremely limited (Autism Daily Newscast 2015; Compton 2015). Therefore, the majority of children with ASD have to rely on government-subsidized private educational center for early invention and therapy session. Meanwhile, for these educational centers which receive limited government funding, their facilities are extremely lag behind their counter-parts in the West or even such neighboring countries and regions as Hong Kong, Japan and Korea.

## 3.2   The Hardware

A pair of an affordable 3D VR glass (around US$12) is attached to a wide-screen Android phone, which are commonly used by many people in China today, as shown in Fig. 2. Figure 3 shows the look of the player wearing the eye glasses.

**Fig. 2.**  The 3D glass (around US$12)

**Fig. 3.**  The player wearing the glass does not need to take off his/her eye glasses

### 3.3 The Software Development

The game was developed using Unity 3D for Android phones.

### 3.4 The Game

Figure 4 shows the screenshots of the game moment as viewed from the player's perspective. The game simulates a 3D room, where pictures of our daily products (as familiar to the children) are displayed on the walls (excluding floor and ceiling), including apple, banana, bed, etc. Head movement from the player is used as the only game control to shift the game's view, with a small yellow dot at the center of it. When player 'look' at an item for a certain time duration (5 s in our current setting), the system will pronounce the item's Chinese name and then disappear from the game (replaced by the starry sky, see the right image in Fig. 4). By 'look' here, we mean the center of the view (yellow dot) points to the item. Note, it is possible that the player is actually not looking straight at the center of the view, such as during the excessive blinking or eye-wandering, both of which might occur due to less visual stimuli exhibited from the images (Sasson and Elison 2012). However, since the aim of our game is not to study children's eye-gaze behaviors, therefore, the item will still disappear when the player is not looking straight at the center of the item block.

**Fig. 4.** Game-playing moment: (left) the player is currently looking at the carrot as highlighted in green, and with a small yellow dot; (right) the carrot disappeared (Color figure online)

## 4 Preliminary Experiment Results

A questionnaire-based study and a pilot experiment are conducted separately in our feasibility study.

## 4.1    Methodology and Participants

In the first study, a questionnaire containing seventeen questions with answers in 7-point Likert scale is used, where a score of 1 for very much dislike, 4 for neutral, and 7 for very much like. The questions can be categorized into four groups: technology exposure (telescope, game, 3D movies, etc.), items children like (fruits, furniture, animals, etc.), activities children like (drawing, playing card, etc.), and a question on health risk (motion/travel sickness).

The questionnaire in Chinese is distributed to parents in an autism educational development center; sixteen parents of children age two to ten fill the questionnaire. Five children are toddler age two to three, and three children are preadolescence age ten.

In the second pilot study conducted four months later, we invite a 12-year-old boy with high-functioning autism and his parent to try the VR game in our lab. The testing on VR game is limited to a two-minute trial after a short pre-adjustment trial (watching a short animated 3D movie), followed by a short picture recognition session. In the picture recognition session, the researchers mix some printed pictures used in the game with unused ones, and ask the participant to identify all pictures seen/selected in the VR game. We also ask the participant some questions.

All activities are video-taped and recorded for analysis. The participant is accompanied by his parent in the whole process, and answers all questions by himself. Their participation is voluntary.

## 4.2    Results

**Questionnaire.** From the questionnaire, only three children out of sixteen have watched 3D movie(s) before, and only one 5-year-old boy likes it very much. However, more than ten children like animated movies and playing games (their answer score is either 6 or 7 in the Likert scale).

Only three children have used telescope but only two toddlers have not used computer. Out of fourteen who have used computer, eleven like it very much, one dislike it, and two are neutral. Hence, we may safely conclude that most children with ASD in this learning center have been moderately exposed to technology, and most of them like it.

With respect to the health risk, none of the parents have observed motion sickness on their children before. Nonetheless, it does not guarantee that using VR equipment may not cause motion sickness.

Finally, on the items and activities the children (dis-)like, a large variation of answers are given, in which some like animals, plants, starry night, drawing, etc. These results are used to help us in selecting the cards/pictures used in the game.

**Pilot testing.** The participant of the pilot testing identifies himself as a good spatial-game player and has used mobile phones and watched 3D movies, but has not used a VR headset before. He has a prior experience of motion sickness, but no symptom is reported during and after the testing.

After the testing, the followings are positively checked in the questionnaire:

- "I can close my eyes and easily picture a scene."
- "I felt involved in the displayed environment."
- "I enjoyed learning in the application."
- "The sound should be softer."

From the recorded video, we observe that the participant understands well the rule of the game in a very short time. After trying the first two pictures he can play very well. We also observe that he stares at buildings and bridges longer than others. However, no special order is followed; which means he is looking at the pictures randomly from one side to another. He also explores the roof of the virtual room.

During the picture recognition session, we observe that he is able to recall all pictures selected by him in the game, and some other pictures shown in the game. It is worthy to note that the participant of this pilot testing is a preadolescent with high-functioning autism who is indistinguishable from children with typical development. In conclusion, the participant enjoys the game and can do the task very well.

From the conversation with the participant's parent, we observe that her primary concern of using VR glasses as a learning tool is its perceived health risk, especially myopia. Note: it is commonly believed by people in China that watching TV or mobile phones causes myopia among children. Hence, wearing VR glasses may only be allowed for a short learning activity (less than 10 min).

## 5   Conclusion and Future Work

Our pilot study documented in this paper contribute to the autism research in China in understanding the first and yet critical question on the acceptability of the use of VR intervention in children with ASD. The future research following this path is to pursue the intertwined associations among eye-gaze pattern, both the density and intensity of visual stimulus in the VR environment, and the word-learning skill. We hope the HCII community could replicate our study and we call for more research in China where the awareness and acceptance of autism remains to be much lower than its western counterparts (Compton 2015).

**Acknowledgements.**   The authors acknowledge the financial support to this project from the Wenzhou-Kean University Student Partnering with Faculty (SpF) Research Program. The authors also thank Tiffany Tang, Charles Zekun Li, and the participants in this study.

## References

Autism Daily Newscast: China Struggles to Understand Autism. Autism Daily Newscast, 25 May 2015. Accessed 12 February 2016

Aresti-Bartolome, N., Garcia-Zapirain, B.: Technologies as support tools for persons with autistic spectrum disorder: a systematic review. Int. J. Environ. Res. Publ. Health **11**, 7767–7802 (2014)

Bellani, M., Fornasari, L., Chittaro, L., Brambilla, P.: Virtual reality in autism: state of the art. Epidemiol. Psychiatr. Sci. **20**, 235–238 (2011)

Cheng, Y., Ye, J.: Exploring the social competence of students with autism spectrum conditions in a collaborative virtual learning environment – the pilot study. Comput. Educ. **54**, 1068–1077 (2010)

Compton, N.: Autism in China: a Silent Epidemic. Special Educational Needs (SEN) Magazine (2015)

Happé, F., Frith, U.: The weak coherence account: detail focused cognitive style in autism spectrum disorders. J. Autism Dev. Disord. **36**(1), 5–25 (2006)

Herrera, G., Alcantud, F., Jordan, R., Blanquer, A., Labajo, G., De Pablo, C.: Development of symbolic play through the use of virtual reality tools in children with autistic spectrum disorders: two case studies. Autism **12**(2), 143–157 (2008)

Iarocci, G., McDonald, J.: Sensory integration and the perceptual experience of persons with autism. J. Autism Dev. Disord. **36**(1), 77–90 (2006)

Kandalaft, M.R., Didehbani, N., Krawczyk, D.C., Allen, T.T., Chapman, S.B.: Virtual reality social cognition training for young adults with high-functioning autism. J. Autism Dev. Disord. **43**(1), 34–44 (2013)

Lovaas, O.I.: Behavioral treatment and normal educational and intellectual functioning in young autistic children. J. Consult. Clin. Psychol. **55**(1), 3–9 (1987)

Lu, M., Yang, G., Skora, E., Wang, G., Cai, Y., Sun, Q.: Self-esteem, social support, and life satisfaction in chinese parents of children with autism spectrum disorder. Res. Autism Spectrum Disord. **17**, 70–77 (2015)

Parsons, S., Mitchell, P., Leonard, A.: The use and understanding of virtual environments by adolescents with autistic spectrum disorders. J. Autism Dev. Disord. **34**, 449–466 (2004)

Parsons, S., Mitchell, P., Leonard, A.: Do adolescents with autistic spectrum disorders adhere to social conventions in virtual environments? Autism **9**, 95–117 (2005)

Randi, J., Newman, T., Grigorenko, E.L.: Teaching children with autism to read for meaning: challenges and possibilities. J. Autism Dev. Disord. **40**(7), 890–902 (2011)

Riva, G.: Virtual reality in psychotherapy: review. Cyberpsychol. Behav. **8**(3), 220–230 (2005)

Sasson, N.J., Elison, J.T.: Eye tracking young children with autism. J. Vis. Exp. **61**, e3675 (2012)

LaViola Jr., J.J.: A discussion of cybersickness in virtual environments. ACM SIGCHI Bull. **32**(1), 47–56 (2000)

Stevenson, R.A., Siemann, J.K., Schneider, B.C., Eberly, H.E., Woynaroski, T.G., Camarata, S.M., Wallace, M.T.: Multisensory temporal integration in autism spectrum disorders. J. Neurosci. **34**(3), 691–697 (2014)

Strickland, D.: Virtual reality for the treatment of autism. Stud. Health Technol. Inform. **44**, 81–86 (1997)

Strickland, D., Marcus, L.M., Mesibov, G.B., Hogan, K.: Two case studies using virtual reality as a learning tool for autistic children. J. Autism Dev. Disord. **26**, 651–659 (1996)

Tang, T.Y., Wang, R.Y., Hui, Y., Huang, L.Z., Chen, C.P.: Supporting collaborative play via an affordable touching + singing plant for children with autism in china. In: UbiComp/ISWC 2015 Adjunct, pp. 373–376. ACM, New York (2015)

Woynaroski, T.G., Kwakye, L.D., Foss-Feig, J.H., Stevenson, R.A., Stone, W.L., Mark, T., Wallace, M.T.: Multisensory speech perception in children with autism spectrum disorders. J. Autism Dev. Disord. **43**(12), 2891–2902 (2013)

# Design of a Mobile Collaborative Virtual Environment for Autism Intervention

Lian Zhang[1(✉)], Megan Gabriel-King[5], Zachary Armento[5],
Miles Baer[5], Qiang Fu[1], Huan Zhao[1], Amy Swanson[2,3],
Medha Sarkar[5], Zachary Warren[2,3], and Nilanjan Sarkar[1,4]

[1] Electrical Engineering and Computer Science Department,
Vanderbilt University, Nashville, USA
lian.zhang@vanderbilt.edu
[2] Treatment and Research in Autism Spectrum Disorder (TRIAD),
Vanderbilt University, Nashville, USA
[3] Pediatrics and Psychiatry Department, Vanderbilt University, Nashville, USA
[4] Mechanical Engineering Department,
Vanderbilt University, Nashville, TN 37212, USA
[5] Computer Science Department,
Middle Tennessee State University, Murfreesboro, TN 37132, USA

**Abstract.** Autism Spectrum Disorders (ASD) are characterized by deficits in social skills and communications. This paper describes a Collaborative Virtual Environment (CVE) on the Android platform designed to investigate the collaborative behaviors and communication skills of children with ASD. The mobile CVE has the advantages of (1) widespread availability, and (2) allowing flexible communication between people. This presented mobile CVE allows two users in different locations to interact and communicate with each other while playing puzzle games on mobile devices. Multiple puzzle games with different interaction patterns were designed in the environment, including turn-taking, information sharing, and enforced collaboration. Audio and video chat were implemented in the environment in order for the geographically distributed players to talk with and see each other. The usability of the environment has been validated through a user study involving five pairs of subjects. Each pair included one child with ASD and one typically developing (TD) child. The results showed that the presented CVE environment may have the potential to improve players' collaborative behaviors and communication skills.

**Keywords:** Collaborative virtual environment · Android game · Autism intervention

## 1 Introduction

Autism Spectrum Disorders (ASD) affect 1 in 68 children in the United States [1]. ASD consists of a range of developmental disorders characterized by deficits in social skills and communications [2]. Many studies have been investigating social skills and communications of children with ASD [3]. However, access to trained autism clinicians is limited and cost associated with traditional therapies is significant. The use of

© Springer International Publishing Switzerland 2016
M. Antona and C. Stephanidis (Eds.): UAHCI 2016, Part III, LNCS 9739, pp. 265–275, 2016.
DOI: 10.1007/978-3-319-40238-3_26

technology, such as virtual environments, may provide an alternative approach to ASD intervention that is more scalable and accessible [4]. Researchers are increasingly exploring virtual environments as potential intervention platforms for children with ASD in their social skills, including facial expression recognition [5] and communications in social tasks [6]. To date, however, preprogrammed and/or confederate avatars have mostly been used in such environments with only one user, which are unrealistic and inflexible [7].

Another paradigm with potential use in ASD intervention can be Collaborative Virtual Environments (CVE). CVEs are distributed, multiplayer involved virtual environments [8], and are more realistic and flexible than traditional virtual environment by allowing interactions and communications among players within the controlled environments. Controlled tasks could be designed within such environments that may ultimately enhance interaction and communication skills of children with ASD without relying on preprogrammed or facilitated interaction. Previous studies using CVEs for autism intervention were PC based environments with limitations in data analysis [9] and lacked simultaneous interaction [10]. The existing multiplayer video games aiming at entertainment and limited in feedback were not useful for educational or skill training purposes for children with ASD. Therefore, we designed a CVE on the Android platform for ASD intervention with the goal to understand and ultimately promote the collaborative interactions and communications of children with ASD.

Because the use of mobile devices is growing exponentially, mobile applications have the potential to increasingly engage children with ASD [11] by creating ubiquitous learning environments [12]. The studies using mobile applications for ASD intervention include emotion recognition [13], social interactions [14], and vocabulary learning [15]. However, these mobile applications are limited in interactions and communications between real people. Our mobile CVE (Fig. 1)—supporting multiple players' interactions and communications in the shared collaborative environment—investigated the collaborative interactions and communications of children with ASD.

**Fig. 1.** Two players using the mobile CVE

The goals of the current research were to: (1) evaluate the usability of the mobile CVE; and (2) investigate the collaborative interactions and the communications of children with ASD when playing puzzle games with their TD peers. This novel environment supports following functionalities:

- Interaction between two geographically distributed players via internet
- Audio and video communication
- Automatic performance and audio recording

## 2  Method

The mobile CVE was designed with Unity3D (www.unity3d.com). The environment, which can be accessed by players using Android mobile devices, allows two players to interact and communicate with each other remotely. A variety of puzzle games were developed that compelled interactions between two players, such as turn-taking, information sharing, and enforced collaboration. The environment supported video and audio communication between the two players. The performance status and dialogue of players were recorded by the CVE system for offline analysis. In order to support these functionalities, a software framework (Fig. 2) was developed with four modules: a game controller module, a network connection module, a communication module, and a data recording module. The game controller module implemented the application logic of the puzzle games. The audio/video chat between two geographically distributed players was supported through the communication module. The network connection module was responsible for transferring the data from game controller and communication modules via the internet. The data recording module recorded locally information related to how players played the game and how they communicated with each other. The functionality and the usability of this mobile CVE has been evaluated by a small user study involving five pairs of players, each consisting of one child with ASD and one TD child.

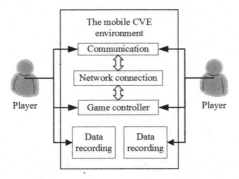

**Fig. 2.** The framework of our mobile CVE

### 2.1  System Design

**Game Controller.** The logic of the mobile CVE was implemented based on a hierarchical and concurrent Finite State Machine (FSM) model, shown in Fig. 3. The

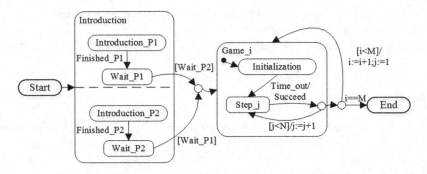

**Fig. 3.** The finite state machine model of the mobile CVE

element of concurrency in the design made it possible for players to reside in different sub-states while still maintaining application synchronization. Take the 'Introduction' state for instance: player1 could stay in the 'Wait_P1' state after he/she finished reading the introduction, while player2 could still read the introduction in the 'Introduction_P2' state. After both players finished reading the introduction, their game states would be rejoined upon exiting the 'Introduction' state. In Fig. 3, M is the total number of puzzle games to be played in a session, which is customizable for different requirements (will be discussed in Sect. 2.2). N is the total steps of one game, which can vary from game to game.

**Table 1.** Game configuration parameters

| Game index | Color visibility | Block controllability | Rotatability | Interaction type |
|---|---|---|---|---|
| 1 | P1 and P2 | P1 in step 1, 3, 5, 7; P2 in step 2, 4, 6 | Auto | Turn-taking |
| 2 | P1 and P2 | P1 in step 3, 4, 7; P2 in step 1, 2, 5, 6 | Auto | Turn-taking |
| 3 | P1 and P2 | P1 and P2 in all steps | Auto | Enforced collaboration |
| 4 | P1 | P2 in all steps | P2 | Information-sharing |
| 5 | P2 | P1 in all steps | P1 | Information-sharing |
| 6 | P1 | P1 and P2 in all steps | P2 | Enforced collaboration |
| 7 | P2 | P1 and P2 in all steps | P1 | Enforced collaboration |
| 8 | Half for P1 and Half for P2 | P1 in step 1, 3, 5, 7, 9; P2 in step 2, 4, 6, 8, 10 | Auto | Turn-taking |

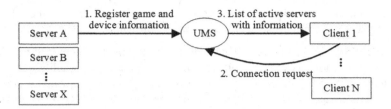

**Fig. 4.** Unity master server (UMS) role

The hierarchical 'Game_i' state defined the logic of each puzzle game in the CVE. In order to study the different collaborative interactions of children with ASD, three types of puzzle games were designed in the CVE: turn-taking games, information sharing games, and enforced collaboration games. In the turn-taking games, players had alternating control of blocks movement. Information sharing games asked players to share color information in order to move the correct blocks. The enforced collaboration games aimed to impose simultaneous interactions of two players. Both players had to move the same block in the same direction at the same time in the enforced collabo-ration games. A considerable amount of communication between the players was required in the enforced collaboration games.

Each game was composed of multiple steps. The steps were generalized and modeled using the 'Step_j' state in Fig. 3. The implementation of the steps were different depending on the configuration of the following parameters: (1) color visi-bility (i.e., which players can see the color); (2) block controllability (i.e., which players can move the block); and (3) block rotatability (i.e., which players can rotate the block). The values of these parameters determined the types of game interaction, shown in Table 1. Game 1 was a turn-taking game, in which two players, P1 and P2, were both able to see the color of blocks. At the first step, player P1 had control of all the blocks. At the next step, P2 had control of all the blocks. They would take turns dragging the block in game 1. The number of steps in each game was seven in all but the last game, which had ten steps.

**Network Connection.** A client-server network architecture was used for the mobile CVE involving two players. The device of one player acted as a server, while the other player's device acted as a client. All the computationally-intensive tasks were imple-mented on the server side. This network architecture has been widely used for two-player mobile games and it is simple and sufficient [16]. The network connection was created via Unity Master Server (UMS) (http://docs.unity3d.com/Manual/net-MasterServer.html), which allowed players to find each other at any time and at any location. The function of the UMS for network connection is shown in Fig. 4. Any player can initiate a game as a server, for example the 'Server A' or the 'Server B' in Fig. 4, by clicking the 'start game' button in the game. The device information (IP address and port number) were registered with the UMS. Other players can connect to one of the active servers, thus becoming a client. The client can send connection requests by clicking the 'connect' button in the game. After receiving this request, the UMS then returns a list of active servers to the client. The returned list contains all pertinent information required for the client to connect to the server. The client then selects one server from the list to create a connection with the selected server.

**Communication.** The communication module was designed to support the audio and video communication between the players. The video chat functionality allowed two players to see each other in real time, which was implemented following the procedure in Fig. 5. The image was captured by the mobile camera in ARGB32 format. The captured image was then encoded into a JPG file, which was amenable to network transfer because it had a small data size and was in serialized format. The Unity remote procedure call (http://docs.unity3d.com/Manual/net-RPCDetails.html) was used for the image data transferring. When the receiving mobile device obtained the transferred data, it was decoded into the RGB24 format and displayed using the Texture2D component (http://docs.unity3d.com/ScriptReference/Texture2D.html). The video was updated with a fixed frequency 12 Hz.

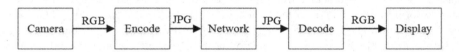

**Fig. 5.** The video chat procedure

The audio chat feature was used for players to talk with each other in real time. This feature was implemented with a procedure similar to the video chat. With both a speaker and microphone on the device, there was an audio feedback problem during the audio chat. Head phones were worn by all players to solve this audio feedback problem.

**Data Recording.** The data recording module records the performance and dialogue data of players in the CVE for the offline analysis. The recorded performance metrics included the success frequency (how many times they succeed per game), game duration, and collaborative movement duration, which were written to a file in real time. The audio data of each player were recorded locally with a frequency of 44.1 KHz. The recorded audio data were written to a file at the very end of all games, and were later transcribed and labeled with some predefined utterance types manually. The utterance types were defined referring to previous literature to evaluate the communication [17, 18], including the words spoken per minute, the frequency of question-asking, the frequency of response, the frequency of spontaneous information sharing, and the frequency social oriented utterance.

## 2.2    Experiment Setup

Five age- and gender-matched pairs of subjects were recruited for a preliminary evaluation of the mobile CVE. Each pair was composed of one child with ASD and one TD child. All the children with ASD had a clinical diagnosis of ASD from a licensed clinical psychologist. The Social Responsiveness Scale, second edition (SRS-2) [19]

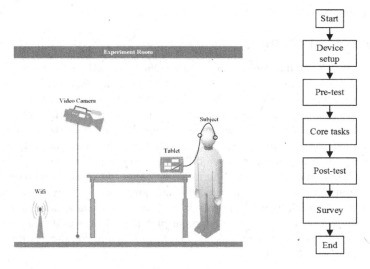

**Fig. 6.** The experiment room layout (left) and the experiment procedure (right).

and Social Communication Questionnaire Lifetime Total Score (SCQ) [20] were completed by for a parent of each child with ASD. The experiments were approved by the Vanderbilt University Institutional Review Board (IRB). The information of all the subjects are summarized in the Table 2.

**Table 2.** Subject characteristics

|  | Age: Mean (Std) | Gender Female/male | SRS-2 total raw score: Mean (Std) | SCQ current total score: Mean (Std) |
|---|---|---|---|---|
| ASD | 10.99 (3.69) | 4/1 | 83.50 (24.96) | 20.25 (10.50) |
| TD | 10.81 (2.32) | 4/1 | 9.80 (7.53) | 0.80 (1.30) |

During the experiment, subjects in a pair sat separately in two different rooms. The layout of the experiment rooms is shown in Fig. 6 (left). One tablet, Nexus 9, and one set of headphones were provided for each subject for the experiment. A video camera recorded the subject and the device during the experiment. Each experiment lasted about 40 min. The experiment procedure is shown in Fig. 6 (right). At the beginning, the devices were given to each subject. Then, subjects completed the pre-test, with one turn-taking game (game 8), and two enforced collaboration games (game 6 and game 7). During the core task, seven puzzle games, from game 1 to game 7, were presented in order. The post-test included the same games as the pre-test. After the post-test, subjects completed a survey regarding their experience with the system and with their partners.

# 3  Results

## 3.1  The System Usability

Five pairs completed the preliminary study. One pair had difficulty to finish the experiment and their data were excluded from analysis. The other four pairs completed the experiment. The network connection was lost during one pre-test. The automatically recorded performance and audio data of game 7 in this pre-test were also lost. However, we recovered the audio data by extracting the audio from the recorded video. The turn-taking game (game 8) and the enforced collaboration games (game 6 and game 7) were analyzed separately since different games required different interactions. Four pairs' data were used for the turn-taking game, the survey analysis, and the communication analysis of the enforced collaboration games. Only three pairs' data were used for the performance analysis in the enforced collaboration games. Even though the video chat was implemented in our mobile CVE, it was disabled during the experiment because it caused data loss and lag. Instead, audio communication was used during the experiment.

## 3.2  Data Analysis

All pairs showed an improved performance during the post-test compared to the pre-test. This meant all pairs succeeded more in both the turn-taking game (game 8), and the enforced collaboration games (game 6 and game 7). In addition, all pairs required less time to finish both turn-taking game, and enforced collaboration games in the post-test. All pairs also demonstrated an increased collaborative movement duration, which was defined as the duration of time players moved blocks together. The increased collaborative duration may indicate improved collaboration between the players. The mean and standard deviation (Std) of all these changes are listed in Table 3. The first row shows that the success frequency increased by 3.25 s on average in game 8, which allowed a maximum of 10 successes, with a standard deviation 1.7.

**Table 3.** Performance changes from pre-test to post-test

| Game index | Variable | Increased/decreased | Mean (Std) |
|---|---|---|---|
| 8 | Success frequency | Increased | 3.25 (1.70) |
| | Time duration (in seconds) | Decreased | 28.00 (18.78) |
| 6 & 7 | Success frequency | Increased | 8.67 (3.06) |
| | Time duration (in seconds) | Decreased | 304.67 (83.94) |
| | Collaborative ratio (in seconds) | Increased | 20.62 (8.55) |

For the communication data, we found some differences between the children with ASD and their TD peers during the pre-test in the enforced collaboration games. In the pre-test, all the children with ASD spoke fewer words than their TD partners in the enforced collaboration games. They also asked fewer questions, but gave more

**Table 4.** Magnitude change in communication from pre-test to post-test

|            | Words         | Questions   | Responses   |
| ---------- | ------------- | ----------- | ----------- |
| Mean (Std) | 39.75 (27.62) | 8.00 (8.66) | 3.00 (2.65) |

responses, compared to their TD partners in the pre-test of the enforced collaboration games. The mean and standard deviation of the absolute value of these differences are listed in Table 4. However, these differences were not observed during the post-test. The changes from the pre-test to the post-test in terms of the communication variables were not found.

The survey from the subjects reflected positive opinions for the environment. From the survey, all subjects enjoyed playing the games. All subjects perceived an improved individual performance in playing the games and increased ease in talking with their partners at the end of the experiments. Each question in the survey was scored on a 5-Likert scale. In terms of enjoying the game, number 1 indicated no enjoyment at all, while number 5 meant very much enjoyment. In terms of their performance in the game and the communication with their partners, number 1 indicated performance/communication became much worse at the end of the experiment, while number 5 meant performance/communication became much better at the end of the experiment. The mean and standard deviation of the survey questions are shown in Table 5.

**Table 5.** Enjoyment in games, improved individual performance and Increased ease of communication with partner

|            | Enjoyment   | Communication | Individual performance |
| ---------- | ----------- | ------------- | ---------------------- |
| Mean (Std) | 4.88 (0.35) | 4.63 (0.74)   | 4.50 (0.53)            |

# 4  Conclusions and Future Works

This paper discusses the design of a CVE on the Android platform for ASD intervention with the goal to improve the collaborative interaction and communications of children with ASD. The environment facilitates the interaction and communication of two players from different locations by playing multiple block games.

Five ASD/TD pairs participated in the preliminary study. The usability of the environment and its functionalities, including the two players' interactions, audio communications, and data recording, have been validated by the preliminary study. The result of the experiments may support the potential of the environment in improving the collaborative interactions and communications of children with ASD.

There were some limitations in the system design and user study in this paper. Only a small sample size were included in our current study. More subjects will be involved for the experiments in the future. The current CVE was evaluated in a small local network, which will be extended to the global network in order for players from any location in the world to gain access. Future work will consist of a closed-loop system using targeted feedback based on the player's communication and collaborative performance.

**Acknowledgment.** This work was supported in part by the National Institute of Health Grant 1R01MH091102-01A1, National Science Foundation Grant 0967170 and the Hobbs Society Grant from the Vanderbilt Kennedy Center.

# References

1. Wingate, M., Kirby, R.S., Pettygrove, S., Cunniff, C., Schulz, E., Ghosh, T., Robinson, C., Lee, L.-C., Landa, R., Constantino, J.: Prevalence of autism spectrum disorder among children aged 8 years-autism and developmental disabilities monitoring network, 11 sites, United States, 2010. MMWR Surveill. Summaries **63**(2), 1–21 (2014)
2. Snoek, C.G., Worring, M., Smeulders, A.W.: Early versus late fusion in semantic video analysis. In: Proceedings of the 13th Annual ACM International Conference on Multimedia, pp. 399–402 (2005)
3. Sundberg, M.L., Partington, J.W.: Teaching Language to Children with Autism and Other Developmental Disabilities. Behavior Analysts Inc., Pleasant Hill (1998)
4. Lahiri, U., Bekele, E., Dohrmann, E., Warren, Z., Sarkar, N.: A physiologically informed virtual reality based social communication system for individuals with autism. J. Autism Dev. Disord. **45**, 919–931 (2015)
5. Kandalaft, M.R., Didehbani, N., Krawczyk, D.C., Allen, T.T., Chapman, S.B.: Virtual reality social cognition training for young adults with high-functioning autism. J. Autism Dev. Disord. **43**, 34–44 (2013)
6. Parsons, S., Mitchell, P.: The potential of virtual reality in social skills training for people with autistic spectrum disorders. J. Intellect. Disabil. Res. **46**, 430–443 (2002)
7. Schmidt, M., Laffey, J., Stichter, J.: Virtual social competence instruction for individuals with autism spectrum disorders: beyond the single-user experience. In: Proceedings of CSCL, pp. 816–820 (2011)
8. Benford, S., Greenhalgh, C., Rodden, T., Pycock, J.: Collaborative virtual environments. Commun. ACM **44**, 79–85 (2001)
9. Millen, L., Hawkins, T., Cobb, S., Zancanaro, M., Glover, T., Weiss, P.L., Gal, E.: Collaborative technologies for children with autism. In: Proceedings of the 10th International Conference on Interaction Design and Children, pp. 246–249 (2011)
10. Stichter, J.P., Laffey, J., Galyen, K., Herzog, M.: iSocial: delivering the social competence intervention for adolescents (SCI-A) in a 3D virtual learning environment for youth with high functioning autism. J. Autism Dev. Disord. **44**, 417–430 (2014)
11. Tanaka, J.W., Wolf, J.M., Klaiman, C., Koenig, K., Cockburn, J., Herlihy, L., Brown, C., Stahl, S., Kaiser, M.D., Schultz, R.T.: Using computerized games to teach face recognition skills to children with autism spectrum disorder: the Let's Face It! program. J. Child Psychol. Psychiatry **51**, 944–952 (2010)
12. Gravenhorst, F., Muaremi, A., Bardram, J., Grünerbl, A., Mayora, O., Wurzer, G., Frost, M., Osmani, V., Arnrich, B., Lukowicz, P.: Mobile phones as medical devices in mental disorder treatment: an overview. Pers. Ubiquit. Comput. **19**, 335–353 (2015)
13. Leijdekkers, P., Gay, V., Wong, F.: CaptureMyEmotion: a mobile app to improve emotion learning for autistic children using sensors. In: IEEE 26th International Symposium on Computer-Based Medical Systems (CBMS 2013), pp. 381–384 (2013)
14. Escobedo, L., Nguyen, D.H., Boyd, L., Hirano, S., Rangel, A., Garcia-Rosas, D., Tentori, M., Hayes, G.: MOSOCO: a mobile assistive tool to support children with autism practicing social skills in real-life situations. In: Proceedings of the SIGCHI Conference on Human Factors in Computing Systems, pp. 2589–2598 (2012)

15. Husni, E.: Mobile applications BIUTIS: let's study vocabulary learning as a media for children with autism. Procedia Technol. **11**, 1147–1155 (2013)
16. Gautier, L., Diot, C.: Design and evaluation of MiMaze a multi-player game on the internet. In: IEEE International Conference on Multimedia Computing and Systems, Proceedings, pp. 233–236 (1998)
17. Charlop-Christy, M.H., Carpenter, M., Le, L., LeBlanc, L.A., Kellet, K.: Using the picture exchange communication system (PECS) with children with autism: assessment of PECS acquisition, speech, social-communicative behavior, and problem behavior. J. Appl. Behav. Anal. **35**, 213–231 (2002)
18. Nunes, D., Hanline, M.F.: Enhancing the alternative and augmentative communication use of a child with autism through a parent-implemented naturalistic intervention. Int. J. Disabil. Dev. Educ. **54**, 177–197 (2007)
19. Constantino, J.N., Gruber, C.P.: The Social Responsiveness Scale. Western Psychological Services, Los Angeles (2002)
20. Rutter, M., Bailey, A., Lord, C.: The Social Communication Questionnaire. Western Psychological Services, Los Angeles (2003)

# A Novel Collaborative Virtual Reality Game for Children with ASD to Foster Social Interaction

Huan Zhao[1]([⊠]), Amy Swanson[2], Amy Weitlauf[2], Zachary Warren[2], and Nilanjan Sarkar[1]

[1] Electrical Engineering and Computer Science Department,
Vanderbilt University, Nashiville, TN 37212, USA
huan.zhao@vanderbilt.edu
[2] Treatment and Research Institute for Autism Spectrum Disorders (TRIAD),
Vanderbilt University, Nashiville, TN 37212, USA

**Abstract.** Children with Autism spectrum disorders (ASD) often suffer from deficits in communication and social interaction, which lead to various social challenges in interacting with peers in collaborative tasks. The application of Collaborative Virtual Environment (CVE) technology in ASD intervention brings advantages in providing a safe, flexible, and collaborative environment. This paper proposes and describes the development of a novel distributed CVE system for playing a series of collaborative games using hand movement that is tracked in real-time via cameras. These games aim to positively impact the social interaction of users. A usability study indicated potential of this system in fostering collaboration and communication skills among children with and without ASD.

**Keywords:** Collaborative virtual environment · ASD intervention · Social interaction and communication

## 1 Introduction

Autism spectrum disorders (ASD), characterized by impairments in communication and social interaction, represent a group of neurodevelopmental disabilities [1–3]. According to the reports of the Centers for Disease Control and Prevention, the number of children with ASD (6–17 years) has steadily increased from 1.16 % in 2007 to 2.00 % in 2012 [4]. In 2012, 1 in 68 children (8 years) was diagnosed with ASD [5]. Children with ASD often display disabilities in developing competence necessary for appropriately interacting with their typically developing (TD) peers in group tasks. Social challenges are even exacerbated as they get older with limited social skills facing more complex social situations. Various intensive ASD interventions have been employed to improve the deficits of social competence for children with ASD. Recently, collaborative virtual reality technology is applied in some ASD interventions enabling multiple individuals in distributed locations to interact with one another within a safe, flexible and collaborative environment. In the CVE-based interventions, individuals with ASD usually experience less anxiety as face-to-face communications

© Springer International Publishing Switzerland 2016
M. Antona and C. Stephanidis (Eds.): UAHCI 2016, Part III, LNCS 9739, pp. 276–288, 2016.
DOI: 10.1007/978-3-319-40238-3_27

are reduced in CVEs [6]. They get rid of physical distance restrictions and can accept the interventions outside the clinic [7]. CVEs are also capable of creating motivating collaborative tasks that inspire participation of children with ASD in the interactive work so as to develop communicative and social interactive skills.

A growing number of studies have begun to explore the influence and effectiveness of CVEs used in ASD interventions. Weiss et al. created a CVE program called Talk-About for children to learn and practice social conversation skills with their partner [8]. Cheng et al. developed a collaborative virtual learning environment (CVLE), where students communicated with a virtual teacher to answer questions according to the context of social scenarios so as to learn social techniques (including social cognition and interaction) [9]. Stichter et al. used a distributed 3D CVLE, iSocial, for youth with high functioning autism (HFA) to complete collaborative tasks (e.g., to design and build a restaurant) in the shared virtual environment [10]. Millen et al. introduced a CVE called Island of Ideas that encouraged students with ASD to take part in participatory design activities [11]. Battocchi et al. employed a puzzle game featuring with enforced collaboration on a tabletop to facilitate cooperative behaviors in children with ASD [12].

Our distributed CVE system, called Hand-in-Hand (HIH) CVE system, aims to provide a flexible and effective interaction environment and eventually foster communicative and interactive behaviors among users through collaborative tasks. Since distributed users cannot "read" partners' intentions through face-to-face observation, they are more likely to talk with one another to share ideas. The nature of collaborative games raise the awareness of the importance of cooperation between users and also requires significant conservations. This system is expected to engage children with ASD in the collaborative tasks implemented with Leap Motion cameras [13], and record performance data as well as conversation audio in real time. In this paper, we present the design of this system and evaluate the efficiency of this system via a usability study. The rest of the paper is organized as follows: Sect. 2 discusses the system structure and game design; Sect. 3 presents the preliminary results of the usability study; and Sect. 4 concludes with a discussion of the contributions and limitations as well as future work.

## 2  HIH CVE System Design

The major goal of this system is to provide a CVE where distant users can play games in a collaborative manner. We first created the CVE that users can access from distant locations via Internet. This CVE was built using Unity [14] and designed as a 3D game space supporting network connection and simultaneous manipulations from distributed users. Next, we designed a series of collaborative games in this CVE with implicit rules to foster social interaction between users. These games integrated with the Leap Motion offer a chance for players to control virtual game elements in the CVE with their hands. Along with these games, a database was developed to collect gaming data including audio data for offline analysis. Figure 1 shows major components of the HIH CVE system. The user interacts with the CVE Application via the Leap Motion controller. Communication Management enables the distant CVE application connection and

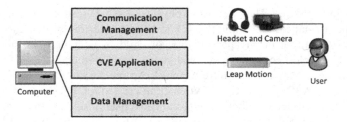

**Fig. 1.** Overall architecture of the HIH CVE system

real-time communication between the users. All the gaming data and audio data of conversation are recorded by the Data Management component.

## 2.1 Collaborative Tools

All the games in this CVE are required to play with Leap Motion controller, which is a gesture-based interactive tool. Instead of traditional input devices such as mouse or keyboard, the Leap Motion was chosen in order to provide a more naturalistic way of manipulating virtual game objects and to make users feel more immersed within this system. We programmed the Leap Motion Controller to develop two virtual collaborative tools (Fig. 2) controlled by hand gestures/motion. The user's actions can be mapped to the behaviors of controlled tools. In the CVE, the user's hand is represented by a circle. When the user's hand (the circle) touches the tool, the user can manipulate the tool. For example, when the user clenches his/her hand, the tool is grasped and can be moved to any location. When the user opens his/her hand, the tool is released.

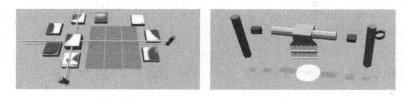

**Fig. 2.** Move Tool (left) and Collection Tool (right)

These two collaborative tools are called *Move Tool* and *Collection Tool*. They were designed to enforce collaborative activities between users in three ways: (a) they require matching efforts from each player, (b) they only function through collaborative operation, and (c) they display the effect of individual operation. Both tools have two handles, each of which is required to be controlled by one user. These tools become functional only when users coordinate their operations on the handles. When using the *Move Tool*, each handle is limited to move in one direction (horizontal direction or vertical direction). Thus each user respectively controls one moving direction of the puzzle piece. As for *Collection Tool*, both handles are prohibited to go beyond a certain distance and users are forced to coordinate their heading directions.

## 2.2  Game Design

The primary part of the CVE application is a series of collaborative games. When we started designing those games, we focused on creating those that (a) can be easy to learn and play, (b) require players to undertake equal work, and (c) have implicit rules for fostering extensive interactions and communications. Therefore, we chose games in the form of collaborative manipulation of objects from one location of the virtual space to another, sometimes in the presence of obstacles. Finally, we designed three such types of collaborative games, where players virtually hold/move/drop the virtual objects using handles via the Leap Motion controllers. These games are called *Puzzle Game*, *Collection Game* and *Delivery Game* (Fig. 3). We modeled these games using Statechart diagrams (Fig. 4) to support hierarchy and concurrency.

**Fig. 3.** Puzzle Game (left), Collection Game (middle) and Delivery Game (right)

*Puzzle Game* requires players to put nine puzzle pieces together to match a target picture. In the Statechart model of Fig. 4 (top), the "TIME" mode records the game time and would end the game after 5 min. The "PUZZLES" mode controls the states of nine puzzle pieces, which have the same low-level mode "Puzzle [Num]". Initially, nine puzzle pieces "Stay" dispersedly in the game space. When both players choose the same piece and grab their handles, the piece would "Move" following the *Move Tool*. When either player releases the handle, the piece would be put down. If the piece is put down at the correct destination, it means the placement of this piece is "Finished". Once all the puzzle pieces reach the correct locations, the game would be ended even before the timeout expires. To win this game, two players are required to collaboratively determine the move order of puzzle pieces and the correct destination of each piece.

Similar to *Puzzle Game*, players bring nine different objects to collection areas where their pictures are shown in the *Collection Game*. Compared to *Puzzle Game*, an additional "Target" mode is added into the model of *Collection Game*. This mode performs the function of randomly displaying one target picture within one of three collection areas every 15 s (defined by "t") or after one object is successfully collected. We created three *Collection Games* with some differences in rules. The Statechart diagram of Fig. 4 (middle) is for the first Collection Game. In the first and second Collection Game, every 15 s, only one target picture is shown. But in the first one, the

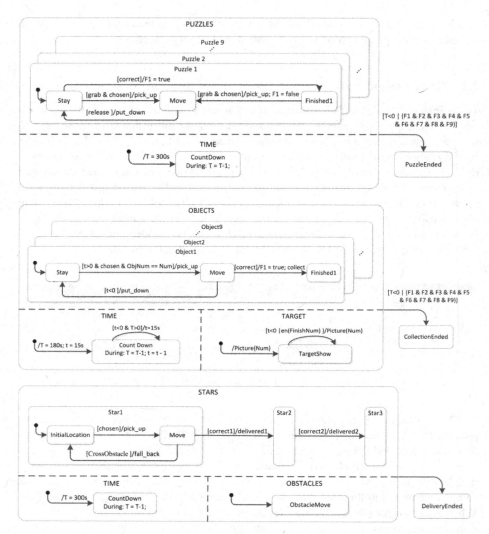

**Fig. 4.** Statechart diagrams modeling the *Puzzle Game* (top), *Collection Game* (middle) and *Delivery Game* (bottom).

target picture is visible to both players, while it is invisible to one of players in the second game. In the third game, two target pictures are shown and each of them is only visible to one player. Accordingly, operation conflict happens when two players head for different targets. In order to win, two players have to share information and make concerted actions.

The goal of *Delivery Game* is to deliver three stars to three blue-star areas surrounded by several obstacles. The Statechart diagram in Fig. 4 (bottom) explains this game. The "OBSTACLES" mode manages the states of obstacles according to the predefined logic. Players are supposed to deliver stars one by one and avoid obstacle areas. The star will fall into the obstacle areas and go back to the "InitialLocation" when crossing these areas. Players are rewarded with different points for three successful deliveries. Therefore, to achieve higher scores within limited time, it is important to make a reasonable delivery order and choose safer and faster paths from several available paths. We also modified the layout of obstacle areas to create three *Delivery Games*. In this type of game, players need to perform collaborative manipulation as well as collaborative path planning.

### 2.3  Communication Management

The word "Communication" here refers to user communication and game connection. Skype [15] is used in this system to support real-time communication between users. As a popular communication application, Skype is easy to install and use, and provides good video and audio quality [16]. The nature of distributed multiplayer games demands real-time synchronization and consistent maintenance of game states on distant computers. We used server-client architecture to implement data exchange across the network between distant CVE applications. The server runs the major programs. Clients connected to the server constantly receive data from the server in order to carry out their own purpose. When running two CVE applications, any one application can be selected as the server, while the other one connects to the server via a specified IP address and plays the client role. As shown in Fig. 5, the server and the client separately process each player input in the form of hand gestures and perform the logic of handle control locally. Any information regarding local actions would then be sent to the server, which carries out game rules according to the information and synchronizes all actions with the world state so as to update the game states. After that, the server propagates the updated data to the client so as to synchronize the game state on both sides.

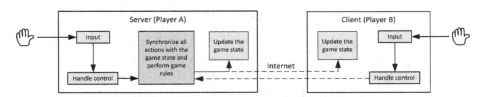

**Fig. 5.** Game data exchange and update between two CVE applications

### 2.4  Data Management

The database collects objective process data, which is indexed by time and stored as *. *csv* files in real time. It also records users' conversation in the form of audio. Based on these data, we can summarize a series of offline quantitative measures to evaluate the performance and interaction of the users (Table 1).

**Table 1.** Measures of users' performance and interaction

| Measures | Description |
|---|---|
| Total play time (s) | The time between the start and the end of one game. It suggests the difficulty of the game for the players. |
| Collaborative operation efficiency (%) | Duration of collaborative operation divided by the total play time. It indicates the prevalence of collaborative activities. |
| Finished objects (/minute) | The number of objects that reached the correct destinations within one minute. It denotes the rate of game completion. |
| Words said by one pair/one player (per minute) | The total number of words that one/two player(s) spoke in one game divided by the total play time. It indicates negotiation between two players. |

# 3 Usability Study

## 3.1 Participants

We conducted a usability study to evaluate the HIH CVE system with 12 participants. This study was approved by the Vanderbilt Institutional Review Board (IRB) and supervised by engineers and ASD therapists. All the participants were first paired based on age and gender and divided into three ASD/TD pairs (three male pairs) and three TD/TD pairs (two male pairs and one female pair). Before the experiment, participants' parents completed the Social Responsiveness Scale, second edition (SRS-2) [17] and Social Communication Questionnaire Lifetime Total Score (SCQ) [18] to quantify the current ASD symptoms of the participants. Participants' detailed information is shown in Table 2.

**Table 2.** Participan Characteristics

| Participants | ASD (n = 3) | | TD 1[a] (n = 3) | | TD 2[a] (n = 6) | |
|---|---|---|---|---|---|---|
| | Mean | SD | Mean | SD | Mean | SD |
| Age (years) | 11.70 | 2.24 | 11.09 | 1.19 | 9.99 | 0.87 |
| SRS-2 total raw score | 115.67 | 8.50 | 44.33 | 33.55 | 6.67 | 9.18 |
| SRS-2 Tscore | 82.67 | 3.21 | 54.33 | 13.58 | 40 | 3.58 |
| SCQ current total score | 26.67 | 6.11 | 10.33 | 13.58 | 1.5 | 2.07 |

[a]TD1 represents the TD participants in the ASD/TD group and TD2 represents those in the TD/TD group.

## 3.2 Procedure

This study was conducted in our two separate experimental rooms (Fig. 6). Paired participants were invited to use the system and complete all the sessions lasting about one hour. Before starting the experiment, experimenters explained the experimental procedure, length and devices to participants and taught them how to use the Leap Motion Controller for interaction.

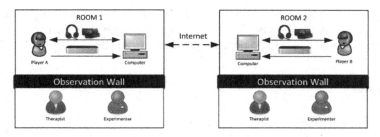

**Fig. 6.** Experimental setup

Participants then went to separate rooms to interact with the system. They would wear the headsets during the whole experiment in order to talk with their partners. As shown in Fig. 7, each participant first took an independent practice game that helped them get familiarized with the handle's operation. The length of this session depended on the abilities of participants. Following the practice session, a brief tutorial of all games informed participants of general game rules and encouraged them to cooperate with one another in the game session. Note that this tutorial did not cover everything; participants still needed to talk with their partners to figure out how to play the games. The game session consists of eight separate games. Experimenters did not provide help for them or intervene during this session. Participants played *Puzzle Games* in pre-test and post-test. These two games used different target pictures with similar visual complexity. Therefore, from the results of the pre-test and post-test, we could compare the change in participants' performance and interaction before and after *training*. After the pre-test, they entered the training part which consisted of three *Collection Games* and three *Delivery Games* to foster social understanding and collaborative skills. As mentioned before, all these games were different in terms of game difficulty or game setting. So participants could be kept interested in the games and negotiation with their partners at all times.

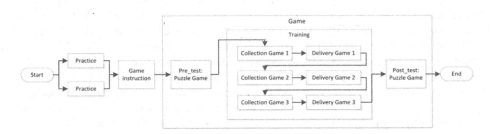

**Fig. 7.** Experimental procedure

At the end of the experiment, participants filled out a questionnaire and received gift cards as compensation. Twelve questions in the questionnaire obtained participants' feedbacks regarding their levels of engagement, performance and communication as well as their perception of the game quality. Seven of the questions were scored on a five-point scale based on self-assessment (where 5 = "like very much", 1 = "not at all"). Four of the questions were answered by choosing one answer from three choices. The last question was optional asking about suggestions for game improvement.

# 4    Results

## 4.1    User Experience

All of the participants completed the entire experiment. They each had prior video game experience and could figure out how to use this system easily. None of them had ever used Leap Motion but most of them could quickly learn how to operate it. Most participants expressed strong curiosity about the Leap Motion device and felt that "the technology is so cool!" Table 3 shows the feedbacks of user experience. Questions 1–7 received mostly positive feedbacks (Mean > 3). Participants perceived the games as interesting and easy to play with their partner. They also thought themselves and their partners did a good job in the games. They even gave highly positive values (Mean > 4.5) regarding the importance of communication and cooperation in the pursuit of success. The only negative value was for "Easy to control handle?" We concluded two likely reasons for the negative feedback: (a) some participants did not place the hand in the appropriate position thus reducing the detection accuracy (e.g. the hand is placed too low, too high or tilted too much), and (b) some participants' hands were too small for the Leap Motion to correctly detect.

From the group perspective, the TD/TD group had a little more fun with the games compared to the ASD/TD group. However, participants with ASD showed relatively deep interest (Mean = 4) in the games, which indicated these games were engaging for them. Additionally, participants in the TD/TD group thought more highly of their partner (Mean = 4) than of themselves (Mean = 3.33), unlike what was seen in the ASD/TD group. It seems that the participants with ASD were especially very satisfied with their performance (Mean = 4.33), while their partners did not rate their performance as highly (Mean = 3.33). This interesting result might speak to some aspects of social manners, such as modesty and praising others. In fact, we found that some TD participants really played very well, but only chose "Good" instead of "Excellent" in self-evaluation. In the TD/TD group, the maximum value for self-evaluation was 4, compared to 5 for partner-evaluation. As for the fourth question, participants with ASD were "optimistic" about cooperation with their partners; however, participants with ASD gave a relatively low value on the importance of communication. As for the cooperation, both groups had the same attitude that it was necessary and important. This seems appropriate as each game was designed to be a collaborative task.

The number of answers to each choice of questions 8–11 were counted and shown in Table 3. Numbers in the brackets below the "ASD/TD" column represent the answers of participants with ASD (the first value) and TD participants (the second value). Most participants agreed that they talked "very often" in the games, not just "when I needed" and believed "Talking with my partner" was the most useful way to learn how to play the games. Both groups gave different opinions on "Did you play better?" The TD/TD group felt "better" by the end. But TD participants in the ASD/TD

**Table 3.** Feedbacks of participants from questionnaires

| Questions: 1-7 | ASD/TD | | | | TD/TD | | | |
|---|---|---|---|---|---|---|---|---|
| | ASD | | TD | | TD | | TD | |
| | Mean | SD | Mean | SD | Mean | SD | Mean | SD |
| Like the games? | 4 | 0 | 3.67 | 0.47 | 4.33 | 0.94 | 4 | 0.82 |
| Did you do well? | 4.33 | 0.47 | 3.67 | 0.47 | 3.33 | 0.94 | 3.33 | 0.47 |
| Did partner do well? | 3.33 | 0.94 | 3.33 | 0.47 | 4 | 0 | 4 | 0.82 |
| Easy to work together? | 4 | 0.82 | 3.33 | 1.25 | 3.33 | 0.47 | 3.67 | 0.94 |
| Easy to control handle? | 2 | 0.82 | 2.33 | 0.47 | 2.33 | 0.47 | 2 | 0.82 |
| Important to talk? | 3.67 | 1.25 | 4 | 0.82 | 4.33 | 0.47 | 4 | 0.82 |
| Important to cooperate? | 4.67 | 0.47 | 4.67 | 0.47 | 4.67 | 0.47 | 4.67 | 0.47 |

| Questions: 8-11 | ASD/TD | Choices | TD/TD |
|---|---|---|---|
| How often did you talk? | 5(2/3) | "Very often" | 4 |
| | 1(1/0) | "Only when I needed" | 2 |
| | 0 | "Very little" | 0 |
| Which was most useful to learn how to play? | 5(2/3) | "Talking with my partner" | 3 |
| | 0 (0/0) | "Reading game instructions" | 2 |
| | 1 (1/0) | "By trying several times" | 1 |
| Did you play better? | 2(2/0) | "We played better by the end" | 4 |
| | 3(0/3) | "Stayed the same" | 2 |
| | 1 (1/0) | "We played worse" | 0 |
| Which was most useful to win? | 6(3/3) | "Working closely with my partner" | 5 |
| | 0 | "My personal performance" | 1 |
| | 0 | "Understanding the game rules" | 0 |

| Question: 12 | ASD/TD | TD/TD |
|---|---|---|
| Suggestions for game improvement (optional) | 2(1/1): It's awesome. /No need. 2(1/1): Change rewarding points. /Use other games. 2(1/1): No answer. | 1: No, it's fine. 1: Same more games. 3: Make handle more controllable. /Use mouse to play. 1: No answer. |

group felt "same" while their partner felt "better." This is reasonable because, from the performance analysis (discussed later in detail), the TD/TD group achieved much more progress than the ASD/TD group. It also suggests that participants with ASD were more pleased with their performance. For the question 11, in accordance with the results for question 7, both groups highlighted the usefulness of "working closely with my partner."

As for the optional question, except for responses related to game design, some participants felt it was a little difficult to control the handle, which indicated that even though they were curious about the new technology of Leap Motion, they could not adapt to it quickly owning to unfamiliarity and the limitations of device.

## 4.2 User Performance

The results regarding user performance are shown in Table 4. The significantly decreased mean play time, increased mean collaborative operation efficiency and finished pieces demonstrate that, on the average, participants could spend less time, cooperate more efficiently, achieve higher rewards, and thus performed better collaboratively in the post-test than in the pre-test. Moreover, participants talked more in the post-test, which was an unexpected finding. This may be an indication that participants still needed or wanted to communicate with each other in our CVE system even after they had become familiar with the games.

**Table 4.** Comparison of participants' performance in pre- and post-test

| Measures | ASD/TD | | | TD/TD | | |
|---|---|---|---|---|---|---|
| | Pre | Post | Diff. | Pre | Post | Diff. |
| Total play time (s) | 300 | 242 | −58 | 300 | 212 | −88 |
| Collaborative operation efficiency (%) | 19 | 24.49 | 5.49 | 18.77 | 39.41 | 20.64 |
| Finished pieces (/minute) | 0.8 | 1.74 | 0.94 | 0.8 | 2.55 | 1.75 |
| Words said by one pair (/minute) | 65 | 78 | 13 | 74 | 104 | 30 |
| Words said by the child with ASD (/minute) | 29 | 41 | 12 | / | / | / |
| Words said by each player (/minute) | 36 | 37 | 1 | 37 | 52 | 15 |

Comparing both groups, we can see that the TD/TD group played better, especially in terms of "collaborative operation efficiency". The TD/TD group communicated more frequently in the post-test by increasing about 30 words per minute. Although corresponding growth in the ASD/TD group is weak, it is worth noting that the participants with ASD had a higher level of communication than their TD partner and demonstrated a similar increase trend (Diff. = 12) as that of TD participants in the TD/TD group (Diff. = 15).

## 5    Conclusion and Future Work

In this paper, we present the development and implementation of a novel distributed CVE system capable of providing a flexible interaction platform for children with ASD and their peers, and collecting quantitative and objective metrics regarding collaborative and communicative performance. The system integrated with the Leap Motion employed a series of collaborative games with implicit interaction rules. Based on participants' feedbacks, they were engaged in these games and motivated to play well, even though they were not well adapted to the use of the Leap Motion device. They also understood the importance of cooperation and communication to win each game and worked hard to achieve success. The real-time communication tool guaranteed flexible and uninterrupted information exchange under the distributed condition. Although current experimental results were limited and we cannot able to generalize the conclusion that children with ASD can improve social competence through our system, the results are promising and demonstrate the potential value of our system in fostering collaboration and communication among children with and without ASD.

In the future, we will refine the system to support better gameplay experience. Considering the limitations of the Leap Motion device, we may adjust its properties based on the children's characteristics or replace it with another input device. We are investigating haptic devices that provide physical contact [19]. We also want to expand the sample size of the user study to obtain the statistical power of results in verifying the influence of this system on children. Additionally, we found that several participants' conversations not only involved contents about games, but also referred to other social information. For example, they asked each other's name, age and the games they played in daily life. Therefore, we plan to analyze the conversation content emerging from the use of this system in order to deeply understand the behaviors of children with ASD.

**Acknowledgment.** This work was supported in part by the National Institutes of Health under Grant 1R01MH091102-01A1. Some virtual objects and pictures in the CVE system were obtained from free online repositories, such as Unity assert store.

# References

1. Baio, J.: Prevalence of Autism Spectrum Disorders: Autism and Developmental Disabilities Monitoring Network, 14 Sites, United States, 2008. Morbidity and Mortality Weekly Report. Surveillance Summaries, vol. 61, no. 3. Centers for Disease Control and Prevention (2012)
2. Kim, Y.S., et al.: Prevalence of autism spectrum disorders in a total population sample. Am. J. Psychiatry **168**(9), 904–912 (2011)
3. Johnson, C.P., Myers, S.M.: Identification and evaluation of children with autism spectrum disorders. Pediatrics **120**(5), 1183–1215 (2007)
4. Blumberg, S.J., et al.: Changes in prevalence of parent-reported autism spectrum disorder in school-aged US children: 2007 to 2011–2012. National health statistics reports, vol. 65, no. 20, pp. 1–7 (2013)
5. Home, C.: Prevalence of Autism Spectrum Disorder Among Children Aged 8 Years— Autism and Developmental Disabilities Monitoring Network, 11 Sites, United States, 2010 (2014)
6. Moore, D., McGrath, P., Thorpe, J.: Computer-aided learning for people with autism–a framework for research and development. Innovations Educ. Teach. Int. **37**(3), 218–228 (2000)
7. Churchill, E.F., Snowdon, D.: Collaborative virtual environments: an introductory review of issues and systems. Virtual Reality **3**(1), 3–15 (1998)

8. Weiss, P.L., et al.: Usability of technology supported social competence training for children on the autism spectrum. In: 2011 International Conference on Virtual Rehabilitation (ICVR). IEEE (2011)
9. Cheng, Y., Ye, J.: Exploring the social competence of students with autism spectrum conditions in a collaborative virtual learning environment–the pilot study. Comput. Educ. **54** (4), 1068–1077 (2010)
10. Stichter, J.P., et al.: iSocial: delivering the social competence intervention for adolescents (SCI-A) in a 3D virtual learning environment for youth with high functioning autism. J. Autism Dev. Disord. **44**(2), 417–430 (2014)
11. Millen, L., et al.: Collaborative virtual environment for conducting design sessions with students with autism spectrum conditions. In: Proceedings of 9th International Conference on Disability, Virtual Reality and Association Technologies (2012)
12. Battocchi, A., et al.: Collaborative Puzzle Game: a tabletop interactive game for fostering collaboration in children with Autism Spectrum Disorders (ASD). In: Proceedings of the ACM International Conference on Interactive Tabletops and Surfaces. ACM (2009)
13. Leap Motion. https://www.leapmotion.com/
14. Unity. https://unity3d.com/
15. Skype. http://www.skype.com/en/
16. Baset, S.A., Schulzrinne, H.: An analysis of the skype peer-to-peer internet telephony protocol. arXiv preprint cs/0412017 (2004)
17. Constantino, J.N., Gruber, C.P.: The Social Responsiveness Scale. Western Psychological Services, Los Angeles (2002)
18. Rutter, M., Bailey, A., Lord, C.: The Social Communication Questionnaire Manual 2003. Western Psychological Services, Los Angeles (2003)
19. Ramstein, C., Hayward, V.: The pantograph: a large workspace haptic device for multimodal human computer interaction. In: Conference Companion on Human factors in Computing Systems. ACM (1994)

# Design for Healthy Aging
# and Rehabilitation

# Home Trials of Robotic Systems: Challenges and Considerations for Evaluation Teams

Ilia Adami[1], Margherita Antona[1(⊠)], and Constantine Stephanidis[1,2]

[1] Institute of Computer Science, Foundation for Research and Technology - Hellas (FORTH), N. Plastira 100, Vassilika Vouton, Heraklion, Crete 70013, Greece
antona@ics.forth.gr
[2] Computer Science Department, University of Crete, Heraklion, Crete, Greece

**Abstract.** In the past decade, the field of social robotics has focused its efforts on robotic systems whose main purpose is to support and elongate independent living at home for the elderly. A quick research on the subject will produce numerous publications on robotic prototypes, on the methodologies used to derive design requirements, and on the results from laboratory based evaluations. Reports on how such systems perform in actual home environments with ever-changing parameters and conditions are scarce and so are reports on what to take into consideration when planning the implementation of such complex evaluations. This paper will discuss some of the challenges that were faced by the experiment team during the home trials of an autonomously moving social robotic system.

**Keywords:** Assistive robots · Elderly · Home trials

## 1 Introduction

There is a growing need to address the worldwide-observed phenomena of population aging and the numerous implications it can create in the existing socioeconomic structures and healthcare frameworks of the affected countries. According to the 2015 UN report [1] on world population ageing, it is estimated that globally the number of older persons (60+) is expected to grow by 56%, by the year 2050. And older persons are projected to exceed the number of children for the first time in 2047. In Europe alone the number of senior citizens (ages from 65 to 80) will rise by nearly 40%. Australia, Japan, and the United States are also experiencing this trend. Moreover, according to the same report, the older population is itself ageing, meaning that the number of people 80 years or over, the "oldest-old" persons, is growing even faster than the number of older persons overall. As pointed out in [13], there will be a tremendous shortage on staff and qualified healthcare personnel in the near future to cater to the needs of the graying population.

Advancements in the Information and Communication Technologies (ICTs), electronics, and robotics, have allowed fields such as tele-healthcare and robotics to

© Springer International Publishing Switzerland 2016
M. Antona and C. Stephanidis (Eds.): UAHCI 2016, Part III, LNCS 9739, pp. 291–301, 2016.
DOI: 10.1007/978-3-319-40238-3_28

explore technological solutions for the support of the elderly, such as tele-monitoring platforms, ambient assisted living environments, robotic assistants, and social assistive robots (SARs). All initiatives seem to share a common goal, namely to find ways to support and elongate the time people can live independently at their homes, while maintaining a good quality of life. Furthermore, solutions are being sought to deal with the usual effects associated with aging such as physical and mental impairments, social isolation, and loneliness.

In the past decade a number of technological prototypes have been developed and evaluated. More often than not, however, these solutions are evaluated in laboratory settings or in the premises of institutions and public spaces. Very few have actually been installed in actual home environments. A long term home trial of an autono-mously moving social robot was conducted in the context of the 7th Framework Pro-gramme European funded project HOBBIT-the Mutual Care Robot[1]. A total of three countries, Austria, Sweden, and Greece, were involved in the HOBBIT project. The main goal of the project was to develop a low cost robotic assistant for the elderly that can move autonomously in a home environment and perform tasks such emergency detection and handling, fall prevention, and providing a "feeling of being safe and supported" [2]. In addition, Mutual Care was one of the core interaction paradigms that were studied in HOBBIT. The first prototype (PT1) of the robot was evaluated by a total of 49 users in laboratory conditions in three countries, Austria, Sweden, and Greece. The results from that first evaluation lead to the development of the final robot prototype (PT2), which was then evaluated in the actual homes of a total of 18 elderly users in these three countries for a total of 3 weeks per user 4. This paper will not focus on the methodologies used for the trials, or on the actual collective results of the trials, which are reported elsewhere [3]. Rather, it will present some of the challenges and lessons learned in organizing and running home trials with four elderly users in the island of Crete in Greece, with the goal of providing practical insights to researchers who plan similar home trials of complex technologies in the future.

## 2    Background

The likelihood for home robots to be adopted by older adults depends greatly on two main factors. Firstly, on how successful these systems are in meeting older adults' needs, and secondly, on how amenable respective users are to robot assistance [21]. Borrowing user requirements techniques from the HCI field (i.e., focus groups, ques-tionnaires, structured interviews, and exploratory studies) has allowed many research teams to investigate the above two factors and on coming up with design guidelines for such robotic systems (i.e., [7, 10, 18–20]). As a result, based on the acquired knowledge on what older users need, a number of robotic prototypes have been developed and showcased in the past years. In their review on social assistive robots in elderly care, Broekens et al. [13] give a number of examples of assistive robots such as Nursebot [12], Care-o-Bot 3 [14], Pearl [15], and PARO [16]. Other more recent examples include

---

[1] http://hobbit.acin.tuwien.ac.at/.

Robear [5], a prototype robot that helps in lifting patients from bed and supporting them in walking which was designed by Riken a Japanese research institute.

However, even though we are seeing numerous prototypes of autonomously moving robotic assistants, not a lot of them have been extensively evaluated under real conditions and outside the controlled environment of a laboratory or an institution (i.e., nursing homes, long term care institutions, schools, etc.). For example, Prakash et al. [7] studied older adults' reactions to a robot appearance (PR2 robot) in the Aware Home Research facility of Georgia Tech, a home-based laboratory that serves as a platform for testing home-based technologies. In a different study with the same robot and the same laboratory, Prakash, Beer et al. studied how robots can assist older people in their medication management [8]. In the context of the EU project SERA, von der Pütten et al. [9] presented the results of the home trials of a stationary robotic companion for the elderly with real users and stated that despite the challenges of conducting home trials, they gained useful insights that traditional laboratory testing wouldn't have been able to give them.

Often, traditional controlled lab settings fail to capture the complexities and richness of the real living environments in which these systems are placed 5. Thus, there is a big gap in the research as to how such complex systems can behave under real conditions where user scenarios don't follow a specific sequence or script and important parameters can shift on a daily basis, and how users interact with them in the long run. Evaluating robotic systems that provide interactive services autonomously in real environments for an extended period of time has always being a challenge in HRI and assistive robots [17]. Apart from the high requirements on the stability and reliability of the system [22], carrying out long-term home trials of complex technological systems with real users is a rather time and resource intense endeavor. There is an ongoing debate on whether field trials in general are worth the effort, with advocates arguing on both sides on the subject; some claim that the added value is questionable [24], while others stress over the fact that field trials can unveil problems impossible to observe under the ideal conditions of a lab setting (i.e., lighting, background noise level, and perfect wireless connectivity, etc.) [4]. Even though our sample of four participants was small, the experience gained from conducting the home trials of HOBBIT in Crete gave us valuable lessons on the challenges and the factors that should be taken into consideration when planning for similar trials in the future. These challenges and considerations are presented in the following sections.

## 3  Recruiting Participants Challenges

Finding elderly candidates that would be willing to participate in long-term evaluations of complex systems in real home environments is a challenging task for multiple reasons. Usually, depending on the type of the study and the user profile it targets, there is a list of inclusion criteria based upon which the participant selection is made. In our case, for example, the inclusion criteria included that the candidate had to be 75 years or older, single-living at home, not suffer from any major illnesses, disabilities or cognitive impairments, and have at least one self-reported (i.e., screening questionnaire) moderate or severe vision, hearing, or mobility related impairment, and be available for the duration of the three-week long evaluation without any extended absences. In addition, the home or flat of the candidate had to be spacious enough to host the robot, have no steps, stairs or other type of levels, and wide enough door passages and corridors for the robot to cross.

As a result, there were many situations where a prospective participant that would fit perfectly the user profile, had to eventually be excluded because his or her home environment was not conducive for the trial. Such constrains may make the recruitment efforts difficult, thus it is strongly recommended for the experiment team to acquire a large number of contacts of prospective candidates initially, even if the evaluation involves a small number of users.

In choosing the best technique to recruit prospective participants, the experiment team should also take into consideration the geographic location where the experiment is going to take place and how this may affect the access to pools of elderly users. In big urban areas it may be easier to find independent living facilities for the elderly and other type of institutions and organizations for the elderly, or make use of publications for pensioners to advertise the experiment. In smaller or more remote geographic areas, such resources may be more limited and thus other venues should be examined at a local level, such as community centers, or personal contacts and referrals. For our home trials in Crete, we collaborated with a local Community Care & Active Ageing Center (Municipality of Heraklion). This care center promotes active ageing to its members by involving them in various social and recreational activities and projects. Our contact there was very helpful in finding us potential candidates that fit the general inclusion criteria and arranged to bring them to our laboratory for a presentation and demonstration of the system.

Giving presentations of the system at community centers, lodges, senior centers, or inviting groups of prospective candidates to the laboratory for a presentation of the system and the goals of the experiment offer a great opportunity for collecting contact information. Respectively, a fun evening at the laboratory, where the experiment can be discussed over coffee, tea, and cookies is a nice ice-breaker and a good opportunity for the prospective participants to get to know the research team and vice versa. Even if the presentation attendees are not interested in participating in the experiment, they may know of others who would be interested [23]. Regardless of whether the presentation takes place at the elderly center or at the laboratory, there are a few factors that the research team should take into account in order to make the most of such events. In the following paragraphs, the considerations on organizing a presentation at the laboratory are discussed.

*Create a Welcoming and Comforting Atmosphere.* The organizer of the event should make sure that the guests seat comfortably during the presentation, and at the right distance from the screen if a slide presentation is used. Snacks and refreshments such as tea, coffee, juice, and water should be offered throughout the presentation.

*Introduction.* After introducing the research team, it is beneficial to give a brief background on the purpose of the entire initiative. This will help the elderly candidates to get a broader perspective on the problem the scientific community is trying to address and how the current project is contributing in moving a step forward towards finding a possible solution. Often elderly people are reluctant to discuss technology matters because their lack of previous experiences with interactive technologies makes them think that they do not have anything of valuable to share. Therefore, it is important to emphasize to them how their insight and opinions, regardless of their exposure to such technologies, can help the researchers in further improvements of such systems for future generations.

*Presentation Material.* The presentation material should be straightforward and the presenter must use non-technical language when describing the system and its capabilities. Dickinson et al. [6] state that using technical words that technology specialists use everyday such as "monitor" or "functionality", can be at best confusing and at worst distressingly unfamiliar, causing the technology to become even more foreign to the potential elderly users and the users to become less confident in participating in the discussion about it. We found that the key is to focus on describing how the robot can help by giving real life examples relevant to everyday common needs of the elderly, rather than explaining the mechanisms that allow it to perform the tasks.

There should be a good balance of keeping the presentation fun but informative, without tiring or overwhelming the elderly audience with too much information. After the presentation ends, the team should allocate some time for an open discussion where answers to any questions about the system or the experiment itself can be given.

*Showcase the System if Possible.* If the event takes place at the laboratory or building where the prototype is housed, it is very helpful to arrange a demonstration of the system. In our case, the majority of the elderly had not seen a robot in real life before and any notion they had was acquired from the TV or science fiction movies, in which the depiction of robots is often unrealistic or even frightening. Having no previous real experience of a robotic system would make anyone reluctant to agree to participate in any type of study, let alone agreeing to host an autonomously moving robot in their homes for an extended period of time. Being able to demonstrate the robotic prototype diminishes the fear of the unknown and closes the gap between expectations and reality. After the demonstration, it is a good idea to encourage the guests to come close and try out the system for themselves. This helps alleviate the pre-established notion that new technologies are difficult to learn or use. After we demonstrated the robot, we asked the guests to come close and try interacting with it. At the beginning they all gathered around it, but were reluctant to engage in any type of interaction. They were unsure and shy about trying it, mostly because they were afraid that they wouldn't manage to operate it or that they would do something wrong and embarrass themselves in front of the others. But after the encouragement from the technician, the most adventurous from the group started interacting with the interface. When the rest of the guests saw their peer interacting with it, they too wanted to try it out. The uncertainty slowly dissipated as the users realized that you don't have to be a scientist or a specialist to be able to operate it and it is indeed designed for the everyday elderly person who may not have any computer experience. By the end of the event, we could hear discussions among the guests as to who would be the best candidate to take the robot home for the trial.

This event helped us communicate the goal of the experiment and gather initial contact information from potential candidates that showed a sincere interest in participating in the home trials of the prototype.

If the prototype of the system is not available for demonstration, then a video showcasing the system or still pictures of it performing various tasks can be shown.

*Prepare Information Leaflets to Give Away at the end of the Presentation.* Printed material with information on the project and its purpose and on details about the overall process of the experiment (i.e., inclusion criteria, duration, type of data that will be collected, etc.), and the team's contact information for interested parties, should be given to each attendee on their way out.

*Communicate the Terms and Conditions of the Experiment.* The communication of the terms and conditions of participating in a home trial experiment to a candidate that has shown interest in participating in the home trial is also a very important stage and should be done with great care by the experiment team, in order to ensure that the candidate has clearly understood all the details about the process of the actual trial before agreeing to participate or signing a consent form. Details about the duration of the experiment, the type of information that is going to be collected (i.e., questionnaires, data logging, interviews, etc.), the measures the team will take to safeguard the privacy of the data collected, the kind of support that is going to be offered during the trials for technical or other type of issues that may arise during the experiment, and the overall process that is going to be followed, should be clarified. It is very important at this stage to also stress that during the trials the participants will be fully supported by the experiment team and that should they decide to stop the trial at any given point for whatever reason, there will be no obligations or repercussions.

The key point is that apart from the fact that it is an ethical obligation of the experiment team to inform the participant about all aspects of the experiment, it is imperative to do so in order to avoid the creation of false expectations by the participant that could lead to serious disruptions during the experiment. Another important point to stress to the prospective participant is that the system that will be installed in his or her home environment is an experimental prototype, which means that technical issues may arise from time to time during the trial. The participant should be given a contact list of the experiment team to contact in case of such occurrences.

## 4    Scheduling of the Experiment

In their paper, Rogers et al. [5] stress that traditional evaluation methods and metrics (derived from laboratory settings) often fail in capturing the complexities of the real world in which systems or technologies are placed and used. In their field trial of a mobile system they concluded that even something as simple as the changing nature of the physical environment, such as the time of year, can have quite significant impact on the user experience. In planning the home trials of the robotic assistant we found this to be very true. The actual timing of the experiment affected not only our recruitment efforts, but in some cases it also affected the users' interaction time with the system.

The season during which the experiment is going to take place can increase the rate of difficulty for the evaluation team. Obviously, a lot of times the selection of the time period that the experiment will take place is determined by factors beyond the team's control, i.e., obligations towards the overall project timeline and deadlines, production, development and deployment timeframes, etc. In our case, the home trials were eventually scheduled for the beginning of summer, with some cascading to the middle of the summer. In the island of Crete, during the summer a lot of elderly people move away from the cities to their villages. This factor affected our recruiting efforts a great deal, simply because a lot of our initial contacts were no longer available for the experiments. As a result, we had to recruit anew, and find candidates that had not participated in any stage of the project before. This doubled the time and effort of the evaluation team, who had to reach new candidates by phone interviews, house visits, face-to-face interviews, etc.

The weather in the summer also seemed to affect the amount of time spent interacting with the robot during the home trials. One of the participants, for example, told us that she would have interacted more with the robot if we had brought it during the winter. She further explained that in the summer, she prefers to sit in her yard where it is cooler and enjoy the good weather. In winter time, she explained, she stays mostly indoors because of the rain and the cold and so she believed that the robot would have been a better distraction for her then. Another user ended up turning off the system for a few days because it emitted extra heat warming up even more the house and making it uncomfortable.

The weather factor had inflicted worries to the team at the beginning of the project, but mostly about the experiments having to take place in the winter time. The research team was worried that asking potential candidates if they would be willing to remove their carpets in the areas the robot would circulate during the cold months of winter would have received a negative response, as area rugs and carpets is a very common way of insulating the home against the cold in Greece.

Apart from the weather, another factor that may affect the scheduling of the experiment is local holidays, religious or non-religious ones, or other local special events during which the prospective users may be absent or have family visiting.

Both temporal conditions and local traditions may affect the scheduling aspects of the trials and the research team must be aware of that in order to take the appropriate measures.

## 5   Considerations When Conducting the Home Trial

In the handbook of usability testing [11], the author describes the characteristics of a good test monitor or facilitator. Some of these characteristics include: being able to form instant rapport with the participant by sizing up each participant's personality and making the person feel comfortable and secure, being a good listener by laying aside personal biases and strong opinions about what she or he is seeing and hearing, being empathic and able to relate to the participant's views and experiences, being flexible and able to understand when to deviate from the test plan if needed. These characteristics are essential for any type of user-based experiment, but even more so for long-term experiments with vulnerable groups such as the elderly. In the following section we discuss issues to take into consideration when conducting home trials.

*Introducing the System to the Elderly Participant.* The introduction of the system to the elderly user is one of the most important phases of the experiment, in which the facilitator has to ensure that the user will feel comfortable and confident in operating the system when left alone with it. In order for this to be achieved, certain factors need to be taken into consideration. The first factor is that each user is unique in how fast he or she can learn a new system, how much new information they can retain in one session, and how much training they need before starting to use it. Before introducing the main operations of the system, the facilitator has to investigate the user's overall experience with interaction methods. For example, all our participants were novice users with no former experience with any kind of interactive systems. Thus, the experiment facilitator had to start from the very basics, such as explaining how to select an option on the "touch screen" mounted on the robot, i.e., how much pressure to apply and how to navigate through the available menu and sub-menus before proceeding to explain more advance operations. Throughout this phase, it is important for the experiment facilitator to be able to recognize signs of fatigue or anxiety by the user, and adjust the training pace accordingly, either breaking down the introduction in smaller sessions, or incrementally introducing each function over the first few days. In addition, having the participant perform the basic functions in the presence of the facilitator ensures to the latter that the user has indeed understood the operation and is comfortable in using it on his or her own. The main point here is for the facilitator to allocate the appropriate time to explain the system to the user in a calm, patient, and straightforward manner.

*Respecting Local Customs.* In their study on the in-home requirements gathering with frail older people, Dickinson et al. [6] stress that it is important to be conscious of the expectations that an older person may have of a guest entering their home as the ritual of hospitality is often integral to a sense of self. For example, even an apparently insignificant action like refusing a cup of tea can make a tremendous difference to the comfort of your host. The hospitality parameter proved to be a very important one during the home trials in Crete, where it is very common for example, even during a short visit to a house for the host to offer refreshments and snacks or to even invite the guest to stay for lunch or dinner depending on the time of the visit. Thus, it was very important for our experiment team when visiting to apply technical support or for the facilitator to conduct any scheduled interview to allocate extra time for such social interactions. Even though such interactions are time consuming, conversations during them proved to be very insightful in understanding the background of the participant and their routines. Furthermore, it was found that during those less structured discussions the participants often offered deeper opinions about modern technologies and their limitations or advantages. For example, during a coffee session with one of the participants, she started talking about how much harder yet simpler life was in the old days compared to modern times, and how she found it disconcerting that the younger generations have become so attached to their phones and other similar technologies often preferring to sit for hours in front of screens instead of enjoying the outdoors.

*Defining the Role of the Researcher.* At the beginning of any type of evaluation, it is essential for the participant to understand that it is the system that is being evaluated and not their performance and that the role of the facilitator of the experiment is just to collect the data. At the same time, it is also important to stress that it is valuable for the experiment team to hear not only the positive aspects of the interaction with the system, but also the negative ones which will lead to further improvements of the system down the line [25]. Whereas in a short evaluation such clarification is usually given once at the beginning, in a long-term evaluation, it may need to be repeated periodically. As the trials progressed and the relationship between the experiment team and the participants grew on a more personable manner, it was noticed on multiple occasions that some participants became worried that if they reported the negative aspects of the robot that it would somehow reflect negatively on us personally or professionally. For example, one of the participants during an interview mentioned something negative and quickly added that perhaps this information should not go on the official report. When the facilitator asked why the participant thought so, the participant said that this information could hurt the performance rating of the team. In this instance, the facilitator had to reassure the participant that the experiment team did not have any personal stake in the system and to reinforce the importance of reporting all aspects of the interaction with the robot in order to draw concrete conclusions on how it can be improved in the future. Facilitators of long-term evaluations should be aware of the possibility of the participants developing similar sentiments and address them appropriately when needed.

## 6 Conclusions

Long-term home trials of complex assistive systems can provide tremendous insights on how users experience living with such systems in their own home environment and they are important for future developments of prototypes. However, the complexity of home trials is often much higher than laboratory-based trials and can lead even experienced HCI researchers into common pitfalls. In this paper, we presented some considerations and suggestions regarding the planning of the execution of such trials, based on our experience from conducting home trials with four elderly participants in Greece. Even though some of the considerations may seem obvious to the reader, they can be easily overlooked as more urgent issues may take precedence in the planning of the evaluations, such as testing and ensuring the prototype system to be evaluated is ready for the trials, choosing or coming up with the appropriate methodologies for collecting quantitative and qualitative data, constructing structured interviews protocols for all evaluators to follow, drawing common guidelines, preparing help manuals for the system, etc. The main conclusion is that no matter how careful the planning is, there is a higher than usual probability of unexpected factors and events to take place during such evaluations and thus the team has to be flexible enough to tackle such events without compromising the integrity of the evaluation.

**Acknowledgments.** Part of this work has been conducted in the context of the Project ICT-HOBBIT "HOBBIT The Mutual Care Robot", funded by the European Commission under the 7th Framework Programme (Grant Agreement 288146). The authors would like to thank the project's partners: ACIN, Technische Universität Wien, AAT Logo AAT, Technische Univervisät Wien, MetraLabs GmbH Neue Technologien und Systeme, Hella Automation GmbH, Lund University, Academy for Aging Research at HB. In addition, the authors would like to thank the "TALOS" Community Care & Active Ageing Center of Heraklion Municipality for their assistance in finding candidates for the PT1 and PT2 trials.

# References

1. United Nations. World Population Ageing, pp. 1–11 (2015)
2. Vincze, M., Zagler, W., Lammer, L., Weiss, A., Huber, A., Fischinger, D., Gisinger, C.: Towards a robot for supporting older people to stay longer independent at home. In: Proceedings of 41st International Symposium on Robotics ISR/Robotik 2014, pp. 1–7. VDE, June 2014
3. Pripfl, J., Körtner, T., Batko-Klein, D., Hebesberger, D., Weninger, M., Gisinger, C., Weiss, A.: Results of a real world trial with a mobile social service robot for older adults. In: The Eleventh ACM/IEEE International Conference on Human Robot Interation, pp. 497–498. IEEE Press, March 2016
4. Rogers, Y., Connelly, K.H., Tedesco, L., Hazlewood, W., Kurtz, A., Hall, R.E., Hursey, J., Toscos, T.: Why it's worth the hassle: the value of in-situ studies when designing ubicomp. In: Krumm, J., Abowd, G.D., Seneviratne, A., Strang, T. (eds.) UbiComp 2007. LNCS, vol. 4717, pp. 336–353. Springer, Heidelberg (2007)
5. http://www.riken.jp/en/pr/press/2015/20150223_2/
6. Dickinson, A., Goodman, J., Syme, A., Eisma, R., Tiwari, L., Mival, O., Newell, A.: Domesticating technology: in-home requirements gathering with frail older people. In: Proceedings of 10th International Conference on Human - Computer Interaction HCI, pp. 827–831 (2003)
7. Prakash, A., Kemp, C.C., Rogers, W.A.: Older adults' reactions to a robot's appearance in the context of home use. In: Proceedings of the 2014 ACM/IEEE International Conference on Human-Robot Interaction, pp. 268–269. ACM, March 2014
8. Prakash, A., Beer, J. M., Deyle, T., Smarr, C.A., Chen, T.L., Mitzner, T.L., Rogers, W.A.: Older adults' medication management in the home: how can robots help? In: 2013 8th ACM/IEEE International Conference on Human-Robot Interaction (HRI), pp. 283–290. IEEE, March, 2013
9. von der Pütten, A.M., Krämer, N.C., Eimler, S.C.: Living with a robot companion: empirical study on the interaction with an artificial health advisor. In: Proceedings of the 13th International Conference on Multimodal Interfaces, pp. 327–334. ACM, November 2011
10. Wrede, B., Haasch, A., Hofemann, N., Hohenner, S., Hüwel, S., Kleinehagenbrock, M., Fritsch, J.: Research issues for designing robot companions: BIRON as a case study. In: Drews, P. (ed.) Proceedings of IEEE Conference on Mechatronics and Robotics, vol. 4, pp. 1491–1496 (2004)
11. Rubin, J., Chisnell, D.: Handbook of Usability Testing: How to Plan, Design and Conduct Effective Tests. Wiley, New York (2008)
12. Matthews, J.T.: The Nursebot Project: developing a personal robotic assistant for frail older adults in the community. Home Health Care Manage. Pract. **14**(5), 403–405 (2002)

13. Broekens, J., Heerink, M., Rosendal, H.: Assistive social robots in elderly care: a review. Gerontechnology **8**(2), 94–103 (2009)
14. Graf, B., Reiser, U., Hägele, M., Mauz, K., Klein, P.: Robotic home assistant Care-O-bot® 3-product vision and innovation platform. In: 2009 IEEE Workshop on Advanced Robotics and its Social Impacts (ARSO), pp. 139–144. IEEE, November 2009
15. Pollack, M.E., Brown, L., Colbry, D., Orosz, C., Peintner, B., Ramakrishnan, S., Thrun, S.: Pearl: A mobile robotic assistant for the elderly. In: AAAI Workshop on Automation as Eldercare, vol. 2002, pp. 85–91, August 2002
16. Wada, K., Shibata, T.: Living with seal robots—its sociopsychological and physiological influences on the elderly at a care house. IEEE Trans. Robot. **23**(5), 972–980 (2007)
17. Kuo, I.-H., Jayawardena, C., Broadbent, E., Stafford, R.Q., MacDonald, B.A.: HRI evaluation of a healthcare service robot. In: Ge, S.S., Khatib, O., Cabibihan, J.-J., Simmons, R., Williams, M.-A. (eds.) ICSR 2012. LNCS, vol. 7621, pp. 178–187. Springer, Heidelberg (2012)
18. Chang, W.L., Šabanovic, S.: Potential use of robots in Taiwanese nursing homes. In: Proceedings of the 8th ACM/IEEE International Conference on Human-Robot Interaction, pp. 99–100. IEEE Press, March, 2013
19. Cesta, A., Cortellessa, G., Giuliani, V., Pecora, F., Scopelliti, M., Tiberio, L.: Psychological implications of domestic assistive technology for the elderly. PsychNol. J. **5**(3), 229–252 (2007)
20. Broadbent, E., Tamagawa, R., Patience, A., Knock, B., Kerse, N., Day, K., MacDonald, B. A.: Attitudes towards health-care robots in a retirement village. Aust. J. Ageing **31**(2), 115–120 (2012)
21. Beer, J.M., Smarr, C.A., Chen, T.L., Prakash, A., Mitzner, T.L., Kemp, C.C., Rogers, W.A.: The domesticated robot: design guidelines for assisting older adults to age in place. In: Proceedings of the Seventh Annual ACM/IEEE International Conference on Human-Robot Interaction, pp. 335–342. ACM, March 2012
22. Hüttenrauch, H., Eklundh, K.S.: Fetch-and-carry with CERO: observations from a long-term user study with a service robot. In: Proceedings of 11th IEEE International Workshop on Robot and Human Interactive Communication, 2002, pp. 158–163. IEEE (2002)
23. Pak, R., McLaughlin, A.: Designing Displays for Older Adults. CRC press, p. 126 (2010)
24. Kjeldskov, J., Skov, M.B.: Was it worth the hassle?: ten years of mobile HCI research discussions on lab and field evaluations. In: Proceedings of the 16th International Conference on Human-Computer Interaction with Mobile Devices & Services, pp. 43–52. ACM, September 2014
25. Nielsen, J.: Usability Engineering. Elsevier (1994)

# Self-Conscious Support on Walking Posture Through Mobile Avatar: Focusing on Women's Frailty Prevention Toward Old Age

Masayuki Anekawa[1]([envelope]), Atsushi Hiyama[2], Sachiko Kamiyama[3],
and Michitaka Hirose[1]

[1] Department of Mechano-Informatics, The University of Tokyo, 7-3-1 Hongo,
Bunkyo-ku, Tokyo 113-8656, Japan
{anekawa,hirose}@cyber.t.u-tokyo.ac.jp
[2] Graduate School of Information Science and Technology,
The University of Tokyo, 7-3-1 Hongo, Bunkyo-ku, Tokyo 113-8656, Japan
atsushi@cyber.t.u-tokyo.ac.jp
[3] The KAITEKI Institute, Inc., 1-1, Marunouchi 1-chome, Chiyoda-ku,
Tokyo 100-8251, Japan
kamiyama.sachiko@mh.kaiteki-institute.com

**Abstract.** An aging population in a society leads to higher expenditure on social security and medical care. To reduce the cost of treatment, it is essential that preventing frailty of nearly aged women by undertaking habitual physical exercise such as walking, since 70 % of national nursing expense is for this cohort. However, if walking activity has performed with bad posture, it will result in musculoskeletal disease. Therefore, a system that supports to correct walking activity is required. In this research, we propose a system that promotes each users walking habits, including daily steps and walking posture. The result of the experiment suggested that Avatar-based gait representation improves the self-consciousness of users' walking posture significantly rather than number-based representation.

**Keywords:** Avatar · Elderly people · Gait · Walk habit · Smart phone

## 1 Introduction

The purpose of this research is to prevent frailty of women toward an advanced age. Japan is experiencing a yearly increase in the proportion of the elderly population. The proportion of the elderly over the age of 65 has exceeded 25 % in 2013 [1], and is expected to increase to 40.5 % by 2055 [2]. Health problems of the elderly in this hyper-aged society are directly linked to the country's financial problems. Social security costs are expected to rise as the number of unhealthy elderly increases. As a result, there is a risk of the essential social support not reaching to the entire populace of nation. Therefore, supporting the promotion of health-related activities for the super-aged society is important.

M. Antona and C. Stephanidis (Eds.): UAHCI 2016, Part III, LNCS 9739, pp. 302–311, 2016.
DOI: 10.1007/978-3-319-40238-3_29

Japanese government's nursing expense reaches 12 trillion yen, and 70 % of this is for women. The need of nursing care is mostly caused by musculoskeletal disease. Though daily exercise is needed for maintaining the function of musculoskeletal system, only 29 % of Japanese women have exercise habit. Friedman et al. suggested that having an exercise habit until an advanced age extends the healthy life expectancy [3].

Walking is the most familiar exercise, and is closely related to the daily life and social activities. It is considered to be suitable for preventing frailty. However, walking in an inappropriate posture may increase the risk of falling in reverse. Hence, it is important to obtain proper walking posture before getting old. In this work, we have focused on building a system to support the long-term posture improvement and increase the number of steps. We have built and validated the system to solve the health problems of women by implementing an application that gives feedback of user's gait and number of steps by using a smartphone.

## 2   Design and Implementation

### 2.1   Study on the Measurement and Learning of Walking Motion

Kojima et al. [4] proposed a system to measure the walking posture without contacting the participants of the experiment. This system has been reported to be effective in the objective attitude presentation. The following are the four parameters to be acquired: the tilt of the back part (slouch); the longitudinal direction of the range of movement of the hands (arm swing); the range of movement of the left and right direction of the foot (horizontal width of the foot); the range of movement in the longitudinal direction of the foot part (stride). This system is able to gather sufficient data to promote a healthy walking habit. Moreover, it has high applicability, given that it does not requires physically contacting the user.

Once the walking posture is acquired, it is imperative to present the data in a recognizable manner for the user to learn the correct walking posture using the measured data. The technique to reflect the attitude data into human-type avatars as a presentation method on the virtual reality space (VRS) is considered valid. Nawahdah and Inoue [5] have reported that presenting the attitude-teaching avatar in VRS has improved the learning efficiency of attitude. Therefore, it is a system that can observe the avatar freely in VRS that is considered to be valid presentation of the measured gait.

### 2.2   Study on Techniques to Support the Habit for Health

Kobayashi et al. [6] have classified the 16 elements involved in motivation by extrinsic or intrinsic, and personal or social. For example, Skill Fitness as intrinsic and personal, Social Contribution as intrinsic and social, Payment as extrinsic and personal, and Social Contract as extrinsic and social motivation have been cited.

**Gamification.** The proposed technique described in the previous section can be effectively applied to the motivation, by gamification. Gamification results in extrinsic and intrinsic motivation by using the mechanics often appearing in games. The following items can be cited as the mechanics that are treated at Gamification.

- Experience: The value experience is stored by the visual display of the various actions. Reward is offered to level up and multiple levels are offered.
- Badge: A badge is given to honor a particular action. Usually, a badge has a variety of types, and it motivates the user to collect more badges.

In addition, when considering Gamification, an avatar is essential. The avatar often mediates the experience value and badge. Avatars are presented to the user to specifically motivate the user. Avatar is the only place in the game world, where the user can associate a strong sense of unity, intimacy, and a feeling of individuality. The clothes and items used for the avatar change in various ways and are factors that motivate the user behavior.

## 2.3   Design

In this study, the function of performing the present posture of the user through an avatar, the function of measuring and presenting the number of steps and the function to support the habit of walking exercise so that above 2 functions provide a long-term effect on the user is proposed as a method in order to wear a healthy walking habit.

## 2.4   Implementation

Precedents in above, which devised to encourage the active participation of the user along with the mention introduce research and products for gait analysis and improvement of the past with the advantage of gait analysis system of the past for its limits It was analyzed. Therefore, in the third section to propose and build an avatar system to help so that the user actually light of these related research is wearing a healthy walking habits.

## 2.5   The Proposed System

**System Overview.** The configuration of the system requires two applications that provide feedback to the user through the avatar based on the pedometer data held in the posture data. Internal data is obtained through an inquiry of attitude data in response to the ID of the server user that stores and delivers the attitude data. The non-contact type mentioned in Sect. 2 is desirable for a conveniently utilizable measurement method of attitude. In this case, it was decided to use a walking measurement system by implemented the Kinect system.

The system comprises mainly of the following three functions. The number of steps presentation function, which counts the number of steps by accessing the motion measurement chip in the smartphone. It is possible to change the degree of obesity of the avatar according to the step count of past days. The posture presentation function, which converts the gait data acquired from an external system, downloaded at any time, to the motion of the avatar. The habit support function, which prompts the user to inculcate healthy walking habits

**Avatar Design.** For providing attitude feedback as a condition, the avatar is required to have human-like features. In addition, the learning of attitude, as seen above, is considered to be freely observed in avatar wear enabled on the VR space. Moreover, there is a need to be careful as to some extent the approach and favorability in reality does not fall into the so-called uncanny valley [7,8], which decreases avatar's familiarity. According to Heike et al. [9] avatars that have minor deformation are easy to use and most preferable.

According to the survey of Banks and Bowman [10] about the relationship between the avatar and the player (user), user's sense of reality, operational feeling and a sense of responsibility in the system depends on whether the user considers the avatar as "object", "myself", "symbiote" or "others." Like the Johnsen et al.'s method [11], it is considered important to increase the sense of responsibility of the user so as to provide a motivation to walk when the avatar gets fat. Therefore avatar should be designed as others.

By the way, the purpose of the this study is not to pursue the detailed modeling of the avatar, but is the development of the avatar system to support the walking habits. Again, it is difficult to produce a character with a sense of intimacy from scratch, and character design is considered to be a field difficult to establish a unified opinion. So based on the above conditions, we chose the Avatar used in this study from existing characters. This time, it is the mascot character "Kokoron" of Shimonoseki, Insurance Department of Yamaguchi Prefecture.

**Pedometer Function.** Step umber presentation function shows user's daily steps in 3 ways: by steps number, by progress bar, by percentage of ratio of today's steps to goal steps.

Real time goal achievement status display: The achievement status is displayed as an image display by the percentage progress bar of the goal. The degree of obesity changes in the avatar. The degree of obesity of the avatar, which is displayed in the system center, depends on the number of steps walked.

Change of avatar's degree of obesity: The degree of obesity of the avatar, which is displayed in the center of display, changes depending on the number of past achievement of goal steps (shown in Fig. 1).

**Posture Presentation Function.** First we need to determine the gait parameters used in this research. Referring to previous studies [4,12–14], gait parameter to be used in the proposed system is composed of following four parameters: slouch – the forward displacement of center of shoulders from center of waist, expressed in millimeters; swing – the ratio of the arm swing width to the ideal

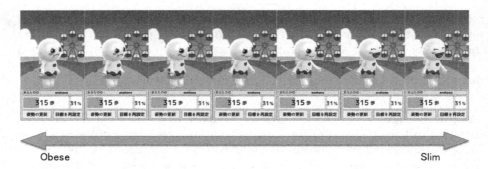

**Fig. 1.** The degree of obesity of the avatar is changed in accordance with the progress in target number of steps

arm swing width, expressed in percentage; swing position – the forward displacement of center of arm swing from the shoulder, expressed in millimeters; stride – the ratio of stride over stride to ideal stride, expressed in millimeters. For the ideal gait referenced in the swing and the stride, instructor's walking motion was captured.

Stepless reflection of the gait data to avatar animation: It is the regeneration of the walking motion of a 3D model of the avatar, in the 3D space created within unity, and reflecting the user's posture data. Attitude data in this system is used as a weight, when it has been digitized by four parameters blending the motion data that does not deviate from the ideal motion data. The motions are blended by Unity [15] mecanim [16].

**Habits Support Function.** Get and loss of avatar parts: Acquiring and/or losing the parts by the upper and lower relationship of each of the attitude parameters and threshold values on receiving an update of attitude.

Regular stimulus presentation using the notification function: The smartphone can be set to notify in advance by specifying the date even when the application is not running. This feature is called push notification. Healthy walking habits can be encouraged by displaying a notification statement to the user by using this feature in this system.

Variability of the target number of steps: There is a possibility that if user set goal step too high, the goal step will be never achieved and the user will stop using the system, because positive feedback isn't given. So we implemented a function to alter the goal number of steps if necessary.

## 3    Experimental Method

In this section, we propose an experiment to verify whether the user can recognize and improve of their walking gait by using proposed system. The purpose of this experiment is to verify if avatar gait representation is more effective than number gait representation, to investigate to which element in application users pay attention, to survey the feasibility of avatar system that promotes walk habit comprehensively.

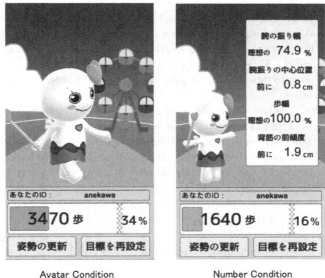

Avatar Condition                    Number Condition

**Fig. 2.** The interface of each representation condition

### 3.1  Experimental Environment

A comparison of the attitude presented by the numerical Avatar was investigated. In both the experiments, participants were presented the attitude and in each of the technique during the orientation, we verified whether the measurement can improve the level of attitude.

The experiments were performed among the participants plan consisting of the following two conditions.

- Avatar condition (Fig. 2 left): The participants of the experiment are presented the attitude that has been reflected in the avatar after the first measurement. The application to be used in the presentation will also be carried out to display the balloon acquisition and loss of exactly the same parts as those described in Sect. 3.
- Number condition (Fig. 2 right): The participants of the experiment are presented with the measurement data after initially extracting the attitude data as a real value. The application to be used in the presentation was modified in the following manner.

- Avatar maintains the T-pose (upright posture with open arms horizontally), and doesn't animate the walking motion.
- Four parameters are arranged numerical display for the window next to the avatar is displayed.
- Even when sliding finger on the screen avatars doesn't rotate.

It should be noted that display of the balloon acquisition and loss of avatar parts also in the numerical conditions is carried out. However balloon position is not adjusted. There were 25 women participants for the experiment with their ages in the range 24–57 years (average age 33.1 years, standard deviation 7.1 years). These participants were the members of the experiment on the same day. There are 12 people as number condition, and 13 people as avatar condition. In addition, we questioned the users by using an alternative formula to judge which of the participants had the most attention towards the function at the time of the attitude presented orally during the hearing after the experiment. The hearing feedback received a reply from 28 people immediately, after the posture presentation of the second measurement. The results are discussed in the next section.

## 4   Results and Discussion

The degree of improvement under each application conditions for each posture is shown in Fig. 3.

The equality of mean slouch improvements between avatar condition and number condition was rejected at a significance level of 0.05 (*) using the Welch t-test. The results of the avatar conditions were excellent, improving the swing position by 19 mm and the stride by 1.8 % more than that the number condition. Focusing on why the significant difference was observed in the slouch, the difference from other parameters is the necessity to be aware of the trunk. Number

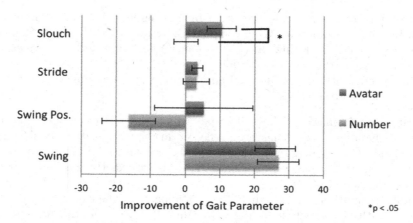

**Fig. 3.** Comparison of Gait parameters improvement between representation conditions

presentation of gait information may be useful in the control of the ends of the body, such as arm swing; But for trunk gait recognition, intuitive representation by the avatar is considered to be more effective.

Among 12 number condition participants, 7 felt that they were paying attention to the numerical value, 3 on the avatar parts, and 2 on the balloon. On the other hand, among 13 avatar condition participants, 4 felt that they were paying attention to the walking motion of the avatar, 7 on the avatar parts, and 2 on the balloon. Figure 4 shows attention distribution of each condition.

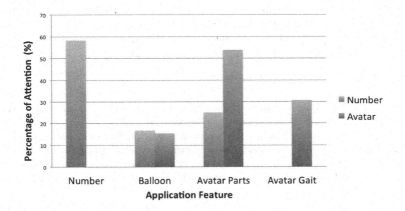

**Fig. 4.** Comparison of attention between representation conditions

It is suggested from the experimental results that the first avatar presentation is much more valid than the numerical presentation in terms of attitude improvement. However, the reason for the consideration of the avatar group is that the attention was focused on the numerical value of a numeric army, while an avatar attitude and parts focused on the same degree. The numerical consideration is the idea that attitude improvement from a schematically macro point of view, which is in effect the acquisition and loss of Avatar attitude is more effective than improving the attitude from an accuracy and microscopic point of view.

## 5   Conclusion and Future Work

It is necessary to improve and maintain the walking habits of women toward an advance age for promoting and maintaining their health. In this study, we developed a smartphone application, My Kokoron, which encourages good walking posture by visualizing an avatar for the users walking habit rather than increasing the number of steps. This application improved the users motivation to exercise by visually presenting the walking motion of the user in the form of an avatar. Moreover, the establishment of continuous walking habits of the user was promoted and incorporated using Gamification. In the study, an experiment was performed to the validity of the proposed application; The avatar attitude representation was found to be effective in improving the posture as opposed to the attitude presented by the numerical value. A system, such as adopting a walking habit by the women that do not actively exercise, is required to greet the bright aging society so as to increase the proportion of the healthy and active elderly.

**Acknowledgments.** This material is based on work funded by S-innovation (Strategic Promotion of Innovative Research and Development) funding under Industry Academia Collaborative R&D Programs administered by the Japan Science and Technology Agency (JST). We are also grateful to Kazuo Kumai, Motohiro Senga and staffs of the health department of Shimonseki city office for their participation in this project.

# References

1. Government Of Japan Cabinet Office. Annual report on the aging society (2014)
2. Kaneko, R.: Population projections for Japan: 2006–2055 outline of results, methods, and assumptions ryuichi kaneko, akira ishikawa, futoshi ishii, tsukasa sasai, miho iwasawa, fusami mita, and rie moriizumi. Japan. J. Popul. 6(1) (2008)
3. Friedman, H.S., Martin, L.R.: The Longevity Project: Surprising Discoveries for Health and Long Life from the Landmark Eight-Decade Study. Hudson Street Press, New York (2011)
4. Kojima, T., Hiyama, A., Miura, T.: Gait analysis and visualization of seniors in virtual environment. In: Proceedings of the Virtual Reality Society of Japan, Annual Conference, vol. 19, pp. 278–281, September 2014 (In Japanese)
5. Nawahdah, M., Inoue, T.: Motion adaptive orientation adjustment of a virtual teacher to support physical task learning. Inf. Media Technol. 7(1), 506–515 (2012)
6. Kobayashi, M., Arita, S., Itoko, T., Saito, S., Takagi, H.: Motivating multigenerational crowd workers in social-purpose work. In: Proceedings of the 18th ACM Conference on Computer Supported Cooperative Work & #38; Social Computing (CSCW 2015), pp. 1813–1824, New York, NY, USA. ACM (2015)
7. Seyama, J., Nagayama, R.S.: The uncanny valley: effect of realism on the impression of artificial human faces. Presence Teleoperators Virtual Environ. 16(4), 337–351 (2007)
8. Mori, M., MacDorman, K.F., Kageki, N.: The uncanny valley [from the field]: robotics & automation. IEEE Mag. 19(2), 98–100 (2012)
9. Heike, M., Kawasaki, H., Tanaka, T., Fujita, K.: Study on deformation rule of personalized-avatar for producing sense of affinity. Trans. Hum. Interface Soc. 13(3), 243–254 (2011)
10. Banks, J., Bowman, N.D.: Close intimate playthings? understanding player-avatar relationships as a function of attachment, agency, and intimacy. In: Selected Papers of Internet Research, vol. 3 (2013)
11. Johnsen, K., Ahn, S.J., Moore, J., Brown, S., Robertson, T.P., Marable, A., Basu, A.: Mixed reality virtual pets to reduce childhood obesity. IEEE Trans. Vis. Comput. Graph. 20(4), 523–530 (2014)
12. Yamada, H., Hiyama, A., Miura, T.: Gait analysis of elderly with wearable devices. In: Proceedings of the Virtual Reality Society of Japan, Annual Conference, vol. 19, pp. 632–635, September 2014 (In Japanese)

13. Tomoyuki, A., Yoshitaka, S., Shuichiro, W., Hirosi, S.: The relationship between the stride time variability, motor ability and fall in community-dwelling elderly people. J. Japan. Phys. Ther. Assoc. **38**(3), 165–172 (2011)
14. Kuwae, Y., Miyoshi, H., Sekine, M., Tsuji, M., Fujimoto, T., Tamura, T.: Verification of low-frequency exercise of requiring support–by monitoring in wearable motion sensors. Japan. Soc. Med. Biol. Eng. **50**(6), 535–542 (2012)
15. Unity. http://unity3d.com/
16. Animate anything with mecanim. http://unity3d.com/jp/learn/tutorials/modules/beginner/live-training-archive/animate-anything

# Senior-Oriented On-Demand Economy: Locality, Matching, and Scheduling are the Keys to Success

Shoma Arita[✉], Atsushi Hiyama, and Michitaka Hirose

The University of Tokyo, 7-3-1 Hongo, Bunkyo, Tokyo 113-8656, Japan
{arita,atsushi,hirose}@cyber.t.u-tokyo.ac.jp

**Abstract.** The world's population is aging at an unprecedented rate. Promoting the engagement of senior workforces is essential to cover the increasing cost of social security and to provide aging workers with a raison d'être. Although many seniors are willing to work, senior workforces, with their waning strength and skills, are not commonly employed. We argue that the on-demand economy is a promising platform for the senior workforce because of the flexibility it provides to these workers. First, we introduce a new classification of on-demand services, distinguishing four groups: property sharing, real-world skills, bargaining of goods, and online crowdsourcing. Next, we discuss key technologies needed to improve support to senior workforce in an on-demand economy. Finally, we build an online consumer-to-consumer matching platform, GBER, where senior workers find local jobs. GBER consists of two functions: a comprehensive help-matching function, and a specialized freelancer-matching function.

**Keywords:** On-Demand economy · Crowdsourcing · Senior workforce · Job matching · Social inclusion · Social engagement

## 1 Introduction

### 1.1 Senior Workforces Will Solve Problems in an Aging Society

The world is facing an unprecedentedly rapid aging of the society. There were 0.9 billion people aged 60 or over by 2015, and this number are estimated to increase to 2.1 billion by 2050 [1]. Not only will the developed countries, which have already experienced an aging society, but developing countries will also face this situation. We conducted our research in Japan, the country that had the highest aging rate, 26 %, in 2015 [2].

The main problem of population aging is the increasing cost of social security, as there will be fewer taxpaying workforces and more non-labor-force population [2]. It is possible to alleviate the decline in labor force by raising the participation of those who have capacity to work, but are currently not working such as the elderly, the young, and the female workers. In this paper, we will argue about engaging the senior workforces.

Encouraging elderly people to work is beneficial not only in financial terms, which is, the reduction of social security costs and the supplementation of the house budget, but it also increases their quality of life (QOL). Many elderly people feel isolated from society after they retire from their job and lose social ties. Their hopes upon retirement

M. Antona and C. Stephanidis (Eds.): UAHCI 2016, Part III, LNCS 9739, pp. 312–323, 2016.
DOI: 10.1007/978-3-319-40238-3_30

are to contribute to society, make new friends and have someone to talk to, have something to live for, and maintain good health [2].

### 1.2   On-Demand Economy as a Suitable Platform for Senior Workers

**Seniors' Requirements on Work.** Although many senior workers are still willing to work, many current jobs do not fulfill these workers' requirements. In Japan, the country with the highest rate of aging, 51 % of the people aged 65–69 were unemployed in 2015. Of them, 25 % still wished to work. The number was 68 % for people aged 70–74 and 84 % for seniors over 75 [2].

The objectives of senior workforce are slightly different from that of the younger generation. Salary is not of the utmost importance to them because for many of them pensions received from the government or companies suffice to support their daily lives. In fact, 70 % of the elderly people have no worries about earning a living [2]. Their average savings are 1.4 times higher than savings in the other age groups [2]. They seek to stay in good health, contribute to society, and talk to people.

The main reasons why companies avoid to hire the elderly are [3]: it is difficult to uniformly deal with them as their individual physical and cognitive strengths differs largely (39 %), the companies are anxious about the workers' health problems (31 %), and the companies want to enforce restructuring of the employees (27 %).

We argue that jobs suitable for elderly workers are jobs in which they can work in vicinity, where their work times are flexible, and can contribute to society [2]. Working full-time and commuting to the office can be exhausting for many senior citizens because of their diminishing physical strength. It is thus desirable that elderly people work anywhere and anytime they like, and their work serves society well.

**Utilizing Senior Workforces in the On-Demand Economy.** The on-demand economy is on the rise and it is a suitable working platform for the elderly. The on-demand economy fulfills the requirements on the elderly on the time, place, and purpose of the job. On-demand economy differs from the traditional market such that customers interact with each other. The companies in this business only facilitate a platform where customers directly sell or buy goods and services.

To give a better illustration of on-demand companies, we introduce three major players in the on-demand economy. Uber [4] is the most successful company that provides on-demand taxi services. Customers summon Uber taxis on their smartphones; they can choose taxis on a map interface that displays a car location retrieved from GPS and the driver's information. The drivers are not the employees; they are freelance drivers who are registered to Uber. Uber makes profit from the margin. Another successful example is Airbnb [5], which offers a matching platform between hosts who want to sublet their rooms and tenants or guests who want to stay in places beside hotels to reduce their expense or to have special experiences.

Uber and Airbnb are actively trying to engage senior workers, recognizing the potential in their experience and responsibility. Uber announced a partnership with Life Reimagined, a company that helps the elderly plan their next step in life. Airbnb announced on the same day that they are welcoming elderly hosts and guests. It is important to note that 25 % of the drivers at Uber are 50 or older, and 50 % of the hosts at Airbnb are over 40, while 10 % of them are over 60. In Japan, 84 % of the elderly are potential providers because they own houses that can be used for renting.

The Minnade-DAISY project [6, 7] is one of the successful examples in involving senior workers in an on-demand service. This project crowdsources micro-tasks that help create accessible books for the blind. A third of all participants are over 60, and they showed more continuity, engagement, and enthusiasm toward the project.

## 2  A Case Study on Senior Workforce in Japan

### 2.1  Seniors' Potential to Work

The reason why we propose the engaging senior workforce is beneficial is based on an assumption that the elderly have both potential and ability to work. Several facts and examples about senior workforces support this assumption.

Current seniors are healthier than ever before. The retirement age in Japan was 55 in the 1980s; it was 61 in 2015 and will be raised to 65 by 2025. One reason is that the average life expectancy is rising to over 80, and people are still in good health under the age of 65. About half of the people over 65 experience subjective symptoms, but only a quarter of them experiences problems in their daily lives. This means that 75 % of the people over 65 are still able to work.

Additionally, seniors own properties and have valuable skills and knowledge, and for frail seniors, sharing or selling their properties is one of the easiest ways to contribute to society. Eighty-four percent of the elderly have their own house, in which they can rent out spare rooms. They have free land for parking space. Also their experience in cooking or childcare can reduce the burden on full-time workers. They have knowledge that young people do not. For example, many seniors work as storytellers in war museums.

Another example is employing senior taxi drivers in advertising local sightseeing spots. Hana-navi [8], which means flower navigation in Japanese, is an application where taxi drivers in Kyoto upload photos of local flowers daily. The database they created attracts many tourists into the region because flower viewing is one of the most popular reasons for trips.

Further, Kamikatsu is a model town for agriculture and commerce cooperation by the elderly. Its population is only about 1,500 and 52 % of the inhabitants are over 65. The elderly workers harvest beautiful leaves for decorating plates and ship them to restaurants all over Japan. Their annual sales are ¥ 260 million (approximately $2.3 million as of February 2015); some workers earn twice the average of Japanese workers.

### 2.2  Reestablishing Local Ties

Many elderly people want to join some group activities [2]; 61 % of the elderly participated in group-activities from their own initiative in 2013, which is 6.2 % higher than in 2003. They feel that they made new friends (48.8 %); they have a sense of fulfillment (46.0 %), and they feel confident about their health condition (44.4 %). Men answered that they contributed to the society (32.7 %), whereas women answered that they could help each other (37.2 %). Another report says that 60 % of the elderly wish to interact with young people [2].

Social isolation of the elderly is one of the biggest problems in an aging society. Although the percentage of the elderly who talk to others more than once a day exceeds 90 % in total, 25 % of the people who live alone only talk to others less than once in three days [2]. Talking has proven to be effective in preventing dementia, which requires expensive treatments. Therefore, it is beneficial for both the elderly and the society to reestablish local bonds and to promote talking in person.

There are many efforts by local governments and nonprofit organizations to recreate local communities. We introduce the first local social networking service (SNS) in Japan, Gorotto-Yacchiro [9], as such an example. Gorotto-Yacchiro is a portal site and the social networking site of Yachiro City. It has blogs, bulletin boards, news, Q&A sections, and links to local company websites. When you log in, you can view friends' updates, join the community, and become a town reporter. Local SNS are not popular among young people because they cannot connect with people outside the city, and it usually has classic, unattractive user interfaces. However, this became popular among senior people who are unfamiliar with IT and do not have friends outside the city. The Ministry of Internal Affairs and Communications is trying to expand local SNSs to many cities in Japan.

## 3 On-Demand Economy for Senior Workforce

### 3.1 New Classification of On-Demand Market

The on-demand economy has been successful so far. The number of the freelance workers in the US surpassed 53 million people, which is 34 % of all labor force, and is expected to exceed 50 % in 2020. More than 60 % of the major US companies will substitute part of its current workforce with freelance work. Companies can reduce their personnel costs by hiring workers only for a period or for certain temporary jobs that require special knowledge. They want to adjust their productivity to the fluctuating market demand; hence, the stable number of employees became a burden. Workers can work flexibly, anywhere and anytime they want. The key motivation factors for free-lance workers are (the percentages in brackets show the rate of affirmative votes in Japan and in the US, respectively): they have more freedom and flexibility in their work lives as they are not constrained by time and place (46 %, 42 %), they can contribute to the family budget (42 %, 37 %), and they can complement their main income pro-fessions (42 %, 68 %).

There are many words used to describe the on-demand economy: sharing economy, peer economy, classified online marketplace, e-commerce, online auction, collaborative economy, and so on. Not only the terms, but also the field of business is wide ranging. Among 180 startup companies of on-demand services in the US, professional services represented the largest segment—43 % of the companies [10]. The second largest segment was home services (36 %), followed by transportation (35 %), food and beverage (25 %), health and beauty (24 %), delivery and logistics (16 %), dining and drinks (14 %), travel and hospitality (9 %), and events (9 %) [10].

In this section, we propose a new classification method that divides the on-demand market into four groups—real-world skills, property sharing, online crowdsourcing, and bargaining of goods—according to the criteria of local vs. global, material vs. immaterial (Table 1). We point out the important aspects of their implementation to senior-oriented services. We believe that local services are more suitable for seniors.

**Property Sharing: Local and Material.** Property sharing represents services where people can lend and borrow properties. The sharing economy has grown widely across many industries worldwide in the past 6 years. The main domains of sharing include cars, money, parking, home goods, food, housing, and clothing—essentially anything people own. Airbnb [5], who is one of the biggest players in this field, earned $800 million a year in 190 countries by providing a platform for renting houses. Spacemarket [11] offers a marketplace to lend spaces like rooms, halls, or even desert islands.

Sharing of properties is a good way for the elderly to earn money because they are usually wealthier than the young. As we discussed earlier in the Airbnb example, many sharing-platform companies try to attract the elderly to make their unused possessions available. This allows even frail people to earn money because sharing does not require physical strength.

However, there are some concerns. The existing regulation makes it difficult for new companies to enter the market. The insurance companies are not willing to offer policies in case of loss or damage to the property. Airbnb is facing a number of lawsuits concerning its responsibilities for accidents and crimes in rented houses. A change in legislation and increased security are needed for these services to evolve. Another concern is that it is difficult for seniors to gain a sense of fulfillment from work because sharing usually does not require special skills.

The scheduling and recommendation functions need to be improved for better user experience. Currently, scheduling functions often cannot prevent double booking and multiple applications. Sharing requires strict time management because a new customer cannot use the property until the previous customer returns on time. In addition, customers usually send applications to multiple providers because they are not sure if property is available. Improving the matching recommendation function could reduce the time customers spend on finding a good and available lender.

**Real-World Skills: Local and Immaterial.** Real-world skills refer to certain jobs that require professional knowledge or skills, for instance, driving, housework, babysitting, caregiving, consulting, and teaching. Tour guiding became popular recently; many seniors offer local tours like nature explorations or history-themed guided tours. We include services for finding friends of similar interests into this group, although they are not accompanied by monetary transactions. This is because the primary goal in this category is matching people to people.

This is the most promising area for the senior workforce because they can play an active role in the local community, utilizing their knowledge and skills to connect people. It triggers high satisfaction among workers because they can make use of their skills and knowledge to improve other people's lives.

Nevertheless, background functions need to be improved. First, there is a safety issue because the worker and the customer meet in person. Some platforms are accused of being a hotbed of crime. Background checks on the workers (and the customers) need to be conducted by requesting credit information and introducing a worker-evaluation system. Second, a scheduling function to support work sharing among multiple workers is needed. Current services are limited to single-worker jobs, but they need to cover more complex jobs. Most jobs are conducted as a cooperation of several people. That is especially true in the senior workforce. We propose a mosaic-type work system [12], where elderly workers share their time and skills to compensate for their lower strength and form a virtual worker. Hence, we need a system that coordinates the schedule of several workers for a single job. Finally, we need to have a matching recommendation function in order to reduce the time workers spend on routine tasks like matching, messaging, payment, commuting, etc. If the time spent on routine tasks was relatively long compared to the actual working time, workers would find the system dull and would not use it again.

**Bargaining of Goods: Global and Material.** The bargaining of goods represents e-commerce websites and Internet auctions. There are two types of e-commerce websites: direct and indirect selling. In direct selling, people sell their own product, but they have to keep some stock at home. In indirect selling, on the other hand, people shop on-demand and ship to the client's address, a certain percentage of which is overseas transactions. Direct selling is a good e-commerce platform for the elderly workers when they sell products that are made as a hobby or are local staples. Popular products as a hobby are paintings, clothes, sundries, and photos.

We need to support the senior sellers who often do not comply with laws and regulations. For example, they sell photos that breach portrait rights or are trademarked or copyrighted. The services need to detect these illegal acts and should provide support for the inexperienced sellers.

**Online Crowdsourcing: Global and Immaterial.** In micro-task crowdsourcing, people perform easy micro tasks such as image labeling, writing short texts, transcribing, data input, data cleansing, etc. Amazon Mechanical Turk [13] is the global leading service in this field. The problem with purely online services is that they are usually underpaid, they require certain IT skills, and the tasks are often monotonous. These are not so attractive for the senior workforce because the elderly are often weak in operating computers and they are more interested in jobs in which they are more socially contributing. Minnade-DAISY [6, 7] was an exceptionally successful project in Japan because it had a good cause—to help the blind. In the future, purely online services will include macro tasks that require more expertise, time, and collaboration such as design, music or video creation, and smartphone application development.

One of the research topics on supporting online crowdsourcing of senior workforce is the automatic detection of stealth marketing and shilling [14]. Senior worker are a likely target because they have lower IT literacy and are easier to deceive.

**Table 1.** Classification of On-Demand Services and Pros and Cons for the elderly workers

|  | Material | Immaterial |
|---|---|---|
|  | **Property Sharing** | **Real-World Skills** |
| **Local** | Lending their properties: cars, rooms, etc.<br>*(US) Airbnb, ParkWhiz, Lending Club,*<br>*(JP) Spacemarket, Anyca,*<br>Pros. Seniors have more properties.<br>    Frail people can earn money.<br>Cons. Law regulation and lack of insurance.<br>    Constant income not ensured.<br>    No skills required.<br>Tech. Current scheduling functions are imperfect.<br>    Search cost for the borrower is high. | Providing Services using Skills and Knowledge<br>*(US) Uber, BlaBlaCar, TaskRabbit, Zaarly, EatWith (JP) Any*<br>*+Times, Time Dollar System, CaSy, Cyta, TimeTicket, Visasq*<br>Pros. Making real world connections in local.<br>    Utilising their experiences and skills.<br>    Works are socially contributing.<br>Cons. Safety management.<br>Tech. Work sharing between multiple workers.<br>    Chores are time consuming: matching,<br>    messaging, payment, commuting, etc. |
| **Global** | **Bargaining of Goods** | **Online Crowdsourcing** |
|  | Selling one's properties or creations in<br>E-commerce or auction websites<br>*(US) Amazon, eBay, iStockphotos (JP) Yahoo! Auction, mercari*<br>Pros. Earn money with their hobbies.<br>    Enjoy shopping with other people's money.<br>    No work time, no commuting.<br>    Sending local staples to the world.<br>Cons. Keeping unsold stocks at home.<br>    Quality control of creations.<br>Tech. Controlling illegal acts: fraud, infringement. | Performing micro-tasks online<br>*(US) Amazon MTurk, Upwork, UserTesting, Fiverr, Be My Eyes,*<br>*99 designs (JP) Lancers, Minnade-Daisy, Kokonara, Shufti*<br>Pros. Work at anytime, in anywhere.<br>    Tasks are often easy to perform.<br>    Special skills in designing and writing.<br>    Personal background checks not required.<br>Cons. Workers are underpaid.<br>    Many tasks are not socially contributing.<br>Tech. Detecting stealth marketing and shill. |

## 3.2 Platform Companies—Comprehensive or Market-Specific

The companies that provide a platform for on-demand services select one or more markets from the list in the previous section. We call comprehensive companies those that run their business in more than one field, and market-specific companies as the ones that focus on one area.

Comprehensive companies are popular among people with low IT literacy, like the elderly. A major example of comprehensive companies is Craigslist [15], the largest classified advertisements website with many sections like jobs, housing, personals, etc. Over 700 cities in 70 countries have Craigslist sites, where overall monthly page views exceed 2 billion. Jimoty [16], the Japanese Craigslist-like web service, has attracted many seniors; 62 % of its users are over 40. These services have traditional bulletin-board interfaces, resembling the dawn of the Internet.

It is ideal to build comprehensive companies employing senior workers because seniors can seek help for anything in one platform. However, comprehensive services pose certain challenges: they require a large number of users for help matching, the evaluation of workers is complex, and the search cost for jobs is relatively high. It is easier for new businesses to start out as target-specific companies for several reasons; it is easier to find users, match demand and supply, and design the website. Further, user satisfaction is more likely to be higher with target-specific services because the probability of matching users to skilled workers is higher.

Several services support startup platform companies in terms of assuring safety, collecting money, protecting privacy, preventing fraud, and company management. These services help startup companies build trust among users. Major services supporting platform companies are the following. Checkr [17] provides automatic background screening of the worker or user with web applications and API. PayPal [18] act as intermediaries for payment processing so that even the platform companies will not know customers' credits and accounts.

### 3.3   On-Demand Services that Focus on Locality

Several related services provide platforms for local work matching. In this section, we introduce a few services that provide insights into which functions are a prerequisite for successful services.

*Flash Volunteer [19].* Flash volunteer is a platform where users can find information on volunteers. Users search for jobs on a map interface, in which the work location is pinned on a map, and a card interface, in which users can leaf through recruitment information by sliding on the screen. Separating information by cities has proven to be a good idea, but it had too little recruitment information for a comprehensive service, and people stopped using it.

*Any + Times [20].* Any + Times offers a matching platform for specialized freelance workers. "Supporters" register on this website according to their specialty, like room cleaning, pet care, cooking, shopping services, etc. This company is a comprehensive service provider, but the services are limited, based on the supporters' specialty.

*Time Dollar System [21].* Time Dollar System is a unique gamification metrics for local voluntary cooperation operated by a nonprofit organization called NALC. Users earn points—1 point per hour—for helping out elderly neighbors. In the future, they can use their points to get voluntary services from others. The service has been successful so far, it now has 125 satellite offices and 30,000 members.

*Peuplade in Paris [22].* Peuplade in Paris is the world's largest community-based social networking service that enhances connections between local people. It has three main functions: (a) *rendez-vous*, where users call for someone to go along with them to events or gatherings; (b) *idées*, where users post their interests and ideas to take action or to seek help such as a classified service; and (c) location search, where users can check other users' location. It is a great example which citizens form real community from an online service.

## 4   Key Technologies that Support the Elderly to Work in On-Demand

As discussed above, services supporting local communities are a hopeful platform for senior labor forces to work in. The elderly can make the most of their knowledge, skills, and ownership. However, some challenges in providing these services still exist:

locality, work of long duration, community identity, and automated recommendation on matching.

The first problem is that many of the current services do not focus on locality, although the physical proximity between the client and the worker is the important factor in sharing services and real-world-skill services. In many services, search is limited to large geographical units. On the other hand, some successful services like Uber [4] and Airbnb [5] offer information on places using map interface with GPS data. Craigslist [15], which is a service that the elderly commonly use, runs separate services in each city. We suggest these matching services have a search function where the search can be limited to the user's vicinity, or a map interface.

The second problem is that current services only match jobs one by one. Many are not built to request the same worker for the same kind of job; hence, the customer royalty is pretty low. In addition, many real-world tasks are complicated and require long-term work involving many people, but there are no major services to support that. Thus, we propose functions that group workers and assign tasks to them in reference to their registered schedule—all in one application.

The third problem is that in the current service setup, workers tend to feel isolated. They usually work alone and do not have the chance to communicate with other freelance workers, which may harm workers' state of mind. As we saw in the example of Peuplade in Paris [22], providing community functions increases worker engagement and improves worker satisfaction.

Finally, the fourth problem is the still high search cost for both workers and clients, especially in comprehensive services. In many services, users need to skim through irrelevant bulletin board posts, which is very time-consuming. We can optimize the search result by filtering according to location and skills. The way the search result is displayed could be modified—from the traditional list of results to map-based or calendar-based display, in line the requirements of the jobs.

## 5    GBER—On-Demand Help Matching Platform Supporting Seniors Working Locally

In this chapter, we introduce the design philosophy and the basic functions of our system GBER. GBER stands for "Gathering Brisk Elderly in the Region." It is an on-demand C2C market platform, where the elderly can find jobs and connect to each other. Each city will own its GBER service, because locality is an important factor in senior workforce engagement. To reduce search cost, we support map-based and calendar-based job search, and job or worker recommendation. We introduce scheduling functions with multiple workers for introducing more complicated macro tasks (Fig. 1).

**The Comprehensive Help-Matching System.** GBER supports a pure consumer-to-consumer platform, where users can seek help by simply choosing their location from the map, and typing the date, price, the number of helpers, and the specification of the help they need. The content of the request can be anything from the classification of the on-demand markets above: real-world skills, property sharing, and bargaining of goods. Those workers who live in the vicinity, or have registered skills or interests similar to the content of the request will receive a notification. Those who do not receive notifications can also find requests on an easy map interface, or on a card interface. When there are multiple offers from the users, the requestor can choose among the applicants After the service, the requestor rates the helpers on a scale from one to ten, The ratings are displayed on each user's profile page.

**The Specialized Freelancers-Matching System.** GBER offers a platform where the registered freelance-workers groups can receive requests from the customers. The interface is similar to the previous comprehensive help matching, but users can only seek help for certain jobs. First, the administrator of the workers group receives a job request from the user. Next, the administrator and the requestor make a contract specifying the price and dates. The administrator selects workers from the group and employs them on the agreed dates. Finally, after the job is completed, workers receive money from the requestor and the ratings of each worker are registered. GBER has a scheduling system, where the administrator can easily select workers for specific tasks.

This system is aimed to cater to the requirements that the elderly place on jobs. Some elderly have the desire to try new things in the second career of their lives. Hence, each group occasionally holds lectures and trainings to welcome new registered workers. In addition to what workers already know, this system creates new job opportunities. Moreover, elderly people like to work in teams for several reasons: they can complement their skills with the help of co-workers; it is easier to take a leave if

**Fig. 1.** (Left) Map-based interface for uploading job information. Workers can search for jobs with similar interface. (Right) Calendar-based interface that support workers' scheduling.

health issues arise; they can control how long they work; they can make friends with the co-workers.

We include specialized tasks as well because it secures the highest number of active users. Comprehensive services fail mainly due to lack of active users and lack of requests, resulting in a negative feedback loop. Workers registered for specialized tasks manifest high loyalty to this service and help the service prosper.

## 6  Conclusion

The world is aging rapidly. Engaging senior workforces is essential in order to cover the increasing cost of social security and to give a purpose in life to workers. Senior workforces are, however, not commonly employed, although many are willing to work despite of their waning strength and skills. We argued that the on-demand economy is a promising platform for the senior workforce as it allows seniors to work anywhere and anytime.

First, we classified on-demand services into four groups according to several criteria—local vs. global, and material vs. immaterial. We pointed out the importance of local services, mainly in the context of sharing of properties and real-world skills, as a suitable platform for elderly workers.

Next, we discussed key technologies that need to be developed in order to support the senior workforce in an on-demand economy. Senior-oriented services should support locality, work of long duration, community identity, and automated recommendation on matching.

Finally, we built an online consumer-to-consumer matching platform, GBER, where senior workers find jobs locally. GBER consists of two functions: a comprehensive help-matching function, and a specialized freelancers-matching function.

**Acknowledgments.** This research was partially supported by the Japan Science and Technology Agency (JST) under the Strategic Promotion of Innovative Research and Development Program.

## References

1. United Nations: World Population Prospects the 2015 Revision. http://esa.un.org/unpd/wpp/Publications/Files/Key_Findings_WPP_2015.pdf
2. Cabinet Office, Government of Japan: Annual Report on Aging Society. http://www8.cao.go.jp/kourei/whitepaper/index-w.html
3. The Japan Institute for Labor Policy and Training: Research on Hiring Senior Workforce. JILPT Research Series No. 67 (2010)
4. Uber: https://www.uber.com/. Accessed 12 Feb 2016
5. Airbnb: https://www.airbnb.com/. Accessed 12 Feb 2016
6. Itoko, T., Arita, S., Kobayashi, M., Takagi, H.: Involving senior workers in crowdsourced proofreading. In: Antona, M., Stephanidis, C. (eds.) UAHCI 2014, Part III. LNCS, vol. 8515, pp. 106–117. Springer, Heidelberg (2014)
7. Kobayashi, M., Arita, S., Itoko, T., Saito, S., Takagi, H.: Motivating multi-generational crowd workers in social-purpose work. In: Proceedings of the 18th ACM Conference on Computer Supported Cooperative Work & Social Computing, pp. 1813–1824 (2015)

8. Hana-navi: http://flowertourism.net/. Accessed 12 Feb 2016
9. Gorotto-Yacchiro: http://www.gorotto.com/. Accessed 12 Feb 2016
10. State of the on Demand Economy Report October 2014. http://kungfu.co/wp-content/uploads/2014/10/on-demand-economy-2015.pdf
11. Spacemarket: https://spacemarket.com/. Accessed 12 Feb 2016
12. Nakayama, M., Hiyama, A., Miura, T., Yatomi, N., Hirose, M.: Mosaic-type work support system using touch screen computers for senior people. In: Proceedings of the 2013 Conference on Computer Supported Cooperative Work Companion, pp. 235–238 (2013)
13. Amazon Mechanical Turk: https://www.mturk.com/. Accessed 12 Feb 2016
14. Baba, Y., Kashima, H., Kinoshita, K., Yamaguchi, G., Akiyoshi, Y.: Detecting inappropriate crowdsourcing tasks using machine learning. In: The 5th Forum on Data Engineering and Information Management, Fukushima, Japan (2013)
15. Craigslist: https://www.craigslist.org/. Accessed 12 Feb 2016
16. Jimoty: http://jmty.jp/. Accessed 12 Feb 2016
17. Checkr: https://checkr.com/. Accessed 12 Feb 2016
18. PayPal: https://www.paypal.com/. Accessed 12 Feb 2016
19. Flash Volunteer: http://www.flashvolunteer.org/. Accessed 12 Feb 2016
20. Any + Times: https://anytimes.co.jp/. Accessed 12 Feb 2016
21. Time Dollar System: http://nalc.jp/jikan/jikan.htm. Accessed 12 Feb 2016
22. Peuplade in Paris: https://peuplade.fr/. Accessed 12 Feb 2016

# Health Training Platform

Clifton Clunie[1], Virgílio Reis[1], Pedro Silva[1], Luís Mendes[1,4],
Carlos Rabadão[1,2], João Barroso[3(✉)], and António Pereira[1,2]

[1] School of Technology and Management,
Computer Science and Communication Research Centre,
Polytechnic Institute of Leiria, 2411-901 Leiria, Portugal
{2151411, 2152269, 2151666}@my.ipleiria.pt,
{lmendes, carlos.rabadao, apereira}@ipleiria.pt
[2] Information and Communications Technologies Unit,
INOV INESC Innovation-Delegation Office at Leiria, Leiria, Portugal
[3] INESC TEC (formerly INESC Porto),
Universidade de Trás-os-Montes e Alto Douro,
Quinta de Prados, 5000-801 Vila Real, Portugal
jbarroso@utad.pt
[4] Instituto de Telecomunicações, Lisbon, Portugal

**Abstract.** People in modern societies have increasingly sedentary lifestyles. They usually do not have time to take part in physical activity on a regular basis. Additionally, due to time constraints, people are consuming more processed and junk foods. This behavior may lead to health issues, such as obesity or cardiovascular disease. On the other hand people are becoming more aware and more interested in doing physical activities, which has resulted in an increase of memberships at gymnasiums. People usually obtain better results in training by having a personal trainer, especially in the beginning, because personal trainers can recommend safer and more effective exercises, as well as provide motivation. Moreover, personal trainers can also play the roles of life coaches or nutritionists. Despite the benefits, having a personal trainer can be difficult. Due to time constraints, it might not be simple to combine both schedules of the personal trainer and the client. In this paper we present a novel health training platform to maximize the personal trainer and client relationship and, therefore, increase the client's well-being. The health training platform allows clients to have sensors connected to their smartphones and send their exercise data to their personal trainer. It also allows personal trainers to observe their clients' evolution and provide feedback. The health training platform has an architecture that allows multiple configurations involving personal trainers, clients and gymnasiums. We have built and tested a prototype of a health training platform.

**Keywords:** Physical activities · Wellbeing · Sensors · Mobile device

## 1 Introduction

Modern lifestyles with demanding and time-consuming jobs, combined with extended periods of time spent on commuting journeys and related traffic jams, all contribute to a lack of free time and can lead to excessive stress. At the end of the day people with this

© Springer International Publishing Switzerland 2016
M. Antona and C. Stephanidis (Eds.): UAHCI 2016, Part III, LNCS 9739, pp. 324–331, 2016.
DOI: 10.1007/978-3-319-40238-3_31

routine usually feel exhausted and tend to be absorbed in their daily tasks. This lack of time also leads to poor nutrition habits as people eat out more often and consume more and more fast food. This factor combined with patterns of no exercise may lead to health issues, such as cardiac diseases, diabetes, etc. Nevertheless, people are starting to become more aware of these issues and, as a result of this awareness, fitness trends have been growing for a couple of years. Nowadays people have several ways to train, depending on what they want to achieve. Users have many options for different types of training, such as weight training, running, CrossFit training, etc. One of the most important factors for success in training is the assistance of a personal trainer, especially during the first sessions. However, getting a personal trainer might not be an easy task since it can be expensive and users have to coordinate their schedule with that of the personal trainer.

It is our belief that the challenges described above can be tackled through the use of technologies which maximize remote interactions between users and their personal trainers. For this purpose, we present a health training platform in the present paper. In short, health training platform users are able to train according to their time and location availability and their exercise results are collected by sensors connected to a mobile device, which are later sent to the personal trainer for evaluation and guidance.

The remainder of the paper is organized as follows: related work is presented in Sect. 2, followed by the architecture in Sect. 3. Section 4 describes the implementation. Section 5 contains the tests. Conclusions and future work are presented in Sect. 6.

## 2  Related Work

As previously mentioned, people's interest in a healthier lifestyle through sports is increasing. However, despite this significant trend, time availability and financial constraints are still problems which limit the practice of physical exercise.

In this section we will describe the most relevant current applications being used by personal trainers, which are then compared to our motivation and proposed work.

The Wello Online Service [1] is a paid online service providing workouts over live video adapted to mobile devices. These live videos allow users to train anywhere. Users may filter these live videos by activity type, days of the week and start time, as well as enroll in sessions, joining a workout group with a trainer.

Another tool for personal trainers and their clients is Fity [2]. The idea of this application is to provide video streaming so the client and the personal trainer can interact with each other. The application also includes other features so that the client can have a complete training session at the moment of the training execution.

The Remote Coach [3] application has an interactive platform where the personal trainer can communicate with its clients and upload special materials that the client would need in order to execute the training session. The application also provides personal trainers with a report tool allowing them to measure different aspects of the users' training.

Despite being very useful resources, there are still some issues to be overcome, such as the lack of flexible solutions that may be used in both gymnasium and non-gymnasium environments. Collected data input can also be improved by using sensors that can automate and facilitate the process. With these concerns in mind, we propose a novel Health Training Platform. The architecture of this new platform is presented in the next section.

## 3   Architecture

The architecture of the novel Health Training Platform includes 3 major entities *(i)* the personal trainer, *(ii)* the clients and *(iii)* the gymnasiums. Due to the structure of the architecture, the scalability and the adaptation to any business model are ensured. For instance, we can have a scenario where a personal trainer interacts directly with clients without requiring a gymnasium or, alternatively, one which includes a gymnasium.

Regarding *(i)* the personal trainers, they are able to access their clients' workouts, interact with the clients by giving them feedback on their activities and motivating them, both in presence and at a distance.

Concerning the *(ii)* the clients, they are able to perform their workout, access the results, and interact with their personal trainer, receiving feedback and asking questions. The interaction with their personal trainer can also be in presence or at a distance. The remote interaction between clients and their personal trainers provide time flexibility, which is extremely important for clients with busy schedules. Remote interaction can also lead to cost reduction, since personal trainers and clients do not have the obligation of meeting in person.

Regarding *(iii)* the gymnasiums, they are optional as personal trainers can directly interact with clients who may perform their workouts in other facilities besides a gymnasium. Nevertheless, the presented architecture includes gymnasiums as an entity that can be present in the business model.

Regarding the procedures, there may be some distinctions depending on the chosen configuration. The clients use their smartphone to collect the data from their training. The smartphone then sends the data to the database server. The location of the database and application server is one of the nuances of the architecture, since it can be either in the cloud or in a gymnasium, depending on the configuration. Besides collecting the data, clients can use their smartphone to access their personal workouts and check on their personals trainer's feedback.

The personal trainers use their smartphones or other connected electronic devices to login into the system and retrieve the data from the database server of its clients. They then send a response to the clients, with adjustments to the training session in order for clients to improve their techniques and exercises.

Figure 1 shows different approaches that can be taken with this project, enhancing its flexibility. It shows the 3 entities – personal trainers, clients and gymnasiums – and the possible interactions between them.

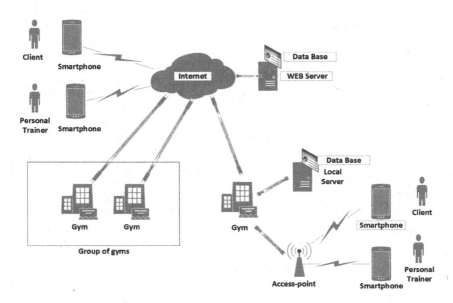

**Fig. 1.** Architecture

The next section presents the implementation of the architecture described above.

## 4    Implementation

For the purpose of implementation, we have developed an application for clients and personal trainers – the client application – and have set up the server for communication between the two applications, using open source tools – the server application. Additionally, we have used SME (*Sistema Móvil de Entrenamiento*) with Arduino microcontroller to gather information from clients. Figure 2 represents a diagram of the implementation. A detailed explanation is included afterwards.

We have set up a virtual machine to implement the server. It was implemented in Laravel Homestead with the pre-packaged Vagrant "box" which allowed for the development of the environment without requiring each tool to be installed. The server was configured as Nginx web server.

The server application was developed in PHP (1). The database was stored in the server and was implemented using MySQL engine. The passwords saved in the database are encrypted using the bcrypt [4] encryption (2).

The HTTP proxy server implementation and the communication with the client application were developed in PHP. The database that was implemented on the server was the MySQL engine (3).

In order to ensure security of the server and client applications, communications were carried out with HTTPS, using a symmetric cipher [5] generated by OpenSSL

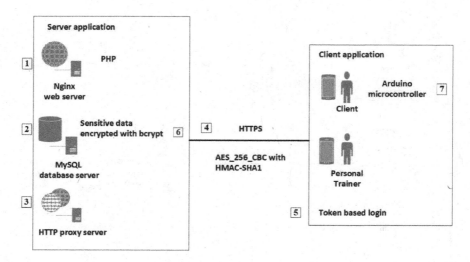

**Fig. 2.** Implementation

certification. Also the communication is encrypted using AES_256_CBC with HMAC-SHA1 for authentication of messages (4).

Additionally, a token is generated each time users perform their login. All the tokens have a limited life period, so that the time the user can use the application is controlled (5). Also the user's password is encrypted with bcrypt [4] and based on the blowfish encryption (6).

As mentioned above, one of the improvements that can be made in training solutions is the method of how data is collected from the clients. In our specific solution we have used SME [6]. We have added a new module to the SME [6] system which allows communication with the server, user token based login and client registration. We have developed it in Java language for the Android platform.

Moreover, the SME system uses the Arduino Microcontroller to connect sensors for evaluating the exercise. The connection between the mobile device and the Arduino [7] microcontroller is performed with a Bluetooth module (Bluetooth RN42) [8]. Figure 3 represents the SME with the Arduino microcontroller.

The sensor that is used to evaluate the performance of the exercises is an ultrasonic sensor (SRF04) [9]. This sensor is capable of generating, transmitting and detecting ultrasound waves. The sensor is attached to a muscle, in this case the bicep. Using the pulses provided by the sensor to the Arduino, it is relatively simple to determine the position of the bicep in relation to the training time (7).

The information that is gathered by the sensor and Arduino [7] is sent to the mobile device and the clients send this information to the personal trainers. The data sent to the personal trainers allow them to be informed of what exercise the clients are doing and how it was executed. Then the personal trainers can send feedback to the clients in order to improve exercise execution or even as a motivational response.

**Fig. 3.** SME with Arduino microcontroller

## 5   Tests

After building the prototype, we performed several tests. Since the human body is extremely complex, we have focused the tests on the bicep muscle, using the curl bicep exercise to verify the angle of the exercise execution.

In order to do so, on the clients' side we have used ultrasonic sensors - SRF04 - which must be calibrated to the training area. The use of two SRF04 sensors allowed us to detect the correct position of the arm when doing the exercise. These two SRF04 sensors gathered the information of the arm in each half second.

The Arduino gets this data from the sensor and converts the ultrasonic sound into a distance in "cm" and sends the data of the exercise execution to the smartphone via Bluetooth. This execution is then sent to the "Health Training Platform" by the users.

Afterwards, on the personal trainers' side, they can access the platform and check the exercise execution and validate if the users executed it correctly, send feedback to the users so they can improve the exercise execution.

As the SME was already developed, we focused the tests on the server and the connection between the smartphone and the server.

The certification applied to test this system uses the AES (Advanced Encryption Standard) [10] with 256 bits and CBC (Cipher Block Chaining) [11] as a mode of operation. The authentication messages used was the HMAC (Hash Message Authentication Code) [12] and SHA1 (Secure Hash Standard) [13].

On the server's side, the data was encrypted with the bcrypt [4] cryptographic method.

## 6   Conclusions and Future Work

In modern societies, people are getting more absorbed by daily tasks such as demanding jobs, child care, household activities and social involvement. This lack of time usually has negative impacts on people's nutrition and exercise habits since they tend to consume more processed and fast food and not practice any physical activity on a regular basis. However, people are becoming aware of this negative impact and are trying to change their habits. Additionally, it is a fact that personal trainer's help promote more successful training sessions. But having a personal trainer can be expensive and it is not affordable for everyone. Therefore, the challenge is to maximize physical activity for populations with time constraints, while simultaneously providing cost-effective training methods.

With this motivation in mind, we have proposed a novel Health Training Platform which stands out by its scalability and flexibility. In short, clients receive their workouts by smartphone, allowing them to practice whenever they have time (in a gymnasium, at home, outdoors, etc.). The results of their workout are sent from an Arduino Microcontroller to a personal trainer. The personal trainer checks the training and sends feedback to the client. This feedback can be to provide some instructions to correct the exercise or give motivation. The client receives the personal trainer's feedback and acts accordingly.

After developing the Health Training Platform architecture, we have built and tested a prototype. The tests have shown that this platform solved the current problem of people who start training and can't have a personal trainer. This kind of system provides a certain freedom to the users to train and manage their time in different ways. The personal trainers' feedback helps the users to improve their training and to achieve their goals.

As for future work, we will apply this platform using a real time system in order to allow the personal trainers to monitor a client in real time in project NanoStima (NORTE-01-0145-FEDER-000016). Other possible improvements is the creation of an application for a personal computer. The objective of that application is to allow several clients to be monitored at the same time by only one personal trainer.

**Acknowledgments.** This work was partially supported by Health Training Platform project of Computer Science Department of School of Technology of Management of Polytechnic Institute of Leiria and Project "NORTE-01-0145-FEDER-000016" financed by the North Portugal Regional Operational Programme (NORTE 2020), under the PORTUGAL 2020 Partnership Agreement, and through the European Regional Development Fund (ERDF).

# References

1. TNW.    http://thenextweb.com/insider/2013/11/05/remote-personal-trainer-service-wello-launches-demand-workouts/#gref
2. FityGo. www.ifity.net, https://www.ifity.net/#/main
3. Coach, R.: www.remotecoachapp.com, https://www.remotecoachapp.com/tour
4. Provos, D.M.N.: A future-adaptable password scheme. In: 1999 USENIX Annual Technical Conference, Monterey, California, USA (1999)
5. Bellare, M., Desai, A., Jokipii, E., Rogaway, P.: A Concrete Security Treatment of Symmetric Encryption, San Diego (2000)
6. Clunie, C.: Desarrollo de una Aplicación Móvil basada en Android utilizando sensores como apoyo al Entrenamiento Personal, Panamá: Technological University of Panama, Computer Systems Engineering Faculty, Computer and Systems Simulation Department (2013)

7. ©2016 Arduino. https://www.arduino.cc/en/Main/arduinoBoardUno
8. Microchip Technology Inc. The Embedded Control Solutions Company®. http://www.microchip.com/wwwproducts/Devices.aspx?product=RN42
9. SRF04 - Ultra-Sonic Ranger, 22 December 2010. http://www.robot-electronics.co.uk/htm/srf04tech.htm
10. Federal Information Processing Standards Publications, advanced encryption standard (AES), 26 November 2001. http://csrc.nist.gov/publications/fips/fips197/fips-197.pdf
11. atsec information security corporation: National Institute of Standards and Technology's, 16 December 2015. http://csrc.nist.gov/groups/STM/cmvp/documents/140-1/140sp/140sp2549.pdf
12. Krawczyk, H., Bellare, R.: HMAC: Keyed-Hashing for Message Authentication, February 1997. https://tools.ietf.org/html/rfc2104
13. National Institute of Standards and Technology, U.S. Federal Information Processing Standard, "NIST," (2015). http://csrc.nist.gov/publications/fips/fips180-4/fips-180-4.pdf

# On Modeling the Quality of Nutrition for Healthy Ageing Using Fuzzy Cognitive Maps

Sofia B. Dias[1]([✉]), Sofia J. Hadjileontiadou[2], José A. Diniz[1],
João Barroso[3], and Leontios J. Hadjileontiadis[4]

[1] Faculdade de Motricidade Humana, Universidade de Lisboa,
Cruz Quebrada, 1499-002 Lisbon, Portugal
{sbalula, jadiniz}@fmh.ulisboa.pt
[2] Hellenic Open University, Praxitelous 23, 10562 Athens, Greece
shadjileontiadou@gmail.com
[3] INESC TEC, Universidade de Trás-os-Montes e Alto Douro,
Vila Real, Portugal
jbarroso@utad.pt
[4] Department of Electrical and Computer Engineering,
Aristotle University of Thessaloniki, 54124 Thessaloniki, Greece
leontios@auth.gr

**Abstract.** Modelling dietary intake of older adults can prevent nutritional deficiencies and diet-related diseases, improving their quality of life. Towards such direction, a Fuzzy Cognitive Map (FCM)-based modelling approach that models the interdependencies between the factors that affect the Quality of Nutrition (QoN) is presented here. The proposed FCM-QoN model uses a FCM with seven input-one output concepts, i.e., five food groups of the UK Eatwell Plate, Water ($H_2O$), and older adult's Emotional State (EmoS), outputting the QoN. The weights incorporated in the FCM structure were drawn from an experts' panel, via a Fuzzy Logic-based knowledge representation process. Using various levels of analysis (causalities, static/feedback cycles), the role of EmoS and $H_2O$ in the QoN was identified, along with the one of Fruits/Vegetables and Protein affecting the sustainability of effective food combinations. In general, the FCM-QoN approach has the potential to explore different dietary scenarios, helping health professionals to promote healthy ageing and providing prognostic simulations for diseases effect (such as Parkinson's) on dietary habits, as used in the H2020 i-Prognosis project (www.i-prognosis.eu).

**Keywords:** Older adults · Healthy ageing · Emotional state · Fuzzy cognitive maps (FCMs) · Quality of nutrition (QoN) · H2020 i-Prognosis

## 1 Introduction

The ageing process is intrinsically complex, driven by multiple causal mechanisms. Ageing affects people in different ways, with a wide variation in age-related physical and mental functioning; healthier ageing, however, can be reached through modifying some

M. Antona and C. Stephanidis (Eds.): UAHCI 2016, Part III, LNCS 9739, pp. 332–343, 2016.
DOI: 10.1007/978-3-319-40238-3_32

lifestyle factors, e.g., being more physically active and/or eating a balanced diet. More specifically, ageing is determined by complex interactions between biological, environmental, sociocultural and economic factors. Nevertheless, factors that contribute to the ageing process, for instance poor nutrition and psychosocial characteristics (e.g., stress), can be modifiable [1]. This includes health and social care professionals, collaborating to (re)educate patients on improving their nutritional intake, as well as monitoring their ongoing nutritional status [2]. Despite significant medical advances, malnutrition remains a significant public health problem of developed countries. There is evidence that the nutritional intake of older people living in care homes is suboptimal, with high levels of saturated fat, salt, and added sugars [3]. Moreover, malnutrition has significant negative impacts on the physical and emotional well-being of older people, including depression, anxiety, and decreased quality of life (QoL) [4]. Optimizing the dietary intake of older adults, though, can prevent nutritional deficiencies and diet-related diseases, improving their QoL. Used by researchers for designing "ideal" diets, the UK Eatwell Plate is basically a pie-chart diagram consisting of five food group segments, the proportions of which are based on the dietary reference values for the population, namely: (i) bread, rice, potatoes, pasta and other starchy foods (Starchy) (33 % of the diet); (ii) fruit and vegetables (F&V) (33 %); (iii) milk and dairy foods (Dairy) (15 %); (iv) meat, fish, eggs, beans and other non-dairy sources of protein (Protein) (12 %) and (v) foods and drinks that are high in fat or sugar, or both (HFHS) (8 %) [5–7].

In an effort to create a model that could incorporate the interdependencies between the five food groups of the UK Eatwell Plate, taking also into account two additional factors, i.e., water (H2O) and the emotional state (EmoS) of the older adults, a Fuzzy-Logic (FL)-based approach is proposed here as a means to provide a generalized measure of the Quality of Nutrition (QoN). In particular, from the methodological point of view, the Fuzzy Cognitive Map (FCM) modelling methodology, introduced by Kosko [8], is adopted here, resulting in the FCM-QoN model. The latter is based on a directed weighted graph consisting of nodes and weighted arcs, acting as a general model for causes and effects, which is derived from cognitive maps, resulting of integration/combination of FL and neural network, which takes the experts' opinions as input and generates the maps [9]. The expert knowledge for the construction of the proposed FCM-QoN model was drawn from a professional panel, involving Portuguese nutrition/diet experts. Various levels of analysis within the FCM-QoN scheme have shown that the proposed model can provide concepts interconnection and causal dependencies representation, contributing to the analysis and behavioural modeling of beneficial dietary habits and emotional states in the field of intelligent early detection and healthy ageing. The latter can be used as paradigms that comply with the scenarios of the i-Prognosis project (www.i-prognosis.eu), which is situated in the area of healthy and active ageing, targeting intelligent early detection and intervention in Parkinson's disease area.

The rest of the paper is constructed as follows: first, a review of the conceptual background related with healthy ageing and the main methodological issues of the FCM is presented, followed by data characteristics and a description of the proposed model. Next, a description of the implementation issues, analysis of the results, along with discussion and interpretation of the findings are provided. Finally, conclusions and future work conclude the paper.

## 2  Background and Methodology

### 2.1  Nutrients Interdependencies with Healthy Ageing and the Eatwell Plate

In general, the nutritional requirements of the older adult are the same as those for the rest of the adult population; however, some specific nutrients interdependencies should be considered, so to form the basis of some recommendations with related interventions that could assist healthy ageing. Focusing at specific nutrient characteristics the following could be noticed:

- FAT: Increased fat intakes are associated with higher levels of overweight and obesity, cardiovascular disease and some forms of cancer and diabetes mellitus. The older population are already at a higher risk of developing these conditions and high fat intakes can intensify this further. This is particularly so for saturated fat (animal type fats) with unsaturated fats (pure vegetable type fats) not being associated with the same risk. From this perspective, older people should eat less fat and in particular less saturated fat [10].
- PROTEIN: As muscle mass decreases in older people they should intake higher protein per kg lean body mass compared to younger adults; however, older people should therefore not eat excessive amounts of protein and their meals should be based around starchy foods [11].
- FIBER (Non-starch polysaccharide (NSP)): People who have a tendency to constipation are particularly encouraged to increase their NSP intake. As a result of slower gut movement, decreased activity levels and side effects of medications, some older people could be considered to be a group who may have a tendency to constipation, thus it is recommended that older people should eat more fiber [12].
- WATER: Older people are at increased risk of dehydration for a number of reasons including increased losses through skin as a result of skin becoming thinner, diminished ability of the kidneys to concentrate urine and a less sensitive thirst mechanism [13]. The effects of dehydration in older people which may impact on deterioration in nutritional status include: increased risk of pressure sores, unpleasant taste in the mouth, drowsiness, confusion, constipation, and increased risk of urinary tract infections. The consequences of dehydration are many and varied and most of these consequences impact on dietary intake and nutritional status. It is therefore essential that fluid intake (e.g., 6–8 glasses per day) is considered when managing the nutritional status of older people.

The above nutrients interdependencies with healthy ageing are considered in the construction of the Eatwell Plate [7, 14]. The latter highlights the different types of food that make up a functional diet, and shows the proportions needed to have a healthy, balanced diet (see Fig. 1).

The Eatwell Plate has been used as a reference with which the diets of different populations can be compared [15–17], for grouping foods in modelling the effects of increasing food prices on diet quality [18], and for designing "ideal" diets [19, 20]. To this end, the Eatwell Plate was used as a recommendation basis of the food group segments adopted here.

## 2.2 The Fuzzy Cognitive Map (FCM) Approach

In a narrow sense, FL is considered a multi-valued logic technique that is imprecise or approximate. In other words, rather than using traditional logic theory where binary sets have a two-valued logic (i.e., true, 1, and false, 0), fuzzy variables have a truth-value between 0 (absolutely true) and 1 (absolutely false). In this way, using linguistic variables that describes the effect each factor in a knowledge system has on the others, FL can be used to convert the effects into values between 0 and 1. Actually, these values can be input into a graphical representation of the system containing all factors with directed lines (edges), revealing the calculated strength of the causal relationship between them. From this perspective, based on binary values, Kosko [8] suggested the use of fuzzy causal functions considering numbers within [-1, 1], modifying, in this way, the Axelrod's cognitive maps perspective and introducing the FCM concept.

In general, the FCM describes a cognitive map model with two main characteristics, namely: (i) causal relationships between nodes are fuzzified; instead of only using signs to indicate positive/negative causality, a number is associated with the relationship to express the degree of relationship between two concepts; and (ii) the system is dynamic involving feedback, where the effect of change in a concept node affects other nodes, which in turn can affect the node initiating the change.

FCMs have gained considerable research interest in several scientific fields from knowledge modelling to decision making [21, 22], resorting to data mining techniques for promoting user's expert knowledge [23–25] and modelling interdependence between concepts in the real-world, by graphically representing the causal reasoning relationships between vague or un-crisp concepts [8, 26, 27]. Overall, the FCM structure can be viewed as an artificial neural network, where concepts are represented by neurons and causal relationships by weighted links or edges connecting the neurons.

FCMs are graphical representations of the relationships between elements of a system, as perceived by "experts", where an expert is any person with knowledge of the system under scrutiny. FCM comprise vertices, representing concepts (C), joined by directional edges, representing causal relationships between concepts. Each connection is assigned a weight $w_{ij} \in [-1,1]$ which quantifies the strength of the causal relationship between concepts $C_i$ and $C_j$ [8]. A positive weight $w_{ij} > 0$ indicates an excitatory relationship, i.e., as $C_i$ increases $C_j$ increases, while a negative weight $w_{ij} < 0$ indicates an inhibitory relationship, i.e., as $C_i$ increases $C_j$ decreases.

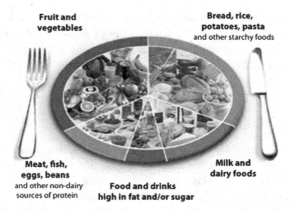

**Fig. 1.** The pie-chart diagram of UK Eatwell Plate consisting of five food group segments [5–7, 14].

## 2.3   The Proposed FCM-QoN Model

In this work, the FCM was initially constructed with the support of the knowledge and experience of the domain experts to determine the cause-effect relationships of the various knowledge representation elements (concept/nodes) of the system under study. In this way, the information regarding the factors/concepts that can contribute to healthy ageing field was gathered from nutritionists/dietitians and relevant literature based on recommendations and guidelines related to factors that contribute to the ageing process [3–7, 11, 14, 16]. The gathered knowledge was presented to four nutritionists/dieticians affiliated to different centers/departments in Lisbon, Portugal. After some discussions/informal interviews with the experts, and taking into account the four aforementioned experts' opinion, eight concepts were identified as the main influencing factors that can contribute to the ageing process of older adults, in order to improve their QoL, namely: Starchy, F&V, Dairy, Protein, HFHS, H2O, EmoS and QoN (output).

In this way, the involved FCM plays the role of a system representation, dismantling the 7 inputs-1 output relations, as represented by the estimated adjacency matrix. This actually reflects the expert's knowledge representation hidden in the IF/THEN fuzzy rules of the FCM-QoN model, yet in a more quantitative way, i.e., in the form of the interconnection weight values.

The eight concepts together form the basic nodes of the FCM-QoN model. The experts describe the influence of one concept on the other using fuzzy rules. In fact, different experts can have different opinions about the causal associations between different pair of concepts. From this perspective, in order to calculate the numerical weight that connects two nodes, the opinions of different experts are combined using an appropriate aggregation function, in order to eliminate subjectivity issues. The produced aggregated output is then defuzzified to rich a numerical weight of the link that connects two concepts; then, the weights of the links connecting the cause and effect

**Table 1.** Construction of the triangle-membership functions and corresponding linguistic weights. Start, peak and end denote the triangle vertices.

|           | Positively | | | Negatively | | |
|-----------|-------|------|------|-------|-------|-------|
|           | Start | Peak | End  | Start | Peak  | End   |
| Very low  | 0.00  | 0.10 | 0.15 | −0.15 | −0.10 | 0.00  |
| Low       | 0.10  | 0.20 | 0.30 | −0.30 | −0.20 | −0.10 |
| Medium    | 0.20  | 0.50 | 0.70 | −0.70 | −0.50 | −0.20 |
| High      | 0.60  | 0.70 | 0.80 | −0.80 | −0.70 | −0.60 |
| Very high | 0.70  | 0.80 | 1.00 | −1.00 | −0.80 | −0.70 |
| Zero      | 0.00  | 0.00 | 0.01 | −0.01 | 0.00  | 0.00  |

nodes of the system are obtained, reflecting the combined opinion of the experts of causal associations between different attributes of the system [28].

In order to exemplify how the experts' opinions on causal relationships are converted into numerical weight values, the following fuzzy rule tries to express the interconnection between the concept HFHS and the output concept QoN:

*"IF the value of the HFHS changes very much THEN the value of the QoN changes very much. Consequently, the effect of HFHS to QoN will be negatively very high."*

The MAX method for the aggregation of the triggered fuzzy membership functions were used. In general, six linguistic weights (i.e., very few, few, moderate, much, very much, zero) (see Table 1) and seven linguistic weights for the case of the Emotional State (i.e., positive2negative, positive2neutral, negative2positive, negative2neutral, neutral2positive, neutral2negative, no effect) were aggregated. Moreover, a seven-level of triangle membership functions $\mu$ (positively very low, positively low, positively medium, positively high, positively very high, zero, negatively very low, negatively low, negatively medium, negatively high, negatively very high) were adopted for the change effect within the range of [-1,1] (see structural triangle characteristics in Table 1). Then the centroid defuzzification method were implemented to calculate the numerical value of the weight in the range [−1, 1] as illustrated in Fig. 2.

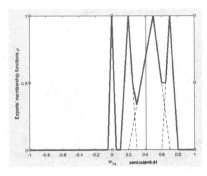

**Fig. 2.** The aggregation of linguistic variables using the MAX method, related with two concepts, namely: EmoS and Protein. The vertical line corresponds to the centroid of the pair (EmoS, Protein) =0.41, denoting weight $w_{74}$ (see also Table 2).

## 2.4   Implementation Issues

The implementation of the whole analysis of the FCM-QoN model was carried out in Matlab 2015a (The Mathworks, Inc., Natick, USA), using custom-made programming code. The visualization of the estimated FCM graph was carried out via a Matlab application, namely FCM-Viewer [29]. The results from the analysis of the afore-mentioned experts' opinions data with the proposed FCM-QoN model are described/discussed in the succeeding section.

# 3   Results and Discussion

## 3.1   The Derived FCM-QoN Structure

Figure 3 depicts the structure of the derived FCM-QoN model, showing the inter-connection between the seven input concepts and the QoN output. The corresponding weights are analytically presented in Table 2.

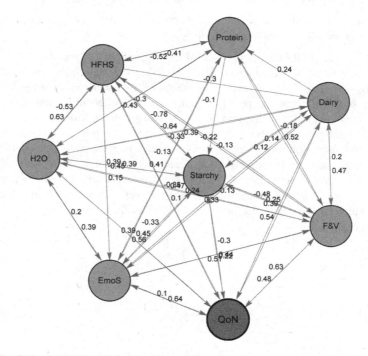

**Fig. 3.** The derived FCM-QoN model with the interconnection weights between the seven input concepts (in orange) and the output QoN (in green), shown in detail in Table 2. (Color figure online)

**Table 2.** The concept interconnection weights of the FCM-QoN model corresponding to the values of the FCM of the Fig. 3.

|         | Starchy | F&V   | Dairy | Protein | HFHS  | H2O   | EmoS  | QoN   |
|---------|---------|-------|-------|---------|-------|-------|-------|-------|
| Starchy | 0       | −0.48 | 0.12  | 0       | −0.64 | 0.39  | −0.33 | −0.30 |
| F&V     | 0.25    | 0     | 0.47  | 0.52    | −0.13 | 0.24  | 0.22  | 0.63  |
| Dairy   | 0.14    | 0.20  | 0     | 0.24    | 0     | 0.39  | −0.13 | 0.39  |
| Protein | −0.10   | −0.18 | 0     | 0       | −0.41 | −0.30 | −0.13 | 0     |
| HFHS    | −0.78   | −0.22 | −0.30 | −0.52   | 0     | −0.53 | −0.45 | −0.35 |
| H20     | 0.39    | 0.47  | −0.33 | −0.43   | 0.63  | 0     | 0.20  | 0.39  |
| EmoS    | 0.45    | 0.51  | 0.33  | 0.41    | 0.15  | 0.39  | 0     | 0.10  |
| QoN     | 0.44    | 0.48  | 0.54  | 0       | 0.10  | 0.56  | 0.64  | 0     |

## 3.2 Analyzing Scenarios

For the constructed FCM-QoN model, a *static analysis* of the domain for establishing the relative importance of concepts, and indirect and total causal effects between concept nodes was conducted. In fact, several previous studies have used a static analysis for identifying important concepts based on network theory, such as centrality [30–32].

As a *first level of analysis*, the causal relationships between the concepts that are directly connected with the QoN, illustrated as orange circles in Fig. 3, are interpreted. In this line, the main concepts are Starchy, F&V, Dairy, HFHS, H2O, EmoS, which are directly connected with the QoN (green circle). Based on the corresponding weights (Table 2), Protein is the only concept that does not (positively/negatively) directly affect the QoN, whereas the latter seems to affect the most (highest value (0.64) of the positive weights of Table 2) the EmoS, and then the H2O (0.56 weight value). These findings indicate the need for attention in the way that emotional well-being of older people (e.g., depression, anxiety, optimism) should be considered as important factor in the field of healthy ageing combined with the adoption of healthy dietary habits. At the same time, due to the increased risk of dehydration in older people (older people lose around 2 L of water per day), fluid intakes should be considered as part of intervention strategies; moreover, the increased risk of constipation in older people means that adequate fluid should be encouraged.

With regard to the highest negative effect, this appears between HFHS and F&V (−0.78), followed by the interdependency between Starchy and HFHS (−0.64). These findings express the interconnection between the F&V with HFHS and Starchy. In general, vegetables are good for healthy ageing, but some of them contain high levels of sugar. Knowing which vegetables have a high glycemic index number and therefore affect the blood sugar faster is valuable information. The higher the glycemic index, the more sugar the food contains and the faster blood sugar will feel the impact. Among the vegetables that are high in sugar, several fall into these categories, namely: roots, sweet peppers, bulbs and starchy vegetables.

As there is a number of interrelationships between the concepts within the FCM-QoN model, there is a potential for feedback cycles to exist within it, whereby a change in one concept can have a cumulative and/or self-sustaining effect.

**Table 3.** The main feedback cycles (24) of the estimated FCM-QoN model (see Fig. 3). Note that these feedback cycles are structured by the concepts that are connected with the QoN.

| No. | Main Feedback Cycles | Cycle Sign |
|---|---|---|
| 1 | *Starchy → H2O → EmoS → QoN → F&V → Starchy* | (+) positive |
| 2 | *Starchy → EmoS → QoN → Starchy* | (−) negative |
| 3 | *Starchy → Protein → F&V → QoN → Starchy* | (−) negative |
| 4 | *F&V → EmoS → QoN → F&V* | (+) positive |
| 5 | *F&V → Dairy → Starchy → QoN → F&V* | (−) negative |
| 6 | *F&V → HFHS → H2O → EmoS → QoN → F&V* | (+) positive |
| 7 | *Dairy → Protein → Starchy → QoN → Dairy* | (+) positive |
| 8 | *Dairy → H2O → QoN → Dairy* | (+) positive |
| 9 | *Dairy → Protein → EmoS → QoN → F&V → Dairy* | (−) negative |
| 10 | *Protein → HFHS → QoN → Dairy → Protein* | (+) positive |
| 11 | *Protein → F&V → QoN → Starchy → Protein* | (−) negative |
| 12 | *Protein → EmoS → QoN → H2O → Protein* | (+) positive |
| 13 | *HFHS → EmoS → QoN → HFHS* | (−) negative |
| 14 | *HFHS → H2O → EmoS → QoN → Starchy → HFHS* | (+) positive |
| 15 | *HFHS → F&V → QoN → HFHS* | (−) negative |
| 16 | *H2O → QoN → Dairy → H2O* | (+) positive |
| 17 | *H2O → EmoS → QoN → Starchy → H2O* | (+) positive |
| 18 | *H2O → Protein → F&V → QoN → H2O* | (+) positive |
| 18 | *EmoS → QoN → F&V → EmoS* | (+) positive |
| 20 | *EmoS → Starchy → Dairy → F&V → QoN → EmoS* | (+) positive |
| 21 | *EmoS → H2O → HFHS → Dairy → QoN → EmoS* | (−) negative |
| 22 | *QoN → Dairy → F&V → H2O → QoN* | (+) positive |
| 23 | *QoN → EmoS → Starchy → QoN* | (−) negative |
| 24 | *QoN → HFHS → F&V → QoN* | (−) negative |

In this way, similarly to the work of [31], the *second level of the static analysis* was adopted, based on studying the characteristics of the weighted directed graph that represents the derived FCM-QoN, using graph theory techniques [33]. In this context, it is our intention to better understand the role of the influential factors of the QoN and to analyze their contribution to self-sustained cycles. From this perspective, the main feedback cycles (24) were identified within the estimated FCM-QoN model, structured by the concepts that are connected with the QoN. The identified main feedback cycles are tabulated in Table 3. Each identified feedback cycle was allocated a positive/negative sign (last column of Table 3), which was determined by multiplying the signs of the arcs present in each feedback cycle [33]. In fact, positive (negative) feedback cycle behavior is that of amplifying (counteracting) any initial change, leading to a constant increase (decrease) in case an increase is introduced to the system [33].

For example, the cycle No. 4 (F&V→EmoS→QoN→F&V) from Table 3 shows that F&V affects EmoS, which affects QoN, which then affects back F&V. This cycle could interpreted as follows: the consumption of F&V could affect the EmoS, which could evoke the QoN, leading back to more consumption of F&V. This cycle exhibits a positive sign (Table 3, last column) and shows how the feedback of FCM-QoN model could contribute in fueling a self-sustaining action (F&V), which has a cumulative effect on other actions, i.e., EmoS and QoN within the derived FCM-QoN model.

In another example of Table 3, i.e., No. 21 (EmoS→H2O→HFHS→Dairy→QoN →EmoS), it is clear that this feedback cycle is not self-sustained, as it is characterized by a negative sign (Table 3, last column), denoting that the combination of the food segments involved, and especially HFHS combined with Dairy, could lead to more negative emotions.

From an overall perspective of the cycles in Table 3, it seems that there is a balance between the number of cycles with positive (14) and negative (10) sign, denoting the opposite effect of various possibilities that could be adopted in the dietary habits. Consequently, following mainly self-sustained cycles, they potentially could promote further the QoN towards healthy nutrition in the silver community.

## 4 Conclusion

In this paper, a new way of modeling the food groups interconnection within the Eatwell Plate, combined with the water and emotional state, for the healthy ageing population was explored. Seen as a holistic and flexible model, the proposed FCM-QoN approach has the potential to surface possibilities and scenarios from different (macro, meso, micro) perspectives, helping nutritionists/dietitians and other health professionals to promote a healthy lifestyle, assisting older adults, in particular, to make better decisions regarding food choices as part of a healthy diet taking into account their emotional state. As a step further, the FCM-QoN model could be examined from a dynamic analysis approach, incorporating the effect of different diseases upon the dietary habits and emotional state, allowing for the simulations of the effects of the diseases on patients' nutrition behavior. This could also assist in the creation of prognostic indices related to the disease early symptoms. The latter is meticulously exploited in the H2020 i-Prognosis project (www.i-prognosis.eu), which is situated in the area of healthy and active ageing, targeting intelligent early detection and intervention in Parkinson's disease area.

**Acknowledgements.** This work has received funding from the EU H2020-PHC-2014-2015/H2020-PHC-2015, grant agreement No. 690494: 'i-Prognosis' project (www.i-progn osis.eu). Moreover, Dr. Dias (first author) acknowledges the financial support by the Foundation for Science and Technology (FCT, Portugal) (Postdoctoral Grant SFRH/BPD/496004/20) and the Interdisciplinary Centre for the Study of Human Performance (CIPER, Portugal). Finally, the authors would like to thank the four nutritionists/dieticians that served as experts in this study.

## References

1. Myint, P.K., Welch, A.A.: Healthier ageing. BMJ **344**, e1214 (2012)
2. Taylor, C.: Looking at malnutrition from the patient's perspective. J. Comm. Nurs. **28**(2), 40–44 (2014)

3. Bamford, C., Heaven, B., May, C., Moynihan, P.: Implementing nutrition guidelines for older people in residential care homes: a qualitative study using normalization process theory. Implement. Sci. **7**, 106 (2012)

4. Arvanitakis, M., Coppens, P., Doughan, L., Van Gossum, A.: Nutrition in care homes and home care: recommendations - a summary based on the report approved by the council of Europe. Clin. Nutr. **28**, 492–496 (2009)

5. Food Standards Agency, Guidelines for use and reproduction of the eatwell plate model. http://www.food.gov.uk/scotland/scotnut/eatwellplate/guidelines

6. Food Standards Agency, the eatwell plate. http://tna.europarchive.org/20100929190231/ http://www.eatwell.gov.uk/healthydiet/eatwellplate/

7. Public Health England in association with the Welsh government, the Scottish government and the Food Standards Agency in Northern Ireland. https://www.gov.uk/government/ publications/the-eatwell-plate-how-to-use-it-in-promotional-material/

8. Kosko, B.: Fuzzy cognitive maps. Int. J. Man Mach. Stud. **24**, 65–75 (1986)

9. Dickerson, J.A., Kosko, B.: Virtual worlds as fuzzy cognitive maps. In: IEEE Virtual Reality Annual International Symposium, pp. 471–477. IEEE Press, New York (1993)

10. Taba, T.V.S., Nezami, B.G., Shetty, A., Chetty, V.K., Srinivasan, S.: Association of high dietary saturated fat intake and uncontrolled diabetes with constipation: evidence from the national health and nutrition examination surve. Neurogastroenterol. Motil. **27**(10), 1389–1397 (2015)

11. Department of Health (DH) Committee on Medical Aspects of Food Policy: Dietary reference values for food energy and nutrients for the United Kingdom. Report on health and social subjects, no. 41, London, HMSO (1991)

12. Gandell, D., Straus, S.E., Bundookwala, M., Tsui, V., Alibhai, S.M.: Treatment of constipation in older people. CMAJ **185**(8), 663–666 (2013)

13. Hodak, S.P., Verbalis, J.G.: Abnormalities of water homeostasis in aging. Endocrinol. Metab. Clin. N. Am. **34**(4), 1031–1046 (2005)

14. Jones, J., Duffy, M., Coull, Y., Wilkinson, H.: Older people living in the community-nutritional needs, barriers and interventions: a literature review, Project Report, Scottish Government Social Research, Edinburgh (2009)

15. Macdiarmid, J., Kyle, J., Horgan, G., Loe, J., Fyfe, M., Johnstone, A., McNeill, G.: Livewell: A balance of healthy and sustainable food choices. WWF-UK, Godalming (2011)

16. Harland, J.I., Buttriss, J., Gibson, S.: Achieving eatwell plate recommendations: is this a route to improving both sustainability and healthy eating? Nutr. Bull. **37**, 324–343 (2012)

17. Department for Environment, Food and Rural Affairs (DEFRA), Family food 2014 report (2015)

18. Jones, N.R.V., Conklin, A.I., Suhrcke, M., Monsivais, P.: The growing price gap between more and less healthy foods: analysis of a novel longitudinal UK dataset. PLoS ONE **9**(10), e109343 (2014)

19. Banks, J., Williams, J., Cumberlidge, T., Cimonetti, T., Sharp, D.J., Shield, J.P.H.: Is healthy eating for obese children necessarily more costly for families? Br. J. Gen. Pract. **62**, e1–e5 (2012)

20. Leslie, W.S., Comrie, F., Lean, M.E., Hankey, C.R.: Designing the eatwell week: the application of eatwell plate advice to weekly food intake. Public Health Nutr. **16**, 795–802 (2012)

21. Lee, S., Yang, J., Han, J.: Development of a decision making system for selection of dental implant abutments based on the fuzzy cognitive map. Expert Syst. Appl. **39**(14), 11564–11575 (2012)

22. Groumpos, Peter P., Karagiannis, Ioannis E.: Mathematical modelling of decision making support systems using fuzzy cognitive maps. In: Glykas, Michael (ed.) Business Process Management. SCI, vol. 444, pp. 299–337. Springer, Heidelberg (2013)

23. Hong, T., Han, I.: Knowledge-based data mining of news information on the Internet using cognitive maps and neural networks. Expert Syst. Appl. 23(1), 1–8 (2002)

24. Kotsiantis, S.B.: Use of machine learning techniques for educational proposes: a decision support system for forecasting students' grades. Artif. Intell. Rev. 37(4), 331–344 (2012)

25. Hadjileontiadou, S.J., Dias, S.B., Diniz, J.A., Hadjileontiadis, L.J.: Fuzzy logic-based modeling in collaborative and blended learning. In: Tomei, E.D. (ed.) Advances in Educational Technologies and Instructional Design (AETID). IGI Global, Hershey (2015)

26. Dickerson, J., Kosko, B.: Virtual worlds as fuzzy cognitive maps. Presence 3(2), 173–189 (1994)

27. Giles, B.G., Findlay, C.S., Haas, G., LaFrance, B., Laughing, W., Pembleton, S.: Integrating conventional science and aboriginal perspectives on diabetes using fuzzy cognitive maps. Soc. Sci. Med. 64(3), 562–576 (2007)

28. Papageorgiou, E.I.: A new methodology for decisions in medical informatics using fuzzy cognitive maps based on fuzzy rule-extraction techniques. Appl. Soft Comput. 11(1), 500–513 (2011)

29. Dias, S.B., Hadjileontiadou, S.J., Hadjileontiadis, L.J., Diniz, J.A.: Fuzzy cognitive mapping of LMS users' quality of interaction within blended-learning environment. Expert Syst. Appl. 42(21), 7399–7423 (2015)

30. Khan, M.S., Quaddus, M.: Group decision support using fuzzy cognitive maps for causal reasoning. Group Decis. Negot. 13(5), 463–480 (2004)

31. Hossain, S., Brooks, L.: Fuzzy cognitive map modelling educational software adoption. Comput. Educ. 51(4), 1569–1588 (2008)

32. Yaman, D., Polat, S.: A fuzzy cognitive map approach for effect-based operations: an illustrative case. Inf. Sci. 179(4), 382–403 (2009)

33. Tsadiras, A.K., Kouskouvelis, I., Margaritis, K.G.: Making political decisions using fuzzy cognitive maps: the FYROM crisis. In: Proceedings of the 8th Panhellenic Conference on Informatics (EPY 2003), vol. 2, pp. 501–510. Thessaloniki, Greece (2001)

# MAGNI: A Real-Time Robot-Aided Game-Based Tele-Rehabilitation System

Srujana Gattupalli[1(✉)], Alexandros Lioulemes[2], Shawn N. Gieser[2],
Paul Sassaman[2], Vassilis Athitsos[1], and Fillia Makedon[2]

[1] VLM - The Vision-Learning-Mining Research Laboratory,
Department of Computer Science and Engineering,
University of Texas at Arlington, Arlington, TX, USA
srujana.gattupalli@mavs.uta.edu, athitsos@uta.edu
[2] HERACLEIA - Human-Center Computing Laboratory,
Department of Computer Science and Engineering,
University of Texas at Arlington, Arlington, TX, USA
{alexandros.lioulemes,paul.sassaman}@mavs.uta.edu,
{shawn.gieser,makedon}@uta.edu

**Abstract.** During the last two decades, robotic rehabilitation has become widespread, particularly for upper limb physical rehabilitation. Major findings prove that the efficacy of robot-assisted rehabilitation can be increased by motivation and engagement, which is offered by exploiting the opportunities of gamification and exergaming. This paper presents a tele-rehabilitation framework to enable interaction between therapists and patients and is a combination of a graphical user interface and a high dexterous robotic arm. The system, called MAGNI, integrates a 3D exercise game with a robotic arm, operated by therapist in order to assign in real-time the prerecorded exercises to the patients. We propose a game that can be played by a patient who has suffered an injury to their arm (e.g. Stroke, Spinal Injury, or some physical injury to the shoulder itself). The experimental results and the feedback from the participants show that the system has the potential to impact how robotic physical therapy addresses specific patient's needs and how occupational therapists assess patient's progress over time.

**Keywords:** HCI · Upper-limb rehabilitation · Gamification

## 1 Introduction

Stroke is the fourth leading cause of death and the leading cause of serious, long term adult disability in the United States, with approximately 795,000 individuals experiencing a new or recurring stroke every year [1]. Numerous studies have discovered that based on the concept of neuroplasticity, the brain's ability to reorganize by forming new neural connections [2, 3], stroke patients' motor function improves with continuous rehabilitation of the extremities affected by hemiparesis [4, 5]. It has been shown

---

MAGNI—The Norse God of strength.

© Springer International Publishing Switzerland 2016
M. Antona and C. Stephanidis (Eds.): UAHCI 2016, Part III, LNCS 9739, pp. 344–354, 2016.
DOI: 10.1007/978-3-319-40238-3_33

that the intensity of training has a positive effect on regaining motor function. This has constituted a main motivation for use of robots in aiding rehabilitation of stroke patients [6, 7].

In this work we contribute technically in building an end-to-end prototype for the user's real-time tele-rehabilitation experience by conducting experiments that allows the therapist to administer the patients remotely through a virtual exer-game. Our algorithmic rehabilitation motion analysis contribution and the empirical studies of health-related information provide an important innovation in the Human Computer Interaction (HCI) community. The upper limb health data captured from the user's whole arm, coordinated with the data visualization of the user's hand, performances, and scores, provides valuable information to physical and occupational therapists for the patient's rehabilitation progress. The data collected will be used to provide input to the therapist for both monitoring the patient's progress over time and for offering recommendations about the next course of treatment. Surveys were given to the subjects to evaluate and deliver feedback on our prototype. The results and conclusions from the surveys will be incorporated in our final system that can potentially be used in a clinical environment to improve the communication and interaction of a therapist and a patient in robot-aided therapy.

We evaluate the users' exercises according to the prescribed therapist exercises using the Barrett WAM Arm [29] in order to capture range of motion of the users' upper limb. The purpose of this assessment tool is to motivate the user to perform some of the exercises, assigned in real-time by the therapist, using a 3D carnival-themed game. The contribution of this work is that wraps the Patient-Robot-Game (PRG) Interaction, Analysis and Database together in an integrated GUI that can be used in real-time by patients and therapists (Fig. 1). Our research presents an innovative tele-rehabilitation system that tracks movements on a highly dexterous robotic platform to evaluate range of motion associated with patient's upper-limbs.

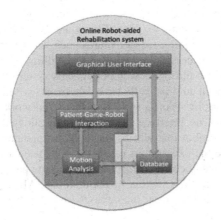

**Fig. 1.** The MAGNI system consists of four crucial parts – A Patient-Robot-Game (PRG) Interaction subsystem, an Analysis and Movement tracking engine, a Graphical User Interface and a Database.

## 2 Related Work

The use of rehabilitation robots began in the late 1990s [8] and offers various benefits over manually supported motor rehabilitation: increased patient motivation; repetitive and intensive movement exercise capability; adjustability of assistance or resistance forces based on patients' progress [9]; and acquisition of data that can be used to objectively quantify the improvement of motor function [10, 11]. Multisite clinical studies have shown that the outcome of robot-aided rehabilitation is at least equal to, and in some aspects better, than the outcome of traditional rehabilitation with a therapist [12].

Rehabilitation robots developed for the upper extremity fall into one of two categories based on their kinematic structure: end-effector type and exoskeleton devices. End-effector type devices were the first of these to be implemented and tested in stroke rehabilitation research due to their more straightforward design [2, 13]. Powered exoskeletons, on the other hand, carry the distinct advantage of enabling both accurate measurement and application of torques to specific joints, as well as precise recording and monitoring of individual joint motion trajectories [14, 15]. Within the context of traditional stroke rehabilitation, the term "engagement" has a variety of meanings. One common interpretation of engagement is motivation for undergoing rehabilitation. An important finding is that highly motivated patients are more likely to attribute themselves a more active role in rehabilitation [16–18]. A strong motivator for the use of robotic devices in rehabilitation is that they facilitate clinical assessment by recording and measuring the kinematics and kinetics of human movements (speed, position and force) with high resolution [19, 20, 30].

Several User Interface (UI) tools have already been developed to be used by therapists. In [21], authors developed a UI to allow therapists to perform balance exercises using a balance board and a motion tracking system for use in fall detection and prevention. The therapist can select which patient, choose which tests to run, and view any important information either instantaneously or later. This system, however, does not have a game-like interface to keep the patient engaged. The authors in [22] provide therapists with a system to view Electronic Health Records (EMR). This system is very extensive providing many features such as viewing and editing patient profiles, adding any notes necessary, scheduling and billing of sessions, and allowing the patient to see results also through a web portal. This system however is not directly linked to a game, nor does it automatically save data from sessions. All information has to be input from the therapist's notes. In [23], authors did work with Autism patients during therapy sessions. The interface developed here allowed therapists to set the order of expressions of a robot that will be displayed to patients from a monitor. The therapist can also change the expressions of the robot by use of a remote control. This system does not automatically collect information about the patients as the information gathered was in the form of notes written by the therapist. Also, there was no interface to view the information about current or previous sessions, but only a single session control interface.

## 3   System Setup

Our game consists of moving one hand to hit a sequence of targets that are placed along an exercise gesture path. To make this more interesting, we borrow the aesthetics from traditional ball-toss carnival games. In these games, you toss a ball at a series of targets (cans, round target, or other visually intriguing objects) in an attempt to knock them down or break them. This is nearly identical to the actions we need the patients to complete. Additionally, as there are a wide variety of visually distinct carnival games with similar goals, we can easily alter the visuals of our virtual carnival game while keeping our gameplay the same. This provides more visual and audio variety to the user keeping them interested for longer.

To provide a large degree of adaptability for therapy sessions, our system utilizes two screens at the same time. One screen is for the patient and displays only the game (Fig. 2 - Left). This screen may be visible by the therapist depending on if he is in the same location/facility as the patient. The second screen (Fig. 2 - Right) allows the therapist to adjust the exercise program in real time by drag and drop of the exercise trajectories in the exercise list on the right side of the screen. Running along the top of the therapist's screen is a horizontally scrollable section that visually shows the sequence of exercises for this session as a series of pictures, placed sequentially in the order that they have been or will be completed. The exercises that have been completed are located on the left side of the list. The exercise currently being performed by the patient is after the completed exercises and is indicated by a yellow border. The exercises that have yet to be completed are located on the right side of the list, after the current exercise. These uncompleted exercises are changeable and can be reorganized at will.

 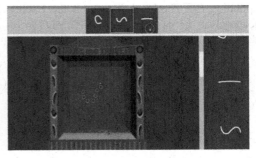

**Fig. 2.** Left – Patient, Game and Robotic Arm interaction, Right – Therapist's screen for online session adaptability that displays duplicate view of the patient's game-play (center), current exercise program (top) and available exercises (right).

## 4  Exercise Analysis

Dynamic time warping (DTW) [24] is a robust algorithm for measuring similarity between two sequences which may vary in time or speed. We use the Multi-Dimensional DTW algorithm for the purpose of measuring the distance between the time-series representations of the exercise trajectories. These trajectories are the spatial coordinates received from the Barrett Arm corresponding to its location at any given time. The authors in [25] have used the same warping technique for sign language recognition and we incorporate the same analysis for measuring the exercise trajectory deviation.

Let $R$ be an exercise trajectory. Here we can represent $R$ as a time series $(R_1, \ldots, R_{|X|})$, where each $R_t$ is the spatial coordinate of the Barrett arm. Given a reference trajectory $R$ and patient trajectory $P$, DTW computes a warping path $W$ that forms correspondences between features of $R$ and $P$:

$$W = ((r_1, p_1), \ldots, (r_{|W|}, p_{|W|}))  \tag{1}$$

Here $|W|$ is the length of the warping path, and pair $(r_i, p_i)$ shows that feature $r_i$ of $R$ corresponds to feature $p_i$ of $P$. The warping path follows rules as shown below:

• Boundary Conditions: This states that the first elements match ($r_1 = 1, p_1 = 1$) and the last elements match ($r_{|W|} = |R|, p_{|W|} = |P|$).

• Monotonicity and Continuity: This states that the alignment cannot go backwards and the alignment cannot skip elements ($0 \le r_{i+1} - r_i \le 1, 0 \le p_{i+1} - p_i \le 1$).

The cost measure $D(W, R, P)$ of a warping path $W$ is the sum of individual local optimal distances $d(R_{ri}, P_{pi})$, corresponding to matching each $R_{ri}$ with the corresponding $P_{pi}$. The local distance is the Euclidean distance between the corresponding features of the two trajectories. The DTW distance between trajectories $R$ and $P$ is defined as the cost of the lowest-cost warping path between $R$ and $P$. We use this

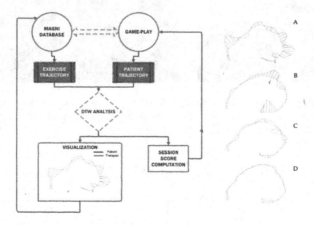

**Fig. 3.** Left - Exercise Analysis Flow Diagram; Right – Patient's recovery progress in four sessions. The score error deviation over sessions are (A) 52.38, (B) 25.83, (C) 8.31 and (D) 7.53

distance to calculate score for the game. This enables accurate score calculations for trajectory time series with similar shapes even if they may be out of phase in the time axis. We visualize the Multi-Dimensional DTW optimal alignment to provide the therapist a better understanding of the patient trajectories' error deviations. Figure 3 above shows the overall flow of the exercise analysis that is performed in our system and an example of the patient's score and recovery progress over multiple sessions.

## 5   Experimental Setup and Results

In Human-Computer Interaction (HCI), role-play is a useful technique to develop an understanding of users' needs and to evaluate design prototypes where access to users or environments is limited. In our work, we use therapeutic role-play [26] technique with our participants in order to gain feedback about the design of our system. Here we imply a procedure similar to the Goldfish bowl role-play technique where there are two participants in the role-play and many observers. We use two participants in the role-play, one as the therapist and the other as the patient. The developers of the system are the active and engaged observers who receive feedback from the participants on the design of the interface and the game-play experience. The system was tested with 10 participants (3 females and 7 males) who actively took part in the therapeutic role-play technique while using our system and then providing feedback by filling out two surveys, namely "MAGNI Game Survey" and "MAGNI Therapist User Interface Survey". Both surveys contained Likert-like questions with 10 points scale with "1" being "Very Easy" and "10" being "Extremely Difficult". Our participants were all students from Computer Science Department with good vision and physical condition. Instructions were given to the participants in order to inform them what are the disabilities of stroke patients related to the arm movement, such that they could successfully participate in such a role-play. Each participant first played the game in the role of the patient and then used the user interface of our system in the role of the therapist.

The hardware that we require for our infrastructure is the Barrett WAM Robotic Arm, a Linux desktop computer to control the Arm, a Windows desktop computer to run the game and contain the database, one projector monitor and networking hardware (LAN cable and router). All experiments of the User Interface were conducted on an Intel i5 4690 CPU @ 3.5 GHz machine with 16 Gigabytes of main memory, running Windows 8.1 with NVIDIA GeForce GTX 780 graphics card.

### 5.1   3D Perception

As the patient smashes each target in the sequence, their arm follows a preset path that equates to performing a therapy exercise. While it is extremely easy to convey the horizontal and vertical position of each target on a 2D screen, intuitively communicating the depth of the targets proved to be more challenging. Our initial attempt at conveying depth was to place thin columns below each target that stretched to the bottom of the game box (Fig. 4 - Left). A column was also attached to the hand position indicator which moved at the same pace/to the same location as the indicator.

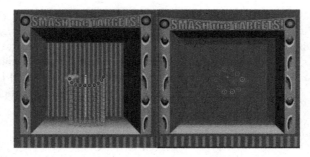

**Fig. 4.** 3D visualization and perception. (a) To the left is the initial 3D attempt. Here, the object illuminated in pink is the target and depth is indicated using columns, (b) To the right is the final depth plane visualization. Here, the target is displayed by green visual cues, depth is indicated using color fields and brightness of a point indicates it's depth relative to the depth plane. (Color figure online)

While this did show how far back in the play-field each item was, the single thin point of contact was often quite far below the target/hand. This required the user to take extra time to repeatedly glance down at the bottom of the play-field then back up to the targets to keep track of where they were located. Additionally, numerous volunteers had trouble understanding how the columns indicated depth.

Our second attempt at conveying depth involved two transparent colored fields (Fig. 4 - Right). Both fields cover the width and height of the play-field. The first field was colored blue and would move to the depth of the current target needing to be hit. The second field was colored orange and would move to the depth of the hand position indicator. As the fields are transparent, it is easy to see both fields at the same time by looking through whatever field is currently in front. The transparency also allows the user to see the targets and hand indicator through the fields. Due to the sheer size of each field, peripheral vision allows the user to see the depth of the current target and hand without looking away from the targets. Most importantly, as the hand moves behind and in front of the current target, the main visible color of the fields will switch between orange and blue depending on whether the hand indicator or the target is in front. This allows the user to intuitively tell if they need to move their hand more to the front or to the back. The tests with participants showed good results for the second way to convey depth, as this system was much more intuitive to understand. The GUI and the 3D video game that the participants used are shown in the following link:

https://www.youtube.com/watch?v=tCjntdBC2BY

## 5.2   Role-Play Survey Results

Table 1 shows some of the questions that were presented during the two surveys. Figure 5 shows the mean value of the results taken from the surveys. This shows that the responses to our game and interface were mostly positive with the lowest mean being approximately 7.40. The higher values may be caused by the participants having prior experience with games and their work in other areas of Computer Science.

**Table 1.** Questions given during survey

| Label | Question |
|-------|----------|
| Q1 | Was it easy to understand the trajectory deviation between the therapist and the patient? |
| Q2 | How easy was it to understand the interface during gameplay? |
| Q3 | How easy was it to keep track of the patient's progress during gameplay? |
| Q4 | Was the calibration phase easy to understand? |
| Q5 | How easy was it to understand how to play? |
| Q6 | How easy was it to understand how to play? |
| Q7 | How easy was it to control the game/hit targets? |

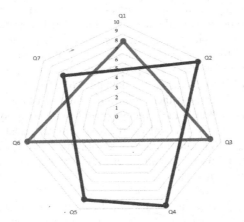

**Fig. 5.** The mean value of the responses from the survey (The red lines correspond to the therapist interface answers and the blue lines with the patient interface). (Color figure online)

The participants also provided additional comments on both the game and interface. The most common response was to grant the therapist the ability to manipulate the graphs. This way, the therapist can pan, rotate, or zoom in on the graph to see certain portions of the graph clearer. Another common response was about the depth perception of the game. Even though the game was a 3D game, it appeared to the participants as if it was 2D, making it difficult to understand the depth of the target. Lastly, participants wanted some additional information when adding or updating patients in the interface, such as user prompts and error messages that pop up and provide additional information.

## 6 Conclusion and Future Work

In this work we combine the robot-assisted rehabilitation with a 3D video game that motivates the user in a GUI operated by therapists and allows them to interact in real-time with the patient. We evaluate the users' exercises according to the prescribed therapist exercises using the robotic arm in order to capture the users' upper limb range of motion and disabilities.

Our prototype demonstrates that 3D game in combination with robotic end-effector enhances the compliance of user by proving motivation to continue through the prescribed exercises. Visualizing the error of patient's exercise trajectory compared to the therapist's recorded reference exercise trajectory helps therapists to understand where the patients had issues during performing exercise that can be addressed in further treatment sessions. Finally, the accurate recovery outcomes exported after each rehabilitation session provide the therapist with the recovery progress of the patient's upper limbs and visual exercise cues in order to plan their next rehabilitation session.

As a future work, we plan to implement the changes recommended by the participants during the survey, especially the manipulation of graphs and improving the depth perception of the game. This will allow a therapist to view the patient's progress in more detail. We also plan to deploy an adaptation module, which will be responsible for the session personalization and adaptation. Each session consists of a certain amount of exercises as prescribed by the therapist. The system will be able to adapt the exercise type and difficulty based on the subject's performance and facial expressions (e.g. pain).

Furthermore, we plan to use the force deviation to apply active motion control to the patients' arm in order to help them gain more control of their motor function. In more advanced stages of rehabilitation, the user will be able to apply forces to move the robotic arm, and the robotic arm will exert an amount of resistance adapted to the specific user's activities [27]. Finally, the usage of remote eye tracking may provide a valuable measurement of users' cognitive engagement and concentration rates over time for smart rehabilitation [28].

**Acknowledgment.** This work is supported in part by the National Science Foundation under award numbers NSF-1338118 and NSF-1055062. Any opinions, findings, and conclusions or recommendations expressed in this publication are those of the author(s) and do not necessarily reflect the views of the National Science Foundation. The authors would like to thank Dr. Fillia Makedon who taught the Special Topics in HCI Course, in which this project was a part of.

# References

1. Lloyd-Jones, D., Adams, R., Carnethon, M., De Simone, G., Ferguson, T.B., Flegal, K., Ford, E., Furie, K., Go, A., Greenlund, K., et al.: Heart disease and stroke statistics—2009 update a report from the american heart association statistics committee and stroke statistics subcommittee. Circulation **119**(3), e21–e181 (2009)
2. Wolf, S.L., Winstein, C.J., Miller, J.P., Taub, E., Uswatte, G., Morris, D., Giuliani, C., Light, K.E., Nichols-Larsen, D., Investigators, E., et al.: Effect of constraint-induced movement therapy on upper extremity function 3 to 9 months after stroke: the excite randomized clinical trial. JAMA **296**(17), 2095–2104 (2006)
3. Green, J.B.: Brain reorganization after stroke. Top. Stroke Rehabil. **10**(3), 1–20 (2003)
4. Jones, T.A., Allred, R.P., Adkins, D.L., Hsu, J.E., O'Bryant, A., Maldonado, M.A.: Remodeling the brain with behavioral experience after stroke. Stroke **40**(3 suppl. 1), S136–S138 (2009)

5. Kwakkel, G., van Peppen, R., Wagenaar, R.C., Dauphinee, S.W., Richards, C., Ashburn, A., Miller, K., Lincoln, N., Partridge, C., Well-wood, I., et al.: Effects of augmented exercise therapy time after stroke a meta-analysis. Stroke 35(11), 2529–2539 (2004)
6. Teasell, R., Bitensky, J., Salter, K., Bayona, N.A.: The role of timing and intensity of rehabilitation therapies. Top. Stroke Rehabil. 12(3), 46–57 (2005)
7. Riener, R., Nef, T., Colombo, G.: Robot-aided neurorehabilitation of the upper extremities. Med. Biol. Eng. Comput. 43(1), 2–10 (2005)
8. Krebs, H.I., Hogan, N., Aisen, M.L., Volpe, B.T.: Robot-aided neurorehabilitation. IEEE Trans. Rehabil. Eng. 6(1), 75–87 (1998)
9. Burgar, C.G., Lum, P.S., Shor, P.C., Van der Loos, H.M.: Development of robots for rehabilitation therapy: the palo alto va/stanford experience. J. Rehabil. Res. Dev. 37(6), 663–674 (2000)
10. Celik, O., O'Malley, M.K., Boake, C., Levin, H., Fischer, S., Reistetter, T.: Comparison of robotic and clinical motor function improvement measures for sub-acute stroke patients. In: IEEE International Conference on Robotics and Automation, ICRA 2008, pp. 2477–2482. IEEE (2008)
11. Celik, O., O'Malley, M.K., Boake, C., Levin, H.S., Yozbatiran, N., Reistetter, T.A.: Normalized movement quality measures for therapeutic robots strongly correlate with clinical motor impairment measures. IEEE Trans. Neural Syst. Rehabil. Eng. 18(4), 433–444 (2010)
12. Klamroth-Marganska, V., Blanco, J., Campen, K., Curt, A., Dietz, V., Ettlin, T., Felder, M., Fellinghauer, B., Guidali, M., Kollmar, A., et al.: Three-dimensional, task-specific robot therapy of the arm after stroke: a multicentre, parallel-group randomised trial. Lancet Neurol. 13(2), 159–166 (2014)
13. Phan, S., Lioulemes, A., Lutterodt, C., Makedon, F., Metsis, V.: Guided physical therapy through the use of the barrett wam robotic arm. In: 2014 IEEE International Symposium on Haptic, Audio and Visual Environments and Games (HAVE), pp. 24–28. IEEE (2014)
14. Perry, J.C., Rosen, J., Burns, S.: Upper-limb powered exoskeleton design. IEEE/ASME Trans. Mechatron. 12(4), 408–417 (2007)
15. Gupta, A., O'Malley, M.K.: Design of a haptic arm exoskeleton for training and rehabilitation. IEEE/ASME Trans. Mechatron. 11(3), 280–289 (2006)
16. Maclean, N., Pound, P., Wolfe, C., Rudd, A.: Qualitative analysis of stroke patients' motivation for rehabilitation. BMJ 321(7268), 1051–1054 (2000)
17. Balaam, M., Rennick Egglestone, S., Fitzpatrick, G., Rodden, T., Hughes, A.M., Wilkinson, A., Mawson, S.: Motivating mobility: designing for lived motivation in stroke rehabilitation. In: Proceedings of the SIGCHI Conference on Human Factors in Computing Systems, pp. 3073–3082. ACM, May 2011
18. Alankus, G., Lazar, A., May, M., Kelleher, C.: Towards customizable games for stroke rehabilitation. In: Proceedings of the SIGCHI Conference on Human Factors in Computing Systems, pp. 2113–2122. ACM, April 2010
19. Mohammadi, A., Tavakoli, M., Marquez, H., Hashemzadeh, F.: Non-linear disturbance observer design for robotic manipulators. Control Eng. Pract. 21(3), 253–267 (2013)
20. Lioulemes, A., Sassaman, P., Gieser, S.N., Makedon, F., Metsis, V.: Self-managed patient-game interaction using the barrett wam arm for motion analysis. In: 8th International Conference on Pervasive Technologies Related to Assistive Technologies, PETRA. ACM, July 2015
21. B. Engineering: Equilibrate. http://balancengineering.com/features-and-benefits/
22. 1st Providers Choice, "Physical therapy emr". http://www.1stprovierschoice.com/physical-therapy-emr.php

23. Goodrich, M.A., Colton, M., Brinton, B., Fujiki, M., Atherton, J.A., Robinson, L., Ricks, D., Maxfield, M.H., Acerson, A.: Incorporating a robot into an autism therapy team. IEEE Intell. Syst. **27**(2), 52–60 (2012)
24. Kruskall, J., Liberman, M.: The symmetric time warping algorithm: from continuous to discrete time warps, string edits and macro-molecules (1983)
25. Wang, H., Stefan, A., Moradi, S., Athitsos, V., Neidle, C., Kamangar, F.: A system for large vocabulary sign search. In: Kutulakos, K.N. (ed.) ECCV 2010 Workshops, Part I. LNCS, vol. 6553, pp. 342–353. Springer, Heidelberg (2012)
26. Matthews, M., Gay, G., Doherty, G.: Taking part: role-play in the design of therapeutic systems. In: Proceedings of the 32nd Annual ACM Conference on Human Factors in Computing Systems, pp. 643–652. ACM (2014)
27. Lioulemes, A.: Adaptive user and haptic interfaces for smart assessment and training. In: Proceedings of the Companion Publication of the 2016 International Conference on Intelligent User Interfaces Companion. ACM (2016) (manuscript has been accepted for publication)
28. McMurrough, C.D., Lioulemes, A., Phan, S., Makedon, F.: 3D mapping of visual attention for smart rehabilitation. In: 8th Interational Conference on Pervasisve Technologies Related to Assistive Technologies, PETRA. ACM, July 2015
29. Product. Retrieved February 29, 2016. http://www.barrett.com/
30. Theofanidis, M., Lioulemes, A., Makedon, F.: A motion and force analysis system for human upper-limb exercises. In: 9th Interational Conference on Pervasive Technologies Related to Assistive Technologies, PETRA. ACM, July 2015

# Connecting Aged Parents with Their Adult Children Over Long Distances: Challenges and a Solution

Chen Guo[✉], Xiaohang Zhang, Zhenyu Cheryl Qian,
and Yingjie Victor Chen

Purdue University, West Lafayette, IN, USA
{guo171,zhan1233,qianz,victorchen}@purdue.edu

**Abstract.** Many elderly people are living apart from their children. We want to develop a system that can reinforce the connection and emotional feelings between aged parents and their children by combing new digital technologies with soft and warm leather material. Through an iterative design process that includes user interview and observation, design exploration, low-fidelity and high-fidelity prototypes, and usability testing, we present a small digital screen attached to an existing leather wallet of the aged parent to receive and display pictures or videos sent from their adult children. By attaching LINK, the old leather wallet serves as an invisible channel, sharing and connecting beautiful family memories without interrupting the private life of either side.

**Keywords:** Gerontology · User-centered design · Tangible interaction design

## 1 Introduction

This paper introduces the motivation, design process, and evaluation outcomes of an interactive device that supports effortless and nonintrusive communications between aged parents and their adult children. According to the U.S. Census Bureau [1], as a consequence of the post-World War II Baby Boom (1946–1964) the proportion of old people aged 65 and over will nearly double to 20 % in 2030, from 14 % in 2012. The fastest-growing group in the United States mirrors that in many other countries. Many elderly people are living apart from their adult children, which increases demand for long-term care.

As an example, a survey conducted across England, Scotland, and Wales shows that almost three-quarters of people over 75 live alone. One in three of them wish to see their children at least weekly; however, almost half of these elders are visited just once every two to six months [2]. It is challenging for seniors to maintain connections with their children, and emotionally it is even more difficult. We want to develop a system that can reinforce the emotional bond between aged parents and their adult children.

Although advanced mobile technology has greatly reconstructed our daily lives, many elderly people find it difficult to use mobile devices because of their decreasing

© Springer International Publishing Switzerland 2016
M. Antona and C. Stephanidis (Eds.): UAHCI 2016, Part III, LNCS 9739, pp. 355–366, 2016.
DOI: 10.1007/978-3-319-40238-3_34

motor and cognitive skills [3, 4]. Failing to "catch up with" their children, the aged parents are often stuck with the traditional telephone communication format, unable to receive updated and enriched information from their children. In the long run, many feel isolated and lonely [5].

Bearing these problems in mind, we want to develop a solution that can facilitate the connections between aged parents and their children by combining new technology with a product that seniors will have no problem adopting and using. Our design process includes semistructured interviewing, observing, brainstorming, low-fidelity and high fidelity prototyping, storyboarding, and usability testing.

## 2 Related Work

The rapid aging of society brings many challenges and serious problems worldwide. Many projects focus on how to connect elderly people with their children over long distances. The Telepathy Lamp [6] is among pioneer projects dealing with emotional communication between elderly parents and children. The authors designed two lamps with colorful LEDs for parents and children. By turning a lamp on or off, users are able to feel the presence of other family members. Researchers in University College London Interaction Centre (UCLIC) designed a device called Silka [7] to support a remote presence by sending "smiles" and "handprints" to enable nonintrusive communication between the households. With the use of poetic communication, an interactive carpet was proposed to display awareness and emotions through sensing and actuation [8]. With technologies including durability, natural movement of tufts, and inaudible hardware, two remote carpets can be connected to create a sense of sharing and copresence through aesthetic interactions.

Previous researches demonstrated that the involvement of elderly end users could contribute to the design process [9, 10]. By means of participatory design sessions, valuable concepts and responses were generated in the conceptual design process [11]. Some researchers explored the collaboration of elderly and children users in two different design stages – the contextual user research and the evaluation of concepts [12]. They stated that a combination of the two user groups played an important role in generating insights into the design process. Researchers should gather information, inspiration, and empathy while working with elderly and children.

Some research measured the usability for elderly and children with digital devices. For example, a study presented that the elderly and children performed better with the tasks of dragging, rotating, and scaling than normal adults did [13]. Another investigation compared two versions of the same Web mail system – linear vs. hypertextual navigation – and found that elderly users obtained better performance results with linear navigation [14]. Some researchers have identified and summarized the major issues when developing technologies for the elderly [15]. Designers should take into consideration the physical and cognitive specificities of this age group and develop adaptive applications that leverage their abilities and views.

## 3    User Needs – an Investigative Research

To identify our design space, we assessed the aged parents' needs by conducting semistructured interviews with 20 residents in three residential care homes. They were all seniors over 75 whose children were living far away. Our investigation explored patterns of communications, living circumstances, favorable products, and attitudes toward technology. We gained some major insights into the user needs.

- **Design for Intimacy at a Distance was Preferable.** Seniors shared similar life patterns broadly, such as having been retired for many years and living alone. Their children had moved away and established their own families. Children living independently outside are unable to contact parents on a daily basis, which leads to seniors' feelings of loneliness and depression. The feeling between parents and children is naturally intimate and full of love. Design for intimacy at a distance could be preferable for aged parents.
- **Don't Want to Disturb Children.** During the interviews, we were touched by learning that most seniors don't want to disturb their children. Elderly people were willing to dedicate time to converse with their children on the phone or text them. However, they thought this kind of contact was intrusive. One participant said, "I don't want to contact my sons a lot since they are now quite busy. I don't want them to say, 'Oh, God. It's my mother again!'" They just wanted to silently pay attention to their children instead of calling them frequently. Another resident said she felt uncomfortable when calling her children because she felt like there was nothing interesting to tell them and she was interrupting their time. This unwillingness to "interrupt" or "disturb" was in part tied up with a desire not to become a burden to the children.
- **Fear of New Technology.** Nearly 80% of the interviewees had no smartphone. They knew nothing about WIFI. Privacy was very important to them. They were afraid to use new technologies. One participant said, "I usually take longer to learn something new. I don't have an iPhone. I'm scared of new technology because things always go wrong. Actually, it's a love-hate relationship." Memory is among the most frequently mentioned challenges for the elderly. They need instructions for using a new device and forget them quickly. Elderly people may take longer to learn how to use a smartphone or a computer. But we did find that swiping images with fingers on the touch screen was very easy for them.
- **The Way to be Involved in Children's Lives is Through Pictures.** Many interviewees mentioned that the common way to be involved in their children's lives is through pictures. Almost all had their children's and grandchildren's pictures in picture frames. They looked at them frequently and showed them to others. Our findings revealed that elderly people preferred using images to communicate over long distances instead of by e-mail and phone calls. One resident said that she used to receive a new picture of her grandchildren every year at Christmas. Pictures allow them to closely follow children's growth and enhance their communication over distances.
- **Special Feelings for Leather Products.** Seniors were especially interested in items that carry stories, e.g., those given by their spouses or purchased on a memorable

trip. They preferred a well-crafted product that had value. We found that seniors had special thoughts for their own leather products that had soft and intimate feelings. Participants expressed that they didn't want to change their old wallets. A leather wallet can keep all the valuables inside a zippered compartment. Leather wallets for elderly people are extremely elegant and stylish, and leather is soft and supple, aging well and slowly under daily wear and tear of regular use.

## 4    Design Process

Based on user studies, we brainstormed intuitive and simple ways for elderly people to get closer with their children. With this in mind, we started to sketch design ideas wildly and presented these initial designs to 20 potential users to collect their eventual feedbacks.

### 4.1    A Smartbelt to Monitor the Well-Being of Senior Adults

The smartbelt concept enables automated and noninvasive monitoring of elderly people with sensors (Fig. 1). It helps children or caregivers maintain a close watch of their parents. The system uses a combination of wireless accelerometer sensors on the belt to monitor the body temperature, heart rate, and respiratory rate of elderly people. An open-source electronics Arduino board [16] is able to process the data and transfer the data via Internet to children's smartphones. A smartphone will upload values to the server and display elderly people's vital status via graphs in real time. If one health vital's datum, such as blood glucose, blood pressure, or heart rate, exceeds a predefined threshold, the app will send an alert to a child's smartphone informing that his/her parents may be in danger. In the meantime, the belt buckle will flash and display the elder's health status with an emergency sign.

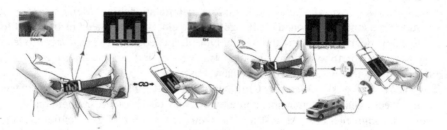

**Fig. 1.** A smartbelt to monitor the well-being of senior adults

The smartbelt received positive feedback from our participants. People considered using it to monitor body data. However, we cannot determine how to track blood pressure data with a remote sensor. If the data are inaccurate, the tool becomes useless. Furthermore, it is inconvenient for senior users to wear one constantly and lower their heads to read the data.

## 4.2    A Leather Shoe Sole with GPS Tracking to Help Find Missing Elderly People

Normal aging is associated with a decline in various memory abilities in many cognitive tasks. One key concern of seniors we interviewed is the experience of memory loss, especially because it is known to be one of the hallmark symptoms of Alzheimer's disease. Apart from diseases, getting lost is another big concern for senior citizens with declining memory. We propose the design of a shoe sole with an embedded global positioning system (GPS) to help senior citizens who are at risk of becoming lost (Fig. 2). A GPS chip is hidden inside the shoe sole. The GPS unit and antenna are on the back of the sole and covered by leather. The antenna picks up signals from satellites necessary for directions. When an elderly person becomes lost, he or she needs only to click on the back of the shoe sole (the heel), and family members or caregivers will receive an alert on a smartphone to show the wearer's location. Family members can also determine a GPS-equipped shoe's location by calling it. The shoe responds by sending a Google map that pinpoints the location. They can then map the location and call emergency help if needed.

**Fig. 2.**  A leather shoe sole with GPS tracking to help find missing elderly people

Many senior users dislike the idea of placing their intimate objects under the feet and having to move the shoe sole from one shoe to another every time they change shoes. So this leather shoe sole concept was also discarded.

## 4.3    A Smartwallet to Update and Display Pictures

During our interview, we found that elderly people like to see value-added products and services with new technologies to help them easily connect with their families over long distances. They also love to view their grandchildren's pictures, basically every day. These desires inspired us to design a smartwallet that allows a projection of images to support social interaction (Fig. 3).

As discussed, elderly people lack the experience of using digital devices. This deficiency inspired us to search for another "smart" way for them to communicate with family members. There is often a space in wallets to put photo IDs. Seniors we interviewed usually fill it with photos of their children or grandchildren. We started to consider digitalizing this element. With Arduino and Wi-Fi, the wallet can directly

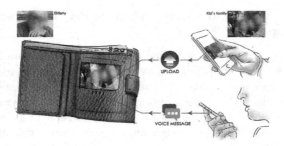

**Fig. 3.** A smart wallet to update and display pictures

receive pictures. The wallet-sized screen will update and display pictures in real time. When a new photo arrives, it will serve as a pleasant morning surprise for senior adults. The interface is simple and requires elderly persons to do nothing. Thus they can see their grandchildren's new pictures every day without waiting for holidays.

The leather wallet concept received positive feedbacks from potential users, who were excited about receiving their children's pictures this way.

## 4.4    A Tangible Sofa to Communicate Touch Over Distance

Living apart and maintaining connection can be a challenge. We wildly brainstormed to push the limits of user experience. Here we propose a tangible leather sofa concept for elderly parents with the intention of bringing on the copresence and allowing parents and children to feel one another's touch. All sofas in a family are connected with the Internet. When an elderly parent sits on the sofa, the body part that touches it will be warmed up if another family

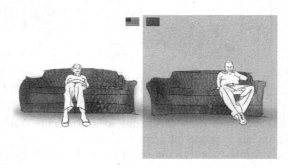

**Fig. 4.** A tangible sofa to communicate touch over distance

member is also sitting on a smart sofa at his or her home (Fig. 4). The touched interface on the sofa will emit a soft heat by infrared rays. The two users will create a bond, and the heat transmitted to the hands increases the duration of the interaction. The technology is already available in the field of infrared heating and offers several integration possibilities. The system will work by a reflection of far-infrared waves that directly heat furniture and human bodies.

Some potential users like the connection with two products, but hesitate about the real experience of soft heat. This technology part is also a huge issue that creates obstacles to our further exploration.

## 5 Storyboards and Scenarios

Based on our research findings, we used our personas to create storyboards and scenarios to illustrate how LINK would be used to help elderly people improve communication over distances (Fig. 5).

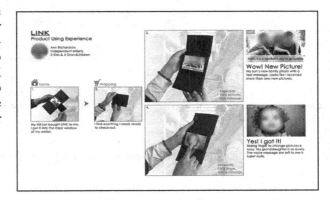

**Fig. 5.** Storyboards and scenarios of LINK

## 6 Low-Fidelity Prototype and Usability Testing

We created a wallet-sized digital screen for the parent end and a mobile application for their adult children (Fig. 6a). Children can use the app to upload pictures to the photo album and send them to LINK (Fig. 6b). The interface of the LINK product is similar to the interface of the LINK app. An album button is on the upper left corner to display the number of left images. On the upper right corner is a text message icon. Aged parents can also listen to the voice message.

We conducted a usability testing study to gain insight into needed design improvements and to identify usability problems for refinement. There are two tasks for the elderly, viewing an image and viewing a video, and three tasks for the children – selecting, uploading, and sending an image. We recruited 5 users to think aloud while performing these tasks. At the same time, we observed and recorded the process to understand their behaviors. The main findings are as follows.

- It was easy to figure out how to swipe images with fingers.
- The album interface was complicated and confused users.
- The font size of album and album numbers was unreadable.
- The paragraph spacing was too small.
- Users would like to see recent images first.

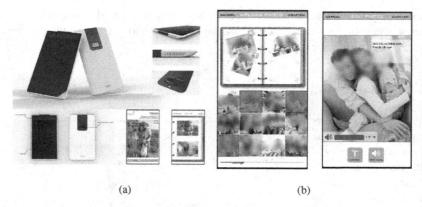

(a)                                    (b)

**Fig. 6.** (a): Low-fidelity of the LINK digital screen. (b): Low-fidelity of the LINK, mobile application.

- Users preferred to view images either horizontally or vertically as they rotated the wallet.
- Users would like to reset the leather wallet or freeze it to go to sleep.
- Users had no idea of how to charge the device.

These findings showed several crucial usability problems and guided us to refine the interface design. We improved the legibility of the interface with bigger pictures and fewer words. We simplified the functions, and the only interaction for elderly people is to use their fingers to swipe pictures. During our interview, we found that users regarded their own old leather wallets as valuable items. Elderly people don't want to change their old wallets. The interface should be quite simple and require elderly people to do nothing.

# 7   High-Fidelity Prototype

We observed the leather wallet market, and found the windows to display pictures or identification cards in the wallet have the same size (originally to show the photo IDs). Designing one electrical card will fit almost all of them. This concerns the digital and physical platforms where the communication takes place and the technologies are used for LINK (Fig. 7).

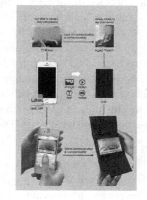

## 7.1   Digital Media

We created a mobile application for the children's end. The interface is simple and easy to use. Children

**Fig. 7.** Product interaction explanation of digital media and physical media.

need to find the unique machine ID of the LINK product and add their parents to the contacts. Then choose images or videos from the photo album and send them to the parent end. Moreover, children can add a text message or a voice message with the image to explain the contents or more greeting sentences.

## 7.2    Physical Media

Leather wallets have great in varieties. As personal items, they deliver messages about people's personality. However, these artifacts cannot convey rich textual information, since they lack the physical storage of storytelling. Thus LINK bridges between the tangible leather wallet and image-based communication (Fig. 7). Considering physical and cognitive abilities of the elderly, LINK has only the input from children and no input from parents, thus reducing the cognitive challenge for the elderly.

LINK receives pictures with text or voice messages and videos from the children's end. The screen will display the incoming images or play videos automatically when the user opens it. Aged parents may receive a delightful surprise when opening the wallet in an early morning. LINK can resize images and crop a horizontal image into a vertical one, or vice versa. Because of age-related vision problems, LINK will read out incoming text messages instead of letting the user read

**Fig. 8.** Product design details of LINK and further explanation of key features.

them. LINK uses different icons to differentiate voice texting and text messaging. On the upper left corner of the screen, the icon will show the number of unread pictures. On the upper right corner of the screen, the icon represents the time of voice messaging. The only activity users need to do is finger swiping – swipe left or right to switch from one image to another. The recent one is always on the top of all the other images.

At the back of LINK are the solar panel and the reset button (Fig. 8). Users need to slide LINK out of the wallet and put it under the sunlight or light to charge it, which encourages the elderly to go outside (Fig. 8). A user can reset LINK after tapping the reset button.

## 7.3    Technologies

LINK is basically a simplified smartphone that only keeps several necessary functions. With a processor, semiconductor memory, LCD, SSD, solar panel, or 4G modem, a digital product is feasible. One of the basic technologies of LINK is the ability to store more pictures. It can connect to a secure cloud server and store a large amount of pictures. A strong and unique password for each device will make personal data more secure.

Another technological aspect of LINK is supporting gestures and touch interactions. With the optical tangible technology, the touch screen will be pressure-sensitive and recognize the swiping method.

## 8  Evaluation

We created a high-fidelity prototype and conducted a usability testing with LINK. We recruited 20 elderly people (the same group in the beginning stage of the user study) and 10 adults who have aged parents or grandparents. We asked them to complete four tasks separately and encouraged them to think aloud during the process.

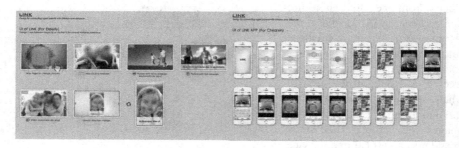

**Fig. 9.** Left: User interface (UI) tasks of the application for the elderly. Right: UI tasks of the leather wallet for children

There were four tasks for aged parents (Fig. 9, left):

- Use LINK in the leather wallet to view an image or a video.
- Find the icon of text messages and voice messages.
- View previous images and open unread ones.
- Charge the leather wallet and reset the device.

There were four tasks for the children (Fig. 9, right):

- Find the unique machine ID of the LINK product and add parents to the contact.
- Upload and send images and videos to parents.
- Add a text message to the image.
- Add a voice message to the image.

We asked participants to answer post-task questionnaires with a Likert scale after the experiments. The questionnaire was based on five usability metrics: ease of use, comprehension, efficiency, clarity of fonts and icons, and satisfaction. The main findings were as follows.

- All adult participants completed all the tasks. Ninety percent of the elderly finished all usability tasks. Only one failed the task of finding the icon of voice messages.
- The two sides both rated the overall tasks easy. Users comprehended each task and were satisfied with the LINK product and its app.
- Aged parents would like to respond to their children through pictures.
- Users would like to see alternative ways to charge the LINK instead of removing it from the leather wallet.

These users are presented from the beginning of the design to the end of the evaluation. They liked communicating with their children through digital pictures in the leather wallet. We may consider their suggestions to add a message-response function to LINK, something we had not considered originally. We also found a new way to charge the leather wallet. By adding a clear thin layer of crystal glass to the screen, users can make the wallet solar powered automatically. However, given the technical difficulty and production costs, we need to conduct research for validation in the next stage.

## 9   Conclusion

As human beings, we naturally dislike being lonely and want to relate with others, especially our loved ones. As an accessory to the leather wallet, the small LINK screen adds new digital values to the old leather material. It further strengthens family values and happiness. Driven by investigative research, our iterative design process makes the manufacturing practice possible. An application of this system will not only produce a high impact on improving elderly's health and wellness and family bonding, but also on many benefits to communities and society.

## References

1. Ortman, J., Colby, S.: The Baby Boom Cohort in the United States: 2012 to 2060. Bureau of the Census, Washington, DC (2014)
2. WRVS report: loneliness amongst older people and impact of family connections. http://bundlr.com/clips/50c84b87b80fc4000200111b. Accessed: 08 Feb 2016
3. Lindley, S.E., Harper, R., Sellen, A.: Designing for elders: exploring the complexity of relationships in later life. In: Proceedings of the 22nd British HCI Group Annual Conference on People and Computers: Culture, Creativity, Interaction, vol. 1, pp. 77–86 (2008)
4. Hope, A., Schwaba, T., Piper, A.M.: Understanding digital and material social communications for older adults. In: Proceedings of the SIGCHI Conference on Human Factors in Computing Systems, pp. 3903–3912 (2014)
5. Karimi, A., Neustaedter, C.: From high connectivity to social isolation: communication practices of older adults in the digital age. In: Proceedings of the ACM 2012 Conference on Computer Supported Cooperative Work Companion, pp. 127–130 (2012)

6. Ying, F., Li, B., Li, Z., Li, X., Tao, J., Gao, S.: Telepathy lamp: remote affective interaction based on ambient metaphor for emotional caring of the elderly. In: 2010 International Conference on System Science, Engineering Design and Manufacturing Informatization (ICSEM), vol. 2, pp. 129–132 (2010)

7. Stawarz, K., Garde, J., McLoughlin, C., Nicolaides, R., Walters, J.: Silka: a domestic technology to mediate the threshold between connection and solitude. In: Proceedings of the 2012 ACM Annual Conference Extended Abstracts on Human Factors in Computing Systems Extended Abstracts, pp. 1309–1314 (2012)

8. Tharakan, M.J., Sepulveda, J., Thun, W., Cheok, A.D.: Poetic communication: interactive carpet for subtle family communication and connectedness. In: Keyson, D.V., Maher, M.L., Streitz, N., Cheok, A., Augusto, J.C., Wichert, R., Englebienne, G., Aghajan, H., Kröse, B. J. (eds.) AmI 2011. LNCS, vol. 7040, pp. 335–339. Springer, Heidelberg (2011)

9. Mitchell, C.T.: Action, perception, and the realization of design. Des. Stud. 16(1), 4–28 (1995)

10. Saritabak, O.D., Demirkan, H.: Involving the elderly in the design process. Archit. Sci. Rev. 41(4), 157–163 (1998)

11. Demirbilek, O., Demirkan, H.: Collaborating with elderly end-users in the design process. In: Collaborative Design, pp. 205–212. Springer, London (2000)

12. van Doorn, F., Gielen, M., Stappers Jan, P.: Involving children and elderly in design research as a combined user group to inform design. Interact. Des. Archit. J. - LxDA, 20, 86–100 (2014)

13. Chang, H.-T., Tsai, T.-H., Chang, Y.-C., Chang, Y.-M.: Touch panel usability of elderly and children. Comput. Hum. Behav. 37, 258–269 (2014)

14. Castilla, D., Garcia-Palacios, A., Miralles, I., Breton-Lopez, J., Parra, E., Rodriguez-Berges, S., Botella, C.: Effect of web navigation style in elderly users. Comput. Hum. Behav. 55, 909–920 (2016)

15. Silva, S.: Developing technologies for the elderly: To whom are we really developing? In: Annual International Conference of the IEEE Engineering in Medicine and Biology Society, pp. 8030–8033 (2015)

16. Arduino - Home. https://www.arduino.cc/. Accessed: 12 Feb 2016

# Design and Evaluation of an Innovative Hazard Warning Helmet for Elder Scooter Riders

Yu-Hsiu Hung[(⊠)], Hua-Cheng Hsu, and Yu-Fang Huang

Department of Industrial Design,
National Cheng Kung University, Tainan, Taiwan
{idhfhung, P36031105, P36034072}@mail.ncku.edu.tw

**Abstract.** Senior people inevitably experience the deterioration of cognitive functions and physical capabilities. Studies showed that elderly people are more likely to be involved in collisions in complex traffic situations. As the number of elder scooter riders is rising around the world, this study presented a hazard warning helmet aimed to help the elderly avoid traffic hazards and possible collisions. Our helmet was designed to provide visual warnings of fast approaching vehicles when elder riders pass through double-parked vehicles. An observational study was conducted to evaluate the effectiveness of the helmet design. Five elderly participants were recruited to wear our helmet and a conventional helmet respectively to interact with 50 double parked vehicles (including cars and scooters). Participants' behavioral reactions were observed and recorded. Results of the study identified four behavioral reactions to double parked vehicles: (1) reducing speed when passing through (without looking back), (2) reducing speed and looking back before passing through, (3) looking in the side mirror before passing through, (4) passing through without taking precaution. Results also showed that participants wearing our helmet were more likely to reduce speed before passing through double parked vehicles than those wearing a conventional helmet. This work has contributions on (1) lowing traffic collision rates, (2) helping elder scooter users be more aware of traffic hazards, and (3) improving elder scooter users' risky behavior.

**Keywords:** Elder · Scooter · Helmet · Warning design

## 1 Introduction

The global population of people aged 65 and older is growing at a fast rate. As population aging becomes a trend in the 21st century, the safety and mobility of all elder road users deserves more attention. In Taiwan, senior citizens accounted for 11 percent of the total population; the country is now moving from an aging society to an aged society [1]. The most common motor vehicles in Taiwan are scooters. Scooters are allowed on most roads (except highways and expressways). Almost one-half of the total population owns a scooter and 70 % of the registered vehicles are scooters [1]. The dense population and limited living spaces make scooter riding a convenient way to travel in and around the

© Springer International Publishing Switzerland 2016
M. Antona and C. Stephanidis (Eds.): UAHCI 2016, Part III, LNCS 9739, pp. 367–374, 2016.
DOI: 10.1007/978-3-319-40238-3_35

cities. The costs of riding scooters (including tax, gas, and maintenance) are lower than those of driving cars, which makes scooters become popular among adults and the elderly.

The patterns of riding a scooter and driving an automobile are quite different. Scooter riding requires less mental resources than automobile driving. However, the risks for riding scooters are much higher than those of driving automobiles [2]. According to You et al. [1], accidents involving scooters contribute to more than 80 % of fatalities in traffic accidents in Taiwan, resulting in more than 2,000 deaths annually. The literature indicates that elderly people are more likely to be involved in crashes, and they are more likely to suffer serious injuries in crashes [3]. The probabilities and consequences of traffic accidents are both higher on elderly people than on young people [2].

The main causes of higher risks of traffic accidents among senior road users include the decreased visual attention, and physical and functional capabilities [4]. Horberry et al. [5] found that, compared with young adults, elder adults are more easily distracted by the surroundings. Braitman et al. [6] and Fofanova and Vollrath [7] also found that elder drivers are less able to deal with complicated road conditions than young drivers. As to the riding behavior, senior road users are more likely to fail to give right of way (due to attention degeneration), leading to traffic collisions [8].

Studies indicated that in order to drive safely senior road users (being aware of their limitations) tend to compensate for their physical degeneration by driving more slowly, driving less at night or during bad weather, or keeping a safe distance behind the vehicle in front [9, 10]. However, these strategies may not always be sufficient to avoid risks and hazards on the road. Traffic accidents still happen constantly. To further lower the probability of traffic accidents, research and technological efforts were made in the industry and the academia. For example, Vashitz et al. [11] developed innovative in-vehicle displays that provide highly informative road safety information to improve traffic safety, especially in tunnels; Yu et al. [12] proposed the use of smart automotive lighting in vehicle safety systems that can detect potential risks in advance and provide early warnings to drivers. In fact, what has been most emphasized was related to automobile safety, not including scooter safety.

In Taiwan, scooters are allowed to travel on the right/slow lanes, but not on the left/fast lanes. It is common that automobiles double park temporarily on the roadside with car signal lights flashing (for quick paying bills/buying groceries etc.). However, this occupies a certain portion of the road/street, oftentimes forcing scooter riders to change the lane to pass through temporarily double parked automobiles. The problem is that traffic accidents/collision could happen during the lane changing if the trailing vehicles cannot react quickly enough due to high speed. The problem may get worse if the involved scooter riders are the elderly. The speed of the elder scooter riders typically is relatively slow, but elder scooter riders are more vulnerable to be hit by any vehicles when changing the lane.

Therefore, to enhance the safety of elder scooter riders, in this study, we developed a hazard warning helmet that can reduce risk taking behavior when elder scooter users attempt to pass through double parked vehicles (considered obstacles in front). In addition, we demonstrated the effectiveness of our helmet through an observational study. This work has contributions on (1) lowing traffic collision rates, (2) helping elder scooter users be more aware of hazards in the surroundings, and (3) improving elder scooter users' risky behavior.

## 2   Design and Development of the Hazard Warning Helmet

The hazard warning helmet design was inspired by the fact that elder scooter riders might be hit by approaching vehicles from the back after being forced to change the lane (for passing through double parked automobiles on the roadside).

As shown in Fig. 1, the helmet consists of four components: (1) LED lights attached to the front end of the fit padding inside the outer shell (to the back of the helmet face shield); (2) The Arduino UNO microcontroller board attached on top of the outer shell of the helmet; (3) two ultrasonic sensors attached to the upper-front and the back of the helmet.

**Fig. 1.** Design of the hazard warning helmet

The upper-front ultrasonic sensor is designed to detect double parked vehicles/obstacles (or traffic cones) standing in the way of a scooter rider. As soon as an obstacle is detected, the upper-front ultrasonic sensor triggers the ultrasonic sensor in the back of the helmet that identifies whether or not there is any moving vehicle approaching the scooter rider from behind. As long as the ultrasonic sensor senses any approaching vehicle, the LED lights will be turned on.

We set the sensing distance of the upper-front ultrasonic sensor to be 17.2 meters. The rationales are: (1) the time required for young adults to respond to a lead car's brake lights is about 1.25 s, and elderly people generally respond 0.3 s more slowly than young people [13]; (2) the average speed of elder scooter riders on the road is 40 km/hr. (from our pilot observations of six elder scooter riders on differing road intersections).

The ultrasonic sensor in the back is used to detect the "speed" and "distance" of any approaching vehicle coming from behind. As long as the distance of the approaching vehicle to the scooter is equal or smaller than the minimal required distance for stopping a vehicle, the ultrasonic sensor would turn on the LED lights. If the speed of an approaching vehicle is relatively high, the LED lights would flash quickly. Given that the human perception-brake reaction time is 1.25 s [13], the minimal required distance for stopping a vehicle can be obtained by detecting the "relative speed" of the approaching vehicle to the elder scooter rider. In addition, the benefit for placing the LED lights on the front end of the fit padding is that the red warning signal can be easily noticed by the scooter rider's eyes.

## 3   Methods

An observational study was conducted to evaluate the effectiveness of the proposed hazard warning helmet.

### 3.1   Participants

Convenience sampling and snowball sampling were used by visiting the community centers in Tainan City, Taiwan. A total of five volunteering male elderly participants (over 65 years old) were recruited. All participants had ridden scooters on a daily basis and had more than 5-year experience of riding scooters. In the study, no monetary rewards were provided to the participants.

### 3.2   Equipment and Variables

The equipment included an open face helmet (with a face shield) and our proposed hazard warning helmet. The independent variable was helmet design (a conventional design vs. our proposed design). The dependent variable was behavioral reactions to double parked vehicles.

### 3.3   Procedure

At the beginning of the study, participants were given the instructions and explanations of the features of our proposed helmet. This study adopted a within subject design. Participants were required to experience both of the helmets (the conventional helmet and the hazard warning helmet). They were asked to wear the helmets respectively and ride their scooters in their pace to pass through 50 obstacles (i.e., double parked vehicles) along the roadside. The obstacles in this study were defined as temporarily double parked automobiles or traffic cones on the roadside, or any slow moving vehicles (including cars, scooters, and bicycles). Because these types of obstacles were common in Taiwan, this study did not manipulate their locations or appearances on the road.

This study selected a busy road (in Tainan City, Taiwan) with a total of six lanes long enough (about 12 km) for experiencing 50 obstacles. All participants were required to begin their riding tasks at the same designated location. The study was conducted between 2 to 5 pm to avoid the rush hour so that participants' true riding and passing through behavior would not be affected by slow traffic.

In the study, there was one experimenter sitting behind every participant, riding with the participant, and counting the number of obstacles. The experimenter carried a wood board for recording the behavioral reactions of every participant when they faced obstacles. In this study, without vehicles approaching the participants from behind, the obstacle would not be counted and the participant's behavior would not be recorded. As soon as a total of 50 obstacles were recorded, the experimenter would notify the participants and let them know they had completed the task.

A Wizard of Oz experimental technique was used where participants interacted with the provided hazard warning helmet that they believed to be autonomous in showing warning signals. The warning signals, in fact, were provided by the experimenter (sitting in the back) if he/she saw any vehicles behind was approaching when participants faced obstacles.

In addition, in order to identify participants' true behavior when interacting with obstacles, the experimenters did not let participants know what behavior we were particularly looking for in the study. However, after completing the riding task, participants were informed about the details of the observational results. Participants had the right to withdraw. They could also determine if the observed data could be used for this study.

# 4  Results and Discussion

Results of the study identified four types of behavioral reactions to roadside double-parked vehicles: (1) reducing speed (without looking back) to pass through, (2) reducing speed and looking back before passing through, (3) looking in the side-mirror before passing through, and (4) passing through without taking precaution.

As shown in Table 1, it appears that when seeing obstacles or double parked vehicles, participants generally passed them through directly no matter which helmet they wore, which accounts for 66 % of all behavioral reactions when wearing our proposed helmet and 91 % of all behavioral reactions when wearing a conventional helmet. Only few participants (no matter which helmet they wore) would look back or look in the side mirror to prevent being hit by approaching vehicles.

Table 1 also revealed that, except passing through without taking precaution (considered risky behavior), most behavioral reactions (three out of four) were all related to reducing speed for avoiding possible collisions. However, the percentages of them to all behavioral reactions were relatively low (mostly less than 25 % no matter which helmet was worn). This suggests that safety awareness was poor among elder scooter riders and thus road safety education is necessary for elder scooter riders. Also, warning design and/or safety measures should be in place to help elder scooter riders avoid risks and hazards on the road.

**Table 1.** Participants' behavioral reactions to and the corresponding # of obstacles (mostly double parked vehicles)

| Participants | Helmet design | Total # of obstacles/double parked vehicles | Behavioral reactions and the corresponding # of obstacles/double parked vehicles | | | |
|---|---|---|---|---|---|---|
| | | | Reducing speed to pass through (without looking back) | Reducing speed and looking back before passing through | Looking in the side-mirror before passing through | Passing through without taking precaution |
| # 1 | New | 50 | 12 | 2 | 0 | 36 |
| | Conventional | 50 | 0 | 0 | 0 | 50 |
| # 2 | New | 50 | 12 | 3 | 13 | 22 |
| | Conventional | 50 | 2 | 0 | 5 | 43 |
| # 3 | New | 50 | 9 | 2 | 0 | 39 |
| | Conventional | 50 | 3 | 2 | 0 | 45 |
| # 4 | New | 50 | 15 | 0 | 13 | 32 |
| | Conventional | 50 | 1 | 1 | 5 | 43 |
| # 5 | New | 50 | 14 | 1 | 0 | 35 |
| | Conventional | 50 | 4 | 0 | 0 | 46 |
| Average | New | 50 | 12.4 (25 %) | 1.6 (3 %) | 5.2 (10 %) | 32.8 (66 %) |
| | Conventional | 50 | 2 (4 %) | 0.6 (1 %) | 2 (4 %) | 45.4 (91 %) |

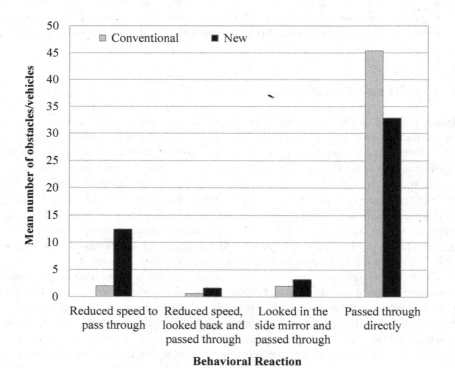

**Fig. 2.** Comparisons of two helmet designs on participants' behavioral reactions when passing through double parked vehicles

Figure 2 compares the two helmet designs on participants' behavioral reactions when interacting with obstacles/double parked vehicles. From Fig. 2, participants wearing our proposed helmet, compared with those wearing a conventional helmet, were more likely to reduce speed of their scooters for passing through obstacles. Moreover, participants wearing our proposed helmet were less likely to pass directly through obstacles/double parked vehicles than those wearing a conventional helmet. The results provided empirical evidence on the effectiveness of our hazard warning helmet in (1) promoting safe riding behavior, (2) inhibiting unsafe riding behavior, and (3) avoiding fast approaching vehicles. It is expected that elder scooter riders wearing our proposed helmet will ride more safely on the roads.

## 5    Conclusions

The purpose of this study was to develop and evaluate a hazard warning helmet that is aimed to help the elderly avoid traffic collisions and accidents. Our proposed helmet consists of four hardware components (the LED lights, the Arduino UNO microcontroller board, and two ultrasonic sensors). This innovative helmet provides visual warnings of fast approaching vehicles when elder riders pass through double-parked vehicles. An observational study was conducted to evaluate the effectiveness of the proposed helmet design. Five elderly participants participated in the study. They were asked to wear our proposed helmet and a conventional helmet respectively to interact with 50 roadside obstacles (mostly double parked vehicles). Results of the study showed that participants wearing our proposed helmet were (1) more likely to reduce speed and (2) less likely to directly pass through double parked vehicles without taking precaution.

Our work demonstrated that our innovative hazard warning helmet is effective in (1) promoting safe riding behavior, (2) inhibiting unsafe riding behavior, and (3) avoiding fast approaching vehicles from behind. Our study found that elder scooter riders tend to have risk taking riding behavior. Road safety education is needed (for example, through posters and social media and community networks, etc.) to enhance safety awareness among elder scooter riders. In addition, from the perspective of product design, designers should put more emphasis on designing products not only to improve the overall wellbeing, but also the health and safety of the elderly.

Our society is stepping into a digital and aging society. Leveraging the power of technology to develop senior-friendly products and devices should become an important consideration for all designers. This study is limited by the number of participants, culture, traffic conditions, environment, and ambient situations (e.g., noises and lighting). More in-depth investigations are required to verify the efficacy of the proposed helmet design in avoiding traffic collisions and hazards. Nevertheless, the results of this study provided insight into designing warning signals for scooter riders.

# References

1. You, S.H., Chang, S.H., Lin, H.M., Tsai, H.M.: Visible light communications for scooter safety. In: Proceeding of the 11th Annual International Conference on Mobile Systems, Applications, and Services, pp. 509–510. ACM, June 2013
2. Chang, H.L., Wu, S.C.: Exploring the mode choice in daily travel behavior of the elderly in Taiwan. J. Eastern Asia Soc. Transp. Stud. 6, 1818–1832 (2005)
3. Guerrier, J.H., et al.: The role of working memory, field dependence, visual search, and reaction time in the left turn performance of older female drivers. Appl. Ergonomics 30, 109–119 (1999)
4. Rodrigues, P.F., Pandeirada, J.N.: Attention and working memory in elderly: the influence of a distracting environment. Cogn. Process. 16(1), 97–109 (2015)
5. Horberry, T., Anderson, J., Regan, M.A., Triggs, T.J., Brown, J.: Driver distraction: the effects of concurrent in-vehicle tasks, road environment complexity and age on driving performance. Accid. Anal. Prev. 38(1), 185–191 (2006)
6. Braitman, K.A., Kirley, B.B., Ferguson, S., Chaudhary, N.K.: Factors leading to older drivers' intersection crashes. Traffic Inj. Prev. 8(3), 267–274 (2007)
7. Fofanova, J., Vollrath, M.: Distraction while driving: the case of older drivers. Transp. Res. Part F: Traffic Psychol. Behav. 14(6), 638–648 (2011)
8. Clarke, D.D., Ward, P., Bartle, C., Truman, W.: Older drivers' road traffic crashes in the UK. Accid. Anal. Prev. 42(4), 1018–1024 (2010)
9. Bauer, M., Adler, G., Rottunda, S., Kuskowski, M.: The influence of age and gender on the driving patterns of older adults. J. Women Aging 15(4), 3–16 (2003)
10. Charlton, J.L., Oxley, J., Fildes, B., Oxley, P., Newstead, S.: Self-regulatory behaviours of older drivers. Annu. Proc. Assoc. Adv. Automot. Med. 47, 181–194 (2003)
11. Vashitz, G., Shinar, D., Blum, Y.: In-vehicle information systems to improve traffic safety in road tunnels. Transp. Res. Part F: Traffic Psychol. Behav. 11(1), 61–74 (2008)
12. Yu, S.H., Shih, O., Tsai, H.M., Wisitpongphan, N., Roberts, R.: Smart automotive lighting for vehicle safety. Commun. Mag. IEEE 51(12), 50–59 (2013)
13. Green, M.: "How long does it take to stop?" methodological analysis of driver perception-brake times. Transp. Hum. Factors 2(3), 195–216 (2000)

# Active and Healthy Ageing Big Dataset Streaming on Demand

Evdokimos I. Konstantinidis[1], Antonis Billis[1],
Charalambos Bratsas[2,3], and Panagiotis D. Bamidis[1,3(✉)]

[1] Medical Physics Laboratory, Faculty of Health Sciences, Medical School,
Aristotle University of Thessaloniki, Thessaloniki, Greece
bamidis@med.auth.gr
[2] Department of Mathematics, Faculty of Exact Sciences,
Aristotle University of Thessaloniki, Thessaloniki, Greece
[3] Open Knowledge Foundation - Chapter Greece, Thessaloniki, Greece

**Abstract.** Designing and conducting user studies and pilot trials within the Active and Healthy Ageing (AHA) domain remains a major challenge for researchers. This work presents the architecture and implementation of an infrastructure for streaming and playing back AHA datasets recorded in ecologically valid environments on demand. The CAC Playback Manager presented in this paper, is a system composed of a number of streaming players delivering data streams to remote clients. This manager simulates the output of sensors that have been previously recorded during a pilot trial or experiment. The recorded output is reproduced (playback) through the CAC-framework communication channel as if the pilot/experiment was conducted now. The CAC Playback Manager exposes its functionality through an API to facilitate researchers in utilizing it. A web application has been developed on top of this API in order to facilitate the study of several use cases presented within this work. Finally, the potential socioeconomic impact of the system is presented.

**Keywords:** Dataset streaming · Dataset playback · Active and Healthy Ageing · Ambient assisted living · Ubiquitous communication technologies

## 1 Introduction and Background

### 1.1 Introduction

Designing and conducting user studies and pilot trials in Active and Healthy Ageing (AHA) remains a major challenge for the researchers [1, 2]. Recognizing the challenging character of this domain and taking into account the socio-economic impact of such studies, Europe shifted a noteworthy portion of funding to large scale pilots in ecologically valid environments or even better in seniors' homes. It is luckily that this domain, consisting a new distinct research area, will be in the foreground for the next decades, demanding technological researchers with expertise on the AHA domain.

Over the last few years, a large number of projects have been working on technological innovations for seniors. Algorithms detecting behavioral changes [3, 4], monitoring and classifying daily indoor/outdoor activities, serious games through

© Springer International Publishing Switzerland 2016
M. Antona and C. Stephanidis (Eds.): UAHCI 2016, Part III, LNCS 9739, pp. 375–384, 2016.
DOI: 10.1007/978-3-319-40238-3_36

contemporary controllers [5] as well as tools assessing seniors' physical and cognitive status [6, 7] have been developed. Small scale trials and case studies [2] were the common methodologies for evaluating these technologies. However, only recently researches started employing large scale trials for producing high accuracy and robust technologies that could be applied in real life settings. In that context, Big Data datasets have been emerged.

However, these datasets usually belong to the project partners and it is only recently that funding bodies have asked for data openness provisions (e.g. H2020 Data Management Plans). Such initiatives target to accelerate design and evaluation of technologies even from SMEs or individual researchers towards market ready innovation. In that context, the cost, the infrastructure and complexity of conducting pilot trials with real users are deterrent factors for designing, testing and evaluating new ideas and tools. On top of this, inexperience or limited knowledge about different stages of piloting with real users (e.g. recruitment, protocol design, ethical issues, technical details, etc.), as well as the need for trust development when seniors are involved, are time and cost consuming barriers.

Consequently, specially designed tools and infrastructures supporting Big Data collection and sharing, are more than essential now than ever before. This work presents the architecture and implementation of an infrastructure for streaming AHA datasets on demand. A large number of datasets ($\sim 1.5$ TB) have been collected within the pilot trials of the USEFIL project carried in the Active and Healthy Ageing Living Lab, an ecologically valid environment resembling a real home environment [8]. A number of elderly volunteers were visiting this environment daily and performing a set of daily activities. The sources of the collected datasets are the Kinect (RGB video and skeleton), as well as, the Wii Balanceboard device (center of balance) and an IP video camera.

## 1.2 Background

To date, several annotated open source datasets have been produced and shared with the research community. Some of them were captured in the patient's homes[1] [9]. The common ways of getting access to such datasets is to download them from a website[2] [10] or even worse to get them stored in physical means (external hard-disk) due to the very large size (>1 TB) or the institution's policy not to provide such datasets through public accessible means. In the same context, although the emergence of tools to explore, publish and share public datasets led to online collections of such tools [11], there is no tool that reproduces a pilot experiment by synchronously playing back a number of different datasets. Nebeling et al. [12] presented Kinect Analysis, a system designed for interaction elicitation studies with support for record-and-replay, visualisation and analysis based on Kinect's depth, audio and video streams. Kinect Analysis enables post-hoc analysis during playback and live analysis with real-time feedback while recording. Nebeling et al.

---

[1] https://archive.ics.uci.edu/ml/datasets/Parkinsons+Telemonitoring.
[2] https://crcns.org/data-sets.

presented that Kinect Analysis in combination with Kinect-Script is useful and effective for a range of analysis tasks, based on a guessability study with 25 users. Finally, they concluded that their implementation could enable researchers to more easily collect, study and share interaction proposals.

In the same context, a number of applications have already been designed for recording and playing back the Kinect channels (RGB, depth and skeleton). The Kinect Stream Saver Application [13], based on the KinectExplorer-D2D, allows users to display and store the Kinect streams. The recording class stores stream data (color, depth, skeleton) to output files in the disk. The Kinect Toolbox[3] includes a set of replay classes that allows recording and replaying of Kinect sessions. As the authors declare: "It is much easier to debug and develop when you don't always have to stand up". Lars Ivar Hatledal[4] developed a system which records a 3D video of a person using the Kinect v2 and plays it back in a 3D environment running in the browser (WebGL and three.js). The recorded file are compressed and uploaded to the browser for playing it back. However, none of the latter implementations stream the recorded datasets through a publish/subscribe architecture where more than one clients could concurrently get access to.

## 2   Materials and Methods

### 2.1   CAC Playback Manager

The CAC Playback Manager presented in this paper, is a system composed of a number of streaming players (start, stop, pause, move time, etc.), delivering data streams to remote clients (developers' app) on demand (Fig. 1). This manager simulates the output (events, video, skeleton streams, etc.) of devices that have been recorded during a pilot trial or experiment. The recorded outputs are reproduced (playback) synchronously through the CAC-framework communication channel (web socket, publish/subscribe based) as if the pilot/experiment was conducted at the moment of the playback session. The CAC-framework ensures that any client (device or application) connected to it gets the streamed information as if it was used during the pilot/experiment even if this client was not there initially. The CAC Playback Manager exposes its functionality through an API to facilitate researchers in utilizing it.

### 2.2   The CAC Framework API and Client Libraries

The Controller Application Communication (CAC) framework [8] (www.cac-framework.com) is a cross device, application independent service providing a number of compatible client libraries [14]. Based on the contemporary websockets communication protocol, the CAC- framework functions as an intermediary, facilitating the connection of a series of controllers and devices (Kinect, Wii Balanceboard, Emotiv, etc.) to

---

[3] http://kinecttoolbox.codeplex.com/.

[4] http://laht.info/record-3d-video-with-kinect-v2-and-play-it-back-in-the-browser/.

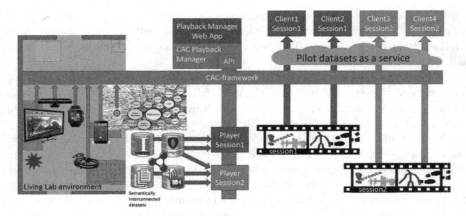

**Fig. 1.** Conceptual architecture representing the flow from the actual pilot trials on the left side to the subsequent playback of the collected datasets on the right.

any applications requesting their input (cf. Fig. 2). Given the number and type of these devices' information (skeleton, video, etc.), the framework is already adapted to high throughput. The framework's design principles align with the Internet of Things (IoT) paradigm following the publish/subscribe architecture witha JSON messages.

Despite the simple and well documented[5] communication protocol of the API, a number of available client libraries can facilitate developers to incorporate the framework's functionality to web applications exploiting the usage of contemporary controllers. Javascript, nodeJS, C# and Python are some of the supported development languages. Taking advantage of these libraries, any application can be easily configured to get access to the streamed information without significant effort or configuration on the device's side.

## 2.3    CAC Playback Player

A CAC Playback Player is a module that communicates with a specific type of dataset (MongoDB, local file, triplestore, etc.) and streams/playbacks the dataset with respect to the acquisition frame rate. Each player utilizes the corresponding CAC client library to stream the recorded dataset through the CAC framework, simulating the source device's functionality. For instance, if a pilot trial was captured by Kinect, the CAC playback player would reproduce the datasets as if the pilot was conducted now. The player's synchronization (frames per second) relies on the datasets' timestamp as well as the requested playback speed.

Each CAC Playback Player exposes a set of commands and properties in order to be managed by the CAC Playback Manager. The properties refer to the CAC server endpoint, streaming session, player status (playing, stopped, paused, cursor position, etc.),

---

[5] http://www.cac-framework.com/files/javascript-api-manual.pdf.

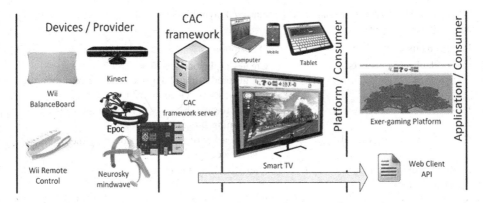

**Fig. 2.** Controller Application Communication (CAC) framework concept

dataset name and type, image and video size. Apart from the properties, a CAC playback player exposes a number of methods pertaining to initializing the player, start/stop/pause streaming, set/move playback cursor position as well as some callback's on streaming finished, connection lost events, etc.

### 2.4 CAC Playback Manager API

The CAC Playback Manager orchestrates and synchronizes a number of streaming players by exposing a number of functionalities in the form of an API, delivering data streams to remote client (developers' app) on demand. It keeps a record of all the alive sessions alongside the corresponding playback players and properties. The manager is responsible for releasing any session resources in case of inactivity (keep-alive message has not been received for more than 15 min). The CAC Playback manager exposes its functionality through a restful API (Table 1). The playback session id, shared and defining a common session among all clients and playback players, is a common parameter for each method of the API.

### 2.5 CAC Playback Manager Web App

The CAC Playback Manager Web App[6] is a web application providing access to the CAC Playback Manager API through an intuitive user interface for non-programmers. The user configures the session id and initiates a playback session. A listbox allows the user to select the datasets while the start, pause and stop buttons correspond to the playback functionalities of the dataset. The user can move the cursor forward/backward or even to a specific date and time. The web app incorporates also a client to illustrate the streamed dataset (Fig. 3: the streamed skeletons on the right and the RGB images on the left are depicted).

---

[6] http://www.cac-framework.com/app.

**Table 1.** CAC Playback Manager API methods. Playback session (psid) parameter is shared among all the methods.

| Restful method | Description |
|---|---|
| CreatePlaybackSession (sesid) | Creates a playback session. This session is registered in the Playback Manager returning the unique Playback session Id (psid) |
| DeletePlaybackSession(psid) | Deletes the playback session and terminates all streaming processes in progress. |
| GetAvailableDatasets (psid) | Returns a list of the existing datasets the user can have access to |
| StartPlaybackSession (psid, DatasetName) | Start streaming the dataset |
| StopPlaybackSession (psid) | Stops streaming and return the playback cursor to the first frame of the dataset |
| PausePlaybackSession (psid) | Pauses streaming without moving the playback cursor |
| MovePlaybackCursor (psid, days, hours, minutes, seconds, millis) | Moves forward/backward the playback cursor according the given time window |
| SetPlaybackCursor (psid, startDatetimeStreaming) | Moves forward/backward the playback cursor to the specified date and time |
| SetPlaybackCursorMilliseconds (psid, startDatetimeMillisecStreaming) | Identical to SetPlaybackCursor with different representation of the data and time |
| UpdateKeepAlive (psid) | Keep-alive signal of the playback session. The Playback Manger terminates a session when a keep-alive signal has not been received for 15 min (to release resources) |

**Fig. 3.** The CAC Playback Manager Web App (http://www.cac-framework.com/app). Skeletons streaming (Right) and RGB Video streaming (Left) are handled by the integrated CAC client.

# 3   Use Cases

The system has already been utilized to support researchers. More specifically it facilitated the development of an algorithm for calculating High Density Regions (HDR) of indoor localization [15]. It was also employed to support the implementation of an algorithm about seniors' skeleton rotation and identification. The exergaming recordings (part of the datasets collection protocol) facilitated the iterative development of the webFitForAll exergaming algorithms [16], improving seniors' experience. Finally, the CAC Playback Manager facilitated the datasets' annotations.

## 3.1   High Density Regions of Indoor Localization

The indoor analytics client [15] is implemented in NodeJS and is based partially on the Node.js CAC-framework client described in [15]. By subscribing to the skeleton streaming channel, the indoor analytics client gets access to the skeletons' center of mass position along with the timestamp, the skeleton id and the corresponding position of the joints, clustering the regions in a room that are more frequently visited by seniors in their home. These High Density Regions are then used for context aware gait analysis.

The CAC Playback Manager was utilized to fine tune the algorithm by feeding the indoor analytics client with datasets collected during pilots conducted in the ecologically valid Active and Healthy Ageing Living Lab in the Lab of Medical Physics in Thessaloniki. Moreover, the developers utilized the datasets to find workarounds on overcoming the computing power constraints (RAM and CPU usage) towards deploying the indoor analytics client in a Raspberry PI 2.

## 3.2   Skeleton Rotation and Identification

A dataset representing a person revolving around his body's axis was captured by a Kinect. This dataset was then used to facilitate the development of an algorithm for coordinating and transforming the skeleton to be vertical to the Kinect's axis. This relies on identifying the skeleton's angle and position offset (Fig. 4).

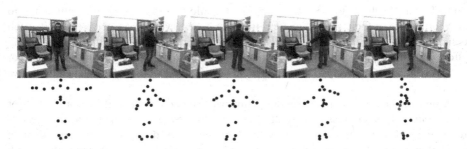

**Fig. 4.** Top: Screenshot of a participant conducting an exergame activity (revolving around his body's axis). Bottom: the skeleton dataset representing the same person.

### 3.3   Exergaming Design and Development

The FitForAll exergaming platform, tailored to seniors, was developed years before, when the contemporary gaming controllers where restricted to the Wii devices [5]. The advent of Kinect made the FitForAll team consider it as a one way, incorporating it in the second version, webFitForAll [16]. The adoption of Kinect opened new ways of navigating throughout the exercises as well as the way these exercises are performed. The recordings of some exergaming sessions performed by 14 people within USEFIL's [17] trials constitute the basis datasets for fine tuning the exercises experience as well as the monitoring assessment algorithms behind the exercises [7].

## 4   Discussion and Conclusions

Our work was motivated from challenges that emerged from pilot trials with elderly people and testing of technologies in the Active and Healthy Ageing domain. Developing and evaluating algorithms and tools by reproducing pilot trials on demand with a time and cost effective way remains a big challenge in the Big Data area.

The work presented in this paper goes beyond the existing implementations that simply record Kinect datasets locally in files replacing the Kinect by playing back these files. Stream Saver Application, Kinect Toolbox and Lars Ivar Hatledal's work have already implemented different recorders for the Kinect's channel. None of these works however uses websockets or other web communication channels for streaming the recorder datasets to more than one clients at the same time. On the other hand, Nebeling et al. [12] did something very similar to our work. However, their work was restricted to Kinect compatibility with no provision for other type of datasets. One step further, the CAC Playback Manager was built with the intention to reproduce ecologically valid pilot trials and experiments on demand by playing back all the available recorded datasets through a unified solution based on web sockets (CAC-framework [8]). For this purpose, a CAC Playback Player is designed for each dataset type, being synchronized by the CAC Playback Manager.

The CAC Playback Manager delivers an API for playing back collected datasets reproducing a pilot trial or experiment conditions. The value of replaying datasets, in a way of reproducing pilot trials as if they were conducted now without requiring seniors to go through the same activities in the same way which is not ecologically valid, is quite large. Needless to say that such a tool allows developers and companies to develop and tune their algorithms and tools 24 h per day, 7 days per week. Although contemporary technology allows such tools and systems to be built without outstanding effort in conjunction with the fact that sharing of recordings and reproduction of analyses is more than appealing in the days of Big Data, such systems have not emerged yet.

Consequently, the work presented in this paper could be considered as a testbed for unexploited ideas and research results (especially for SMEs and small research groups for which the cost for pilot trials is most of the times deterrent) with considerable innovation potential, against market entrance failure. From a different perspective, such a system could be part of the curriculum in engineering educational institutes creating experienced early engineering researchers in the Active and Healthy Ageing domain. Needless to say that the socio-economic benefits of this in conjunction with the acceleration of new ideas evaluation in real settings are more than significant. Finally, the reproduction of pilot trials, could contribute to the creation of an innovation ecosystem able to transform ideas and knowledge into socio-economic value, accelerating the market entrance.

**Acknowledgements.** The work has been co-funded by the Horizon 2020 Framework Programme of the European Union under grant agreement no 643555. For more details, please see http://www.uncap.eu.

# References

1. Antoniou, P.E., Konstantinidis, E.I., Billis, A.S., Bamparopoulos, G., Tsatali, M.S., Siountas, A., Bamidis, P.D.: Instrumenting the eHome and preparing elderly Pilots - the USEFIL approach. In: Bamidis, P.D., Tarnanas, I., Hadjileontiadis, L., Tsolaki, M.N. (eds.) Innovations in the Diagnosis and Treatment of Dementia (2015)
2. Billis, A.S., Kartsidis, P., Garyfallos, D.-K.G., Tsatali, M.S., Karagianni, M., Bamidis, P.D.: Ecologically valid trials of elderly unobtrusive monitoring: analysis and first results. In: 4th International Workshop on Artificial Intelligence and Assistive Medicine, Pavia, Italy, pp. 32–41 (2015)
3. Bamidis, P.D., Konstantinidis, E.I., Billis, A.S., Siountas, A.: Reviewing home based assistive technologies. In: Bamidis, P.D., Tarnanas, I., Hadjileontiadis, L., Tsolaki, M.N. (eds.) Innovations in the Diagnosis and Treatment of Dementia (2015)
4. Billis, A.S., Papageorgiou, E.I., Frantzidis, C.A., Tsatali, M.S., Tsolaki, A.C., Bamidis, P.D.: A decision-support framework for promoting independent living and ageing well. IEEE J. Biomed. Health Inform. **19**, 199–209 (2015)
5. Konstantinidis, E.I., Billis, A.S., Mouzakidis, C.A., Zilidou, V.I., Antoniou, P.E., Bamidis, P.D.: Design, implementation, and wide pilot deployment of FitForAll: an easy to use exergaming platform improving physical fitness and life quality of senior citizens. IEEE J. Biomed. Health Inform. **20**, 189–200 (2016)
6. Bamidis, P.D., Fissler, P., Papageorgiou, S.G., Zilidou, V., Konstantinidis, E.I., Billis, A.S., Romanopoulou, E., Karagianni, M., Beratis, I., Tsapanou, A., Tsilikopoulou, G., Grigoriadou, E., Ladas, A., Kyrillidou, A., Tsolaki, A., Frantzidis, C., Sidiropoulos, E., Siountas, A., Matsi, S., Papatriantafyllou, J., Margioti, E., Nika, A., Schlee, W., Elbert, T., Tsolaki, M., Vivas, A.B., Kolassa, I.-T.: Gains in cognition through combined cognitive and physical training: the role of training dosage and severity of neurocognitive disorder. Front. Aging Neurosci. 7 (2015)
7. Konstantinidis, E.I., Antoniou, P.E., Bamidis, P.D.: Exergames for Assessment in Active and Healthy Aging - Emerging Trends and Potentialities. In: Proceedings of the 1st International Conference on Information and Communication Technologies for Ageing Well and e-Health, pp. 325–330. SCITEPRESS - Science and Technology Publications (2015)
8. Konstantinidis, E.I., Antoniou, P.E., Bamparopoulos, G., Bamidis, P.D.: A lightweight framework for transparent cross platform communication of controller data in ambient assisted living environments. Inform Sci. **300**, 124–139 (2014)

9. Tsanas, A., Little, M.A., McSharry, P.E., Ramig, L.O.: Accurate telemonitoring of Parkinson's disease progression by noninvasive speech tests. IEEE Trans. Biomed. Eng. **57**, 884–893 (2010)
10. Teeters, J.L., Harris, K.D., Millman, K.J., Olshausen, B.A., Sommer, F.T.: Data sharing for computational neuroscience. Neuroinformatics **6**, 47–55 (2008)
11. Open Knowledge Foundation Germany: Open Data Tools, Tools to Explore, Publish and Share Public Datasets. http://opendata-tools.org/
12. Nebeling, M., Ott, D., Norrie, M.C.: Kinect analysis: a system for recording, analysing and sharing multimodal interaction elicitation studies. In: 7th SIGCHI Symposium on Engineering Interactive Computing Systems. ACM (2015)
13. Dolatabadi, E.: Kinect Stream Saver Application. https://kinectstreamsaver.codeplex.com/
14. Konstantinidis, E.I., Antoniou, P.E., Billis, A., Bamparopoulos, G., Pappas, C., Bamidis, P.D.: Leveraging web technologies to expose multiple contemporary controller input in smart TV rich internet applications utilized in elderly assisted living environments. In: Stephanidis, C., Antona, M. (eds.) UAHCI 2014, Part III. LNCS, vol. 8515, pp. 118–128. Springer, Heidelberg (2014)
15. Konstantinidis, E.I., Bamidis, P.D.: Density based clustering on indoor kinect location tracking: A new way to exploit active and healthy aging living lab datasets. In: 2015 IEEE 15th International Conference on Bioinformatics and Bioengineering (BIBE), pp. 1–6. IEEE, Belgrade, Serbia (2015)
16. Konstantinidis, E.I., Bamparopoulos, G., Bamidis, P.D.: Moving real exergaming engines on the web: the webFitForAll case study in an active and healthy ageing living lab environment. IEEE J. Biomed. Health Inform. (2016). doi:10.1109/JBHI.2016.2559787
17. Artikis, A., Bamidis, P.D., Billis, A., Bratsas, C., Frantzidis, C., Karkaletsis, V., Klados, M., Konstantinidis, E., Konstantopoulos, S., Kosmopoulos, D., Papadopoulos, H., Perantonis, S., Petridis, S., Spyropoulos, C.S.: Supporting tele-health and AI-based clinical decision making with sensor data fusion and semantic interpretation: the USEFIL case study. In: International Workshop on Artificial Intelligence and NetMedicine, p. 21 (2012)

# Augmented Live Communication Workspace Platform to Assist and Utilize Cognitive Abilities of Senior Workers

Akihiro Kosugi[1](✉), Shogo Nishiguchi[2], Masahiko Izumi[3],
Masatomo Kobayashi[1], Atsushi Hiyama[3], and Michitaka Hirose[3]

[1] IBM Research – Tokyo, 19-21 Nihonbashi Hakozaki-cho,
Chuo, Tokyo 103-8510, Japan
{alkosugi,mstm}@jp.ibm.com
[2] Osaka University, 1-3 Machikaneyama, Toyonaka, Osaka 560-8531, Japan
nishiguchi.shogo@irl.sys.es.osaka-u.ac.jp
[3] The University of Tokyo, 7-3-1 Hongo, Bunkyo, Tokyo 113-8656, Japan
{masa,atsushi,hirose}@cyber.t.u-tokyo.ac.jp

**Abstract.** Live communication over long distances is indispensable for seniors, and tools have evolved to improve the sense of presence: sight is added by video and robots represent bodies at remote locations. Emerging technologies that assist cognitive abilities may improve the communication quality beyond reality. However, they have been independently developed and cannot be integrated easily. This results in not only raising the development cost but also hampering new technology being installed in this area. Therefore, we propose a platform for remote and live communication that supports portable and fast data transfer connections as fundamental functions and possesses a plug-in framework that enables features to be extended dynamically on the basis of a common interface. In this paper, we explain the design of this platform and describe some plug-in based applications and scenarios built on it as examples validating the concept.

**Keywords:** Senior workforce · Remote communication · Tele-presence robot · Agent conversations · Physical devices · Augmented reality · Cognitive assistance · Accessibility · Plug-ins · WebRTC

## 1 Introduction

Quality of communication is important to put collaborative work into practice. Face-to-face conversation enables much faster comprehension than delayed communication with static documents, hence we consider meeting in person when we are frustrated with written communication. The richness of information in live communication enables us to more efficiency read emotions and situations, which results in higher quality of understanding. However, these requirements of communicating in person kept away people who had barriers to travelling, including the elderly, from working in important situations. Hence they desired tools for live communication overcoming distance to participate in collaborations in a practical way.

© Springer International Publishing Switzerland 2016
M. Antona and C. Stephanidis (Eds.): UAHCI 2016, Part III, LNCS 9739, pp. 385–394, 2016.
DOI: 10.1007/978-3-319-40238-3_37

Technologies or products fulfilling this demand has been coming closer to imitating face-to-face conversations and have evolved a richness of information to expand the degree of thorough and clear understanding and sense of presence. A video conferencing system allows us to view remote sites, and tele-presence robots represent bodies at these remote sites. Recently, vision technologies and sensory devices are also evolving and assisting the comprehension of situations.

However, those technologies have been independently developed without common protocols or re-usable interfaces. This situation has inhibited developers from integrating one product with another or distributing effectual implementation to the applications that contextually have features that would benefit from it. For example, when we want to apply a voice command operation set of one application to another, we need to look for the API providing the interface accessing the voice stream of the participants and then see if we can port the implementation to it. Furthermore, this scenario is premised on the application allowing access to those resources, but some do not have any programmable interface [2].

Therefore, we propose a platform for remote and live communication in which features can be extended flexibly. In this platform, features are developed as plug-in components so that they can be assembled and re-used with each other, guaranteeing portable and fast data transfer connection among remote sites.

In this paper, after reviewing the related works, we describe the design of the platform and applications using it as proof of concept. We also discuss the possible integrations and then present our conclusion.

## 2    Related Works

### 2.1    Technologies that Help Live Communication

In addition to the auditory conversation with phones, video conferencing has been prevalent since Skype [1] was released. It also extended a platform of applications using the Internet and liberated people from using physical phones. Such live communication using audio and video has become ubiquitous, and now the expansion in the medium source and expression is beginning. Nowadays, various types of tele-presence robots provide different experience on top of video conferences. Double [3] and Beam [4] can be driven remotely, while Kubi [5] pans and tilts its face on a table. The anonymized face of OriHime [6] encourages patients who cannot leave the hospital or home to communicate with others outside through it [7]. Technologies that are categorized as "tele-existence" cover the expressions of the five senses. TELESAR V [12] shares tactile information of an avatar. Kissenger [13] is a pair of mobile phone devices that enables the users to kiss each other remotely and helps them to maintain intimate relationships.

Aside from remote communication, technologies that analyze or sense real-time data are evolving. Speech recognition is used to set a caption on the video for better comprehension for people who have difficulty hearing [14]. Vision technology that recognizes features of a face [11] is utilized to make visually impaired people aware of people approaching them. There are even some prototypes extracting emotion from facial expressions [10], or replacing/deforming the user's image to a favored one [15, 16] in real-time. Digital Audio Controller enables turning on/off the volume from multiple audio sources to pick up and focus on what the listener should/wants to hear [17].

### 2.2 Platforms that Help Making Application for Communication

OpenTok [18] and SkyWay [19] are used to build live communication services such as a video chat application and remote console of tele-presence robots [3, 5]. OpenTok initially used their proprietary protocol on Adobe Flash, but both frameworks now use WebRTC [23] for transmission protocol layer. These platforms are used for the applications beyond video conferencing but still do not have the framework in which features can be extended or re-used dynamically.

Each robot requires specific software to design its behavior. The Robot Engine [20] is a platform to design behavior of any type of humanoid robots. f3.js [21] is an attempt to capsulate the embedded devices (microcomputer, sensor, and actuator) as programmable components so that the developer integrates them using a single programming language (JavaScript). These platforms are made for the local devices, but will also be useful to extend the capability of the people working from remote places.

## 3   Platform

Here we propose a platform for live communication in which we can develop and add features extensibility. We prototyped this platform and developed components for the live communication. Applications consisting of those components on this platform were used during a remote ICT lecture course among senior citizens [22]. In this section, we describe key components and the design of this platform.

### 3.1   WebRTC

WebRTC [23] is a W3C Editor's Draft (as of January 2016) standard for peer-to-peer (P2P) connection using browsers. In addition to video and audio channels, it has a data channel with which the application transfers general data.

To achieve a sense of reality during communication with remote sites, the speed of data transmission is critical. To achieve faster network connections, the route to the destination should preferably have as few nodes as possible. This was one reason we chose the P2P transmission standard. Because the ICT lecture course was held at an all-purpose meeting room in a public community center, we had to set up the equipment in a limited amount of time for the class every single time. Hence we wanted to reduce the steps and machines for the preparation in order to start the class quickly, and the less dependency on the proprietary tool of WebRTC allowed us to reduce the number of prerequisites or machines to be installed or launched.

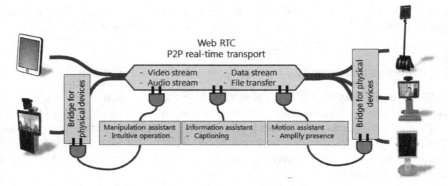

**Fig. 1.** Overview of the platform

## 3.2   Implementing Features as Pluggable Extensions

Figure 1 shows the diagram of how the components that represents individual feature are arranged in the platform. The platform on the basis provides a component that manages connections using WebRTC. The connections initiated by this manager have interfaces so that the other components can write and read the data. The connection is established in peer to peer, and the data is transmitted with less latency. This benefits the components that are handling real-time data in the application. These components are loosely coupled by an event publish-subscribe pattern, so that the features for individual application can be extended/woven dynamically.

Components supposed to be arranged within this platform vary: not only the bridge of a camera device as an audio and video source but also the bridge for physical devices to realize the body remotely; an interaction assistant that helps manipulation of those devices; and an informational assistant such as speech recognition to give captions or minutes of what is said in the meeting.

## 3.3   Bridge for the Physical Devices

Web browser, one of the prerequisites of this platform, is almost ubiquitous, but we sometimes need to overcome its limitations, such as cross domain restrictions or limited access to outside resources. The serial communication is one of them, but it is the most popular way to communicate with the physical devices such as actuators or sensors. To drive robots from the components in the platform, we implemented one server running on the same computer of the browser using Node.js [24] as a communication proxy with physical devices. This server communicates with the components in the platform using a web socket and transfers commands/response data to/from the serial port. We also made a basic component capsuling this series of exchanges with this server, so that it can be re-used for the other components that need to take control of physical devices.

## 4   Application

Here we describe applications as example implementations using this platform and some possible combination scenarios.

### 4.1   Cogi: A Tele-presence Robot with "Observation Window"

Cogi is a tele-presence robot that is controlled by the movement of the operator's head on the basis of the concept of "observation window" motif [25]. Cogi was built on this platform and used by the main lecturers during the experiment of remote ICT lecture courses among senior citizens [22]. As basic functions, this platform has two components: "vc.pero" is the manager of connections, and "vc.video" makes video and audio stream from a camera device. We made an embeddable video conference component from them and used it to make an application for lecturers with integrated view from multiple camera sources at the remote site. In addition, we added components to build the console application for Cogi: "vc.htrack" represents "observation window" behavior, and "vc.cogi" handles serial communication for the robot. "vc.htrack" subscribes the image from "vc.video" and locates the position of the controller's head. Then it calculates the rotation angle of the controller's head and transmits it to the robot through "vc.cogi" to make it follow the operator's head. Meanwhile, it transmits that angle to the remote site through "vc.pero", and then the "vc.htrack" at the remote site forwards it to "vc.cogi" so that the robot at the remote site faces the place the operator intended (Fig. 2).

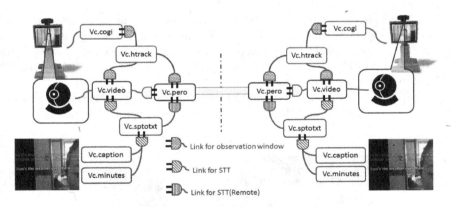

**Fig. 2.**  Assembly example: application for tele-presence robot (Cogi) (Color figure online)

This "observation window" mechanism helped senior lecturers to control the robot at the remote site without heavy cognitive load, even while they were conducting the class. Additionally, "vc.htrack", which is the implementation of this mechanism, can be applied to other types of robots of similar capability such as Kubi [5] or OriHime [6] just by adding bridge implementation for individual devices as replacement of "vc.cogi".

Cogi also has features of adding captions from the conversation and taking minutes. For these features, we prepared three additional components: "vc.sptotxt", which extracts the text from the spoken voice using Speech to Text (STT) service; "vc.caption", which shows the text recognized by "vc.sptotxt" on the screen; and "vc.minutes", which saves the history of the recognized text and has UI to show and edit it. Both "vc.caption" and "vc.minutes" subscribe to the single instance of "vc.sptotxt" to reduce the footprint. Some browsers do not allow voice data to be extracted from a remote audio stream, so we added an additional fix on "vc.sptotxt" to send the command to call the STT service at the remote site and pass it back just by re-using "vc.pero". This demonstrates the advantage of plug-in based development in which features are componentized with portability.

## 4.2  Virtual Agent Mocoro Follows and Facilitates Communication

Mocoro (Fig. 3) is a virtual avatar that listens to people and conducts the communication with its affordance. It acts in motion with its Kawaii [26] appearance in accordance with the context of the conversation. Mocoro has two panels at the bottom of the screen to show assistive information such as the aim of the meeting, pictures, and so on. Mocoro is built on this platform and re-uses the same STT extension of Cogi ("vci.sptotxt") to understand what the people are discussing. In addition, it has a morphological analyzer using Kuromoji [27] to extract keywords and Text-to-Speech (TTS) extension to reply to people vocally. With those components, it can have a simple conversation: it answers vocally when it is asked its name, shows a pre-registered photo on the information panel when it is requested by voice, and displays the keywords recognized in the talk in a tag-cloud form on the information panel.

Elderly people often have high level knowledge or skills in a particular area, but they might not have experience of teaching. When the teachers are not used to conducting classes, they probably do not support the students who are catching up with the contents. This possibly results in worse comprehension of the class, and Mocoro is designed to aid the speakers in this area.

Nonverbal information is important to understand people [28]. However, it is not conveyed well enough through the display. People who are not used to talking in front

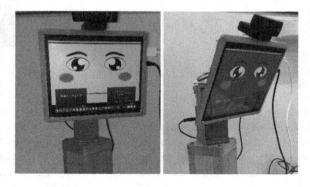

**Fig. 3.**  Virtual agent Mocoro. (Left shows normal face, and right shows confused face.)

of audiences are likely to speak too fast to be understood because they feel pressured and nervous. Therefore, the speed of speech must be appropriately controlled. In addition, the teacher should not stutter much because students will be irritated and less engaged in the class. However, it is difficult for novice teachers to realize this by themselves. Mocoro is placed beside the main screen that the teacher is facing during the class, and, in such cases, it reflects the confusion or irritation of the students on the other side. Mocoro gradually changes the color of its face from pink to blue and hangs its head little by little if the teacher speaks too fast or stutters a lot. Mocoro does not speak to the teacher aloud to avoid interrupting the class. Instead, it shows the estimated feelings of students quietly and moderately. When the teacher notices Mocoro is looking down with a very pale face, he/she asks it "Are you all right?" Then, it looks up and replies "Yes, I am okay but you speak too fast for me." In this way, Mocoro reminds the teachers that they should speak at a more moderate pace for the students, and consequently, we expect they will come to correct themselves naturally.

Mocoro can also be used in multipurpose meetings. When a meeting proceeds fast, some attendees may be unable to follow the contents. However, they sometimes hesitate showing that they missed something and pretend they understand even, or especially, when that meeting is important and all of them need to have common understanding. Mocoro works for such cases: it listens to the participants and estimates the speed of the transition in the topics by counting the number of the keywords extracted using the STT and morphological analyzer component. If too many topics are discussed in a short time, it explicitly warns that the above problem might occur by moving its head and changing the color of its face.

These embodiments of affordance by action of Mocoro are leveraged by the components of this platform and will portably be applied to other scenarios regardless of whether the participants are joining remotely or not.

### 4.3 Magnify the Sound of the Remote Site Using "Observation Window"

Acoustic zooming [17] was named "Zoomap" and optimized for the experiment of remote ICT lecture courses among senior citizens [22]. It assists lecturers' comprehension about what the students at the remote site are saying by magnifying the volume of some audio sources and diminishing the others. Each student's voice is captured by a microphone on the headset. Lecturers use tablets on which the level of the volume of each source is visualized with a location and select the area for which the audio source should be magnified (Fig. 4).

When Zoomap was introduced, one lecturer told the students that he was now able to "see" the sound in the remote class room and could catch what the students were saying even when they were speaking in subdued voices. As can be seen from here, Zoomap was positively accepted by the lecturers and effectively helped them to understand what was going on at the remote site during the class. However, we also observed that some lecturers were not able to use it, especially when they were busy conducting the class. We concluded that this was because operating it using the tablet required increased cognitive load.

**Fig. 4.** View of the remote room (left) and zoomap UI on the tablet (right)

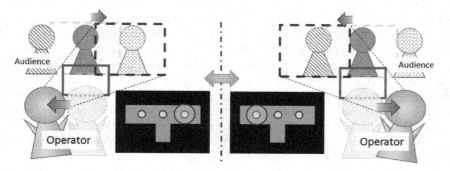

**Fig. 5.** Magnify the audio by "look into" motion

We hereby suggest introducing an observation window motif of Cogi to select the audio source to be magnified. For example, when the lecturer looks into it from the right-hand side, the voice of the student on the left side of the remote site is magnified, and vice versa (Fig. 5). In this way, lecturers do not need to use their hand to listen to the place at which they are looking. Zoomap uses direct connection to transfer the volume level of the audio sources and the command to magnify them, which can be replaced with the P2P data channel of this platform using "vc.pero".

## 4.4    Morphing the Representation or Expression of the Communication

Vision technologies are evolving, and some studies are showing the possibility of extracting the features of the face [10] and morphing it in real-time [16]. When we integrate those vision technologies into the live and remote communication, we might even be able to augment the communication more than we do when face to face. In fact, one of the reasons OriHime [7] is popular with the patients who cannot move from their hospital beds is because its anonymized face covers their real appearance in bed. Also, when we suggested a simplified configuration of a remote lecture system [22] for senior lecturers so that they can conduct classes from home, some female lecturers were concerned that they would need to make themselves up carefully even at home. When this kind of morphing can be woven onto the video stream, it may remove the hesitation in communication in such cases.

## 5  Possible Future Considerations

For various devices being mixed in one place, we need to consider the conflict between the fundamental nature of the device and the application scenario. For example, there will be some conflict in taking turns to use robots when multiple participants take part in a meeting session, because most tele-presence robots are designed to be used by a single user. We might have a conventional resolution using UIs such as buttons on the screen to "raise a hand", but some interaction in which the robot automatically chooses who takes control would be desired in practical use.

Also, some common framework will be needed on morphing the feature in accordance with the setup on the remote peer. Cogi basically uses robots in both peers (one tracks the face of the controller, and the other at the remote peer moves in accordance with the motion of the controller) but has the option of a simplified setting mode when there is no robot at the controller site. We transmitted the information about how the remote peer is set up in the initial handshake phase, but some standard or common implementation that describes the attributes of a remote environment like the profiles of Bluetooth would be preferable.

## 6  Conclusion

We proposed a portable and extensible platform for live remote communication and described our prototype as an example of how it can be utilized.

We expect this platform to improve actualization of the ICT helping people to communicate and work together over distances by not only saving on the development cost but also drawing the channel to introduce new technology into this area. Consequently, we will be able to communicate with others regardless of the distance with a certain sense of reality or beyond by augmenting cognitive ability, which will help the people who face barriers to travelling to work practically. Optimization of working resources in the community is important in rapidly aging societies, and the concept of this platform will help dig up hidden talent and resources.

**Acknowledgements.** This research was partially supported by the Japan Science and Technology Agency (JST) under the Strategic Promotion of Innovative Research and Development Program. We thank all the participants of the experiments.

## References

1. Skype. http://www.skype.com/
2. FaceTime. http://www.apple.com/ios/facetime/
3. Double. http://www.doublerobotics.com/

4.  Beam. https://suitabletech.com/
5.  Kubi. https://www.revolverobotics.com/
6.  OriHime. http://orihime.orylab.com/
7.  How the Japanese robot avatar OriHime fights loneliness. https://www.techinasia.com/orihime-robot-fights-loneliness
8.  Siri. http://www.apple.com/ios/siri/
9.  Kinect. http://www.xbox.com/en-US/xbox-one/accessories/kinect-for-xbox-one
10. IntraFace. http://www.humansensing.cs.cmu.edu/intraface/
11. Jeni, L.A., Girard, J.M., Cohn, J.F., Kanade T.: Real-time dense 3D face alignment from 2D video with automatic facial action unit coding. In: Automatic Face and Gesture Recognition (FG) 11. IEEE (2015)
12. Fernando, C.L., Furukawa, M., Kurogi, T., Hirota, K., Kamuro, S., Sato, K., Minamizawa, K., Tachi, S.: TELESAR V: TELExistence surrogate anthropomorphic robot. In: SIGGRAPH 2012, Article 23. ACM (2012)
13. Samani, H.A., Parsani, R., Rodriguez, L.T., Saadatian, E., Dissanayake, K.H., Cheok, A.D.: Kissenger: design of a kiss transmission device. In: Proceedings of DIS 2012, pp. 48–57. ACM (2012)
14. Automatic captions in Youtube. https://googleblog.blogspot.jp/2009/11/automatic-captions-in-youtube.html
15. Dale, K., Sunkavalli, K., Johnson, K.M., Vlasic, D., Matusik, W., Pfister, H.: Video face replacement. In: Proceedings of SIGGRAPH Asia 2011, Article 130, 10 pp. ACM (2011)
16. Realtime face deformation. https://auduno.github.io/clmtrackr/examples/facedeform.html
17. Izumi, M., Kikuno, T., Tokuda, Y., Hiyama, A., Miura, T., Hirose, M.: Practical use of a remote movable avatar robot with an immersive interface for seniors. In: Stephanidis, C., Antona, M. (eds.) UAHCI 2014, Part III. LNCS, vol. 8515, pp. 648–659. Springer, Heidelberg (2014)
18. OpenTok. https://tokbox.com/
19. SkyWay. https://nttcom.github.io/skyway/en/index.html
20. Bartneck, C., Soucy, M., Fleuret, K., Sandoval, E.B.: The robot engine - making the unity 3D game engine work for HRI. In: Proceedings of RO-MAN 2015, pp. 431–437. IEEE (2015)
21. Kato, J., Goto, M.: Form follows function(): an IDE to create laser-cut interfaces and microcontroller programs from single code base. In: Proceedings of UIST 2015 Adjunct., pp. 43–44. ACM (2015)
22. Takagi, H., Kosugi, A., Ishihara, T., Fukuda, K.: Remote IT education for senior citizens. In: Proceedings of W4A 2014, Article 41. ACM (2014)
23. WebRTC. https://www.w3.org/TR/webrtc/
24. Node.js. https://nodejs.org/en/
25. Kosugi, A., Kobayashi, M., Fukuda, K.: Hands-Free collaboration using telepresence robots for all ages. In: Proceedings of CSCW 2016. ACM (2016)
26. Cheok, A.D.: Kawaii/cute interactive media. In: Cheok, A.D. (ed.) Art and Technology of Entertainment Computing and Communication, pp. 223–254. Springer, New York (2010)
27. Kuromoji. http://www.atilika.org/
28. Burgoon, J.K., Guerrero, L.K., Floyd, K.: Nonverbal Communication. Allyn & Bacon, Boston (2010)

# Perceptual Information
# of Home-Use Glucose Meters for the Elderly

Hsin-Chang Lo$^{(\boxtimes)}$, Wan-Li Wei, and Ching-Chang Chuang

Department of Product Design, Ming Chuan University, Taoyuan, Taiwan
{lohc,wanliwei,ccchuang}@mail.mcu.edu.tw

**Abstract.** Home-use glucose meters provide a simple real-time means for diabetic mellitus patients to monitor their blood sugar. However, there are still many interface design defects in current glucose meter products which can easily cause operation errors. The aim of this study is to identify the perceptional information of commercial home-use glucose meter interfaces for the elderly. First, three aspects of perception information of glucose meters was examined, consisting of the behavioral information (BI), assemblage information (AI), and conventional information (CI) of glucose meters. Then, five elderly test subjects older than 65 years who never used home-use glucose meters before were recruited to perform usability tests in order to identify perceptional information. The results demonstrated that five parts should be used, and nine assembly processes should be operated during glucose measurement. The application for assembly-disassembly ability is required for the part-part category; the AI and CI provide effective support for this application. The critical factors that may cause operation errors involved lancing devices and test strips rather than glucose meters. Possible reasons for this might arise from poor design of product perceptual information or unclear symbols. The conclusion is that product designers should provide more perception information, especially in terms of AI, to assist elderly users to understand how to use home-use medical devices such as glucose meters.

**Keywords:** Perceptual information · Elderly · Glucose meter

## 1   Introduction

According to the International Diabetes Federation (IDF), 8.3 % of adults, the equivalent of 382 million people, suffered from diabetes in 2013. In 25 years, that number of patients will be over 592 million, with the prevalence rate of growth from the current 6.4 % to 7.7 % [1]. Self-monitoring of blood glucose is a useful means of controlling blood sugar [2], which provides diabetic patients and their medical caregivers an instant and easy way to record blood glucose changes. Blood glucose measurement can be difficult and annoying. For people with limited dexterity such as arthritis or neuropathy, injured or malformed hands, or who live with multiple sclerosis, Parkinson's disease, or muscular dystrophy, simply holding a meter steady or loading a test strip or lancing device can be challenging. Users want to conduct blood glucose measurement before picking a meter: work the lancing device, handle the strips and meter buttons, and

© Springer International Publishing Switzerland 2016
M. Antona and C. Stephanidis (Eds.): UAHCI 2016, Part III, LNCS 9739, pp. 395–402, 2016.
DOI: 10.1007/978-3-319-40238-3_38

dispose of everything properly. It can be tough for these users to insert a test strip into the meter, too [3]. A previous study also reported that crucial factors that caused operation errors involved the lancing devices and the test strips rather than the glucose meters themselves. These errors occurred when users did not realize that the lancing device cap should be snapped open but not be unscrewed or pulled [4].

Norman [5] stated that affordance provides strong cues to the operations of objects. For example, by looking at them, users know that plates can be pushed by hand, and knobs can be turned with fingers. Furthermore, the affordance of an object can be specified by perceptual information [6]. Therefore, the physical features are the information that relays possible behaviors to users. In addition to physical properties, symbols, icons, indexes, texts and such are used to illustrate the functions and operations of a product. Symbols and/or icons must be represented in an appropriate form to facilitate the perception and recognition of their underlying meaning [7]. Therefore, the aim of this study is to realize the perceptional information of commercial home-use glucose meter interfaces for the elderly. The results are expected to provide useful information for interface design of home-use medical devices.

## 2   Method

### 2.1   Subjects and Instrumentation

Five seniors above the age of 65 were recruited in this study. The average age was 73.8 years old, ranging from 65 to 79 years old. None of the subjects had upper limb disabilities or cognitive impairment, and none had any experience using home-use glucose meters. A commercial home-use glucose meter (Rightest® Blood Glucose Monitoring System GM300, Bionime, as Fig. 1) was chosen for the experiments.

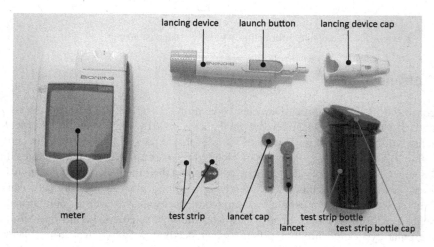

**Fig. 1.**  The glucose meter (Rightest® Blood Glucose Monitoring System GM300)

The five typical operation tasks are: a. changing lancet, b. inserting a strip to turn on the meter, c. lancing, d. waiting for the result and e. discarding lancet (Table 1).

**Table 1.** Home-use glucose meter operation tasks [4]

| Tasks | Sub-tasks |
|---|---|
| a. changing lancet | a.1 open the lancing device cap |
| | a.2 insert the lancet |
| | a.3 remove the lancet cap |
| | a.4 close the lancing device cap |
| | a.5 load the lancet |
| | a.6 adjust the lancing depth |
| b. inserting a strip to turn on the meter | b.1 open the test strip bottle caps |
| | b.2 take a test strip |
| | b.3 close the test strip bottle caps |
| | b.4 insert a test strip into the meter |
| c. lancing | c.1 wipe the lancing area with an alcohol pad |
| | c.2 hold the lancing device firmly against the finger |
| | c.3 press the launch button |
| | c.4 use test strip to sample blood |
| d. waiting for the result | d.1 read the result from the meter |
| | d.2 dispose the test strip |
| e. discarding lancet | e.1 open the lancing device cap |
| | e.2 remove the lancet |
| | e.3 close the lancing device cap |

*lancet needles were removed in advance.

## 2.2 Experimental Protocols

First, the researchers explain the glucose meter operation instructions to the subjects, and allowed them to practice with the meter for 10 min. The researchers would then explain the test procedures, operation tasks and things to be aware of during

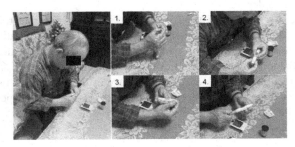

**Fig. 2.** One subject operating the home-use glucose meter (1 - task a.2; 2 - task a.4; 3 - task a.5; 4 - task a.6)

experiments. Subjects operated the glucose meter with no time limit (Fig. 2). After the experiments were finished, subjects were asked to fill in personal information and represent the reasons for any difficulties that they encountered after completing the tasks.

## 2.3   Perceptual Information in Operating Product

Chen and Lee [8] proposed that perceptual information includes behavioral information (BI), assemblage information (AI) and conventional information (CI), which play different roles in facilitating user-product interaction. BI refers to the physical properties of an object: form, material and size that correspond to body size and capacities for users. AI indicates that object-object relationships offer not only a physical constraint for a device's operation, but also a visual cue as information for operational behaviors. CI refers to the signs and texts on products that aid and support users to be aware of the functionalities of each product directly, as well as the experiences, knowledge and cultures of users. In this study, users were asked to identify whether each part of the glucose meter used met the AI, BI or CI requirements through task analysis. Four-fifths agreed that confirm the part was identified to have associated perceptual information.

## 3   Results

### 3.1   Language and Icon Attributes

The types of perceptual information presented for each part can be extracted, and are shown in Table 2. For example, part (A), the lancing device cap, provides BI to indicate that a user must grasp the cap with their fingers and open it in sub-task (a.1), open the lancing device cap. In addition, the same part provides BI and AI to indicate to users how to assemble the part (A) to part (G), the glucose meter. But if the user does not touch the parts, it shows only AI but not BI. For example, where Part (J), the strip slot, is concerned, a user is required to insert the test strip into the slot of the glucose meter, but not to touch the slot during sub-task (b.4), insert a test strip into the meter. Therefore part (J) provides only AI. The remaining parts were classified in accordance with the above principles.

From Table 2, we found that the BI, AI and CI played different roles in assisting users to operate home-use glucose meters. Different perceptual information might occur in one part simultaneously, and one part might be found in different sub-tasks. The perceptual information plays different roles in presenting specific applications for user-product interaction. Table 3 shows a summary of the perceptual information that the subjects encountered while performing the tasks, and how such perceptual information specified the application.

**Table 2.** Analysis of information of home-use glucose meter for the tasks

| Parts | Action-Perceptual information matrix | | | | Content |
|---|---|---|---|---|---|
| | Behavioral and body region | BI | AI | CI | |
| (A) Lancing device cap | a.1 Grasp with finger | | | | Support with finger |
| | a.4 Grasp with finger | | | | Support with finger; Physical matching |
| | c.2 Cap touch sampling finger tip | | | | |
| | e.1 Grasp with finger | | | | Support with finger |
| | e.3 Grasp with finger | | | | Support with finger; Physical matching |
| | information index | 4 | 4 | 0 | |
| (B) Lancing device | a.1 Grasp with hand | | | | Support with Hand |
| | a.2 Grasp with hand | | | | Support with Hand |
| | a.4 Grasp with hand | | | | Support with Hand; Physical matching |
| | a.5 Grasp with hand | | | | Support with Hand |
| | a.6 Grasp with hand | | | | Support with Hand |
| | c.2 Grasp with hand | | | | Support with Hand |
| | e.1 Grasp with hand | | | | Support with Hand |
| | e.2 Grasp with hand | | | | Support with Hand |
| | e.3 Grasp with hand | | | | Support with Hand |
| | information index | 9 | 0 | 0 | |
| (C)Launch button | c.3 Switch with finger | | | | Support with finger; Symbol |
| | information index | 1 | 0 | 1 | |
| (D)Loaded lever | a.5 Grasp with finger and pull | | | | Support with finger; Symbol |
| | information index | 1 | 0 | 1 | |
| (E) Lancet | a.2 Grasp with finger and insert in | | | | Support with finger; Physical matching |
| | a.3 Grasp with finger and fix | | | | Support with finger |
| | e.2 Grasp with hand | | | | Support with Hand |
| | information index | 3 | 2 | 0 | |
| (F) Lancet cap | a.3 Pinch and unscrew with finger | | | | Support with finger; Shape |
| | e.2 Grasp with finger | | | | Support with finger; Material |
| | information index | 2 | 1 | 2 | |
| (G) Strip | b.2 Take from bottle | | | | Support with finger |
| | b.4 Grasp with finger | | | | Support with finger; Physical matching; Symbol |
| | c.4 Sampling with strip | | | | Symbol |
| | d.2 Grasp with finger | | | | Support with finger |
| | information index | 3 | 2 | 2 | |
| (H) Strips bottle cap | b.1 Open with finger. | | | | Support with Hand |
| | b.3 Close with finger | | | | Support with Hand |
| | information index | 2 | 2 | 1 | |
| (I) Strips bottle | b.1 Grasp with hand | | | | Support with Hand |
| | b.2 Grasp with hand | | | | Support with Hand |
| | b.3 Grasp with hand | | | | Support with Hand |
| | information index | 3 | 0 | 0 | |
| (J) Strip slot | b.4 Put strip into slot | | | | Physical matching |
| | d.2 Take strip out of slot | | | | |
| | information index | 0 | 1 | 0 | |
| (K) Glucose meter | b.4 Grasp with hand | | | | Support with Hand |
| | d.1 See the index | | | | |
| | d.2 Grasp with hand | | | | Support with Hand |
| | information index | 2 | 0 | 0 | |

**Table 3.** Parts - perceptual information - application (A: AI; B: BI; C: CI)

| Parts | Perceptual information | Number of operation | Affordance conditions |
|---|---|---|---|
| A | (B B B B) (A A A A) | 5 | Grasp ability; Assembly ability |
| B | (B B B B B B B B) | 2 | Grasp ability; Assembly ability |
| C | (B) (C) | 1 | Press ability; Functionality |
| D | (B) (C) | 1 | Pull ability; Operation direction |
| E | (B B B) (AA) | 1 | Pinch ability; Grasp ability; Assembly ability; Operation direction |
| F | (B B) (A) (C C) | 2 | Pinch ability; Functionality; Operation direction |
| G | (B B B) (A A) (C C) | 4 | Pinch ability; Assembly ability |
| H | (B B) (A A) (C) | 2 | Pinch ability; Assembly ability |
| I | (B B B) | 4 | Grasp ability |
| J | (A) | 2 | Assembly ability |
| K | (B B) | 4 | Grasp ability |

# 4   Discussion and Conclusion

## 4.1   Behavioral Information

In this study, almost all the parts were provided with BI information, however users were not able to identify the correct meaning of each part via its shape and material. Part (A), the lancing device cap, provides disassembly information. However, the transparent material of the cap resulted in user confusion as to the correct position for opening the cap. Users did not know where to pull and open the cap, and therefore could not finish the task. Part (C), the launch button, and part (D), the loaded lever, provide consistent shape and color, therefore prompting the user to realize that these parts' function is "button" or "lever" which can be pulled or pressed.

## 4.2   Assemblage Information

Some assembly processes are required for the operation of the blood glucose meter, such as replacing the lancing device cap, inserting the lancet into the slot of the lancing device, and inserting the test strip into the meter. Parts provide the correct AI that can guide users to assemble two corresponding parts, but this is related to whether the parts are able to provide the correct assembly information. For example, part (A), the lancing device cap, and its assembly with part (B), the lancing device, is designed to be equipped in a certain direction and angle, and both parts must be aligned for correct assembly. Such deliberate design might cause inconvenience for the elderly. Elderly patients may not be aware of the feature of part shape because of visual degeneration, and as a result, these parts cannot be accurately assembled easily. Previous studies also mention that the lancing devices often had different shapes and colors to distinguish the devices and its cap, which provided AI that the lancing device and the cap were detachable. However, the information of how to detach the cap was not clear [4].

### 4.3   Conventional Information

In this study, lancing devices adopt red line to represent blood sampling depth. Most Users state that they cannot clearly determine the skin puncture depth when operating sub-task (a.6), adjusting the lancing depth. Abstract images may not be able to assist elderly patients to understand this. In addition, Part (C), the launch button, and part (D), the loaded lever, also provide CI. Even if elderly users can accurately understand the above two parts with BI, enough to distinguish between the two, they may not be able to confirm that the "launch button" serves to launch the lancet, and the "loaded levers" serves to load the lancet.

Hsiao et al. [9] define that a symbol is one of affordance properties to represent the function of a product part. Perceiving the functionality of a product might be related to users' cultures and experiences. Therefore, users have to learn which affordances will satisfy particular goals, and they need to learn to attend to the appropriate aspects of the visual environment [10].

## 5   Conclusion

This study recruits elderly test subjects to operate home-use glucose meters and identify the perceptual information provided by each part of the meter. It is concluded that the application for assembly-disassembly ability is required for the part-part category, and AI and CI provide effective support for this application. The crucial factors that may cause operation errors involved lancing devices and test strips, rather than the glucose meters themselves. The possible reasons for these errors might arise from poor design of product perceptual information or unclear symbols. This study therefore suggests product designers provide more perception information, especially AI, in order to assist elderly users to understand how to use home-use medical devices such as glucose meters.

**Acknowledgement.** The authors appreciate Chiu Shu-Yueh and the participation of elder adults. This work was sponsored under grant MOST 103-2410-H-130-050 - by the Ministry of Science and Technology, Taiwan.

## References

1. International Diabetes Federation (IDF) (2013). http://www.idf.org/
2. Nyomba, B.L., Berard, L., Murphy, L.J.: Facilitating access to glucometer reagents increases blood glucose selfmonitoring frequency and improves glycemic control: a prospective study in insulin-treated diabetic patients. Diabet. Med. **21**, 129–135 (2004)

3. Diabetesforecast    (2011).    http://www.diabetesforecast.org/2011/jan/2011-blood-glucose-meter-special-features.html
4. Lo, H.C., Tsai, C.L., Lin, K.P., Chuang, C.C., Chang, W.T.: Usability evaluation of home-use glucose meters for senior users. Commun. Comput. Inf. Sci. **435**, 424–429 (2014)
5. Norman, D.A.: The Design of Everyday Things. MIT Press, London (1990)
6. McGrenere, J., Ho, W.: Affordance: clarifying and evolving a concept. In: Proceedings of Graphics Interface 2000 Conference. Lawrence Erlbaum Associates Press, Montreal (2000)
7. Rogers, Y., Sharp, H.: Interaction Design: Beyond Human-Computer Interaction. Wiley, New York (2002)
8. Chen, L.H., Lee, C.F.: Perceptual information for user-product interaction: using vacuum cleaner as example. Int. J. Des. **2**, 45–53 (2008)
9. Hsiao, S.H., Hsu, C.F., Lee, Y.T.: An online affordance evaluation for product design. Des. Stud. **33**, 126–159 (2012)
10. Eysenck, M.W., Keane, M.T.: Cognitive Psychology, 4th edn. Psychology Press, New York (2000)

# Developing a System for Post-Stroke Rehabilitation: An Exergames Approach

Arsénio Reis[1], Jorge Lains[5], Hugo Paredes[2(✉)], Vitor Filipe[2],
Catarina Abrantes[4], Fernando Ferreira[3], Romeu Mendes[4],
Paula Amorim[5], and João Barroso[2]

[1] Universidade de Trás-os-Montes e Alto Douro, Vila Real, Portugal
ars@utad.pt
[2] INESC TEC and Universidade de Trás-os-Montes e Alto Douro,
Vila Real, Portugal
{hparedes,vfilipe,jbarroso}@utad.pt
[3] 2C2T/Universidade do Minho, Guimarães, Portugal
fnunes@det.uminho.pt
[4] Research Center in Sports Sciences, Health and Human Development,
CIDESD, GERON Research Community
and Universidade de Trás-os-Montes e Alto Douro, Vila Real, Portugal
{abrantes,rmendes}@utad.pt
[5] CMRRC Rovisco-Pais, Tocha, Portugal
{jorgelains,paulaamorim}@roviscopais.min-saude.pt

**Abstract.** Stroke episodes are a major health issue worldwide for which most patients require an initial period of special rehabilitation and functional treatment, involving medical doctors and specialized therapists, followed by ambulatory physiotherapy exercise. In this second period most do not fulfil the prescribed recovery plan, resulting in setbacks in their recovery. This paper reports on the design of a methodology to develop a system to support the ambulatory rehabilitation therapy, providing constant feedback to the clinicians, by means of an information system platform, and maintaining the patient motivation by using an exergames approach to design and deliver the therapy exercises to the patient.

**Keywords:** Stroke rehabilitation · Motor therapy · Body motion analysis

## 1 Introduction

Every year 15 million people suffer a stroke, worldwide. From these, 5 million die and another 5 million are left with permanent disability, becoming a burden to the family, to the National Health Service and, in general, to the community [1]. In 2010, the absolute numbers of people with first stroke (16.9 million), stroke survivors (33 million), stroke-related deaths (5.9 million), and Disability-Adjusted Life Year (DALY) lost (102 million) were high and had significantly increased since 1990 (68 %, 84 %, 26 %, and 12 % increase, respectively), with most of the burden (68.6 % incident strokes, 52.2 % prevalent strokes, 70.9 % stroke deaths, and 77.7 % DALYs lost) in low-income and middle-income countries [37].

© Springer International Publishing Switzerland 2016
M. Antona and C. Stephanidis (Eds.): UAHCI 2016, Part III, LNCS 9739, pp. 403–413, 2016.
DOI: 10.1007/978-3-319-40238-3_39

The central hospitals of rehabilitation medicine have multiple valences, providing special rehabilitation and functional reeducation cares, with emphasis on stroke patient treatment and spinal cord injury treatments, due to the various aspects and constraints related to their limitations. In the initial phase of the physical rehabilitation, patients require a strong monitoring and therapists support with close proximity, in most cases due to their limitations and low autonomy. During their recovery, the patients' progress evaluation is carried out by medical doctors and specialized therapists, albeit with some degree of subjectivity, using scales and other assessment instruments to characterize the evolution of these patients.

The application of technology in health care has attracted, from a long time, the engineering attention and support to assist the therapy process, such as the case of gait analysis. Due in large part to the great changes in technology, particularly in optical motion capture systems and information extraction through digital image analysis. These systems have been created to support health professionals in the evaluation recovery process of patients, and to help to improve the level of the physical recovery of people. Some research demonstrates that exergames (video games which integrate exercise and gaming entertainment) can generate some general health benefits and also positive effects in increasing the recovery process in some diseases. The level of motor and functional recovery after the occurrence of a stroke is characterized by a great individual variability.

Some motor functions recover quickly, while others may remain indefinitely with permanent deficits. A large part of the motor function recovery occurs within the first three months after the occurrence of the vascular event, and after six months only small improvements are expectable, but these improvements can be functionally significant. For some patients recovery of motor function can continue for a long period.

After the initial recovery process in central specialized hospitals, patients have medical discharge, but they have to continue the recovery process. Usually, a set of exercises is prescribed, and can be performed in proximity physiotherapy centers, or by themselves in their own homes, in attempt to continue to improve their recovery. These periods that patients spend at home are essential both for economic and resource management reasons, and, or by social and emotional personal reasons.

After this recovery period in ambulatory, patients return to the central hospital facilities for evaluation, and since medical discharge there is no interaction or feedback to the medical doctors or central hospital. According to recent studies, in most cases, either for economic reasons or because of family and social low support, the patients do not fulfil the recovery plan. Consequently, setbacks occur in the recovery process, worsening the quality of life and, in some situations, patients need to return to the hospital for another period of time.

In this context, we propose a set of research and development activities, with the following main objectives:

- Application of information and communication technologies in the development of a prototype of a system focused on the upper limb rehabilitation of post stroke patients using exergames and natural interaction, in attempt to establish a link between central level (i.e. specialized hospitals) and patients recovery process at home or in proximity centres.

- Design and implement an intervention program to a group of post stroke patients randomly divided into experimental group (technology aided care) and control group (usual care).
- Validation of the results of the previously mentioned prototype and program with the results of medical assessment of the post-stroke patient.

The system development is associated with the specific objectives of procedural generation of the levels of exergames based on medical prescriptions and the capabilities to be exercised, dynamically adapted to the state and progression of the patient; capture of body movements and extraction of gesture information; nonintrusive acquisition of complementary biomedical signals; and biomedical and biomechanical metrics generation.

The system will be implemented using an evolutionary development model at the Rovisco Pais Medical Rehabilitation Center (CMRRC-Rovisco Pais), which will have the support of the Research Unit of the centre during the first eighteen months of the project. After the development phase, the system will be set up at the patients homes appointed by CMRRC-Rovisco Pais and will be tested and evaluated by patients and by health experts of this centre over the following months under project NanoStima (NORTE-01-0145-FEDER-000016). At the same time, relevant changes or adjustments will be introduced.

## 2   State of the Art

In the last two decades there has been an increase in the absolute number of people with new stroke (68 %), post-stroke survivors (84 %) and DALY (12 %) 23 [4]. Although the ratios incidence/mortality came to decline in the last two decades, there has been an increasing overhead in terms of the annual absolute number of stroke victims, the number of post-stroke survivors and DALY, especially in countries with low and middle incomes. Estimates from the Global Burden of Diseases, Injuries, and Risk Factors Study (GBD 2010) ranked stroke as third most common cause of disability-adjusted life-years (DALYs)2 worldwide in 2010 [38].

After a stroke various capacities can be affected, inter alia, language, personality and memory. The classic description of motor deficit in the acute phase of a stroke often points the predominant involvement of the upper limb, and its less favourable recovery comparatively to the leg. Spontaneous motor recovery of upper limb after stroke is generally limited to the first six months of injury, during which the rehabilitation medicine may have an active role, in a facilitating sense.

Traditional methods require intensive rehabilitation after a stroke, accompanied by physical therapists, therapies and specialized equipment. In recent years there has been an increase in the costs associated with these treatments [5], which has led to a decrease in demand for treatment sessions, which, in turn, has reflects in the rehabilitation process. One potential solution to the problem is based on the use of home-based exercise in virtual reality systems. Virtual reality has been shown as an effective means when used in the rehabilitation training. This approach, combined with technology of serious games contributes to the increase of the stimuli and the patient's motivation indices to meet the rehabilitation programs [6].

Research has shown that digital games improve elders' physical health, in aspects as diverse as physical balance, balance confidence, functional mobility, executive function and processing speed [7]. The last decade has witnessed the increasing use of games that employ the motor skills of players, including elders, for physical rehabilitation, treatment and diagnosis [8,9]. The use of such games, dubbed "exergames" [10] has been shown to have a positive effect on the physical outcome of elders 11. In particular, stroke rehabilitation using low-cost motion detection is a recent focus of research, with applications both on rehabilitation methods and serious games [12]. Several research efforts focused on the evaluation of Kinect's spatial accuracy specifically for stroke rehabilitation purposes. Limitations of current research are its focus on sets of gross movements, with more specific diagnostic movements sets needed; and the need to complement Kinect's accuracy limitations, on detection of internal shoulder joints rotation and fine motor skills (ibid.). A recent survey comparing therapy outcomes for post-stroke adults between motion-detection virtual reality (VR) and conventional therapy has shown that VR rehabilitation yields moderately improved outcomes, and called for better control of participation measures, and motivational components of therapy [13]. The motivational aspects can be tackled by the entertainment component brought about by exergames, rather than plain VR therapy. This motivational factor, or engagement, can address a major barrier to rehabilitation: patient nonadherence. Research points out that game design, in aspects such as choices, rewards, and goals, leads to increase in motivation/engagement [14].

This design aspects add on the basic design guides and should address the principles of motor recovery and learning: meaningful task; intensive and repetitive practice; close-to-normal movements (including bilateral exercises); muscle activation driving practice of movement; focused attention/motivation; and training specificity, variability and progression [31–34].

Procedural content generation is a commonly used term to describe a methodology that seeks to produce automatically, rather than manually, any kind of media content (models, textures, sounds, objects, etc.) through a set of techniques, computer algorithms and a certain degree of randomness. The concept of procedural content generation is not new in the gaming domain. One of the first use cases emerged in the 80's, called Elite.

There is a set of distinct techniques for procedural content generation for digital games [15]. Some of these techniques can be used to generate game levels [16] in a way to adapt the game design, automatically, to the distinct needs of a specific problem, namely it can be used to adapt to a specific therapy. The success in engaging the player is also connected to the way the gameplay adapts her/him. Therefore, some recent research is focused on adapting the gameplay, dynamically, to the players' needs [17]. The game design should enforce the training shaping (specificity, variability and progression) assuring: immediate feedback concerning movements; individualized tasks; prompting and cueing; and progressive increase in the difficulty of the tasks [35, 36].

Motion tracking or Motion Capture (MoCap) records human body's kinematic data with high accuracy and reliability. It has been started as analysis tool in biomechanics research in the 1970 s, however as the technology matured, it was expanded in several fields: robotics, human computer interaction (HCI), cinema, and video games, and virtual reality. Nowadays MoCap is very useful in medical science and sports applications to analyse human movement and gait.

Optical motion capture systems utilize data captured from image sensors to obtain the 3D position of subject's body joints. Traditionally data acquisition was implemented using special markers attached to an actor; however, emerging techniques and research in computer vision leaded to the development of the markerless approach. Because in vision-based markerless human motion capture technology, users are not required to wear a special costume and no markers need to be attached to the human body, this new technology provides a very attractive solution for the movement analysis in patients with stroke.

In markerless systems, the image features such as colors, edges, shapes, and/or depth are used to track human skeletal and estimate accurately the 3D body joints positions. Microsoft Kinect is one of such capture systems, which uses computer vision algorithms to detect and track human body from the sequences of depth images. It enables users to control and interact with electronic devices, through a natural user interface using gestures and spoken commands. Several studies identify the Kinect's potential for use in rehabilitation [19,20].

## 3   Methodology

The methodology aligns the expected positive effects, correlating the key research challenges with specific research activities. The results of these research activities may provide new insights into the distance monitoring of rehabilitation patients and the ability of technology to support patients to fulfil their rehabilitation plan.

We expect several positive effects of the use of exergames for rehabilitation:

(1) Patients motivation: exploring the entertaining aspect of rehabilitation, as literature suggests that the age group, of stroke patients, falls within the strategy of usage of serious games for exercise;

(2) Socialization: a social network of stroke patients with matching motor skills enhancing the group capability to pursuit their objectives, following gamification patterns;

(3) Personalized exergames with adaptation to user capabilities: the exergames are generated to each user from the clinical prescription and adapted to the users' attitude and execution of the exercises correcting their positions and movements.

The System will mimic the exercises used in specific Physical therapy interventions, improving the motor function (fine and gross), speed and grip strength related to arm-hand activities focused in intensive high repetitive task-oriented and task-specific training in all post stroke phases [22]. Therefore, we expect to contribute positively to the recuperation of patients due to an increase of the number of hours of specialized therapy thanks to its availability at every moment at their homes.

## 3.1   Objectives and Research Activities

The specific objectives are described in the following list, as well as the research activities designed to assure their fulfillment. Specific objectives:

**(O1)** the development of a prototype of a system focused on the upper limb rehabilitation of post stroke patients using exergames and natural interaction, establishing a link between central level centres and patients when they are recovering at home or in proximity centres;

**(O1.1)** procedural generation of the levels of exergames based on medical prescriptions and the capabilities to be exercised, dynamically adapted to the state and progression of the patient;

**(O1.2)** capture of body movements and extraction of gesture information;

**(O1.3)** non-intrusive acquisition of complementary biomedical signals;

**(O1.4)** generation of biomedical and biomechanical metrics.

**(O2)** application of an intervention program to a group of post-stroke patients randomly divided into experimental group (SelfTherapy) and control group (usual care);

**(O3)** validation of the results of SelfTherapy with the results of medical assessment of the post-stroke patient.

The research activities with a focus on testing and evaluation:

**(R1)** Exercise motivation and Serious games;

**(R2)** Evaluating smart clothes for physiological monitoring with embedded electronics;

**(R3)** Body motion capture and biomechanics analysis;

**(R4)** Integration and visualization platform;

**(R5)** Tests and evaluation.

The objective (O1.1) is primarily supported by research work to be developed on research activity 1 and the objectives (O1.2) and (O1.3), are respectively addressed by research activities 2 and 3. Research activity 4 comprises the integration of work carried on research activities 1, 2 and 3, in order to attain the objective (O1.4) and consequently the aggregation of the work to achieve the overall objective (O1). The consolidation of objectives O2 and O3 are addressed in research activity 5, also ensuring a continuum of evaluation by users and experts' feedback crosswise involved in research activities 1, 2, 3 and 4.

## 3.2   Development

Methodologically a user-centred development will be followed, based on the ISO 9241-210: 2010, with strong relations between the research team and the potential project stakeholders, linking the identified requirements with the user needs. This design approach also aims to improve patients' motivation and engagement, without compromising the goals of therapy. We will combine the Lukosch et al.'s method [18] with low-tech prototype methods of participatory design, which enable faster feedback loops and diminish risk [21]. Functional prototype generation and testing will be performed in each cycle in two steps: first using fast prototyping tools for a quick feedback loop with the participation of experts. After experts approve the prototype, different system actors will be involved in the testing, to further refine the prototype iteratively. Four combinatory cycles are defined for the development process:

**(C1) Core features:** analysis, where typical methods (therapist interviews, literature review) are combined with therapist participation to establish design criteria, via brainstorming sessions known as Group Decision Room and role-playing sessions to enhance context awareness; conceptualization of objectives O1.1, O1.2 and O1.3 and low-fidelity prototyping of concepts; demonstration of the technology possibilities to the users; testing and requirements gathering of multimodal interfaces for achieving the stated features.

In research activities 1, 2 and 3 single low fidelity demonstrators will be created. In such demonstrators users should perceive the capital gains and individual impacts of serious games, body motion capture, gesture recognition and textiles with embedded electronic that the project aims to develop and integrate. In research activity 4 the system usage storyboard will be developed, considering the various use cases and players of the system. This storyboard will be validated in tests set within research activity 5, which will be consequently mapped into use cases diagrams. The activities outlined which involve interaction with the system actors are framed in research activity 5 and will be conducted in the laboratory at CMRRC-Rovisco Pais. During this cycle there is interdependence between research activity 1 and research activity 5, overlooking the definition of the principles and metrics to be used for exercises and therapies classification that can be mutually accepted by therapists, clinicians, and data captured during the game execution (game analytics).

**(C2) Multimodal interfaces:** Synthesis of the criteria, yielding a provisional design; Simulation via generation of a low-tech prototype, which will enable experts and developers to test the designs, detect misunderstandings, and refine concepts, yielding a refined system design; first interactions in the laboratory, enhancing the assessment of user needs and their capabilities to the use of technology overlooking the refinement of the interaction potential and user experience.

Functional prototypes will be implemented, developing the demonstrators established in the previous cycle and reflecting the needs and expectations stated in the tests. In research activity 1 serious game prototypes will be developed integrating game mechanics adapted to the rehabilitation plan prescribed by clinicians, a generation module and dynamic adaptation of the levels of these games given the capacity to exercise the patients according to the good practice defined a set of standardized exercises established and validated for rehabilitation of stroke patients. An application prototype of a t-shirt with embedded sensors to capture biological data will be developed at this stage in research activity 2. In research activity 3 libraries to capture body movements and gestures extraction will be developed and exploited standards for representation of the collected data. Note that all demonstrators and prototypes developed during this cycle in research activities 1, 2 and 3 are standalone, without any kind of integration between them. The definition of integration API and low-fidelity prototypes of different user interfaces (mobile, web and set top device) will be developed during this cycle on research activity 4. In research activity 5 different tests on the developed functional demonstrators will be coordinated and a database of therapies and exercises classified according to the metrics defined in the previous cycle will be developed.

(C3) **User interaction and user experience:** development of a full-system; laboratory testing with users for real-scenario test preparation. This cycle is characterized by the integration of the various components developed in different research activities, with a strong interdependence between all research activities. Thereby in the research activities 1, 2 and 3, the specified integration API will be used under the coordination of the research activity 4 to connect the all system. In these research activities usability tests and developed mechanisms will also be defined to improve the user experience through an internal module (in-game assessment) to capture the game data (game analytics). In research activity 4, the integration process will be coordinated and defined the orchestration model following storyboard set on cycles (C1) and (C2). As in previous cycles, the interaction tests with system actors are set at research activity 5 and will be conducted in lab environment at CMRRC-Rovisco Pais.

(C4) **End user testing in real scenario:** tests involving a small group of users that during a three months period will have the system installed in their homes, simulating an actual usage environment and allowing the team to understand the system impacts. Two groups of patients will be considered: an intervention group that will use the system during the period of 3 months; a control group that will not use the system. Patients will be observed before and after the period in ambulatory by physicians who follow them, as detailed in the planning description of research activity 5.

The coordination of the tests with users in a real scenario will be performed on research activity 5, setting the overall system evaluation policy. Sectorially, for each of the research activities and according to the established objectives metrics analysis and appropriate quantifiers to the specific needs assessment will be defined.

A group of patients classified with mild/moderate stroke after hospital admission and baseline tests will receive 3 months of a "routine" physiotherapy by a specialized hospital therapist. After hospital discharge and new testing, patients will be randomly assigned in a control group (CG) or intervention group (IG). The control group will continue physiotherapy on ambulatory conditions (e.g. rehabilitation centers), and the intervention group will continue physiotherapy on ambulatory conditions plus the same exercise in the system platform in a home-based condition during more 3 months.

The recovery process assessment will be tested with the following tools:

1. Brunnstrom recovery stage [24];
2. Enjalbert recovery stage;
3. Wolf Motor Function Test [25];
4. Box and Block Test [26];
5. Stroke Impact Scale [27];
6. Action Research Arm Test [28];
7. Fugl-Meyer Scale [29];
8. Short form (36) health survey (SF-36) [31].

The methodology presented and the defined plan are articulated in the following cycle/research matrix, which summarizes the entire process.

| Research Cycles | Cycle 1 (C1) Core Features | Cycle 2 (2) Multimodal Interfaces | Cycle 3 (C3) User interaction and user experience | Cycle 4 (C4) End user testing in real scenario |
|---|---|---|---|---|
| Research activity 1 Exercise motivation and Serious games | - Core requirements specification; - Low fidelity prototype of serious games; - Motivation strategies evaluation; - Group decision room; - Role playing sessions; - User technology demonstration. | - Implementation of standalone serious games functional prototypes; - Development of module for dynamic generation and adaptation of game levels; - Prototype testing with experts and users; - Usability requirements identification; - Analysis of prototypes user experience level. | - Prototype refinement; - Integration with the body motion capture libraries; - Integration with the biomechanics analysis libraries; - Integration with the platform. | - Identification of the serious games testing objectives; - Definition of analysis metrics; - Analysis of the results; - Task results evaluation and objectives achievement. |
| Research activity 2 Design and production of t-shirt for physiological monitoring with embedded electronics | - Typical biotype characterization; | - Physical, chemical and comfort assessment; - Raw material specification; - Fabric production. | - Physical and chemical testing; - Integration with the platform. | - Prototype production; - Identification of the physiological monitoring testing objectives; - Definition of analysis metrics; - Analysis of the results; - Task results evaluation and objectives achievement. |
| Research activity 3 Body motion capture and biomechanics analysis | - Stroke recovery anatomic key points identification; - Adapted model for body tracking specification; - Impacts of Stroke in standard biomechanical models; - body motion capture low fidelity prototype development; - Suitability evaluation of adapted biomechanical models for stroke patients. | - Development of body motion capture libraries; - Gesture extraction; - Pattern exploration for body motion and gesture data and metadata representation; - Implementation of functional demonstrators of the libraries; - Prototype testing with experts and users; - Usability requirements identification; - Analysis of prototypes user experience level. | - Library refinement; - Integration with the platform. | - Identification of the body motion libraries testing objectives; - Definition of analysis metrics; - Analysis of the results; - Task results evaluation and objectives achievement. |
| Research activity 4 Integration and visualization platform | - Storyboard for system usage; - System requirements specification; - Coarse-grained architecture design; - Use cases design. | - Specification of integration API; - Low fidelity prototypes of user interfaces: mobile, web, set top unit; - Prototype evaluation. | - Implementation of the specified and validated user interfaces prototypes; - Definition of the orchestration model; - Coordination of the integration process; - Development of a functional prototype of the platform. | - Platform preparation for field testing; - Identification potential failures and definition of contingency plan; - Technical supervision of field tests; - Task results evaluation and objectives achievement. |
| Research activity 5 Tests and evaluation | - Identification of stroke rehabilitation therapy and exercises taxonomy; - Classification metrics for therapy and exercises; - Coordination of brainstorming sessions with users and experts; - Coordination of low fidelity prototype testing. | - Exercise and therapy database design; - Coordination of field tests with the developed functional demonstrators. | - Usability tests planning; - Coordination of usability tests; - Recommendations for enhancing usability and user experience. | - Global coordination of field testing; - Sample characterization; Data collection; - Analysis results; - Overall assessment of the project. |

# 4    Conclusion

The development of a system following this methodology should assure a low cost, user friendly and motivational/behavioral solution that aggregates three elements in the rehabilitation of post-stroke patients: recognition of body movements and gestures; instrumented textiles; and adaptive serious games and gamification strategies.

Regarding the overall benefits of the system, we expect to demonstrate that the passive monitoring strategy abdicates of clinical-patient interactions in the ambulatory period, creates an indirect relationship between the two, based on notifications and allowing early intervention in situations of default and/or reversal of the patient's condition. The gamification approach should ensure an easy adoption of the system as well as a user readiness by the patients as end-users.

A key aspect for the success of this methodology is the consortium which will develop the various research activities, including the software prototype. It is such an interdisciplinary proposal, that we came to the conclusion that this consortium should have deep insight in the areas of technology, health, rehabilitation and post-stroke treatment.

**Acknowledgements.** This work is funded by: Project "NORTE-01-0145-FEDER-000016" is financed by the North Portugal Regional Operational Programme (NORTE 2020), under the PORTUGAL 2020 Partnership Agreement, and through the European Regional Development Fund (ERDF).

# References

1. WORLD HEALTH ORGANIZATION Stroke, Cerebrovascular accident (2015). (http://www.emro.who.int/health-topics/stroke-cerebrovascular-accident/index.html). (Accessed on January 2015)

2. Lozano, R., Naghavi, M., Foreman, K., et al.: Global and regional mortality from 235 causes of death for 20 age groups in 1990 and 2010: a systematic analysis for the Global Burden of Disease Study 2010. Lancet **2012**(380), 2095–2128 (2012). [PubMed: 23245604]

3. Murray, C.J.L., Vos, T., Lozano, R., et al.: Disability-adjusted life-years (DALYs) for 291 diseases and injuries in 21 regions, 1990–2010: a systematic analysis for the Global Burden of Disease Study 2010. Lancet **2012**(380), 2197–2223 (2010). [PubMed: 23245608]

4. Feigin, V.L., Lawes, C.M., Bennett, D.A., Barker-Collo, S.L., Parag, V.: Worldwide stroke incidence and early case fatality reported in 56 population-based studies: a systematic review. Lancet Neurol. **2009**(8), 355–369 (2009). [PubMed: 19233729]

5. Pricewaterhouse Coopers Health Research Institute: Behind the Numbers. In: Medical cost trends for 2009

6. Garcia, J.A., Navarro, K.F., Schoene, D., Smith, S.T., Pisan, Y.: Exergames for the elderly: Towards an embedded Kinect-based clinical test of falls risk. In: Studies in Health Technology and Informatics, vol. 178. Health Informatics: Building a Healthcare Future Through Trusted Information (2012)

7. Zhang, F., Kaufman, D.: Physical and cognitive impacts of digital games on older adults a meta-analytic review. J. Appl. Gerontology, 0733464814566678 (2015)

8. Marcus, B.H., Nigg, C.R., Riebe, D., Forsyth, L.H.: Interactive communication strategies: implications for population-based physical-activity promotion. Am. J. Prev. Med. **19**, 121–126 (2000)

9. von Bruhn Hinné, T., Keates, S.: Using motion-sensing remote controls with older adults. In: Stephanidis, C. (ed.) Universal Access in HCI, Part II, HCII 2011. LNCS, vol. 6766, pp. 166–175. Springer, Heidelberg (2011)

10. Vaghetti, C.A.O., Botelho, SSCdC: Virtual learning environments in physical education: a review of the use of Exergames. Ciências Cognição **15**, 76–88 (2010)

11. Larsen, L.H., Schou, L., Lund, H.H., Langberg, H.: The physical effect of exergames in healthy elderly—a systematic review. Games Health J. Res. Dev. Clin. Appl. **2**(4), 205–212 (2013)

12. Webster, D., Celik, O.: Systematic review of Kinect applications in elderly care and stroke rehabilitation. Assessment **23**, 26 (2014)

13. Lohse, K.R., Hilderman, C.G., Cheung, K.L., Tatla, S., Van der Loos, H.M.: Virtual reality therapy for adults post-stroke: a systematic review and meta-analysis exploring virtual environments and commercial games in therapy. PLoS ONE **9**(3), e93318 (2014)

14. Lohse, K., Shirzad, N., Verster, A., Hodges, N., Van der Loos, H.M.: Video games and rehabilitation: using design principles to enhance engagement in physical therapy. J. Neurologic Phy. Ther. **37**(4), 166–175 (2013)

15. Hendrikx, M., Meijer, S., Van Der Velden, J., Iosup, A.: Procedural content generation for games: a survey. ACM Trans. Multimedia Comput. Commun. Appl. (ACM TOMCCAP), **9** (1) (2013)

16. Dormans, J.: Level design as model transformation: a strategy for automated content generation. In: Proceedings of the 2nd International Workshop on Procedural Content Generation in Games (PCGames 2011) (2011)

17. Lopes, R., Bidarra, R.: Adaptivity challenges in games and simulations: a survey. IEEE Trans. Comput. Intell. AI Games **3**(2), 85–99 (2011). doi:10.1109/TCIAIG.2011.2152841

18. Hondaori, H.M., Khademi, M.: A review on technical and clinical impact of Microsoft Kinect on physical therapy and rehabilitation. J. Med. Eng. (in Press). http://dx.doi.org/10.1155/2014/846514

19. Webster, D., Celik, O.: Systematic review of Kinect applications in elderly care and stroke rehabilitation. J. NeuroEng. Rehabil. **11**, 108 (2014)

20. Lukosch, H., van Ruijven, T., Verbraeck, A.: The participatory design of a simulation training game. In: Proceedings of the Winter Simulation Conference, p. 142 (2012)
21. Pereira, L.L., Roque, L.: Towards a game experience design model centered on participation. In: CHI 2012 Extended Abstracts on Human Factors in Computing Systems, pp. 2327–2332. ACM (2012)
22. Veerbeek, J.M., van Wegen, E., van Peppen, R., Jan, P., van der Wees, E., Hendriks, M.R., Kwakkel, G.: What is the evidence for physical therapy poststroke? a systematic review and meta-analysis. PLOS One **9** (2014)
23. Lewis, J.R.: IBM computer usability satisfaction questionnaires: psychometric evaluation and instructions for use. Int. J. Hum.-Comput. Interact. **7**(1), 57–78 (1995)
24. Naghdi, S., Ansari, N.N., Mansouri, K., Hasson, S.: A neurophysiological and clinical study of Brunnstrom recovery stages in the upper limb following stroke. Brain Injury **24**, 1372–1378 (2010)
25. Mcculloch, K., Cook, E.W., Fleming, W.C., Novack, T.A., Taub, E.: A reliable test of upper extremity ADL function. Arch. Phys. Med. Rehabil. **69**, 755 (1988)
26. Mathiowetz, V., Volland, G., Kashman, N., Weber, K.: Adult norms for the box and block test of manual dexterity. Am. J. Occup. Ther. **39**, 386–391 (1985)
27. Duncan, P.W., Wallace, D., Lai, S.M., Johnson, D., Embretson, S., Laster, L.J.: The stroke impact scale version 2.0 - Evaluation of reliability, validity, and sensitivity to change. Stroke; a journal of cerebral circulation **30**, 2131–2140 (1999)
28. Lyle, R.C.: A performance test for assessment of upper limb function in physical rehabilitation treatment and research. Int. J. Rehabil. Res. Internationale Zeitschrift fur Rehabilitationsforschung Revue internationale de recherches de readaptation **4**, 483–492 (1981)
29. Fugl-Meyer, A.R., Jaasko, L., Leyman, I., Olsson, S., Steglind, S.: The post-stroke hemiplegic patient. A method for evaluation of physical performance. Scand. J. Rehabil. Med. **7**, 13–31 (1975)
30. McHorney, C.A., Ware Jr, J.E., Lu, J.F., Sherbourne, C.D.: The MOS 36-item Short-Form Health Survey (SF-36): III. Tests of data quality, scaling assumptions, and reliability across diverse patient groups. Med. Care **32**, 40–66 (1994)
31. Pekna, M., et al.: Stroke **43**(10), 2819–2828 (2012)
32. Arya, K.N., et al.: J Bodyw Mov Ther. **15**(4), 528–537 (2011)
33. Daly, J.J., Ruff, R.L.: Sci. World J. **20**(7), 2031–2045 (2007)
34. Hosp, J.A., Luft, A.R.: Neural Plast. **2011**, 871296 (2011)
35. Taub, E., Uswatte, G., Pidikiti, R.: Constraint-induced movement therapy: a new family of techniques with broad application to physical rehabilitation—a clinical review. J. Rehabil. Res. Dev. **36**, 237–251 (1999)
36. Taub, E., Uswatte, G., Elbert, T.: New treatments in neuroRehabilitation founded on basic research. Nat. Rev. Neurosci. **3**, 228–236 (2002)
37. Feigin, V.L., et al.: Global and regional burden of stroke during 1990–2010: findings from the Global Burden of Disease Study 2010. Lancet **383**(9913), 245–254 (2014)
38. Murray, C.J.L., Vos, T., Lozano, R., et al.: Disability-adjusted life-years (DALYs) for 291 diseases and injuries in 21 regions, 1990–2010: a systematic analysis for the Global Burden of Disease Study 2010. Lancet **380**, 2197–2223 (2012)

# Comparative Study of Tangible Tabletop and Computer-Based Training Interfaces for Cognitive Rehabilitation

Kyuye Song[1,2], Sekwang Lee[3], Sung-Bom Pyun[3],
and Laehyun Kim[1,2(✉)]

[1] Center for Bionics Korea Institute of Science and Technology,
Seoul, Republic of Korea
{gl4501,laehyunk}@kist.re.kr
[2] Department of HCI and Robotics,
University of Science and Technology, Daejeon, Republic of Korea
[3] Department of Physical Medicine and Rehabilitation,
Korea University College of Medicine, Seoul, Republic of Korea
insu5812@gmail.com, rmpyun@korea.ac.kr

**Abstract.** Computer-based training (CBT) has lately been applied for the cognitive rehabilitation of stroke patients. However, most CBT programs do not consider body movement, which is important for cognitive rehabilitation because body movement (action) and thought (mind) are deeply correlated. Based on the coupling of action and mind, we propose a tangible tabletop-based training (TTBT) platform, E-CORE. We conducted a comparative study between E-CORE (TTBT) and RehaCom (CBT), for which we recruited eight patients as participants. We used the performance score yielded by the Intrinsic Motivation Inventory (IMI), the System Usability Scale (SUS), and the Questionnaire for User Interaction Satisfaction (QUIS) for quantitative analysis, and observation and semi-structured interviews as tools for qualitative analysis. Even though the user group was comparatively small, we found that E-CORE (TTBT) increases patients' motivation for rehabilitation.

**Keywords:** Cognitive rehabilitation · Stroke · User interfaces · Tangible tabletop · Computer-based training

## 1 Introduction

Approximately 800,000 people suffer strokes each year [1]. Stroke survivors can experience various impairments of their motor, sensory, and cognitive skills [2]. These defects result in disabilities related to concentration, memory, simple mathematical computations, and spatial visualization and orientation [3, 4]. In such cases, cognitive training can help improve stroke patients' cognitive functions and help slow deteriorating cognitive impairments [5, 6]. Studies on animal as well as humans have shown that intensive and repetitive training helps reduce impairment in stroke patients [7]. Motivation is an important factor in the effects of cognitive rehabilitation training. Motivated patients tend to participate more actively in rehabilitation programs because

M. Antona and C. Stephanidis (Eds.): UAHCI 2016, Part III, LNCS 9739, pp. 414–424, 2016.
DOI: 10.1007/978-3-319-40238-3_40

they consider rehabilitation to be a means of recovery [8]. Rehabilitation programs can integrate gaming features into rehabilitation training to enhance patients' motivation. Furthermore, gaming features-based rehabilitation has been reported to enhance motivation in adults patients undergoing physical, cognitive, and occupational therapy following a stroke [9]. However, the role of body movement in cognitive rehabilitation of previous training program has not been studied as extensively. Body movements should be considered when designing a cognitive training program because human actions (body) and thoughts (mind) are intimately connected [10]. With regard to the coupling of human action and thought in cognitive rehabilitation, we propose tangible tabletop-based training (TTBT), which relies on physical manipulation and cognitive tasks, as superior to conventional computer-based training (CBT), which involves the use a keyboard and mouse for cognitive rehabilitation. We conduct a comparative study to establish the superiority of TTBT over CBT programs.

In this paper, we make the following assumptions: First, there is a statistical preference for TTBT in terms of test scores for motivation and usability. Second, there is a correlation between MMSE (Mini-mental State Examination) and the motivation score on IMI (Intrinsic Motivation Inventory).

## 2 Background and Related Work

In this section, we review existing work related to the comparison of input interfaces in cognitive rehabilitation.

### 2.1 Traditional Physical Object-Based Training

Traditional cognitive training using physical tools, such as shapes and images, is a typical method in therapy. Training using physical tools is familiar to patients, and has the advantage of immediate feedback. However, there are limitations due to the cost of setting up the tool and the variety of training content [11]. In addition, in traditional rehabilitation it is difficult to evaluate the patient's performance objectively.

### 2.2 Computer-Based Training (CBT)

Computer-based training (CBT) can provide real-time performance feedback and personalized programs [12]. Although CBT was developed to solve problems with traditional cognitive training interfaces, limitations in it persist. Patients are not familiar with computer interfaces and find it difficult to use a mouse and keyboard-based panel interface [13, 14]. An instance of a CBT program is RehaCom, shown in Fig. 1.

**RehaCom:** RehaCom is a cognitive training program developed to enhance concentration, memory, and visualization. The system comprises a keyboard and a mouse panel [15]. It allows easy and more extensive access to its record as numerous hospitals use it.

**Fig. 1.** RehaCom as an instance of computer-based training for cognitive rehabilitation

## 2.3    Tangible Tabletop-Based Training (TTBT)

The bulk of research on cognitive rehabilitation has focused on specific cognitive domain effects such as attention and memory [11, 12]. A TUI (tangible user interface) allows users to interact with a digital device through the manipulation of commonplace objects using a computer system [16, 17]. The physical interaction with real objects can improve the quality of training for patients who need cognitive and/or motor rehabilitation [18].

**E-CORE (Embodied Cognitive Rehabilitation System):** Based on the concept of embodied cognition, E-CORE is a novel cognitive rehabilitation system that can delay or prevent cognitive problems using tangible objects and a tabletop interface to train patients to perform activities of daily living (ADL) [19]. Examples of tangible objects are shown Fig. 2. Compared with computer-based training (CBT) that involves singular mental tasks using keyboard and mouse, E-CORE can reinforce the coupling of body movement and cognition. Embodied cognitive rehabilitation helps improve patients' cognitive functions while they enjoy the relevant exercises. In this study, we report on the development of a cookie-making game as part of the instrumental ADL. The task involves creating the shape of cookies using a cookie cutter, calculating the proper temperature of the oven to bake them, moving the cookies, serving syrup using a brush, and sprinkling toppings on the cookies from containers.

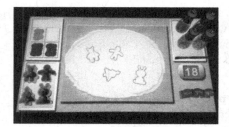

**Fig. 2.** E-CORE system as a tangible tabletop-based training for cognitive rehabilitation

# 3   Experiment

## 3.1   Participants

The eight participants of our study were stroke inpatients (four females and four males) from a hospital. They were recruited according to criteria for the Mini-mental State Examination (MMSE). Patients who scored between 12 and 26 on the MMSE were considered suitable for the experiment. In addition, the participants could move their upper limbs, as the two interfaces being compared required the ability in subjects to move their upper limbs in order to grasp objects and push buttons. We received informed consent for all procedures was obtained from each participant and caregiver, and the study was approved by institutional review board of Korea University Anam Hospital. The range of the participants' MMSE scores varied from 13 to 26 (M = 19.75 ± 4.83). The range of their ages was 48 to 78 years (M = 64.25 ±13.26). This information is shown in Table 1.

**Table 1.** General Characters of Participants

| Subject# | Charateristics | | | | | |
| | Gender | Age (y) | Affected side | Diagnosis | MMSE | Academic level |
|---|---|---|---|---|---|---|
| 1 | F | 74 | Right· | Rt. PCA territory infraction | 16 | Less than a high school |
| 2 | M | 74 | Left | Lt. MCA, ACA territory infarction | 14 | High school graduates |
| 3 | M | 49 | Right | Rt. BG ICH | 23 | Less than a high school |
| 4 | F | 78 | Right | Rt. F-T-P SDH | 13 | Less than a high school |
| 5 | M | 49 | Left | SAH with IVH | 23 | High school graduates |
| 6 | F | 67 | Right | Rt. cerebellar ICH with IVH | 26 | Less than a high school |
| 7 | M | 75 | Right | Rt. Lat. Medullary infarction | 23 | Less than a high school |
| 8 | F | 48 | Right | Lt. MCA territory infarction | 20 | High school graduates |

## 3.2    Settings

To compare the levels of motivation and usability of body movement in E-CORE (TTBT) and CBT, we chose RehaCom as the CBT program. The methods used for task assessment are shown in Fig. 3. We set-up our study in an enclosed space as this allowed for a controlled environment for the study that could be replicated. Moreover, RehaCom (CBT) and E-CORE (TTBT) were placed apart in the environment. Therefore, the evaluation of experiments on each proceeded independently of the other.

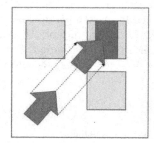 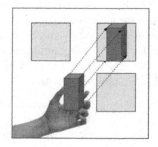

**Fig. 3.** Inputs in the cognitive training task: 2D inputs, such as a mouse or a keyboard in the CBT program (left) and 3D inputs, such as tangible objects in the TTBT program (right)

## 3.3    Measures

The MMSE score was used to screen patients and find a correlation in motivation or usability test scores. In this study, we used several types of quantitative and qualitative methods. The factors that were studied are shown in Table 2.

We recorded participants' statistics, such as reaction time, error rate, and verbal reactions, to identify user engagement and preferences [20]. As post-questionnaires, we used the Intrinsic Motivation Inventory (IMI), the System Usability Scale (SUS), and the Questionnaire for User Interaction Satisfaction (QUIS) to evaluate the participants' motivation and usability of body movement, and the usability of the two cognitive rehabilitation interfaces [21, 22]. All scores were compared using the Wilcoxon signed-rank test because of the small number of participants.

# 4    Results

Data for our study were collected in a number of ways. A quantitative analysis of the results are based on a statistical analysis of patients' responses to the questionnaires (IMI, SUS, QUIS) and performance results. A qualitative analysis of observations was conducted by using our video and audio records, and semi-structured interviews were used to contextualize the quantitative findings.

**Table 2.** The factors of RehaCom (CBT) and E-CORE (TTBT)

| Factors | CBT (RehaCom) | TTBT (E-CORE) | |
|---------|---------------|---------------|---|
| **Attention** | Attention and concentration training session | Following the in-struction at each step | |
| **Memory** | Memorize the position of cards | Memorize cookie shape and color of syrup and toppings | |
| **Calculation** | Calculation train-ing session | Calculate the bak-ing temperature | |
| **Factors** | **CBT (RehaCom)** | **TTBT (E-CORE)** | |
| **Execution** | Pointing or pressing the button and using joystick | Using the cookie cutter, serving the syrup, and sprin-kling toppings | |
| **Spatial operations** | Spatial operation and 2D operation training session | Recognizing the rotation of shape | |

## 4.1 Motivation

The level of motivation was calculated by IMI, QUIS, error rate, observation, and verbal reaction.

**Motivation Inventory (IMI):** The IMI score of the TTBT was significantly higher than that of CBT, especially for "Interest" (TTBT: M = 3.5, $SD$ = 1.3; CBT: $M$ = 1.88, $SD$ = .98), ($z$ = 2.414, $P$ < .05) and "Perceived choice" (TTBT: $M$ = 3.38, $SD$ = .43; CBT: $M$ = 1.88, $SD$ = .32), ($z$ = 2.15, $P$ < .05), whereas the "Pressure/Tension" score of TTBT was lower than that of CBT (TTBT: $M$ = 1.62, $SD$ = .22; CBT: $M$ = 3.75, $SD$ = .13), ($z$ = 2.59, $P$ < .05).

**User Interaction Satisfaction (QUIS):** The QUIS scores of the TTBT focusing on "User learnability" were higher than the CBT scores (TTBT: M = 4.75, $SD$ = 0.38;

CBT: $M = 3.5$, $SD = 0.84$), ($z = 2.04$, $p < .05$). However, there was no significant difference between the systems in terms of the other factors.

**Error Score:** The error sore was transformed five-point Likert scale from 0 to 100 game score (0 ∼ 20  - > 4;   21 ∼ 40  - > 3;   41 ∼ 60- > 2;   61 ∼ 80- > 1; 81 ∼ 100- > 0). The errors in the execution and spatial operations of the CBT (execution: M = 3.13, SD = .99; spatial operations: M = 2.75, SD = 1.17) were significantly higher than those for the TTBT score (execution: M = 1.25, SD = 1.04; spatial operations: M = .88, SD = .83), (execution: $z = 2.42$, $p < .05$; spatial operations: $z = 2.13$, $p < .05$). The results are shown in Fig. 4.

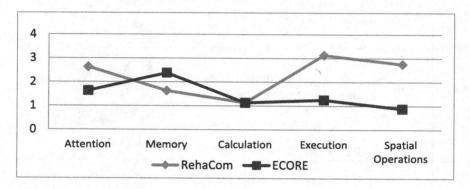

**Fig. 4.** Error score of both interfaces

**Observation and Verbal Reactions:** The methods focused on user preferences and motivation. In order to identify the preference among patients between the CBT and TTBT interfaces, we conducted semi-structured interview after the sessions. Most participants commented that both cognitive training interfaces were effective. They said that since they did not know exactly how each system worked, they preferred E-CORE's tools, which were more familiar to them. A few participants mentioned that they disliked using both digital interfaces due to their unfamiliarity with computers.

## 4.2    Usability and Body Movement

The usability and body movement of the interfaces were calculated through SUS, reaction time, observation, and verbal reaction

(a) **System Usability Scale (SUS):** The SUS score was calculated on a scoring form, and ranged from 0 to 100. The SUS score of TTBT ($M = 48.75$, $SD = 22.6$) was little higher than that of CBT ($M = 46.25$, $SD = 11.10$), whereas no significant differences were found in the SUS evaluation ($z = .281$, $p = .779$).

**Reaction Time (RT):**    Except for the calculation stage, the reaction times of all stages of the CBT were higher than those of TTBT. In particular, we found that the reaction time of "Execution" and "Spatial operation" of the CBT (execution:$M$ = 3469.258, $SD$ = 249.10; Spatial operation: $M$ = 4041.5, $SD$ = 208.3) were significantly higher than those of TTBT (Execution: $M$ = 1353.38, $SD$ = 97.10; Spatial operations: $M$ = 1614.25, $SD$ = 139.2), (Execution: $z$ = 2.52, $P$ < .05; Spatial operations: $z$ = 2.51, $P$ < .05). The results are shown in Fig. 5.

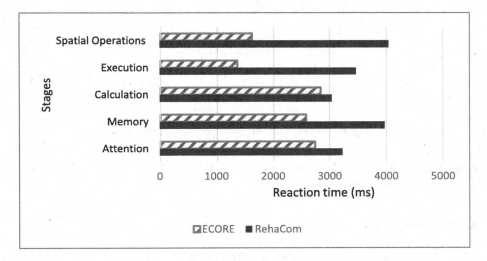

**Fig. 5.** Reaction time of both interfaces

**Observation and Verbal Reactions:** Observations were focused on physical manipulation, which were hypothesized to be important in cognitive rehabilitation using a coupling of the body and the mind [13]. We assumed that most participants would start concerning the input tool such as panel keyboard and cookie cutter. However, we observed that participants were interested in the tabletop display due to its conspicuous color and shape. While working with RehaCom (CBT), participants had difficulty using the panel keyboard even though we had explained how to use it. They preferred pointing to the display rather than using the panel keyboard. However, participants were easily able to use the tools to cut and bake cookies in E-CORE (TTBT). They reported finding that cookie-making tools, such as the cookie cutter, the brush, and the topping container, were familiar to them from daily life. Observational analysis revealed that participants were much more active and intuitive in terms of body movement (action) in cognitive training on E-CORE than on RehaCom.

### 4.3 Correlation Between MMSE and IMI, QUIS Score

MMSE and IMI scores were normalized to analyze the correlation. The MMSE score had a strong positive correlation with the IMI score of TTBT (Interest: r = .82, p < .01; Perceived competence: r = .717, p < .05; Perceived choice: r = .856, p < .01; pressure: r = -.815, p < .05). Further, we found a positive correlation of MMSE scores with

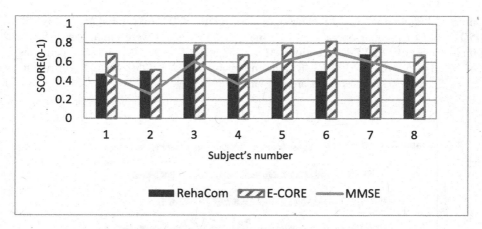

**Fig. 6.** MMSE with IMI scores of both interfaces

both interfaces for "User learnability" in QUIS (CBT: $r = .73$, $p < .05$; TTBT: $r = .68$, $p < .05$). The results are shown in Fig. 6.

# 5    Discussion

## 5.1    Motivation and Usability of Body Movement

We found that the participants perceived the feedback from TTBT interesting. The TTBT interface using a tabletop system appeared to be more powerful in terms of visual, aural, and tactile feedback than the CBT interface. In previous study, the tabletop system has been shown to be compatible with a multimodal feedback interface [23]. Further, we found that since the tangible objects used in TTBT were familiar to participants from everyday life, they found it easier to use TTBT than CBT [24].

## 5.2    MMSE Score and Motivation

The MMSE score is related to factors affecting patients' motivation in the TTBT interface. If participants had high MMSE scores, they had determined that the level of motivation provided by the TTBT interface was high. Based on observation of their verbal reactions, we concluded that the participants' positive motivational reaction to TTBT reflects the fact that the E-CORE (TTBT) task engages body movement to a greater extent, consistently with its use in ADL, than RehaCom (CBT). Therefore, since patients with high MMSE scores considered E-CORE (TTBT) an effective rehabilitation training tool, they were motivated to train with it. They found the tools provided by the former easier to handle and more interesting [8]. Furthermore, this indicates that MMSE scores and physical impairment are related. For example, grasping or rotating an object might be difficult for a patient with a low MMSE score following disability of physical movement [25]. In addition, the "learnability" score of

QUIS for both interfaces was positively correlated with MMSE scores. Patients with high MMSE scores recognized the importance of training in treating cognitive problems. That is, they were highly motivated to get better, which is important for rehabilitation.

## 6  Conclusion

In this study, even though the sample size used in our experiments was small, we found that E-CORE (TTBT) increases patients' motivation for rehabilitation. Because E-CORE involves intuitive body movement to manipulate tangible objects, the participants of our experiments were motivated to perform cognitive training tasks using our system. We also found that several patients with high MMSE scores perceived the E-CORE (TTBT) system to be motivating because of the novel forms of therapy that it uses; therefore, they preferred TTBT as a cognitive training program. In the future, we intend to adjust the game level and substantially redesign the components of the E-CORE system on the basis of the results of this study. Finally, we plan to conduct a longitudinal study by using E-CORE as a cognitive training system in the clinical field.

**Acknowledgement.** Authors would like to thank the volunteers for participating in this study. This study was partly supported by Institute for Information & communications Technology Promotion (IITP) grant funded by the Korea government (MSIP, 10045452), and the National Research Foundation (NRF) of Korea and the Korea government (MSIP, NRF-2015M3C7A1065049).

## References

1. National Stroke Association (2000). http://www.stroke.org. Accessed 28 July 2015
2. Belleville, S.: Cognitive training for persons with mild cognitive impairment. Int. Psychogeriatr. **20**, 57–66 (2008)
3. Diller, L., Weinberg, J.: Differential aspects of attention in brain-damaged persons. Percept. Mot. Skills **35**, 71–81 (1972)
4. Diller, L., Weinberg, J.: Hemi-inattention in rehabilitation and the evolution of a rational remediation program. In: Weinstein, E.A., Freidland, R.P. (eds.) Advances in Neurology. Raven Press, New York (1977)
5. Belleville, S.: Cognitive training for persons with mild cognitive impairment. Int. Psychogeriatr. **20**, 57–66 (2008)
6. Faucounau, V., Wu, Y.H., Boulay, M., De Rotrou, J., Rigaud, A.S.: Cognitive intervention programmes on patients affected by mild cognitive impairment: a promising intervention tool for MCI? J. Nutr. Health Aging **14**, 31–35 (2010)
7. Nudo, R.J.: Neural substrates for the effects of rehabilitative training on motor recovery after ischemic infarction. Science **272**, 1791–1794 (1996)
8. Maclean, N., Pound, P., Wolfe, C., Rudd, A.: Qualitative analysis of stroke patients' motivation for rehabilitation. BMJ **321**(7268), 1051–1054 (2000)

9. Jack, D., Boian, R., Merians, A., Tremaine, M., Burdea, G., Adamovich, S., et al.: Virtual reality -enhanced stroke rehabilitation. IEEE Trans. Neurol. Syst. Rehabil. Eng. **9**, 308–318 (2001)

10. Klemmer, S.R., Hartmann, B., Takayama, L.: How bodies matter: five themes for interaction design. In: Proceedings of the 6th Conference on Designing Interactive Systems, pp. 140–149. ACM, June 2006

11. Reis, A., Petersson, K.M., Castro-Caldas, A., Ingvar, M.: Formal schooling influences two-but not three dimensional naming skills. Brain Cogn. **47**, 397–411 (2001)

12. Herrera, C., Chambon, C., Michel, B.F., Paban, V., Alescio-Lautier, B.: Positive effects of computer-based cognitive training in adults with mild cognitive impairment. Neuropsychologia **50**(8), 1871–1881 (2012)

13. Barnes, D.E., Yaffe, K., Belfor, N., Jagust, W.J., DeCarli, C., Reed, B.R., Kramer, J.H.: Computer-based cognitive training for mild cognitive impairment: results from a pilot randomized, controlled trial. Alzheimer Dis. Assoc. Disord. **23**(3), 205 (2009)

14. Lányi, C.S., Geiszt, Z., Magyar, V.: Using IT to inform and rehabilitate aphasic patients. Inf. Sci. J. **9**, 163–179 (2006)

15. Schuhfried GmbH: RehaCom catalogue. GmbH, December 2009. http://www.schuhfried.at/fileadmin/pdf_eng/catalog_RehaCom_en.pdf

16. Ullmer, B., Ishii, H.: Emerging frameworks for tangible user interfaces. IBM Syst. J. **39**, 915–931 (2000)

17. Sitdhisanguan, K., Dechaboon, A., Chotikakamthorn, N., Out, P.: Comparative study of WIMP and tangible user interfaces in training shape matching skill for autistic children. In: TENCON 2007 IEEE Region 10 Conference, pp. 1-4. IEEE, October 2007

18. Annett, M., Anderson, F., Goertzen, D., Halton, J., Ranson, Q., Bischof, W.F., Boulanger, P.: Using a multi-touch tabletop for upper extremity motor rehabilitation. In: Proceedings of the 21st Annual Conference of the Australian Computer-Human Interaction Special Interest Group: Design: Open 24/7, pp. 261–264. ACM, November 2009

19. Jung, J., Kim, L., Park, S., Kwon, G.H.: E-CORE (Embodied COgnitive REhabilitation): a cognitive rehabilitation system using tangible tabletop interface. In: Pons, J.L., Torricelli, D., Pajaro, M. (eds.) Converging Clinical & Engi. Research on NR, vol. 1, pp. 893–897. Springer, Heidelberg (2013)

20. Ericsson, K.A., Simon, H.A.: Verbal reports data. Psychol. Rev. **1980**(87), 215–251 (1980)

21. Bangor, A., Kortum, P.T., Miller, J.T.: An empirical evaluation of the system usability scale. Int. J. Hum. Comput. Interact. **24**(6), 574–594 (2008)

22. Chin, J.P., Diehl, V.A., Norman, K.L. Development of an instrument measuring user satisfaction of the human-computer interface. In: Proceedings of the SIGCHI Conference on Human Factors in Computing Systems, pp. 213–218. ACM, May 1988

23. Leitner, M., Tomitsch, M., Költringer, T., Kappel, K., Grechenig, T.: Designing tangible table-top interfaces for patients in rehabilitation. In: CVHI (2007)

24. Marques, T., Nunes, F., Silva, P., Rodrigues, R.: Tangible interaction on tabletops for elderly people. In: Anacleto, J.C., Fels, S., Graham, N., Kapralos, B., Saif El-Nasr, M., Stanley, K. (eds.) ICEC 2011. LNCS, vol. 6972, pp. 440–443. Springer, Heidelberg (2011)

25. Arsic, S., Konstantinovic, L., Eminovic, F., Pavlovic, D., Popovic, M.B., Arsic, V.: Correlation between the quality of attention and cognitive competence with motor action in stroke patients. BioMed Res. Int. **2015** (2015)

# Content Analysis of Specialist Interviews During the Design of Cervical Collar Devices for Elderly Patients with Central Cord Syndrome

Wan-Ting Tsai[1], Kevin C. Tseng[1,2(✉)], and Po-Hsin Huang[1]

[1] Product Design and Development Laboratory,
Department of Industrial Design, College of Management,
Chang Gung University, Taoyuan, Taiwan, ROC
ktseng@pddlab.org
[2] Healthy Aging Research Centre, Chang Gung University,
Taoyuan, Taiwan, ROC

**Abstract.** This study aimed to analyze the design of cervical collar devices for elderly patients with central cord syndrome during physical therapy-based rehabilitation and to summarize related patient needs. To design a cervical collar device that met patient needs, a physician and patients who had worn a cervical collar for more than three months were both interviewed to collect opinions from a professional perspective and from user experience. A qualitative analysis of the content of the interview was then conducted to characterize an optimal cervical collar device for elderly patients with central cord syndrome during rehabilitation. The analytical results showed that cervical collar device development should focus on comfort and fixity.

**Keywords:** Central cord syndrome · Cervical collar · Content analysis · Participative design · Rehabilitation

## 1 Introduction

Central cord syndrome (CCS) is the most common traumatic phenomenon. A study by Brodell et al. (2015) found that patient age and complications affected patient mortality. There are many causes for CCS. A study by Aito et al. (2007) found that the causes of injury included traffic accidents (57 %), falling (36 %), and sports (7 %). Generally, treatments for CCS include both surgical and non-surgical treatments, and a cervical collar is required for neck fixation in either case. Burl et al. (1992) tested the walking balance of healthy young women wearing a protective cervical collar, and the results showed that a cervical collar did not affect the walking balance of healthy young woman. However, according to a study by Waters et al. (1994), most patients with CCS need an assisting device to help them walk safely, and training for walking and gait should be provided by a physical therapist during the rehabilitation of CCS patients to improve their torso balance and stability (Michelle 2015). A study by Miller et al., (2013) found that, when a test subject wore a rigid cervical collar and performed

© Springer International Publishing Switzerland 2016
M. Antona and C. Stephanidis (Eds.): UAHCI 2016, Part III, LNCS 9739, pp. 425–435, 2016.
DOI: 10.1007/978-3-319-40238-3_41

activities such as putting on socks, putting on shoes, reading, eating, walking upstairs, and walking downstairs, the restriction to the neck due to a rigid collar was similar to that due to a soft collar. Theoretically, the restriction of neck motion by a rigid cervical collar should be greater than that of a soft cervical collar, but the results of their study showed a similar restriction for both the rigid collar and the soft collar. In 2013, Evans et al. (2013) compared the fixity of elongated flexion, lateral bending and rotation for five types of cervical collars, including the Aspen®, Philadelphia®, Vista®, Miami J®, and new Miami J® collars, and their experimental data showed that the Vista® collar was superior to the other collars in various tests. In that study, researchers measured the range of neck motion when a test subject was wearing a cervical collar. They found that, in lateral bending, the neck fixity of the Vista® cervical collar was not superior. According to a study by Karason et al. (2014) the Miami J® collar is appropriate for emergency and long-term treatment, while the Vista® is appropriate for long-term treatment. Thus, when a CCS patient needs to wear a cervical collar while simultaneously performing rehabilitation activities, the utility of commercially available collar devices is questionable. If a collar device cannot provide sufficient utility, it may cause patients to be inconvenienced or to have a bad experience.

Thus, the present study aimed to develop a collar device that is suitable for elderly patients with CCS during rehabilitation and that assists with rehabilitation and slowly trains the basic functions of the neck. To assess whether a prototype collar device can meet the needs of elderly patients with CCS during rehabilitation, this study used a semi-structured questionnaire to collect the professional opinion of a physician and the opinions of experienced users who had been wearing the cervical collar device for more than three months. Language analysis was conducted for the obtained interview contents to identify the most-desired features of the cervical collar. This study is divided into four sections. The first section is the research background and motivation, the second section is the design of the cervical collar, the third section is the content analysis of the interview and discussion, and the last section is the conclusion.

## 2   Design of the Cervical Collar Device

In this study, patient needs and questions about the cervical collar device were first collected from patients using interviews. A prototype of the cervical collar was then designed based on user needs in concert with a literature review and participative design. The professional opinion of a physician and the opinions of experienced users were integrated into the prototype design of the cervical collar, which was in line with the biomechanical principles of a cervical brace. The supporting sites were on the upper chest to the jaw and occipital. The supports at these sites enhanced the stability of the cervical collar. The cervical collar must remain at the center of the head while avoiding concentrated pressure on the skin at any of the contacting sites; the contact pressure should be evenly distributed. In a study by Miller et al. (2010a, b), a Vista® collar that allowed six adjustable heights with 1.5-cm increments was used, and it was found that the height of the collar device was related to its fixity for the neck. The test for the Vista® collar was to adjust the height using the upper limb knob on the front panel of the collar so that it could fit users of different heights. The height-adjustment function was not available with the Miami J® collar, which instead offered different sizes to fit users with different neck heights and sizes. In the future, our work will attempt to implement a design with different heights based on the characteristics of the rack structure and the original hexagonal mesh at different densities. The changes in height will result in different levels of fixity for users in different situations, recapitulating the difference between the Vista® collar and the Miami J® collar. A hexagonal mesh was used because of its good mechanical and geometrical properties, as a hexagonal structure provides a high strength-to-weight ratio (Zhang et al. 2015). CCS may result in upper-limb movement being more difficult than lower-limb movement (McKinley et al. 2007). Therefore, the prototype cervical collar in this study was designed to be fixed from the front to the rear with the assistance of another person. The frame of the prototype collar body is constructed of ABS (acrylonitrile butadiene styrene). An isometric view of the overall appearance of the prototype design is shown in Fig. 1. The rear panel of the prototype collar is shown in Fig. 2. The entire collar device was then assembled with its different parts and structures. The main parts and structures are listed with their functions in Table 1.

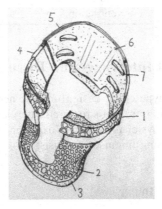

**Fig. 1.** Isometric view of the overall appearance of the prototype collar design

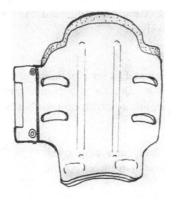

**Fig. 2.** The rear panel of the prototype collar

**Table 1.** Nomenclature and functions of different parts of the collar device

| No. | Name | Description |
|-----|------|-------------|
| 1 | Main part of the front panel | Constructed of hexagonal mesh and can be assembled with or without the supporting part of the front panel (2). |
| 2 | Supporting part of the front panel | Mainly constructed of hexagonal mesh and can be removed from the main part of the front panel (1). |
| 3 | Cushions | Used at pressure-bearing sites in the jaw, the rear of the neck, and the thoracic areas to avoid direct skin contact with the hard material of the main part. |
| 4 | Buckle | Allows fixation of the device. |
| 5 | Main part of the rear panel | Provides protection and fixation for the back of the neck. |
| 6 | Booster strip of the rear panel | Located on both sides of the spine to prevent patient lean-back. |
| 7 | Air hole | For ventilation. |

## 3  Content Analysis of Interviews and Discussion

To assess whether the prototype collar design met the needs of elderly patients with CCS during their rehabilitation, a semi-structured interview was conducted with one professional rehabilitation physician and two experienced patients. The interview content was then analyzed using linguistic analysis.

### 3.1  Physician and Patient Interviews

The interview questions were pre-designed. The physician responded according to his expertise, while the patients answered the questions based on their experience using the cervical collar device. Information about the interviewees is shown in Table 2. The researchers recorded each interview verbatim, and the interview content was then analyzed using linguistic analysis.

(1) Physician respondent

The interviewed physician was Doctor Xu Jialin, of the Department of Rehabilitation, Li Shin Hospital, Taiwan. Dr. Xu is a clinical physician with experience in elderly rehabilitation and in applied research on prostheses and assistive devices.

(2) Patient respondents

The interviewed patients had been diagnosed with CCS and had experienced wearing a collar device for more than three months.

**Table 2.** Information about the interview respondents

| Physician | | |
|---|---|---|
| *Name* | *Expertise* | *Experience* |
| Xu Jialin | General rehabilitation, elderly rehabilitation, application of prostheses and other assistive devices | Department of Rehabilitation, Li Shin Hospital |
| **Patients** | | |
| *Pseudonym* | *Situation* | *Collar device* | *Duration of collar use* |
| Chen Yihan | Long-term occupational upward-looking posture for fruit harvesting, which led to compression on the nerves that caused hand weakness; underwent surgery | Vista® | Approximately six months |
| Li Xincheng | Long-term occupational posture led to compression on the nerves, causing hand numbness and inflexibility; underwent surgery. | Vista® | Approximately six months |

(3)  Interview tools

Information for this study was collected in the context of formal interviews. The physician interview consisted of three aspects. The first aspect included questions related to the rehabilitation of elderly patients with CCS; the second aspect included questions related to elderly patients with CCS and their use of an existing collar; and the third aspect included questions related to professional ideas and suggestions for the prototype collar design described in this study. The patient interviews also consisted of three aspects. The first aspect included questions related to problems that were encountered during rehabilitation when wearing the collar; the second aspect included questions related to comments about the collar that was currently being worn; and the third aspect included questions related to patient opinions and suggestions for the prototype collar design described in this study. Consent to photograph and to record audio (and video if needed) during the interview was obtained from the respondents in advance.

(4)  Interview content organization and analysis

In this study, the content analysis method was used for evaluation. In this method, content may be obtained from mail, diaries, newspapers, novels, articles, and symbols. Content analysis then seeks to convert the original contents of a file into data. In this study, the recorded audio file of the interview was first converted into a verbatim manuscript, which was then encoded for analysis.

The implementation procedures in this study were as follows: (a) the recorded audio file of the interview was converted into a verbatim manuscript; (b) the text in the manuscript was classified according to the part of speech of each word, as judged by the meaning of each phrase, and the part-of-speech classification included an analysis of word frequency; (c) for all content, numbers, punctuations, and meaningless words were eliminated, while the frequencies of the remaining verbs, nouns and adjectives were calculated, and similar categories were combined to form major categories based on the meaning of the phrases; and (d) in the major categories, the frequency of the text was used to infer the relative importance of each corresponding phrase in the physician and patient interviews, and the exact meaning of each expression was extracted.

Content analysis of the patient interviews allowed us to extract patient impressions of the current commercial products and their expectations for the prototype collar device. Similarly, content analysis of the physician interview allowed us to extract his professional opinions and the key features of the prototype collar design in this study. The suggestions of the physician provided a more specific direction for the prototype collar design and its future application.

## 3.2     Results of the Interview Analyses

### 3.2.1     Content Analysis of the Patient Interview

In the patient interview content analysis, the phrase density was 1.12. According to the part-of-speech classification published by the Ministry of Education, the word properties, part of speech, frequency and percentage were sorted (Table 3).

The content analysis results for the patient interviews revealed 34 nouns, 16 adjectives, and 37 verbs. The statistical analysis of the part-of-speech frequency was manually performed. During the statistical process, the error was verbatim-checked against the original manuscript. Finally, 13 phrases that were highly related to the topic of this study

**Table 3.** Content analysis of the patient interviews: parts of speech

| Notional word | | Part of speech | Frequency | Percentage |
|---|---|---|---|---|
| | | Noun | 34 | 23 |
| | | Adjective | 16 | 11 |
| | | Verb | 37 | 25 |
| | | Adverb | 10 | 7 |
| | | Pronoun | 9 | 6 |
| | | Quantifier | 2 | 1 |
| Functional word | Relative | Preposition | 1 | 1 |
| | | Conjunction | 6 | 4 |
| | Modal particle | Interjection | 1 | 1 |
| Punctuation | | , | 23 | 16 |
| Number | | Roman numeral | 8 | 5 |

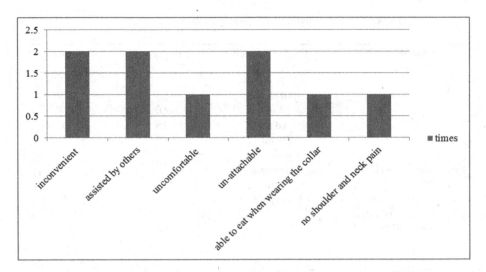

**Fig. 3.** Results of the content analysis for the patient interview

were selected from the total patient interview content and classified into seven primary categories for frequency analysis. The analytical results are shown in Fig. 3.

The frequently encountered phrases "inconvenient" (2 times), "uncomfortable" (1 time), and "un-attachable" (2 times) were classified as sensations of patients when using the collar and accounted for 71.4 % of the phrases. Meanwhile, "assisted by others" (1 time), "able to eat when wearing the collar" (1 time), and "shoulder and neck pain" (1 time) were classified as needs of the patients while using the collar and accounted for 28.6 % of the phrases. Because the sensations of patients when using the collar accounted for 71.4 % of the phrases, this result implies that sensations are of most concern to the patients, followed by the needs of patients in using the collar device, which accounted for 28.6 % of the phrases.

### 3.2.2   Content Analysis of the Physician Interview

In the content analysis of the physician interview, the phrase density was 0.62. According to the part-of-speech classification published by the Ministry of Education, the word properties, parts of speech, frequency and percentage were sorted (Table 4).

The content analysis results for the physician interview showed 84 nouns, 64 adjectives, and 69 verbs. The statistical analysis of the part-of-speech frequency was manually performed. During the statistical process, the error was verbatim-checked against the original manuscript. Finally, 371 phrases that were highly related to the topic of this study were selected from the total content of the physician interview, and they were classified into 15 primary categories for frequency analysis. The analytical results are shown in Fig. 4.

The frequent phrases "patients with CCS" (2 times) and "elderly" (3 times) were classified as the objects of collar usage and accounted for 22.7 % of the phrases; "assisted by others" (3 times), "rehabilitation" (2 times), "comfort" (7 times) and "fixity"

**Table 4.** Content analysis of the physician interview: parts of speech

| Notional word | | Part of speech | Frequency | Percentage |
|---|---|---|---|---|
| | | Noun | 84 | 23 |
| | | Adjective | 64 | 17 |
| | | Verb | 69 | 19 |
| | | Adverb | 15 | 4 |
| | | Pronoun | 15 | 4 |
| | | Quantifier | 7 | 2 |
| Functional word | Relative | Preposition | 4 | 1 |
| | | Conjunction | 19 | 5 |
| | Modal particle | Interjection | 9 | 2 |
| Punctuation | | , | 66 | 18 |
| | | . | 9 | 2 |
| Number | | Roman numeral | 8 | 2 |
| Unclassifiable | | English/Oral argument | 2 | 1 |

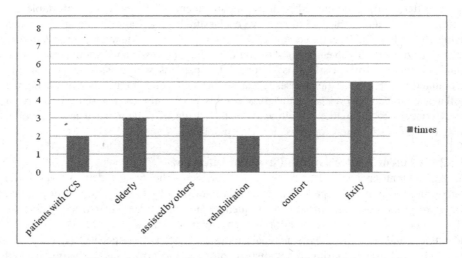

**Fig. 4.** Phrase frequencies after content analysis of the physician interview

(5 times) were classified as patient needs when using a collar and accounted for 77.3 % of the phrases. As the needs of the patient during collar use accounted for 77.3 % of the total phrases, this is the topic of greatest concern for the physician.

## 3.3  Discussion

This study, we attempted to develop a prototype collar for elderly patients with CCS during their rehabilitation. Both a professional physician and actual collar users were interviewed. The collar design was based on user needs and was then modified and improved according to the opinions of the physician as a result of the follow-up interview. The results of the physician interview and the patient interviews were discussed. First, content analysis of the patient interviews showed that the interview contents included (1) patient sensations when using the collar and (2) the needs of patients with respect to the collar. The two patients were interviewed indoors during the summer. The patients were both wearing Vista® collars, and their feelings about the collars were mainly that they were hot and oppressive with the chest support, thereby causing discomfort and inconvenience during some activities. Assistance of others was often needed. The collar needs to be taken off for cleaning after long-term use, and it requires occasional adjustment to ensure comfort. Thus, the Velcro fixing strap must be repeatedly pulled on and off; after time, wear may render the strap un-attachable. Next, content analysis was performed for the physician interview. The results of the analysis included (1) the objects of collar usage and (2) the needs of the patients with respect to the collar. For the objects of collar usage, it was clear that the collar designed in the present study is for "patients with CCS" and "elderly" users. The common characteristic of these two groups is that they are unable to flexibly operate their hands. Therefore, the important parts of the collar must be designed to be large and easily operated. The patients' needs with respect to collar use included the "assistance of others", "rehabilitation", "comfort", and "fixity". As the users are not able to flexibly operate their hands, the assistance of others is typically needed to put on the collar. If the important parts of the collar are large and easy to operate, people can easily explain their use to patients at the time of operation, thus reducing difficulties in communication. As the collar is designed for use during patient rehabilitation activities, the physician recommended that the collar should fit the neck as perfectly as possible and that a multi-piece collar will work better. For optimal comfort and fixity, the contact sites of the collar at the jaw, sternum, and occipital regions must be considered. The collar should be fixed at the unmovable sites; the comfort of the collar is mainly judged by whether a patient experiences pain when wearing the collar. Finally, the physician made positive comments about the conceptual collar design proposed by the investigators, but he also reminded the researchers to pay attention to the materials used. Certain materials can be considered to increase the performance of the collar.

In summary, the hexagonal structure concept in the present study is promising. The collar design is expected to combine comfort and fixity, especially for the supporting sites where pressure is applied. In future improvements of the collar, this concept will be further discussed.

# 4 Conclusion

In this study, a cervical collar device was designed for elderly patients with CCS during physical therapy-based rehabilitation. First, the respective literature relating to collar devices, elderly patient rehabilitation and CCS were reviewed and collected. Based on interviews with actual patients, user needs and usability issues related to cervical collar devices were better understood. Content analysis was performed on the interview content as a reference for the design of the conceptual prototype collar. In this study, in addition to considerations from the user perspective, a professional physician was also interviewed to further discuss potential collar problems from a professional perspective. Thus, the design of the prototype collar can better meet the needs of elderly patients with CCS during rehabilitation, providing a safer and more comfortable user experience. In the future, this study will enhance the collar design with a hexagonal mesh structure to better suit elderly patients.

**Acknowledgements.** This work was supported in part by the Ministry of Science and Technology, Taiwan, ROC under Contract MOST 103-2628-H-182-001-MY2, and by the Healthy Aging Research Centre, Chang Gung University (fund no. EMRPD1F0301, CMRPD1B0331, and CMRPD1B0332). The funders had no role in study design, data collection and analysis, decision to publish, or preparation of the manuscript.

# References

Brodell, D.W., Jain, A., Elfar, J.C., Mesfin, A.: National trends in the management of central cord syndrome: an analysis of 16,134 patients. Spine J. **15**(3), 435–442 (2015)

Aito, S., D'andrea, M., Werhagen, L., Farsetti, L., Cappelli, S., Bandini, B., Di Donna, D.: Neurological and functional outcome in traumatic central cord syndrome. Spinal Cord **45**(4), 292–297 (2007)

Burl, M.M., Williams, J.G., Nayak, U.S.: Effects of cervical collars on standing balance. Arch. Phys. Med. Rehabil. **73**(12), 1181–1185 (1992)

Waters, R.L., Adkins, R.H., Yakura, J.S., Sie, I.: Motor and sensory recovery following incomplete tetraplegia. Arch. Phys. Med. Rehabil. **75**(3), 306–311 (1994)

Michelle, J.A.: Re: Central Cord Syndrome Treatment & Management, 12 February 2015. http://emedicine.medscape.com/article/321907-treatment. (Retrieved)

Miller, C.P., Bible, J.E., Jegede, K.A., Whang, P.G., Grauer, J.N.: Soft and rigid collars provide similar restriction in cervical range of motion during fifteen activities of daily living. Spine **35**(13), 1271-1278 (2010a)

Evans, N.R., Hooper, G., Edwards, R., Whatling, G., Sparkes, V., Holt, C., Ahuja, S.: A 3D motion analysis study comparing the effectiveness of cervical spine orthoses at restricting spinal motion through physiological ranges. Eur. Spine J. **22**(1), 10–15 (2013)

Karason, S., Reynisson, K., Sigvaldason, K., Sigurdsson, G.H.: Evaluation of clinical efficacy and safety of cervical trauma collars: differences in immobilization, effect on jugular venous pressure and patient comfort. Scand. J. Trauma, Resuscitation Emerg. Med. **22**(1), 37 (2014)

Howard-Wilsher, S., Irvine, L., Fan, H., Shakespeare, T., Suhrcke, M., Horton, S., Song, F.: Systematic overview of economic evaluations of health-related rehabilitation. Disabil. Health J. **9**(1), 11–25 (2016)

Zhang, X., Xia, Y., Wang, J., Yang, Z., Tu, C., Wang, W.: Medial axis tree—an internal supporting structure for 3D printing. Comput. Aided Geom. Des. **35**, 149–162 (2015)

Miller, C.P., Bible, J.E., Jegede, K.A., Whang, P.G., Grauer, J.N.: The effect of rigid cervical collar height on full, active, and functional range of motion during fifteen activities of daily living. Spine **35**(26), E1546-E1552 (2010b)

McKinley, W., Santos, K., Meade, M., Brooke, K.: Incidence and outcomes of spinal cord injury clinical syndromes. J. Spinal Cord Med. **30**(3), 215 (2007)

# Interactive Searching Interface
# for Job Matching of Elderly Workers

Hiroshi Yamada[1(✉)], Kaoru Shinkawa[2], Atsushi Hiyama[1],
Masato Yamaguchi[3], Masatomo Kobayashi[2], and Michitaka Hirose[1]

[1] The University of Tokyo, 7-3-1 Hongo, Bunkyo, Tokyo 113–8656, Japan
{h_yamada, atsushi, hirose}@cyber.t.u-tokyo.ac.jp
[2] IBM Research - Tokyo, 19-21 Hakozaki, Nihonbashi, Chuo,
Tokyo 103–8510, Japan
{kaoruma, mstm}@jp.ibm.com
[3] Circulation Co., Ltd., 2-2-1 Marunouchi, Chiyoda, Tokyo 100–0005, Japan
yamaguchi@circu.co.jp

**Abstract.** In the aging Japanese society, most elderly people still have enough
energy to work and have the potential to become essential labor forces. A job
matching method that can allocate their unique abilities is required. However,
the current job matching relies on each recruiter's tacit knowledge, and the
recruiter assigns only specific candidates to work profiles. In this paper, we
propose an interactive job matching system that can reflect the recruiter's tacit
knowledge and help search for diverse elderly workers for each work profile.
The results indicate that interactions of the proposed system can improve the
matching diversity by retrieving recruiters' tacit knowledge. When there is a
work profile in which it is difficult to extract appropriate keywords, our interactions become most effective.

**Keywords:** Job matching · Elderly workers · Resume · Interactive information
retrieval

## 1 Introduction

Japanese society is rapidly aging. It is estimated that the percentage of Japanese people
over the age of 65 will be 40.5 % in 2055 [1]. According to research on desired
retirement age, about 30 % of respondents indicated that they want to continue working
as long as possible [2]. In addition, if 40 % of the unemployed elderly Japanese
workers can work with average work productivity, the resultant positive economic
effect for Japanese society is calculated to reach about 22.6 trillion Japanese yen.
Therefore, promoting elderly people working is important in the aging society.

In order to do this, there are basically two current issues. One issue is that the
current job matching relies on the recruiter's tacit knowledge. Elderly people have
experiences and knowledge from their earlier lives that young people do not have.
Because of these experiences and knowledge, their skills are much more varied. In
addition, the skills required are different for each work profile. Therefore, knowledge
about each worker's skill and the required skills for each work profile are important.

© Springer International Publishing Switzerland 2016
M. Antona and C. Stephanidis (Eds.): UAHCI 2016, Part III, LNCS 9739, pp. 436–445, 2016.
DOI: 10.1007/978-3-319-40238-3_42

However, this knowledge is the tacit knowledge of recruiters, and it cannot be transmitted to others easily.

The second issue is that only specific candidates are assigned to each work profile. The number of candidates that one recruiter can remember is limited, and this decreases work opportunities for elderly people. Thus, a job matching system that can search all candidates and match diverse candidates is required.

In this paper, we focus on these two problems and propose an efficient interactive job matching system that can retrieve recruiter's tacit knowledge and match diverse candidates by the recruiter's interaction with the system. Recruiters change the weights of skills for each work profile and search for appropriate elderly workers interactively.

## 2   Related Work

### 2.1   Job Matching by Computer

**Natural Language Processing.** Yi et al. matched resumes and work profiles by using the structured relevance model. They looked into the accuracy of correct candidates being matched among the top 1,000 estimated candidates for each work profile and found that it was improved by 14 %. [3]. However, when they examined the accuracy among the top five candidates, it became less than 20 %. Therefore, in terms of matching the varied skills of elderly people, the matching accuracy was insufficient. Lavrenko et al. estimated similarities of documents with no training data [4]. However, this method is difficult to implement as work profiles and resumes are relatively short texts and typically contain words specific to a particular industry. Miura et al. estimated the skills of seniors through matching elderly people's resumes and job requests using the frequency of words [5, 6]. Our own research has led us to conclude that this method is effective. However, if only the frequency of words is implemented, matching diverse candidates is difficult, as the context of sentences in a resume cannot be utilized.

**Implementation of Attribute Information.** Kakuda et al. attached tags for working lists and candidate lists and conducted a simulation and evaluation to determine the cost of the job matching [7]. Lavrenko et al. estimated the attribute information of a candidate by using the ones of other candidates [8]. Attribute information is implemented as recruiter's tacit knowledge in the current job matching. In order to utilize the job matching system in business, this tacit knowledge should be integrated into the system.

### 2.2   Job Matching with the Intervention of Humans

**Comparison of Job Matching Between Computers and Humans.** Hoffman et al. verified that the candidates matched by a computer had worked longer than the ones matched by a recruiter [9], and Kuncel et al. verified that a computer could match candidates 25 % better than a recruiter [10]. However, if the job matching is conducted only by computers, candidates would definitely find ways to make their resumes effective for defined algorithms, and then candidates would not be matched accurately [11].

**Interactive Search with Collaboration of Computers and Humans.** Singh et al. created a system called PROSPECT in which resumes and job requests are automatically matched and recruiters can conduct filtering interactions by adding search options [12]. However, interactions are limited just to adding or deleting keywords that have been retrieved from resumes. Therefore, it is difficult to deal with the various types of resumes that have different content depending on the business. Reflecting the importance of detailed information in resumes would be required for the interactions.

In job matching, humans are considered effective for specifying what skills are needed for each work profile [11] while computers are better at classifying all candidates in a short time. In order to utilize the strong points of both computers and humans, using computers for paring down candidates and humans for deciding final candidates will be important.

### 2.3    Knowledge from Related Works

The works discussed above are effective for analyzing the skills of candidates and conducting job matching between people and jobs. We also follow previous researches on the point of analyzing resumes and attaching tags to people and jobs. However, as yet there has been no research that reflects the recruiter's tacit knowledge about important skills for work profiles. Our work differs from the related works in that we actually utilize a prototype in a recruitment scenario and implement the recruiter's tacit knowledge for job matching by interactions with our proposed system. In this research, we expand upon our past job matching method [13] and attempt to match diverse candidates for each work profile.

## 3    Proposed System

### 3.1    Methodology

The methodology of the proposed system is shown in Fig. 1. Our system is currently being used by recruiters at Circulation Co., Ltd. The system usage is as follows:

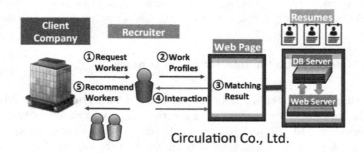

**Fig. 1.** System methodology

(1) The recruit information is sent from the client company.
(2) Recruiters send work profiles to our system.
(3) Candidates who are matched to work profiles are shown on our Web page.
(4) On the basis of the matching results, recruiters interact with the system and decide the candidates who ultimately match the work profiles.
(5) Recruiters introduce the matched candidates to the client company.

For the evaluation of our system, the resumes of about 2,500 elderly candidates are used.

## 3.2    Implementation

The proposed system is a Web application based on HTML5 and JavaScript. This system accesses the search engine and the database through AJAX communications. It enables users to search candidates' resumes using a job description written in natural language. The system extracts keywords from the job description text by tokenizing sentences and filtering noun words on the basis of the morphological analysis results. Dictionaries and stop words are defined on the basis of feedback from users. Keyword scores are calculated from the average of term scores included in the top 100 documents matched by the query. Term scores are returned from Solr/Lucene using the BM25 similarity algorithm [14] and calculated by the following Eq. (1). BM25 scoring utilizes both term frequency and document length normalization.

$$Score(D, Q) = \sum_{i=1}^{n} IDF(q_i) \cdot \left( \frac{f(q_i, D) \cdot (k_1 + 1)}{f(q_i, D) + k_1 \cdot \left( 1 - b + b \cdot \frac{|D|}{avgdl} \right)} \right) \qquad (1)$$

The Eq. (1) shows the BM25 score of a document $D$, for a given query $Q$ containing keywords. $q_1, \ldots, q_n$. $(q_i, D)$ is $q_i$'s term frequency in the document $D$, $|D|$ is the length of the document $D$ in words, and $avgdl$ is the average document length in the text collection. $k_1$ and $b$ are free parameters, and we used Lucene's default value $k_1 = 1.2$, $b = 0.75$ for this experiment. $IDF(q_i)$ is the inverse document frequency weight of the query term computed by

$$IDF(q_i) = \log \frac{1 + N - n(q_i) + 0.5}{n(q_i) + 0.5} \qquad (2)$$

The similarity of the resume to the work profile, $M$, is calculated as the sum of the score of the extracted top 10 keywords. The similarity $M$ is normalized to make the maximum score be 10. All matched candidates are plotted in a scatter diagram and descriptions of the top 10 candidates are listed in the application.

The top 10 keywords are listed in the application with a slider bar. Users can delete, add, and change the weights of the keywords to adjust the query. On the basis of user modified keyword settings, the system will generate a Solr query and execute it. The scatter diagram and list of top 10 candidates are dynamically updated and users can interactively change the keyword weights to find appropriate candidates. These scores are plotted on the y-axis of the scatter diagram.

### 3.3  Three-Axis Scoring Algorithm

In addition to the full-text search, we introduced another scoring algorithm to search resumes using three axes: Contents, Category, and Position. According to recruiters, these three axes comprise the most frequently considered information during job matching. Figure 2 shows how to utilize selected tags.

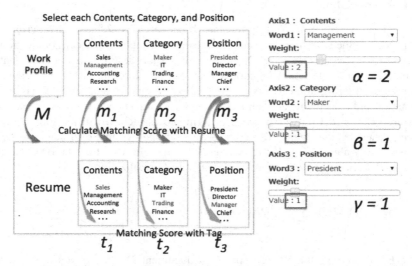

**Fig. 2.** Selection of three-axis values and weights (Left: three-axis values, Right: weights)

As shown in the left side of Fig. 2, recruiters choose Contents, Category, and Position tags that are appropriate for the work profile. In the case of the left side of Fig. 2, Management is chosen as Contents, Maker is chosen as Category, and President is chosen as Position. The matched scores of these chosen tags with the resumes are calculated by Eq. (1), and each score is defined as $m_1$, $m_2$, and $m_3$. The weights of the chosen tags are defined as $\alpha$, $\beta$ and $\gamma$ In the case of the right side of Fig. 2, Contents weight $\alpha = 2$, Category weight $\beta = 1$, and Position weight $\gamma = 1$. Each resume also has three-axis tags. The matching scores between the chosen tags and the resume's tags are defined as $t_1$, $t_2$, and $t_3$. These variables ($t_1$, $t_2$, $t_3$) reflect recruiters' opinions for the matching score. Calculation methods of $t_1$ (Contents), $t_2$ (Category), and $t_3$ (Position) are as follows.

– $t_1$ (Contents)
  Contents code (5- or 6-digit number) is divided into three parts (e.g., 20102 −> $a = 2$, $b = 01$, $c = 02$). If $a$ of the selected tag and that of the resume's tag are

the same, then $a_{score} = 1$, otherwise, $a_{score} = 0$. Similarly, if both $b$s are the same, then $b_{score} = 6$, otherwise, $b_{score} = 0$. Similarly, if both $c$s are the same, then $c_{score} = 3$, otherwise, $c_{score} = 0$. Variable $t_1$ is defined as $t_1 = a_{score} + b_{score} + c_{score}$. By this definition, $t_1$ varies in four kinds of numbers: 10 ($t_{11}$), 7($t_{12}$), 1($t_{13}$), and 0($t_{14}$).

- $t_2$ (Category)
  Category code (4-digit number) is divided into two parts (e.g., 1203 $\rightarrow a = 12$, $b = 03$). If $a$ of the selected tag and that of the resume's tag are the same, then $a_{score} = 7$, otherwise, $a_{score} = 0$. Similarly, if both $b$s are the same, then $b_{score} = 3$, otherwise, $b_{score} = 0$. Variable $t_2$ is defined as $t_2 = a_{score} + b_{score}$. By this definition, $t_2$ varies in three kinds of numbers: 10($t_{21}$), 7($t_{22}$), and 0($t_{23}$).

- $t_3$ (Position)
  Positions are divided into four rank numbers ($rank = 1, 2, 3, $ and 4). If the rank number of the chosen tag, $rank_{ch}$, is bigger than that of resume, $rank_{re}$, then $t_3 = 10$. In other cases, $t_3$ is defined as $t_3 = 10 - 3 \times (rank_{re} - rank_{ch})$. By this definition, $t_3$ varies in five kinds of numbers; 10($t_{31}$), 7($t_{32}$), 4($t_{33}$), 1($t_{34}$), and 0($t_{35}$).

## 3.4 Interaction and Visualization

In order to retrieve the recruiter's tacit knowledge, three kinds of interactions can be conducted. The first interaction is deleting the listed candidates. If the recruiter deletes one of the listed candidates, the next matched candidate on the list is shown. The second interaction is adding, deleting, and weighing keywords. The recruiter can freely add, delete, and weigh the extracted top 10 keywords. The third interaction is selecting and weighing three-axis tags. As stated in Sect. 3.3, the recruiter selects and weighs tags that are appropriate for the work profile.

In order to understand the matching results and identify the diverse candidates effectively, results are shown in a 2D graph. X and Y-axes are:

X-axis: $\sqrt{(\alpha p_1)^2 + (\beta p_2)^2 + (\gamma p_3)^2}$

Y-axis: $M$

Variables $p_1$, $p_2$, and $p_3$ are defined by using $m_i$ and $t_i$ ($i = 1, 2, $ and $3$), which are defined in Sect. 3.3. This definition is adopted for the visual discrimination of the results. Variables $p_1$, $p_2$, and $p_3$ are calculated in the following equations:

$$\begin{cases} p_i = t_{ij} & (if\ t_i = t_{ij}, j = 1) \\ p_i = t_{ij} + m_i \times (t_{i(j-1)} - t_{ij})/10 & (if\ t_i = t_{ij}, j \geq 2) \end{cases} \quad (3)$$
$$1 \leq i \leq 3,\ 1 \leq j \leq 5,\ i \in N,\ j \in N$$

By using these variables $p1$, $p2$, and $p3$ and weight variables $\alpha$, $\beta$, and $\gamma$, the X-axis shows the score from the interactions by the recruiter and the Y-axis shows the similarity of the resume to the work profile $M$. Both axis numbers are normalized so that the maximum becomes 10.

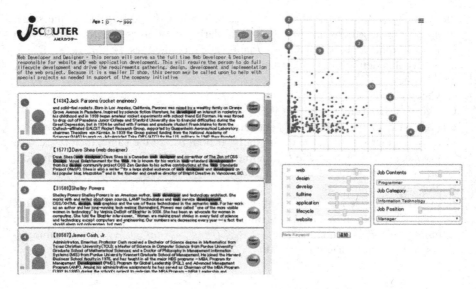

**Fig. 3.** System visualization after interactions

Figure 3 shows a 2D graph visualization after interactions. The data shown in the figure is dummy personal data fetched from Wikipedia. Each dot represents a candidate whose resume is registered in our system. When a mouse cursor hovers over a dot, detailed information of the candidate is displayed. When a dot is clicked, the detailed resume of the candidate is shown. A red dot indicates that the distance from the origin of coordinates is the farthest, while the distance of blue ones is second to tenth and gray ones are below the tenth. When the distance of a dot from the origin of coordinates is farther, that candidate is considered well matched. In Fig. 2, the three dots labeled 1, 4, and 7 are candidates whose matching scores (Y-axis) are low but whose Contents, Category, and Position (X-axis) scores are high. These candidates may not be matched before interactions but may be well matched from the recruiter's point of view. In this way, the matching results that reflect the recruiter's tacit knowledge about candidates and work profiles are visualized after interactions.

# 4   Evaluation

In order to collect data for the analysis, we need this system to be used in an actual business. The initial prototype evaluation was conducted with the director of Circulation Co., Ltd., which is a recruiting agency in Japan. We received direct feedback on the system including feature requests for utilization in real projects. The system was developed with an agile development approach: namely, we obtain feedback, develop, test, and deploy iteratively so that all feedback can be reviewed and collected in a short amount of time.

After the initial experiment and improvements based on feedback from the director, the system was deployed for an experiment with real projects. About 2,500 elderly candidates' resumes were registered in our system and two recruiters were assigned to use this system with real work profiles. The way of searching for candidates is to query with full-text first, and if no candidate is found, the recruiters will conduct the interactions discussed in Sect. 3.4 until they find the appropriate candidates. Selected candidates considered to be well-matched workers are marked as "Best matched" or "Probably matched". The number of these candidates is used as the criteria for evaluating the efficiency of the interactions with the system.

# 5    Results and Discussion

## 5.1    Interaction Effect

The evaluation results were collected after the first week of the experiment. The recruiters queried 12 real work profiles and selected 38 candidates in total. Figure 4 shows the number of candidates found before and after interaction. The system returns a summary of the top 10 candidates for each result. Therefore, selected candidates who were below the tenth position in the initial query are regarded as being unfound. These unfound candidates came into the selection scope because of interactions. For candidates marked as "Best matched", 4 out of 10 candidates were newly found by interactions. For candidates marked as "Probably matched", 8 out of 28 candidates were newly found by interactions. The reason for this is as follows. The interactions of our proposed system rely on the knowledge of the user. In order to conduct interactions, the user is required to estimate the skills of each work profile. Therefore, recruiters who have knowledge about the job matching can get positive results by doing interactions. This suggests that our interface can retrieve the recruiter's tacit knowledge for job matching and successfully match diverse candidates.

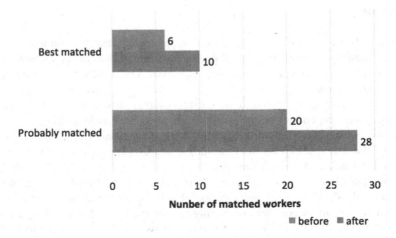

**Fig. 4.** Number of matched candidates before and after interactions (Color figure online)

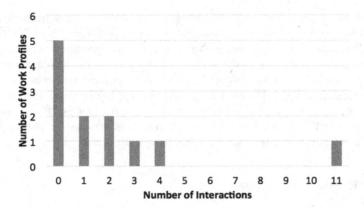

**Fig. 5.** Number of interactions for each work profile

## 5.2   Number of Interactions

Figure 5 shows the number of interactions for each work profile. The user conducted interactions until appropriate candidates were found. In Fig. 5, five out of 12 work profiles had no interactions. This means that appropriate candidates were found in the first query execution. One reason for this is that the work profile query contained a proper noun, namely, a specific company name. Since there was only one resume that contained this specific word, no additional interaction was required. The other reason is that the extracted top 10 keywords were appropriate and the system was able to return the expected result in the initial query. In this case, all keywords had the same weight. In Fig. 5, there is a work profile for which 11 interactions were conducted. Among those interactions, ten of the 11 were about deleting candidates from the list. This suggests that the extracted top 10 keywords were not appropriate.

## 6   Conclusion

In this research, we created an interactive job matching system that can match diverse elderly candidates and work profiles. We proposed three kinds of interactions for the list of candidates, extracted keywords, and three axes. The results demonstrate that the recruiters' tacit knowledge was effectively retrieved and diverse candidates were matched by conducting the interactions. The results also show that the effectiveness of our system varies depending on the work profile and that it is less effective for work profiles that contain specific words such as company names. Our future work is as follows. (1) Further research on work profiles is needed. The number of work profiles should be increased and the relationships between the similarity of each work profile and the number of candidates marked as "Best matched" or "Probably matched" need to be analyzed. (2) Personality information should be included in our system. The impression the recruiters get after conducting job interviews with the candidates needs to be weighed and retrieved. The axes for the impressions should be described similar to three axes (Contents, Category, and Position) we conducted in this experiment.

**Acknowledgements.** This material is based on work funded by S-innovation (Strategic Promotion of Innovative Research and Development) under Industry Academia Collaborative R&D programs administered by the Japan Science and Technology Agency (JST). We are also grateful to Circulation Co., Ltd. for their great help.

# References

1. Kaneko, R., Ishikawa, A., Ishii, F., Sasai, T., Iwasawa, M., Mita, F., Moriizumi, R.: Population projections for Japan: 2006–2055 outline of results, methods, and assumptions. Jpn. J. Popul. **6**, 76–114 (2008)
2. Cabinet Office, Government of Japan: Awareness survey about the elderly people's participation motivation to a community (2013). http://www8.cao.go.jp/kourei/ishiki/h25/sougou/zentai/pdf/s2-1.pdf
3. Yi, X., Allan, J., Croft, W.B.: Matching resumes and jobs based on relevance models. In: SIGIR2007, pp. 809–810 (2007)
4. Lavrenko, V., Croft, W.B.: Relevance-based language models. In: SIGIR2001, pp. 120–127 (2001)
5. Miura, T., Hiyama, A., Kobayashi, M., Takagi, H., Yatomi, N., Hirose, M. Investigation on work motivation of Japanese seniors and skill discovery from their resumes. In: SII2013, pp. 190–197 (2013)
6. Miura, T., Kobayashi, M., Hiyama, A., Takagi, H., Hirose, M.: Skill discovery and matching based on feature words extraction from senior people's resumes. IEICE Tech. Rep., vol. 112, pp. 55–59 (2012)
7. Kakuda, T., Ono, A., Mine, T.: Matching between people and job with bidirectional feedback. IEICE Tech. Rep., vol. 112, pp. 13–18 (2012)
8. Lavrenko, V., Yi, X., Allan, J.: Information retrieval on empty fields. In: NAACL-HLT, pp. 89–96, (2007)
9. Hoffman, M., Kahn, L.B., Li, D.: Discretion in hiring. Working Paper 21709, National bureau of economic research (2015). http://www.nber.org/papers/w21709
10. Kuncel, N.R., Klieger, D.M., Connelly, B.S., Ones, D.S.: Mechanical versus clinical data combination in selection and admissions decisions: a meta-analysis. J. Appl. Psychol. **98**, 1060–1072 (2013)
11. Kuncel, N.R., Klieger, D.M., Ones, D.S.: In hiring, algorithms beat instinct. Harv. Bus. Rev. **92**(5), 32 (2014)
12. Singh, A., Catherine, R., Visweswariah, K., Chenthamarakshan, V., Kambhatla, N.: PROSPECT: a system for screening candidates for recruitment. In: CIKM2010, pp. 659–668 (2010)
13. Yamada, H., Hiyama, A., Yamaguchi, M., Kobayashi, M., Hirose, M.: Job matching interface for searching elderly workers. In: LIFE2015 (2015)
14. BM25 similarity. https://lucene.apache.org/core/5_4_0/core/org/apache/lucene/search/similarities/BM25Similarity.html

# Universal Access to Media and Games

# The Effect of Feedback in a Computerized System of Puzzle Completion Tasks

Nirit Gavish[1(✉)], Hagit Krisher[1], and Guy Madar[2]

[1] ORT Braude College, Karmiel, Israel
{Nirit,hevenzur}@braude.ac.il
[2] Technion – Israel Institute of Technology, Haifa, Israel
guy.madar@gmail.com

**Abstract.** The explosive growth of computerized systems aimed at improving cognitive functions has rised the question of provision of feedback to trainees during the training. In order to address some of the issues regarding feedback, two studies were performed in computerized systems for puzzle completion tasks. The first study questioned whether the mere knowledge that feedback is available should produce a motivational effect, creating a psychological state of mind that could improve training and transfer. We tested this hypothesis among 76 undergraduate students using a puzzle replication task. The results demonstrated that performance was improved among trainees who are given the opportunity to receive feedback compared with those for whom feedback is not available. The second study evaluated the effect of a complementary audio feedback (CAF) in a 50-piece puzzle completion task among 53 undergraduate students. Results demonstrated that the difference between the higher achievers and the lower achievers was larger in the CAF group compared to the Control group. In addition, while the Control group used a planning strategy more, the CAF group used a trial and error strategy more. Hence, CAF which is in the low-level of feedback is not recommended for the weaker performers.

**Keywords:** Feedback · Executive functions · Motivation · Puzzle · Auditory feedback

## 1 Introduction

Neurological findings on the plasticity of the human brain and its ability to acquire and improve cognitive skills (much more than once thought possible) [1] have produced what Owen et al. [2] called the "multimillion-pound industry" (pp. 775) of computerized systems aimed at training the brain and improving cognitive functions. The explosive growth of this industry is also fueled by the rising number of elderly people and their desire to maintain their cognitive abilities [3], as well as advancements in our knowledge about learning deficits and attention disorders such as ADHD ([4, 5]).

An important question that must be addressed when designing computerized training systems concerns the provision of feedback to trainees during the training. Feedback is information provided by an agent – whether a teacher, a book, a program, etc. – about aspects of a learner's performance or understanding. In a sense, then,

© Springer International Publishing Switzerland 2016
M. Antona and C. Stephanidis (Eds.): UAHCI 2016, Part III, LNCS 9739, pp. 449–459, 2016.
DOI: 10.1007/978-3-319-40238-3_43

feedback should be a straightforward reflection of the individual's performance [6]. However, the effects of feedback are not straightforward. Feedback can improve performance by providing the trainee with information that can serve as a basis for error correction [7]. On the other hand, several studies have suggested that learners may become dependent on the feedback they receive, and in consequence fail to take in or effectively use other sources of information. The dependence on feedback creates over-confidence and blocks the development of learners' intrinsic processing capacity, so that they become unable to detect errors themselves, or (for example) to process proprioceptive information in motor tasks – a phenomenon known as the guidance hypothesis ([7, 8]).

In addition, with the advance in technology, designing systems can take advantage of the opportunity to add complementary feedback channels for the performance various visual-spatial tasks. Adding complementary feedback channels to a visual-spatial task, and especially an auditory feedback, is supported by evidence from several studies which demonstrate that using both the visual and auditory channels for presenting information improves performance compared to the use of a single modality ([9–13]). However, although adding a complementary audio feedback to a visual-spatial task has the potential to be beneficial for performance and learning, several studies have demonstrated the in some cases this is not helpful, and sometimes it is even distractive. Audio feedback of earcones was found to be detrimental to response time in a drag-and-drop task [14]. Additional audio and haptic feedbacks in a menu-selection task harmed performance because of overloading the users with superfluous and distractive information [15]. An auditory feedback in a virtual reality insertion task deteriorated completion time, because it made participants to pay extra, unnecessary attention to collisions [16]. It seems that the benefit of a complementary auditory feedback is questionable.

In order to address some of these concerns, two studies were performed in computerized systems for puzzle completion tasks. The first study addressed the issue of training executive functions. Executive functions are the high-level cognitive skills – e.g., attention, self-control, working memory, and abstract thinking – involved in planning, organizing, and executing lower-level cognitive tasks. The first study questioned whether it may be possible to harness the motivational effects of feedback without risking the potential negative effects explained by the guidance hypothesis. This could be the case if the motivational power of feedback is derived simply from its being available, as distinct from any effect of actually drawing on feedback for guidance during training. The result should be improved performance among trainees who are given the opportunity to receive feedback compared with those for whom feedback is not available, even if the former rarely or never take up the feedback offer. We tested this hypothesis among 76 undergraduate students using a puzzle replication task.

The second study evaluated the effect of a complementary audio feedback in a 50-piece puzzle completion task. During the puzzle completion task, each time the participants composed a piece correctly he got a visual feedback, since the piece was stuck together with the other pieces. The complementary auditory feedback was a "beep" sound when the piece was composed correctly. Trainees were invited to two consecutive sessions, in each of them they were asked to complete three puzzles as quickly as possible. Fifty-three undergraduate students were randomly assigned to the two training groups: Complementary Auditory Feedback (CAF) group, who received the auditory feedback during the task; and a Control group, who did not receive the auditory feedback. We hypothesized that the CAF group will develop different performance strategies compared to the Control group.

## 2    Study 1: Feedback Availability

### 2.1    Method

**Design and Experimental Task.** Several tasks were evaluated from a computerized training system developed by Mindri (http://www.mindri.com). The chosen task was a simple puzzle replication task using a variety of geometric shapes (see Fig. 1). Trainees were invited to two training sessions, held a week apart, in each of which they were asked to complete four 4-piece puzzles and eleven 9-piece puzzles. In the second session they were also given a transfer test, which required them to complete five 16-piece puzzles using a set of identical geometric shapes (see Fig. 2). To ensure that trainees would focus on improving their executive function skills, they were instructed to complete each task as efficiently as possible (i.e., using the smallest possible number of rotations and moves). They were also told that their payout for the session would depend on their performance across the entire set of tasks.

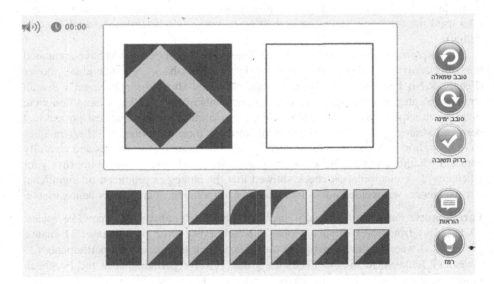

**Fig. 1.** The experimental puzzle completion task

**Fig. 2.** The transfer test task

Participants were randomly assigned to two between-participants groups: with and without the option of receiving feedback (the Feedback and No Feedback groups respectively). The feedback option showed participants the most efficient way to complete their most recent move. Because the task was relatively simple, most trainees with the feedback option chose to use it only once, or not at all. The data of trainees who used the feedback option more than once were excluded from the analysis (see below).

The experiment initially followed a 2X2 factorial design that would have compared the effects of two types of feedback: specific feedback on individual moves (Feedback/No Feedback) and more general feedback about the participant's overall strategy (Strategy/No Strategy). Half the participants in each feedback condition were told that an expert trainer had evaluated their performance in the first session and had prepared strategies that would help them improve their performance. The strategies were very short and very general (e.g., "Try to think through your moves and carefully consider whether a piece matches before placing it in the frame. This will improve your efficiency"). A manipulation check showed that the strategies produced no significant effects. Hence, we decided not to include this manipulation as an independent variable.

**Participants.** Participants initially included 88 undergraduate students (59 males, 29 females) from ORT Braude College, Israel. Forty-three participants (31 males, 12 females) were randomly assigned to the Feedback group, and 45 participants (28 males, 17 females) to the No Feedback group. Twelve participants in the Feedback group were excluded from the analysis because they used the suggested system's feedback at least twice in at least one of the two sessions. Hence, the final sample comprised 76 participants, of whom 31 (21 males, 10 females) were in the Feedback group.

## 2.2    Results

The main dependent measures in both the main task and the transfer test were the number of excess rotations and moves performed when completing the puzzles. These were calculated by subtracting the minimum required rotations and moves for each puzzle from the number actually performed. Task duration was also calculated, although participants were not instructed to complete the task as fast as possible.

To analyze the results for the main tasks, a repeated-measures ANOVA was conducted, with feedback condition (Feedback/No Feedback) as the between-participants independent variable and the training session (first or second) as the within-participants independent repeated measure. Separate ANOVAs were conducted for the transfer test and the pencil-and-paper visual perception test, with feedback condition as the between-participants independent variable.

**Main Task.** With respect to excess moves in the main task, the effect of training session was significant ($F(1,74) = 4.74$, $p = 0.03$, *partial eta squared* = 0.06): participants made fewer excess moves in the second session ($M = 17.12$, $SE = 3.57$) compared to the first session ($M = 21.26$, $SE = 3.97$). The effect of feedback condition was also significant ($F(1,74) = 6.23$, $p = 0.02$, *partial eta squared* = 0.08): participants in the Feedback group made fewer excess moves ($M = 10.08$, $SE = 5.62$) compared to the No Feedback group ($M = 28.30$, $SE = 4.66$). The interaction between training session and condition was not significant ($F(1,74) = 0.65$, $p = 0.42$, *partial eta squared* = 0.01).

The question arises whether the results would have been similar had we included those participants who were dropped from the analysis because they took advantage of the feedback option twice or more in either session (suggesting that they might have been weaker performers). We therefore ran a second repeated measures ANOVA with the addition of these 12 participants. The results confirmed the previous findings. Again, the effect of training session was significant ($F(1,86) = 5.40$, $p = 0.02$, partial eta squared = 0.06), with fewer excess moves made in the second session ($M = 17.59$, $SE = 3.16$) compared to the first ($M = 21.37$, $SE = 3.46$). The effect of condition was also significant ($F(1,86) = 7.54$, $p = 0.01$, *partial eta squared* = 0.08), with fewer excess moves made in the Feedback condition ($M = 10.66$, $SE = 4.59$) compared to the No Feedback condition ($M = 28.30$, $SE = 4.49$). As before, the interaction between training session and condition was not significant ($F(1,86) = 1.36$, $p = 0.25$, *partial eta squared* = 0.02).

With respect to excess rotations, the effect of training session was significant ($F(1,74) = 33.87$, $p < 0.001$, *partial eta squared* = 0.31): fewer excess rotations were performed in the second session ($M = 17.56$, $SE = 2.65$) compared to the first ($M = 28.97$, $SE = 3.30$). The effect of condition was not significant ($F(1,74) = 2.42$, $p = 0.12$, *partial eta squared* = 0.03), nor was the interaction between training session and condition ($F(1,74) = 0.29$, $p = 0.66$, *partial eta squared* = 0.003).

The pattern of results for mean duration is similar to the pattern for mean extra rotations. The effect of training session was significant ($F(1,74) = 125.96$, $p < 0.001$, partial eta squared = 0.63): participants needed less time to complete the task in the second session ($M$ = 505.49 s, $SE$ = 16.70) compared to the first ($M$ = 667.26 s, $SE$ = 23.64). The effect of feedback condition was not significant ($F(1,74)$ = 3.01, $p$ = 0.09, partial eta squared = 0.04), nor was the interaction between training session and condition ($F(1,74)$ = 0.27, $p$ = 0.61, *partial eta squared* = 0.004).

**Transfer Test.** In the transfer test, the effect of feedback condition on excess moves was very close to significance ($F(1,74)$ = 3.75, $p$ = 0.057, *partial eta squared* = 0.05): fewer excess moves were made in the Feedback condition ($M$ = 6.16, $SE$ = 4.08) compared to the No Feedback condition ($M$ = 16.42, $SE$ = 3.39). As before, to evaluate whether excluding the participants who took advantage of the feedback option twice or more in either session affected the results, we ran a second ANOVA with the addition of these 12 participants. In this analysis the effect of feedback group was even more significant ($F(1,86)$ = 6.46, $p$ = 0.01, *partial eta squared* = 0.07), with fewer excess moves in the Feedback condition ($M$ = 4.98, $SE$ = 3.22) compared to the No Feedback condition ($M$ = 16.42, $SE$ = 3.15).

The effect of feedback condition on mean excess rotations in the transfer test was not significant ($F(1,74)$ = 0.17, $p$ = 0.68, *partial eta squared* = 0.002).

The effect of feedback condition on mean duration was not significant ($F(1,74)$ = 1.91, $p$ = 0.17, *partial eta squared* = 0.02).

## 2.3    Discussion and Conclusions

Overall, the current findings suggest that in computerized training systems for executive functions, simply making feedback available, even if most trainees are likely to make little use of it, can have strong influence on both training and performance. This finding should be evaluated further using other tasks and in other domains, to examine its robustness for future computerized training system design recommendations and guidelines.

The current findings are interesting in light of research about the extent to which priming – i.e., exposing individuals to a particular stimulus – can affect participants' behavior and performance in different situations. For example, Bargh et al. [17] found that "participants whose concept of rudeness was primed interrupted the experimenter more quickly and frequently than did participants primed with polite-related stimuli," while "participants for whom an elderly stereotype was primed walked more slowly down the hallway when leaving the experiment than did control participants" (p. 230). Steele and Aronson [18] showed that African Americans who were primed with a negative stereotype about their intellectual ability performed more poorly in intellectual tests than similar black participants who were not so primed. Likewise, Dijksterhuis and Van Knippenberg [19] reported that priming the stereotype of a professor or the trait "intelligent" improved participants' performance on a general knowledge test, while priming the stereotype of soccer hooligans or the trait "stupid" reduced their performance. In a similar manner, the mere knowledge that feedback is available may prime trainees with the motivational effect of feedback, creating a psychological state of mind that may improve training and transfer.

## 3  Study 2: Complementary Auditory Feedback

### 3.1  Method

**Design and Experimental Task.** Participants were randomly assigned to two between-participants groups: CAF group, who received an auditory feedback during the puzzle completion task: a "beep" sound when the piece was composed correctly; and a Control group, who did not receive the auditory feedback. Both groups got a visual feedback, which was the appearance of a piece as stuck together with the other pieces when it was composed correctly.

The experimental task entailed computerized puzzles composed of various pictures. The site used for the task was http://thejigsawpuzzles.com/Waterfalls-jigsaw-puzzle (see Fig. 3). Participants had to select a piece with the mouse and move it to the correct place in the puzzle. No rotations were needed. Clicking on the upper right icon displayed the entire picture, and clicking on it again closed the picture. A watch displaying the time elapsed from the beginning of each puzzle was located in the bottom right corner. When the puzzle was completed successfully the watch stopped. Participants in the CAF group used headphones. Participants faced a 20-pieces puzzle for practice (without headphones for the both groups) and 6 50-pieces puzzles (3 in the first day of the experiment and 3 in one week afterward). A transfer task with an additional 50-pieces puzzle (without headphones for the both groups) was given to both groups. The 8 puzzled used in the study were identical for all participants. Participants were told to complete the puzzles as quickly as possible.

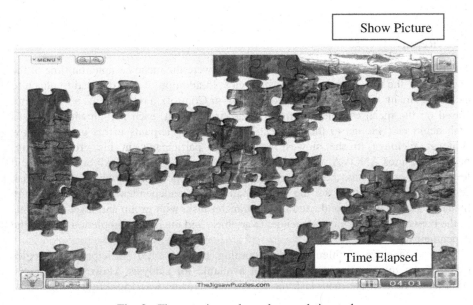

**Fig. 3.** The experimental puzzle completion task

**Participants.** Participants included 53 undergraduate students (33 males, 20 females) from ORT Braude College, Israel. Twenty-seven participants (16 males, 11 females) were randomly assigned to the CAF group, and 23 participants (17 males, 9 females) to the Control group. The average participants' age was 25.4, with a range of 20 to 30. All participants had normal or corrected-to-normal visual acuity.

**Performance Strategies.** During the two session, participants' actions when completed the 50-pieces puzzles were recorded and analyzed. Specifically, six performance strategies were analyzed. For each session, each participant scored "0" or "1" for every strategies, "1" if he used it and "0" if not. Below is the list of strategies and the measures:

1. Displaying Picture: Displaying the picture by clicking the icon. Participants who clicked the icon to display the picture at least twice got the score of 1.
2. Separating the frame: Separating the frame parts from the other parts. Participants who separated at least 5 parts of the frame in at least one puzzle got the score of 1.
3. Connecting the frame: Starting from connecting the frame parts before connecting the body of the puzzle. Participants who connected no more 5 parts of the body before completing connecting the frame in at each of the puzzles got the score of 1.
4. Connecting to the frame: Connecting puzzle parts to the frame. Participants who connected at least 5 parts to the frame before connecting the other puzzle parts in at least one puzzle got the score of 1.
5. Gathering parts: Gathering parts according to colors or patterns. Participants who gathered at least 5 parts in at least one puzzle got the score of 1.
6. Trial and Error: Trying to connect parts by trial and error. Participants who tried to connect at least one part to at least 5 places in the puzzle in at least one puzzle got the score of 1.

## 3.2    Results

The main dependent measures for the main task were the mean completion time of the puzzles and the use of each of the 6 strategies. In addition, it was decided to attach to each participant, in addition to his group (CAF or Control), a rating of his achievement. Based on the mean completion times in the first session, each participants scored as high achiever (belongs to the quickest half of the participants in his group) or low achiever (belongs to the slowest half of the participants in his group). A repeated-measures ANOVA was conducted, with group condition (CAF or Control) and level (high or low) as the between-participants independent variable, and the task session (first or second) as the within-participants independent repeated measure. Separate ANOVA was conducted for the transfer task, with group and level conditions as the between-participants independent variables, and the mean completion time as the dependent measure.

Due to technical problems while recording, the data on 7 participants' strategies usages from the Control group was not available for analysis. However, the mean completion time in the main task for these 7 participants was 15.90 min compared to

16.00 min for the rest 19 participants, hence it was decided to continue with the analysis also these data were missing.

**Main Task.** *Mean completion time (in minutes).* The effect of session was significant ($F(1,49) = 82.95$, $p < 0.001$, *partial eta squared* = 0.63): mean completion time was shorter in the second session ($M = 14.86$, $SD = 3.67$) compared to the first session ($M = 17.86$, $SD = 4.83$). The effect of group was not significant ($F(1,49) = 1.47$, $p = 0.23$, *partial eta squared* = 0.03). As expected, the effect of level was significant ($F(1,49) = 91.11$, $p < 0.001$, *partial eta squared* = 0.65): mean completion time for the high level ($M = 13.25$, $SD = 1.80$) was shorter compared to the low level ($M = 19.47$, $SD = 3.08$). The interaction between group and level was significant ($F(1,49) = 6.68$, $p = 0.01$, *partial eta squared* = 0.12): the difference between higher achievers ($M = 12.80$, $SD = 1.69$) and lower achievers ($M = 20.71$, $SD = 3.01$) in the CAF group was greater than the difference between higher achievers ($M = 13.70$, $SD = 1.86$) and lower achievers ($M = 18.23$, $SD = 2.71$) in the Control group, see Fig. 2. In addition, the interaction between session and level was also significant ($F(1,49) = 21.49$, $p < 0.01$, *partial eta squared* = 0.31): the difference between higher achievers ($M = 14.00$, $SD = 1.94$) and lower achievers ($M = 21.74$, $SD = 3.56$) in the first session was greater than the difference between higher achievers ($M = 12.51$, $SD = 2.08$) and lower achievers ($M = 17.21$, $SD = 3.21$) in the second session. The other interactions were not significant: the interaction between session and group ($F(1,49) = 0.03$, $p = 0.86$, *partial eta squared* < 0.001), and the triple interaction session X group X level ($F(1,49) = 0.42$, $p = 0.52$, *partial eta squared* = 0.01).

*Mean strategies usage.* Below are the main analysis of the strategy usage.

Strategy #2: Separating the Frame. The effect of session was not significant ($F(1,42) = 0.57$, $p = 0.46$, *partial eta squared* = 0.01). In contrast, the effect of group was significant ($F(1,42) = 3.91$, $p = 0.06$, *partial eta squared* = 0.13): 63.0 % ($SD = 48.7$ %) from the participants in the CAF group used this strategy, compared to 89.5 % ($SD = 31.1$ %) from the participants in the Control group. The effect of level was not significant ($F(1,42) = 0.82$, $p = 0.37$, *partial eta squared* = 0.02). The interaction between group and level was not significant ($F(1,42) = 0.001$, $p = 0.92$, *partial eta squared* < 0.001), nor the interaction between session and level ($F(1,42) = 0.23$, $p = 0.64$, *partial eta squared* = 0.01), the interaction between session and group ($F(1,42) = 0.51$, $p = 0.48$, *partial eta squared* = 0.01), and the triple interaction session X group X level ($F(1,42) = 0.31$, $p = 0.58$, *partial eta squared* = 0.01).

Strategy #6: Trial and Error. The effect of session was not significant ($F(1,42) = 0.19$, $p = 0.66$, *partial eta squared* = 0.005). In contrast, the effect of group was significant ($F(1,42) = 4.59$, $p = 0.04$, *partial eta squared* = 0.10): 59.3 % ($SD = 46.9$ %) from the participants in the CAF group used this strategy, compared to only 36.8 % ($SD = 48.9$ %) from the participants in the Control group. The effect of level was not significant ($F(1,42) = 0.81$, $p = 0.37$, *partial eta squared* = 0.02). The interaction between group and level was not significant ($F(1,42) = 2.39$, $p = 0.13$, *partial eta squared* = 0.05), nor the interaction between session and level ($F(1,42) = 0.94$, $p = 0.34$, *partial eta squared* = 0.02), the interaction between session and group

$(F(1,42) = 0.50$, $p = 0.59$, *partial eta squared* $= 0.01$), and the triple interaction session X group X level $(F(1,42) = 3.83$, $p = 0.06$, *partial eta squared* $= 0.08$).

**Transfer Test.** *Mean completion time (in minutes).* The effect of group was not significant $(F(1,49) = 0.63$, $p = 0.43$, *partial eta squared* $= 0.01$). The effect of level was significant $(F(1,49) = 38.43$, $p < 0.001$, *partial eta squared* $= 0.44$): mean completion time for the high level $(M = 3.91$, $SD = 0.68$) was shorter compared to the low level $(M = 5.21$, $SD = 0.88$). The interaction between group and level was significant $(F(1,49) = 5.00$, $p = 0.03$, *partial eta squared* $= 0.09$): the difference between higher achievers $(M = 3.76$, $SD = 0.58$) and lower achievers $(M = 5.52$, $SD = 0.95$) in the CAF group was greater than the difference between higher achievers $(M = 4.06$, $SD = 0.77$) and lower achievers $(M = 4.89$, $SD = 0.70$) in the Control group.

## 3.3    Discussion and Conclusions

The differences in performance between the CAF and Control groups, though the effect of group was not significant, we did find that, both for the main task and the transfer task, the difference between the higher achievers and the lower achievers was larger in the CAF group compared to the Control group. It seems that the CAF helped the better performers but deteriorated the performance of the weaker ones. Most interestingly, this effect was dominate also in the transfer task, when the CAF was not supplied. It can be assumed that participants who got CAF developed different performance strategies, which persisted also without its existence.

Indeed, a closer look at the strategies used by the two groups reveals some differences between the groups. While the Control group used the strategy of separating the frames parts from the other puzzle parts more, the CAF group used trial and error strategy more. It can be speculated that since the CAF emphasized immediate, short-term result, it caused participants to lower their level of pre-planning (for example, by separating the frame parts) and focus more on trying to maximize short-term achievements (for example, by trial and errors). In general, this behavior was less helpful for the weaker performers, maybe because it distracted them from the long-term goal of completing the entire puzzle.

To sum, the conclusion from the current study are that CAF which is in the low-level of feedback is not recommended for the weaker performers, as it caused them to adopt less effective strategies which are focused more on the short-term goals. Designer of modern system should be, therefore, careful when augmenting the visual-spatial task with CAF. It should be noted that the task which was chosen for this study, a puzzle task, requires planning, and it is possible that with simpler tasks this finding will not be evident. Future research should evaluate the robustness of this finding.

**Acknowledgments.** This research was supported in part by ORT Braude Research Committee, Israel.

# References

1. Buonomano, D.V., Merzenich, M.M.: Cortical plasticity: from synapses to maps. Annu. Rev. Neurosci. **21**, 149–186 (1998)
2. Owen, A.M., Hampshire, A., Grahn, J.A., Stenton, R.R., Dajani, S., Burns, A.S., Howard, R. J., Ballard, C.G.: Putting brain training to the test. Nature **465**, 775–779 (2010)
3. Stern, Y., Blumen, H.M., Rich, L.W., Richards, A., Herzberg, G., Gopher, D.: Space fortress game training and executive control in older adults: a pilot intervention. Aging Neuropsychol. Cogn. **18**, 653–677 (2011)
4. Kieling, C., Goncalves, R.R.F., Tannock, R., Castellanos, F.X.: Neurobiology of attention deficit hyperactivity disorder. Child Adolesc. Psychiatr. Clin. N. Am. **17**, 285–307 (2008)
5. Steinhausen, H.C.: The heterogeneity of causes and courses of attention deficit/hyperactivity disorder. Acta Psychiatr. Scand. **120**, 392–399 (2009)
6. Hattie, J., Timperley, H.: The power of feedback. Rev. Educ. Res. **77**(1), 81–112 (2007)
7. Salmoni, A.R., Schmidt, R.A., Walter, C.B.: Knowledge of results and motor learning: a review and critical appraisal. Psychol. Bull. **5**, 355–386 (1984)
8. Schmidt, R.A., Young, D.E., Swinnen, S., Shapiro, D.C.: Summary of knowledge of results for skill acquisition: support for the guidance hypothesis. J. Exp. Psychol. Learn. Memory Cogn. **15**, 352–359 (1989)
9. Brooks, L.: The suppression of visualization by reading. Q. J. Exp. Psychol. **19**, 289–299 (1967)
10. Frick, R.: Using an auditory and a visual short-term store to increase digit span. Mem. Cogn. **12**, 507–514 (1984)
11. Mayer, R.E., Anderson, R.B.: Animations need narrations: an experimental test of dual-coding hypothesis. J. Educ. Psychol. **83**, 484–490 (1991)
12. Mayer, R.E., Anderson, R.B.: The instructive animation: helping students build connections between words and pictures in multimedia learning. J. Educ. Psychol. **84**, 444–452 (1992)
13. Mayer, R.E., Sims, V.K.: For whom is a picture worth a thousand words? extension of a dual-coding theory of multimedia learning. J. Educ. Psychol. **86**, 389–401 (1994)
14. Vitense, H.S., Jacko, J.A., Emery, V.K.: Multimodal feedback: an assessment of performance and mental workload. Ergonomics **46**, 68–87 (2003)
15. Cockburn, A., Brewster, S.: Multimodal feedback for the acquisition of small targets. Ergonomics **48**(9), 1129–1150 (2005)
16. Lecuyer, A., Megard, C., Burkhardt, J.M., Lim, T., Coquillart, S., Coiffet, P., Graux, L.: The effect of haptic, visual and auditory feedback on an insertion task on a 2-screen workbench. In: Proceedings of the Immersive Projection Technology Symposium (2002)
17. Bargh, J.A., Chen, M., Burrows, L.: Automaticity of social behavior: direct effects of trait construct and stereotype activation on action. J. Pers. Soc. Psychol. **71**(2), 230–244 (1996)
18. Steele, C.M., Aronson, J.: Stereotype threat and the intellectual test performance of African Americans. J. Pers. Soc. Psychol. **69**(5), 797–811 (1995)
19. Dijksterhuis, A., Van Knippenberg, A.: The relation between perception and behavior, or how to win a game of trivial pursuit. J. Pers. Soc. Psychol. **74**(4), 865 (1998)

# A Framework for Generation of Testsets for Recent Multimedia Workflows

Robert Manthey[(✉)], Steve Conrad, and Marc Ritter

Department of Computer Science Junior Professorship Media Computing,
Technische Universität Chemnitz, StraßE der Nationen 62, 09111 Chemnitz, Germany
{robert.manthey,steve.conrad,marc.ritter}@informatik.tu-chemnitz.de
http://www.tu-chemnitz.de/informatik/mc

**Abstract.** Our framework offers solution approaches for that inadequacy to be overcome. An abstract description define each test case, its transformation to the designated target platforms as well as the operations and parameters to be processed within the evaluation in such a way that it is independent of any platform. The control of our automated framework workflow is based on Python and Apache Ant which trigger the execution of the described definitions with the result that different tools can be used flexible and purpose-dependent.

We conduct an visual error detection evaluation of FFmpeg, Telestream Episode and Adobe Media Encoder. This consists the creation of single uncompressed images based on the definitions of the test patterns in POV-Ray. After that, they are merged together to video samples which form the platform dependent instances of the test cases. All of these videos are processed with different codecs and encoding qualities during the evaluation. The results are compared with its uncompressed raw material or other test cases.

The evaluation shows that the identical test case video file results in visual strongly different outcomes after the encoding. Furthermore some created test cases cause complete losses of the raw information data, ringing artefacts at contrast edges and flicker effects.

**Keywords:** Framework · Multimedia · Quality analysis · Testing

## 1 Introduction

Today, a massive amount of video and multimedia data is processed. Cameras observe systems in manufacturing, food production and car traffic. They provide information in autonomous driving cars and advanced driver assistance systems as well as entertainment systems. In a similar way audio and further data are used and sometimes combined to one file or a group of files to make multimedia data. The amount of that data grows as rapid as the their complexity. The resolution increases to HD and more, they get 5.1 to 22.2 surround sound, as well as 3D or 360-degree. The field of application expands form TV and computer screens to huge projectors and small smartwatch like devices. But commonly the

© Springer International Publishing Switzerland 2016
M. Antona and C. Stephanidis (Eds.): UAHCI 2016, Part III, LNCS 9739, pp. 460–467, 2016.
DOI: 10.1007/978-3-319-40238-3_44

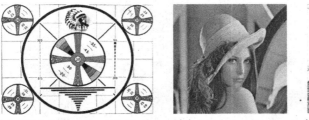 

(a) RCA Indian-head test image      (b) Lena test image      (c) Frame of the Flower test video

**Fig. 1.** Commonly used test images and test video

examination of accessibility, correctness, performance and especially quality will be done with old, small size single media samples like Fig. 1a[1], Fig. 1b[2] and Fig. 1c[3] from last century, reaching SD with stereo sound at most.

In principle thereby different steps of a processing chain (Fig. 2) are processed, in order to improve the data, to store them or to show them. Each step has thereby its own characteristics and adds errors, which can be noticed e.g. as picture artefacts shown in Fig. 3. The type of artefacts and their frequency of occurrence are heavily addicted to numerous parameters like the transcoding system, its implementation and settings as well as the input data. Different test patterns exists for different types of image artefacts and due to the innumerable amount of artefacts, they should prompt as many as possible artefact types and make them detectable.

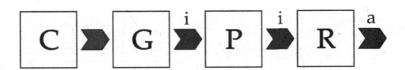

**Fig. 2.** Processing chain for images "C, input from camera; G, grab image (digitize and store); P, preprocess; R, recognize (i, image data; a, abstract data)."[1]

Many artefacts are nevertheless not detectable, since they will not appear in a single test pattern. They are results of movements, quick image switching or other conditional image transformations which appears in image sequences like videos.

Testsets should not only cause the expected errors, but also make them clearly visible and detectable. In case of single images or nature movies it is e.g. difficult to see slight color differences or single pixel errors. Furthermore in some areas

---

[1] http://sipi.usc.edu/database/download.php?vol=misc&img=4.2.04.
[2] http://www.forensicgenealogy.info/contest_206_results.html.
[3] http://media.xiph.org/video/derf/y4m/flower_cif.y4m.

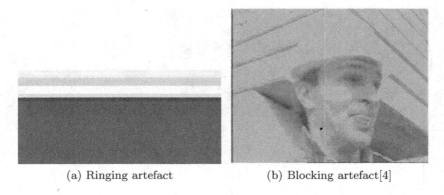

(a) Ringing artefact                    (b) Blocking artefact[4]

**Fig. 3.** Common artefacts in digital images

like image understanding [3], image retrieval or digital archiving [2] the testsets have to be as compact as possible since otherwise extensive tests would hardly or not at all be possible with such an amount of data. Facing these problems we conceptualized a highly flexible synthetic testset, which was adapted to these specific purposes.

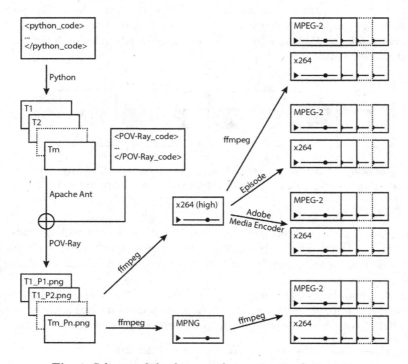

**Fig. 4.** Schema of the framework to generate the testsets

## 2    Framework Structure

To generate a synthetic, versatile and flexible testset which is able to detect designated picture artefacts, it is necessary to use a highly adaptable framework from
first to last as proposed in Fig. 4. As the fundament we need a vectorized description of the different test patterns like the Scene Description Language used in
the open source raytracing software POV-Ray. This abstract scene description is
based on parameters and coordinates whereby it is independent from the desired
resolution, aspect ratio and file format. Due to this it is easily possible to change
the testset or add further test cases in order to adapt the test pattern to changed
purposes. In the next step we defined the test cases through the scene description parameters within a Python script which generates the workflow control
file. This control file is constructed in such a way that all, a selective amount
and even single test cases can be created. It uses Apache Ant to call POV-Ray
and to pass the parameters to them. These test cases serve as the input data for
the programs to test and as the original material for the comparison with the
transcoded results.

## 3    Testset Generation

We used the description language of the raytracing renderer POV-Ray to define
a set of test pattern in a abstract, target and size independent way as shown
in Fig. 5a. At the same time a set of descriptions is defined with the Python
programming language to form the test sequences (Fig. 5b) as well as the way
to handle there execution through the planned program. This forms an Ant-
based control[4] file to allow parallel as well as independent execution of each
test (Fig. 5c). Further processing steps can be accomplished if planned program
needs it to handle the input, as shown in Fig. 4 for cases listed in Table 1.

   The created test patterns can be divided in four groups of pattern designs.
The first pattern design is a Cartesian grid structure of square blocks, which are
provided in edge lengths of 1, 4, 5, 8 and 10 pixels. Except for the 1-pixel-design,
the pattern sequences also exist in a rotating version. The images of the second
pattern design are composed of 1, 2 or 4 rectangular sections. Additionally the
2-section-sequence are translated perpendicular to their separation line. The 4-
section-sequences are also rotating. The third group contains images with stripes
in widths of 1, 4, 5, 8 and 10 pixels, which also are rotated and translated in
various ways. The last category of test patterns shows a Siemens star in different
sizes and with a different number of beams, which are available in a rotating
version as well.

   Every test pattern sequence exists in four different resolutions, two commonly
used and two unusual ones. On the one hand $1920 \times 1080$ as a high frequently
used resolution for videos and movies as well as for displays and video projectors.
On the other hand $1024 \times 768$ as an old-standard but still used resolution e.g.
in smaller displays, netbooks and mobile devices. Besides we constructed two

---

[4]  https://ant.apache.org/.

```
#while(siemens_beam_count_temp < siemens_beam_count)
polygon {  4,
  <0.0, 0.0, -50>,
  <0, siemens_radius, -50>,
  <sin(1/siemens_beam_count*pi)*siemens_radius,
   sqrt(siemens_radius*siemens_radius -
   (sin(1/siemens_beam_count*pi)*
   siemens_radius*sin(1/siemens_beam_count*pi)*siemens_radius)
   ), -50>,
  <0.0, 0.0, -50>
  texture{
    pigment{ color rgb<0,0,0>}
    finish{ ambient 1.0 diffuse 0.0 }
  }
  rotate<0,0,90-(360*siemens_beam_count_temp/siemens_beam_count)>
  #if (rotation = 1)
    rotate<0,0,abs(360-clock*2)>
  #end
  #declare siemens_beam_count_temp = siemens_beam_count_temp + 1;
 }
#end
```

(a) Generic POV-Ray code to generate the siemens star

```
<target name="40007_povray">
    <exec executable="bin\pvengine64.exe">
        <arg line="Output_File_Name=
        siemens_40007_1920_1080_beams16_size3_rot0\
        Output_File_Type=N
        Initial_Frame=0
        Final_Frame=359
        Initial_Clock=0
        Final_Clock=359
        Width=1920
        Height=1080
        Declare=rotation=0
        Declare=siemens_size=3
        Declare=siemens_beam_count=16
        /RENDER siemens.pov /EXIT"/>
    </exec>
</target>
```

(b) Definition of a testcase showing a siemens star without rotation

```
<target name="40007_ffmpeg">
  <exec executable="ffmpeg.exe">
    <arg line="-i siemens_40007_1920_1080_beams16_size3_rot0\
    40007_mpng.avi
    -vcodec libx264
    -framerate 25
    -r 25
    -y
    -b 400000
    -s 1920x1080
    output_ffmpeg\siemens_40007_1920_1080_beams16_size3_rot0\
    40007_x264_400000.avi"/>
  </exec>
  <exec executable="ffmpeg.exe">
    <arg line="-i siemens_40007_1920_1080_beams16_size3_rot0\
    40007_mpng.avi
    -vcodec libx264
    -framerate 25
    -r 25
    -y
    -b 1500000
    -s 1920x1080
    output_ffmpeg\siemens_40007_1920_1080_beams16_size3_rot0\
    40007_x264_1500000.avi"/>
  </exec>
```

(c) Definition of the execution of a testcase with 400 kBit/s and 1.5 MBit/s with FFmpeg

**Fig. 5.** Sample of the control element to generation a testcase with rotation and its execution

**Table 1.** Usability of image sequences as direct input data

| Encoder | Image sequences usable |
|---|---|
| FFmpeg | ✓ |
| Episode Engine | × |
| Adobe Media Encoder | × |

resolutions out of prime numbers: $1009 \times 631$ with an usual aspect ratio of about $16 : 10$ and $997 \times 13$ with an uncommon aspect ratio of about $77 : 1$. Moreover each test pattern were generated in five different color sets: A grayscale set, a color set that consists the six complementary colors red, green, blue, cyan, magenta and yellow, a set whereby all $16,777,216$ colors of the RGB color space are randomly changing and two green color sets. These permutations finally result in over 900 test cases with different structures, transformations, colors and resolutions.

Every test case sequence is made of 360 images of every of these test cases whereby the appropriated transformations and colors change from frame to frame. We used *FFmpeg 2015*, *Telestream Episode 6.4.6* and *Adobe Media Encoder CC 2015.0.1(7.2)* to combine and to transcode the respective 360 frames into different video formats with various qualities. We used the video codecs H.264/x264, which is employed on Blu-ray Discs, in the digital 'satellite TV broadcast standard DVB-S2 as well as in internet movies and in MP4 files for mobile devices, and MPEG-2, which serves as video format e.g. for DVDs and digital TV broadcast. The test sequences were transcoded to videos with bit rates of 400 kBit/s and 1.5 MBit/s, which are the minimum speed for high quality video calling respectively the recommended speed for HD video calling in Skype, in addition 4.976 MBit/s, 31.668 MBit/s and 83.11 MBit/s, which are the lowest and the highest possible bit rate in DVB-T as well as the highest in

(a) Original strip pattern

(b) Pattern dissolution with spots          (c) Substantial spots in the pattern

**Fig. 6.** The strip sample (a) rotating around the picture center leads with FFmpeg, H.264 and 1 MBit/s to the results in (b) and (c). It shows up different unevenly arising spots in varying intensity and with complete dissolution of the original pattern in the first.

DVB-C, and 15 MBit/s, which is e.g. equal to the MPEG-2 Main Level bit rate. Refresh rate and resolution were not changed during the transcoding process.

## 4    Experimental Results and Discussion

The generated test sequences are processed by the video encoders and empirically examined for remarkable events. The results show that huge single colored structures as well as fence-like vertical or horizontal structures are good encodable. In contrast to that the strip-like content as well as the siemens star pattern

(a) Original siemens star with cutout marking

(b) Central part of the result frame 1

(c) Central part of the result frame 7

(d) Central part of the result frame 15

**Fig. 7.** The motionless siemens sample (a) leads with Episode Engine, MPEG-2 and 1.5 MBit/s to the results in (b), (c) and (d). After the substantial artefact formation in first frame, a frame-wise quality improvement followed and leads to (c). The next frame (d) show substantial artefacts again and starts a new sequence of improvement with relative good quality conditions in the end.

will create clearly visible artefacts as shown in Figs. 6 and 7. Some are disturbing like in Fig. 6c whereas others impaired the whole image as Fig. 6b.

A further effect of video test sequences is shown in Fig. 7. Still standing similar frames will be modified by the video encoding process and a not existing movement is created.

## 5 Future Work

In this paper we proposed a new framework for generation of testset for multimedia systems. Since the description of the tests is separated, the applicability of the framework appears very flexible in creating arbitrary testsets and there execution in different environments. We show that the generated testsets can be usable to search for badly influencing effects of performance and quality. We show cases which are too complex to be detected with old-style test images and video sequences.

The next steps incorperate further more complex test patterns, composite sequences to address more artefacts. Test patterns with sound as well as 3D and embeded metadata are to be added. An automatic preliminary investigation of the results could be used to find candidates of problematic testcases. An application to other fields of image processing like robustness research in the field of pedestrian detection can be possible.

**Acknowledgments.** This work was partially accomplished within the project *localizeIT* (funding code 03IPT608X) funded by the *Federal Ministry of Education and Research* (Bundesministerium für Wissenschaft und Forschung, Germany) in the program of *Entrepreneurial Regions InnoProfile-Transfer*.

## References

1. Davies, E.: Machine Vision. Morgan Kaufmann, San Francisco (2005)
2. Manthey, R., Herms, R., Ritter, M., Storz, M., Eibl, M.: A support framework for automated video and multimedia workflows for production and archive. In: Yamamoto, S. (ed.) HCI 2013, Part III. LNCS, vol. 8018, pp. 336–341. Springer, Heidelberg (2013)
3. Ritter, M.: Optimization of algorithms for video analysis: a framework to fit the demands of local television stations. In: Eibl, M. (ed.) Wissenschaftliche Schriftenreihe Dissertationen der Medieninformatik, vol. 3, pp. i-xlii, 1–336. Universitätsverlag der Technischen Universität Chemnitz, Germany (2014). http://nbn-resolving.de/urn:nbn:de:bsz:ch1-qucosa-133517
4. Wiegand, T., Sullivan, G.J., Bjntegaard, G., Luthra, A.: Overview of the h.264/avc video coding standard. IEEE Trans. Circuits Syst. Video Technol. **13**(7), 560–576 (2003)

# The Effects of Background Color, Shape and Dimensionality on Purchase Intentions in a Digital Product Presentation

Rafał Michalski[✉] and Jerzy Grobelny

Faculty of Computer Science and Management,
Wrocław University of Technology, Wrocław, Poland
{rafal.michalski,jerzy.grobelny}@pwr.edu.pl
http://RafalMichalski.com
http://JerzyGrobelny.com

**Abstract.** The presented study explores diverse ways of demonstrating the product in a digital way, e.g. in big digital outdoor telebims, monitors situated in supermarkets or electronic shops available on the Internet. Three different factors were examined in a laboratory based experiment: product presentation background colors (red, green, and blue), presentation shape (sharp versus rounded edges) and presentation dimensionality (two and three dimensional). The potential customers expressed their purchase intentions towards various product presentation variants by means of pairwise comparisons. The analysis of data collected from 51 persons revealed the statistical importance of all three examined factors along with the significance of dimensionality and shape interaction. Subjects preferred rounded options more than these with sharp edges only. The three dimensionally looking package was better liked than its two dimensional counterpart. Participants favored also blue background color over the red and green ones.

**Keywords:** Digital signage · Two and three dimensions · Package design · Roundedness · Purchase intensions · AHP

## 1 Introduction

In today's digitized world people more and more often come across virtual presentations of products rather than real objects. It frequently happens, especially in electronic shops, that customers make their buying decisions based only on a digital appearance of an article. There were numerous studies in a marketing field regarding traditional ways of demonstrating goods and many of them concerned products packages (e.g. Richardson et al. 1994 and lately Valajoozi and Zangi 2015 or Werle et al. 2016). The general review in this area may be found in the work of Azzi et al. (2012). Among basic packaging functions one may find the following (Rundh 2005; Robertson 2006): containment, protection, convenience, and communication. Naturally, the last role is crucial in a digitized product presentation and has recently also been subject to scientific investigation (e.g. Deliza et al. 2003; Harris et al. 2011 and recently Grobelny and Michalski 2015).

© Springer International Publishing Switzerland 2016
M. Antona and C. Stephanidis (Eds.): UAHCI 2016, Part III, LNCS 9739, pp. 468–479, 2016.
DOI: 10.1007/978-3-319-40238-3_45

There is a variety of package features that may influence the consumer preferences and as a result purchase intentions. It seems that one of the most important characteristics in this context may be connected with the application of specific color schemes. The color has been identified as an important factor influencing peoples' perception in various fields, for instance, in general psychology (Granger 1955; Guilford and Smith 1959), or in human factors (Christ 1975). The importance of the background color in a digital presentation was also examined in the work of Middlestandt (1990) or Grobelny and Michalski (2011). One may also find a few papers in the marketing area dealing directly with the product digital presentation. For instance, Rebollar et al. (2012) examined the impact of various artificially prepared chewing gum packages involving warm, cold and grey colors on consumer expectation and willingness to buy whereas Grobelny and Michalski (2015) focused only on two colors: pink and grey. In light of Schloss et al. (2013) findings this direction is worth following as the color effect is frequently moderated by other experimental factors.

The shape of packages is considered as important factor influencing customers' product perception as well and was subject to examination by multiple researchers. Particularly intriguing is the general effect of preferring curved contours and shapes over the edgy ones which was observed in a series of previous experiments (e.g. Becker et al. 2011; Westerman et al. 2013).

In real environment the packages presenting products to consumers have always three dimensional shapes. However, in a digital space articles are usually demonstrated as two dimensional pictures. These images may depict products or services either in a flat two-dimensional way or mimics three-dimensional objects. Thus, it is noteworthy to verify if such factor influences subjects' willingness to buy. It is quite hard to find research articles that investigate this dimensionality effect in the digital product presentation context however, some studies from a general psychology suggest that people could prefer 3D looking versions over the 2D ones. Murrey et al. (2002) showed by means of the brain imaging technique that the perception of 3D shapes results in lower activity in human primary visual cortex. This suggests that such an object is easier processed which can lead to higher preferences. Similar results were provided by Norman et al. (2004).

In view of the brief literature review presented above, this study focuses on the influence of virtual product presentation differentiated by the background color, shape, and dimensionality on the perceived willingness to purchase a smartphone.

## 2   Method

### 2.1   Participants

There were 24 (47 %) males and 27 females (53 %) voluntarily engaged in the current investigation. All of them were undergraduate students of the Wrocław University of Technology (Poland), aged from 18 to 24 years with the average of 20.6 years and standard deviation equal to 1.5.

## 2.2   Variables and Experimental Design

A number of pictures presenting a fictitious smartphone on a digital package prototype were created for the purposes of the present investigation. For clarity, the design included only basic components that are associated with the packaging, that is: the product picture and its imaginary name. These items were identical for all conditions. The prepared digital product presentations were differentiated by three independent variables, namely the background color of the presentation, two or three dimensional appearance, and sharp or rounded edges. Exemplary conditions are shown in Fig. 1.

**Fig. 1.**  Exemplary experimental conditions used in the current study

The background color was specified on three basic colors: blue, green, and red. The specific color parameters were selected in such a way that the perceptual differences between them were comparable. Thus, we took advantage of the CIE Lab color system (Robertson 1977) to choose colors with a similar Euclidean distance between them. The detailed color characteristics for these colors both in the CIE Lab space and in RGB system are provided in Table 1.

**Table 1.**  Detailed specification of background colors used in the present experiment

| Color name | Color sample | RGB | CIE Lab |
|:---:|:---:|:---:|:---:|
| **Blue** | | #AFD9E2 | (84,-12,-9) |
| **Green** | | #CDD796 | (84,-11,30) |
| **Red** | | #FFC1C1 | (84, 23,  9) |

A mixture of the three independent variables Background color (Blue, Green, Red) × Dimensionality (Two and Three dimensional appearance) × Shape (Rounded versus Sharp presentation) gives twelve unique experimental conditions. As the within subjects design was employed each subject assessed all the product presentation variants.

## 2.3   Apparatus, Dependent Measures, and Experimental Procedure

Custom made software supported the whole experimental procedure which involves pairwise comparisons of stimuli within the framework of Analytic Hierarchy Process (AHP, Saaty 1977, 1980).

The examination started with informing subjects about objectives of the research. After the consent of participating in the experiment they provided some basic data about themselves. Then, participants were asked to rate which of the two presented at a time product digital presentations would increase their willingness to buy. The conditions' pairs were displayed in a random order. The condition's left-right location was also set randomly. An example of such a comparison is demonstrated in Fig. 2.

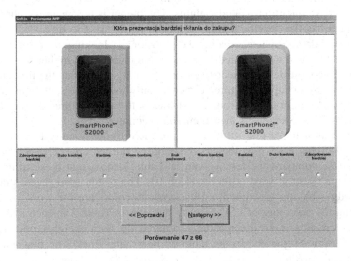

**Fig. 2.** An exemplary, single comparison displayed by the experimental software

Apart from presenting digital versions of product packages, the application registered subjects' responses in the database and computed the final subjective hierarchy of examined conditions. The calculations were performed according to the AHP procedure and resulted in obtaining two types of dependent measures, that is, preference weights used for determining conditions' priorities and consistency ratios (CR) allowing for controlling the coherence of subjects' responses.

The experiments were conducted on personal computers and monitors with software and hardware having the same technical characteristics and settings, located in teaching laboratories under the same lighting conditions. Specific procedures of eliciting users' preferences applied in this study may be found in Michalski (2011).

# 3 Result

## 3.1 Basic Statistical Characteristics

Out of 51 subjects participating in this study the results of two were excluded from further analysis since their responses' inconsistencies measured by CR were higher than .25. Additionally, a one way analysis of variance was apply to test whether there are any differences between consistency levels for males and females. Although the mean CR values for women were slightly lower than for men, the discrepancy was not statistically significant $F(1, 49) = 1.62$, $p = .21$.

A final hierarchy of the examined product presentations is put together in Table 2 and graphically illustrated in Fig. 3. The ranking is based on the average scores of the perceived purchase intentions called weights. The bigger is the mean weight the higher positive impact has the specific condition on the willingness to buy.

The obtained data shows that the three dimensionally looking, rounded presentation with a blue background was decidedly best with the mean value higher by almost 40 % percent than the condition in the second place. One may notice that the first three places in the hierarchy are occupied by three dimensionally looking presentations. It can also be observed that conditions with rounded shapes both two and three dimensional seem to be generally better perceived than their sharp counterparts.

Figure 1 demonstrates that in all cases the three dimensionally looking presentations received higher rates than their corresponding flat variants. The performed LSD Fischer pairwise comparisons tests, given in Table 3 show that these differences are statistically significant at least at the level of .01. The results also reveal that variants with sharp edges having green and red background colors are the worst perceived.

Presenting the outcomes of LSD Fischer statistics in Table 3 in such a way that the experimental conditions are decreasingly ordered by their weights one may easily identify four groups separated in the table by horizontal lines. The first one contains only one member *Blue background color–Sharp edges–Three dimensional shape* which was meaningfully better rated than any other condition. There is a similar pattern in the second, third, and fourth group. The differences within a group are statistically irrelevant while differences between members of a given cluster differ considerably with members of other groups.

## 3.2 Analysis of Variance

A classic, three-way analysis of variance (Color × Shape × Dimensionality) was used to formally test whether the examined factors statistically significantly influence potential customers' mean purchase intentions. The obtained Anova outcomes are put together in Table 4. The data show statistically meaningful effects of all three investigated factors and a considerable impact of the *Shape × Dimensionality* interaction on the average willingness to buy level.

Mean weights for all significant effects are graphically demonstrated in Figs. 4–7 where vertical bars denote .95 confidence intervals. The mean weights visible in Fig. 4 clearly suggest higher purchase intentions for presentations with a blue background color as compared with the variants having either green or red background colors.

**Table 2.** Final hierarchy of examined conditions based on mean weights of the purchase intentions. Standard deviations in brackets.

| Hierarchy | Condition | | Mean weight (SD) |
|---|---|---|---|
| 1. | 1. Blue Round 3D | | .1491(.0597) |
| 2. | 9. Red Round 3D | | .1072(.0569) |
| 3. | 5. Green Round 3D | | .1031(.0559) |
| 4. | 2. Blue Round 2D | | .0951(.0379) |
| 5. | 3. Blue Sharp 3D | | .0931(.0419) |
| 6. | 10. Red Round 2D | | .0789(.0537) |
| 7. | 6. Green Round 2D | | .0695(.0372) |
| 8. | 7. Green Sharp 3D | | .0679(.0372) |
| 9. | 4. Blue Sharp 2D | | .0673(.0338) |
| 10. | 11. Red Sharp 3D | | .0673(.0330) |
| 11. | 12. Red Sharp 2D | | .0508(.0240) |
| 12. | 8. Green Sharp 2D | | .0507(.0264) |

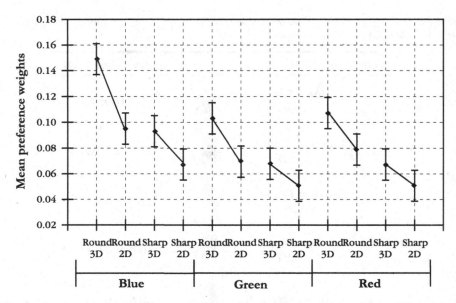

**Fig. 3.** Average purchase willingness weights for all experimental conditions. Vertical bars denote 0.95 confidence intervals.

**Table 3.** LSD Fischer pairwise comparisons probabilities between all experimental conditions. (Between MS = .00186, df = 576).

| | BR3 | RR3 | GR3 | BR2 | BS3 | RR2 | GR2 | GS3 | BS2 | RS3 | RS2 | GS2 |
|---|---|---|---|---|---|---|---|---|---|---|---|---|
| **BR3** | × | .001* | .001* | .001* | .001* | .001* | .001* | .001* | .001* | .001* | .001* | .001* |
| **RR3** | | × | .64 | .17 | .11 | .001* | .001* | .001* | .001* | .001* | .001* | .001* |
| **GR3** | | | × | .36 | .25 | .006* | .001* | .001* | .001* | .001* | .001* | .001* |
| **BR2** | | | | × | .82 | .064** | .003* | .002** | .001* | .001* | .001* | .001* |
| **BS3** | | | | | × | .10** | .007* | .004* | .003* | .003* | .001* | .001* |
| **RR2** | | | | | | × | .28 | .205 | .183 | .18 | .001* | .001* |
| **GR2** | | | | | | | × | .85 | .80 | .79 | .031* | .031* |
| **GS3** | | | | | | | | × | .95 | .94 | .050* | .049* |
| **BS2** | | | | | | | | | × | .99 | .057** | .057** |
| **RS3** | | | | | | | | | | × | .059** | .058** |
| **RS2** | | | | | | | | | | | × | .99 |
| **GS2** | | | | | | | | | | | | × |

*p < .05; **p < .1; df–degrees of freedom; MS–mean sum of squares; First character denotes the background color, the second: sharp or rounded edges, and the number: 2 or 3 dimensional shape

In order to check if the differences between individual factor levels are meaningful, an additional LSD Fischer' post-hoc analysis was conducted. Its results are given in Table 5 and indicate statistically significant discrepancies between blue-green and blue-red background colors whereas there is no difference between conditions with green and red background colors.

**Table 4.** Three-way (Color × Shape × Dimensionality) analysis of variance results

| Effect | SS | df | MS | F | p | $\eta^2$ |
|---|---|---|---|---|---|---|
| Color | .094 | 2 | .047 | 25 | <.0001* | .081 |
| Shape | .17 | 1 | .17 | 93 | <.0001* | .14 |
| Dimensionality | .13 | 1 | .13 | 68 | <.0001* | .10 |
| Color × Shape | .0054 | 2 | .0027 | 1.5 | .24 | |
| Color × Dimensionality | .0086 | 2 | .0043 | 2.3 | .101 | |
| Shape × Dimensionality | .013 | 1 | .013 | 7.0 | .0085* | .012 |
| Color × Shape × Dimensionality | .002 | 2 | .00087 | .47 | .62 | |
| Error | 1.1 | 576 | .0019 | | | |

*p < .05; df–degrees of freedom; SS–sum of squares; MS–mean sum of squares; η2–partial eta-squared

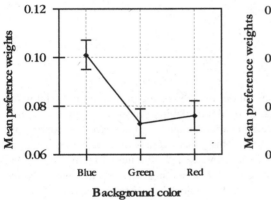

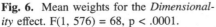

**Fig. 4.** Mean weights for the *Background color* effect. F(2, 576) = 25, p < .0001.

**Fig. 5.** Mean weights for the *Presentation Shape* effect. F(1, 576) = 93, p < .0001.

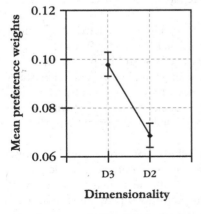

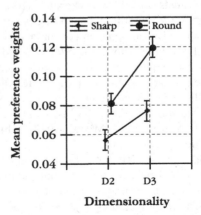

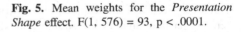

**Fig. 6.** Mean weights for the *Dimensionality* effect. F(1, 576) = 68, p < .0001.

**Fig. 7.** Mean weights for the *Dimensionality × Shape* interaction. F(1, 576) = 7.0, p < .012 (Color figure online).

Figures 5 and 6 confirm initial observations made in the previous section and indicate considerably higher mean scores for rounded shapes of product presentations versus the sharp ones, and decidedly better perception of three dimensionally looking presentations as compared with their two dimensional counterparts. The *Dimensionality × Shape* interaction shown in Fig. 7 reveals that the roundedness effect is stronger for three dimensionally looking presentations than for the 2D ones.

**Table 5.** LSD Fischer post-hoc analysis probabilities for the *Background color* factor. (Between MS = .00186, df = 576).

|        | Blue | Green | Red |
|--------|------|-------|------|
| Blue   | ×    | <.0001[*] | <.0001[*] |
| Green  |      | ×     | .46 |
| Red    |      |       | × |

[*] p < .0001

# 4  Discussion and Conclusions

The current study explores various ways of demonstrating the product in a digital way, which is nowadays very common e.g. in outdoor telebims, monitors showing digital signage messages to potential consumers in supermarkets or electronic shops operating through Internet. The outcomes presented in this paper suggest that the way of product digital presentation significantly affect the expressed willingness to buy an article. More specifically, all of the main examined factors including *Background color*, *Shape*, and *Dimensionality* considerably influenced the subjects' product perceptions.

The best scores received for the blue background color are consistent with the results provided by Middlestandt (1990) where pens presented on a blue background were higher rated than demonstrated against a red background. The bigger willingness to buy products with blue backgrounds was also reported by Ngo et al. (2012) in relation to bottles of still and sparkling water.

This effect is also partly in concordance with investigations conducted in the field of general psychology by Granger (1955) and Guilford and Smith (1959) that showed the general preference of blue over green and green over red. In the present investigation the red background color was more preferred than green, but the difference was statistically insignificant Table 5. Moreover, so decisive blue background preference over other examined colors may be connected with associating this color with competence Labrecque and Milne (2012) which may suite the perception of the smartphone.

Rebollar et al. (2012), in turn, presented that subjects preferred chewing gum packaging in warm (red and yellow tints) colors, more than the cool once (purple-green tints). However, these finding cannot be fully compared with the current study because they used a combination of two colors and smooth transitions between them for a particular package design while we applied uniform background colors.

Rebollar et al. (2012), in addition, showed that purchase willingness is more influenced by the color of the packaging than by its format. This is in contrast with findings of the present experiment indicating that the background color effect is the least important (compare partial eta-squared values from Table 4). The difference may probably be attributed to different natures of the examined products.

The presentation *Shape* factor significantly differentiated the perceived willingness to buy revealing much higher mean rates to rounded conditions. This outcome was rather expected and is consistent with previous studies reporting bigger preferences both for two dimensional curved lines (Ngo et al. 2012; Westerman et al. 2013) as well as three dimensional shapes (Becker et al. 2011). They also support findings derived on the general psychology ground (e.g. Bar and Neta 2006). Such a result may be explained by anthropological associations of edgy objects with a threat posed by knifes, axes, spears etc.

The *Dimensionality* effect revealed markedly bigger purchase intentions for three dimensionally looking presentations.

Such a result is in concordance with the neurophysiologic findings showing reduced activity in the primary visual cortex while recognizing three dimensional looking shapes (Murray et al. 2002). It seems that real life experiences, where packages are three dimensional objects, could have affected consumers' expectations regarding product digital presentation. On the other hand, the obtained result may be to some degree surprising. One could presume that two dimensional curvatures as simpler objects would require less attentional effort than 3D shapes and thereby be better liked. Favoring the three dimensional conditions could be explained to some extent in light of the results reported by John et al. (2011). The authors, by examining 2D and 3D objects demonstrated that shape understanding is better in a 3D perspective view, whereas manipulating and judging objects relative positions were better performed in 2D views. Thus, probably, consumers could faster identify 3D-like presentation as a real product package than in case of two dimensional variants. This smaller perceptual endeavor could have translated to higher purchase intentions.

It is worth noticing that the obtained in the current investigation Shape ($\eta^2 = .14$) effect size can be categorized according to Cohen (1988) as large while Dimensionality ($\eta^2 = .10$) and Color ($\eta^2 = .081$) effect sizes as medium. The lowest importance is attributed to the Shape $\times$ Dimensionality effect size ($\eta^2 = .012$) which can be described as small. Despite this, the significant interaction between Dimensionality and presentation Shape is still interesting since it indicates that the examined factors may be interdependent. In this case, the Shape factor influence is amplified by the Dimensionality effect.

One should take into account various limitations concerned with the presented results when extending or generalizing them on other situations. First, the participants represented a very specific group of people: young, undergraduate students and the obtained finding may not apply to other populations. It should be also noted that though the number of males and females was comparable, this effect was neither controlled nor analyzed. This could have had some impact on the subjective responses especially regarding the Background color factor since there are studies showing gender differences in this regard (e.g. Grobelny and Michalski 2015).

Some future investigations may be directed to compensate the abovementioned drawbacks and extend the ecological validity of the obtained outcomes by conducting experiments with real packages and in real circumstances. Some additional studies can be focused on different types of products to whether the results would be similar.

Despite these shortcomings, the current study results increase our knowledge about human visual behavior in a specific marketing context. It may also be assumed that subjective responses examined in the present experiment will affect the real purchase decisions. Therefore knowing the described in the current study findings and applying them during the design process would not only extend our knowledge about processing visual information by potential consumers but also be beneficial for practitioners.

**Acknowledgments.**  The work was partly financially supported by the Polish National Science Center grants no. 2011/03/B/HS4/03925.

# References

Azzi, A., Battini, D., Persona, A., Sgarbossa, F.: Packaging design: general framework and research agenda. Packag. Technol. Sci. **25**(8), 435–456 (2012). doi:10.1002/pts.993

Bar, M., Neta, M.: Humans prefer curved visual objects. Psychol. Sci. **17**(8), 645–648 (2006). doi:10.1111/j.1467-9280.2006.01759.x

Becker, L., van Rompay, T.J.L., Schifferstein, H.N.J., Galetzka, M.: Tough package, strong taste: the influence of packaging design on taste impressions and product evaluations. Food Qual. Prefer. **22**(1), 17–23 (2011). doi:10.1016/j.foodqual.2010.06.007

Christ, R.E.: Review and analysis of color coding research for visual displays. Hum. Factors: J. Hum. Factors Ergon. Soc. **17**(6), 542–570 (1975). doi:10.1177/001872087501700602

Cohen, J.: Statistical Power Analysis for the Behavioral Sciences, 2nd edn. Erlbaum, Hillsdale (1988)

Deliza, R., Macfie, H., Hedderley, D.: Use of Computer-Generated Images and Conjoint Analysis to Investigate Sensory Expectations. J. Sensory Stud. **18**(6), 465–486 (2003). doi:10.1111/j.1745-459X.2003.tb00401.x

Granger, G.W.: An Experimental Study of Colour Preferences. J. Gen. Psychol. **52**(1), 3–20 (1955). doi:10.1080/00221309.1955.9918340

Grobelny, J., Michalski, R.: Various approaches to a human preference analysis in a digital signage display design. Hum. Factors Ergon. Manuf. Serv. Ind. **21**(6), 529–542 (2011). doi:10.1002/hfm.2029

Grobelny, J., Michalski, R.: The role of background color, interletter spacing, and font size on preferences in the digital presentation of a product. Comput. Hum. Behav. **43**, 85–100 (2015). doi:10.1016/j.chb.2014.10.036

Guilford, J.P., Smith, P.C.: A System of Color-Preferences. Am. J. Psychol. **72**(4), 487 (1959). doi:10.2307/1419491

Harris, J.L., Thompson, J.M., Schwartz, M.B., Brownell, K.D.: Nutrition-related claims on children's cereals: what do they mean to parents and do they influence willingness to buy? Public Health Nutr. **14**(12), 2207–2212 (2011). doi:10.1017/S1368980011001741

John, M.S., Cowen, M.B., Smallman, H.S., Oonk, H.M.: The use of 2D and 3D displays for shape-understanding versus relative-position tasks. Hum. Factors: J. Hum. Factors Ergon. Soc. **43**(1), 79–98 (2001). doi:10.1518/001872001775992534

Labrecque, L., Milne, G.: Exciting red and competent blue: the importance of color in marketing. J. Acad. Mark. Sci. **40**(5), 711–727 (2012). doi:10.1007/s11747-010-0245-y

Michalski, R.: Examining users' preferences towards vertical graphical toolbars in simple search and point tasks. Comput. Hum. Behav. **27**(6), 2308–2321 (2011). doi:10.1016/j.chb.2011.07. 010

Middlestadt, S.E.: The effect of background and ambient color on product attitudes and beliefs. Ad. Consum. Res. **17**(1), 244–249 (1990)

Murray, S.O., Kersten, D., Olshausen, B.A., Schrater, P., Woods, D.L.: Shape perception reduces activity in human primary visual cortex. Proc. Nat. Acad. Sci. **99**(23), 15164–15169 (2002). doi:10.1073/pnas.192579399

Ngo, M.K., Piqueras-Fiszman, B., Spence, C.: On the colour and shape of still and sparkling water: insights from online and laboratory-based testing. Food Qual. Prefer. **24**(2), 260–268 (2012). doi:10.1016/j.foodqual.2011.11.004

Norman, J.F., Todd, J.T., Orban, G.A.: Perception of three-dimensional shape from specular highlights, deformations of shading, and other types of visual information. Psychol. Sci. **15** (8), 565–570 (2004). doi:10.1111/j.0956-7976.2004.00720.x

Rebollar, R., Lidón, I., Serrano, A., Martín, J., Fernández, M.J.: Influence of chewing gum packaging design on consumer expectation and willingness to buy. an analysis of functional, sensory and experience attributes. Food Qual. Prefer. **24**(1), 162–170 (2012). doi:10.1016/j. foodqual.2011.10.011

Richardson, P.S., Dick, A.S., Jain, A.K.: Extrinsic and intrinsic cue effects on perceptions of store brand quality. J. Mark. **58**(4), 28–36 (1994). doi:10.2307/1251914

Robertson, A.R.: The CIE 1976 color-difference formulae. Color Res. Appl. **2**(1), 7–11 (1977). doi:10.1002/j.1520-6378.1977.tb00104.x

Robertson, G.L.: Food packaging: principles and practice. Taylor & Francis/CRC, Boca Raton (2006)

Rundh, B.: The multi-faceted dimension of packaging: marketing logistic or marketing tool? Brit. Food J. **107**(9), 670–684 (2005). doi:10.1108/00070700510615053

Saaty, T.L.: A scaling method for priorities in hierarchical structures. J. Math. Psychol. **15**(3), 234–281 (1977). doi:10.1016/0022-2496(77)90033-5

Saaty, T.L.: The Analytic Hierarchy Process. McGraw–Hill, New York (1980)

Schloss, K.B., Strauss, E.D., Palmer, S.E.: Object color preferences. Color Res. Appl. **38**(6), 393–411 (2013). doi:10.1002/col.21756

Valajoozi, M.R., Zangi, N.O.: A review on visual criteria of pure milk packaging for parents and their children (case study: Tehran, Iran). Brit. Food J. **118**(1), 83–99 (2015). doi:10.1108/BFJ-12-2014-0425

Werle, C.O.C., Balbo, L., Caldara, C., Corneille, O.: Is plain food packaging plain wrong? Plain packaging increases unhealthy snack intake among males. Food Qual. Prefer. **49**, 168–175 (2016). doi:10.1016/j.foodqual.2015.12.007

Westerman, S.J., Sutherland, E.J., Gardner, P.H., Baig, N., Critchley, C., Hickey, C., Zervos, Z.: The design of consumer packaging: Effects of manipulations of shape, orientation, and alignment of graphical forms on consumers' assessments. Food Qual. Prefer. **27**(1), 8–17 (2013). doi:10.1016/j.foodqual.2012.05.007

# Inspecting the Quality of Educational Video Artefacts Employed in Speech-Language Pathology Telerehabilitation: A Pilot Study

Dijana Plantak Vukovac[1](✉), Tihomir Orehovački[2],
and Tatjana Novosel-Herceg[3]

[1] Faculty of Organization and Informatics, University of Zagreb, Pavlinska 2,
42000 Varaždin, Croatia
dijana.plantak@foi.hr
[2] Department of Information and Communication Technologies, Juraj Dobrila
University of Pula, Zagrebačka 30, 52100 Pula, Croatia
tihomir.orehovacki@unipu.hr
[3] VaLMod Speech-Language Pathology Centre,
Ante Starčevića 25, 42000 Varaždin, Croatia
tatjana.novoselherceg@gmail.com

**Abstract.** Information and communication technology, particularly multimedia technology and the Internet, are commonly employed in the assessment, treatment and education of speech-language and communication disorders. Considering that video artefacts supplement or replace the speech therapist and can be used in both synchronous and asynchronous settings, they represent an important part of an online therapy. This paper presents a part of an ongoing research regarding the use of video in speech-language online therapy. The aim of the paper is threefold. First, we describe how video artefacts have been designed in accordance with the principles of multimedia learning and subsequently employed in telerehabilitation of pediatric speech disorder (dyslalia). Second, we introduce a set of quality attributes which significantly affect the success of the implementation of educational video artefacts in speech-language pathology (SLP) online therapies. Finally, we present and discuss the results of a pilot study carried out with an objective to examine the perceived quality of educational video artefacts applied in SLP telerehabilitation.

**Keywords:** Quality evaluation · Educational video artefacts · Speech-language pathology telerehabilitation · Dyslalia

## 1 Introduction

Relevant literature on telerehabilitation in speech-language pathology (SLP) provides a lot of evidence of applying information and communication technology, particularly multimedia technology and the Internet, in the assessment, treatment and education of speech-language and communication disorders. In recent systematic review of 103 papers that investigated the use of telehealth in speech, language and hearing sciences, 85.5 % of the studies indicated that SLP telehealth has advantages over the

© Springer International Publishing Switzerland 2016
M. Antona and C. Stephanidis (Eds.): UAHCI 2016, Part III, LNCS 9739, pp. 480–491, 2016.
DOI: 10.1007/978-3-319-40238-3_46

non-telehealth procedures [15]. There are an increasing number of research studies that support the effectiveness of remote assessment (e.g. [9, 28]) or online SLP therapy that is equal to or better than face-to-face service (e.g. [4, 12]). Some studies also indicated user satisfaction with applied online SLP services (e.g. [28]).

Delivery of SLP remote services is provided by combining synchronous and asynchronous technologies such as e-mail, photos, audio, video, etc. Video presents an important part of an online therapy since it supplements or replaces the therapist and can be used in both technologies' settings. It can be used for synchronous real-time interactions between the patient and the therapist by employing videoconferences, or asynchronously presented as video recordings of therapy demonstrations during treatment or post-treatment. Our previous study had shown that activities that include engagement of video in SLP online services are among top three preferred activities for both clients and therapists [25].

Video is gaining more attention in recent years in educational settings, particularly with the introduction of massive online courses like those implemented in Coursera or Udacity e-learning platforms. When direct tutoring and mentoring of an online teacher is not available, video is used as a replacement for face-to-face lesson delivery, enabling multiple playbacks of a lesson. Video also increases student's motivation to continue with the lesson [3]. Studies had shown that the appropriate design of multimedia learning materials, including educational video, has positive effects on learning (e.g. [1, 7, 11]). The same premise could be applied to educational video employed in speech-language telerehabilitation: design and creation of a video demonstration of a particular therapy (exercise) according to design principles should promote learning of concepts and foster automatization of skills, whether it is a case of learning how to pronounce a sound/word or how to breathe while speaking. Thus the ultimate goal of any educational video design should be a delivery of high-quality instructional videos that achieve their purpose.

Over the years, video quality has been measured from various aspects. Technical aspect of the quality includes factors like video resolution, bitrate, compression, buffering ratio or bandwidth [5]. User aspect includes factors such as user perceived quality, user engagement, content popularity, etc. [5]. Pedagogical aspect of video quality is particularly important in educational videos and is related to video length, content type, speaking rate, production style, etc. [8] as well as video design that includes factors like animation, narration, integration of pictures, type and position of on-screen text or integration of subtitles [1, 2].

According to the recent international standard [10], quality in general refers to the degree to which a piece of software meets stated and implied needs when used under specified conditions. In that respect, quality is considered to be one of the essential factors that contribute to the acceptance of software applications including artefacts resulting from their use. Since it is a systematic process of measuring the relevance of software features [6], the process of quality evaluation is commonly applied with an objective to determine whether any usability issues are appearing during the interaction with the software as well as for the purpose of inspecting diverse facets of user experience. While recent HCI literature offers a number of different advances in the field in terms of models, methods, and standards meant for evaluating different dimensions of quality in the context of social web applications [16, 21, 22], games [19] and educational artefacts created with Web 2.0 applications [24], studies related to the quality assessment in the SLP environment are in general fairly scarce. The set forth findings encouraged us to initiate a research on the design of the framework that would facilitate the design of educational artefacts and quality evaluation of educational artefacts employed in SLP telerehabilitation.

The aim of this paper is threefold. First, we will describe how video artefacts have been designed in accordance with the principles of the cognitive theory of multimedia learning [13] and subsequently employed in telerehabilitation of pediatric speech disorder (dyslalia). Second, we will introduce a set of quality attributes which significantly affect the success of the implementation of educational video artefacts in online SLP therapies. Finally, we will present and discuss findings of an empirical pilot study conducted with an aim to explore the perceived quality of educational video artefacts applied in SLP telerehabilitation.

The remainder of this paper is structured as follows. The next section offers a brief overview of recent and relevant studies in the field. Details on employed research methodology are provided in the third section. The results of the conducted pilot study are presented in the fourth section. Contributions, limitations, and future research directions are discussed in the last section.

## 2  Background to the Research

Mayer's Cognitive Theory of Multimedia Learning (CTML) offers the foundation for efficient design of multimedia learning materials. CTML is based on three scientific assumptions about how human minds works [13]: (1) *dual-channel* assumption which states that humans possess two separate channels: visual/pictorial channels for processing visual input and auditory/verbal channels for processing auditory input, (2) *limited-capacity* assumption which states that humans' working memory is limited in the amount of information it can process in each channel at one time, and (3) *active-processing* assumption which states that active learning happens when humans actively pay attention, organize incoming information and integrate them with other knowledge. These assumptions were the basis for the creation of twelve principles of multimedia learning, i.e. instructional features of multimedia lessons that underpin meaningful learning. For instance, multimedia principle states that learning is better when pictures are presented together with the spoken words, while the signaling principle states that learning is better when essential material is highlighted in the multimedia lesson [13, 14].

Meaningful learning requires substantial learning processing that also involves building connections among visual and verbal information. For example, learning material can show an animation during which a narrator explains what is happening in the animation, so both visual and verbal channels are occupied. Since the capacity of working memory is limited for processing information in each channel at one time, cognitive load can occur when total intended processing of information exceeds the learner's cognitive capacity [14]. If cognitive processing does not serve instructional goal, e.g. lesson contains interesting but irrelevant information, or is caused by confusing instructional design or layout, an *extraneous cognitive overload* takes place [13, 14]. Typical example for this is a background instrumental music during auditory presentation of essential learning information, which results with overload in auditory channel and possible inability of learner to pay attention to learning material.

Mayer has proposed five principles to reduce extraneous cognitive load in multimedia presentations [13, p. 86]: (1) *coherence principle* – exclude extraneous words, sound or graphics, (2) *signaling principle* – highlight essential words or graphics, (3) *redundancy principle* – exclude redundant captions from narrated animation, (4) *spatial contiguity principle* – place essential words next to the corresponding graphics, and (5) *temporal contiguity principle* – present the corresponding words and pictures simultaneously. These principles can also be applied in the design of educational videos. Bouki et al. have been exploring redundancy principle in videos and how redundant information in videos, e.g. on-screen text and subtitles affects learners' attention and comprehension [2]. One of the results from their qualitative research with eye-tracking method indicates that if the textual information, handled by the visual channel, does not conflict with the auditory information, handled by the auditory channel, then subjects can easily process both visual and auditory messages. A research by Arguel and Jamet shed light on spatial contiguity principle: they examined the influence of video on learning outcomes and found out that students who had been learning from a combination of video and static pictures performed better in the assessment than those learning only from video presentations [1]. This suggests that it is better to design videos with static pictures in the vicinity of videos, in contrast to videos without them, particularly when pictures emphasize the key stages of a procedure presented in the video.

Video is also recognized as the essential part of speech-language telepractice [25, 27], but to our knowledge, there are no researches on the video design employed in SLP online therapy. Recommendations on a video design are mainly oriented towards technical aspects of recording and delivering video online, e.g. usage of video formats that can be viewed on various devices, operating systems and browsers; short video length; customization of video regarding its size on the screen, or recommendations on services for video upload [27]. Thus, one of the goals of this paper is to present how principles of multimedia learning can be applied in the design of instructional videos employed in SLP therapy of pediatric speech disorder, with emphasis on principles that reduce extraneous cognitive load.

## 3    Methodology

In order to inspect the quality of educational video artefacts employed in speech-language pathology telerehabilitation, the following sub-goals of our research were defined:

- design and development of educational video artefacts for the therapy of pediatric speech sound disorder (dyslalia) according to the principles of CTML,
- design and implementation of an instrument for measuring the quality of educational video artefacts applied in SLP therapy,
- conducting a pilot study to examine the perceived quality of educational video artefacts for telerehabilitation of dyslalia,

- conducting the main study with control and experimental group to examine the video quality and outcomes of online SLP therapy of dyslalia employing educational videos.

This paper presents the methodology for and findings of the first three sub-goals.

## 3.1    Design and Development of Educational Video for SLP Therapy

Recording, design and development of the video artefacts have been accomplished at the Faculty of Organization and Informatics of the University of Zagreb, Croatia, in cooperation with two speech-language therapists from the local SLP centre. The SLP therapists have suggested dyslalia therapy since it is feasible to be prepared in the form of educational video artefacts. Dyslalia is a speech sound disorder which is often present in a native language of preschool or early years school child, but sometimes in adult age as well. The disorder is manifested as sound or phoneme that is either not produced, not produced correctly, or not used correctly, e.g. pronunciation of the sound R in the word "rabbit" might be produced like "wabbit". The SLP therapists included in the pilot research suggested preparation of educational videos for the sounds S upon the availability of the test participants with that sound disorder. Together with a research leader, they have prepared storyboards for video recording and editing.

A typical SLP therapy for correcting the sound S (and many other sounds) consists of a set of exercises in which the client (child or adult) repeats the sound in all positions in the word - at the beginning, in the middle, at the end and close to a vowel. During the exercise (or therapist's assessment), incorrect pronunciation can be observed, so a special case exercise should be performed to correct the mispronunciation before continuing to the next exercise. In order to cover all cases for the sound S, twelve videos have been recorded or the following four videos for each sound position: (1) demonstration of the sound S at the beginning/in the middle/at the end of the word, (2) repeating exercise of the sound S at the beginning/in the middle/at the end of the word, (3) demonstration of errors when pronouncing the sound S at the beginning/in the middle/at the end of the word, and (4) demonstration of the sound S used in a combination with the vowels at the beginning/in the middle/at the end of the word.

In order to produce professional like videos, video recordings were made in an improvised recording studio with two speech-language therapists, one of whom has served as a demonstrator and the other as a narrator. The demonstrator was recorded against a green backdrop with three digital video cameras placed on the tripods using different close-up shots: *enface* close-up, *enface* extreme close-up and *profile* extreme close-up, in order to record all the necessary details of the mouth and tongue position while pronouncing the sound S. Post-production was made in Adobe Premiere CS6 video editing software. For the purpose of the pilot research, only three videos with the sound S at the beginning of the word were edited.

Every video consisted of the following logical parts: introductory part with copyright information and the project's logo; title of the video; announcement part narrated by the demonstrator who explained the content of the video; the main content with a demonstration or exercise shown in various close-up shots; the demonstrator's wrap up with the announcement about the next video; and scrolling credits part at the end of the video.

Video editing was done in accordance with five CTML principles to reduce extraneous cognitive load:

- *Coherence principle*: copyright information about the video is important from the aspect of video creators, but are not directly associated with the instructable content. In order to avoid diverting an attention from the exercise, copyright information, logo graphics and short music were not added throughout the video, but only at the beginning and/or the end of the videos.
- *Signaling principle*: visual and auditory signaling were added to guide viewer's attention to the key elements of performing the pronunciation of the sound S. Visual signaling was provided in the form of arrows, accented text or other visual clues (see Fig. 1), while auditory signaling was provided in the form of vocal emphasis and music during the introductory and credits parts.
- *Redundancy principle*: concurrent video/animation and on-screen text are considered redundant information that overloads the visual channel, so this combination was avoided in most parts of the video. However, the redundancy principle was violated in two cases: when transcribed narration was placed next to the narrator's face in order to give additional information to parents on how to produce a specific sound (see Fig. 2), and when *enface* extreme close-up and *profile* extreme close-up were placed in the same scene; both for the reason to allow pausing of the video playback in key position moments.
- *Spatial contiguity principle:* visual clues are presented near the corresponding parts of the video in order to avoid visual cognitive load (see Fig. 1).
- *Temporal contiguity principle*: the narrator simultaneously explains the demonstration of the position of mouth or tongue, so information is processed in both visual and auditory channel.

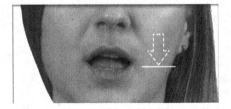

**Fig. 1.** Signaling and spatial contiguity principles

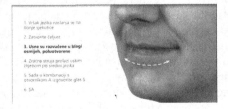

**Fig. 2.** Violation of redundancy principle

## 3.2   Design of an Instrument for Measuring Quality of Educational Video Artefacts Applied in SLP Therapy

Drawing on the literature review related to the assessment of various dimensions of quality including usability [21, 22, 24], user experience [18, 21], quality in use [17, 21], and success [20, 21], an initial set of 26 attributes was generated. In order to examine their adequacy for measuring the quality of video artefacts employed in SLP therapies, an empirical study was carried out [23]. Seven attributes which have not met the cut-off values of two content validity indicators were omitted from further analysis. The remaining pool of 19 attributes was enhanced with additional attribute that deals with particularities of video artefacts. The final post-use questionnaire was composed of 110 items designed for measuring facets of 20 quality attributes in the context of video artefacts used for the purpose of SLP therapies. Considering the items assigned to attributes *accessibility* and *portability,* they were renamed *flexibility* and *displayability,* respectively. The answers were scored on a four-point Likert scale (1 – strongly agree, 4 – strongly disagree). Each attribute was measured with between three and nine items. For the purpose of data analysis, the value of a particular quality attribute was operationalized as a sum of responses to the assigned items.

## 3.3   Research Design of the Pilot Study

Nine parents who had an appointment with their children in the local SLP centre have agreed to participate in the pilot study after they were briefly introduced with the idea of online SLP therapy and a research goal to examine video quality. They have signed an informed consent and filled out the web questionnaire about their usage of ICT and preferences regarding SLP therapies provided online. The children were previously examined by a speech therapist, who had determined dyslalia disorder with the sound S. After the therapist's evaluation, the therapy started with the therapist's demonstration of pronouncing the sound S at the beginning of the word. Nowadays, many parents, with the therapist's approval, record (by means of the smartphone, camera or camcorder) the therapist's demonstration and the way he/she sets the sound. That was also the case with all parent participants in the pilot study. Finally, the therapist wrote down the prescribed therapy on practicing the pronunciation in the child's notebook and once more informed the parents about the whole procedure and how they are going to work with the child at home. Parents were instructed to practice pronunciation with a child on classical way at least for 2–3 days before accessing online SLP therapy. The therapy with edited videos was embedded into a learning management system and all parents received login information along with the instructions how to use the video by means of e-mail. Parents were also asked to fill-out the post-questionnaire after using the videos with their children for at least two times.

# 4  Results

**Participants.** Five out of nine parents have accessed online SLP therapy with their children. The majority of parents (80 %) were female, whereas all the children were male. The children ranged in age from five to eight (M = 5.40, SD = 1.517). At the time the pilot study took place, the participants originated from three different Croatian counties. When the employment of information and communication technology is considered, 60 % of them are using desktop computers, 60 % of them are utilizing laptops, 40 % are applying tablets, 80 % are employing smartphones, 40 % are using web cams, 40 % are utilizing headphones, 20 % are applying microphones, 60 % are employing digital cameras whereas 20 % of them are using digital camcorders. The majority of respondents (60 %) are using computers at their homes for up to two hours. The same percentage of parents are consuming the Internet on a daily basis.

When the reasons for attending the speech-language therapies are taken into account, all the children were diagnosed with dyslalia disorder, 20 % of them also had undeveloped speech disorder, and 20 % of them also had stuttering disorder. The majority of parents (80 %) expressed their readiness to perform occasional online therapies at their homes. Regarding the manner in which parents are willing to take part in online therapies, 20 % of parents are willing to carry out online exercises only for the duration of the therapy and only if speech therapist is going to monitor the activities of their child, 60 % of parents are ready to conduct online exercises during and upon completion of the therapy, with or without the speech therapist's supervision, and only 20 % of parents are willing to continue to perform online exercises after the end of the therapy without the speech therapist's supervision.

Considering the form of online therapies, all pilot study participants reported they would like to use it in the form of video artefacts, 20 % of parents are interested in therapies in the form of an online game, 40 % of them would like to practice it in the form of a game installed on a smartphone or a tablet, 60 % of them are willing to conduct online therapy through interaction with the speech therapist via video link, and 40 % of parents want to use the calendar with appointments with the therapist.

When the parents were asked how they would like to monitor their child's progress in online speech therapy, all of them answered they want to have an insight into the conducted therapies and into the assignments the child needs to complete until the next appointment with the speech therapist, also 60 % of them are willing to help their child improve his speech skills by playing a computer game which monitors progress over a certain period of time, and 60 % of them are ready to check the completion of the assignments executed at home until the next appointment with the therapist.

**Findings.** The analysis of the collected data revealed that study participants strongly agreed (92 %) and agreed (8 %) on items which indicate that video artefacts precisely and accurately display how to pronounce particular sounds (*correctness*). It was also discovered that parents strongly agreed (73.33 %) and agreed (26.67 %) on items which denote that the content of video artefacts is complete and clear (*coverage*). According to the results of the pilot study, respondents strongly agreed (90 %) and agreed (10 %) on items designed for evaluating the level to which the content of video artefacts is trustworthy and reliable (*credibility*). Parents also strongly agreed (80 %) and agreed (20 %) on items which imply that video artefacts are beneficial in terms of treating speech and language disorders (*usefulness*). The results of data analysis indicate that pilot study subjects strongly agreed (90 %) and agreed (10 %) on items which denote they have a positive stand on the employment of video artefacts in SPL therapies (*attitude*). On the other hand, parents strongly agreed (65 %), agreed (32.50 %), and disagreed (2.50 %) on items which imply that they intend to continue to use video artefacts for speech disorder rehabilitation purposes and recommend them to others who have some kind of speech disorder (*continuance intention*). It was also found that respondents strongly agreed (54.29 %) and agreed (45.71 %) on items which indicate that video artefacts have met parents' expectations (*satisfaction*).

The analysis of data gathered by means of post-use questionnaire uncovered that participants strongly agreed (80 %), agreed (15 %), and disagreed (5 %) on items which denote that users can adjust video artefacts to their needs (*customizability*). Parents reported they strongly agreed (80 %), agreed (14.29 %), and disagreed (5.71 %) on items which imply that it is easy to become proficient in employing video artefacts (*ease of use*). Pilot study subjects strongly agreed (80 %) and agreed (20 %) on items which denote that video artefacts are designed in a way that users cannot make a mistake in pronouncing a particular sound (*error prevention*).

On the other hand, it was discovered that parents strongly agreed (28.57 %), agreed (60 %) and disagreed (11.43 %) on items which indicate that video artefacts are visually appealing (*aesthetics*). Moreover, respondents strongly agreed (33.33 %) and agreed (66.67 %) on items which denote that the use of video artefacts represents a unique approach to treatment of speech disorders (*uniqueness*). It was also discovered that parents strongly agreed (20 %), agreed (50 %), and disagreed (30 %) on items which imply that the use of video artefacts for the purpose of rehabilitating speech disorders successfully absorbs patients' attention (*playfulness*). Pilot study participants reported they strongly agreed (36.67 %), agreed (33.33 %), disagreed (13.33 %), and strongly disagreed (16.67 %) on items which indicate they are using video artefacts for telerehabilitation purposes because they were recommended by the speech therapist (*social influence*).

According to pilot study results, parents strongly agreed (40 %), agreed (40 %), disagreed (13.33 %), and strongly disagreed (6.67 %) on items which denote that the use of video artefacts enable monitoring the implementation of SLP therapies (*trackability*). It was also found that respondents strongly agreed (35 %), agreed (40 %), disagreed (15 %) and strongly disagreed (10 %) on items which imply that online therapies with the use of video artefacts do not differ significantly from "classical" SLP therapies (*familiarity*). The analysis of gathered data has shown that parents strongly agreed (56.67 %), agreed (33.33 %), and disagreed (10 %) on items which indicate that video artefacts are usable for treating various speech and language disorders (*flexibility*). Study participants reported they strongly agreed (56 %), agreed (40 %), and disagreed (4 %) on items which denote that the use of video artefacts does not differ significantly among web browsers and devices that have Internet connection (*displayability*). It was also revealed that parents strongly agreed (40 %), agreed (16 %), disagreed (12 %), and strongly disagreed (32 %) on items which imply that video artefacts are available to everyone and every time they need them (*availability*).

Finally, pilot study participants strongly agreed (71.11 %) and agreed (29.89 %) on items which indicate that video artefacts are professionally prepared and modernly designed (*overall quality*).

# 5   Discussion and Concluding Remarks

This paper introduced an approach to the design of educational video artefacts employed in speech-language telerehabilitation of dyslalia. Video design and production have been prepared in accordance with the principles of the cognitive theory of multimedia learning that reduces extraneous cognitive load. This approach was chosen because of the similarities of online learning that applies video artefacts and learning that happens during an SLP therapy. While four of CTML principles (coherence, signaling, spatial contiguity and temporal contiguity principle) were applied to the design of SLP video artefacts, the redundancy principle was violated. One part of the artefact was designed with concurrent video, narration and on-screen text due to the fact that video will be observed both by a child who cannot read, and a parent who might need additional written instructions on how to produce a particular sound.

Video artefacts have been examined in an empirical pilot study with five children and their parents. After interactions with video artefacts, parents have evaluated the video quality with a post-use questionnaire. The findings of the study indicate that edited videos were of very high quality and prepared professionally. However, some aspects of the quality were less favorable, like visual appeal and the quality of audio (noise and metal sound were noticeable in one video). In addition, video artefacts were found neither entertaining nor available (due to the fact that users should log in to be able to view video). Parents have expressed a strong positive attitude towards the employment of video artefacts in SLP therapies and confirmed that videos have met their expectations. However, parents' intention to continue to use video artefacts was not that high, which might suggest the lack of motivation or the lack of time for telerehabilitation. Considering there are neither standards on the design of educational videos in general [2], nor strong evidence about the outcomes of online treatment of dyslalia [26], particularly the one that employs video, we believe that findings presented in this paper significantly add to the extant body of knowledge and establish a background for further theoretical and empirical advances in the field of dyslalia telerehabilitation.

Taking into account that reported findings emerged from an empirical pilot study, several limitations must be acknowledged. Although parents of the children with speech disorder are a representative sample of video artefacts users, a heterogeneous sample in terms of age, gender, and type of speech disorder could have importantly different perception about the quality of video artefacts used in SLP telerehabilitation. The second limitation deals with the sample size. Five individuals may be sufficient for presenting the results of the pilot study, but to draw sound conclusions, the research needs to involve more participants. The last limitation is that the results cannot be generalized to all types of speech disorders but only to those related to the pronunciation of the sound S. Having that in mind, the empirical results should be interpreted carefully.

The results of the pilot study have revealed several directions for enhancing the quality of video artefacts. However, a deeper insight into the quality and the usage of video artefacts would be achieved with a qualitative research, which would enable us to observe interactions of the child and parents with the videos and the system into which the videos were embedded. In that respect, our future work efforts will be focused on: (1) inclusion of control and experimental group of patients which would enable us to further explore the video quality in accordance with different production styles; (2) measuring the efficiency of online SLP therapy of dyslalia employing educational videos; and (3) validation of an instrument for evaluating the quality of video artefacts in SLP telerehabilitation.

# References

1. Arguel, A., Jamet, E.: Using video and static pictures to improve learning of procedural contents. Comput. Hum. Behav. **25**(2), 354–359 (2009)
2. Bouki, V., Economou, D., Angelopoulou, A.: Cognitive theory of multimedia learning and learning videos design: the redundancy principle. In: Proceedings of the 29th ACM International Conference on Design of Communication, SIGDOC 2011 (2011)
3. Bravo, E., Amante-Garcia, B., Simo, P., Enache, M., Fernandez, V.: Video as a new teaching tool to increase student motivation. In: Proceedings of 2011 IEEE Global Engineering Education Conference, pp. 638–642 (2011)
4. Carey, B., O'Brian, S., Onslow, M., Packman, A., Menzies, R.: Webcam delivery of the camperdown program for adolescents who stutter: a phase I trial. Lang. Speech Hearing Serv. Sch. **43**(3), 370–380 (2012)
5. Dobrian, F., Sekar, V. Awan, A., Stoica, I., Joseph, D., Ganjam, A., Zhan, J., Zhang, H.: Understanding the impact of video quality on user engagement. In: Proceedings of the ACM SIGCOMM 2011 Conference, pp. 362–373 (2011)
6. Gena, C., Weibelzahl, S.: Usability engineering for the adaptive web. In: Brusilovsky, P., Kobsa, A., Nejdl, W. (eds.) Adaptive Web 2007. LNCS, vol. 4321, pp. 720–762. Springer, Heidelberg (2007)
7. Gligora Marković, M., Kliček, B., Plantak Vukovac, D.: The effects of multimedia learning materials quality on knowledge acquisition. In: Proceedings of the 23rd International Conference on Information Systems Development, pp. 140–149. Faculty of Organization and Informatics, Varaždin (2014)
8. Guo, P.J., Kim, J., Rubin, R.: How video production affects student engagement: an empirical study of MOOC videos. In: Proceedings of the first ACM Conference on Learning @ Scale Conference, pp. 41–50 (2014)
9. Hill, A.J., Theodoros, D., Russell, T., Ward, E.: Using telerehabilitation to assess apraxia of speech in adults. Int. J. Lang. Commun. Disord. **44**(5), 731–747 (2009)
10. ISO/IEC 25010: Systems and software engineering - Systems and software Quality Requirements and Evaluation (SQuaRE) - System and software quality models (2011)
11. Lou, S., Lin, H., Shih, R.C., Tseng, K.H.: Improving the effectiveness of organic chemistry experiments through multimedia teaching materials for junior high school students. Turk. Online J. Educ. Technol. **11**(2), 135–141 (2012)
12. Mashima, P.A., Birkmire-Peters, D.P., Syms, M.J., Holtel, M.R., Burgess, L., Peters, L.J.: Telehealth: voice therapy using telecommunications technology. Am. J. Speech-Lang. Pathol. **12**(4), 432–439 (2003)

13. Mayer, R.E.: Multimedia Learning. Cambridge University Press, New York (2009)
14. Mayer, R.E., Moreno, R.: Nine ways to reduce cognitive load in multimedia learning. Educ. Psychol. **38**(1), 43–52 (2003)
15. Molini-Avejonas, D.R., Rondon-Melo, S., de La Higuera Amato, C.A., Samelli, A.G.: A systematic review of the use of telehealth in speech, language and hearing sciences. J. Telemed. Telecare **21**(7), 367–376 (2015)
16. Orehovački, T.: Perceived quality of cloud based applications for collaborative writing. In: Pokorny, J., et al. (eds.) Information Systems Development – Business Systems and Services: Modeling and Development, pp. 575–586. Springer, Heidelberg (2011)
17. Orehovački, T.: Proposal for a set of quality attributes relevant for Web 2.0 application success. In: Proceedings of the 32nd International Conference on Information Technology Interfaces, pp. 319–326. IEEE Press, Cavtat (2010)
18. Orehovački, T., Al Sokkar, A.A., Derboven, J., Khan, A.: Exploring the hedonic quality of slow technology. In: CHI 2013 Workshop on Changing Perspectives of Time in HCI (2013). http://bib.irb.hr/datoteka/617623.workshop_paper_final3.pdf
19. Orehovački, T., Babić, S.: Inspecting quality of games designed for learning programming. In: Zaphiris, P., Ioannou, A. (eds.) LCT 2015. LNCS, vol. 9192, pp. 620–631. Springer, Heidelberg (2015)
20. Orehovački, T., Babić, S., Jadrić, M.: Exploring the validity of an instrument to measure the perceived quality in use of Web 2.0 applications with educational potential. In: Zaphiris, P., Ioannou, A. (eds.) LCT 2014, Part I. LNCS, vol. 8523, pp. 192–203. Springer, Heidelberg (2014)
21. Orehovački, T., Granić, A., Kermek, D.: Evaluating the perceived and estimated quality in use of Web 2.0 applications. J. Syst. Softw. **86**(12), 3039–3059 (2013)
22. Orehovački, T., Granollers, T.: Subjective and objective assessment of mashup tools. In: Marcus, A. (ed.) DUXU 2014, Part I. LNCS, vol. 8517, pp. 340–351. Springer, Heidelberg (2014)
23. Orehovački, T., Plantak Vukovac, D., Novosel-Herceg, T.: Educational artefacts as a foundation for development of remote speech-language therapies. In: Vogel, D., et al. (eds.) Transforming Healthcare Through Information Systems. Lecture Notes in Information Systems and Organisation. Springer, Heidelberg (2016)
24. Orehovački, T., Žajdela Hrustek, N.: Development and validation of an instrument to measure the usability of educational artifacts created with Web 2.0 applications. In: Marcus, A. (ed.) DUXU 2013, Part I. LNCS, vol. 8012, pp. 369–378. Springer, Heidelberg (2013)
25. Plantak Vukovac, D., Novosel-Herceg, T., Orehovački, T.: Users' needs in telehealth speech-language pathology services. In: Proceedings of the 24th International Conference on Information Systems Development, pp. 1–12. Harbin Institute of Technology, Harbin (2015)
26. Theodoros, D.G.: Speech-language pathology and telerehabilitation. In: Kumar, S., Cohn, E. R. (eds.) Telerehabilitation, pp. 311–323. Springer, London (2013)
27. Towey, M.: Speech therapy telepractice. In: Kumar, S., Cohn, E.R. (eds.) Telerehabilitation, pp. 101–123. Springer, London (2013)
28. Ward, E., Crombie, J., Trickey, M., Hill, A., Theodoros, D.G., Russell, T.G.: Assessment of communication and swallowing postlaryngectomy: a remote telerehabilitation trial. J. Telemed. Telecare **15**(5), 232–237 (2009)

# Simplifying Accessibility Without Data Loss: An Exploratory Study on Object Preserving Keyframe Culling

Marc Ritter[1]([✉]), Danny Kowerko[1], Hussein Hussein[1], Manuel Heinzig[1],
Tobias Schlosser[1], Robert Manthey[1], and Gisela Susanne Bahr[2]

[1] Junior Professorship Media Computing, Technische Universität Chemnitz,
09107 Chemnitz, Germany
{marc.ritter,danny.kowerko,hussein.hussein,manuel.heinzig,
tobias.schlosser,robert.manthey}@informatik.tu-chemnitz.de
[2] Department of Biomedical Engineering, Florida Institute of Technology,
Melbourne, FL 32901, USA
gbahr@fit.edu

**Abstract.** Our approach to multimedia big data is based on data reduction and processing techniques for the extraction of the most relevant information in form of instances of five different object classes selected from the TRECVid Evaluation campaign on a shot-level basis on 4 h of video footage from the BBC EastEnders series. In order to reduce the amount of data to be processed, we apply an adaptive extraction scheme that varies in the number of representative keyframes. Still, many duplicates of the scenery can be found. Within a cascaded exploratory study of four tasks, we show the opportunity to reduce the representative data, i.e. the number of extracted keyframes, by up to 84 % while maintaining more than 82 % of the appearing instances of object classes.

**Keywords:** Multimedia analysis · Duplicate detection · Human inspired data reduction algorithms · Data reduction strategies · Big data · Object detection · Instance Search · Rapid evaluation

## 1 Introduction

A more recent challenge in the area of accessibility engineering is how to cope with large volumes of data. Approaches to the analysis of audiovisual big data are usually based on data reduction and processing techniques that focus on the extraction of the most relevant information. On closer consideration, such kind of information usually appears in the form of objects that occur within a specific shot, whereas we denote a shot as a continuous recording in time and space [1]. In order to retrieve such valuable objects, two essential steps need to be accomplished: A decomposition of the structure of a video into homogeneous sequences of images (shots) that is often followed by a more distinct content-based analysis focusing on the detection or recognition of specific objects. However, this

© Springer International Publishing Switzerland 2016
M. Antona and C. Stephanidis (Eds.): UAHCI 2016, Part III, LNCS 9739, pp. 492–504, 2016.
DOI: 10.1007/978-3-319-40238-3_47

procedure opens a spot for a vast reduction of data by allowing the selection of representative keyframes on a shot-level basis that are further processed as a surrogate in place for the remaining frames in the very same shot. Over more than a decade, a lot of efforts within the scientific community around the international *Text Retrieval Evaluation Campaign on Videos* (TRECVid) [2], annually organized and held by the *National Institute of Standards and Technologies* (NIST, US), have led to advanced methods in structural and content-based analysis in the task of *Instance Search* that nowadays yield reasonable results. The major objective is to locate instances of a given object class. This becomes outstandingly challenging, since the object class is mainly provided by four sample images and a descriptive text string of the class. Since the requested object class is unknown prior to the appearance of the search query and the search systems are not allowed to be trained on the class requested, there is a need to adapt the knowledge base of the system on-line once the search query becomes available. A principle capability of adaption is also necessary, since the object class requested may alter their appearance far beyond the four given query samples: E.g. the period of TRECVid 2014 contained an object query (topic ID 9103) that was named *a curved plastic-bottle of ketchup*. During the course of the series the ketchup container changed from a tall and slim bottle of ketchup into a small and bulbous bottle. A lot of the participants use a variety of different methods to reduce the number of frames for object extraction. All have in common that they try to greatly reduce the amount of data. For example, *Alvi et al.* [3] extract one image per second and *Feng et al.* [4] resize it to 75 %, while *Yao et al.* [5] select every 15th frame. In contrast to those methods that extract a constant number of keyframes in a specific interval, our contribution focuses on a more adaptive scheme (Sect. 2) that tries to reduce the number of frames in a shot by selecting a different amount of keyframes with respect to the length of the shots and their overall distribution. This method has already been successfully applied within past evaluation periods (cf. to *Ritter et al.* [6,7]). The necessary master shot boundaries are officially provided by NIST as a result of an automated boundary shot detection algorithm on video footage of 464 h from the British soap *BBC EastEnders*. Despite the application of this adaptive method, still a vast number of duplicates from the same scenery with a lot of overlapping contents is extracted. In order to investigate such shot-based duplicate keyframes, we use a large sample from the TRECVid 2015 BBC *Instance Search* dataset. An intellectual way to identify duplicated keyframes is to investigate the extracted frames for common objects. This can be regarded as a challenging task, since no objects in the fore- or background should be removed by accident in order to prevent a loss of information for further processing. Within a cascaded empirical study in Sect. 3, we are going to ask the participants to identify the keyframes with the same objects and to remove the duplicated ones respectively. We will use multiple sequential tasks that build on each other in order to intensify the efforts of the cognitive workload of the participants. Furthermore, in Sect. 4 we are interested to learn about the criteria for the intellectual process of duplicate removal with removal constraints in order to compare them to results from tra-

**Table 1.** Summary of the data set that builds the base of our experiments.

| Data set | Subset of TRECVid BBC EastEnders | |
|---|---|---|
| Video resolution | 768 × 576 px anamorphic | |
| Omnibus video files | # 114 | # 163 |
| Duration | 01:54:20 h | 01:57:49 h |
| Size | 1.25 GB | 1.29 GB |
| Keyframe resolution | 928 × 512 px | |
| Keyframe format | 24 Bit JPEG | |
| # Keyframes | 5,428 | 4,921 |

ditional methods from the field of image similarity computation using different measures. The general prevention of a loss of objects will be limited to a number of five different object/topic categories that originate from the past evaluation campaign period. Our developed annotation and evaluation tools [8–10] create a convenient baseline for the investigations involved.

## 2   System Architecture, Data Extraction Scheme, and Data Setup

In the following paragraphs, we introduce the origin, the construction scheme, and characteristic properties for the image data that provides the base for the further experiments of the study.

**Data Setup:** Our primary data source is derived from the video footage of the TRECVid 2015 *Instance Search* task. This data set consists of recordings from the *BBC Series EastEnders*, a daily soap running in the UK since 1985 featuring various indoor and outdoor settings in more than 26 filming locations with a huge variety of objects used as background decoration. As the production and release of such daily episodes tends to be a bit hasty and time pressured, the footage is not very well edited from time to time. As a consequence, even basic cineastic standards for image quality are missed, resulting for instance in an imperfect white balance and brightness level. The given video collection contains 244 so called omnibus episodes, which means that a number of episodes are glued together to form one big two hour long sequence without any interruptions caused by intro, outro or advertisements. The videos are recorded with 25 frames per second in an anamorphic format, which has the effect of standard algorithms grabbing a 4:3 image that appears visually distorted and therefore has to be stretched to 16:9 to achieve visual regularity. We also remove black borders that appear around the image content in order to prevent distractions in the visual cognition of the test subjects. The main goal in the TRECVid *Instance Search* task is to automatically detect appearances of objects ("instances") in the given data set. In each years evaluation period, there are 30 so called "topics" consisting of four example pictures and a very brief description of what can be

**Table 2.** Five object topics from the TRECVid *Instance Search 2015 task* [12] to be retrieved by the participants in Task 3 and 4 of the study.

| 9130 | 9131 | 9150 | 9154 | 9156 |
|------|------|------|------|------|
| | | | | |
| a chrome napkin holder | a green and white iron | this IMPULSE game | this neon Kathy's sign | a 'DEVLIN' lager logo |

seen in the pictures or whether a particular specification of the object is needed. This also comprises additional properties like slight differences that manifest for instance in different colors of a shirt or vest. The search targets can be of any kind and are not limited by any means. Persons as well as small physical things or even particular houses or landmarks can be of interest. Some of them are easy to perceive by a human, some appear quite challenging. Whereas the first two tasks are concerned with duplicate removal, the latter tasks focus on the intellectual retrieval of five different topics. Therefore, we must assure that those objects appear in the video footage chosen for our experiments. Therefore, we analyze the ground-truth distribution of object appearances in specific shots for all 30 topics provided by NIST for the last years iteration of TRECVid. Due to a very time-consuming and mentally exhausting annotation process, the hand-truth distribution only contains results from an inspected fraction of all available shots. However, the intellectually annotated instances of all topics are to be considered as rare cases and are not spread uniformly in the data set. By using analytical methods, we found that the five relevant object categories in this contribution (see Table 2) mostly occur together in the videos with the numbers 114 and 163 with a total of 111 instances. This is why we select both videos for our experiment. The data properties are shown in Table 1.

**Adaptive Keyframe Extraction Scheme:** Since the data is recorded with 25 frames per second, it leads to potentially 90,000 images per hour that potentially contain objects of interest. Given the limits of human attention, evaluating such huge numbers of pictures turns out as a very challenging task. Therefore, we developed an approach to automatically reduce the data by a significant factor while losing a minimum of semantic information. The essential knowledge we have to keep are objects that are present in the video footage. When looking at the given data from that point of view, a cinematic characteristic can be noticed: During a shot, the objects that appear are mostly stable. That is, because in the small time window where a camera is directed approximately at the same scenery, usually things in the background do not move and are present for a plenty of subsequent frames. This leads to the assumption, that it is sufficient to look at one representative picture (that we refer to as keyframe) per shot. In practice this assumption does not hold strictly due to camera twists, slow turns or object movements, which lead to a change of the depicted area and consequently the objects in it. To respect this factor, we propose a scheme that extracts a various number of keyframes from each shot to represent temporal object variances. Following a simple but logical approach, the most representative frame to extract is the one in the middle of a shot. As stated before, this is only sufficient for very short shot durations. To represent the whole temporal outline, we also extract a frame from the start and the end of each shot. Sometimes the duration of a shot gets extensively large (20 s and more). In such cases we can no longer be sure that the filmed scenery does only change slightly, which could lead to lost objects when only extracting the three frames mentioned above. In order to still keep all existing objects, we introduce yet another level of extraction, where two more frames are picked at 25 % and 75 %, in between the existing positions. We finally end up with a scheme, that extracts one keyframe when the length of the shot is lower than two seconds, 5 keyframes when its 5 s or longer and 3 keyframes in between. The selected intervals are resulting from an analysis of the shot length distribution (cmp. to *Ritter et al.* [6, p. 3]). Applied to the selected video footage, this leads to a reduction from 167,750 potential to 5,428 representative frames for the first test video 114 while reducing 171,075 frames to 4,921 keyframes on video 163, which is a diminution by approximately a factor of more than 30.

## 3   Experiments and Results

In the following, we investigate the extracted keyframe data set from the previous section by our study in order to explore the potential for the reduction of duplicates while preserving relevant object instances.

**Method:** Five persons (age $\mu = 32.6$ and $\sigma = 7.9$, male, expertise in computer science or physics) participated in the exploratory study that consists of four major tasks (the first three tasks are building upon and complementing each other). Due to its dependent nature, the amount of data varies between the participants in both of the inner tasks. *Task 1* uses the total amount of 10,349 keyframes whereas *Task 4* operates on shots that contain at least two representative frames per shot adding up to 8,881 keyframes in total. The first task intents to eliminate unusable keyframes in which no objects are found due to poor quality, monochromaticity or blurred pictures as well as to keep usable keyframes with identifiable objects. The second task aims to sort out duplicate keyframes in shots from which at least more than one keyframe was extracted. The keyframes with the same objects are removed (culled), whereas keyframes with different objects are preserved. The third task attempts to search for objects in the remaining keyframes from the second task. We used five different objects from the TRECVid 2015 *Instance Search* evaluation campaign database. The fourth task seeks for the same objects which are used in the third task.

- *Task 1* removes keyframes which don't contain any useful information, i.e. no objects can be found in the pictures. The maximal search time is limited to 45 min per video.
- *Task 2* comprises the removal (culling) of shot-based duplicate keyframes that seem to contain the same objects without changes. The search time is limited to multiples of 20 min sprints being followed by a break of 5 min.
- After removing unusable and duplicated keyframes in the previous tasks, *Task 3* aims to spot five instances of different object categories on a shot-level basis. Every participant searched for three different objects; in total each object category is searched by three different users. The search time is limited to 10 min sprints followed by a break of 5 min. The objects used in this study are shown in Table 2.
- *Task 4* aims to retrieve the object topics from *Task 3* by using the complete set of keyframes used before the *Task 1* in order to compare the working speed as well as the quality & quantity between this task on the one and the other three tasks on the other hand. Every participant searched for instances of exactly one specific object category. The search mode is equal to the previous task.

In addition, answers to the following questions are retrieved from the participants for each task:

- Information comprising criteria or individual reasoning about the elimination of unusable keyframes and the preservation of useful keyframes.
- Identification or individual reasoning of criteria that led to the maintenance or deletion of shot-based duplicate keyframes.
- Impressions showing the experience in object recognition as well as the advantages and disadvantages of the search process.
- Discovery of individual differences or opinions between the test people.

Humans usually adapt to patterns while dealing with larger amounts of data resulting in an acceleration of the task completion time. In order to counter such effects and also relieve fatigue, we split the participants into two groups: We join two participants (P2 and P4) in the first group and the other three (P1, P3, and P5) into a second group and reverse the processing order of keyframe data sets for the both groups in *Task 1, 2,* and *4*. Due to the large reduction in the number of keyframes in the previous tasks, we didn't provide any order for *Task 3*.

**Evaluation of the Study:** The completion times, numbers of culled images, and remaining images for the four tasks of the exploratory study are shown in Tables 3 and 4. *Task 1* detected a very small number of unusable keyframes with an average of 16 and a standard deviation of 5 as shown in Table 3. The participants performed the task with a varying accuracy. P1 and P5 are the slowest participants, however, P1 removed only one keyframe on average, whereas P5 found the largest number

**Table 3.** Completion times $(t_1, t_2)$ of *Task 1+2* in seconds as well as numbers of culled images $(c_1, c_2)$ and remaining images $(r_1, r_2)$ for the data sets *Video 114* and *Video 163* of the participants (P1–P5). The initial data set contained the same $10,349$ images for every participant being reduced by the results of the first task.

| | Video 114 | | | Video 163 | | | Task 1 | | | | | |
|---|---|---|---|---|---|---|---|---|---|---|---|---|
| | $t_1$ | $c_1$ | $r_1$ | $t_2$ | $c_2$ | $r_2$ | $\mu_t$ | $\sigma_t$ | $\mu_c$ | $\sigma_c$ | $\mu_r$ | $\sigma_r$ |
| P1 | 1,144 | 0 | 5,428 | 1,237 | 2 | 4,919 | 1,190.5 | 65.8 | 1.0 | 1.4 | 5,173.5 | 359.9 |
| P2 | 690 | 6 | 5,422 | 678 | 10 | 4,911 | 684.0 | 8.5 | 8.0 | 2.8 | 5,166.5 | 361.3 |
| P3 | 513 | 18 | 5,410 | 774 | 23 | 4,898 | 643.5 | 184.6 | 20.5 | 3.5 | 5,154.0 | 362.0 |
| P4 | 736 | 10 | 5,418 | 725 | 17 | 4,904 | 730.5 | 7.8 | 13.5 | 4.9 | 5,161.0 | 363.5 |
| P5 | 1,260 | 44 | 5,385 | 900 | 30 | 4,887 | 1,080.0 | 254.6 | 37.0 | 9.9 | 5,136.0 | 352.1 |
| Ø | | | | | | | 865.7 | 104.2 | 16.0 | 4.5 | 5,158.2 | 359.8 |

| | Video 114 | | | Video 163 | | | Task 2 | | | | | |
|---|---|---|---|---|---|---|---|---|---|---|---|---|
| | $t_1$ | $c_1$ | $r_1$ | $t_2$ | $c_2$ | $r_2$ | $\mu_t$ | $\sigma_t$ | $\mu_c$ | $\sigma_c$ | $\mu_r$ | $\sigma_r$ |
| P1 | 7,139 | 2,675 | 1,923 | 5,754 | 2,649 | 1,532 | 6,446.5 | 979.3 | 2,662.0 | 18.4 | 1,727.5 | 276.5 |
| P2 | 4,900 | 2,752 | 1,846 | 3,950 | 2,707 | 1,475 | 4,425.0 | 671.8 | 2,729.5 | 31.8 | 1,660.5 | 262.3 |
| P3 | 3,418 | 2,856 | 1,736 | 1,534 | 2,693 | 1,485 | 2,476.0 | 1,332.2 | 2,774.5 | 115.3 | 1,610.5 | 177.5 |
| P4 | 3,883 | 2,876 | 1,719 | 2,538 | 2,750 | 1,428 | 3,210.5 | 951.1 | 2,813.0 | 89.1 | 1,573.5 | 205.8 |
| P5 | 3,760 | 2,949 | 1,606 | 2,740 | 2,818 | 1,357 | 3,250.0 | 721.2 | 2,883.5 | 92.6 | 1,481.5 | 176.1 |
| Ø | | | | | | | 3,961.6 | 931.1 | 2,772.5 | 69.4 | 1,610.7 | 219.6 |

of unusable keyframes with an average of 37 keyframes. Some reasons given by test subjects for the deletion of keyframes are unsharp pictures, blurred objects, and compression artifacts. The number of keyframes detected as duplicates and therefore being removed from the data set in *Task 2* is 2,772 keyframes on average. The completing time of this task varied strongly between participants. With 2,476 s, P3 appears as the fastest participant in almost all tasks. The participants detected duplicate keyframes that for instance don't contain changes in objects or don't show other objects in the fore- and background by slight camera movements. Individual results showing the distribution of remaining keyframe numbers of P1 to P5 in absolute values are depicted in Fig. 1 which tends to be homogeneous between all participants with a standard deviation of less than 15 % on average. Moreover, participants tend to have individual preferences for a specific keyframe number, like 0 and 2. The domination of keyframes 0, 2 and 4 over 1 and 3 results from the fact that a vast number of shots consist of only three keyframes enumerated with the labels "0", "2" and "4". As each keyframe is selected using the keys 1 to 5 on the keyboard, the participants use individual favourite keys in case of similar images for the sake of time. In conclusion, the average of 1,611 remaining keyframes approximately equals to 16 % of the data set used in the study yielding a data reduction potential of more than 84 %. With 3,961 s on average, the working time is about 4.5 times higher than in the previous task greatly reflecting the cognitive challenge of finding duplicates while preserving any objects. In addition, *Task 3* searched for instances of the five topics in the data set remainder from the previous tasks and

**Table 4.** Completion times ($t_1$, $t_2$) of *Task 3+4* in seconds as well as the numbers of shots containing object instances found ($h_1$, $h_2$) of the participants (P1–P5). The initial data sets for *Task 3* contained the remaining individual sets from *Task 2* of every participant in contrast to the 8,881 keyframes that contain at least two keyframes per shot in *Task 4*.

| | $TopicID$ | Video 114 | | Video 163 | | Task 3 | | | | | |
| | | $t_1$ | $h_1$ | $t_2$ | $h_2$ | $\sum_t$ | $\mu_t$ | $\sigma_t$ | $\sum_h$ | $\mu_h$ | $\sigma_h$ |
|---|---|---|---|---|---|---|---|---|---|---|---|
| | 9150 | 666 | 8 | 840 | 17 | 1,506 | 753.0 | 123.0 | 25 | 12.5 | 6.4 |
| P1 | 9154 | 836 | 1 | 536 | 4 | 1,372 | 686.0 | 212.1 | 5 | 2.5 | 2.1 |
| | 9156 | 847 | 4 | 812 | 16 | 1,659 | 829.5 | 24.7 | 20 | 10.0 | 8.5 |
| | 9130 | 570 | 21 | 425 | 4 | 995 | 497.5 | 102.5 | 25 | 12.5 | 12.0 |
| P2 | 9131 | 580 | 0 | 420 | 7 | 1,000 | 500.0 | 113.1 | 7 | 3.5 | 4.9 |
| | 9156 | 516 | 2 | 440 | 14 | 956 | 478.0 | 53.7 | 16 | 8.0 | 8.5 |
| | 9131 | 423 | 4 | 291 | 10 | 714 | 357.0 | 93.3 | 14 | 7.0 | 4.2 |
| P3 | 9154 | 351 | 1 | 284 | 0 | 635 | 317.5 | 47.4 | 1 | 0.5 | 0.7 |
| | 9156 | 296 | 4 | 232 | 11 | 528 | 264.0 | 45.3 | 15 | 7.5 | 4.9 |
| | 9130 | 467 | 19 | 256 | 3 | 723 | 361.5 | 149.2 | 22 | 11.0 | 11.3 |
| P4 | 9131 | 371 | 10 | 312 | 6 | 683 | 341.5 | 41.7 | 16 | 8.0 | 2.8 |
| | 9150 | 329 | 7 | 236 | 11 | 565 | 282.5 | 65.8 | 18 | 9.0 | 2.8 |
| | 9130 | 344 | 20 | 308 | 4 | 652 | 326.0 | 25.5 | 24 | 12.0 | 11.3 |
| P5 | 9150 | 304 | 8 | 297 | 15 | 601 | 300.5 | 4.9 | 23 | 11.5 | 4.9 |
| | 9154 | 250 | 1 | 181 | 2 | 431 | 215.5 | 48.8 | 3 | 1.5 | 0.7 |
| | Ø | | | | | 868.0 | 434.0 | 76.7 | 15.6 | 7.8 | 5.7 |

| | $TopicID$ | Video 114 | | Video 163 | | Task 4 | | | | | |
| | | $t_1$ | $h_1$ | $t_2$ | $h_2$ | $\sum_t$ | $\mu_t$ | $\sigma_t$ | $\sum_h$ | $\mu_h$ | $\sigma_h$ |
|---|---|---|---|---|---|---|---|---|---|---|---|
| P1 | 9130 | 1,391 | 20 | 1,124 | 3 | 2,515 | 1,257.5 | 188.8 | 23 | 11.5 | 12.0 |
| P2 | 9154 | 713 | 1 | 1,080 | 5 | 1,793 | 896.5 | 259.5 | 6 | 3.0 | 2.8 |
| P3 | 9150 | 577 | 6 | 599 | 17 | 1,176 | 588.0 | 15.6 | 23 | 11.5 | 7.8 |
| P4 | 9156 | 533 | 4 | 643 | 14 | 1,176 | 588.0 | 77.8 | 18 | 9.0 | 7.1 |
| P5 | 9131 | 956 | 16 | 543 | 9 | 1,499 | 749.5 | 292.0 | 25 | 12.5 | 4.9 |
| | Ø | | | | | 1,631.8 | 815.9 | 166.7 | 19.0 | 9.5 | 6.9 |

achieved a completing time of 434 s per omnibus episode, whereas the execution time of *Task 4* is almost twice as long as shown in Table 4. This indicates that the object recognition based on the deletion of unusable and duplicates keyframes can be more quickly performed than on the whole data set. We recognize an affordable loss of around 18 % in accuracy in the number of retrieved instances between both tasks from 9.5 to 7.8 on average and a similar behavior in the standard deviations can be explained by high number of eliminated duplicates in addition to common human errors that usually occur by working on such complex tasks. The experience in object recognition reported by participants showed that this is task was perceived as a very tiring one, where the attention decreases without breaks. The participants report a focus on specific scenes or locations in order to retrieve the object more quickly. Some problems encountered by the participants are the search

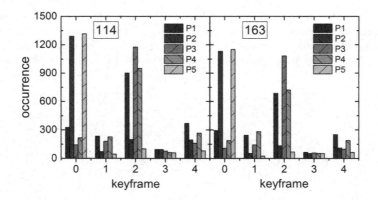

**Fig. 1.** Keyframe number selection statistics from *Task 2* of all five participants (P1–P5) for omnibus videos 114 and 163.

for small objects which took a long searching time compared to large objects. The poor quality of the images was given as one major reason.

## 4  Comparison of Intellectual Selections with Computational Similarity Measures

The combination of culled and remaining images of *Task 2* contains information about *human* categorization into quasi-similar and dissimilar, a binary classification represented by 1 and 0 in the following. It is used to assign both values for each image combination within a shot, represented as elements $M_{ij}$ of a similarity matrix M which is shown in Fig. 2 for three typical shots from *video 114*. A drawback of our selection method is that for shots with 5 keyframes and 2, 3 or 4 selected images, we cannot assign 9, 7 or 4 human similarity values, exemplified in shot 1,009 of Fig. 2 by using the label "ND" (not determined). In shots with three keyframes and two selections, two ND fields remain, while selecting 1 or 3 images results in 3 similarity values of type 1 or 0, respectively. Furthermore, the comparison matrix is symmetric $(M = M^T)$ since the order of comparing two images does not play a role $(M_{ij} = M_{ji})$. The respective values were omitted together with diagonal elements (self comparison) $M_{ii}$ for clarity in Fig. 2. For shots with 3 or 5 keyframes, we eventually extract a maximum of 3 or 10 values. With the given number of shots and keyframes, the raw data of *video 114 and 163* allow a maximum of 5,998 + 5,937 = 11,935 image comparisons giving a maximum of 59,675 comparisons of human and computational similarity. Due to the selection effect in *Task 1* and the above mentioned "ND" cases, the expected values will be lower, dominated by the information loss of the "ND" problem. The derivation of the computational similarity values using the FUZZ metric from ImageMagick[1] will be described in the following. Therefore

---

[1] http://www.imagemagick.org, 02-29-2016.

| Similarity → | | HUMAN | | | | | FUZZ | | | | |
|---|---|---|---|---|---|---|---|---|---|---|---|
| Keyframe → | | 0 | 1 | 2 | 3 | 4 | 0 | 1 | 2 | 3 | 4 |
| 1000 | | | | | | | | | | | |
| 0 | | - | | | | | - | | | | |
| 2 | | 1 | | - | | | 0.08 | | - | | |
| 4 | | 1 | | 1 | | - | 0.09 | | 0.08 | | - |
| 1009 | | | | | | | | | | | |
| 0 | | - | | | | | - | | | | |
| 1 | | 0 | - | | | | 0.22 | - | | | |
| 2 | | ND | ND | - | | | 0.22 | 0.13 | - | | |
| 3 | | ND | ND | ND | - | | 0.22 | 0.13 | 0.11 | - | |
| 4 | | ND | ND | ND | ND | - | 0.21 | 0.14 | 0.12 | 0.11 | - |
| 1012 | | | | | | | | | | | |
| 0 | | - | | | | | - | | | | |
| 1 | | 0 | - | | | | 0.18 | - | | | |
| 2 | | 0 | 0 | - | | | 0.27 | 0.26 | - | | |
| 3 | | 0 | 0 | 0 | - | | 0.23 | 0.24 | 0.25 | - | |
| 4 | | 0 | 0 | 0 | 0 | - | 0.32 | 0.32 | 0.31 | 0.28 | - |

**Fig. 2.** Similarities as determined by participants (HUMAN) compared to a typical computational similarity metric (FUZZ) for 3 representative shots of *video 114* with either 3 or 5 keyframes are illustrated for shot 1,000; 1,009 and 1,012. Red boxes mark the corresponding choices of P1. Fields with "ND" refer to HUMAN similarity that could not be determined automatically in *Task 2*. (Color figure online)

the chosen evaluation criterion is the FUZZ metric, which calculates the difference between two given images pixel by pixel, adding up the squared distortions and normalizing the total of it. Formally:

$$FUZZ = \sqrt{\frac{1}{N} \sum_{i=1}^{N} (c_i - \bar{c}_i)^2} \tag{1}$$

Given two images $c$ and $\bar{c}$ of size $N$ pixel, let $c_i$ and $\bar{c}_i$ denote the respective ones in comparison. Those are calculated separately for each color channel and eventually averaged. From the similarity matrices presented in Fig. 2, the human and computational equivalent elements are combined to a scatter plot shown in Fig. 3 on the top left. The anti-correlation of the 23 selected data points clearly supports the hypothesis that FUZZ metric and human similarity follow a common trend. Low FUZZ values represent high similarity as the definition of FUZZ relies on the difference between two images, see Eq. 1. Note that for shot 1,009, the ND values have manually been determined as follows: $M_{2,0} = M_{3,0} = M_{4,0} = 0$ and $M_{2,1} = M_{3,1} = M_{4,1} = M_{3,2} = M_{4,2} = M_{4,3} = 1$. In conclusion the 3 example shots imply a strong consistence of human and computational similarity. Expanding this concept to the data to all 5 participants and all shots/keyframes selected in *Task 2*, for *videos 114 and 163*, we obtained 2,962 and 1,937 FUZZ values categorized by humans with type 0, as well as 18,884 and 21,313 type 1 rated FUZZ values whose probability density distributions are shown in Fig. 3, bottom. The dominance of 1 indicates the existence of a majority of shots with 3 or 5 similar keyframes. However, the individual as well as the sum distributions of *videos 114 and 163* show merely the same trend. FUZZ metric values closer to 0 than 0.4 are distinctly more often selected by human beings as similar keyframes. Still, all distributions overlap considerably. Defining a simple FUZZ threshold value is inappropriate to automatically remove duplicate type images within the data set analyzed in this study.

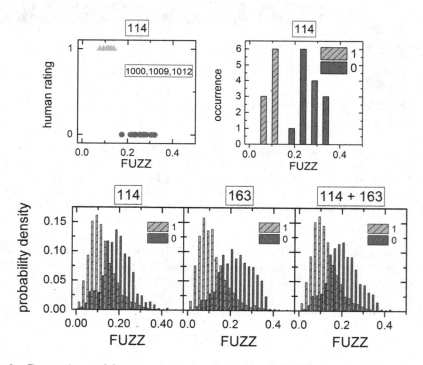

**Fig. 3.** Comparison of human and computational similarity metrics. Top: A non-overlapping anti-correlation is shown for the 3 exemplary shots of Fig. 2 with 23 data points. Bottom: Normalized histograms from the data of all participants for both videos, each including more than 20,000 HUMAN-FUZZ similarity pairs.

# 5    Summary and Future Work

In conclusion, we demonstrated that within a total experiment time of about 12 h and 5 participants more than 45,000 human-computer image similarity comparisons have been derived. The obtained overlapping histogram distributions (cmp. to Fig. 3) of human and computational similarities resemble those of other problems like face detection. Therefore, ensemble-based machine learning techniques like boosting are promising to further separate duplicates in an automated manner, reliably reducing the amount of data used in big data evaluation campaigns like TRECVid with a small loss of information. The binary annotation and classification tool [10] has proven beneficial over all 4 tasks in order to create statistically sound data sets within a reasonable period of time. Furthermore, 36 additional shots amongst five topics could be identified in both videos that were not contained in the ground-truth information provided by NIST. Future work focuses on the identification of the *not determined* values of the similarity matrices, a modification of *Task 2* will potentially increase the total number of human-computer image similarity pairs considerably.

**Acknowledgments.** This work was partially accomplished within the project *localizeIT* (funding code 03IPT608X) funded by the *Federal Ministry of Education and Research* (BMBF, Germany) in the program of *Entrepreneurial Regions InnoProfile-Transfer*. Programme material is copyrighted by the BBC.

# References

1. Ritter, M.: Optimierung von Algorithmen zur Videoanalyse: Ein Analyseframework für die Anforderungen lokaler Fernsehsender. In: Wissenschaftliche Schriftenreihe Dissertionen der Medieninformatik (3), TU Chemnitz, 336 pp. (2014)
2. Smeaton, A.F., Over, P., Kraaij, W.: Evaluation campaigns and trecvid. In: ACM International Workshop on Multimedia Information Retrieval, pp. 321–330 (2006)
3. Alvi, M., Khan, M.U.G., Sadiq, M., Aslam, M.: University of Engineering & Technology, Lahore, The University of Sheffield at TRECVID, (2011) Observation of strains: Instance Search. In: TRECVID Workshop 2015, Gaithersburg, Maryland, 5 pp. (2015)
4. Feng, Y., Dong, Y., Wu, Y., Bai, H., Cen, S., Liu, B., Wang, K., Liu, Y.: BUPT & ORANGELABS (OrangeBJ) AT TRECVID 2014: INSTANCE SEARCH. In: TRECVID Workshop 2014, 10–12 November 2014, Orlando, Florida, USA, 9 pp. (2014)
5. Yao, L., Ye, M., Liu, D., Shao, R., Liu, T., Liu, J., Wang, Z., Liang, C.: WHU-NERCMS at TRECVID2015: Instance Search task. In: TRECVID Workshop (2015)
6. Ritter, M., Heinzig, M., Herms, R., Kahl, S., Richter, D., Manthey, R., Eibl, M.: Technische Universität Chemnitz at TRECVID Instance Search 2014. In: TRECVID Workshop 2014, 10–12 November 2014, Orlando, Florida, 8 pp. (2014)
7. Ritter, M., Rickert, M., Juturu Chenchu, L., Kahl, S., Robert, H., Hussein, H., Heinzig, M., Manthey, R., Bahr, G.S., Richter, D., Eibl, M.: Technische Universität Chemnitz at TRECVID Instance Search 2015. In: TRECVID Workshop (2015)

8. Ritter, M., Eibl, M.: An extensible tool for the annotation of videos using segmentation and tracking. In: Marcus, A. (ed.) HCII 2011 and DUXU 2011, Part I. LNCS, vol. 6769, pp. 295–304. Springer, Heidelberg (2011)

9. Storz, M., Ritter, M., Manthey, R., Lietz, H., Eibl, M.: Annotate. Train. Evaluate. A unified tool for the analysis and visualization of workflows in machine learning applied to object detection. In: Kurosu, M. (ed.) HCII/HCI 2013, Part V. LNCS, vol. 8008, pp. 196–205. Springer, Heidelberg (2013)

10. Ritter, M., Storz, M., Heinzig, M., Eibl, M.: Rapid model-driven annotation and evaluation for object detection in videos. In: Antona, M., Stephanidis, C. (eds.) UAHCI 2015 Part I. LNCS, vol. 9175, pp. 464–474. Springer, Heidelberg (2015)

11. Forsyth, D.A., Malik, J., Fleck, M.M., Greenspan, H., Leung, T., Belongie, S., Carson, C., Bregler, C.: Finding pictures of objects in large collections of images. In: International Workshop on Object Recognition for Computer Vision, pp. 335–360 (1996)

12. Over, P., Awad, G., Michel, M., Fiscus, J., Kraaij, W., Smeaton, A.F., Quenot, G., Ordelman, R.: TRECVID 2015-an overview of the goals, tasks, data, evaluation mechanisms and metrics. In: Proceedings of TRECVID 2015, NIST, USA (2015)

# Audio Description of Videos
# for People with Visual Disabilities

Agebson Rocha Façanha[1(✉)], Adonias Caetano de Oliveira[1],
Marcos Vinicius de Andrade Lima[2],
Windson Viana[2], and Jaime Sánchez[3]

[1] Federal Institute of Education,
Science and Technology of Ceará (IFCE), Fortaleza, CE, Brazil
{acessibilidadevirtual,agebson}@ifce.edu.br
[2] Federal University of Ceará (UFC), Fortaleza, CE, Brazil
adonias.ifce@gmail.com, marcos.engsoft@gmail.com,
windson@virtual.ufc.br
[3] Universidad de Chile, Santiago, Chile
jsanchez@dcc.uchile.cl

**Abstract.** Audio description can be defined as an activity of linguistic mediation that transforms visual to verbal, allowing for a better comprehension of scenes when there is no dialog between personages. In this paper, we present the conception, development, and an initial usability evaluation of a software suite for audio description. The proposal pursues to facilitate and widen a comprehension of videos for people with visual disabilities by using synthesized voice. We developed a video player– ADVPlayer – that synchronizes the original video with a second audio containing a TTS version of an audio description script. We evaluated the usability of ADVPlayer with students with visual impairment in two South American countries. This evaluation revealed a high comprehension and acceptance in terms of satisfaction and confidence.

**Keywords:** Accessibility · Digital video · Audio description

## 1 Introduction

Modern society experiences a time of intensive access to digital media. Entertainment, education, work, in short, almost all daily activities of the modern citizen are influenced by digital media. One of the most successful media is digital video, which is broadcasted on digital TV, shared on social websites (e.g., Vimeo), or distributed on physical media as DVD and Blu-Ray.

Most digital videos, however, are inaccessible to people with visual impairment. According to the World Health Organization, 285 million people with visual disabilities are estimated in the whole world. 40 million of them are totally blind. The majority (90 %) live in developing countries, such as, Brazil and India [5]. These people face daily difficulties. Nowadays, they also have to deal with a socio-cultural exclusion from the digital world, since they do not have guarantees of access to visual content. The

M. Antona and C. Stephanidis (Eds.): UAHCI 2016, Part III, LNCS 9739, pp. 505–515, 2016.
DOI: 10.1007/978-3-319-40238-3_48

majority part of the productions released in digital media (e.g., films, TV series, and popular Youtube videos) does not have accessibility features.

An attempt to reduce this exclusion recommends the addition of a narration of the scenes. This technique is known as audio description, and it adds a second audio to the original one. Audio description can be defined as an activity of linguistic mediation, a mode of inter-semiotic translation that transforms visual to verbal, allowing for a comprehension of scenes when there is no dialog between personages. The idea is to add descriptions of the video visual elements, which are essential for understanding the dialogues and scenes that contain a strong visual character [6]. However, many videos do not have this accessibility feature, due to the economic costs of the audio description production.

Some initiatives exist to provide audio description of films and digital television shows. In many cases, the audio descriptions are made grace to accessibility laws (e.g., Brazil federal law n° 5.296). However, these initiatives contemplate a small portion of digital videos. This problem is even greater if we analyze the digital videos available on the Web (e.g., news websites, video sharing platforms like Youtube and Vimeo).

For a task of this magnitude, a possible approach is to rely on the help of virtual communities, and use systems that assist the process of creating and playing audio description. Sites for collaborative creation of movie subtitles illustrate the potential of the approach. The Opensubtitles.org site is one such example. However, the quality of the audio descriptions should not be compromised in this process.

In recent years, the synthesized voice technologies showed strong growth in performance and effectiveness. They provide the "transformation" of a text into "human" voices. Text-To-Speech (TTS) software is a key component in the functioning of accessibility technologies targeting users with visual impairment, such as: screen readers [2], software to aid Web navigation [2], virtual keyboards [3], and, accessible digital games [1, 4].

In this context, our research goal is to explore the voice synthesized technologies in order to maximize and accelerate the production of audio descriptions. With this approach, we believe it will increase the number of accessible digital videos to the visually impaired.

In this paper, we present the conception, development and initial usability evaluation of a software suite for audio description. We developed a video player– ADVPlayer – that synchronizes the video with a description script (textual file similar to SRT, which contains metadata such as: description time, configuration of the synthesized voice, and scene description). In fact, ADVPlayer executes a second audio generated from a TTS, which is a speech version of a description script. This is a more flexible and low cost approach comparing with the conventional audio description production process (i.e., with human voice recording).

The remainder of this paper is organized as follows: Sect. 2 presents related work on audio description. The ADVPlayer suite, and its design, and development processes are described in Sect. 3. Section 4 presents the usability evaluation implemented with students' with visual impairment from two South American countries. Finally, we conclude the paper with final considerations and future work in Sect. 5.

## 2   Related Work

Research on the development of assistive technologies for digital video is relatively recent. They propose to minimize the task effort of audio description [8–10]. For instance, researchers of the work [8] recommend the use of a tool to support the audio descriptors' work: the Subtitle Workshop software. This tool is focused on producing video subtitles. Subtitle Workshop uses the SRT (Subrip subtitle format) for storing the audio description information. The researchers' goal was to speed up the process of traditional audio description by using their tool. However, the approach is still requiring a human audio description recording.

Researches of Kobayashi et al. focus on removing the audio description recording phase [6]. The authors analyzed the acceptability of speech synthesizers for this task. Analyses were performed with audio in English and Japanese. They conducted a major study of 115 participants with visual impairment during an exhibition of assistive technologies in Japan. The aim was to compare the quality of human audio description with the quality of synthesized audio description. Despite the superiority of human narration, most participants admitted that their quality of life could be enhanced with synthesized narrations. Good digital tools following this approach could increase the number of online video with audio description.

Our research follows some of the Kobayashi's findings. We propose a set of tools that assist the production, sharing, and execution of synthesized audio description.

## 3   Synthesized Audio Description

We propose tools to support a Synthesized Audio Description approach. Our research provides audio description with a lower cost because it does not require studio recording of the audio description voices. The approach relies on speech synthesis of what should be narrated. The main objective is to facilitate understanding when no audio dialogues exist between characters, similar to what happens in traditional audio description. The key component of this proposal is a video player that executes a second audio by using a TTS synthesizer. ADVPlayer supports AVI video files (Audio Video Interleave), which originally does not have accessibility features. ADVPlayer synchronizes the original digital video with speech synthesis of a text file. This file contains the audio description and their execution times.

Figure 1 shows the main components of ADVPlayer and its execution process. The system input is composed of two files: a text file with audio descriptions (.adv), which follows the standard used by movie subtitle files (SRT), and the original video file. ADVPlayer has three main modules: (i) a digital media player, to read and reproduce the original video; (ii) a synchronizer to read the descriptions and to invoke the speech synthesizer, which will turn them into voice, and (iii) the TTS software itself.

According to Zuffo and Pistori [7], the speech synthesis is the generation of sound signals that reproduce the equivalent words in a given natural language. Synthesize voice applications are designed to imitate human speech. In the case of ADVPlayer, we used the eSpeak TTS for this task.

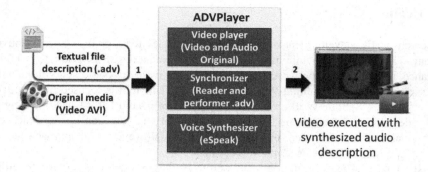

**Fig. 1.** ADVPlayer components

## 3.1   Audio Description Text File (.ADV)

The description file (.adv) contains the descriptions that provide a good video under-standing by people with visual impairment. During a video execution, ADVPlayer reads (.adv) text and passes it as parameter to the eSpeak TTS, following a pre-established synchronism time. The text is converted into synthesized speech, and, then, synchronized with the video.

The ADV format is similar to Subrip Subtitles format (SRT)[1]. The SRT has four parts: (i) the subtitle number; (ii) the time that the subtitle appears on the screen (in hour: minute: second: millisecond format), and the time it will disappear; (iii) the subtitle text; and finally (iv) one blank line, which has the purpose of separating subtitles.

We extended the SRT format in order to support synthesized audio description. We added a new line, which contains two parameters: the synthesized speech rate and the volume of the synthesized voice (line N of Fig. 2). The speech rate parameter indicates

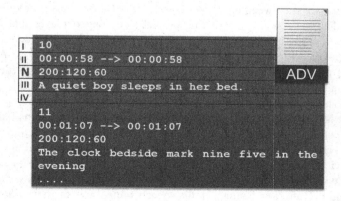

**Fig. 2.** ADV file example

[1] http://en.wikipedia.org/wiki/SubRip.

the execution speed of the audio description. Its acceleration can avoid overlapping of dialogues. This feature also acts to accelerate longer descriptions in shorter periods of time, without, however, losing the audio description understanding (very useful in audio description of action movies).

People with visual impairment are habituated to listening to the synthesized voice at fast speeds. The volume parameter allows for overlapping the environment sound of the original video. Thus, the synthesized audio description can be better understood. Figure 2 shows an excerpt from an ADV file containing an audio description example.

W3C proposes TTML[2] as standard to represent timed text on the Web. However, we chose to extend SRT, since there is on the Internet a large community of people who produce subtitles of movies, series, and other videos. All these virtual communities are familiar with the SRT format. Our hypothesis is that it will be easier for them to collaborate in the creation of synthesized audio descriptions.

The use of files ".adv" makes possible a constant improvement in the quality of audio descriptions. Changes can be made only by modifying the content of ".adv" files (descriptions, synchronization time, and/or volume). This is quite different from the recorded audio description. Upon completion of the audio description and the video distribution, one cannot update the descriptions without dealing with a substantial financial impact.

**Fig. 3.** (a) ADV Editor screenshot; (b) ADVPlayer playing Rocky movie; (c) a blind user testing our approach

[2] http://www.w3.org/TR/ttaf1-dfxp/.

## 3.2   ADVEditor and ADVPlayer

The ".adv" files can be written with any text editor (e.g., Windows Notepad). Nonetheless, we created a tool, named ADVEditor for assisting this editing process. This application allows for inserting textual descriptions and the specification of the speed, volume, and tone of the synthesized voice. The tool includes a video player to facilitate the visualization, testing, and edition of the order of the descriptions inserted.

Figure 3 shows a ADVEditor screenshot. The tool was developed using Java SE. The Standard Widget Toolkit (SWT) was used to implement graphic elements accessible to screen readers. We also used the DirectShow Java (DSJ) API for media reproduction.

Descriptions should always be positioned in times when there is no dialogue between the characters, giving a better understanding of the video by the visually impaired. ADVEditor assists in this process by providing the audio description editor test and simulation features.

Once created the ".adv" file, the user can open the ADVplayer program and provides information on the video he wants to run in sync with the audio description. The ADVPlayer tool synchronizes the video execution with reading the descriptions. In addition, it uses the user's preferences specifications to change the type and volume of the synthesized voice. The ADVPlayer tool was developed using the same ADVEditor technologies.

Figure 3 also shows the ADVPlayer software running. After the ADVPlayer program is opened, the user must: (1) load the description file (.adv); (2) point out the media that contains the video to be played; and (3) select the play button to start playing. The synthesized audio description system will be enabled automatically once the ADVplayer program is loaded.

ADVplayer is a free software and requires for its operation the Windows platform (Windows XP or above). It has its current version in beta testing and is used by a small group of people with visual impairment. The tool can be downloaded at: http://adv-acessibilidade.rhcloud.com.

## 3.3   Improving the Quality of Audio Description

We have created a web page[3] to promote communities of audio description editors. The goal is to ensure the maintenance of quality of descriptions, and increase the available number of films and videos (e.g., translations into other languages).

On the website, people can share new descriptions, propose improvements, and qualify the descriptions already available (through a ranking system). Our website follows the W3C accessibility guidelines.

In this way, we hope that in a short time the number of available titles will grow rapidly through the power of virtual communities. This behavior is already happening in web sites that provide video subtitles (movies, series and other videos).

---

[3] http://adv.ifce.edu.br/.

# 4 Usability Evaluation

We performed an initial usability testing to determine the technology acceptance and get new ideas and suggestions for improvements of the ADV Player prototype. We use a 3 min video of the film Monsters, Inc. to acclimate users. Then, we used focal group techniques[4] to discover, analyze, and validate it by observing users. We perform sessions with eight people with visual disabilities, which had distinct levels of understanding of the topic addressed. This initial evaluation revealed a high comprehension and acceptance in terms of satisfaction and confidence with synthetized audio description.

The ADVEditor prototype was introduced to three audio description specialists using the brainstorming techniques to know how they make the description and their interests in producing descriptions using the application. Diverse suggestions to improve the tools were highlighted. We corrected some aspects of our applications and made its internationalization for Portuguese, English and Spanish.

After taking into account these aspects, we implemented an assessment usability test of ADVPlayer. Tests were made with 19 students with visual disabilities in two South American countries (Brazil and Chile). The tests seek to measure the effectiveness of the ADVPlayer implementation and also to quantify the acceptance of synthesized audio description.

## 4.1 Sample

The sample was composed by 19 students with visual impairment. The sample was non-probabilistic, selected for convenience. They were students of three specialized institutions on people with visual disabilities: Escuela de Ciegos Santa Lucia, the Col-lege Hellen Keller and the Blind Association of Ceará). The first school is Chilean and others are Brazilian schools.

The sample has:

- 8 men and 11 women
- Age from 6 to 47 years old
- 4 were totally blind e 15 had low vision

12 users had prior knowledge of what was an audio description, although, only seven users have watched a video with this feature. Six of the users reported watching movies with audio only. 4 of them were completely blind and 2 had low vision (with serious vision impairment). Other users have reported watching videos with both image and audio features.

Regarding the use of TTS, 9 of them did not use screen readers, eight use the JAWS screen reader, and two of them prefer the NVDA reader, always with male voices.

---

[4] Focal group methodology is a sampling process that seeks to obtain qualitative information given the perceptions reported by participants during discussion meetings.

## 4.2    Materials

We decided to use slices of 15 min from the beginning of films to evaluate the ADVPlayer. The goal was to reduce the time of the test sections. We created .ADV files of three films: "The Book Thief", "The Fault in Our Stars", and "Inside Out". All descriptions have been prepared by people with training in scripts for audio description, supervised by a consultant with visual impairment. Figure 4 shows the group of descriptors using the ADVEditor. The complete audio descriptions of the movies are now available at the project Web site.

**Fig. 4.**  Audio descriptors are writing and reviewing (.adv) files on ADVEditor

## 4.3    Instruments

In all sessions, we administered a questionnaire with four parts. The first one has a pre-collection questionnaire with personal information to draw a profile of the target users studied (results are summarized in Sect. 4.1). The other parts are related to pos-collection, usability feedback, and movie comprehension.

The questionnaire was developed and implemented in order to discover, analyze and validate, from observations of the user group, requirements for the improvement and implementation of ADVPlayer software. The pre-collection allows for knowing each user's profile. The post-collection measures the impact of using audio description with the synthesized speech.

Usability part of the questionnaire was designed following the works [11, 12]. The questionnaire was created guided by the following metrics:

P1 - The audio descriptions are clear and objective, avoided me an erroneous interpretation of the scene. (CONFIDENCE)

P2 - The amount of information transmitted during the silence interval is appropriate. (SATISFACTION)

P3 - The audio volume of the audio descriptions are appropriate to each situation. (SATISFACTION)

P4 - The audio tone is appropriate for each situation. (SATISFACTION)

P5 - The type of TTS and the speed rate of the synthesized voice are appropriated to the original movie audio.

P6 - The audio description allows imagining the movie scenes. (RELEVANCE)

P7 - Watch the movie with synthesized audio description convinced me to watch other movies with this feature. (MOTIVATION)

P8 - I feel more pleasured watching the video as a result of the audio descriptions.

P9 - I can understand information that was previously only visual. (CONFIDENCE)

To measure the degree of agreement, we used a Likert scale, ranging from 1 (completely disagree) to 5 (completely agree).

The last part of the questionnaire asks about users' understanding on the movie. It contains questions about the environment of the scenes, the time when the story happened, what and who were the characters, and the identification of the clothes they wore.

### 4.4    Procedure

The tests were implemented according to the following methodology:

(1) Each session has 4–6 students, who were informed about the purpose of the synthesized audio description, and how ADVPlayer works;
(2) They chose one of the three films for the group session;
(3) Next, the group watched a stretch of about 15 min of the film;
(4) At the end, we applied to each of them a questionnaire to get their opinion, usability feedback, and understanding of the film.

The main purpose of this structure was to obtain qualitative results of validation and acceptance. The perceptions reported by participants during the sessions can lead us to a better implementation of the tool in the school environment. Additionally, this structure allows for elucidating new requirements of the proposed software. Figure 5 illustrates one of the sections.

**Fig. 5.** Two photos illustrating the usability section implemented in Chile

### 4.5    Results

From the observations and reports obtained from participants in the experiment, we realized that there is a high satisfaction and confidence in the use of audio description technology with voice synthesis. We can highlight as relevant points of the questionnaires results:

1. 94.7 % of users understood the audio description for the section film (P1 and P2) and, more specifically, they were able to understand information that was previously only visual (P9).
2. The audio volume (P3) and the type of TTS (P5) were points of disagreement among some users (10.5 % and 31.5 %, respectively). This indicates the need for greater flexibility in movie playback. We are already working to add voice choice and speed in ADVPlayer.
3. The use of the synthesized audio description stimulated the creativity of users (P6) and the search for other videos with audio description (P7); which is a technology acceptance indicator.
4. We realized that the lack of experience of some users with TTS technology had an impact on the assessment of the speed of the voice. 73.68 % of users reported the voice speed was normal, but, 26.3 % of them considered it too fast.

## 5 Discussion and Conclusion

Studies on synthesized audio-description are still incipient, especially, research on romance languages (e.g., Portuguese, Spanish). However, it is patent this approach is a good alternative to make accessible a lot of visual productions, such as films, series, documentaries, concerts, for people with visual impairment.

The main features of our proposal are: (i) we provide a collaborative creation of the audio-descriptions, since it is based on virtual communities; (ii) the approach allows a constant improvement in the quality of available descriptions; (iii) ADVPlayer uses various types of synthesized voices; and, finally, (iv) we allow users to customize the running speed of the audio description.

Initial usability results of our approach indicate that most users comprehended the information described during the video, they could understand information that before was only visual. The voice speed and the audio volume were aspects of disagreements of users indicating a need for a higher flexibility of these functionalities in the video executions. Also, the use of audio description with synthesized voice stimulated the creativity of diverse users and the search for other videos with audio description evidencing the technology acceptance.

The research is in progress now considering port ADV Player to mobile platforms, such as Android and iOS. As future work, we also plan to make ADVPlayer Web versions. Regarding ADVEditor, we are planning to build a recommendation feature able to detect, through video content processing, silence moments adequate to insert audio descriptions.

Furthermore, a collaborative web site to share description files is being developed. It allows for sharing diverse films, making them fast accessible. The approach opens more options to this population to access to digital media, which contributes to their cultural, social and school inclusion. Finally, we believe that research on synthesized audio description may expand its potential for other populations, such as people with intellectual disabilities, elderly, and dyslexics.

**Acknowledgments.** This paper was partially funded by the Program of Scientific Cooperation called STIC-AmSud-CAPES program/CONICYT/MAE. The sponsored project is entitled Knowing and Interacting while Gaming for the Blind (KIGB), 2014. The research was also funded by the Fondo Nacional de Desarrollo Científico y Tecnológico (FONDECYT), Fondecyt 1150898; and the Basal Funds for Centers of Excellence, FB0003 project, from the Associative Research Program of CONICYT.

The desktop and Web applications have been developed with the support of MCTI-SECIS/CNPq No. 84/2013 - Assistive Technology project, registered under grant number 458825/2013-1.

# References

1. Garcia, F.E., de Almeida Neris, V.P.: Design guidelines for audio games. In: Kurosu, M. (ed.) HCII/HCI 2013, Part II. LNCS, vol. 8005, pp. 229–238. Springer, Heidelberg (2013)
2. Hakobyan, L., Lumsden, J., O'Sullivan, D., Bartlett, H.: Mobile assistive technologies for the visually impaired. Surv. Ophthalmol. **58**(6), 513–528 (2013). ISSN:0039-6257
3. Façanha, A.R.; Araújo, M.D.C., Viana, W., Pequeno, M.C.: LêbrailleTWT. In: The 18th Brazilian Symposium on Multimedia and the Web (2012). São Paulo/SP. Proceedings of the 18th Brazilian Symposium on Multimedia and the Web - WebMedia 2012, vol. 1, pp. 313–320. ACM Press, New York (2012)
4. Milne, L.R., Bennett, C.L., Ladner, R.E.: VBGhost: a braille-based educational smartphone game for children. In: Proceedings of the 15th International ACM SIGACCESS Conference on Computers and Accessibility (ASSETS 2013). ACM, New York (2013)
5. WHO. World Health Organization. Universal eye health: a global action plan 2014–2019. Disponível em: http://www.who.int/blindness/AP2014_19_English.pdf. Acesso em: 26 Nov 2015
6. Kobayashi, M., O'Connell, T., Gould, B., Takagi, H., Asakawa, C.: Are synthesized video descriptions acceptable? In: Proceedings of the 12th International ACM SIGACCESS Conference on Computers and Accessibility (ASSETS 2010), pp. 163–170. ACM, New York (2010)
7. Zuffo, F., Pistori, H.: Tecnologia Adaptativa e Síntese de Voz: Primeiros Experimentos. Anais do V Workshop de Software Livre - WSL. Porto Alegre, 2–5 de Junho 2004
8. Magalhães, C.M., Araújo, V.L.S.: Metodologia para elaboração de audiodescrições de museus baseada na semiótica social e na multimodalidade. Revista Latinoamericana de Estudiosdel Discurso **12**, 31–56 (2012)
9. Gagnon, L., Foucher, S., Heritier, M., Lalonde, M., Byrns, D., Chapdelaine, C., Turner, J., Mathieu, S., Laurendeau, D., Tan Nguyen, N., Ouellet, D.: Towards computer-vision software tools to increase production and accessibility of video description for people with vision loss. Univers. Access Inf. Soc. **8**(3), 199–218 (2009)
10. Campos, V.P., Araujo, T.M.U., Souza Filho, G.L.: CineAD: Um Sistema de Geração Automática de Roteiros de Audiodescrição. In: Simpósio Brasileiro de Sistemas Multimídia e Web (WebMedia), 2014, João Pessoa. WebMedia (2014)
11. Sánchez, J.: Software Usability for Blind Children Questionnaire (SUBC). Usability evaluation test, University of Chile (2003)
12. Sánchez, J.: End-user and facilitator questionnaire for Software Usability. Usability evaluation test. University of Chile (2003)

# Changes in Brain Blood Flow by the Use of 2D/3D Games

Masumi Takada[1], Yuki Mori[2], Fumiya Kinoshita[3],
and Hiroki Takada[2,3(✉)]

[1] Faculty of Rehabilitation Nursing,
Chubu Gakuin University, 2-1 Kirigaoka, Seki, Gifu 501-3993, Japan
[2] Department of Human and Artificial Intelligent Systems, Graduate School
of Engineering, University of Fukui, 3-9-1 Bunkyo, Fukui 910-8507, Japan
takada@u-fukui.ac.jp
[3] Department of Information Engineering, Graduate School of Information
Science, Nagoya University, Furo-cho, Chikusa-Ku, Nagoya 464-8601, Japan

**Abstract.** Recently, with the rapid progress in image processing and three-dimensional (3D) technology, stereoscopic images are not only seen on television but also in theaters, on game machines, etc. However, symptoms such as eye fatigue and 3D sickness may be experienced when viewing 3D films on displays and visual environments. The influence of stereoscopic vision on the human body has been insufficiently understood; therefore, it is important to consider the safety of viewing virtual 3D content. In this study, we examine whether exposure to 3D video clips affects the human body such as brain blood flow. Subjects viewed 3D video clips on the display of portable game machines, and time series data of their brain blood flow was measured by near-infrared spectroscopy (NIRS) with use of FOIRE-3000 (Shimazu Co. Ltd., Kyoto). Our results showed oxyhemoglobin tended to increase throughout the cerebral cortex while operating the game machines on the 3D display in comparison with the 2D display.

**Keywords:** 3D video · Visually induced motion sickness (VIMS) · Near infrared spectroscopy (NIRS) · Brain blood flow

## 1 Introduction

The opportunity to see stereoscopic images has increased with the recent spread of 3D TVs and game machines, but these images may have a negative influence on the human body. Specific influences include eye fatigue and visually induced motion sickness. There are various theories of the developmental mechanism of these symptoms which has not been clarified, but the sensory conflict theory is generally known [1]. However, the development of all cases of sickness cannot be explained with this theory, and current knowledge about the influence of stereoscopic images on the body is insufficient.

Near-infrared spectroscopy (NIRS) utilizes the property of hemoglobin which absorbs near infrared light, and it is capable of noninvasively measuring the blood

M. Antona and C. Stephanidis (Eds.): UAHCI 2016, Part III, LNCS 9739, pp. 516–523, 2016.
DOI: 10.1007/978-3-319-40238-3_49

volume in the body. Applying this to the brain, changes in brain blood flow within a 2–3 cm range from the scalp can be measured, and activated local regions can be detected. Thus, NIRS is a test capable of noninvasively detecting the time-course of overall reactivity to activation of the cerebral cortex in subjects in a natural state [2–8]. In NIRS, changes in the hemoglobin level are calculated from the values of irradiation and detection lights, but the distance (effective optical path length) that the light actually forwarded in the head tissue is not measurable at present. The generally used unit of measurement for NIRS values is the product of the hemoglobin concentration and length, such as [mM·mm] (hemoglobin concentration length).

In this study, to increase knowledge about the influence of stereoscopic images on the body, we focused on 3D game machines. To play NINTENDO 3DS (Nintendo, Kyoto) used in the experiment, operation of the controller while gazing at stereoscopic images displayed on a small screen is necessary. In addition, 2D and 3D images can be instantly switched by operating a knob on the side of the screen. Thus, we investigated changes in brain blood flow while playing a game using 2D and 3D displays by measuring NIRS.

## 2  Materials and Methods

### 2.1  Experimental Method

The subjects were eight healthy young persons (22.8 ± 0.9 years old (mean ± standard) with no past medical history of diseases of the ear or nervous system. The experiment was sufficiently explained to the subjects and written consent was obtained beforehand.

For NIRS, FOIRE-3000 (SHIMADZU, Kyoto) was used. Channels were arranged as follows: 1–12ch on the frontal lobe, 13–24ch on the left temporal lobe, 25–36ch on the right temporal lobe, and 37–48ch on the occipital lobe (Fig. 1). The probe caps to fix the channels were set to the bilateral preauricular points, plane α covering the nasion (root of the nose), and plane β parallel to plane α. The distance between planes α and β was 3 cm, and plane β was present vertically upward of plane α. The occipital lobe was fixed so as to set the center of the probe cap to the inion in the occipital region (external occipital protuberance) (Fig. 2).

For the 3D game machine, NINTENDO 3DS (Nintendo, Kyoto) was used. NINTENDO 3DS adopted the parallax barrier method, and the liquid crystal screen was 3.53-inch (76.8 mm width × 46.08 mm length). For the game software, TETRiS® (BANDAI NAMCO GAMES, Tokyo), which is relatively simple to operate, was selected from general games.

The subjects sat on a chair and played the game in a comfortable position. They first played TETRiS® for 60 s using the 2D display (early 2D), and continued the game for 60 s using the 3D display (3D). The displayed was then returned to 2D and the game was continued for 30 s (late 2D). Regarding this procedure as one set, NIRS was measured while they continuously played 5 sets. Changes in the oxygenated hemoglobin level over the early 2D, 3D, and late 2D periods in the above 5 trials were recorded at 12 channels on the frontal, occipital, and temporal lobes at 7.7 Hz.

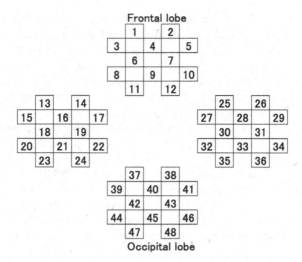

**Fig. 1.** Channel arrangement

**Fig. 2.** Probe cap attachment

## 2.2　Investigation Items

Regarding the oxygenated hemoglobin level determined by NIRS, the high-frequency component was smoothed by the mean movement every 5 s and the average of the five trials, and the integrated values in the 60s-early 2D, 60s-3D, and 30s-late 2D periods were calculated for each channel. To compare early 2D and 3D, the integrated value in late 2D was doubled and recorded. Increases in brain blood flow from early 2D to 3D and from 3D to late 2D were calculated using the formula below:

early 2D − 3D increase[mM · mm] = integrated values in the 3D [mM · mm]
− early 2D[mM · mm]

3D − late 2D increase[mM · mm] = integrated values in the late 2D[mM · mm]
− 3D[mM · mm]

The oxygenated hemoglobin level on NIRS was compared between early 2D and 3D and between 3D and late 2D using the Wilcoxon signed-rank sum test setting the significance level at $p < 0.05$.

## 3   Results

The value at each channel was compared between early 2D and 3D and between 3D and late 2D using the Wilcoxon signed-rank sum test. Channels at which significant changes were observed were colored in Figs. 3 and 4.

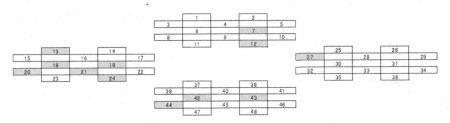

**Fig. 3.** Channels at which significant changes were observed between early 2D and 3D

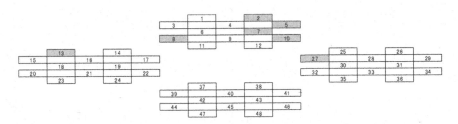

**Fig. 4.** Channels at which significant changes were observed between 3D and late 2D

On the comparison between early 2D and 3D, in the frontal lobe, the 3D integrated value was significantly greater in 3D at ch17 and ch12. In the left temporal lobe, the integrated value was significantly greater in 3D at ch13, ch18–ch21, and ch24. In the right temporal lobe, the integrated value was significantly greater in 3D at ch27. In the occipital lobe, the integrated value was significantly greater in 3D at ch42–ch44.

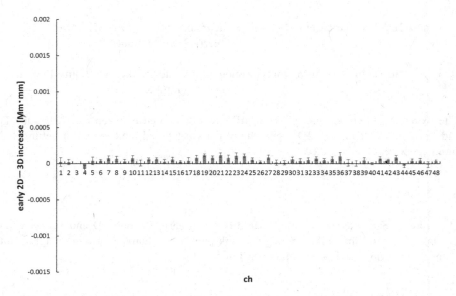

**Fig. 5.** Changes in the oxygenated hemoglobin level from early 2D to 3D [Mm·mm]

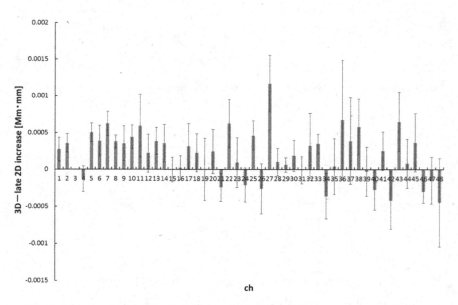

**Fig. 6.** Changes in the oxygenated hemoglobin level from 3D to late 2D [Mm·mm]

On the comparison between 3D and late 2D, the integrated value was significantly greater in late 2D at ch2, ch5, ch7, ch8, and ch10 in the frontal lobe. In the left and right temporal lobes, the integrated value was significantly greater in late 2D at ch13 and ch27. No significant difference was noted in the occipital lobe.

Increases in brain blood flow from early 2D to 3D and from 3D to late 2D are shown in Figs. 5 and 6 (values at ch3 were not presented due to measurement failure). Brain blood flow increased from early 2D to 3D at many channels. The increase in brain blood flow from 3D to late 2D was greater than that from early 2D to 3D, but a sharp reduction in brain blood flow was observed in several channels.

## 4  Discussion

From early 2D to 3D, brain blood flow increased at many channels, suggesting that the blood oxygenated hemoglobin level in the brain increases while playing the 3D game compared to that while playing the 2D game. However, brain blood flow also increased from 3D to late 2D at several channels, for which two reasons are considered: The influence of 3D images remains for a specific time after switching 3D to 2D, or the increase was due to concentration on the operation of the game and thinking. The increase turned to a decrease in ch21, ch24, ch26, ch31, ch34, ch39, ch40, ch42, ch46, and ch48, suggesting that the influence of 3D images was marked at these channels.

In the frontal lobe, a significant difference between early 2D and 3D was noted at ch17 and ch12, and a significant difference between 3D and late 2D was noted at ch2, ch5, ch7, ch8, and ch10. An increase in ch12 was also noted between 3D and late 2D, and blood flow consistently increased from early 2D to late 2D at many channels. Since the frontal lobe controls psychogenesis, such as emotion, attention, thinking, and voluntary movement, brain blood flow may have continued to increase due to thinking and concentration on the game operation [9–11].

In the occipital lobe, a significant difference between early 2D and 3D was noted at ch42–ch44. No significant difference was noted on a comparison between 3D and late 2D. Therefore, the oxygenated hemoglobin level increased in the occipital lobe when 2D was switched to 3D. The oxygenated hemoglobin level turned to decrease at ch42 from 3D to late 2D, suggesting that it was markedly influenced by 3D images. Since the visual area responsible for vision is present in the occipital lobe [9–11], it may have been strongly influenced when 2D was switched to 3D.

In the temporal lobe, on a comparison between early 2D and 3D, the integrated value was significantly higher in 3D at ch13, ch18–ch21, and ch24 in the left temporal lobe. On the comparison between 3D and late 2D, the integrated value was significantly higher in late 2D at ch13, but differences at other channels became insignificant. In addition, the oxygenated hemoglobin level tended to increase from 2D to 3D in the left temporal lobe but turned to decrease from 3D to late 2D at some channels, being markedly influenced by 3D images. Various sensory areas are present in the left temporal lobe, and, in contrast to the right temporal lobe which memorizes sounds and shapes, the left temporal lobe memorizes and understands speech [9–11]. Since TETRiS® is a game requiring thinking, 3D images may have a large influence on the left temporal lobe.

## 5 Conclusion

Aiming at increasing knowledge about the influence of stereoscopic images on the body, we focused on a 3D game machine. Changes in brain blood flow while playing the game were compared between playing using the 2D and 3D displays by measuring NIRS.

On the comparison between early 2D and 3D, the integrated value was significantly greater in 3D at ch17 and ch12 in the frontal lobe. In the left temporal lobe, the integrated value was significantly greater in 3D at ch13, ch18–ch21, and ch24. In the right temporal lobe, the integrated value was significantly greater in 3D at ch27. In the occipital lobe, the integrated value was significantly greater in 3D at ch42–ch44. On the comparison between 3D and late 2D, in the frontal lobe, the integrated value was significantly greater in late 2D at ch2, ch5, ch7, ch8, and ch10. In the left, right temporal lobe, the integrated value was significantly greater in late 2D at ch13 and ch27. No significant difference was noted in the occipital lobe.

A marked increase in brain blood flow was noted in the frontal, occipital, and left temporal lobes. In the frontal lobe, brain blood flow consistently increased from early 2D to late 2D at many channels. Since the frontal lobe controls psychogenesis, such as emotion, attention, thinking, and voluntary movement, brain blood flow may have continued to increase due to thinking and concentration on the game operation. In the occipital and left temporal lobes, brain blood flow increased from early 2D to 3D, and no significant difference was noted between 3D and late 2D. The visual area responsible for vision is present in the occipital lobe, and various sensory areas are present in the left temporal lobe. Thus, sensory areas, such as the visual area, may have been activated when playing the game with 3D images compared to activation by 2D.

**Acknowledgements.** This work was supported in part by the Japan Society for the Promotion of Science, Grant-in-Aid for Scientific Research (C) Number 26350004 and Research Activity Start-up Number 50760998.

## References

1. Saito, S.: Safety image for all: the evaluation method and international standard. J. Inst. Image Inf. Telev. Eng. **58**, 1356–1359 (2004)
2. Fukuda, M., Mikuni, M.: A study of near-infrared spectroscopy in depression. J. Clin. Exp. Med. **219**, 1057–1062 (2006)
3. Zardecki, A.: Multiple scattering corrections to the Beer-Lambert Law. Proc. SPIE **1983**, 103–110 (1983)
4. Wray, S., Cope, M., Delpy, D.T., Wyatt, J.S., Reynolds, E.O.: Characterization of the near infrared absorption spectra of cytochrome AA 3 and hemoglobin for the non-invasive monitoring of cerebral oxygenation. Biochemica et Biophysica A **933**, 184–192 (1988)
5. Elwell, C.E., Cooper, C.E., Cope, M., Delpy, D.T.: Performance comparison of several published tissue near-infrared spectroscopy algorithms. Anal. Biochem. **227**, 54–68 (1995)
6. Hoshi, Y., Tamura, M.: Detection of dynamic changes in cerebral oxgenation coupled to neural function during mental work in man. Neurosci. Lett. **150**, 5–8 (1993)

7. Kato, T., Kamei, A., Takashima, S., Ozaki, T.: Human visual cortical function during photic stimulation monitoring by means of near-infared spectroscopy. J. Cereb. Blood Flow Metab. **13**, 516–520 (1993)
8. Hazeki, O., Tamura, M.: Quantitative analysis of hemoglobin oxygenation state of rat brain in situ by near-infrared spectroscopy. J. Appl. Physiol. **64**, 796–802 (1988)
9. Sugihara, I.: Audition and equilibrium. In: Sakai, T., Kawahara, K. (eds.) Normal Structure and Function of Human Body, vol. 9, Nervous System 2, pp. 66–77. Nihon-Ijishinpo, Tokyo (2005)
10. Netter, F.H.: Netter Atlas of Human Anatomy, 6th edn. Saunders Elsevier, Philadelphia (2014)
11. Dox, I.G., Melloni, B.J., Eisner, G.M., Melloni, J.: Illustrated Medical Dictionary, 4th edn. Collins Reference, Glasgow (2001)

# Universal Access to Mobility and Automotive

# Predictive Pointing from Automotive to Inclusive Design

Bashar I. Ahmad[1(✉)], James K. Murphy[1], Patrick M. Langdon[2],
and Simon J. Godsill[1]

[1] Signal Processing and Communications Laboratory (SigProC),
Department of Engineering, University of Cambridge, Cambridge, UK
{bia23, jm362, sjg30}@cam.ac.uk
[2] Department of Engineering, Engineering Design Centre (EDC),
University of Cambridge, Cambridge, UK
pml24@cam.ac.uk

**Abstract.** With interactive displays, such as touchscreens, becoming an integrated part of the modern vehicle environment, predictive displays have emerged as a solution to minimize the effort as well as cognitive, visual and physical workload associated with using in-vehicle displays. It utilises gesture tracking in 3D as the basis of an input modality enabling interface component acquisition (pointing and selections). Nevertheless, the predictive display technology has the potential to facilitate and assist human computer interaction for motion impaired users, for example, those with cerebral palsy, tremors and spasms, in various scenarios. It also has a wider application in inclusive design addressing general ranges of impairments, such as those arising from ageing. This paper explores the potential of this promising technology and proposes that a predictive display, which was developed to aid drivers in a situationally induced impairment due to using non-driving interfaces in a moving car, can be applicable to the health induced impairment arising from perturbations due to physical movement disorders. It is concluded that 3D predictive gesture tracking can simplify and expedite target acquisition during perturbed pointing movements due to a health/physical-capability impairment.

**Keywords:** Interactive displays · Bayesian inference · Target assistance · Motor impairment · Endpoint prediction · Inclusive design

## 1 Introduction and Background

Interactive displays, such as touchscreens, are becoming increasingly prevalent in the modern vehicle environment, progressively replacing traditional in-vehicle mechanical controls such as switches, knobs and buttons [1, 2]. This is due to their ability to present large quantities of information related to in-vehicle infotainment systems, facilitate intuitive interactions via free hand pointing gestures (particularly for novice users) and offer additional design flexibilities (for example, the display can be adapted to the context of use via a reconfigurable Graphical User Interface GUI) [1–4]. However, undertaking a free hand pointing gesture to acquire (pointing and select) a target on the display, e.g. a GUI icon, requires dedicating a considerable amount of

© Springer International Publishing Switzerland 2016
M. Antona and C. Stephanidis (Eds.): UAHCI 2016, Part III, LNCS 9739, pp. 527–537, 2016.
DOI: 10.1007/978-3-319-40238-3_50

attention (visual, cognitive and physical) that would be otherwise available for driving [4], with potential safety implications [5]. Due to road and driving conditions, the user pointing gesture can be subject to high levels of perturbations leading to erroneous on-screen selections [6]; attempts to rectify an incorrect selection or adapting to the noisy environment can lead to even more distractions, i.e. Situationally Induced Impairment and Disability (SIID). Therefore, intent-aware displays [7], which can infer, notably early in the free hand pointing gesture, the intended on-screen item can simplify and expedite the selection task (even under perturbations). They can significantly improve the usability of in-car touchscreens by reducing distractions and workload associated with interacting with them.

Additionally, with the proliferation of the increasingly ubiquitous touchscreen technology in everyday use, target acquisition (pointing and selection) on a graphical user interface has become part of modern life and a frequent Human-Computer Interaction (HCI) task. Pointing reliability and accuracy is of a key importance for the design of effective GUI. This has triggered an immense interest in approaches that model pointing movements and assist the pointing task by reducing the cursor pointing time and improving its accuracy [8–22]. This can be achieved via pointing facilitation techniques, such as increasing the size of the target icon, altering its activation area, dragging the cursor closer to the target, etc. However, such strategies can be effectively applied only if the intended GUI item is known *a priori* [11–17]. Such studies focus on pointing via a mouse or mechanical-device in a 2D set-up to select a GUI icon(s) and often focus on able-bodied computer users in a stationary input situation. However, the pointing-selection task can be particularly challenging or even overwhelming at times for users with a motion-visual impairment [17–22], i.e. due to Health Induced Impairment and Disability (HIID). For example, in [18] a method that is based on an advanced state-space particle filter technique is used to smooth the 2D pointing mouse cursor trajectory such that it compensates for HIID-related-perturbation leaving the cursor to move only in the intended direction.

On the other hand, inclusive design is a user-centered approach that examines designed product features with particular attention to the functional demands they make on the perceptual, thinking and physical capabilities of diverse users, including those with impairments and ageing. Inclusion refers to the quantitative relationship between the demand made by design features and the capability ranges of users who may be excluded from the use of the product because of those features [25]. Therefore, formulating solutions that facilitate HCI for people with a wide range of HIID, including those that arise from age and not only severe forms of physical disability, is crucial. Most importantly, an inclusive design approach extends beyond the scope of conventional usability methods as it must accommodate extremes of capability range or situational contexts of task or stress, that are not normally accommodated by product design. A predictive display presents itself in this context as a means to extend the usability of the interactive displays to a diverse population of users, for example motion impaired or able-bodied users, elderly or young users, expert or non-expert users as well as situationally impaired users.

The transferability of HCI solutions for HIID to SIID scenarios (and vice versa), was proposed in [22, 23]. It assumes that any human user can be impaired (disabled) in their effectiveness by characteristics of their environment, the task and the design of the

GUI. Such impairment may take the form of perceptual, cognitive and physical movement functional limitations, which translate into inability [18, 25]. For instance, attempting to enter text on an in-car touchscreen (e.g. for navigation) whilst driving in an off-road environment presents difficulties in perceiving the interface for multiple tasks (seeing on-screen icons, outside driving environment and vehicle controls), performing the attentional tasks necessary for safe driving (track/correct vehicle movement, maintaining car controls as well as monitor/correct semantic an texting task), and carrying out the required physical movements (pointing, pressing, steering, braking, etc.).

Figures 1 and 2 depict 2D and 3D pointing trajectories for several on-screen selection tasks, respectively. In the former, several mouse cursor trajectories pertaining to two users (one suffers from severe motor impairment) carrying out a number of target acquisitions on a computer screen using a mechanical mouse. Figure 2 displays the 3D pointing gesture track recorded by a gesture-tracker (namely Leap Motion Controller) whilst a user interacts with a touchscreen in a car under different road/driving conditions. This clearly demonstrates the similarities between perturbations in the pointing movement due to situational (especially when a car is driven on a harsh terrain) and health induced impairments. Thus, solutions devised for predictive in-vehicle displays can be applied to tackle HIID perturbations in the pointing movement.

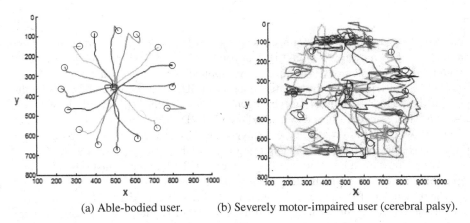

(a) Able-bodied user.    (b) Severely motor-impaired user (cerebral palsy).

**Fig. 1.** 2D mouse cursor tracks to acquire on-screen GUI icons (classical Fitt's law task, ISO 9241) for an able-bodied user and a user suffering from cerebral palsy [18].

The developed predictive display for automotive applications utilises a gesture tracker, which captures, in real-time, the pointing hand/finger location(s), in conjunction with probabilistic inference algorithms to determine the intended destination on the interactive surface (e.g. touchscreen). The prediction results for each of the GUI selectable icons are subsequently used to decide on the intended endpoint and accordingly alter the GUI to assist the selection process. Several such pointing gesture trackers, which can accurately track, in real-time, a pointing gesture in 3D, have

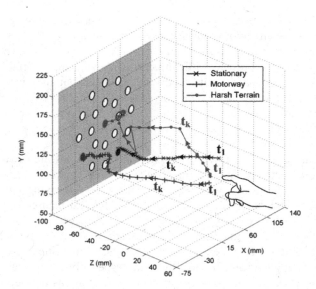

**Fig. 2.** Full pointing finger-tip trajectory during several pointing gestures aimed at selecting a GUI item (circles) on the touchscreen interface surface (blue plane), under various road conditions [7]. Arrows indicate the direction of travel over time, starting at $t_1 < t_k$. (Color figure online)

emerged lately, e.g. Microsoft Kinect, leap motion controller, and Nimble UX. They are motivated by a desire to extend HCI beyond traditional keyboard input and mouse pointing. The Bayesian destination predictor applied here relies on defining a Hidden Markov Model (HMM) of the pointing motion in 3D, effectively capturing the influence of the intended endpoint on the finger/hand movement [7]. This is distinct from previous HCI research on endpoint prediction in 2D scenarios, e.g. [11–15], which often follow from Fitt's law type analysis and uses a static setting/model. The Bayesian HMM approach permits capturing the variability among users as well as the noise of the movement tracking sensor via Stochastic Differential Equations (SDE) that represent the destination-motivated pointing motion in 3D.

The remainder of this paper is organised as follows. In the next section, we describe the adopted Bayesian intent inference framework used in the predictive displays and outline the flexibility of this formulation. Pilot results from the automotive domain are shown in Sect. 3. Finally, the applicability of predictive displays in inclusive design is discussed in Sect. 4 and conclusions are drawn.

## 2 Bayesian Intent Inference with Hidden Markov Models

Bayesian inference with HMM allows the flexible modelling of the pointing motion with either HIID or SIID via a stochastic differential equation. The variability in the pointing movement, e.g. due to the user behavior and/or impairment, can be introduced through the noise element of the state (position, velocity, acceleration, etc.) evolution equation.

Additionally, the noise generated from the employed sensor, e.g. a particular gesture tracker, can be incorporated via the measurement noise in the observation equation. Most importantly, the statistical filter utilised to infer the state or intent/final destination of the tracked object (e.g. mouse cursor in 2D or pointing finger for free hand pointing gestures) can be applied to the same class of motion models (e.g. Kalman filtering for linear models) despite changing the adopted pointing movement process/model. The effectiveness of the state-space-modelling for removing unintentional impairment-related pointing movement were demonstrated in [17, 18, 26]. Nevertheless, the main objective of employing HMM in predictive displays is to determine the icon the user intends to select on the display as early as possible; removing unintentional HIID/SIID-related pointing movement, although desirable, is not essential.

## 2.1 Destination Motion Models

Since the pointing motion is intrinsically driven by the endpoint (i.e., the intended on-screen icon), destination-reverting models such as the linear Mean Reverting Diffusion (MRD) and Equilibrium Reverting Velocity (ERV) models can be suitable for predictive displays under health or situationally induced impairments. Following the integration of their respective SDEs and assuming that the intended destination is $\mathcal{D}_i$, linear destination reverting models can be expressed by

$$\mathbf{s}_{i,k} = \mathbf{F}_{i,k}\mathbf{s}_{i,k-1} + \boldsymbol{\kappa}_{i,k} + \mathbf{w}_k, \ i = 1, 2, \ldots, N \tag{1}$$

where $\mathbf{s}_{i,k-1}$ and $\mathbf{s}_{i,k}$ are the hidden model state vectors at two consecutive time instants $t_{k-1}$ and $t_k$. For example, the state $\mathbf{s}_{i,k}$ can include the true pointing-finger location in 3D and other higher order motion dynamics such as velocity as in the ERV case. Matrix $\mathbf{F}_{i,k}$ is the state transition and $\boldsymbol{\kappa}_{i,k}$ is a time varying constant (both are with respect to the $i^{th}$ destination $\mathcal{D}_i$), and the motion model dynamic noise is $\mathbf{w}_k$. Therefore, for $N$ possible endpoints on the display (i.e. selectable GUI icons), $N$ such models can be constructed. The (also linear) observation model is given by

$$\mathbf{m}_k = \mathbf{H}_k\mathbf{s}_{i,k} + \mathbf{n}_k \tag{2}$$

where $\mathbf{n}_k$ represents the noise introduced by the sensor. For more details on the destination reverting models and their characteristics, the reader is referred to [7, 27].

To demonstrate the ability of the destination reverting models to capture a wide range of possible pointing behaviors in 3D, Fig. 3 depicts several possible velocity profiles of the pointing finger (during target acquisition tasks via free hand pointing gestures) as per the ERV motion model. Each of these plots is obtained by setting a different value for the damping parameter of the ERV model along the $x$, $y$ and $z$ axes via $\mathbf{F}_k$ in (1). The figure clearly illustrates that by using ERV, a range of possible pointing velocity profiles can be modelled, for example, reflecting the motor-ability and/or reach of a user interacting with a touchscreen positioned at a considerable distance from the seating positions such as with an in-vehicle interactive display for

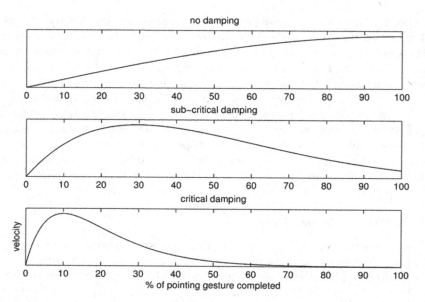

**Fig. 3.** Velocity profile of the pointing-finger during a free hand pointing gesture as per the ERV motion model, various damping terms are applied [7].

controlling the infotainment system. It is noted that the bottom plot in Fig. 3 resembles the expected velocity profile of the point gestures of an in-car touchscreen user without any impeding HIID or SIID.

## 2.2 Intent Inference

Predictive displays aim to establish, in real-time, the likelihood of each of the selectable icons of the displayed GUI being the intended destination of the undertaken pointing task (e.g. of a pointing gesture). For example, at time instant $t_k$ where the available pointing object (finger/cursor) observations (positions) are $\mathbf{m}_{1:k} = \{\mathbf{m}_1, \mathbf{m}_2, \ldots, \mathbf{m}_k\}$, the system calculates

$$\mathcal{P}(t_k) = \{P(\mathcal{D}_i = \mathcal{D}_I | \mathbf{m}_{1:k}), i = 1, 2, \ldots, N\}. \tag{3}$$

The intended destination, which is unknown *a priori*, is notated by $\mathcal{D}_I$ such that $\mathcal{D}_I \in \mathbb{D} = \{\mathcal{D}_1, \mathcal{D}_2, \ldots, \mathcal{D}_N\}$. It is noted that the location of the items in $\mathbb{D}$ are known, however, no assumptions are made on their distribution-layout. After evaluating $\mathcal{P}(t_k)$ in (1), a simple intuitive approach to establish the intended destination at $t_k$ is to select the most probable endpoint via

$$\hat{I}(t_k) = \arg \max_{\mathcal{D}_i \in \mathbb{D}} P(\mathcal{D}_i = \mathcal{D}_I | \mathbf{m}_{1:k}) \tag{4}$$

Decision criterion other than (4) can be applied. For the linear destination reverting models, Kalman filters can be used (one per nominal destination) to calculate $P(\mathcal{D}_i = \mathcal{D}_l | \mathbf{m}_{1:k})$ in (3) as per [7, 27]. Adopting nonlinear motion or observation models can lead to advanced statistical inference methods such as sequential Monte Carlo or other related methods [28] being required for online filtering.

### 2.3   Smoothing Noisy Trajectories

The results of the $N$ statistical filters applied to determine (3) can be utilised to remove the unintentional perturbations-impairment-related movements as shown in [7]. However, in certain scenarios (e.g. infrequent severe perturbations) where it is desirable to maintain a simple linear motion model for the intent inference functionality, a pre-processing step/stage can be added such that the raw pointing data is filtered, e.g. using a particle filter [18, 26]. The filtered track is subsequently used by the destination inference module.

## 3   Pilot Results

Figure 4 depicts selected pilot results of using a predictive display in an automotive context. The benefits are assessed in terms of the technology ability to reduce the effort/workload associated with interacting with an in-vehicle display. In this scenario, a gesture tracker is employed to produce, in real-time, the locations of the pointing hand/finger in 3D, which are then utilised by the intent predictor. Here, the predictive display auto-selects the intended on-screen icon once a particular level of inference certainty is achieved (the user need not touch the touchscreen surface to make a selection). This figure shows the measured subjective workload using NASA TLX forms when the prediction and auto-selection capability is on and off. In the latter case, the experiment becomes a conventional task of interacting with a touchscreen where completing a selection operation entails physically touching the intended on-screen icon. Figure 4 illustrates that the predictive display system can reduce the workload of interacting with an in-vehicle display by nearly 50 %, therefore, significantly simplifying and facilitating the on-screen target acquisition task via free hand pointing gestures.

Figures 5 and 6 demonstrate the ability of a sequential Monte Carlo method, namely the variable rate particle filter, to remove highly non-linear perturbation-related pointing movements when interacting with a touchscreen via free hand pointing gestures or selecting icons of a GUI displayed on a computer screen using a mechanical mouse, respectively. The raw cursor movement data in Fig. 6 is for a user that suffers from cerebral palsy. The figure exhibits the confidence ellipses obtained from the sequential Monte Carlo filter, which has visibly removed the health-induced-impairment-related jumping behavior of the mouse cursor position and can assist identifying the user's

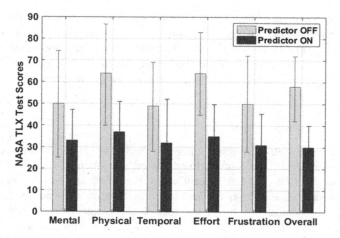

**Fig. 4.** Workload scores (NASA TLX) for interacting with touchscreen in a vehicle with and without the predictive functionality (with auto-selection) for 18 participants. (Color figure online)

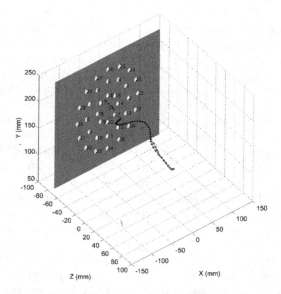

**Fig. 5.** 3D pointing gesture trajectory before (black) and after (red) applying a variable rate particle filter [26]. (Color figure online)

intended destination (despite the ambiguity of the raw pointing data). On the other hand, unintentional situational-induced-impairment-related pointing finger movements are successfully removed in Fig. 6.

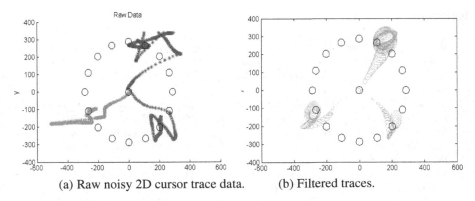

(a) Raw noisy 2D cursor trace data.        (b) Filtered traces.

**Fig. 6.** Filtering noisy mouse cursor trajectories due to HIID using a particle filter and showing the confidence ellipses [18]; units on the axes are pixels.

## 4   Conclusions and Future Work

Consideration of the effectiveness of measures intended for situational impairment, such as when using a touchscreen in a moving vehicle over a badly maintained road (a perturbed environment) have shown that probabilistic predictors can bring significant gains in SIID. This strongly suggests that similar gains can be achieved in a health induced impairment scenario. That is to say that spasm, weakness, tremor and athetosis may be mitigated or eliminated by the predictive approach based on automotive algorithms/applications we describe. In particular, motion impaired users, who may have difficulty pointing and selecting on touchscreens will benefit not only from prediction and automated selection (i.e. auto-selection as in Fig. 4), but also from the reduction of workload reported by the automotive trial participants, reliably measured using NASA TLX scores.

Additionally, from an inclusive design perspective [29] the predictive display technology may greatly benefit those with age related or mild physical or perceptual impairments by enhancing performance in pointing-selection and reducing the associated workload. Mild functional impairments such as physical, visual, hearing reach and stretch and cognitive may be accommodated. The adopted predictive techniques are also applicable to special purpose designs for more extreme impairment and disability. Experimental studies will initially require the same tasks, modified for floor effects from physically impaired participants. However, these will be superseded by trials of the same algorithms and detection technologies with interfaces in mobile displays, walking scenarios, wheelchair use and on public transportation. Finally, it is noted that predictive displays are particularly flexible in terms of incorporating additional sensory data or input modalities when available, e.g. eye-gaze or voice-based commands, via the Bayesian framework described in Sect. 2.

# References

1. Burnett, G.E., Porter, J.M.: Ubiquitous computing within cars: designing controls for non-visual use. Int. J. Hum. Comput. Stud. **55**(4), 521–531 (2001)
2. Harvey, C., Stanton, N.A.: Usability Evaluation for In-vehicle Systems. CRC Press, Boca Raton (2013)
3. Burnett, G.E., Lawson, G., Millen, L., Pickering, C.: Designing touchpad user-interfaces for vehicles: which tasks are most suitable? Behav. Inf. Technol. **30**, 403–414 (2011)
4. Jaeger, M.G., Skov, M.B., Thomassen, N.G., et al.: You can touch, but you can't look: interacting with in-vehicle systems. In: Proceedings of the SIGCHI Conference on Human Factors in Computing Systems, pp. 1139–1148 (2008)
5. Klauer, S.G., Dingus, T.A., Neale, V.L., Sudweeks, J.D., Ramsey, D.J.: The impact of driver inattention on near-crash/crash risk: an analysis using the 100-car naturalistic driving study data. National Highway Traffic Safety Administration, DOT HS 810 5942006 (2006)
6. Ahmad, B.I., Langdon, P.M., Godsill, S.J., Hardy, R., Skrypchuk, L., Donkor, R.: Touchscreen usability and input performance in vehicles under different road conditions: an evaluative study. In: Proceeding of the 7th International Conference on Automotive User Interfaces and Interactive Vehicular Applications (AutomotiveUI 2015), Nottingham, UK, pp. 47–54 (2015)
7. Ahmad, B.I., Murphy, J., Langdon, P.M., Godsill, S.J., Hardy, R., Skrypchuk, L.: Intent inference for pointing gesture based interactions in vehicles. IEEE Trans. Cybern. **46**(4), 878–889 (2015)
8. Mackenzie, S.: Fitts' law as a research and design tool in human-computer interaction. J. Hum. Comput. Interact. **7**, 91–139 (1992)
9. Kopper, R., Bowman, D.A., Silva, M.G., McMahan, R.P.: A human motor behavior model for distal pointing tasks. Int. J. Hum Comput Stud. **68**, 603–615 (2010)
10. Meyer, D.E., Smith, J.E., Kornblum, S., Abrams, R.A., Wright, C.E.: Optimality in human motor performance: ideal control of rapid aimed movements. Psychol. Rev. **8**, 340–370 (1988)
11. McGuffin, M.J., Balakrishnan, R.: Fitts' law and expanding targets: experimental studies and designs for user interfaces. ACM Trans. Comput. Hum. Interact. **12**(4), 388–422 (2005)
12. Murata, A.: Improvement of pointing time by predicting targets in pointing with a PC mouse. IJHCI **10**(1), 23–32 (1998)
13. Wobbrock, J.O., Fogarty, J., Liu, S., Kimuro, S., Harada, S.: The angle mouse: target-agnostic dynamic gain adjustment based on angular deviation. In: Proceedings of the SIGCHI Conference on Human Factors in Computing Systems, pp. 1401–1410 (2009)
14. Asano, T., Sharlin, E., Kitamura, Y., Takashima, K., Kishino, F.: Predictive interaction using the Delphian desktop. In: Proceedings of the ACM Symposium on User Interface Software and Technology. ACM, pp. 133–141 (2005)
15. Lank, E., Cheng, Y.-C.N., Ruiz, J.: Endpoint prediction using motion kinematics. In: Proceedings of the SIGCHI Conference on Human factors in Computing Systems, pp. 637–646 (2007)
16. Ziebart, B., Dey, A., Bagnell, J.A.: Probabilistic pointing target prediction via inverse optimal control. In: Proceedings of the ACM International Conference on Intelligent User Interfaces, pp. 1–10 (2012)
17. Ahmad, B.I., Langdon, P.M., Bunch, P., Godsill, S.J.: Probabilistic intentionality prediction for target selection based on partial cursor tracks. In: Stephanidis, C., Antona, M. (eds.) UAHCI 2014, Part III. LNCS, vol. 8515, pp. 427–438. Springer, Heidelberg (2014)

18. Langdon, P., Godsill, S., Clarkson, P.J.: Statistical estimation of user's interactions from motion impaired cursor use data. In: Proceedings of the 6th International Conference on Disability, Virtual Reality and Associated Technologies (ICDVRAT 2006), Esbjerg, Denmark (2006)
19. Keates, S., Hwang, F., Langdon, P., Clarkson, P.J, Robinson, P.: Cursor measures for motion-impaired computer users. In: Proceedings of the Fifth International ACM Conference on Assistive Technologies – ASSETS, New York, pp. 135–142 (2002)
20. Wobbrock, J.O., Gajos, K.Z.: Goal crossing with mice and trackballs for people with motor impairments: performance, submovements, and design directions. ACM Trans. Accessible Comput. (TACCESS) 1(4), 1–37 (2008)
21. Gajos, K.Z., Wobbrock, J.O., Weld, D.S.: Automatically generating user interfaces adapted to users' motor and vision capabilities. In: ACM symposium on User interface software and technology, pp. 231–240 (2007)
22. Biswas, P., Langdon, P.: Developing multimodal adaptation algorithm for mobility impaired users by evaluating their hand strength. Int. J. Hum. Comput. Interact. 28, 576–596 (2012)
23. Sears, A., Lin, M., Jacko, J., Xiao, Y.: When computers fade: pervasive computing and situationally induced impairments and disabilities. In: Proceedings of HCI International, pp. 1298–1302 (2003)
24. Newell, A.F., Gregor, P.: Human computer interfaces for people with disabilities. In: Handbook of Human Computer Interaction, pp. 813–824 (1997). ISBN: 0-444-1862-6
25. Langdon, P., Persad, U., Clarkson, P.J.: Developing a model of cognitive interaction for analytical inclusive design evaluation. Interact. Comput. 22, 510–529 (2010)
26. Ahmad, B.I., Murphy, J.K., Langdon, P.M., Godsill, S.J.: Filtering perturbed in-vehicle pointing gesture trajectories: improving the reliability of intent inference. In: Proceedings of IEEE International Workshop on Machine Learning for Signal Processing (MLSP 2014) (2014)
27. Ahmad, B.I., Langdon, P.M., Hardy, R., Godsill, S.J.: Intelligent intent-aware touchscreen systems using gesture tracking with endpoint prediction. In: Antona, M., Stephanidis, C. (eds.) UAHCI 2015. LNCS, vol. 9176, pp. 3–14. Springer, Heidelberg (2015)
28. Godsill, S., Vermaak, J.: Models and algorithms for tracking using trans-dimensional sequential Monte Carlo. In: Proceedings of the IEEE International Conference on Acoustics, Speech, and Signal Processing (ICASSP 2004), pp. 973–976 (2004)
29. Langdon, P., Thimbleby, H.: Inclusion and interaction: designing interaction for inclusive populations. Interact. Comput. 22, 439–448 (2010)

# Online Engagement Detection and Task Adaptation in a Virtual Reality Based Driving Simulator for Autism Intervention

Dayi Bian[1(✉)], Joshua Wade[3], Zachary Warren[4,5,6],
and Nilanjan Sarkar[1,2]

[1] Department of Electrical Engineering, Vanderbilt University,
Nashville, TN, USA
{dayi.bian, nilanjan.sarkar}@vanderbilt.edu
[2] Department of Mechanical Engineering, Vanderbilt University,
Nashville, TN, USA
[3] Department of Computer Science, Vanderbilt University, Nashville, TN, USA
[4] Department of Pediatrics and Psychiatry, Vanderbilt University,
Nashville, TN, USA
[5] Department of Special Education, Vanderbilt University, Nashville, TN, USA
[6] Vanderbilt Kennedy Center, Treatment and Research Institute of Autism
Spectrum Disorders, Vanderbilt University, Nashville, TN, USA

**Abstract.** Individuals with Autism spectrum disorder (ASD) have difficulty functioning independently on essential tasks that require adaptive skills such as driving. Recently, computer-aided technology, such as Virtual Reality (VR), is being widely used in ASD intervention to teach basic skills to children with autism. However, most of these works either do not use feedback or solely use performance feedback from the participant for system adaptation. This paper introduces a physiology-based task adaptation mechanism in a virtual environment for driving skill training. The difficulty of the driving task was autonomously adjusted based on the participant's performance and engagement level to provide the participant with an optimal level of challenge. The engagement level was detected using an affective model which was developed based on our previous experimental data and a therapist's ratings. We believe that this physiology-based adaptive mechanism can be useful in teaching driving skills to adolescents with ASD.

**Keywords:** Virtual Reality (VR) · Driving simulator · ASD intervention · Dynamic difficulty adjustment (DDA) · Physiological signals · Machine learning · Affective computing · Human computer interaction

## 1 Introduction

Autism spectrum disorder (ASD) has a high prevalence rate of 1 in 68 children in the US [1] and is associated with high familial and societal cost [2, 3]. Individuals with ASD have difficulty functioning independently on essential tasks that require adaptive skills such as driving [3], which is crucial for independent living in developed countries.

© Springer International Publishing Switzerland 2016
M. Antona and C. Stephanidis (Eds.): UAHCI 2016, Part III, LNCS 9739, pp. 538–547, 2016.
DOI: 10.1007/978-3-319-40238-3_51

Although there is no single accepted treatment or known cure for ASD, there is a growing consensus that skill training and educational intervention programs can significantly improve long-term outcomes for individuals with ASD and their families [4, 5]. A growing number of studies have been investigating applications of computer-aided technology [6–11], including Virtual Reality (VR) platforms, for ASD intervention. However, most of these studies do not provide feedback or solely use participants' performance or explicit user feedback as primary means of evaluation.

Task difficulty can induce a variety of cognitive workload and affective states [12]. A task that is beyond an individual's capability can be overwhelming and cause anxiety while a task that does not utilize the skill of a person might result in boredom. An individual under the states of anxiety or boredom will focus less on their tasks, learn less, be less productive, and be more prone to errors [13]. Minimizing anxiety and boredom during a task can help people maintain a high level of engagement, perform well, and learn efficiently. To provide users with an optimal level of challenge, dynamic difficulty adjustment (DDA) is used to automatically alter the task difficulty in real-time by monitoring user state. Compared to strictly performance-based feedback, physiology feedback can be more efficient in providing optimal challenge to users, increasing their engagement and improving their performance [14].

The present study introduced a VR-based adaptive driving skill training system which automatically adjusted its difficultly levels based on participants' engagement levels and performance metrics. The engagement detection model was developed by training on data that was collected from our previous study where we recorded physiological signals and engagement labels [15]. Off-the-shelf driving simulators were not suitable for this study because we needed to design new driving tasks with embedded intervention rules as well as to integrate the simulator with real-time physiological recording and engagement detection modules. To the best of our knowledge, none of the commercial driving simulators offer these flexibilities.

We believe that by utilizing physiology-based engagement detection to adjust difficulty levels in a VR-based driving system, our proposed system can be used more effectively for driving skill training of individuals with ASD.

## 2    System Overview

The proposed VR-based driving environment with adaptive response technology comprised of (1) a VR-based driving task module; (2) a real-time physiological data acquisition module; and (3) an individualized DDA module utilizing a physiology-based engagement prediction mechanism (Fig. 1).

### 2.1    VR-Based Driving Task Module

In this study, we used desktop VR applications because they are accessible, affordable and potentially minimize cyber sickness for this especially-sensitive ASD population [16]. Unity (www.unity3d.com), a commercial VR design platform, was used to design the VR environment. Within Unity, we developed a graphical user interface, created

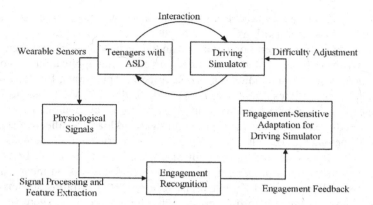

**Fig. 1.** System framework overview

behaviors for vehicles, pedestrians and traffic lights, designed the driving scenario and embedded customized driving rules.

The task difficulty can be adjusted by modifying several game parameters, such as responsiveness of the brake pedal, accelerator pedal, steering wheel, intensity of light in the environment etc. Detailed information of these parameters are presented in Table 1. The values of these parameters for different difficulties were chosen based on the average performance of the participants in our previous study. The parameters related to difficulty levels were grouped into two categories. One category is car controllability, which contains the responsiveness of the brake pedal, accelerator pedal and steering wheel. These are also the main factors that affect the difficulty of the game. The other category is environment, which contains speed for agent vehicles and the intensity of light in the environment. Each category has three difficulty levels from easy to hard. By combining these two categories, we have nine different difficulty states, among which the switching mechanism adjusts the difficulty.

## 2.2  Physiological Data Processing Module

Physiological response for an individual can be utilized to assess one's affective states [17]. The physiological data were collected using the Biopac MP150 physiological data acquisition system (www.biopac.com) with a sampling rate of 1000 Hz. Using hardware API provided by Biopac, we developed a customized physiological data acquisition program, in which we integrated socket-based communication with the Unity program to automatically record event information and time stamps. In this study, three physiological signals were investigated, which were photoplethysmogram (PPG), galvanic skin response (GSR) and respiration (RSP). These signals were measured by using light-weight, non-invasive wireless sensors. PPG and GSR were measured from toes instead of fingers in order to reduce the motion artifact from driving. Respiration was measured by using a respiration belt tied around the participant's abdomen.

The engagement model was developed offline using physiological data and therapist's labels from our previous study [15]. Therefore, it is necessary that the patterns

**Table 1.** Difficulty parameters

| Group | Parameters | Domain | Easy difficulty | Medium difficulty | Hard difficulty |
|---|---|---|---|---|---|
| Car Controllability | Responsiveness of brake pedal | [0.35, 1] | 1 | 0.675 | 0.35 |
| | Responsiveness of the accelerator pedal | [1, 1.5] | 1 | 1.25 | 1.5 |
| | Responsiveness of the steering wheel | [1, 3.75] | 1 | 1 | 3.75 |
| Environment | Intensity of light in the environment | [0.01, 0.5] | 0.5 | 0.226 | 0.01 |
| | Speed of agent vehicles | [0.85, 1.75] | 0.85 | 1.35 | 1.75 |

of emotional responses remain stable across participants. Although different patterns of emotional responses have been found in psychophysiological studies, Stemmler [18] argues that they are due to context deviation specificity. Since, in the current study, the engagement is elicited in the same context (the driving task), inter-participant variability should be low. Nevertheless, to further reduce this variability, three minutes' physiological data during a period of rest were acquired as a baseline. The raw physiological signals from our previous study were preprocessed to remove motion artifacts and noise. After preprocessing, the data were subsampled 10-fold. Subsampling can significantly reduce computation time for feature extraction, which is very crucial in real-time closed-loop systems. A set of features, which were highly correlated with engagement, were selected for training an engagement detection model [15]. After feature extraction, several machine learning algorithms from the Waikato Environment for Knowledge Analysis (WEKA) [19] toolkit were used to build the engagement detection model. Ten-fold cross-validation was used to validate the model. In the end, the Random Forest algorithm, which had the highest accuracy (84.72 %), was chosen to develop the engagement model.

In our proposed closed-loop driving scenario, the driving task program and engagement detection module communicated via sockets over a local area network (LAN). When defined events, like start of trial, end of trial, failure, success etc., occurred, a JSON (http://www.json.org) string containing the time stamp and event message was sent to the physiological data acquisition module. Event makers were recorded with the physiological data for future offline analysis. In the beginning of the experiment, three minutes of baseline data were recorded. After the baseline recording, baseline data were processed to get the baseline features. Every three minutes, the driving task sent an event marker to the engagement detection module to trigger detection. The engagement detection module acquire three minutes' data before this trigger. These data were preprocessed and ten selected features were extracted. The baseline features were subtracted from the features of the three minutes' data to offset environment and subject difference. Then these features were fed into the Random Forest model to predict the engagement level. A binary label, "HIGH" or "LOW", was sent to the driving task program via the socket. Then the difficulty adjustment module took over and made the decision to switch the task difficulty (Fig. 2).

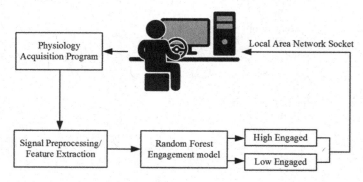

**Fig. 2.** Physiological data processing module

## 2.3 Difficulty Adjustment Module

**Performance-Sensitive System (PS).** For the PS, a task-switching mechanism adjusts the difficulty states based on participants' performance metric alone. When a participant's performance is "Good" (Case 1), the task progression continues step-wise while the task difficulty level increases based on the state flow representation shown in Fig. 3. On the other hand, if a participant's performance is "Poor" (Case 2), the task progression continues step-wise while decreasing the task difficulty level. The switch mechanism continues until Case 1 reaches the most difficult level or Case 2 reaches the easiest level (Fig. 3).

**Engagement-Sensitive System (ES).** For the ES, however, the task switching mechanism is not only based on participants' performance but also his/her engagement level. In other words, in order to move up to higher difficulty levels, the participant must not only perform "Good" in the task, he/she must also be "High Engaged" in the task. In the ES, we fuse performance metrics and engagement levels to make the decision regarding the next step (Table 2). In some cases, the switching strategy is intuitive: If a participant is "High Engaged" and performs "Good", the system increases the difficulty level based on the finite state machine representation. On the other hand, if a participant is "Low Engaged" and performs "Poor", the system decrease the difficulty level. However, in the other two cases, where the engagement and performance metrics does not agree with each other, the switching strategy is harder to define. We give performance more priority for these cases. For case 2 in Table 2, in which engagement is "High" but performance is "Poor", the system recommends decreasing the difficulty level. For case 3, when a participant is "Low Engaged" but performs "Good", the difficulty level remains the same at least until next adjustment. At the next

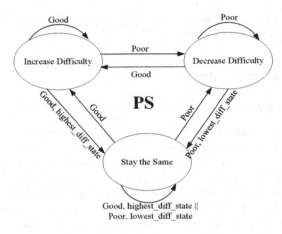

**Fig. 3.** Performance-Sensitive System difficulty switching state flow. (highest_diff_state: system at highest difficulty state, lowest_diff_state: system at lowest difficulty state).

**Table 2.** Engagement-Sensitive System cases

|            | Engagement | Performance | Action                   |
|------------|------------|-------------|--------------------------|
| Case 1     | High       | Good        | Increase difficulty      |
| Case 2     | High       | Poor        | Decrease difficulty      |
| Case 3a/3b | Low        | Good        | Same/Decrease difficulty |
| Case 4     | Low        | Poor        | Decrease difficulty      |

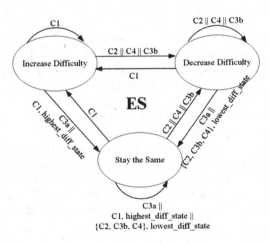

**Fig. 4.** Engagement-Sensitive System difficulty switching state flow. (highest_diff_state: system at highest difficulty state, lowest_diff_state: system at lowest difficulty state, C1, C2, C3a, C3b, C4 are explained in Table below).

adjustment point, if the participant is still "Low Engaged" and performs "Good", the system decreases the difficulty level (Fig. 4).

# 3 Method and Procedure

## 3.1 Experimental Setup

The VR driving environment was run on a server-grade machine that could provide high quality rendering for graphics, while the peripheral physiological signals were acquired and processed in parallel on a separate. Both machines communicated over the LAN using TCP/IP. The VR driving task was presented on a 24-inch flat LCD panel (at resolution 1980 × 1080). Participants interacted with the driving environment using a Logitech G27 driving controller that was mounted on a specially-designed play-seat [20, 21]. The experiment was conducted in a laboratory with two rooms separated by one-way glass for observation. The researcher sat in the outer room.

## 3.2 Participants

We have recruited 4 teenagers with ASD for this phase of study. One of them is female. All participants had a clinical diagnosis of ASD from a licensed clinical psychologist as well as scores at or above clinical cutoff on the Autism Diagnostic Observation Schedule [22]. The Institutional Review Board (IRB) approval for conducting the experiment was sought and obtained.

## 3.3 Procedure

The participants were randomly assigned to either PS or ES. Each participant completed a 90-min session in one visit. At the start of each session, physiological sensors were placed on the participant's body by a trained experimenter. Participants watched a short video which explained basic instructions and game controls. After the tutorial, the participant was asked to remain calm and relaxed for three minutes during which physiological baseline data were collected. Participants also receive three minutes of practice driving in which there were no pedestrians and no other vehicles in the VR environment. This practice period allowed participants to familiarize themselves with the game controls and virtual environment.

After the three-minute practice, participants began the driving assignment. Through the assignment, participants followed the navigation system and tried to obey traffic rules. Disobeying any traffic rules (i.e., running a red light) caused a performance failure. Time duration for the assignment varied from 30 to 40 min depending on the participant's performance. A post-task survey was completed once the participant finished the assignment.

# 4  Results and Discussion

Four participants were recruited for a pilot study evaluation of the system and all of the participants completed the experiment. Two participants were assigned to the PS group and the other two were assigned to the ES group. The driving task ran smoothly according to the participants' responses; all of the participants reported that they "enjoyed the game" or "enjoyed the game a lot". Importantly, all of the participants reported noticing that the task difficulty changed during the driving task, demonstrating that the driving task difficulty can be successfully manipulated by tuning the difficulty parameters we have chosen. The performance data, such as steering wheel angle, gas and brake pedal usage, driving speed, and failure times, were recorded to hard disk in various formats (e.g., time series and event log). These data could be analyzed to evaluate participants' driving behavior.

Physiological measures including PPG, GSR and RSP were recorded and assessed during the driving task. These data were divided into three minute's windows. After preprocessing, a set of features were extracted from these windows and corrected through baseline features subtraction. These sets of features were then fed into the Random Forest engagement model to measure the average engagement level for each participant during the task. Although we cannot draw conclusion regarding differences between the PS and ES groups due to the small sample size, it is encouraging that all subjects, regardless of group affiliation, demonstrated higher engagement characteristics for a majority of the task duration ($M = 77.79\ \%,\ SD = 4.63$). In addition, the average engagement levels reported from the post-task survey support the acceptability of the system (Table 3).

**Table 3.** Engagement statistics from engagement model and post-task survey

| Participant ID | Percentage of "High Engaged" output from engagement model | Engagement level from post-task survey* |
|---|---|---|
| PS01 | 77.78 | 5 |
| PS02 | 73.84 | 4 |
| ES01 | 84.30 | 5 |
| ES02 | 75.25 | 5 |
| Mean | 77.79 | 4.75 |
| Std | 4.63 | 0.5 |

*The post-task survey used a 5-Likert Scale, where 1 means not engaged and 5 means highly engaged.

One advantage of our system is that it does not rely on direct input from the user; this is advantageous because the user may not be aware of his/her level of engagement during the task and may not have the time or the extra cognitive capability to provide such information. Another advantage is that the engagement detection module and DDA module are independent of the simulation software package and thus can be applied to any learning scenario—not merely driving training. The engagement level predictions are sent as JSON strings over TCP/IP, which can be read and applied generically. Once the difficulty levels are defined for a given task, the difficulty switch logic can be applied based on the performance and engagement level of the user.

DDA is a valuable mechanism for maintaining consistent levels of engagement in people using a system. As wearable physiological sensors such as smart watches become more popular and less invasive, passive systems which make use of the user's affective states will become easier to implement, more reliable, and more common-place. In this paper, we presented our system based on the physiology-based DDA mechanism, which uses the user's engagement level and performance to dynamically adjust the difficulty level of the driving task. We demonstrated that our system is reliable and robust. Future work will focus on conducting a larger user study in order to make conclusion about the superiority of the ES system over the PS system.

**Acknowledgement.** We gratefully acknowledge the support provided by the National Institute of Health Grant 1R01MH091102-01A1 to perform the presented research.

# References

1. CDC, Prevalence of Autism Spectrum Disorder Among Children Aged 8 Years—Autism and Developmental Disabilities Monitoring Network, 11 Sites, United States, 2010 (2014)
2. Ganz, M.L.: The Costs of Autism, pp. 475–502. CRC Press, New York (2006)
3. Chasson, G.S., Harris, G.E., Neely, W.J.: Cost comparison of early intensive behavioral intervention and special education for children with autism. J. Child Fam. Stud. **16**(3), 401–413 (2007)
4. Rogers, S.J.: Empirically supported comprehensive treatments for young children with autism. J. Clin. Child Psychol. **27**(2), 168–179 (1998)
5. Palmen, A., Didden, R., Lang, R.: A systematic review of behavioral intervention research on adaptive skill building in high-functioning young adults with autism spectrum disorder. Res. Autism Spectrum Disord. **6**(2), 602–617 (2012)
6. Welch, K.C., Lahiri, U., Liu, C., Weller, R., Sarkar, N., Warren, Z.: An affect-sensitive social interaction paradigm utilizing virtual reality environments for autism intervention. In: Jacko, J.A. (ed.) HCI International 2009, Part III. LNCS, vol. 5612, pp. 703–712. Springer, Heidelberg (2009)
7. Lahiri, U., Warren, Z., Sarkar, N.: Dynamic gaze measurement with adaptive response technology in Virtual Reality based social communication for autism. In: 2011 International Conference on Virtual Rehabilitation (ICVR). IEEE (2011)
8. Lahiri, U., et al.: Design of a virtual reality based adaptive response technology for children with autism. IEEE Trans. Neural Syst. Rehabil. Eng. **21**(1), 55–64 (2013)
9. Lahiri, U., Warren, Z., Sarkar, N.: Design of a gaze-sensitive virtual social interactive system for children with autism. IEEE Trans. Neural Syst. Rehabil. Eng. **19**(4), 443–452 (2011)
10. Liu, C., et al.: Online affect detection and robot behavior adaptation for intervention of children with autism. IEEE Trans. Robotics **24**(4), 883–896 (2008)
11. Tartaro, A., Cassell, J.: Using virtual peer technology as an intervention for children with autism. Towards Universal Usability: Designing Computer Interfaces for Diverse User Populations, vol. 231, p. 62. Wiley, Chichester (2007)
12. Giakoumis, D., et al.: Identifying psychophysiological correlates of boredom and negative mood induced during HCI. In: B-Interface (2010)

13. Pekrun, R., et al.: Boredom in achievement settings: Exploring control–value antecedents and performance outcomes of a neglected emotion. J. Educ. Psychol. **102**(3), 531 (2010)
14. Rani, P., Sarkar, N., Liu, C.: Maintaining optimal challenge in computer games through real-time physiological feedback. In: Proceedings of the 11th international conference on human computer interaction (2005)
15. Dayi, B., et al.: Physiology-based affect recognition during driving in virtual environment for autism intervention. In: 2nd International Conference on Physiological Computing Systems (2015)
16. Bellani, M., et al.: Virtual reality in autism: state of the art. Epidemiol. Psychiatr. Sci. **20**(03), 235–238 (2011)
17. Sarkar, N.: Psychophysiological control architecture for human-robot coordination-concepts and initial experiments. In: IEEE International Conference on Robotics and Automation, Proceedings, ICRA 2002. IEEE (2002)
18. Stemmler, G., et al.: Constraints for emotion specificity in fear and anger: The context counts. Psychophysiology **38**(2), 275–291 (2001)
19. Hall, M., et al.: The WEKA data mining software: an update. ACM SIGKDD explorations newsletter **11**(1), 10–18 (2009)
20. Bian, D., Wade, J.W., Zhang, L., Bekele, E., Swanson, A., Crittendon, J.A., Sarkar, M., Warren, Z., Sarkar, N.: A novel virtual reality driving environment for autism intervention. In: Stephanidis, C., Antona, M. (eds.) UAHCI 2013, Part II. LNCS, vol. 8010, pp. 474–483. Springer, Heidelberg (2013)
21. Wade, J., Bian, D., Fan, J., Zhang, L., Swanson, A., Sarkar, M., Weitlauf, A., Warren, Z., Sarkar, N.: A virtual reality driving environment for training safe gaze patterns: application in individuals with ASD. In: Antona, M., Stephanidis, C. (eds.) UAHCI 2015. LNCS, vol. 9177, pp. 689–697. Springer, Heidelberg (2015)
22. Lord, C., et al.: The autism diagnostic observation schedule—generic: a standard measure of social and communication deficits associated with the spectrum of autism. J. Autism Dev. Disord. **30**(3), 205–223 (2000)

# An Inclusive Design Perspective on Automotive HMI Trends

Mike Bradley$^{(\boxtimes)}$, Patrick M. Langdon, and P. John Clarkson

Engineering Design Centre, University of Cambridge, Cambridge, UK
{mdb54, pml24, pjcl0}@cam.ac.uk

**Abstract.** This paper looks at recent trends in automotive human machine interfaces, with a lens of evaluation from an inclusive design perspective. The goal of Inclusive Design is to ensure that the population of potential users for a product or service is maximised. Until relatively recently, automotive human machine interfaces (HMI's) have excluded and caused difficulties for users due to visibility, reach and force required to operate controls. Over the last 15 or so years however, there has been a significant increase in control and display location, interface types and integration of functions, as well as dramatically increased potential functionality due to in-vehicle emergent technologies. It is suggested that this increase in interface unfamiliarity for a driver will cause significant difficulty and potential exclusion, due to the demands of learning and conflicts in expectation. The effects on this trend in the context of an ageing population and automated driving technologies are discussed.

**Keywords:** Inclusive design · Exclusion audit · Older user · Usability · HMI · Automotive · ADAS · Autonomous driving

## 1   Background

### 1.1   Inclusive Design and Exclusion Calculation

Inclusive design researchers have attempted to understand which characteristics of interactions cause difficulty and exclusion for people in general and specifically for people with capability impairments [1]. It has been demonstrated that adoption of inclusive design tools and processes during the design and development of mainstream products and services can not only improve the uptake for those with capability impairment, but also improve the user experience for those who do not consider themselves impaired [2].

One of the tools used to evaluate the inclusivity of a user journey, is the Inclusive Design Toolkit's Exclusion Calculator [3]. The proportion of the adult UK population who are unable to achieve certain interactions due to degradation of perceptual and motor skill performance is estimated by comparison of task demand to capability data collected in 1996/7 The Disability Follow-Up Survey [4]. For example, the exclusion calculator can estimate the percentage of UK adults who would not be able to read a small sized font used on a display by comparison to whether the task would be possible by someone who can read a newspaper headline, someone who can read a large print

© Springer International Publishing Switzerland 2016
M. Antona and C. Stephanidis (Eds.): UAHCI 2016, Part III, LNCS 9739, pp. 548–555, 2016.
DOI: 10.1007/978-3-319-40238-3_52

book, or someone who can read ordinary newsprint. By use of similar comparisons, the calculator helps estimate a prediction of the proportion of the UK adult population excluded through the visual, hearing, thinking, dexterity, reaching and locomotion demands of the interaction required to achieve a goal. This enables an assessment to be carried out on a specified user journey which provides a percentage of the UK population who are unable to complete some of the tasks, at an individual task level or aggregated to reflect the complete user journey. By extension, this population exclusion is a proxy measure for difficulty that fully-abled users would be likely to experience also. However, it is recognised that there is a need to develop the cognitive part of the exclusion calculator to allow a more comprehensive assessment of exclusion caused by the thinking required particularly to address the load caused by unfamiliarity in digital interfaces [5]. For some people interacting with technology, it is the learning requirements that cause the most exclusion [6, 7]. In some of the studies conducted on digital interface tasks have shown that this can provide an impenetrable barrier particularly for older and novice users of digital technology interfaces [8]. From previous research, experience with particular interaction patterns combined with the cognitive ability to apply learning in one interface to another potentially unrelated interface are key to an 'inclusive' experience with a new interface [9]. Clearly the learning and trial and error approach are related to the cognitive aspect of interacting with an interface, but the data accessed by the exclusion calculator is not directly comparable [5]. So whilst accurate quantification for cognitive exclusion is not possible with the exclusion calculator, there is evidence that its use is able to identify potential issues.

Some of this evidence was provided during a recent training exercise for corporate clients. A design engineer from the Pharmaceutical industry commented that carrying out an exclusion audit over a 2 hour period with a group of 4 trainees, had elicited the top 3 concerns that had taken hundreds of thousands of dollars to elicit using conventional user trials. However, clearly further research would be needed to validate this.

## 1.2    Ageing Driver Population

It is well documented that in the developed world, populations are ageing partially as a result of increased life expectancies and partly due to historic population anomalies such as those that precipitated the baby boomer generation. In the UK for example, the group aged 85 and older is forecast to increase by over 100 % from 2016 to 2036 (data drawn from [10]). As a result of this, some premium models of vehicles sold in developed markets, the average age of the buyer can be as high as 70, and across one premium vehicle brand has seen its average age of US buyers rise by 10 years in just 13 years: from 51 in 2000 [11], to 61 in 2013 [12].

Ageing is known to affect capability of human beings in vision, hearing, cognition, dexterity and locomotion [3]. A very familiar example is 'age related long-sightedness' (presbyopia) which starts to affect people over the age of 40, which makes adjusting the focal length of the eye to near distances more difficult, and therefore can cause exclusion in situations where reading glasses are not worn, or varifocal lenses are inappropriate.

An ageing driver population therefore needs vehicle interfaces to be designed inclusively, to ensure that manufacturers are able to sell their products to many of the consumers, particularly in developed markets.

### 1.3    Automotive HMI's Through the Years

Since the car was invented, over 100 years ago, there has been a slow convergence of placement location, direction-of-motion and logic of operation of both primary and secondary driving controls. For example, in the 1930's the UK vehicle manufacturer Alvis used to position the accelerator (throttle) in between the clutch and brake pedals (see Fig. 1), and since then the convention of accelerator pedal being positioned to the right of the brake pedal has been consistently applied in production vehicles. It has long been recognised that this consistency provides drivers with the ability to leap from one vehicle into another, and be able to have a 'near transfer' [13]. The near transfer allows the procedural knowledge that a driver will have had from their driver education and experience to bring to bear successfully on a new vehicle. Whilst drivers do expect to make some accommodation to an unfamiliar vehicle, critical primary driving controls would not be expected to change position dramatically, and hitherto, in the main they have not.

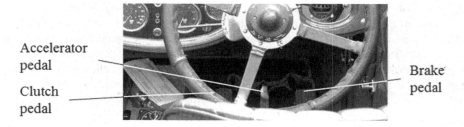

**Fig. 1.** 1933 Alvis 12 interior showing worn metal accelerator pedal visible through steering wheel, between darker clutch (left) and brake (right) pedals. Picture attribution: Steve Glover, reproduced under creative commons attribution 2.0 generic license.

## 2    Recent Developments in Automotive HMI's

However, there is a trend that some secondary, and less-frequently-used primary driving controls have begun to change location, mode of operation and logic. An example of this would be the handbrake, parking or emergency brake control, which in many markets was relatively consistently located on the centre transmission tunnel, between the driver and front passenger occupant. It would be activated by pulling upwards on the large lever, which would raise the lever to an inclined position with an associated increase in force proportional to the force applied to the braked wheels. It was deactivated by pulling up on the lever whilst depressing the end lock button, then lowering the lever back to the horizontal position. The difficulties and exclusion caused by this system were due to the potentially high forces required to pull on the lever, to generate sufficient braking force, and then the high forces required to release the brake when someone stronger had previously set it.

The technology that has altered this interaction is known as an Electronic Parking Brake (EPB) and its sister feature, Hill Start Assist (HSA). This technology applies the braking force with electric power, and so the interfaces have changed from mechanical levers to become electronic switches, or in some vehicle or usage cases, made redundant as the vehicle can activate them autonomously. However, the implementation of switch locations and operating logic across different brands and models has caused significant diversity (see Fig. 2). Some manufacturers locate them on the dashboard (instrument panel), others on the centre console (where the handbrake lever traditionally was located), and others have combined them with gear lever controls [13]. They have been implemented to be automatically applied and released for example to provide the HSA functionality, to simply mimicking the functionality of the mechanical system, requiring driver activation and deactivation. The switch operation has also diverged with some requiring a 'pull', and others a 'push', to activate the brake. This technology has removed the exclusion and difficulty posed by the biomechanical force required to operate the lever. Instead, it introduces a cognitive learning and recalling task for knowing where the controls are, understanding the modes of operation for an individual vehicle driving experience. In addition there is the potential challenge of attempting to learn a mental model which will apply across all the varieties of EPB that a driver may experience, whilst not becoming reliant on one behaviour when it may become inappropriate in another vehicle. This may not be easy for some drivers to do, without the potential for making significant errors.

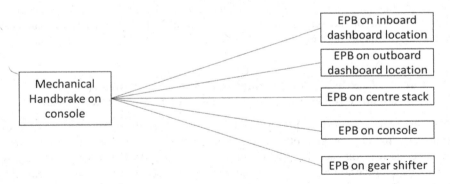

**Fig. 2.** Divergence of control location for Electronic Parking Brake (EPB) from conventional mechanical handbrake lever.

Automotive manufacturers are under considerable market pressure to add features to their vehicles as consumers are often seduced by the promise of new functionality, and marketers look to new features to draw attention to sell the product. However, the HCI community has long recognised that added functionality nearly always brings a reduction in usability. Since the advent of the screen-based menu functionality in modern vehicles, the number of features able to be integrated is almost infinite. Manufacturers have taken advantage of this to provide extensive consumer customisation and functionality. However the use of such systems often requires some level of digital experience and exposure to the interaction patterns from the digital world.

Recently, through the increasing complexity of functions available and the consequent desire to integrate them into standalone electronic HMI units, secondary controls have started to diverge in terms of their interaction patterns, locations and the mental models required to operate them. This was most markedly seen with the BMW iDrive HMI system introduced in 2001 into the E65 7 Series sedan. This system replaced large numbers of discrete buttons on the dashboard and console, with a sophisticated haptic rotary and joystick action controller in the centre console and an associated display screen at the top of the dashboard. This interface implicitly assumed that drivers would learn to use the system, either from a position of relative digital naivety, or more hopefully by extension of prior digital interface experiences, if they experienced 'near-transfer'.

Since then partly as a result of increased function automation, and Advanced Driver Assistance Systems (ADAS) becoming available, some other primary driving controls have also been affected, such as gear shifters, and adaptive and conventional cruise controls. The development of more ADAS and autonomous features seems very likely to further increase the complexity and diversity of the available functions that the driver is able to interact with.

The HMI technologies through which these functions can be accessed has also evolved, such as touchpads, touchscreens, haptic controllers and gestural interfaces, such that now there is for the first time a significant divergent effect on the consistency of control placement, direction-of-motion and logic of operation even for features that drivers are familiar with. If new functionality additionally extends this divergence of control location, interaction and mode of operation, then this can only further increase the learning demand on a driver.

## 2.1    Causes of Exclusion for Automotive Heating, Ventilation and Air Conditioning (HVAC) Controls – Manual Electro-Mechanical Type

HVAC controls are considered to be secondary driving controls, i.e. they are used by the driver while driving, but not as a part of the primary driving task. Thus they should not unnecessarily distract the driver from the driving task. However, they are also sometimes required to be operated beyond just that for occupant comfort, for example to ensure that the driver's view is clear through the windshield/windscreen and other windows and not obscured by frost or misting.

Prior assessments of conventional electro-mechanical manual HVAC controls conducted (see Fig. 3) by the Engineering Design Centre have suggested that the reasons for difficulty and exclusion are predominantly caused by visual obscuration and legibility of labels on the instrument panel surface, reach to some of the controls located furthest from the driver, and forces can be a problem for mechanically only activated controls. It is believed most drivers are either sufficiently familiar with the symbols used to label the controls, or are able to work out what the symbols mean in the context of the other cues. However, the frequency of interaction for these sorts of controls is dependent on the functionality required and the variability of the ambient weather conditions. In colder climates, heating controls are needed to operate potentially safety critical demisting functions, and the system response is subject to the vehicle's engine heating the coolant fluid. So adjustment of the temperature, distribution and fan settings may be required to achieve comfort and demisting functions. In hotter climates, the air conditioning function, temperature and distribution controls, may remain relatively static, and the only the fan speed adjusted to accommodate, for example to a hot vehicle having been parked in the sun. This frequency of use is what the electronic automated HVAC controls attempt to resolve.

**Fig. 3.** A typical manual HVAC control layout

## 2.2 Causes of Exclusion for Automotive HVAC Controls – Automatic Electronic Type

In the attempt to reduce the need for the driver to adjust the HVAC controls, in this example of an automatic electronic interface, the temperature can be set for both the passenger and the driver independently, and the fan speed and distribution (where the air is directed in the vehicle) are controlled automatically. However, this type of HVAC control introduces another significant layer of potential cognitive demand due to the complexity of available functions, the modal nature of some of the sub-systems and the unfamiliarity of some of the labels. So whilst the temperature adjustment is achieved relatively easily by use of the appropriate rotary control, adjustment of fan and distribution is achieved only by more complicated repeated pressing of small push button controls. In this particular example (see Fig. 4) there are also reflection issues impairing the legibility of the display symbols and characters.

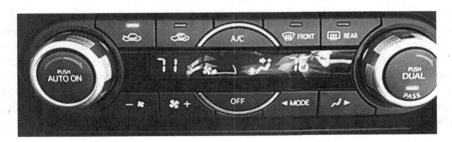

**Fig. 4.** An example of an electronic HVAC control layout

A further trend from some manufacturers has been to integrate the HVAC, audio and satellite navigation functions into one display and control system, which potentially provides more space for legibility of labels and icons, however also presents even more of a cognitive challenge in terms of modality and system comprehension.

## 3   Future Gazing: Advanced Driver Assistance System (ADAS) and Autonomous Feature Integration

If the trend of divergence continues, drivers will be unable to leap into an unfamiliar (such as a rental or loan) vehicle and drive without requiring re-training to operate even some of the most basic of features. Some drivers may be unwilling or unable to make the re-learning transition, and hence become excluded. As ADAS features become more prevalent, and more expected by drivers, this has the potential to cause significant problems both in the learning to operate, and understanding of operation of such features.

In additional risk of accommodating to these helpful features, may prove problematic in situations where the feature is no longer available for them. For example, anecdotal evidence would suggest that many drivers are becoming reliant on parking aid auditory warnings, particularly for reverse parking manoeuvres. If then they are faced with driving a vehicle that doesn't have this feature, and if they are not conscious of it at the time of parking, they may revert to a behaviour that is dependent on the technology to remind them when to stop the vehicle. Extrapolating from this scenario to that for assistance systems which work at higher speeds to help the driver, when not present or active for the driver, have more dire potential consequences.

In contrast to this trend, an alternative path does exist. Previous work [14] engaged users who would not normally be consulted in a deep dialogue, found out their specific needs and difficulties and then linked those with technologies that can help with those needs and developed appropriate interfaces that required very little learning and were highly intuitive. In that instance the older user group identified unintended speeding in the context of speed cameras was an important issue. The solutions of a visual speedometer display showing speed in the context of the speed limit, and a haptic accelerator to give a virtual detent at the speed limit, showed that useful technology could be implemented in a usable unchallenging way, without causing undue cognitive complexity.

Given that the world population is predicted to continue to age, full autonomy would appear to offer both a commercial and humanitarian opportunity to those who struggle with mobility for disability, confidence, capability or for financial reasons. However, the current trajectory for the implementation of the interfaces providing partial autonomy, would suggest that a radical rethink is required to ensure that those who stand to gain the most from the ability to travel easily without being able to drive, are actually able to benefit from full autonomous road transportation. Or perhaps more hopefully, this is a temporary state of affairs before the interaction task is reduced through full automation, to merely asking a car to take you to your destination?

**Acknowledgements.** This work was carried out at the University of Cambridge's Engineering Design Centre, within the Inclusive Design Group.

# References

1. Clarkson, P.J., Coleman, R.: History of inclusive design in the UK. Appl. Ergon **46**, 235–247 (2015)
2. Hosking, I., Waller, S., Clarkson, P.J.: It is normal to be different: applying inclusive design in industry. Interact. Comput. **22**(6), 496–501 (2010)
3. Waller, S., Williams, E., Langdon, P.: Quantifying exclusion for tasks related to product interaction. In: Langdon, P.M., Clarkson, P.J., Robinson, P. (eds.) Designing Inclusive Interactions: Inclusive Interactions Between People and Products in Their Contexts of Use, pp. 57–68. Springer, London (2010)
4. Department of Social Security. Social Research Branch, "Disability Follow-up to the 1996/97 Family Resources Survey." Colchester, Essex: UK Data Archive (2000)
5. Bradley, M., Langdon, P., Clarkson, P.J.: Assessing the inclusivity of digital interfaces - a proposed method. In: Antona, M., Stephanidis, C. (eds.) UAHCI 2015. LNCS, vol. 9175, pp. 25–33. Springer, Heidelberg (2015)
6. Waller, S.D., Bradley, M.D., Langdon, P.M., Clarkson, P.J.: Visualising the number of people who cannot perform tasks related to product interactions. Univers. Access Inf. Soc. **12**(3), 263–278 (2013)
7. Bradley, M., Lloyd, A., Barnard, Y.: Digital Inclusion: is it time to start taking an exclusion approach to interface design? In: Contemporary Ergonomics, Keele (2010)
8. Murad, S., Bradley, M., Kodagoda, N., Barnard, Y., Lloyd, A.: Using task analysis to explore older novice participants' experiences with a handheld touchscreen device. In: Anderson, M. (ed.) Contemporary Ergonomics and Human Factors 2012, pp. 57–64. CRC Press (2012)
9. Langdon, P.M., Lewis, T., Clarkson, P.J.: Prior experience in the use of domestic product interfaces. Univers. Access Inf. Soc. **9**(3), 209–225 (2009)
10. UK Population Projections. http://www.neighbourhood.statistics.gov.uk/HTMLDocs/dvc21 9/pyramids/index.html. (Accessed on 20 Feb 2016)
11. USATODAY.com - Automakers try to get in sync with kids today. http://usatoday30. usatoday.com/money/autos/2001-02-06-young-buyers.htm. (Accessed on 21 Feb 2016)
12. Frohlich, T.C.: Cars With the Oldest Buyers. http://247wallst.com/special-report/2014/10/ 02/cars-with-the-oldest-buyers/4/. (Accessed on 21 Feb 2016)
13. The Science and Art of Transfer. https://www.researchgate.net/publication/2398428_The_ Science_and_Art_of_Transfer. (Accessed on 28 Feb 2016)
14. Keith, S., Bradley, M., Goodwin, R., Kolar, I., Whitney, G., Wicks, C., Wilson, J.: Exploring speed limit compliance from the older driver perspective. In: Myerson, J., Bilsland, C., Bichard, J.-A. (eds.) Designing with people: strategies, stories and systems for user participation in design. Royal College of Arts, London (2007)

# Uncertainty and Mental Workload Among Wayfinding Strategies

Yi Chia Chien, Po An Tsai, Yu Ting Lin, Ssu Min Wu,
Kuan Ting Chen, Yu Ting Han, and Philip Hwang[✉]

National Taipei University of Technology, Taipei, Taiwan
{tokyo199203, jack78419, rock81222,
rockwu79, guantingdesign, fhjqwefa}@gmail.com,
phwang@mail.ntut.edu.tw

**Abstract.** Taiwan welcomed 8 million international visitors in 2013. In a study by Chang Hsuan Hsuan [3], subjects had 38 % failure rate in three wayfinding tests. It is obvious that travelers require guidance from time to time during the journey. Normally, travelers use maps; however once feeling uncertainty, they would seek for excessive reassurance from others [2].

This study summarized wayfinding strategies into two kinds. The first one is "turn-by-turn strategy", in which travelers ask for directions as primary wayfinding information. The second is "map strategy", in which visitors employ a map for wayfinding. As providing tourists with a piece of map seems to be a regular practice, this study intended to challenge it by examining efficiency, frequency of information inquiry and mental workload in the wayfinding journeys.

In the experiment, we employed "participant observation" and recorded wayfinding process of subjects such as wayfinding behavior and reassurance time and location.

Research findings are as follows:

Those using "turn-by-turn strategy" save time of journey, in other words, they are faster reach the destination than that of "map strategy".

Those using "turn-by-turn strategy" inquired wayfinding information less frequently, which means less frequently bothered by intolerance of uncertainty.

Locating the position on the map is the major factor for those applying "map strategy" who have high frequency of reading map, and minor for navigation.

**Keywords:** Wayfinding · Navigation · Anxiety · Intolerance of uncertainty

## 1 Research Motivation and Purpose

To reduce the negative impact for travelers such as frequency of anxiety generated, this study identifies wayfinding behavior and travelers' mental workload by using "turn-by-turn strategy" and "map strategy" which can be applied in unknown environments if the target direction is known.

Research aims:

Sorting and comparing wayfinding strategies / Integrating literatures about frequency of information inquiry of travelers.

© Springer International Publishing Switzerland 2016
M. Antona and C. Stephanidis (Eds.): UAHCI 2016, Part III, LNCS 9739, pp. 556–565, 2016.
DOI: 10.1007/978-3-319-40238-3_53

Reasoning wayfinding behavior, which enables travelers reaching destinations with lower mental workload and less time. When intolerance of uncertainty (IU) increases, travelers tends to check their map/device again. This study aims to investigate the time taken for tourists to develop intolerance of uncertainty due to the inability to navigate, and to determine key factors for the time spent to reach destination.

## 2   Literature Review

When international travelers in an unfamiliar city to their tourist, the most people use map who accounts for 46 % of all experiments, and in these people also have 51 % would ask people for help, and another 35 % don't use the map just by ask people. The rest 19 % do not rely on these two [3].

Results show most travelers are really depend on local people's help and assistance even they have the map. It shall be noted that the travelers are on the right way as usual, they just have no self-confidence.

### 2.1   Wayfinding Behavior

Wayfinding is also defined as a behavior with purposiveness, directionality, and motivation. Passengers can choose and follow the designed path through different information and methods, than move to another place [1, 6].

The involved scope of the wayfinding, as how travelers to use the information, how to know where they are and move forward to the destination, how return to the starting point, and so on.

Travelers who want to find way have 21 % would carry map, 15 % would by landmarks, 9 % would use tourist guide book, and only 6 % would use GPS. So in this study, the first group of participants ask natives, the other group only can use map for wayfinding instead of Google map. The affiliated institutions are to be listed directly below the names of the authors. Multiple affiliations should be marked with superscript.

### 2.2   The Factor Affecting Wayfinding

The factor affecting wayfinding can be divided into external and internal factors [10–13, 18–21]. External factors including the complexity of the space environment, which affect the results of wayfinding is "the number of decision points", and it's depending on space complexity. Overmuch crossroads or complex moving lines both will increase the wayfinding difficulty. Most external factors can't improve in short time because it along with urban development arising.

The internal factors affecting wayfinding are many [7], like personal qualities, such as comprehension, emotion, sense of direction, preference wayfinding strategies, etc. People's own innate characteristics and ability is difficult to improve by design, but which strategies option is better, what factors can increase confidence and reduce anxiety is designers can observe and improve.

## 2.3    Wayfinding

According to Gary E. Burnett [5], route guidance systems can be classified according to the means by which information is displayed –see Fig. 1.

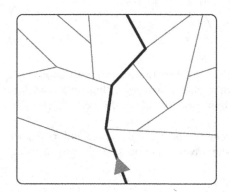 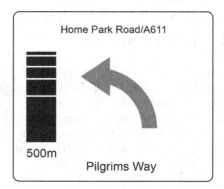

**Fig. 1.** Examples of route guidance systems: map-based and turn-by-turn-based (basic)

Map-based - the driver is presented with a scrolling map and the vehicle's current location is indicated by an icon. Early route guidance systems (e.g. the American ETAK™, early versions of Bosch TravelPilot™) did not offer a specific route for the driver to follow, and have been referred to by Parkes et al. [17] as 'route navigation systems.

Turn-by-turn based- The driver is given instructions (using symbols and often voice messages) relating to the location and direction of each manoeuver. A system's processor can choose how much information is extracted from the digitised map, how this is allocated between the modalities and how the information is then represented.

Route guidance strategy also can used on wayfinding by walk, this study divided subjects into two groups, one is defined as "turn-by-turn strategy", in which travelers ask natives for way-finding information, the other is "map strategy", in which visitors employ a map for way-finding.

## 2.4    Confidence and Anxiety

The individual's wayfinding confidence will influence on their feelings, wayfinding decisions and judgment [4, 16, 22]. Lacking of confidence is prone to anxiety, and it may affect the performance of wayfinding. This study is assumed the wayfinding confidence is inversely proportional to the probability of lost in unfamiliar environment, and is directly proportional to the probability of reaching destination.

## 2.5   Intolerance of Uncertainty and Mental Workload

Intolerance of uncertainty (IU) is one of the Obsessive-Compulsive Disorder (OCD)-related dysfunctional beliefs, and is linked to compulsive checking [15]. Uncertainty usually with anxiety together, difference between the two is Intolerance of uncertainty affect cognition, anxiety affect mood [7].

Parrish & Radomsky and other researchers assumed excessive reassurance seeking is for preventing uncertain disaster. For instance, people will think "if I don't do something to check, like seeking excessive reassurance, there will be a disaster". This behavior can lower anxious temporarily, therefore, people are willing to seek excessive reassurance.

"Workload" covers a broad spectrum of activity, but in "mental workload" we limit these activities to the primarily mental and physical coordination ones, such that muscular fatigue is not an important factor [9].

The main aim of this study is to find out the factor which influence confidence and produce anxiety.

# 3   Research Methods

To compare "turn-by-turn strategy (ask for route)" and "map strategy (reading map)", experiments conducted should show significant difference in mental workload and tolerance in anxiety tolerance frequency.

## 3.1   Measurement

In the experiment, there were twelve subjects who have never been to the task location. They were divided into two groups, and every subject had to finish task alone. In each task, there were one observer with a subject, recording the process by camera in 10-20 m away from the subject.

Subjects in the first group used "turn-by-turn strategy", which means travelers mostly ask whoever they can find for destination information. While subjects in the other group had to rely on "map strategy", in which visitors did not have interaction with other people but only the map.

The research method was "participant observation", in which we recorded a video, observing difference between two strategies. According to the results from experiment, we may calculate the minimum anxiety tolerance frequency in wayfinding process, and factors affecting the frequency.

## 3.2   Procedure

Normally, the task route should not be too easy to achieve or too short. According to a study by Jian Liang Liou and Ting-Wei Wu, the acceptable walking distance for ordinary people is approximately $400 \sim 800$ m. In addition, it must be a regular tourist Route.

From the above suggestions, we chose a task route from "MRT Houshanpi Station" to "Raohe Street Night Market", about 1 km along Fig. 2.

**Fig. 2.** Task route (source: google map)

From an interview with an observer (turn-by-turn strategy), it is noticed that a subject asked for people more frequently while taking more turns. It was seasoned to correlate with disturbing the sense of direction.

A subject (turn-by-turn strategy) expressed that, during the experiment, if he got an uncertain sign such as walking along certain direction for 5 min, he would feel quite unreliable. Nevertheless, once he was given a sign as traffic light or a convenience store, he had great confidence to find it and executed the next step. He also indicate that asking people for the destination is not only for knowing the destination but for knowing where he was.

Thus it is significant to have recognizable signs while finding destination in an unfamiliar area.

# 4    Analysis

In the experiment, subjects are divided into two groups to complete the wayfinding task, one group use "map strategy", the other use "turn-by-turn strategy". Then, record the time respectively when subjects reading map or asking directions. Identify the difference between two strategies, and analysis the time interval of rechecking and asking direction respectively. Task Analysis of Using Map Strategy for Wayfinding.

## 4.1    Task Analysis of Using Map Strategy for Wayfinding

In the experiment of map strategy, frequency of reading map consider as checking frequency, 6 subjects participated in this experiment, the frequency of map reading is: 68, 30, 28, 21, 12, 16, and the average of spent time is 20:36 min (Table 1).

**Table 1.**  Results of map strategy

| Experimental groups | Subjects number | Frequency of map reading | Spent time |
|---|---|---|---|
| Using map strategy for wayfinding | A | 68 | 17:50 min |
| | B | 30 | 20:21 min |
| | C | 28 | 26:03 min |
| | D | 21 | 16:46 min |
| | E | 12 | 20:36 min |
| | F | 16 | 23:20 min |
| | average of spent time | | 20:36 min |

There're some extremely short and long interval among the Time Interval Record (Fig. 3):

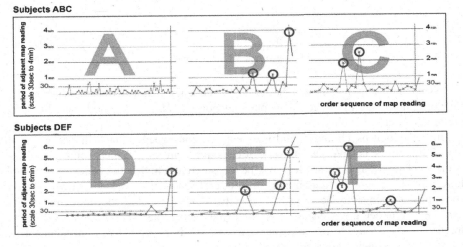

**Fig. 3.**  Time interval record (subjects A-F) (Color figure online)

As the Fig. 3 above shows, if the time interval is shorter than 30 s, the information called short-term memory. In the situation of no recheck and no rehearsal, the duration of short-term memory seems to be between 15 and 30 s [8].

Peak position (marked as blue circle) is "Attention Span". Attention span is the amount of concentrated time one can spend on a task without becoming distracted. Most educators and psychologists agree that the ability to focus attention on a task is crucial for the achievement of one's goals. From interview with subjects after the experiments, it is revealed that subjects have a tendency to remember a series of order after reading a map. Once finish this task or feel anxious, they will repeat this action for several times until reaching the destination. The time before peak may represent the path is simple, therefore, the subjects didn't need to ask for the information, and it took longer time before feeling uncertainty. The time span of the above action is described as frequency of "intolerance of anxiety" [2]. As shown by graph, the average cycle of intolerance of anxiety is 2 min 44 s.

## 4.2 Task Analysis of Using Turn-by-Turn Strategy for Wayfinding

In the experiment of turn-by-turn strategy, subjects would ask for direction as checking frequency when they being intolerance of uncertainty. 6 subjects participated in this experiment, the frequency of ask for directions is: 3, 3, 5, 2, 2, 3, and the average of spent time is 19:26 min (Table 2).

**Table 2.** Results of Turn-by-turn Strategy

| Experimental groups | Subjects number | Frequency of ask for directions | Spent time |
|---|---|---|---|
| Using turn-by-turn strategy for wayfinding | G | 3 | 18:55 min |
| | H | 3 | 16:40 min |
| | I | 5 | 25:09 min |
| | J | 2 | 17:00 min |
| | K | 2 | 23:20 min |
| | L | 3 | 18:00 min |
| | average of spent time | | 19:26 min |

As the Fig. 4 above shows, there will be tendency that a period of adjacent destination inquire getting longer. This phenomenon can also be psychological literature "reinforcement" to explain.

In behavioral psychology, reinforcement is a consequence that will strengthen an organism's future behavior whenever that behavior is preceded by a specific antecedent stimulus. This strengthening effect may be measured as a higher frequency of behavior, longer duration, greater magnitude, or shorter latency. The behavior with positive consequences tends to be repeated, and the behavior called "Reinforcement. For example: A father gives candy to his daughter when she picks up her toys. If the frequency of picking up the toys increases, the candy is a positive reinforcement (to reinforce the behavior of cleaning up).

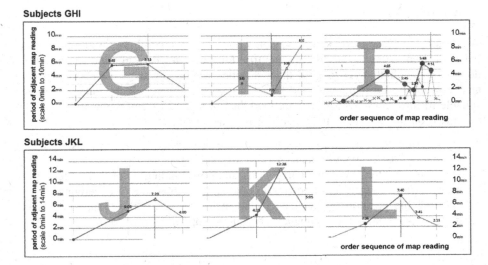

**Fig. 4.** Time interval record (subjects G-L)

In the task of using turn by turn-strategy for wayfinding, the behavior of "finish the indication from other" is reinforcement, when subjects finish the indication successfully would produce confidence, and anxiety will decrease so it makes time of feeling intolerance of uncertainty longer.

In this experiment, period of adjacent destination inquire is about 5 min.

### 4.3   Summary of Experiment

According to the experiment result, the time of using map strategy is longer than using turn-by-turn strategy. Furthermore, the rechecking times of using map strategy is more than using turn-by-turn strategy, in other words, the mental workload of reading a map is higher (Table 3).

**Table 3.** Comparison of Two Strategies

|  | Average of spent time | The rechecking times | Period of intolerance of uncertainty |
|---|---|---|---|
| Using map strategy for wayfinding | 20:36 min | 29 | 2:44 min |
| Using turn-by-turn strategy for wayfinding | 19:26 min | 3 | 5:00 min |

# 5  Conclusion

Wayfinding is every traveler will happen when they in unfamiliar environment, this behavior also necessary to do in the trip for promote Taiwan tourism industry, designers can think how to give them a better wayfinding experience. This paper analyze "turn-by-turn strategy" and "map strategy", compare which strategy is more suitable for use and has lower mental workload in unfamiliar environment.

Based on the synthetic study result above, the study found out:

1. Those using "turn-by-turn strategy" save time of journey, in other words, they are faster reach the destination than that of "map strategy".
2. Those using "turn-by-turn strategy" inquired wayfinding information less frequently, which means less frequently bothered by intolerance of uncertainty.
3. Locating the position on the map is the major factor for those applying "map strategy" who have high frequency of reading map, and minor for navigation.

# References

1. Allen, G.: Cognitive abilities in the service of wayfinding: a functional approach. Prof. Geogr. **51**(4), 555–561 (1999)
2. AnxietyBC, How to Tolerate Uncertainty. http://www.anxietybc.com/sites/default/files/ToleratingUncertainty.pdf
3. Chang, H.-H.: Study of Wayfinding Behavior of Independent International Travelers in an Unfamiliar City. Department of Leisure and Recreation Administration, Ming Chuan University, Taipei (2013)
4. Cooke-Simpson, A., Voyer, D.: Confidence and gender differences on the mental rotations test. Learn. Individ. Differ. **17**(2), 181–186 (2007)
5. Burnett, G., Smith, D., May, A.: Supporting The Navigation Task: Characteristics Of 'Good' Landmarks, 3–4 (2002)
6. Golledge, R.G.: Human wayfinding and cognitive maps. In: College, R.G. (ed.) Wayfinding Behavior: Cognitive Mapping and Other Spatial Processes, pp. 1–45. Johns Hopkins University Press, Baltimore (1999)
7. Hund, A.M., Minarik, J.L.: Getting from here to there: spatial anxiety, wayfnding strategies, direction type, and wayfnding efficiency. Spat. Cogn. Comput. **6**(3), 179–201 (2006)
8. James, W.: The Principles of Psychology, vol. 2. Macmillan, New York (1890)
9. Jex, H.R.: Measuring mental working: problems, progress and promises. In: Hancock, P.A., Meshkati, N.M. (eds.) Human Mental Workload, pp. 5–40. Elsevier, Amsterdam North-Holland (1988)
10. Kato, Y., Takeuchi, Y.: Individual differences in wayfinding strategies. J. Environ. Psychol. **23**(2), 171–188 (2003)
11. Kitchin, R.M.: Cognitive maps: what are they and why study them? J. Environ. Psychol. **14**(1), 1–19 (1994)
12. Kozlowski, L.T., Bryant, K.J.: Sense of direction, spatial orientation, and cognitive maps. J. Exp. Psychol. Hum. Percept. Perform. **3**(4), 590–598 (1977)
13. Lawton, C.A.: Gender differences in wayfinding strategies: relationship to spatial ability and spatial anxiety. Sex Roles **30**(11/12), 765–779 (1994)

14. Lawton, C.A., Kallai, J.: Gender differences in wayfinding strategies and anxiety about wayfinding: a cross-cultural comparison. Sex Roles **47**(9/10), 389–401 (2002)
15. Liao, Y.-Y.: The Role of Intolerance of Uncertainty, Desire for Control, and Sense of Control on Compulsive Checking. Department of Psychology, National Taiwan University (2014)
16. Moe, A., Pazzaglia, F.: Following the instructions! effects of gender beliefs in mental rotation. Learn. Individ. Differ. **16**(4), 369–377 (2006)
17. Parkes, A.M.: Data capture techniques for RTI usability evaluation. In: Advanced Telematics in Road Transport - the DRIVE Conference, vol. 2, pp. 1440–1456. Elsevier Science Publishers B.V., Amsterdam (1991)
18. Passini, R.: Wayfinding design: logic, application and some thoughts on university. Des. Stud. **17**(3), 319–331 (1996)
19. Prestopnik, J., Roskos-Ewoldsen, B.: The relations among wayfinding strategy use, sense of direction, sex, familiarity and wayfinding ability. J. Environ. Psychol. **20**(2), 177–191 (2000)
20. Schmitz, S.: Gender-related strategies in environmental development: effects of anxiety on wayfinding in and representation of a three-dimensional maze. J. Environ. Psychol. **17**(3), 215–228 (1997)
21. Walmsley, D.J., Jenkins, J.M.: Mental maps, locus of control and activity: a study of business tourism in Coffs Harbour. J. Tourism Stud. **2**(2), 36–42 (1991)
22. Wraga, M., Duncan, L., Jacobs, E.C., Helt, M., Church, J.: Stereotype susceptibility narrows the gender gap in imagined self-rotation performance. Psychon. Bull. Rev. **13**(5), 813–819 (2006)

# Navigating the Workplace Environment as a Visually Impaired Person

Jimena Gomez[1]([⊠]), Patrick M. Langdon[2], and P. John Clarkson[1]

[1] Engineering Design Centre (EDC), University of Cambridge, Cambridge, UK
{jlg55,pjcl0}@cam.ac.uk
[2] Department of Engineering, University of Cambridge, Cambridge, UK
pml24@cam.ac.uk

**Abstract.** An inclusive workplace environment should be comfortable and functional for all of its users. Over the past decade, workplace environments have changed to offer more flexible spaces in a variety of ways and locations. Modern office designs blend different working and social spaces, which include, for example, modular workstations, corridors, furniture, non-traditional layouts and open spaces. In this way, workplaces are designed to offer spaces for the effective collaboration of staff and to optimize work practices by promoting spontaneous and free-flowing communication. However, new design tendencies often lead to greater complications in moving around the workplace. Such complications may affect all workers, but they will mainly affect those with sight loss who experience extra difficulties in pursuing their target destination.

**Keyword:** Visual impairments

## 1 Introduction and Background

Workplaces are usually characterized by outdoor/indoor spaces full of equipment, plants, modules, offices and floor levels. Most of the time, they are also composed of smaller fragmented spaces, often with limited spatial information and many direction changes [1]. Thus, workplace navigation 'requires explicit decision-making such as selecting routes to follow and orientation towards non-perceptible landmarks and scheduling the trips' [2]. As a result, if a person does not have previous common knowledge and visual input about the building structure and space, the navigation experience is a complex and stressful task.

Studies of spatial navigation in absence of vision have been approached from diverse perspectives and disciplines such as engineering, psychology and neuroscience. This vast research has contributed to increase our understanding of spatial knowledge acquisition, spatial behavior, cognitive mapping, and technological devices among others topics. Despite these advances, there is still a lack of consensus regarding the mechanisms underlying spatial navigation by visually impaired people as well as an overreliance on the potential of technological solutions [3]. It broadly recognized that our daily movements in large and small-scale environments are mainly guided by our visual perception [4]. However, some people also use nonvisual modalities to construct more sophisticated spatial representations [5].

M. Antona and C. Stephanidis (Eds.): UAHCI 2016, Part III, LNCS 9739, pp. 566–576, 2016.
DOI: 10.1007/978-3-319-40238-3_54

Researchers have widely assumed that sighted and blind people develop similar abilities for acquiring spatial knowledge. However, there is a lack of clarity regarding the spatial learning processes behind navigation performance. Visually impaired people have to cope with the daily challenge of finding their way around built environments. They can easily be disoriented and intimidated as a result of the difficulties they experience in interpreting the built environment [5].

## 1.1    Acquisition of Knowledge Navigation

We are constantly navigating indoor and outdoor environments in order to reach a destination. This navigation process usually involves planning and executing a series of decisions that, according to Montello, [6] encompass wayfinding and locomotion, which are components of spatial decision-making. Locomotion calls for immediate responses to environmental features such as avoiding obstacles or stepping over corners. This corresponds to 'orientation', a common term used in visually impaired literature. As such, locomotion and/or orientation refer to a group of invariably egocentric responses acquired by the observer's body. On the contrary, wayfinding (frequently mentioned as 'mobility' in visually impaired literature) underpins a transitory (short-term) and permanent (long-term) reasoning of mental representations in a person's immediate and remote environment that adopt reference frames acquired directly from experiences (allocentric) [7].

Throughout the navigation process, people learn environmental features that they may use to establish a frame of reference known as a 'landmark'. Afterwards, they construct routes by connecting each landmark. This 'route stage' enables the person to begin to create 'mini-maps' that 'are locally, but not globally coherent' [8]. They will then subsequently integrate these mini-maps to develop a bigger 'cognitive map' of an objective frame of reference. Finally, the survey knowledge stage enables an individual to draw a line distance between two points. In this sense, we can identify three main components in the acquisition of navigational knowledge as follows (Table 1):

**Table 1.** Components involved in the acquisition of navigational knowledge

| |
|---|
| **Landmark:** the visual representation of structures or elements in the landscape that people identify as unique points to guide themselves [9]. |
| **Route:** the sequential process description from one point to another in the environment. This involves all the landmarks at which an action (e.g. turning right or going straight on) should be taken [10]. |
| **Survey knowledge:** refers to graphics or image-like representations of the entire geographic area such as maps of a location or a layout of all the elements of a place and the spatial relationship between them [9, 12] |

## 1.2    People with Sight Loss and the Navigation Process

Certainly, 'landmarks make the wayfinding task more simple' [6] because human beings use them as reference points to navigate themselves, especially in unfamiliar places. The non-visually impaired person will use clues (landmarks) to find their way in an unfamiliar indoor environment. These clues will be, for example, information given by other people, indoor maps or any other wayfinding services that provide a location. As such, empirical evidence suggests that most people naturally tend to set out specific reference points that help them to explore their environment by fixing a landmark as a base to navigate their surroundings. Indeed, whenever they get lost or they want to start over to go in a different direction, they return to the base. Likewise, when they feel familiar with an area, they move from one landmark to another to navigate through larger spaces. In this way, vision therefore plays a significant role in acquiring spatial knowledge to create routes. Furthermore, 'spatial cognition' changes as a result of direct experience in the environment [11]. In this sense, more experience leads to more survey and route knowledge [12, 13].

In contrast, visually impaired people set out landmarks based on their hearing, tactile, and olfactory capabilities by fixing as reference points door movements, the number of people around them, the quality of air (fresh or more concentrated), restaurants, kitchens, etc. They also find small details such as light contrasts produced by windows, lamps, or the wall and floor colors helpful. Likewise, people with sight loss use their cane as a tactile tool to acquire spatial information. They also learn about the environment they are in by identifying the differences between narrow or broad corridors, stairs, floor textures, and obstacles in their path-route [13]. In this way, a common problem for visually impaired people when faced with independent navigation in the workplace is the lack of information that they are provided with in order to make decisions about routes to move from one point to another. In general, existing navigation systems do not provide accurate guidance, and non-visually impaired people offer instructions based on their visual capabilities, which are insufficient for the visually impaired.

A non-visually impaired person will therefore use traditional frameworks of spatial knowledge to produce survey knowledge (cognitive maps) [14]. However, individuals with sight loss use different strategies to acquire spatial navigation knowledge, for example audible representation. Acquiring different types of spatial information is based in spatial learning that is mainly formed by experiences and depends on the reliability of the cues provided by each perceptual modality (e.g. the ability to identify an object's location) [5, 15–17]. A visually impaired person will develop skills to compensate for their lack of visual representations by encountering specific information in the built environment.

As explained above, 'people use landmarks when they give route directions to anchor actions in space or to offer confirmation that the right track is still being followed' [18]. We use environmental information instruction (both verbal and pictorial) to facilitate our navigation in the workplace or any other indoor facility. As such, the two following questions arise: 'What factors do visually impaired workers find useful in acquiring spatial information?' And, 'To what extent do these factors influence the navigation process?'

The aim of the current study was to evaluate what workplace features visually impaired people value when they are navigating their surroundings and environments and how they manage unfamiliar spaces to orientate themselves inside workplace facilities. This information enabled us to clarify whether people with sight loss prefer tactile, audible or olfactory representations when creating landmarks.

This study was conducted by reviewing relevant literature in order to gain knowledge from previous research on spatial navigation from multiple perspectives. We then designed a pilot study to explore the factors that influence the spatial learning and spatial behavior of visually impaired people [17, 19].

## 2 Method

The aim of this study was to learn about the navigation experience of Chilean visually impaired workers in unfamiliar indoor spaces. We attempted to gain knowledge of what factors influence their acquisition of spatial knowledge which enables them to navigate through their workplace. A triangulation strategy consisting of a small pilot study divided into two phases was designed to firstly capture the self-reported information provided by visually impaired workers through a qualitative analysis and secondly to explore the factors influencing the way in which they acquire knowledge to improve their navigation process. In this way, for the first phase, we conducted semi-structured interviews to identify the conceptual factors that the participants reported as relevant aspects influencing their navigation process. In addition, we carried out a second quantitative analysis to assess the factors they reported as relevant in acquiring spatial navigation. Therefore, in order to analyse the self-reported experiences of visually impaired workers themselves, a semi-structured questionnaire was designed where participants freely talked about their navigation process in familiar and unfamiliar environments in their workplaces, and a subsequent online survey was applied to quantify and explore the factors that influenced their acquisition of spatial knowledge.

**Sampling and Measurement.** For the qualitative study, we interviewed 2 males, aged 41 and 35, and 1 female, aged 27. They were all Chilean customer service workers who talked to us about their navigation process experiences. In addition, using Qualtrics Survey Software, we randomly distributed a closed questionnaire to members of the Chilean National Union of and for Blind People (UNCICH). The questionnaire assessed the relevant conceptual factors identified in the preliminary qualitative study. The questionnaire consisted of 67 questions of which 28 were rated on a seven-point Likert Scale. We tested the reliability of our results by using Cronbach's alpha, and all of the data was above 0.7. This confirmed that the questions we had designed were reliable.

We randomly sent the online questionnaire by email to 55 members of the organization. However, only 26 members completed the questionnaire. By analyzing the data achieved, we found that the scale used had a good internal consistency, with a Cronbach alpha coefficient of 859. However, some of the issues explored in the questionnaire were not considered be worthy of retention; therefore these items were removed before going on to the exploratory factor analysis.

**Data Collection.** This study was carried out from 15 December 2015 to 15 January 2016. 55 electronic questionnaires were randomly sent by email to members of the Chilean National Union of and for Blind People. The participants were selected from the members of the Union who were currently working in private or public organisations.

26 questionnaires were completed, and the respondents were 53.8 % female and 46.2 % male (see Table 2 for further demographic details of the participant profile).

**Table 2.** Demographic data

| Variable | Frequency | Percentage |
|---|---|---|
| Age | | |
| 21–30 | 4 | 15.4 |
| 31–40 | 8 | 30.8 |
| 41–50 | 11 | 42.3 |
| 51–60 | 3 | 11.5 |
| Workplace Size | | |
| Small building (less than 4 floors) | 9 | 34.6 |
| Academic campus | 7 | 26.9 |
| Large building (more than 4 floors) | 10 | 38.5 |
| Working Time | | |
| Full time | 11 | 42.3 |
| Part time | 6 | 23.1 |
| Flexible time | 9 | 34.6 |
| Visual impairment | | |
| Blindness | 18 | 69.2 |
| Low vision | 8 | 30.8 |
| Age of Impairment | | |
| 0–1 | 7 | 26.9 |
| 2–14 | 8 | 30.8 |
| 15–44 | 11 | 42.3 |
| Education | | |
| Postgraduate | 4 | 15.4 |
| Undergraduate | 12 | 46.2 |
| High school | 9 | 34.6 |
| Primary school | 1 | 3.8 |

# 3  Data Analysis from the Qualitative Study

## 3.1  Preliminary Findings from the Qualitative Data Study

We explored the data collected using a thematic analysis in its simplest form. This allowed us to create categories that were subsequently assessed in the quantitative analysis. In the analysis, we coded words and phrases that allowed us to identify the categories associated with the acquisition of spatial knowledge described in the existing literature.

**Landmarks.** The qualitative study showed that those who had low vision fixed similar landmarks to those who were completely blind, giving strong value to contrasts of color and light. Participants stated that they made their navigation easier by identifying obstacles or things such as lifts, doors, stairs, floor textures, corners, darkness, and even the people around them. In addition, they remarked that they usually fix landmarks by remembering where an obstacle is located, the difference in the texture of the floor, or by smelling, for example, air fresheners, food, humidity, or any other recognisable odors. The participants also mentioned that they used audible information to fix reference points, for example environmental noises produced by printers, telephones operators, and even people's conversations. They explained that they even learn about indoor spatial environments by identifying the air temperature which enables them to recognize, for example, halls, open spaces, corridors, doors or entrances. Another relevant factor mentioned by the participants to construct spatial knowledge was texture differences on the floor which helped them to remember where they were or to follow a route.

**Route Construction.** The participants explained that it took them about one month to learn the route from the building entrance to their workstation. This task became more complex if any change in the route took place; if furniture was moved from its original position, for example, they were forced to look for alternative routes, and this was extremely confusing for them. The participants also stated that they preferred to avoid new routes; they usually followed the known paths, even though they may be considered longer or more complex by non-visually impaired people. They also clarified that they do not need information such as how many stairs they should go up or down, but rather they need to know, for example, whether there are stairs in front of the lift, if the toilet is on the right-hand side of the stairs, if the kitchen on the left-hand side of the lifts, and so on. In addition, they suggested that if audio or tactile guidance is provided, it should be allocated in standard places, otherwise it would be impossible for them to find. They said, for example, that they frequently have trouble finding bells and door opening buttons. Thus, if the tactile, audible or olfactory signals are not perceptible to them, they will be useless at providing them with any information.

**Survey Knowledge.** The participants explained that usually they are not given clear instructions on how to get places, and that sighted people often do not understand what kind of instructions are most helpful to them. They also said that it took them a long time to get to know the workplace and some of the participants even disclosed that they only knew how to get to the essential areas such as the workstation, kitchen, toilet, lifts, and the way out.

The participants also suggested that braille is an old-fashioned system which does not help them gain information about their surroundings. Although braille is often used and put forward as an appropriate system to help blind people access lifts, for example, very few people use it (either because they have never learnt the system or because they find other ways more useful, such as knowing the position of the lift number required in the panel). The participants believed that in general there is a lack of knowledge and awareness of their real capabilities to acquire spatial knowledge, because audible guidance which tells a person loudly which floor they are on is more useful to visually impaired people than any braille-based information.

Lastly, when the participants were asked about travel assistance aids such as tactile maps, they thought that, in theory, they could be useful to help them learn about an area, but that the tactile maps they had come across had not been fully usable because they needed someone explain the map to them, and the symbols used by the designers. They mentioned that there are no standard codes or symbols used to understand maps, so they usually have to rely on someone with vision to explain the map to them; they cannot use the map independently. Therefore, they suggested that tactile maps should include audible information that helps them to understand the tactile information without asking for help (Fig. 1).

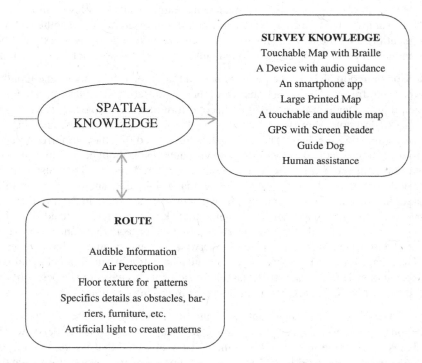

**Fig. 1.** Set of variables grouped in the three components mentioned as influencing the acquisition of spatial knowledge.

**General categories to be tested in the quantitative analysis**

## 4  Data Analysis from Quantitative Study

**Preliminary Findings.** Out of all of the participants, only 46.2 % had learnt braille, with a higher number of females than males. In addition, among those who read braille, 19.2 % never used it and 15.4 % used it less than once in a month to read labels, for example in medicines. 50 % of those who learnt braille were blind from birth, and

50 % of those who had acquired their visual impairment never learnt the system (Table 3).

**Table 3.** Crosstabulation: age of acquiring visual impairment vs. ability to read braille

**Crosstab**

| | | | Read Braille | | |
|---|---|---|---|---|---|
| | | | Yes | No | Total |
| Age of Visual Impairment | 0 -1 | Count | 6 | 1 | 7 |
| | | % within Read Braille | 50.0% | 7.1% | 26.9% |
| | 2 -14 | Count | 2 | 6 | 8 |
| | | % within Read Braille | 16.7% | 42.9% | 30.8% |
| | 15 - 44 | Count | 4 | 7 | 11 |
| | | % within Read Braille | 33.3% | 50.0% | 42.3% |
| Total | | Count | 12 | 14 | 26 |
| | | % within Read Braille | 100.0% | 100.0% | 100.0% |

**Exploratory Categorical Factor Analysis CATPCA.** We had a large number of variables which were mostly ordinal; thus an Exploratory Factor Analysis was employed, using Categorical Principal Component Analysis (CATPCA). This technique enabled us to reduce a large number of variables and therefore facilitate our understanding of the relationship between the factors analysed and the acquisition of spatial knowledge. SPSS was used to analyse the survey data. We got 26 valid cases and no missing value. The analysis was based on positive integer data. We analysed the mean, standard deviation, skewness and kurtosis to test normality; however this assumption was not achieved. To run the analysis from the menu we chose Analyze > Dimension Reduction > Optimal Scaling.

Three groups of categories were created to explain the acquisition of spatial knowledge through landmarks, survey knowledge and travel aids (Table 4). All variables were non-parametric (Fig. 2).

## 5    Results

There is no missing value for all the variables tested. We assessed the stability of the CATPCA solutions for the subsets with regard to (a) total percentage of variance accounted for and Cronbach's alpha (b) the loadings and (c) the category quantifications in order to assess the appropriateness of the choice of the optimal scaling level, of the number of dimensions and of the component structure of spatial knowledge. In addition we investigated whether or not the three components defined in our qualitative

**Table 4.** Model Summary

| Dimension | Cronbach's alpha | Variance accounted for | | |
|---|---|---|---|---|
| | | Total (Eigenvalue) | % of variance | Rotation[a] |
| 1 | .953 | 9.739 | 57.289 | 11.005 |
| 2 | .627 | 2.441 | 14.357 | 3.433 |
| 3 | .514 | 1.937 | 11.396 | 2.832 |
| Total | .987[b] | 14.117 | 83.042 | |

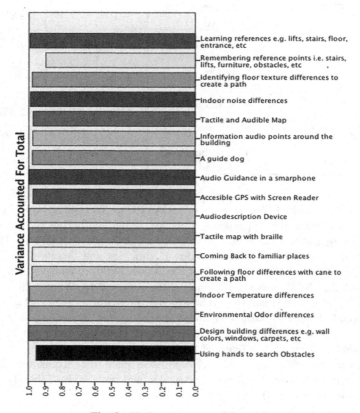

**Fig. 2.** Variance accounted for total.

analysis effectively influenced the spatial knowledge acquisition. The results of a three dimensional solution with ordinal transformation explains 83.042 % of the variance. The percentage of variance accounted for (PVAF) for the first dimension is the highest (57.289 %); almost triple the PVAF for the second dimension (14.357 %) and the third dimension (11.396 %). The variance accounted for the first dimension is equal to .57289 × 13 = 7.45, with .14357 × 13 = 1.87 for the second dimension and

11296 × 13 = 1.5 % for the third dimension. The largest Eigenvalue is 9.739 with a Cronbach's alpha of .953. The following table shows the factors that may be associated with the acquisition of spatial knowledge for visually impaired people in the workplace (Table 5).

**Table 5.** Factors influencing spatial knowledge

| |
|---|
| Accessible GPS with Screen Reader |
| Following floor differences with cane to create a path |
| Coming Back to familiar places |
| A guide dog |
| Identifying floor texture differences to create a path |
| Audiodescription Device |
| Audio Guidance in a smarphone |
| Design building differences e.g. wall colors, windows, carpets, etc |
| Remembering reference points i.e. stairs, lifts, furniture, obstacles, etc |
| Indoor noise differences |
| Using hands to search Obstacles |
| Indoor Temperature differences |
| Tactile map with braille |
| Learning references e.g. lifts, stairs, floor, entrance, etc |
| Environmental Odor differences |

## 6 Conclusions and Future Work

This study aimed to identify the component structure of spatial knowledge self-reported by a group of visually impaired Chilean workers. Using nonlinear analysis for ordinal variables we created variables which, in the qualitative analysis, appeared to be relevant themes to construct spatial knowledge. These subjective themes reported by the participants were subsequently measured in an exploratory analysis that showed us that visually impaired people do not consider the use of white sticks as important to create landmarks, but rather they are an accessory which they believe to be absolutely necessary. In addition, the findings confirm that spatial knowledge acquisition is not influenced by demographic variables such as gender, age or education. However, the age of acquiring the impairment and the vision acuity (the degree of sight loss) do have an influence in the navigational process. Those who were blind from birth appeared to be more confident in creating audible landmarks, and those who had acquired their impairment still attempted to fix visual references such as stairs, colour contrasts or building designs.

Although important findings have been made from this study, further analysis must therefore be performed to confirm the relationship between the components identified and spatial knowledge acquisition. As such, a next step may be to conduct a structural equation model to establish the component structure. In addition, taking into consideration the limited number of participants, our results cannot be generalised to a broader population without extending this analysis to a greater number of individuals.

# References

1. Becker, F.D., Steele, F.: Workplace by Design: Mapping the High-Performance Workscape. Jossey-Bass Publishers, San Francisco (1995)
2. Brunner-Friedrich, B., Radoczky, V.: Active landmarks in indoor environments. In: Bres, S., Laurini, R. (eds.) VISUAL 2005. LNCS, vol. 3736, pp. 203–215. Springer, Heidelberg (2006)
3. Giudice, N.A., Legge, G.E.: Blind navigation and the role of technology. In: Helal, A., Mokhtari, M., Abdulrazak, B. (eds.) The Engineering Handbook of Smart Technology for Aging, Disability, and Independence, pp. 479–500. Wiley, New York (2008)
4. Goldin, S.E., Thorndyke, P.W.: Simulating navigation for spatial knowledge acquisition. Hum. Factors 4(24), 457–471 (1982)
5. Golledge, R.G.: Geography and the disabled: a survey with special reference to vision impaired and blind populations. Trans. Inst. Br. Geogr. 18, 63–85 (1993)
6. Henson, A., et al.: When do we integrate spatial information acquired by walking through environmental spaces? In: Cognitive Science Society (2011)
7. Hintzman, D.L., O'Dell, C.S., Arndt, D.R.: Orientation in cognitive maps. Cogn. Psychol. 13, 149–206 (1981)
8. Karimi, H.A.: Indoor Wayfinding and Navigation. CRC Press, Oakville (2015)
9. May, A.J., et al.: Pedestrian navigation aids: information requirements and design implications. Pers. Ubiquit. Comput. 7(6), 331–338 (2003)
10. Watermeyer, B.: Towards a Contextual Psychology of Disablism. Routledge, London (2013)
11. Thorndyke, P.W., Hays-Roth, B.: Differences in spatial knowledge acquired from maps and navigation. Cogn. Psychol. 14, 580–589 (1982)
12. Quesnot, T., Roche, S.: Quantifying the significance of semantic landmarks in familiar and unfamiliar environments. In: Fabrikant, S.I., Raubal, M., Bertolotto, M., Davies, C., Freundschuh, S., Bell, S. (eds.) COSIT 2015. LNCS, vol. 9368, pp. 468–489. Springer, Heidelberg (2015). doi:10.1007/978-3-319-23374-1_22
13. Schinazi, V.R., Thrash, T., Chebat, D.-R.: Spatial navigation by congenitally blind individuals. Wiley Interdisc. Rev. Cogn. Sci. 7, 37–58 (2016)
14. Timpf, S.: Ontologies of wayfinding: a traveler's perspective. Netw. Spat. Econ. 2(1), 9–33 (2002)
15. Golledge, R.G., Spector, N.A.: Comprehending the urban environment: theory and practice. Geogr. Anal. 10(4), 305–325 (1978)
16. Montello, D., Sas, C.: Human factors of wayfinding in navigation (2006)
17. Tinti, C., et al.: Visual experience is not necessary for efficient survey spatial cognition: evidence from blindness. Q. J. Exp. Psychol. 59, 1306–1328 (2006)
18. Nishisato, S., et al.: Optimal scaling and its generalizations: I. Methods. Dept. of Measurement and Evaluation, Ontario Institute for Studies in Education, Toronto (1972)
19. Langdon, P., Thimbleby, H.: Inclusion and interaction: designing interaction for inclusive populations. Interact. Comput. 22, 439–448 (2010)

# The Impact of Orientation and Mobility Aids on Wayfinding of Individuals with Blindness: Verbal Description vs. Audio-Tactile Map

Eleni Koustriava, Konstantinos Papadopoulos,
Panagiotis Koukourikos, and Marialena Barouti[✉]

University of Macedonia, Thessaloniki, Greece
marialenab90@gmail.com

**Abstract.** The aim of the present study was to examine if a verbal description of an urban area or an audio-tactile map would support the development of an effective cognitive route that could be used consequently for detecting specific points of interest in the actual area. Twenty adults with blindness (total blindness or only light perception) took part in the research. Two O&M aids were used: verbal descriptions and audio-tactile maps readable with the use of a touchpad device. Participants were asked to use each aid separately to encode the location of 6 points of interest, and next to walk within the area with the scope of detecting these points. The findings proved that an individual with visual impairments can acquire and use an effective cognitive route through the use of an audio-tactile map, while relying on a verbal description entails greater difficulties when he/she comes into the physical environment.

**Keywords:** Blindness · Touchpad · Audio-tactile aid · Orientation and mobility

## 1 Introduction

Individuals with visual impairments face significant challenges traveling in the physical environment. Independent movement is directly connected to the quality of someone's life and thus orientation and mobility issues are always listed on the top priorities of research in the field.

The belief of inferiority of individuals with visual impairment in spatial abilities has an impact on their life, as usually, they are excluded from many employment opportunities [1]. Many work places require actions which are considered to be improper or inaccessible for individuals with visual impairment (e.g. operating a computer, driving a car) [1]. Similarly, difficulties in transition to their workplace are believed to entail reduced independence and activity in limited spaces [1].

Individuals with blindness are facing significant difficulties during their orientation and mobility in space. The majority of the researchers that examined spatial performance of individuals with visual impairments and sighted individuals came to the conclusion that visual experience influences decisively spatial behavior [2–4] Moreover, blindness has a negative impact on the development of blind people's spatial skills [4–6].

© Springer International Publishing Switzerland 2016
M. Antona and C. Stephanidis (Eds.): UAHCI 2016, Part III, LNCS 9739, pp. 577–585, 2016.
DOI: 10.1007/978-3-319-40238-3_55

Orientation, wayfinding and cognitive mapping are prerequisite skills to manage novel spatial environments. Wayfinding involves the ability to learn and recall a route as well as to update one's orientation as he/she moves along the route [7]. Wayfinding is one aspect of the spatial knowledge arisen from cognitive mapping [8].

Even in modern cities, wayfinding is difficult for an individual with blindness [9]. Vision plays a chief role in comprehending the spatial structure of an environment [10] and as such, individuals with blindness seem to face difficulties in the acquisition of concepts relevant to spatial relationships [11]. Nevertheless, it has been argued that even individuals who are congenitally blind are able to form mental representations based mainly on tactile and acoustic stimuli [12, 13].

These mental representations, stored in the long-term memory are called cognitive maps and determine the behavior of individuals with blindness in a space [14]. More specifically, cognitive maps are symbolic structures which reflect spatial knowledge and lead individuals with blindness take crucial decisions, related to where to move to, how to move and which path to follow [15]. However, all information available on the cognitive maps of an individual with blindness is in dynamic relation with the individual's experience and they together contribute to planning and decision making related to movement in space [16]. Individuals with visual impairment can create a mental map through the use of vestibular, haptic, auditory, and even olfactory information and locomotion [17, 18].

According to [11], the conceptualization of the environment depends mainly on three interrelated types of experiences which are visual, acoustic, and tactile (combined with motor activities). Individuals with blindness, in order to form their own cognitive maps, compensate the lack of vision by gathering experiences for space through other senses. Touch and hearing are the main senses through which individuals with blindness acquire knowledge about the structure and the content of an environment [19, 20].

It is impossible for people with blindness to collect the external visual stimuli from the environment or to use conventional maps. Therefore, the provision of spatial information through tactile aids is important [21, 22]. The usefulness of tactile maps for spatial knowledge by individuals who are blind has been demonstrated in several studies [23, 24]. Maps constitute a significant orientation and mobility aid supporting the absolute and relative localization of streets and buildings as well as the estimation of directions and distances between two points [25]. The view provided from a tactile map can replace to some extent, the visual view of the environment [26].

Verbal descriptions refer to descriptions of the layout of an area or instructions of how someone could travel within an area, and may contain information relative to landmarks, routes and techniques for specific situations etc. [27]. The value of verbal descriptions in developing spatial knowledge is disputable because they may embed complex or unknown concepts, they may contain imprecisions [27], or even entail memory load and as such, verbal descriptions subject to time restrictions. A main advantage provided by verbal aids is that the information provided on these issues is more detailed compared to tactile maps. Furthermore, verbal aids do not require braille skills [27].

Assistive technology plays a fundamental role in education and everyday life of individuals with blindness [28, 29]. Assistive technology has recently shown great strides in the field of non-visual access to information for individuals with blindness [30].

In case of audio-tactile maps, information can be represented by tactile graphics, audio symbols, tactile symbols, audio-tactile symbols (combined e.g. a tactile symbol that when a user touches it, he can hear additional information) and Braille labels. That allows a vast amount of information to be presented in auditory modality.

Research data reveal that coexistence and adaptation of auditory and tactile information has been proved significant to the success of an application for spatial knowledge with respect to the satisfaction of individuals with blindness [25]. The comparison of an audio-tactile map with a tactile map demonstrated that interactive audio-tactile maps are more usable and preferred by the users [31].

Audio-tactile maps become available with the use of technological devices, such as the touchpad [32]. The benefits of combining audio and tactile information with the use of relative device have been reviewed in MICOLE project [33].

The study of how people build spatial knowledge through multisensory applications can contribute significantly to the improvement and redesign of similar approaches in the future [14]. Quite an optimistic prospect is that in future the low cost of tactile devices will allow individuals with blindness to have their own multimodal map system at their home [34].

## 2   Study

The aim of the present research was to examine if a verbal description of an urban area or an audio-tactile map would support the development of an effective cognitive route that could be used consequently for detecting specific points of interest in the actual area. A comparison of the effectiveness of the two aids was an objective of this study.

The present study is part of an extended research which aims at examining whether spatial knowledge structured after an individual with blindness had studied a map of an urban area, delivered through different aids (a verbal description, an audio-tactile map with the use of a touchpad device, and an audio-haptic map with the use of a force feedback haptic device) could be used for wayfinding and detection of specific points of interest in the area.

### 2.1   Participants

A basic criterion to include a participant in the study was not to have other disabilities, apart from visual impairments. Twenty adults with blindness (total blindness or only light perception) took part in the research. The sample consisted of 15 males and 5 females. The age ranged from 19 years to 61 years (M = 31.75, SD = 10.70). The visual impairment was congenital for 9 participants and acquired for the rest 11 participants – in 4 out of these 11 participants vision loss occurred at the first year of life.

The participants were asked to state the way of their daily move in outdoor places, by choosing one of the following: (a) with the assistance of a sighted guide, (b) sometimes myself and sometimes with the assistance of a sighted guide, and (c) myself, without any assistance. Moreover, the participants were asked to indicate the frequency of their independent movement using a 5-point likert scale: always, usually, sometimes, seldom, or never. According to their answers, 14 participants move without the assistance of a sighted guide and 6 participants sometimes with assistance, sometimes all by themselves. Moreover, 10 participants stated that they "always" move independently, 8 stated "usually", 1 participant stated "sometimes", and 1 participant stated "seldom".

As far as their Orientation and Mobility (O&M) training is concerned, 15 participants stated that they have participated in O&M training sessions, while 5 participants have never been trained in O&M. The training for 12 out of those 15 participants endured from 10 to 100 h in total, while just 3 of the participants have been trained in O&M for more than 100 h. Moreover, 7 participants declared that they have "never" read tactile graphics or maps, 10 participants that they "rarely" have read tactile graphics, 2 participants that they have read tactile graphics "a few times" and 1 participant that he/she has read "many times" tactile graphics. None of the participants had ever used and audio-tactile map.

## 2.2 Instruments

Two O&M aids were developed for the aims of the experiment: verbal descriptions (maps) and audio-tactile maps readable with the use of a touchpad device. Specifically, three maps depicting three different areas of the Thessaloniki city (areas around the city center with apartment buildings and stores) were developed for each of the two types of O&M aid (verbal description and audio-tactile map). All areas had approximately the same extend and included 5 blocks each. Maps consisted of streets, points of interest and the locations that are extremely dangerous for people with blindness. The number of points of interest was 6 and was the same on each map. The 3 maps were slightly different concerning the degree of difficulty.

The verbal description aid included 3 audio files (.mp3 files), one for each map. Verbal descriptions were initially written in text and subsequently were converted into audio files via TextAloud software (NextUp Technologies). The voice used was Loquendo Afroditi (Greek voice). The verbal descriptions included information for the streets, the six points of interest, the dangerous locations, and the boundaries of the map.

For the study of audio-tactile maps, IVEO (ViewPlus) touchpad tactile device was used. Touchpad is an educational device for individuals with visual impairments, which combines audio and tactile stimuli in order to enrich visual information. The audio-tactile aid consisted of three tactile maps, one for each area, and the corresponding computer files (SVG files). Maps were printed on microcapsule paper using the PIAF machine. Audio-tactile maps included streets, points of interest, dangerous locations and soundscape for intersections. The soundscape of intersections was recorded in real time using a Stereo Dat-Mic microphone (TELINGA) and a ZOOM H4n-Handy Recorder. For the study of audio-tactile maps a personal computer was connected to the touch-tablet. Headphones connected to personal computer were used for the listening of verbal descriptions.

## 2.3   Procedures

Participants were asked to use each aid separately to encode the location of 6 points of interest, and next to walk within an area with the scope of detecting these points. During the phase of aid use, each participant tried to form a cognitive map that would help him/her to move within an area and precisely locate 6 points of interest during the second phase that was executed in this same area (in the physical environment).

The selection of the map to be studied was based on a cyclic procedure, with the first participant listening to the verbal description of the first area, the second participant listening to the verbal description of the second area, and so on. Moreover, the first participant was reading the audio-tactile map of the second area, the second participant reading the audio-tactile map of the third area, and so on. Furthermore, not all the participants started the procedure by listening to the verbal description. On the contrary, half of them began with reading the audio-tactile map. The cyclic procedure was followed so as to decrease the potential effect due to the ease or the difficulty of the studied map, as well as to avoid a possible learning effect influence.

The participant had 15 min at his/her disposal in order to use the aid (verbal description or audio-tactile map) but he/she could stop the procedure earlier, if he/she considered that he/she had fully finished the study. The second phase of the procedure, i.e. the independent movement within the area with the scope of locating the 6 points of interest, began 10 min after the end of the first phase, due to the relocation of the researcher and the participant to the actual area of the studied map. Initially, the researcher placed the participant at the starting point of the area. The participant was asked to navigate in the area without any help, choose his/her own orientation and route, as well as to define the correct position of as more of the six points of interest as he/she could. The route followed by each participant was noted by the researchers. The participant had at his disposal a maximum time span of 20 min but he/she could stop searching for the points of interest earlier, either if he/she had found all six points of interest or if he/she could not recall any other information from the mental map he had formed during the first phase.

In cases of emergency and only when the blind participant was on danger the code word "freeze" was told by the researcher in order to freeze the navigation of the participant. Moreover, the researcher did not provide any assistance to the participant in relation to his/her navigation, unless the participant chose a direction in a street that set himself/herself out of the area of the map. In that case, the researcher relocated the participant back into the specified area, noted the mistake and the participant continued his/her navigation.

The comparison of the two aids was processed with reference to 4 variables: (a) number of sections (the parts of a street from intersection to intersection) with points of interest crossed by the participant, (b) number of sections with points of interest that were not crossed by the participant, (c) number of sections that were crossed by the participant more than once, and (d) whether the participant followed the ideal route, or not. As the ideal route was defined the one that if followed, the participant would have met all the 6 points of interest, it would be the shortest possible route, while it would be unnecessary for the participant to traverse a section more than once.

# 3 Results

Initially, the scores of the following 4 variables were calculated: (1) 'sections crossed' which represents the number of sections with points of interest crossed by the participant, (2) 'sections non-crossed' which represents the number of sections with points of interest that were not crossed by the participant, () 'sections crossed' which refers to the number of sections that were crossed by the participant more than once, and 4) 'perfect route' which refers to whether the participant followed the ideal route, or not (this variable was calculated through the scores 0 = not, and 1 = yes). The mean and standard deviation (SD) of scores for each one of the two aids are presented in Table 1. Each correct or wrong answer was scored to 1. The sections including points of interest were 7 in average for each of the 3 maps.

**Table 1.** Mean and standard deviation (SD) of the crossed sections (with points of interest), non-crossed sections (with points of interest), repeated sections, and following the perfect route.

|                      | Verbal description | | Audio-tactile map | |
|----------------------|------|------|------|------|
|                      | Mean | SD   | Mean | SD   |
| Sections crossed     | 5.10 | 1.77 | 5.75 | 1.77 |
| Sections non-crossed | 1.75 | 1.41 | 1.40 | 1.39 |
| Sections repeated    | .95  | .89  | .40  | .75  |
| Perfect route        | .10  | .31  | .65  | .49  |

The implementation of repeated-measures ANOVAs revealed significant differences for the variables: 'Sections repeated' [$F (1, 19) = 5.487$, $p < .05$], and 'Perfect route' [$F (1, 19) = 23.222$, $p < .01$].

The analysis of the results indicated that the participants followed the ideal route statistically significant fewer times after they had listened to the verbal description that they had read the audio-tactile map. In this same case, it seems that participants crossed the same section/s more than once. In addition, the participants appear to have crossed more sections with points of interest after they had read the audio-tactile map than listened to the verbal description. However, this difference is not statistically significant.

Interesting enough are the findings concerning the differences in the variable 'perfect route'. The number of the participants they followed the 'perfect route' using the verbal description was 2, while the participants following the 'perfect route' after they had read the audio-tactile map were 13.

# 4 Conclusions

In the present study, the cognitive maps of individuals with blindness were examined after they had listened to a recorded verbal description and they had explored an audio-tactile map using a touch pad device. This research is significant twofold: not only the comparison of a verbal description with an audio-tactile map has not been met in the field, but also the assessment of cognitive maps in the physical environment (instead of laboratory conditions) which reflects a real situation is generally avoided [35].

According to the results, an individual with blindness can acquire and use an effective cognitive map through reading an audio-tactile map. However, relying on a verbal description before entering an unknowing area entails challenges. The participants' performance was significantly better in the spatial tasks after they had read the audio-tactile map than in the case of listening to the verbal description. It seems that following an ideal route i.e. meeting all the 6 points of interest, detecting the shortest possible route and being quick by avoiding walking repetitions of sections, becomes an easier task after the preparation with an audio-tactile map. This proves not only, that audio-tactile maps constitute an effective orientation and mobility aid but also, that they provide much more support compared to verbal descriptions.

Previous research has also proved that audio-tactile map result in adequate spatial knowledge [36].

A possible explanation of the dominance of audio-tactile maps over verbal description could be the advantages of combining tactile and auditory stimuli, on one hand, and the drawbacks of verbal descriptions, on the other. Taking these results into consideration, it could assumed that audio-tactile maps combining significant advantages of tactile maps with auditory information enable more efficiently the individual with visual blindness when he/she arrives to physical environment. Verbal description appears to be a weaker tool for wayfinding and points of interest detection in the physical environment. This means that while combining tactile and auditory information may consequently lead to a more complete concept [37], verbal descriptions may embed complex or unknown concepts, contain imprecisions, or even entail memory load [27].

The findings of the present study contribute to the understanding of issues concerning the development of cognitive maps in individuals with blindness. These findings are specifically significant in the case of familiarization with a novel area and the consequent creation of a new cognitive map. Thus, the results of the study have implications for both educators and orientation and mobility specialists.

# References

1. Kitchin, R.M., Blades, M., Golledge, R.G.: Understanding spatial concepts at the geographic scale without the use of vision. Prog. Hum. Geog. 21(2), 225–242 (1997)
2. Papadopoulos, K., Koustriava, E.: The impact of vision in spatial coding. Res. Dev. Disabil. 32(6), 2084–2091 (2011)
3. Papadopoulos, K., Koustriava, E., Kartasidou, L.: The impact of residual vision in spatial skills of individuals with visual impairments. J. Spec. Educ. 45(2), 118–127 (2011)
4. Papadopoulos, K., Barouti, M., Charitakis, K.: A University indoors audio-tactile mobility aid for individuals with blindness. In: Miesenberger, K., Fels, D., Archambault, D., Peñáz, P., Zagler, W. (eds.) ICCHP 2014, Part II. LNCS, vol. 8548, pp. 108–115. Springer, Heidelberg (2014)
5. Koustriava, E., Papadopoulos, K.: Mental rotation ability of individuals with visual impairments. J. Vis. Impair. Blin. 104(9), 570–574 (2010)

6. Koustriava, E., Papadopoulos, K.: Are there relationships among different spatial skills of individuals with blindness? Res. Dev. Disabil. **33**(6), 2164–2176 (2012)

7. Blades, M.: Wayfinding theory and research: the need for a new approach. In: Mark, D.M., Frank, A.U. (eds.) Cognitive and linguistic aspects of geographic space, pp. 137–165. Springer, Netherlands (1991)

8. Golledge, R.G.: Wayfinding Behavior: Cognitive Mapping and Other Spatial Processes. Johns Hopkins University Press, Baltimore (1999)

9. Gaunet, F., Briffault, X.: Exploring the functional specifications of a localized wayfinding verbal aid for blind pedestrians. Simple and structured urban areas. Hum. Comput. Interact. **20**, 267–314 (2005)

10. Thinus-Blanc, C., Gaunet, F.: Representation of space in blind persons: vision as a spatial sense? Psychol. Bull. **121**(1), 20–42 (1997)

11. Warren, D.H.: Blindness and Children: An Individual Differences Approach. Cambridge University Press, Cambridge (1994)

12. Ungar, S., Blades, M., Spencer, C.: The construction of cognitive maps by children with visual impairments. In: Portugali, J. (ed.) The Construction of Cognitive Maps. Kluwer Academic Publishing, Dordrecht (1996)

13. Papadopoulos, K., Koustriava, E., Kartasidou, L.: Spatial coding of individuals with visual impairment. J. Spec. Educ. **46**(3), 180–190 (2012)

14. Kitchin, R.M.: Cognitive maps: what are they and why study them? J. Environ. Psychol. **14**, 1–19 (1994)

15. Jacobson, R.D., Kitchin, R.M.: Assessing the configurational knowledge of people with visual impairments or blindness. Swansea Geogr. **32**, 14–24 (1995)

16. Jacobson, D., Lippa, Y., Golledge, R.G., Kitchin, R., Blades, M.: Rapid development of cognitive maps in people with visual impairments when exploring novel geographic spaces. IAPS Bull. People-Environ. Stud. (Special Issue on Environmental Cognition) **18**, 3–6 (2001)

17. Steyvers, F.J.J.M., Kooijman, A.C.: Using route and survey information to generate cognitive maps: differences between normally sighted and visually impaired individuals. Appl. Cogn. Psychol. **23**, 223–235 (2009)

18. Morash, V.: Connell Pensky, A.E., Urqueta Alfaro, A., McKerracher, A.: A review of haptic spatial abilities in the blind. Spat. Cogn. Comput. **12**, 83–95 (2012)

19. Jacobson, R.D., Kitchin, R.M.: GIS and people with visual impairments or blindness: exploring the potential for education, orientation, and navigation. Trans. GIS **2**(4), 315–332 (1997)

20. Lahav, O., Mioduser, D.: Construction of cognitive maps of unknown spaces using a multi-sensory virtual environment for people who are blind. Comput. Hum. Behav. **24**(3), 1139–1155 (2008)

21. Papadopoulos, K.: A school program contributes to the environmental knowledge of blind. Br. J. Vis. Impair. **22**(3), 101–104 (2004)

22. Papadopoulos, K., Karanikolas, N.: Tactile maps provide location based services for individuals with visual impairments. J. Location Based Serv. **3**(3), 150–164 (2009)

23. Ungar, S., Blades, M., Spencer, C.: The role of tactile maps in mobility training. Br. J. Vis. Impair. **11**(2), 59–61 (1993)

24. Espinosa, M.A., Ochaita, E.: Using tactile maps to improve the practical spatial knowledge of adults who are blind. J. Vis. Impair. Blin. **92**(5), 338–345 (1998)

25. Brock, A., Truillet, P., Oriola, B., Picard, D., Jouffrais, C.: Design and user satisfaction of interactive maps for visually impaired people. In: Miesenberger, K., Karshmer, A., Penaz, P., Zagler, W. (eds.) ICCHP 2012, Part II. LNCS, vol. 7383, pp. 544–551. Springer, Heidelberg (2012)

26. Golledge, R.G.: Tactual strip maps as navigational aids. J. Vis. Impair. Blin. **85**, 296–301 (1991)

27. Bentzen, B.L.: Orientation aids. In: Blash, B.B., Wiener, W.R., Welsh, R.L. (eds.) Foundations of Orientation and Mobility, vol. 1, pp. 284–316. AFB Press, New York (1997)

28. Maor, D., Currie, J., Drewry, R.: The effectiveness of assistive technologies for children with special needs: a review of research-based studies. Eur. J. Spec. Needs Educ. **26**(3), 283–298 (2011)

29. Brown, D.J., McHugh, D., Standen, P., Evett, L., Shopland, N., Battersby, S.: Designing location-based learning experiences for people with intellectual disabilities and additional sensory impairments. Comput. Educ. **56**, 11–20 (2011)

30. Abu Doush, I., Pontelli, E., Simon, D., Son, T.C., Ma, O.: Making Microsoft Excel™: multimodal presentation of charts. In: 11th International ACM SIGACCESS Conference on Computers and Accessibility, pp. 147–154. ACM, New York (2009)

31. Brock, A., Jouffrais, C.: Interactive audio-tactile maps for visually impaired people. Accessibility Comput. **113**, 3–12 (2015)

32. Holmes, E., Jansson, G.: A touch tablet enhanced with synthetic speech as a display for visually impaired people's reading of virtual maps (1997). http://www.dinf.ne.jp/doc/english/Us_Eu/conf/csun_97/csun97_060.html

33. MICOLE: D6: Report of the Design and Evaluation of Basic Multimodal Navigation Tools (2006). http://micole.cs.uta.fi/deliverables_public/index.html

34. Brock, A., Truillet, P., Oriola, B., Jouffrais, C.: Usage of multimodal maps for blind people: why and how. In: ITS 2010 ACM International Conference on Interactive Tabletops and Surfaces, pp. 247–248. ACM, New York (2010)

35. Kitchin, R.M., Jacobson, R.D.: Techniques to collect and analyze the cognitive map knowledge of persons with visual impairment or blindness: issues of validity. J. Vis. Impair. Blin. **91**, 360–376 (1997)

36. Papadopoulos, K., Barouti, M.: The contribution of audio-tactile maps to spatial knowledge of individuals with visual impairments. In: Kouroupetroglou, G. (ed.) Proceedings of International Conference on Enabling Access for Persons with Visual Impairment - ICEAPVI-2015, pp. 141–146. Greece, Athens (2015)

37. Landau, S., Russell, M., Erin, J.N.: Using the talking tactile tablet as a testing accommodation. RE: view **38**(1), 7–21 (2006)

# GatePal – Universal Design for Airport Navigation to Allow Departing Travellers to Stay Informed

Yilin Elaine Liu[✉], Christina Harrington, Sarah Melgen,
and Jon Sanford

Georgia Institute of Technology, Atlanta, USA
{y.elaineliu, cnh}@gatech.edu,
{sarah.melgen, jon.sanford}@coa.gatech.edu

**Abstract.** Airports are challenging for travellers with disabilities and senior travellers with functional limitations due to the complexity of terminal environments and the variety of activities (e.g. navigation, check-in, security check) required for one to successfully depart or arrive. Without sufficient information associated with the context of airport environments, travellers with disabilities and functional limitations are not able to plan their activities or efficiently navigate through terminals and surrounding areas. For departing travellers, time is the most important contextual information due to constraints and potential barriers. Without providing the necessary information about the time it takes to complete each activity, especially when navigating, travellers with disabilities and functional limitations are not able to plan or anticipate any upcoming situations. This paper introduces a universal mobile application called GatePal that was designed based on the results of a preliminary user study and utilizes universal design principles to assist travellers with diverse abilities with navigation at airports.

**Keywords:** Decision making · Universal design · Indoor navigation · Information access

## 1 Introduction

In the United States, approximately 18.7 % of the population has at least one type of disability [1] and 61 % of the 44.7 million older adults have at least one basic activity limitation [2]. These disabilities and functional limitations can have a profound negative impact on people's ability to travel and, as a result, they usually experience more physical and psychological travel difficulties [3]. Airports, as complex public transportation structures, are full of challenges for travellers to successfully plan and carry out activities such as navigation, check-in, or baggage claim when departing and arriving [4]. In order to enable people with disabilities and functional limitations to travel by public transportation equitably, airports are required to comply with the Americans with Disabilities Act (ADA) to make the environment accessible by providing a variety of amenities such as accessible restrooms and elevators. However, these regulations primarily address the needs of people with mobility impairments, and

© Springer International Publishing Switzerland 2016
M. Antona and C. Stephanidis (Eds.): UAHCI 2016, Part III, LNCS 9739, pp. 586–594, 2016.
DOI: 10.1007/978-3-319-40238-3_56

only reduce a small number of the environmental challenges faced by these individuals as well as those with other types of disabilities.

Challenges posed by navigation and planning of routes to various destinations still exist and are not addressed by the ADA [16]. The planning of routes and location of activities are traditionally informed by informational signage and airport/airline support staff. When information is missing, ambiguous (e.g., is confusing to someone who is unfamiliar with terminology) or cannot be perceived (e.g., is not seen by someone with a vision loss or distracted by a child), the airport becomes inaccessible to these travellers. For example, without providing information about the location of elevators in a visible and clear way, travellers with mobility impairments will not be able to access other levels, which is often required to get from the ground transportation to the departure gates or from the gates to baggage claim.

At airports, situational/contextual information such as the flight schedules and the navigation information always go hand-in-hand. The separation of navigation and situational information makes it difficult for travellers to anticipate any impact of navigation choices on the over-all situation. The importance of providing information regarding navigation and activity planning to satisfy travellers' needs has been brought up in previous research studies [17–19]. Among these studies, travellers all expressed strong needs for information in regard to time such as up-to-date flight schedules, flight delays [18, 19] and quick check-in/baggage arrival [17]. Typically, important directional information comes from airport staff who not only tell travellers the required activities to get on a plane, but also the location of important services and destinations (e.g. gate direction, bathrooms, check-in counters). Airport staff were observed as playing a key role in balancing queues at airports in order to minimize waiting time for individual travellers [19]. In this case, airport staff have pre-planned routes for travellers and provided them with the critical information to support successfully navigating that route. Planning is important because it allows travellers to anticipate potential barriers, and make decisions about making their way through the airport. Planning is especially important for travellers with disabilities as they often require more time and special accommodations compared to travellers without disabilities. As a result, they are less able to compensate for unexpected route changes or delays, such as gate changes or long waiting times in security. It thus becomes more important for them to be aware of the situation and make alternative decisions on their activities [20]. Providing sufficient information to support the planning of activities and routes for travellers with disabilities enables them to be prepared for navigating in unfamiliar environments and situational changes that can impact route planning to activity destinations. Unfortunately, there are few studies that have examined the informational needs of people with disabilities or have attempted to provide the information from an activity planning perspective. More effort is required to identify their needs and provide them with the information to enable them to use the airport equitably.

In addition to the separation of navigation and situational information, ineffective communication of information also creates barriers for travellers with disabilities. For example, travellers with sensory disabilities have difficulty perceiving information provided by signage and FIDs. Although those travellers can ask airport staff for help with the information, the limited number of airport staff precludes this from being an effective and efficient way of communicating information. As a result, information that is tailored towards their disabilities is needed when navigating and participating in different activities.

In order to facilitate travellers' navigation and participation in activities at airports, a system is needed that not only provides information about navigation, but also provides contextual information such as the time required for each activity to facilitate the proper planning and execution of airport activities. To achieve that, a universal design approach has been used to investigate the information needs of travellers with diverse abilities regarding the environment and the activity planning at airports. A navigation application has been designed based on the results of the investigation and universal design principles to support travellers' activities. In this paper, the universally designed navigation system is presented and the process of designing this system is detailed. We discuss our method of data collection and the ways in which this information guided our design decisions. Lastly, we discuss the future development and testing of this application.

## 2    Current Pedestrian Navigation Solutions

Current pedestrian navigation systems have used various approaches including different technologies and applications to solve wayfinding problems for people with and without disabilities. For people with visual impairments or those who are blind, pedestrian navigation systems have been developed with a specific focus on audio input and output as an accessible means of communicating information [10–12]. With audio output as the primary approach to communicating navigation information, many systems are less effective and efficient for people without visual impairments. In contrast, pedestrian navigation systems designed for people without disabilities have focused more on presenting navigation information graphically, which makes them unusable for people with visual impairments [12, 13, 15]. Whereas the emergence of off-the-shelf smartphones with built-in navigation capability and accessible I/O features has made designing such a system technically feasible, studies are needed to better understand the information needs of airport travellers with disabilities in order to design such a system to be useful and usable by all travellers.

## 3    Method

A user study was conducted to investigate the needs of older adult travellers and travellers with disabilities for three types of information: (1) time-related situational information (flight schedules and delays, time for going through security, etc.); (2) distance to destinations (length of a route from point A to point B); and (3) points of interest (POIs), such as restrooms, shops, restaurants. This data collection was a part of a large wayfinding study funded by the National Research Council to develop wayfinding guidelines for people with disabilities and older adults in airports. The study took place at the Austin-Bergstrom International Airport where participants were debriefed on their

**Table 1.** Demographic Information. Gender: M- Male; F- Female. User Group: HI- Hearing impairments; VI- Visual impairments; MI- Mobility impairments; O- Older adults without disability.

| Participant | 1 | 2 | 3 | 4 | 5 | 6 | 7 | 8 | 9 | 10 | 11 | 12 |
|---|---|---|---|---|---|---|---|---|---|---|---|---|
| Gender | M | F | M | F | F | M | F | F | F | F | F | F |
| Age | 50 | 70 | 74 | 56 | 57 | 32 | 39 | 62 | 69 | 70 | 48 | 54 |
| User Group | HI | MI | O | HI | MI | VI | MI | VI | O | O | VI | MI |

departing experience. By doing it in situ, it allowed participants to have more direct and up-to-date recall of using the airport.

### 3.1 Participants

A total of 12 participants with functional limitations were enrolled, including 3 people with visual impairments, 4 people with mobility impairments, 2 people with hearing impairments and 3 older adults (Table 1). It is worth noting that participant 11 has both visual and hearing impairments and she was counted as visually impaired since she has an implant to facilitate her hearing and did not require an interpreter for communication.

### 3.2 Data Collection

The participants were first asked to rank the order of importance of the three types of information (time, distance, and POI). This was followed by an interview to identify specific reasons for their ranking and preferences of obtaining and using the information provided. It was expected that some participants would consider time and distance to be the same concept since the distance from point A to point B could reflect the time spending on walking if the walking speed was known. To avoid possible misunderstanding, researchers explicitly explained at the beginning of the study that the time-related information refers to flight schedules and delays, and waiting time at the security. The result was analysed and used to develop the universal design criteria for designing an airport navigation system.

## 4   Results

### 4.1   Results from the User Study

Over all, participants considered *time* and *distance* as being the most important information to obtain. Point of interest, on the other hand, was ranked as less important than time and distance. There were 7 out of 12 participants who ranked *time* as the most important information, and there were 5 out of 12 participants ranked *distance* as the most important information. Most of the participants ranked POI as the least important information compare to *time* and *distance*. Detailed distribution of type of information, and rankings of importance level can be found in Fig. 1.

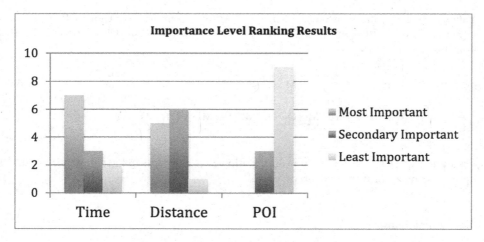

**Fig. 1.** Results of importance level rankings for the three types of information

In the interview session, not all participants were able to provide specific reasons for their rankings for each type of information. Among those who provided specific reasons, the importance level rankings of time and distance were interrelated in some cases. These cases were marked with "(I)". Detailed reasons provided by participants for their rankings can be found in Table 2.

**Table 2.** Detailed reasons for the rankings

| Reasons for ranking time as the (most) important information to know | Reasons for ranking distance as the (most) information to know |
|---|---|
| P2 did not care about the distance because she was using a power chair (I) | P3 said he always go to airport early so time does not matter that much. So he picked distance (I) |
| P4 thought the flight information at the counter might not update | |
| P5 mentioned that the security "eats up" the time and it is really crucial when it's pre-boarding | |
| P9 mentioned that for most of the time she did not go to the airport early so she wanted to keep track of time. She mentioned the WAZE app she used in which it will say there's 10 min away for xxx | |

During the interview, several themes regarding the preferences, the planning strategy and other concerns popped up and they were considered relevant to the access and use of information, thus were worth reporting.

**Preferences for when to obtain the information:** Three (3) participants mentioned that they wanted to know the information about the airport ahead of time (P7, P8, P12). The information they wanted to obtain ahead of time included, but was not limited to information about the locations of accessible restrooms and wheelchair service and the time it took to complete certain activities. P7 explicitly mentioned that if someone were using a wheelchair, it would take different amount of time for one to get to the gate. This kind of information should be provided a day before the actual air trip.

**Use of strategy to plan activities:** Strategy wise, 5 participants mentioned that they would go to the gate first and then explore the airport (P3, P7, P9, P10, P12). If they had extra time when they arrived at the gate, they would go for snacks or restrooms.

**Inaccessible information:** There were 3 participants mentioned that they wanted to know the information about the flight status change (P1, P4, P6). All of them have sensory disabilities that P1 and P4 are with hearing loss and P6 is with vision loss. Their sensory disabilities have prevented them from accessing the schedule change information that was presented through the audio announcements or the displays at the gate.

**Location information for accessible amenities:** There were 4 participants expressed the concern of not knowing the location of accessible bathrooms. (P2, P5, P7, P12) All of them have mobility impairments that they are wheelchair users.

### 4.2 Discussion of the User Study Results

Considering the relatively small size and one concourse linear layout of the Austin airport, the locations of many points of interest were fairly straightforward and uncomplicated. As a result, participants generally took relatively less effort to obtain the POI information because POIs were relatively obvious. This might be the reason for the skewed result that the straightforwardness of the POI information presented at Austin airport might prevent participants from realizing the importance of obtaining POI information. In addition, the size of the airport might affect the ranking of importance level for distance. Within this airport, the distance information can easily be anticipated based on the perceived size.

## 5    Design of the System

### 5.1    Task Analysis

In order to provide time-related information, a task analysis was performed to investigate the time consumption of required activities for departing at airports. Three types of time-related information were identified: (1) walking time (time required for walking from point A to point B); (2) waiting time (time required for waiting in lines); and (3) working time (time required for agents or travellers to work on activities). In Fig. 1, the 3 types of time are illustrated for travellers who either check in online and go straight to security (type 1), travellers who check in at an agent (type 2), and travellers who need to check in at kiosks and check their bags (type 3) (Fig. 2).

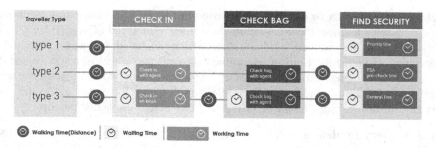

**Fig. 2.** Task analysis in terms of time consumption

## 5.2   Overview of GatePal

Following the task analysis the design team worked to ideate a system that would support airport navigation with an emphasis on making users aware of the time required to get from point to point. GatePal is an iBeacon-based indoor navigation system that provides step-by-step navigation information and real-time contextual and situational information to allow travellers to make route decisions based on time and distance. GatePal was universally designed to address the needs of all travellers. It includes specific accessibility information for travellers with disabilities as well as multimodal ways of providing input and feedback to convey information. A detailed description of each design feature is presented in the following section.

## 5.3   Design Features

**Design Feature 1.** Different route options for accommodating different needs. GatePal provides different route options based on several route characteristics and present all the route options in a consistent way of time. It allows travellers to successfully make route choices that are accommodating their needs and stay informed of the context.

**Design Feature 2.** Flexibility in navigation information presentation. GatePal provides different options for information communication. Travellers are able to choose the navigation information to be presented through text and map in different levels of details.

**Design Feature 3.** Different navigation modes for different strategies. GatePal provides "get to gate" mode and "explore" mode to support travellers' use of different strategies when navigating. Travellers are able to choose between following step-by-step information to their gate and exploring the airport environment on their own. They can switch between these two modes at anytime they want (Fig. 3).

**Fig. 3.** Selected GatePal screenshots

## 6 Discussion and Future Work

There is great value in a navigation application that utilizes a universal design approach for concept generation and development. By considering all end users up front, mobile application systems such as GatePal have the ability to benefit a wide range of users in various contexts, all while providing a seemingly equitable experience.

This paper describes the rational for and the design of a universal navigation system that supports older adult travellers and travellers with diverse abilities to become aware of the context and situation in order to navigate through airports. Currently, the design phase of GatePal is complete and it is under development for implementing some of the design features to technically prove the concept. The next step is to implement the key design features and get it tested with users to further investigate its utility and usability. The results of user studies will be used for designing the next iteration of GatePal.

## References

1. Brault, M.W.: Americans with disabilities: 2010. Curr. Popul. Rep. **7**, 131 (2012)
2. National Center for Health Statistics: US. Health, United States, 2014: With special feature on adults aged, pp. 55–64 (2015)
3. Yau, M.K.S., McKercher, B., Packer, T.L.: Traveling with a disability: more than an access issue. Ann. Tourism Res. **31**(4), 946–960 (2004)
4. Popovic, V., Kraal, B. J., Kirk, P. J.: Passenger experience in an airport: an activity-centred approach. Proceedings of IASDR 2009, pp. 1–10 (2009)
5. Xiong, H., Fan, C., Zhu, X., Shu, W., Zhang, Z., Ji, Q.: Research and de-sign on passengers traffic information services mode of Hongqiao transport hub. Int. J. Bus. Manage. **5**(4), 194 (2010)
6. Burdette, D., Hickman, M.: Investigation of information needs of depart-ing air passengers. Transp. Res. Rec. J. Transp. Res. Board **1744**, 72–81 (2001)
7. Fodness, D., Murray, B.: Passengers' expectations of airport service quality. J. Serv. Mark. **21**(7), 492–506 (2007)
8. Churchill, A., Dada, E., De Barros, A.G., Wirasinghe, S.C.: Quantifying and validating measures of airport terminal wayfinding. J. Air Transport Manage. **14**(3), 151–158 (2008)

9. Jonnalagedda, A., Pei, L., Saxena, S., Wu, M., Min, B. C., Teves, E., Dias, M. B.: Enhancing the Safety of Visually Impaired Travelers in and Around Transit Stations (2014)
10. Golledge, R.G., Klatzky, R.L., Loomis, J.M., Speigle, J., Tietz, J.: A geographical information system for a GPS based personal guidance system. Int. J. Geog. Inform. Sci. 12(7), 727–749 (1998)
11. Ran, L., Helal, S., Moore, S.: Drishti: an integrated in-door/outdoor blind navigation system and service. In: Proceedings of the Second IEEE Annual Conference on Pervasive Computing and Communications, PerCom 2004, pp. 23–30. IEEE (2004)
12. Walker, B.N., Lindsay, J.: Navigation performance with a virtual auditory display: effects of beacon sound, capture radius, and practice. Hum. Factors: J. Hum, Factors. Ergon. Soc. 48(2), 265–278 (2006)
13. Baus, J., Krüger, A., Wahlster, W.: A resource-adaptive mobile navigation system. In: Proceedings of the 7th International Conference on Intelligent User Interfaces, pp. 15–22. ACM (2002)
14. Han, D., Jung, S., Lee, M., Yoon, G.: Building a practical Wi-Fi-based indoor navigation system. IEEE Pervasive Comput. 13(2), 72–79 (2014)
15. Radaha, T. R., Johnson, M. E.: Mobile Indoor Navigation Application for Airport Transits (2013)
16. Raman, S.: Airport accessibility for travellers with disabilities. J. Airport Manage. 5(3), 239–244 (2011)
17. Gupta, R., Venkaiah, V.: Airport passengers: their needs and satisfaction. SCMS J. Indian Manage. 12(3), 46 (2015)
18. Burdette, D., Hickman, M.: Investigation of information needs of departing air passengers. Transp. Res. Rec. J. Transp. Res. Board 1744, 72–81 (2001)
19. Zhang, H., Ruff, L., Strawderman, L., Usher, J. M., Jackson, B.: Understanding passengers' use of airports from a system usability perspective. In: IIE Annual Conference. Proceedings, p. 1. Institute of Industrial Engineers-Publisher (2011)
20. Sami, K., Ari, V.: Public transport real time information in Personal navigation systems for special user groups. In: 11th ITS World Congress, p. 6. Nagoya, Japan (2004)

# Development of an Audio-Haptic Virtual Interface for Navigation of Large-Scale Environments for People Who Are Blind

Lotfi B. Merabet[1(✉)] and Jaime Sánchez[2]

[1] Laboratory for Visual Neuroplasticity, Massachusetts Eye and Ear Infirmary,
Harvard Medical School, Boston, MA, USA
lotfi_merabet@meei.harvard.edu
[2] Department of Computer Science, University of Chile,
Blanco Encalada 2120, Santiago, Chile
jsanchez@dcc.uchile.cl

**Abstract.** We are investigating cognitive spatial mapping skills in people who are blind through the use of virtual navigation and assessing the transference of acquired spatial knowledge in large-scale, real-world navigation tasks. Training is carried out with a user-centered, computer-based, navigation software platform called Haptic Audio Game Application (HAGA). This software was developed to assist in orientation and mobility (O&M) training by introducing blind users to a spatial layout of a large-scale environment through immersive and simulation-based virtual navigation. As part of a self-directed, free exploration strategy, users interact with HAGA in order to navigate through a simulated indoor and outdoor virtual environment that represents an actual physical space. Navigation is based on the use of iconic and spatialized auditory cues and vibro-tactile feedback so as to build a cognitive spatial map of the surrounding environment. The ability to transfer acquired spatial information is then assessed in a series of physical navigation tasks carried out in the actual target environment explored virtually.

**Keywords:** Multimodal interfaces · Blind · Spatial cognition · Navigation

## 1 Introduction

The formal instruction of navigation skills in blind users (referred to as orientation and mobility, or O&M training), is geared at developing strategies to assist with route planning, updating information regarding one's position, and reorienting to reestablish travel as needed [1]. The resultant mental representation of the surrounding external space is referred to as a cognitive spatial map [2–4]. For a blind individual, hearing and touch remain the principal modalities for sourcing information regarding the surrounding environment. In terms of navigation, information captured through sound and touch is essential for developing an awareness of relative orientation and distance, as well as obstacle detection and avoidance [5–7]. The theoretical underpinnings related to spatial abilities and navigation skills in blind individuals have been the subject of intense debate (see [8]). For example, as profoundly blind individuals cannot access

M. Antona and C. Stephanidis (Eds.): UAHCI 2016, Part III, LNCS 9739, pp. 595–606, 2016.
DOI: 10.1007/978-3-319-40238-3_57

spatial information through visual channels, it has been largely assumed that they (especially children that are born blind) have cognitive difficulties in representing spatial environments [9] and consequently, possess impaired navigation skills. However, more recent evidence has shown that blind individuals exhibit equal [10] and in some cases, even superior [11] navigation performance when compared to sighted individuals under experimental testing conditions.

Given these contradictory findings, one has to ask whether difficulties in developing cognitive spatial constructs are due uniquely to the effect of visual deprivation itself (and related developmental factors such as the timing and profoundness of vision loss) or, do they also reflect an incomplete or inflexible acquisition of necessary spatial information through other sensory channels? From an education and rehabilitation standpoint, we argue that what is missing is a more efficient way to access, manipulate, and transfer acquired spatial information for the purposes of navigation; a gap that could be potentially closed through the use of novel and immersive forms of assistive technology.

## 1.1   Virtual Environments and Creating Spatial Mental Maps Through Sound and Touch

Considerable interest has arisen regarding the educative and training potential of virtual reality and computer based video games [12, 13]. Specifically, it has been suggested that the open structure and self-directed discovery of information inherent in virtual reality environments improves contextual learning and the transfer of situational knowledge and awareness (consider as a prototypical example, the success of flight simulators for pilot training) [14, 15]. Successfully leveraging these advantages in the education and rehabilitation arenas would have immense appeal and could potentially facilitate the learning of demanding tasks, and further promote the transfer of acquired skills beyond the constraints of the training context itself [13, 16, 17]. Parallel to this potential application, is the fact that the communications and entertainment industries have driven many technical advances (both software and hardware) such as extreme detailed graphics, highly realistic sounds, as well as tactile and motion feedback joystick controllers; all of which are aimed at generating a greater sense of environmental "immersion" for the user. Based on this premise, we propose that virtual environments can provide a blind individual the possibility to interact with complex contextual information through the use of non-visual sensory modalities. Extended to the case of navigation, a well-designed virtual environment could allow access to crucial spatial information for the purposes of surveying and planning of routes, simulation of travel, and the playing out of hypothetical navigation scenarios. By interacting with auditory and tactile sensory cues that describe the spatial layout of an environment (for example, heading information provided by text to speech (TTS), iconic and spatialized stereo cues for identifying the spatial location of an object, or pulsatile vibrations felt in the hands when an obstacle is hit), a blind user can learn the spatial layout of a complex environment via "structural discovery". Key to this user-centered approach, is the fact that spatial information is acquired within context, and in a highly dynamic and interactive manner that greatly engages the user so as to construct a cognitive spatial map of that area in an efficient "off-line" manner. Once the spatial information is acquired, the individual can then translate this knowledge for the purposes of enhanced navigation skills once they arrive to the actual environment to be explored.

Previous work with blind individuals has shown that spatial information obtained through novel computer-based approaches including audio [18–21] and tactile/ haptic [22–24] modalities leads to the generation of cognitive spatial maps that, in turn, may be useful for the purposes of navigation. Furthermore, combined sensory exploration (i.e. using touch and audio) may lead to an even greater capture of contextual information. Indeed, the perceptual advantage of overlapping multisensory inputs is well established in the psychophysical literature. For example, overlapping multisensory information can enhance object saliency by improving the likelihood of detecting and identifying a sensory event and accelerating perceptual reaction times (see [25] for review). By leveraging these principles, our investigative effort has gone through an evolution of ideas with the ultimate goal of developing computer based software for users who are blind and for the purposes of enhancing navigation-related and spatial cognitive skills. One early approach was the development of "Audio-Doom". This was an auditory-based computer game centered on the popular "first-person shooter" game "Doom" (Id Software) and was developed to promote computer interaction in blind children. Using simple iconic audio cues (for example, door knocks and footsteps), a blind user can acquire contextual spatial information and navigate through a predetermined labyrinth of corridors and obstacles. Following game play, blind users (particularly children) were able to construct (using Lego® blocks) a physical representation of the route they navigated with great accuracy [26] (see Fig. 1 A). This led to the intriguing possibility that blind users who interact with a virtual world that represents a real indoor environment (e.g. a building) can not only create a mental map of its spatial layout, but also transfer this knowledge for the purposes of navigating in the actual target environment presented in the software. This lead to the development of Audio-based Environment Simulator (AbES) (see Fig. 1B). We completed a series of studies and found that blind individuals (both of early and late onset) were able to use contextual and audio-based spatial cues to explore and accurately learn the spatial layout of an indoor environment for which they were previously unfamiliar. Furthermore, the spatial information learned off-line could be transferred to navigation tasks carried out within the real physical space represented in the virtual environment [27–30].

Based on this proof of principle (and as a next step towards creating a truly viable and robust assistive technology for the purpose of enhancing navigation skills in blind users), we have created Haptic Audio Game Application (HAGA); a third generation virtual environment simulator with the following design features: (1) greater immersive sensory experience with full 3D sound and tactile/haptic feedback (allowing for more robust acquisition and interaction with spatial contextual information), (2) rapid prototyping of any large scale environment desired (including indoor and outdoor), and (3) wide deployment on a variety of technology platforms and operating systems (including PC, Mac, and mobile Android, iOS). Finally, HAGA was designed to be used by blind individuals with profound vision loss and could also be modified for use in individuals with low vision (see Fig. 1C).

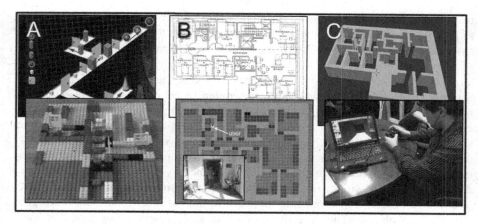

**Fig. 1.** (**A**) With AudioDoom, early blind children use simple iconic and spatialized sound cues to navigate a complex labyrinth of corridors and obstacles (see background figure). The accuracy of the cognitive spatial map resulting from exploration and game play is demonstrated by their ability to construct (using Lego pieces) a physical representation of the target labyrinth (foreground figure). (**B**) With AbES, this approach was expanded to real-world indoor spaces (e.g. corridors and rooms of a building). This allows a blind user to learn the spatial layout of an unfamiliar building (background: building floor plan, foreground: rendering in AbES, inset: user navigating in the target building). (**C**) Using the Unity game engine software platform, virtually any desired environment (indoor and outdoor) can by quickly rendered (in this case, the corresponding indoor floor plan of the building depicted in B was rendered in approximately 3 h; background figure). Audio and tactile/haptic sensory information can be accessed using peripheral interfaces (headphones and Xbox controller with rumble vibration; foreground figure) to create a greater immersive experience during exploration. The Unity software platform was used to create the HAGA software for this study.

## 1.2   Innovation and Current Gaps in Knowledge

Through the development and assessment of this software, we are attempting to address gaps, barriers, and questions of fundamental importance related to the rehabilitation and development of navigation skills in individuals who are blind. First, it is notable that the field of O&M (and blind rehabilitation in general) typically has not benefited from extensive and rigorous outcomes-based research. This includes systematic evaluations to compare the effectiveness of various assistive technologies and teaching strategies. Thus, the establishment of evidence-based best practices are clearly needed. Second, with current advances in neuroscience and modern day brain imaging methodologies (such as functional magnetic resonance imaging, or fMRI), we are in a position to uncover the neurophysiological mechanisms and identification of "neural biomarkers" that are related to behavioral performance. Specifically, carrying out virtual navigation studies in the MRI scanner environment can help identify important brain networks associated with enhanced navigation skills and further, relate this to potentially important factors such as age, previous visual experience, as well as learning and training strategies. As part of our ongoing investigation, we completed a brain imaging study in blind individuals that were asked to navigate in a large scale, indoor virtual environment using audio-based spatial cues. We found that while performing navigation tasks, blind individuals showed brain activation patterns within areas known to be implicated with spatial processing; very similar to that of individuals with normal vision. Furthermore, individual navigational abilities appeared to be related to the utilization of different brain network structures [31]. Thus, by characterizing factors that influence brain activity, we may gain important insight with regards to how spatial navigation skills are learned and ultimately taught in the blind community.

These gaps in knowledge may be due to the fact that the combination of novel assistive technology development and clinical outcomes-based studies have not been extensively pursued. We propose to address these gaps through the development of (1) assistive technology that is more in-line with today's digital-driven approaches in accessing information and leveraging the educative potential of virtual reality-based learning, and (2) employing clinical trial-inspired study design features (e.g. randomization and masked assessments) to evaluate the efficacy of these assistive technologies.

## 2  Approach, Design, and Preliminary Results

### 2.1  Development and Refinement of the Current HAGA Prototype

Our current prototype (HAGA) represents a progressive evolution of a concept; namely, that non-visual sensory cues (i.e. audio and tactile) can be used as a means to acquire crucial sensory information and knowledge regarding the spatial layout of an environment. Interacting with this information in a controlled, safe, self-directed, and a motivating manner leads to behavioral gains that are not typically seen in more didactic or rote-based learning strategies. It is important to note that this proposed assistive technology is not meant (nor can it) replace traditional O&M training but rather, it is meant to serve as a complement. Compared to other approaches (such as tactile maps or GPS based systems), it has the advantage of allowing for self-directed exploration and survey prior to travel (and potentially real-time exploration when deployed on a mobile platform). The interaction is engaging and dynamic, beyond what is typically provided by verbal instruction or using a tactile map (which may be limited in terms of its accessibility). At the same time, it is not limited to outdoor environment use as is the case of GPS based systems. Finally, our approach encourages learning and promotes strategy development, rather than supporting device dependency and over-reliance.

Based on our previous findings, a survey of available assistive technology, and feedback from potential end users, and teachers of O&M, we have incorporated the following innovative features in our next generation platform Haptic Audio Game Application (HAGA): (1) a design to promote dynamic interaction and survey of spatial information using a self-directed exploratory strategy, (2) greater immersive sensory experience with full 3D sound and tactile/haptic feedback allowing for more robust acquisition and interaction with spatial contextual information (including high contrast visual environments for use with individuals with low vision), (3) mapping of complex, large scale, indoor and outdoor environments with multiple routes of travel, (4) adapted functionality to collect data within a neuroimaging scanner, including TTS commands and automated sequential loading of target routes and paths for block design data acquisition (typical for fMRI experiments). Finally, the use of the Unity game engine development software (http://unity3d.com/) allows for: (1) high stability and rapid prototyping of virtually any large scale, indoor and outdoor environment desired and with high ecological validity, (2) wide deployment on a variety of technology platforms and operating systems (including PC, Mac and mobile Android, iOS), and (3) no cost for development and support within an engaging open community forum with over 1 million developers (Fig. 2).

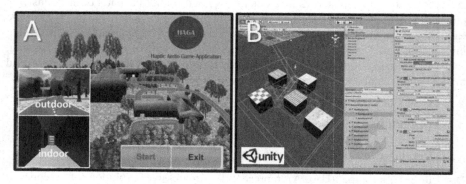

**Fig. 2.** (A) Haptic Audio Game Interface (HAGA) is a full 3D rendering of the indoor and outdoor campus (see inset figures) of the Carroll Center for the Blind. (B) the Unity gaming engine used to create HAGA allows for any environment to be rapidly rendered and audio sounds and tactile feedback to added for the purposes of exploring a large-scale environment.

Prior to assessing the effectiveness of the HAGA device, we carried out a usability evaluation of our current HAGA prototype. This was a combination of expert analysis and a series of user case studies (i.e. focus group of potential end users), the goal of which was to refine the usability of the device by identifying the most important features to be implemented and potential problems to be resolved prior to commencing the behavioral evaluation study. The expert usability analysis represents a formal evaluation of the device and typically separates technical factors (relating to system design and hardware/software considerations) from usability factors (relating to interface design and user experience). This serves to guide the development of the prototype by ensuring that good human-computer interaction principles are followed and that user-centered design is adopted from the onset. The formal report serves initially as a feedback loop for iterative software development efforts. Once finalized, the system design is then benchmarked against actual data to ensure key usability principles are retained and has evolved into the most usable and acceptable device possible. The second stage is a series of user case studies (i.e. focus groups) conducted with the refined prototype. Feedback on its acceptability, the success of the user interface and application design choices will be assessed through a three-part post-test questionnaire. The self-report questionnaire contains both closed-ended statements asking users to provide answers on a 1 to 7 Likert scale, as well as open-ended questions to elicit unformatted feedback regarding the system. The questions focus on three areas:

(i) prototype user-interface design (user feedback on the hardware, input/output devices including the audio and vibro-tactile interface), (ii) scenario design (addressing common issues specific to navigation needs such as devising alternate strategies if the device fails), and (iii) overall acceptability (to determine the overall user-centered success of the system). Although the evaluation typically contains only a small number of participants and is still on-going, the combination of expert usability analysis and user case series is a well-established approach in isolating the main problems related to user-centered design. In general, an estimated 3-5 participants are needed to identify over 75 % of user interface problems in usability [32].

## 2.2   Navigation with HAGA

The spatial layout of the target environment is learned through self-directed navigation using HAGA. Specifically, blind participants use a combination of keyboard strokes and/or a joystick (an Xbox[TM] controller with "rumble" vibration feature) to move through the virtual environment (see Fig. 1C). Each step in HAGA is meant to represent one typical step in real physical space. Footstep sounds are used to help the user determine how fast they are moving, and what surface materials they are walking on (e.g. hard sole sounds on cement, soft sole sounds on carpet, crushing leaves on grass). Iconic spatialized audio cues are delivered after every step taken to help the user gain a sense of the spatial layout of objects and rooms surrounding them and their relative orientation (e.g. a door knocking sound in the left stereo channel is heard as the player walks past a door on their left, walking by the cafeteria elicits a Doppler-like effect of chatter noises and clanging dishes). These iconic and spatialized sounds serve as "audio beacons" or landmarks to help the user capture the overall layout of the area. At any time, the user can also query "what is front of me?" and "where am I?" via key strokes to access TTS information identifying obstacles as well as heading cues for various exits and buildings. Vibratory feedback (rumble feature of the joystick) is used to alert the user of obstacles encountered and using varying pulsing frequencies identifies their orientation relative to that obstacle (i.e. high frequency for head-on and lower frequency while strafing). Orientation information is based on clock hour headings (i.e. "12" is straight ahead) and "beeps" for every 30° of turning angle, to provide a consistent egocentric based frame of reference during navigation. Finally, given that the virtual environment is rendered using a gaming engine that creates a visual first person 3D perspective, there is also the possibility to incorporate high contrast, high magnification visual features that can be used by individuals with low vision.

## 2.3   Subject Recruitment and Testing Environment

Testing will be carried out at the Carroll Center for the Blind (Newton, MA) where clients with profound vision loss and low vision are continuously enrolled throughout the year. The campus covers an area over 430,000 sq ft and has multiple sidewalk and road paths communicating between 4 large buildings (Fig. 3A). For the behavioral assessment, early and late blind as well as low vision individuals (based on current

WHO definitions; males and females aged between 14 and 45 years old) will be invited to participate in the study. Causes of blindness will vary between subjects however, retinopathy of prematurity, optic nerve hypoplasia, and macular degeneration will likely be common causes. Early blind subjects will be defined as individuals with profound visual deprivation occurring before the age of three (i.e. before language development). The lower limit for late blind will be defined as 14 years old. These age limit definitions have been used in previous investigations as a means to dichotomize the effect of prior visual experience on development (see [33] for discussion).

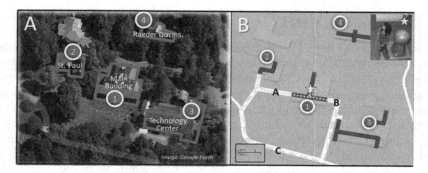

**Fig. 3.** Preliminary results with HAGA used for the purposes of learning the indoor and outdoor spatial layout of the Carroll Center campus. **(A)** Aerial view of campus showing the 4 main buildings and possible routes. **(B)** Results from a navigation task assessment in an early blind individual following exploration and route learning with HAGA. Possible outdoor (white) and indoor (blue) routes are shown. Starting from the meeting point in the main building (star), the participant was able to successfully navigate to the entrance of the St. Paul building (path "A", time: 1 min, 32 s). In a second task, the same individual was able to navigate from the starting point (star) to the entrance of the technology center (path "B", time: 1 min, 15 s). In a second set of navigation tasks, the same participant was asked to find an alternate path from the entrance of the technology center to the St. Paul building (i.e. not crossing through the main building). This was accomplished successfully despite not being explicitly taught the route (see path "C", time 2 min: 33).

## 2.4  Real-World Navigation Task Assessment and Preliminary Results

Eligible participants will be introduced to the HAGA software and familiarized with the function keys and controls. Each participant will interact with HAGA for 90 min (3, 30 min or 2, 45 min sessions) over a 2 day period. This training time was determined based on previous and current pilot study work and deemed as sufficient to allow a user to explore the entire campus. During the training period (i.e. HAGA exploration), early and late blind participants will be blindfolded to minimize possible confounding due to residual visual function.

After the training sessions, participants will then be evaluated on their understanding of the campus layout by carrying out a series navigation tasks (indoor and outdoor) on the Carroll Center campus. For this behavioral assessment phase, all participants will be blindfolded to minimize possible confounding related to residual visual function on navigation task performance. Subjects will be allowed to use a cane as a means of mobility assistance and remain blindfolded throughout the assessment. Subjects will also be followed by an experienced investigator filming the path taken and to ensure their safety, as well as provide further task instructions. On a first level assessment (task 1), navigation performance will be assessed by carrying out a series of 10 predetermined origin-target routes presented in random order. The routes will be of comparable difficulty in terms of distance (comprising of both indoor and outdoor components) and complexity (i.e. number of turns and potential obstacles) and a maximum travel time of 6 min will be allowed. For each path, the subject will be brought to a specific starting point and told to navigate to a target destination using the shortest route possible. In a second level assessment (task 2), participants will be escorted (by a sighted guide) from a point of origin to a target location on campus. They will then be asked to navigate back to the point of origin using an alternate path (i.e. reminiscent of what is referred to in O&M as a "drop-off" task). Again, a series of 10 predetermined origin-target paths (presented in a random order) will be carried out and a maximum travel time of 6 min will allowed for each route.

This later set "drop off" tasks will serve as a means to assess how well the subject can mentally manipulate their cognitive map for the purposes of determining alternate routes (note a counterbalanced design between the two tasks will be carried out in order to minimize the potential of a learning or "carry over" effects from sequential task assessments). For these behavioral assessments, the primary outcome of interest will be mean success in completing the origin-target route pairs (expressed as percent correct). Secondary outcomes will include mean time to destination (quantified by absolute travel time to target as well as preferred walking speed [34, 35]), and route accuracy (quantified by the number of extra turns and unintended collisions [36]). This evaluation approach has been used successfully to quantify performance in similar navigation studies investigating the effectiveness of assistive technology (e.g. [21, 37]). Navigation performance will be scored by a second investigator following the study participant. Timing commences once the participant takes their first step and stops when they verbally report that they have arrived at the target destination.

In a pilot study, an early blind participant (previously unfamiliar with the Carroll Campus) freely interacted with HAGA for 45 min and was asked to navigate a series of pre-determined origin-target paths and alternate routes. Preliminary results carried out with this early blind participant suggest that following exploration using HAGA, they were able to transfer their acquired spatial knowledge by successfully arriving to a series of target destinations. Furthermore, when asked to find an alternative route, they were able to do so despite never being explicitly taught the existence of the path (Fig. 3B). This later observation has important practical and safety implications for O&M in general. Consider the situation where an individual has to find an alternative route when a known path from memory is inaccessible. An individual that has a more robust cognitive understanding of inter-spatial relationships that characterize their surrounding environment will be able to devise and access alternative paths when needed.

## 3  Discussion and Conclusions

We are investigating cognitive spatial mapping skills in people who are blind through the use of virtual navigation and assessing the transference of acquired spatial knowledge in large-scale, real-world navigation tasks. Towards this goal, we have developed a user-centered, computer-based, navigation software platform called Haptic Audio Game Application (HAGA). Using a combination of both iconic and spatialized auditory cues and vibro-tactile feedback, a user is able to survey and build a cognitive spatial map of the surrounding environment. Preliminary testing suggests that a blind user can transfer acquired spatial information as assessed by their performance on a series of physical navigation tasks carried out in the actual target environment that was explored virtually.

While the investigation is ongoing, we believe the strength of the study is related to (1) the user-centered and (2) evidence-based clinical trial designs being employed. By implicating potential end-users of the software early in the design and refinement, we are more likely to develop assistive technology that will enjoy greater adoption by the blind community. Second, by implementing evidence-based study design principles in the evaluation of navigation performance, we are in a position to better evaluate the true efficacy of the software for its intended purpose and avoid the effect of potential confounders such prior visual experience and familiarity with technology on observed performance.

We are also cognizant of potential limitations with this study. For example, we have found it necessary to place an upper limit on the time allotted for navigation task assessment. While this has not been an issue in our past studies, participants in this study will be navigating in a much larger environment (including outdoor spaces) and thus there is the risk that a greater number of unsuccessful and timed out runs will occur. In general, this can be avoided by established a rigorous training program and evaluating participants performance on virtual navigation tasks prior to moving to the physical navigation assessments. By ensuring that a minimal level of performance and understanding of the spatial layout are achieved, testing in the actual physical environment can be more robust and reliable.

In summary, our interest in developing an interface that combines audio and tactile/haptic sensory information, and indeed, this is a core design feature of the next generation assistive device proposed here. From a rehabilitation standpoint, this study has the potential of developing into a relatively simple, novel, engaging and cost effective means to supplement classic O&M training for the blind. In line with our goal of developing this approach as a viable assistive technology tool, we are also looking at expanding this platform to model public spaces and environments such as airports and public transit systems.

**Acknowledgement.** This work was supported by an NIH/NEI RO1 GRANT EY019924 (Lotfi B. Merabet) and also funded by the Chilean National Fund for Scientific and Technological Development, Fondecyt HYPERLINK "tel:1150898" 1150898; and the Basal Funds for Centers of Excellence, FB0003 project, from the Associative Research Program of CONICYT, Chile. (Jaime Sánchez). The authors would like to thank the research participants, as well as Rabih Dow, Padma Rajagopal and the staff of the Carroll Center for the Blind (Newton MA, USA) for their support in carrying out this research.

# References

1. Blasch, B.B., Wiener, W.R., Welsh, R.L.: Foundations of Orientation and Mobility, 2nd ed., xx, 775 p. AFB Press, New York (1997)
2. Landau, B., Gleitman, H., Spelke, E.: Spatial knowledge and geometric representation in a child blind from birth. Science 213(4513), 1275–1278 (1981)
3. Strelow, E.R.: What is needed for a theory of mobility: direct perception and cognitive maps–lessons from the blind. Psychol. Rev. 92(2), 226–248 (1985)
4. Tolman, E.C.: Cognitive maps in rats and men. Psychol. Rev. 55(4), 189–208 (1948)
5. Ashmead, D.H., Hill, E.W., Talor, C.R.: Obstacle perception by congenitally blind children. Percept. Psychophys. 46(5), 425–433 (1989)
6. Ashmead, D.H., et al.: Spatial hearing in children with visual disabilities. Perception 27(1), 105–122 (1998)
7. Thinus-Blanc, C., Gaunet, F.: Representation of space in blind persons: vision as a spatial sense? Psychol. Bull. 121(1), 20–42 (1997)
8. Pasqualotto, A., Proulx, M.J.: The role of visual experience for the neural basis of spatial cognition. Neurosci. Biobehav. Rev. 36(4), 1179–1187 (2012)
9. Axelrod, S.: Effects of early blindness; performance of blind and sighted children on tactile and auditory tasks, ix, 83 p. American Foundation for the Blind, New York (1959)
10. Loomis, J.M., Klatzky, R.L., Golledge, R.G.: Navigating without vision: basic and applied research. Optom. Vis. Sci. 78(5), 282–289 (2001)
11. Fortin, M., et al.: Wayfinding in the blind: larger hippocampal volume and supranormal spatial navigation. Brain 131(Pt 11), 2995–3005 (2008)
12. Bavelier, D., Green, C.S., Dye, M.W.: Children, wired: for better and for worse. Neuron 67 (5), 692–701 (2010)
13. Bavelier, D., et al.: Brains on video games. Nat. Rev. Neurosci. 12(12), 763–768 (2011)
14. Dede, C.: Immersive interfaces for engagement and learning. Science 323(5910), 66–69 (2009)
15. Shaffer, D.W., et al.: Video games and the future of learning. Phi Delta Kappan 87, 104–111 (2005)
16. Lange, B., et al.: Designing informed game-based rehabilitation tasks leveraging advances in virtual reality. Disabil. Rehabil. 34, 1863–1870 (2012)
17. Mayo, M.J.: Video games: a route to large-scale STEM education? Science 323(5910), 79–82 (2009)
18. Giudice, N.A., Bakdash, J.Z., Legge, G.E.: Wayfinding with words: spatial learning and navigation using dynamically updated verbal descriptions. Psychol. Res. 71(3), 347–358 (2007)
19. Ohuchi, M., et al.: Cognitive-map formation of blind persons in a virtual sound environment. In: Proceedings of the 12th International Conference on Auditory Display, London, UK (2006)
20. Riehle, T.H., Lichter, P., Giudice, N.A.: An indoor navigation system to support the visually impaired. Conf. Proc. IEEE Eng. Med. Biol. Soc. 1, 4435–4438 (2008)
21. Legge, G.E., et al.: Indoor navigation by people with visual impairment using a digital sign system. PLoS ONE 8(10), e76783 (2013)
22. Johnson, L.A., Higgins, C.M.: A navigation aid for the blind using tactile-visual sensory substitution. Conf. Proc. IEEE Eng. Med. Biol. Soc. 1, 6289–6292 (2006)
23. Lahav, O.: Using virtual environment to improve spatial perception by people who are blind. Cyberpsychol. Behav. 9(2), 174–177 (2006)

24. Pissaloux, E., et al.: Space cognitive map as a tool for navigation for visually impaired. Conf. Proc. IEEE Eng. Med. Biol. Soc. **1**, 4913–4916 (2006)
25. Driver, J., Noesselt, T.: Multisensory interplay reveals crossmodal influences on 'sensory-specific' brain regions, neural responses, and judgments. Neuron **57**(1), 11–23 (2008)
26. Sanchez, J., Lumbreras, M.: 3D aural interactive hyperstories for blind children. Int. J. Virtual Reality **4**(1), 20–28 (1998)
27. Connors, E.C., et al.: Virtual environments for the transfer of navigation skills in the blind: a comparison of directed instruction vs. video game based learning approaches. Front. Hum. Neurosci. **8**, 223 (2014)
28. Connors, E.C., et al.: Action video game play and transfer of navigation and spatial cognition skills in adolescents who are blind. Front. Hum. Neurosci. **8**, 133 (2014)
29. Connors, E.C., et al.: Development of an audio-based virtual gaming environment to assist with navigation skills in the blind. J. Visualized Exp. JoVE **73** (2013)
30. Merabet, L.B., et al.: Teaching the blind to find their way by playing video games. PLoS ONE **7**(9), e44958 (2012)
31. Halko, M.A., et al.: Real world navigation independence in the early blind correlates with differential brain activity associated with virtual navigation. Hum. Brain Mapp. **35**(6), 2768–2778 (2014)
32. Shneiderman, B., Plaisant, C., Jacobs, S.: Designing the User Interface: Strategies for Effective Human-Computer Interaction, 5th edn. Addison Wesley, Boston (2009)
33. Merabet, L.B., Pascual-Leone, A.: Neural reorganization following sensory loss: the opportunity of change. Nat. Rev. Neurosci. **11**(1), 44–52 (2010)
34. Beggs, W.D.: Psychological correlates of walking speed in the visually impaired. Ergonomics **34**(1), 91–102 (1991)
35. Soong, G.P., Lovie-Kitchin, J.E., Brown, B.: Preferred walking speed for assessment of mobility performance: sighted guide versus non-sighted guide techniques. Clin. Exp. Optom. **83**(5), 279–282 (2000)
36. Hartong, D.T., et al.: Improved mobility and independence of night-blind people using night-vision goggles. Invest. Ophthalmol. Vis. Sci. **45**(6), 1725–1731 (2004)
37. Kalia, A.A., et al.: Assessment of indoor route-finding technology for people with visual impairment. J. Vis. Impairment Blindness **104**(3), 135–147 (2010)

# Combining NFC and 3D Mapping to Enhance the Perception of Spatial Location for the Blind

Tânia Rocha[✉], Hugo Fernandes, Hugo Paredes, and João Barroso

INESC TEC and Universidade de Trás-os-Montes e Alto Douro,
Vila Real, Portugal
{trocha,hugof,hparedes,jbarroso}@utad.pt

**Abstract.** In this paper a 3D map solution combined with a mobile phone application is presented. This solution enables blind users to perceive their spatial location from tactile stimulation, but also contextual information from a mobile application that provides this information via mobile phone, using audio. In the proposed model, 3d map sections embedding NFC technology support the application scenario described in this work.

**Keywords:** Assistive technologies · Blind users · Navigation · 3D mapping · NFC

## 1 Introduction

Since 1990, the American Disability Act (ADA) determines that environments must be accessible to people with disabilities (Bentzen 2007; ADA 1990). In 1993, the United Nations (UN) publishes The Standard Rules on the Equalization of Opportunities for Persons with Disabilities, by focusing on accessibility and valuing it as a key area for equal participation (UN, 1993).

However, blind people are one of the most vulnerable groups of people with regard to physical accessibility. It is considerably difficult to define and specify navigation systems not only because of the risk of collision due to insufficient information but also for the complexity and time spent on planning alternative routes around obstacles (Loomis et al. 2007).

Visual disability has a major impact on individuals' quality of life, not only in their ability to work and develop personal relationships but most importantly regarding their mobility. There are 285 million people with visual impairments, worldwide (WHO 2014). Specifically, 39 million are blind people and 246 million suffer from low vision. According to World Health Organization (WHO), in their International Classification of Diseases, version 10, there are four levels of visual function: normal vision, moderate visual impairment, severe visual impairment and blindness (WHO 2010).

Due to the specific characteristics of their disability, blind people cannot interpret visual stimulus. That stimulus is very important for the interpretation of information about their spatial location. At the same time, navigation systems are generally designed to be used by people without disability, i.e., having no stimuli impairment. The blind are not the only group of people with difficulties in navigation and way

M. Antona and C. Stephanidis (Eds.): UAHCI 2016, Part III, LNCS 9739, pp. 607–615, 2016.
DOI: 10.1007/978-3-319-40238-3_58

finding. Elderly people are one of those groups (Hess 2005; Kirasic 2002), as well as the visually impaired (Helal et al. 2001; Golledge et al. 1996), dementia or Alzheimer's diseases (Rosenbaum et al. 2005; Pai 2006). Therefore, it is commonly accepted that there is a need to study solutions that can overcome the spatial barriers by creating forms of tactile learning, with the same goal. Blind people can very easily recognize three-dimensional shapes through tactile sensations (Teshima 2010).

In this context, we present a navigation solution for special location recognition based on 3D maps and NFC technology under development in project CE4BLIND (UTAP-EXPL/EEI-SII/0043/2014). This solution is aimed to allow blind users to perceive their spatial location from the tactile stimulation, but also with the use of an application that provides spatial information via mobile phone. To present this solution the paper is structured as follow: a background section where the main concepts about navigation for the blind are exposed, the proposed model and its description (3D maps features and NFC technology and finally some conclusions and future work.

## 2   Navigation for the Blind

Broadly, a navigation system consists of an artefact that enables a user to follow a predetermined path between an explicit origin and destination. Thus, the system needs to know the person's position and orientation, continuously, according to the environment and through to the final destination (Aslan and Krüger 2004; Rieser 2007). Furthermore, an effective navigation aims to ensure the best path based on a specific variable, such as: shortest distance, time, minimum cost, type of road, etc. (Teshima 2010).

In the literature we can find several research contributions using Geographic Information Systems (GIS) and Global Positioning System (GNS) -based navigation systems for the visually impaired (Golledge et al. 2004; Helal et al. 2001; Ponchillia et al. 2007; Blake 2011), as analyzed in the work of Teshima (2010). Some present non-visual spatial displays, for example: auditory (Kim et al. 2000; Marston et al. 2007); haptic (Loomis et al. 2007; Marston et al. 2007); and/or virtual acoustic displays (Kim and Song 2007).

Another technology used is Radio Frequency Identification (RFID) tagging. It is a solution presented in different studies (Willis and Helal 2005). However, some authors, such as Liao (2012) highlighted the disadvantages of this technology: an RFID information grid requires a short range communication (7 to 15-cm) and high density of tags (30 cm or 12 in apart) (Liao 2012).

Other studies proposed several assistive technologies to provide navigation assistance to the blind. For example, Wilson et al. (2007) presented a wearable audio navigation system that uses GPS technology, digital compass, cameras and a light sensor to transmit 3D audio cues that could help, not only the blind, but also the visually impaired (Wilson et al. 2007). Other example was a wearable tactile belt that has GPS, compass, inertial sensor, battery and small motors (Zelek and Holbein 2008). This belt provided effective navigational help for people with or without disabilities. Kim et al. (2010) presented an electronic cane with an integrated camera, ZigBee wireless radio and a RFID tag reader (Kim et al. 2010).

In their work, Voženílek et al. (2009) analysed characteristics of interpretation and perception of geospace by using tactile maps based on 3D printing. In this context, they present three types of tactile maps (all maps were coloured):

- "Map of type A is a tactile map printed by 3D printing technology (Contex 3D printers) as traditional relief tactile map with 5 mm thick background using both positive and negative relief with labelling by Braille letters.
- Map of type B is an inverse form of tactile map printed by 3D printing technology which will be used for casting type A tactile maps.
- Map of type C is a sound tactile map derived from map of type A posed onto box with digital voice records of geoinformation (attributes, navigations etc.) activated by touch on maps surface" (Voženílek et al. 2009).

Smartphone applications to assist the blind people are not a newly technology implemented. Liao (2012) presented a work that uses this equipment to help the blind at signalized intersections (Liao 2012).

Tactile Graphics, Touch graphics and the University of Buffalo presented a project that uses a similar technology to the one that is proposed here. A 3D mapping system which works with the tactile sense. In this project, 3D building models were developed on a horizontal map with sensing wires connected to a computer which helps users to localize places. Users must put their fingers on the buildings and the system reads the pressure sending signals to a computer which responds with an auditory stimulus, announcing the building's name and its particular paths (Fig. 1) (Tactile graphics et al., ONLINE).

**Fig. 1.** 3D map from tactile graphics, touch graphics and the University of Buffalo (Tactile graphics et al., ONLINE).

## 3   The Proposed Model

In the model proposed in this work two technologies are combined: 3D mapping and Near Field Communication (NFC), one that provides tactile stimulus and another which stimulates the auditory sense, respectively. A more detailed description is presented in the following sections. The objective is to enhance the spatial perception of the blind.

The overall setup assumes that the location of the user is estimated from a combination of several inputs, namely Global Navigation Satellite System (GNSS) and Radio Frequency Identification (RFID). The user carries an electronic white cane, such as the white cane developed in the Blavigator prototype (Faria et al. 2010; Fernandes et al. 2013a, b) which senses tags on a specific area of interest (such as touristic locations). The tags are placed on a topology that consists of connected lines and clusters, which globally compose a network of safe paths and points of interest. Locally, physically placed on each point of interest, a QR-code also provides information regarding each specific spot.

However, the current model is focused on the contribution that 3D mapping can give while creating a mental map of the environment, before the navigation itself occurs.

Concerning the 3D mapping, it can be created from the existing blueprints or floor plans and modelled with a 3D tool (software). In Fig. 2, we can see the first version of the proposed model with several elements modelled (Fig. 2).

**Fig. 2.** First version model of 3D maps

The second version was created with the intention of simplifying the model (Fig. 3).

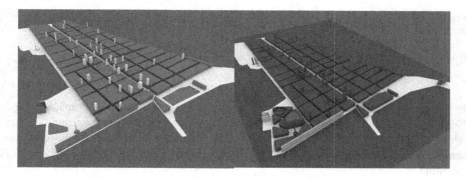

**Fig. 3.** First version model of 3D maps

The different heights of the various points of interest enable easy and fast tactile interpretation by a blind user, combining different textures of the various elements for a better memorization and usability of the attached label, which identifies the areas of special interest (Fig. 4).

**Fig. 4.** View details of the distinctive elements cemeteries (before textures)

The implementation of this map (or sculpture) creates extended visual value also for sighted users, without any visual impairment, as it provides an excellent catalogue, grouped by different colours, on the available points of interest in the infrastructure that can be visited. This accessible 3D map was designed with focus on universal design.

Specifically, the main objective was to create a 3d model to help blind people in their spatial perception. In this context, a plant in Computer Aided format was used. However, this blueprint needed to be adapted to ensure our modelling needs.

First, a graphic tool was used to erase unnecessary elements (such as adjacent buildings and urban furniture). This step was very important to highlight important areas and hide others, not so important. It was important to define the level of detail of the model because it is believed that too much detail could lead to an enormous amount of elements to be perceived, thus confusing the blind user. Also, with this software other elements were added to delimit the model (such as: background, map limits, and sections) and other complex elements which had to be redesigned following the original route. Areas with similar elements were joined into groups in order to facilitate their future recognition. All this redesign was made to simplify the model and making it 'lighter', providing a model that is as "low poly" as possible (Fig. 5).

After this process, the file was exported to an 3d modelling software. In this software the model was resized (width: 84 cm, length: 118 cm and height: 4 cm). After creating the solid faces, they were subsequently extruded with different values for each group (previously defined) in order to be properly recognized, according to the different types of elements. The maximum height size was defined to 4 cm.

As the model was designed as a universal design model, it is intended to be used as a guide for all tourists (not only for the blind), so different colors and textures were added to the different elements.

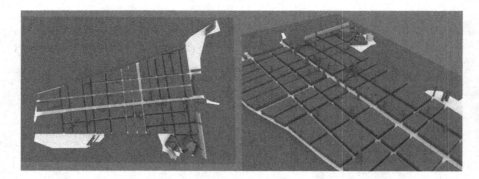

**Fig. 5.** Top view details

In terms of audio information, the model proposes the use of NFC technology embedded on the physical map to provide audio feedback. Near field communication (NFC) is a set of communication protocols that enable devices to establish communication by bringing them close to each other (4 cm, on average). Pervasive computing research has explored the potential benefits of creating a connection between the information that can be stored on the virtual world and elements that are present in the physical world (Want 2011). Typical applications are the communication of two devices for file sharing. Another application is the use of a mobile device to read an NFC enabled credit card, or tag. The latter is the feature used in the model proposed.

Using an NFC reader embedded on the electronic white cane, the blind can use the cane to obtain contextual information about each specific point of interest, marked in the map. The audio information is delivered by a mobile application, using information stored on the NFC tags. The NFC tags are placed physically on the 3D map, on strategic places regarding special points-of-interest, as Fig. 6 suggests. This helps the user on creating a mental map of the expected features to visit, or to expect, on the environment on which he intends to navigate.

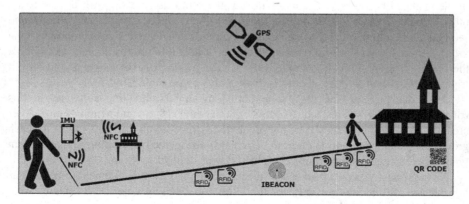

**Fig. 6.** Global model of the use of the technologies (3D mapping, NFC, RFID, iBeacon).

# 4   Conclusions and Future Work

This paper presented a model to enhance the perception of spatial location for the blind, combining NFC technology and 3D mapping. After analysing different, related, work and the technologies they presented as options an innovative solution is presented to connect new and old technologies that are believed to be an interesting and usable solution for blind people to use. In this context, as future work, the design of the textures and usability testing with the blind users will be made.

**Acknowledgments.** The paper is supported by the project CE4blind- Context extraction for the blind using computer vision, with project reference UTAP-EXPL/EEI-SII/0043/2014, a research grant with reference SFRH/BD/89759/2012.

# References

ADA - American Discrimination Act. To establish a clear and comprehensive prohibition of discrimination on the basis of disability (1990). Retrieved from https://www.gpo.gov/fdsys/pkg/STATUTE-104/pdf/STATUTE-104-Pg327.pdf. Accessed 10 Feb 2016

Aslan, I., Krüger, A.: The Bum Bag Navigator (BBN): an advanced pedestrian navigation system. In: Proceedings of AIMS 2004, Nottingham, U.K. (2004). Retrieved from: http://w5.cs.uni-sb.de/~baus/aims04/cameraready/P3.pdf. Accessed 10 Feb 2016

Bentzen, B.L.: Making the environment accessible to pedestrains who are visually impaired: policy research. In: Rieser, J.J., Ashmead, D.H., Ebner, F., Corn, A.L. (eds.) Blindness and Brain Plasticity in Navigation and Object Perception, pp. 313–333. Psychology Press, New York (2007)

Blake, L.: Proving his point. Star Tribune article (2011). Retrieved from: http://www.startribune.com/local/west/114846184.html?elr=KArksUUUoDEy3LGDiO7aiU. Accessed 11 Jan 2016

Faria, J., Lopes, S., Fernandes, H., Martins, P., Barroso, J.: Electronic white cane for blind people navigation assistance. In: World Automation Congress (WAC), pp. 1–7. IEEE, September 2010

Fernandes, H., Faria, J., Lopes, S. Martins, P., Barroso, J.: Electronic white cane for blind people navigation assistance. In: Proceedings of the World Automation Congress 2010, Kobe (2010)

Fernandes, H., Faria, J., Martins, P., Paredes, H., Barroso, J.: RFID mesh network as an infrastructure for location based services for the blind. In: Kurosu, M. (ed.) HCII/HCI 2013, Part V. LNCS, vol. 8008, pp. 39−45. Springer, Heidelberg (2013a)

Fernandes, H., Filipe, V., Costa, P., Barroso, J.: Location based services for the blind supported by RFID technology. In: 5th International Conference on DSAI2013 - Software Development and Technologies for Enhancing Accessibility and Fighting Info-exclusion, Vigo, Spain (2013b). Computer Science Journal, Elsevier

Golledge, R.G., Marston, J.R., Loomis, J.M., Klatzky, R.L.: Stated preferences for components of a personal guidance system for non-visual navigation. J. Vis. Impair. Blindness **98**(3), 135–147 (2004)

Golledge, R.G., Gärling, T.: Cogntive maps and urban travel. In: Hensher, D.A., Button, K.J., Haynes, K.E., Stopher, P.R. (eds.) Handbook of Transport Geography and Spatial Systems. Elsevier, Amsterdam (2004). chap. 28

Helal, A., Moore, S., Ramachandran, B.: Drishti: an integrated navigation system for visually impaired and disabled. In: Proceedings of the 5th International Symposium on Wearable Computer, Zurich, Switzerland (2001). Retrieved from: http://www.icta.ufl.edu/projects/publications/wearableConf.pdf. Accessed 20 Dec 2015

Hess, T.M.: Memory and aging in context. Psychol. Bull. **131**(3), 383–406 (2005)

Kim, Y., Kim, C.-H., Kim, B.: Design of an auditory guidance system for the blind with signal transformation from stereo ultrasonic to binaural audio. Artif. Life Robot. **4**(4), 220–226 (2000)

Kim, C.-G., Song, B.-S.: Design of a wearable walking-guide system for the blind. In: Proceedings of the 1st International Convention on Rehabilitation Engineering; Assistive Technology: in Conjunction with 1st Tan Tock Seng Hospital Neurorehabilitation Meeting, Singapore (2007)

Kirasic, K.C.: Age differences in adults' spatial abilities, learning environmental layout, and wayfinding behavior. Spat. Cogn. Comput. **2**(2), 117–134 (2002)

Klatzky, R.L., Beall, A.C., Loomis, J.M., Golledge, R.G., Philbeck, J.W.: Human navigation ability: tests of the encoding-error model of path integration. Spat. Cogn. Comput. **1**, 31–65 (1999)

Liao, C.-F.: Using a Smartphone App to Assist the Visually Impaired at Signalized Intersections. Final Report. Minnesota Traffic Observatory Laboratory. Department of Civil Engineering. University of Minnesota (2012)

Loomis, J.M., Golledge, R.G., Klatzky, R.L., Marston, J.R.: Assisting way finding in visually impaired travelers. In: Allen, G.L. (ed.) Applied Spatial Cognition: From Research to Cognitive Technology, pp. 179–203. Lawrence Erlbaum Associates, Mahwah, N.J. (2007)

Marston, J.R., Loomis, J.M., Klatzky, R.L., Golledge, R.G.: Nonvisual route following with guidance from a simple haptic or auditory display. J. Vis. Impair. Blindness **101**(4), 203–211 (2007)

Pai, M.C.: The neuropsychological studies of dementias in Taiwan: focus on wayfinding problems in Alzheimer's patients. Acta Neurol. Taiwan **15**(1), 58–60 (2006)

Rieser, J.J., Ashmead, D.H., Ebner, F., Corn, A.L.: Blindness and Brain Plasticity in Navigation and Object Perception. Psychology Press, New York (2007)

Rosenbaum, R.S., Gao, F., Richards, B., Black, S.E., Moscovitch, M.: Where to? remote memory for spatial relations and landmark identity in former taxi drivers with alzheimer's disease and encephalitis. J. Cogn. Neurosci. **17**(3), 446–462 (2005). The MIT Press

Ponchillia, P., Rak, E., Freeland, A., LaGrow, S.J.: Accessible GPS: reorientation and target location among users with visual impairments. J. Vis. Impair. Blindness **101**(7), 389–401 (2007)

Tactile graphics, Touch graphics & University of Buffalo (ONLINE). My engineering website (2015). Retrieved from: http://www.myengineering.net/technology/3d-map-talks-to-help-blind-people-find-their-way/. Accessed 16 Dec 2015

Teshima, Y.: Three-dimensional tactile models for blind people and recognition of 3D objects by touch: introduction to the special thematic session. In: Miesenberger, K., Klaus, J., Zagler, W., Karshmer, A. (eds.) ICCHP 2010, Part II. LNCS, vol. 6180, pp. 513–514. Springer, Heidelberg (2010)

Voženílek, V., Kozáková, M., Šťávová, Z., Ludíková, L., Růžičková, V., Finková, D.: 3D printing technology in tactile maps compiling (2009). Retrieved from: http://icaci.org/files/documents/ICC_proceedings/ICC2009/html/refer/8_4.pdf. Accessed 16 Dec 2015

Want, R.: Near field communication. IEEE Pervasive Comput. **10**(3), 4–7 (2011)

WHO-World Health Organization. Visual impairment and blindness. Fact Sheet n 282 (2014). Retrieved from: http://www.who.int/mediacentre/factsheets/fs282/en/. Accessed 16 Jan 2016

WHO-World Health Organization. International Statistical Classification of Diseases and Related Health Problems (ICD-10 -Vol. 2) (2010)

Willis, S., Helal, S.: RFID information grid for blind navigation and wayfinding. In: Ninth IEEE International Symposium on Wearable Computers, pp.34–37, Galway, Ireland (2005)

Wilson, J., Walker, B.N., Lindsay, J., Cambias, C., Dellaert, F.: SWAN: system for wearable audio navigation. In: Proceedings of the 11th International Symposium on Wearable Computers, Boston, MA (2007). Retrieved from: http://sonify.psych.gatech.edu/publications/pdfs/2007ISWC-Wilson-et-al-submitted.pdf. Accessed 10 Jan 2016

UN – United Nations. Declaração dos direitos das pessoas com deficiência (1975). Retrieved from: http://adg.org.pt/DECLAR. Accessed 10 Jan 2016

Zelek, J.S., Holbein, M.: Wearable tactile navigation system. US Patent Application number: 11/707,031. Publication number: US 2008/0120029 A1 (2008)

# Identifying Urban Mobility Challenges for the Visually Impaired with Mobile Monitoring of Multimodal Biosignals

Charalampos Saitis[✉] and Kyriaki Kalimeri

ISI Foundation, Turin, Italy
{charalampos.saitis,kyriaki.kalimeri}@isi.it

**Abstract.** In this study, we aim to better the user experience of the visually impaired when navigating in unfamiliar outdoor environments assisted by mobility technologies. We propose a framework for assessing their cognitive-emotional experience based on ambulatory monitoring and multimodal fusion of electroencephalography, electrodermal activity, and blood volume pulse signals. The proposed model is based on a random forest classifier which successfully infers in an automatic way the correct urban environment among eight predefined categories (AUROC 93 %). Geolocating the most predictive multimodal features that relate to cognitive load and stress, we provide further insights into the relationship of specific biomarkers with the environmental/situational factors that evoked them.

**Keywords:** Visual impairment · Multimodal · Data fusion · EEG · EDA · BVP · Classification · Stress · Cognitive load · Urban mobility

## 1 Introduction

Mobility in urban areas can be a challenging and emotionally stressful task for visually impaired people (VIP), especially when navigating in unfamiliar environments. Despite an increasing number of assistive technologies that help individuals with sight loss to augment their spatial awareness and wayfinding abilities when in move, very few systems provide a high degree of independence beyond known environments that would allow VIP to significantly achieve mobility and integrate in everyday active life [14,17]. Placing the visually impaired in the center of attention and exploiting recent developments in physiological computing and wearable wireless sensor devices, an extensive study was designed to better understand how people with sight loss perceive and interact with the urban space as manifested in their management of cognitive load and stress.

Orientation and mobility (O&M) in humans heavily relies on sight, which provides instantaneous, effortless access to anticipatory (e.g., stairs, turns, signs) and proactive (e.g., moving people, poles) information at various distances simultaneously [20]. Visually impaired pedestrians learn to obtain critical environmental information primarily through touch (sensing the ground surface with a white

© Springer International Publishing Switzerland 2016
M. Antona and C. Stephanidis (Eds.): UAHCI 2016, Part III, LNCS 9739, pp. 616–627, 2016.
DOI: 10.1007/978-3-319-40238-3_59

cane) and hearing (identifying and localising events and landmarks through sound). Mobility challenges can be summarized in four main problems: avoiding objects or obstacles (e.g., pedestrians, tree branches, improperly parked cars); detecting ground level changes (e.g., stairs, pavement edge or incline); negotiating street crossings (e.g., lack of curbs, traffic lights or sound signalling); and adapting to light variation (e.g., abrupt changes between different environments) [13,24]. Although these problems generally diminish with increased experience of an environment, they still make travelling in unfamiliar settings particularly challenging, often preventing VIP from going outdoors altogether.

Despite a significant amount of research on understanding the perceptual and neurocognitive mechanisms by which people with sight loss access and process wayfinding information [8], there is still little practical knowledge of how the management of mental load and stress relates to the wayfinding process itself. This is a critical aspect of designing mobility technologies that has only recently been considered essential in developing an understanding of how environmental factors affect the cognitive-emotional states of the VIP [27]. Two studies in the early 1970s suggested that some form of psychological rather than physical stress is responsible for increased heart rate in visually impaired versus sighted pedestrians [21,28]. More recently, examination of electrodermal activity [18] and electroencephalography [19] signals recorded from VIP during outdoor travel has shown that they experience psychological stress when walking on busy shopping streets, passing through large open areas, and crossing junctions.

Electrodermal activity (EDA) and heart rate (HR) are well-known indicators of physiological arousal and stress activation in affective computing and human-computer interfaces [5,25]. EDA is more sensitive to emotion related variations in arousal as opposed to physical stressors, which can be better reflected in the HR signal. Measurements of blood volume pulse (BVP), originally used to monitor HR, can also reflect transient processes in arousal and cognitions [22]. Electroencephalography (EEG), on the other hand, can provide neurophysiological markers of cognitive-emotional processes induced by stress and indicated by changes in rhythmic patterns of brain activity [15,16].

Taking advantage of the inherent and complementary properties of the EEG, EDA and BVP signals, this paper presents a multimodal approach to automatic inference of environmental conditions affecting VIP when navigating outdoors using a random forest classifier and features extracted from the three signals. The goal of the study was to discover biomarkers that can be used to detect shifts in emotional stress and cognitive load between different urban environments and situations. Aligning this information with GPS coordinates, we further studied the relationship of specific biomarkers with the environmental/situational factors that evoked them.

## 2    Design and Materials

A route was charted in the city centre of Reykjavik in Iceland (see Fig. 1) with the assistance of caretakers and O&M instructors to take the VIP through situations where different levels of stress were likely to occur. Accordingly, the

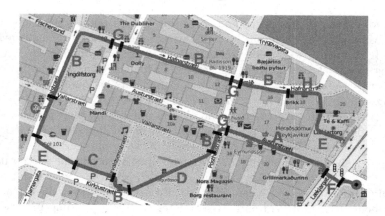

**Fig. 1.** A map of the charted route in the city centre of Reykjavik in Iceland using the OpenStreetMap (OSM) collaborative project (https://www.openstreetmap.org/). Letters depict the different urban environments reported in Table 1; black bars indicate where they start/end; the red-black dot shows the starting point of the walk. (Color figure online)

route comprised eight distinct urban environments representable of a variety of mobility challenges, which can be grouped in three higher-level categories (see Table 1). The route was approximately 1 km long and took on average 13 min 44 s to walk (range = 9–19 min).

Eight VIP with different degrees of sight loss participated in the study (5 female; average age = 39 yrs, range = 22–51 yrs; relevant demographic characteristics are reported in Table 2). To help make them feel comfortable and safe, they were encouraged to walk as usual using their white canes and were accompanied by their familiar O&M instructor. Participants reported having no general health issues. They were instructed to avoid smoking normal or e-cigarettes and consuming caffeine or sugar (e.g., coffee, coke, chocolate) approximately 1 h prior to the walk. Recruitment was based on volunteering and all VIP were capable of giving free and informed consent. The study was approved by the National Bioethics Committee of Iceland. All data was anonymized before analysis.

EEG was recorded using the Emotiv EPOC+, a mobile headset with 16 passive electrodes registering over the 10–20 system locations AF3, F7, F3, FC5, T7, P3 (CMS), P7, O1, O2, P8, P4 (DRL), T8, FC6, F4, F8, and FC4 (sampling rate $f_s$ = 128 Hz). Given the practical constraints involved in an outdoor mobility study, EPOC+ was chosen because it provides a good compromise between performance (i.e., number of channels and scientific validity of the acquired EEG signals) and usability (i.e., outdoor portability, preparation time and user comfort) with respect to other commercial wireless EEG systems [1,9–11].

Along with the Emotiv headset, participants were asked to wear the Empatica E4 wristband [12]. E4 measures the EDA signal through 2 ventral (inner) wrist electrodes ($f_s$ = 4 Hz) and the BVP through a dorsal (outer) wrist

**Table 1.** Descriptions and mobility challenges of the different urban environments along the charted route.

|   | Environment | Objects | Ground | Surroundings |
|---|---|---|---|---|
| A | Shopping street | People, ads, chairs, tables, poles | ramps | |
| B | Small street | People, poles, ads | ramps | Blocked passageway |
| C | Narrow alley | People, chairs, tables, street ads, trash bins, flower planters | stairs going down | parked cars |
| D | Urban park | People, tree branches, poles, flower planters | | blocked passageway |
| E | Open space | People, flower planters | stairs going up | blocked passageway |
| F | Crossing main road with traffic lights | People | | |
| G | Crossing small street without traffic lights | People | uneven pavement, detecting edges | |
| H | Construction alley | People | ramps | construction |

photoplethysmography (PPG) sensor ($f_s = 64$ Hz). The wristband also includes an infrared thermopile sensor and a 3-axis accelerometer. E4 is currently the only commercial multi-sensor device developed based on extended scientific research in the areas of psychophysiology and physiological computing. Additionally, it has a cable-free, watch-like design, which makes it easier and more aesthetically pleasant to wear, and thus better fitted to use in outdoor measurements as compared to other wearable devices. Participants were asked to wear the wristband on the non-dominant hand to minimize motion artifacts related to handling the white cane [5].

Participants walked the charted route twice for training purposes. Directions were only provided during the first walk to help the VIP familiarize with the route. They were instructed to avoid unnecessary head movements and hand gestures as well as talking to their O&M instructor unless there was an emergency. Video and audio were registered by means of a smartphone camera to facilitate data annotation (observing behaviours across the different urban environments) and synchronization (start/end of walk, urban environments and obstacles). In addition, GPS coordinates were logged via a Garmin GPSMAP-64s unit at a rate of 1 registration per second. At the end of the second walk, participants were asked to describe stressful moments along the route.

**Table 2.** Demographic characteristics of participants and their every day mobility patterns.

| ID | Age | Degree (time) of sight loss[a] | Travel alone outdoors | Travel alone in unfamiliar routes | Mobility aid |
|----|-----|-------------------------------|----------------------|-----------------------------------|--------------|
| P1 | 51 | 3 (> 3 yrs old) | Almost daily | Very seldom | Cane, dog |
| P2 | 36 | 3 (< 3 yrs old) | Almost daily | Almost daily | Cane |
| P3 | 45 | 4 (at birth) | Almost daily | Very seldom | Cane |
| P4 | 28 | 4 (at birth) | Weekly | Very seldom | Cane |
| P5 | 41 | 4 (at birth) | Almost daily | Weekly | Cane |
| P6 | 22 | 3 (> 3 yrs old) | Almost daily | Weekly | None |
| P7 | 44 | 5 (at birth) | Almost daily | Very seldom | Cane, dog |
| P8 | 50 | 2 (at birth) | Almost daily | Almost daily | Cane |

[a]1: vision is less than 30 % and more than 10 %; 2: vision is less than 10 % and more than 5 %; 3: vision is less than 5 % and more than being able to count fingers less than one meter away; 4: not being able to count fingers less than one meter away; 5: no light perception (WHO ICD-10 version:2016).

# 3    Data Analysis and Experiments

The goal of the data analysis was to explore features and markers from the collected brain and body signals which can be used to detect cognitive load and stress in humans during outdoor physical activity. While the relationship between unimodal physiological signals and psychological arousal has been studied extensively, the detection of stress from fusing multimodal biosignal streams has not been comparatively investigated. Specifically, the analysis focused on EEG (all 14 channels), EDA, and BVP data.

## 3.1    Signal Processing and Feature Extraction

The Emotiv EPOC+ system involves a number of internal signal conditioning steps. Analogue signals are first high-pass filtered with a 0.16 Hz cut-off, pre-amplified, low-pass filtered with a 83 Hz cut-off, and sampled at 2048 Hz. Digital signals are then notch-filtered at 50/60 Hz and down-sampled to 128 Hz prior to transmission. In this study, the EEG data obtained from the headset was time-domain interpolated using the Fast Fourier Transform (FFT) to account for missing samples due to connectivity issues. Interpolated signals were then normalized to decrease inter-individual variance. For each of the 14 channels, the power spectral intensity (PSI) [23] in each of the $\delta(0.5-4\,\text{Hz})$, $\theta(4-7\,\text{Hz})$, $\alpha(7-12\,\text{Hz})$, and $\beta(12-30\,\text{Hz})$ bands was computed using the PyEEG open source Python module [2]. The PSI of the $k$th band is defined as

$$\text{PSI}_k = \sum_{i=|N(f_k/f_s)|}^{|N(f_{k+1}/f_s)|} |X_i|,\ k = 1, 2, \ldots, K-1$$

where $f_s$ is the sampling rate, $N$ is the time series length, $|X_1, X_2, \ldots, X_N|$ is the FFT of the series, and $K$ is the total number of bands. In total, 56 EEG features were computed.

A measurement of skin conductance (SC) is characterized by two types of behaviour: short-lasting phasic responses (SCRs; can be thought of as rapidly changing peaks) and a long-term tonic level (SCL; can be thought of as the underlying slow-changing level in the absence of phasic activity). Another characteristic is the superposition of subsequent SCRs (i.e., one SCR emerges on top of the preceding one), typically observed in states of high arousal [5]. Skin conductance data obtained from the E4 was first low-pass filtered (1st order Butterworth, $f_c = 0.6$ Hz) to remove steep peaks stemming from artifacts and subsequently min-max normalized to reduce inter-individual variance [7]. Conditioned SC signals were then decomposed into continuous components of phasic and tonic EDA using a deconvolution-based method implemented in Ledalab, a Matlab based toolbox [4]. Six features were extracted: number of SCRs (hereinafter SCRs), sum of their amplitudes (AS), average phasic EDA (PA), maximum phasic EDA (PM), time-integrated phasic EDA (ISCR), and mean tonic EDA (TonicMean).

The BVP signal recorded by the E4 PPG sensor is preprocessed on board using a proprietary motion artifact removal technique [12]. No further conditioning was implemented and the reported data (i.e., BVP amplitude) was used directly as a feature of cardiovascular activity.

## 3.2   Classification Design

In order to identify automatically the affective meaning of an urban space based on biosignals recorded from VIP walking through it, we postulated the study as a supervised classification process. A widely-used ensemble learning method for classification was employed, namely Random Forest (RF) classifier [6], selected due to its ability to deal with possibly correlated predictor variables as well as because it provides a straightforward assess of the variable importances. For each of the distinct environments described in Table 1, each time point of the corresponding biosignal data was annotated based on a binary schema per second, where "1" signalled the presence of the participant in the given environment at the given time point and "0" otherwise.

A series of experiments were designed to assess and compare the predictive power of each modality (EEG, EDA or BVP) as well as of their fusion in a feature-level basis, in both single-class and multi-class scenarios (see Table 3). The adjustment of the two most important parameters of RF was performed by means of grid search parameter estimation with 5 fold cross validation. We exploited the effect of the number of estimators $[150, 300, 600]$ as well as the effect of the maximum number of features $[.5, 1, 2] * \sqrt{NumberOfFeatures}$. Overall, the optimum number of estimators was 300 and the maximum number of features was set equal to the total number of features for each experiment.

For each experiment we estimated the relative rank (i.e. depth), as emerged from the "Gini" impurity function, of each feature in order to assess the rela-

**Table 3.** Definitions of the classification models assessed for the prediction of each environment independently (single-class scenario) or all environments at the same time (multi-class scenario).

| | |
|---|---|
| Exp. I | Single-class classification using as predictors the unimodal features of EEG power spectral intensity ($N = 56$) |
| Exp. II | Single-class classification using as predictors the unimodal features extracted from the EDA ($N = 6$). |
| Exp. III | Single-class classification using as predictors the unimodal raw EDA and BVP signals ($N = 2$). |
| Exp. IV | Single-class classification using feature-level multi-modal fusion of EEG, EDA, and BVP features ($N = 63$). The prediction is made on single-class binary target variables as before. |
| Exp. V | Multi-class classification using feature-level multi-modal fusion of EEG, EDA, and BVP features ($N = 63$). |

tive importance of that feature to the predictability of the target variable [6]. We trained one model for each of the single-class cases and one for the multi-class experiment following a 5 folds cross-validation schema, where the 80 % of the data points were used for training and the 20 % for testing, with data shuffling in order to avoid dependencies in consecutive data points. The best model is chosen as the one that maximised the area under of the receiver operating characteristic (AUROC) weighted statistic, taking into account the lack of balance between the labels.

## 3.3   Results

Table 4 summarises the AUROC weighted metric for all the experiments. Both modalities (Exps. I–III) are predictive of the distinct environments, however, the fusion of the two modalities gave particularly high results, not only in the one-versus-all scenario (Exp. IV) but also in the multi-class classification (Exp. V). Figure 2a depicts the weighted ROC curves of the latter in an one-against-all binary scenario, assessing the qualitative performance of each class. Interestingly, we note that the model performs equally well for all classes showing proof of its stability.

Figure 2b depicts the ten most predictive features of Exp. V. The feature importances were estimated also for all experiments and the most predictive ones appear always with the highest ranks. Interestingly, we note that the features related to skin conductance are the most predictive, with spectral power of the $\beta$ brainwaves further dominating predictions. Although real-time EEG acquisition may be subject to very noisy signals, this finding is in line with the neuroscientific literature. A recent study on cognition and cortical activity after mental stress demonstrated that low amplitude beta waves with multiple and varying frequencies are often associated with active, busy, or anxious thinking and active concentration [3]. Another study confirmed that in subjects with high stress both baseline EEG (low frequency wave) and EEG during a stressful task

**Table 4.** Classification AUROC weighted metric for all the environments across the various experiments. Exp. IV with feature fusion at level base outperforms all other models almost in all environments closely followed by Exp. II. The reported numbers refer to the mean AUROC over all folds in percentile and in parenthesis the standard deviation is reported.

| Environment | Exp. I | Exp. II | Exp. III | Exp. IV | Exp. V |
|---|---|---|---|---|---|
| Construction alley (H) | 90 (0.9) | 96 (1.5) | 84 (1.0) | **97 (1.1)** | |
| Crossing main road (F) | 82 (2.0) | 93 (0.7) | 84 (2.0) | **94 (0.7)** | |
| Crossing small street (G) | 65 (2.9) | **83 (1.6)** | 71 (2.9) | 74 (3.0) | |
| Narrow alley (C) | 74 (1.2) | 87 (0.6) | 79 (1.5) | **89 (1.1)** | |
| Open space (E) | 77 (1.4) | **88 (1.4)** | 76 (0.7) | **88 (0.7)** | |
| Shopping street (A) | 83 (1.1) | 92 (0.3) | 84 (1.1) | **95 (0.4)** | |
| Small street (B) | 80 (0.8) | 85 (1.1) | 75 (0.6) | **89 (1.0)** | |
| Urban park (D) | 76 (1.0) | 89 (0.6) | 83 (1.4) | **93 (1.3)** | |
| All environments | | | | | 93 (0.5) |

(high frequency wave) were beta waves [16]. Theta waves were also observed during the stressful task and attributed to frustration and disappointment. This finding is in line with the fourth most important feature in the multi-class classification, which is a $\theta$ wave.

## 3.4  Visualising Biomarker Density Distributions

To better understand the properties of the most predictive features that emerged from the classification experiments as well as the intensity of the cognitive-emotional responses they express, we assigned feature values to pairs of latitude and longitude coordinates based on recorded timestamps and assessed their geographical distributions by means of weighted kernel density estimation.

The recorded GPS traces were subject to noise due to our request for high sampling rate (1 Hz), therefore each trace was corrected by its Euclidean projection onto a reference route. The high sampling rate allowed us to immediately observe increased concentrations of GPS points when the VIP had to cross a main road (environment F, see Table 1), pass along parked cars in a narrow alley after the urban park (C), walk up and down stairs (E), or pass through a narrow area between construction works (H). In fact, these are the same situations reported as stressful by the participants themselves at the end of the study. Geographic information methods offer great promise in objectively measuring and studying the relationship of biomarkers to human behaviour in terms of physical and transport-related activity.

Let $\{\mathbf{x}_1, \mathbf{x}_2, \ldots, \mathbf{x}_n\}$ be an independent random sample drawn from some distribution with density function $f(\mathbf{x})$ defined on $\mathbb{R}^d$. The (multivariate) weighted kernel density estimate of $f$ is defined in [26] as:

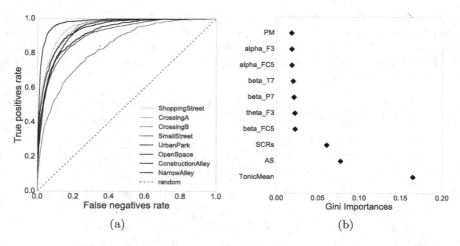

(a)                                          (b)

**Fig. 2.** (a) One against all ROC curves for each one of the classes in Exp. V. The overall AUROC weighted metric for the multi-class classification of environments is 93(0.5) and, importantly, the trained model seems able to learn equally well all the different environments. (b) Feature importances in Exp. V. Mean tonic EDA (TonicMean), number of SCRs (SCRs) and the sum of their amplitudes (AS) emerged as indicative features also in Exps. II–IV.

$$\hat{f}_H(\mathbf{x}) = \frac{1}{n} \sum_{i=1}^{n} w(\mathbf{x}_i, \mathbf{w}) \, K_H(\mathbf{x} - \mathbf{x}_i)$$

where $K$ is a kernel function, $H > 0$ is a symmetric $d \times d$ matrix which controls the bandwidth (or smoothing) of the estimate, $K_H(\mathbf{x}) = |H|^{-1/2} K(H^{-1/2} \mathbf{x})$, and $w$ is a function weighting each data point in the sample with a value from $\mathbf{w} \in \mathbb{R}^m$, $m \leq d$. A popular choice for $K$ is the Gaussian (or normal) kernel, which was also applied here.

The three most predictive features were mean tonic EDA (TonicMean), number of SCRs (SCRs) and the sum of their amplitudes (AS). For each of them, using the values as weights ($w$ with $m = 1$) for GPS coordinates ($\mathbf{x}$ with $d = 2$) and a bandwidth of $H(\mathbf{x}) = 0.0008$, helped estimate the feature-weighted density of GPS points on a $500 \times 500$ grid, and based on this generate a contour plot for each participant. Figure 3 shows the resulting contours aggregated for all participants and plotted on top of an OSM map (the darker the colour, the higher the density of the distribution). Locations of increased stress-elicited arousal along the different urban settings of the route are clearly illustrated.

## 4    Conclusions

This study presents a framework for assessing the emotional experience of people with sight loss, while navigating in unfamiliar outdoor environments based

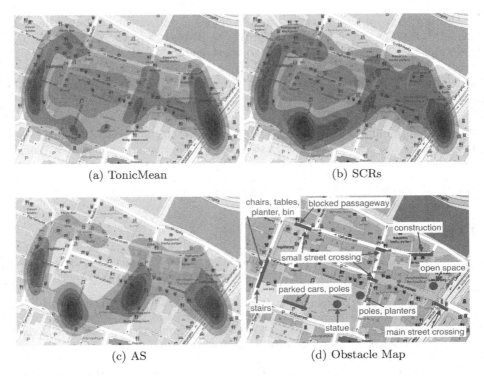

(a) TonicMean

(b) SCRs

(c) AS

(d) Obstacle Map

**Fig. 3.** Contour plot of the kernel density distribution along the charted route in the city centre of Reykjavik in Iceland. GPS coordinates were weighted according to the three most predictive features: mean tonic EDA (TonicMean), number of SCRs (SCRs) and the sum of their amplitudes (AS). The darker the colour is, the higher the density of the distribution is. The lower right figure describes the types of obstacles and situations that evoked increased stress.

on ambulatory monitoring and fusion of multimodal biosignal data. Different urban scenarios were compared, aiming to address the robustness of the model as well as emerging differences in the perception and interaction of the VIP with their surroundings. The high prediction rate (93 % AUROC weighted) is highly encouraging of this approach and, interestingly, the most predictive features of stress and cognitive load indicate as stressful "hotspots" (Fig. 3) scenes that coincide perfectly with the self-reported stressful situations experienced by the participants.

Among the limitations of the study is of course the recording precision of the mobile EEG headset as well as the limited number of participants which does not allow for an in depth analysis of specific stressors in each category of sight loss. Moreover, even if the city of Reykjavik does not present the complexity of big metropolitan areas, the charted route was designed in order to combine some of the busiest streets and most challenging settings reported by the VIP.

Future steps of this research study includes a refinement of the predictive model, extending the categories according to Table 1, as well as expanding to indoor navigation scenarios. Such findings hopefully pave the way to mobile technologies that take the concept of navigation one step further, accounting not only for the shortest path in an urban route but also for the less stressful and safer one.

**Acknowledgments.** The research leading to these results has received funding from the European Union's Horizon 2020 Research and Innovation programme under grant agreement No 643636 "Sound of Vision." The authors wish to thank the administration and O&M instructors at the National Institute for the Blind, Visually Impaired, and Deafblind in Iceland for their valuable input and generous assistance.

# References

1. Badcock, N.A., Mousikou, P., Mahajan, Y., de Lissa, P., Thie, J., McArthur, G.: Validation of the emotiv EPOC EEG gaming system for measuring research quality auditory ERPs. PeerJ **1**:e38 (2013)
2. Bao, F.S., Liu, X., Zhang, C.: PyEEG: an open source Python module for EEG/MEG feature extraction. Comput. Intell. Neurosci. **2011**, e406391 (2011)
3. Baumeister, J., Barthel, T., Geiss, K., Weiss, M.: Influence of phosphatidylserine on cognitive performance and cortical activity after induced stress. Nutr. Neurosci. **11**(3), 103–110 (2008)
4. Benedek, M., Kaernbach, C.: A continuous measure of phasic electrodermal activity. J. Neurosci. Methods **190**, 80–91 (2010)
5. Boucsein, W.: Electrodermal Activity, 2nd edn. Springer, New York (2012)
6. Breiman, L.: Random forests. Mach. Learn. **45**(1), 5–32 (2001)
7. Cacioppo, J.T., Tassinary, L.G.: Inferring psychological significance from physiological signals. Am. Psychol. **45**(1), 16–28 (1990)
8. Cattaneo, Z., Vecchi, T., Cornoldi, C., Mammarella, I., Bonino, D., Ricciardi, E., Pietrini, P.: Imagery and spatial processes in blindness and visual impairement. Neurosci. Biobehav. Rev. **32**, 1346–1360 (2008)
9. David, H.W., Whitaker, K.W., Ries, A.J., Vettel, J.M., Cortney, B.J., Kerick, S.E., McDowell, K.: Usability of four commercially-oriented EEG systems. J. Neural Eng. **11**, 046018 (2014)
10. Debener, S., Minow, F., et al.: How about taking a low-cost, small, and wireless eeg for a walk? Psychophysiology **49**, 1449–1453 (2012)
11. Ekandem, J.I., Davis, T.A., Alvarez, I., James, M.T., Gilbert, J.E.: Evaluating the ergonomics of BCI devices for research and experimentation. Ergonomics **55**, 592–598 (2012)
12. Garbarino, M., Lai, M., Bender, D., Picard, R.W., Tognetti, S.: Empatica E3 - a wearable wireless multi-sensor device for real-time computerized biofeedback and data acquisition. In: EAI 4th International Conference Wireless Mobile Communication Healthcare (Mobihealth), pp. 39–42 (2014)
13. Geruschat, D.R., Smith, A.J.: Low vision for orientation and mobility. In: Wiener, W.R., Welsh, R.L., Blasch, B.B. (eds.) Foundations of Orientation and Mobility. History and Theory, vol. I, 3rd edn. AFB Press, New York (2010)

14. Giudice, N.A., Legge, G.E.: Blind navigation and the role of technology. In: Helal, A., Mokhtari, M., Abdulrazak, B. (eds.) The Engineering Handbook of Smart Technology for Aging, Disability, and Independence, pp. 479–500. John Willey & Sons, Hoboken (2008)

15. Hosseini, S.A., Naghibi-Sistani, M.B.: Classification of emotional stress using brain activity. In: Gargiulo, G.D., McEwan, A. (eds.) Applied Biomedical Engineering, pp. 313–336. InTech, Rijeka (2011)

16. Jena, S.K.: Examination stress and its effect on EEG. Int. J. Med. Sci. Public Health **11**(4), 1493–1497 (2015)

17. Marston, J.R., Golledge, R.G.: The hidden demand for participation in activities and travel by persons who are visually impaired. J. Vis. Impairment Blindness **97**(8), 475–488 (2003)

18. Massot, B., Baltenneck, N., Gehin, C., Dittmar, A., McAdams, E.: EmoSense: an ambulatory device for the assessment of ANS activity–application in the objective evaluation of stress with the blind. IEEE Sensors J. **12**(3), 543–551 (2012)

19. Mavros, P., Skroumpelou, K., Smith, A.H.: Understanding the urban experience of people with visual impairments. In: Proceedings of GIS Research UK 2015, pp. 401–406. Leeds, 15–17 April 2015

20. Millar, S.: Understanding and Representing Space: Theory and Evidence from Studies with Blind and Sighted Children. Clarendon, Oxford (1994)

21. Peake, P., Leonard, J.A.: The use of heart rate as an index of stress in blind pedestrians. Ergonomics **14**(2), 189–204 (1971)

22. Peper, E., Harvey, R., Lin, I.M., Tylova, H., Moss, D.: Is there more to blood volume pulse than heart rate variability, respiratory sinus arrhythmia, and cardiorespiratory synchrony? Biofeedback **35**(2), 54–61 (2007)

23. Quiroga, R.Q., Blanco, S., Rosso, O.A., Garcia, H., Rabinowicz, A.: Searching for hidden information with Gabor Transform in generalized tonic-clonic seizures. Electroencephalogr. Clin. Neurophysiol. **103**, 434–439 (1997)

24. Quiñones, P.A., Greece, T.C., Yang, R., Newman, M.W.: Supporting visually impaired navigation: a needs-finding study. In: ACM CHI Conference Human Factors Computing Systems, pp. 1645–1650. Vancouver, BC, 7–12 May 2011

25. Turner, J.R.: Cardiovascular Reactivity and Stress: Patters of Physiological Response. Springer, New York (1994)

26. Wand, M.P., Jones, M.C.: Kernel Smoothing. Chapman & Hall, London (1995)

27. Welsh, R.L.: Improving psychosocial functioning for orientation and mobility. In: Wiener, W.R., Welsh, R.L., Blasch, B.B. (eds.) Foundations of Orientation and Mobility. Instructional Strategies and Practical Applications, vol. 2, 3rd edn. AFB Press, New York (2010)

28. Wycherley, R.J., Nicklin, B.H.: The heart rate of blind and sighted pedestrians on a town route. Ergonomics **13**(2), 181–192 (1970)

# Usability and Safety of a HUD During Powered Chair Navigation: A Pilot Study

Katie Seaborn[1](✉), Yutaka Satoh[2], and Deborah I. Fels[3]

[1] University of Toronto, Toronto, Canada
kseaborn@mie.utoronto.ca
[2] National Institute of Advanced Industrial Science and Technology,
Tsukuba, Japan
yu.satou@aist.go.jp
[3] Ryerson University, Toronto, Canada
dfels@ryerson.ca

**Abstract.** Ensuring that mixed reality spaces are inclusive to those who have motor impairments requires evaluating and, if necessary, modifying existing technology for the assistive mobility devices they use. Heads-up displays (HUDs) are a common facilitator of virtual augmentations on physical reality, especially for motor vehicles. However, little research to date has explored the efficacy of such displays for powered chairs, which is paramount to ensure safety and effectiveness of use. In this pilot study, we compared (a) transparency of the display (transparent, semi-transparent, and opaque) and (b) presentation mode of the information (text, icon, and text + icon) through dynamic powered chair navigation tasks in a controlled course setup. We found no difference for workload and error among transparency and presentation styles, but a significant difference between presentation styles on delay. These results will be evaluated in full through an mixed reality platform with powered chair users.

**Keywords:** Head-up display · Powered wheelchair · Navigation · Mixed reality · Inclusive design

## 1 Introduction

Virtual, mixed, and augmented reality has become more widely used due to the advent of less expensive and more powerful (and often smaller and more lightweight) technologies that can facilitate a range of interactive experiences involving real and virtual spaces. Similarity, knowledge of and interest in promoting and creating inclusive technologies and spaces for people of varying abilities has gained stead. Researchers and practitioners are now exploring the possibilities afforded by the convergence of these trends for different areas of application, such as health, education, and entertainment.

One point of exploration is mixed reality as a training and entertainment platform for people who use powered chairs, including electric wheelchairs and mobility scooters. At face value, mixed reality is a natural choice for this user group: the use of powered mobility aids implies large space and movement, characteristics that pair well

© Springer International Publishing Switzerland 2016
M. Antona and C. Stephanidis (Eds.): UAHCI 2016, Part III, LNCS 9739, pp. 628–638, 2016.
DOI: 10.1007/978-3-319-40238-3_60

with the notion of virtual augmentations merged with physical space. However, this raises the question of what display and interaction technologies—head-up displays? Tablets? Glasses? Head-mounted displays? etc.—are best suited for this user group.

As personal power-operated motor vehicles, powered chairs bear several similarities to road vehicles: like cars, trucks and vans, powered chairs require manual operation of controls for driving and navigation in a dynamic context (movement in a non-stationary, somewhat unpredictable environment) that makes demands of the user's physical, perceptual, and cognitive abilities [1]. In the past few decades, windshield-based HUDs have been explored as a way of presenting virtually-augmented information to users of motor vehicles. While it is possible that such displays are suitable during powered chair use, very little research has explored this, and no known research to date has evaluated which, if any, existing augmented reality technologies are the most suitable.

In this paper, we present initial findings from a pilot study that evaluated the feasibility and usability of two a tablet + mirror HUD with three transparency options —transparent, semi-transparent, and opaque—based on navigation task (e.g. turn left at the next corner) and presentation style (text, icon, or text + icon). Our goal was to discover which version of the display, if any, is suitable for powered chair use, especially while the chair is being operated, and whether use of the display was effective and safe during driving operations and navigation tasks.

## 2  Related Work

While displays and interfaces to facilitate mixed reality for powered and non-powered chair users is not well researched, we can draw from two related areas: displays for virtual reality and mobility impaired people, and HUDs for motor vehicles.

### 2.1  Displays for Virtual and Augmented Reality

Augmented and virtual reality fall within the mixed reality continuum, which is defined by pure virtuality and pure reality opposite ends [15]. In augmented reality, virtual augmentations are merged into/onto physical space. In virtual reality, environments are purely virtual, with no physical augmentations or spaces involved. Thus, the technologies used to facilitate each have different requirements. Augmented reality displays require that some aspect of reality is experienced synchronously with some aspect of virtuality. The Nintendo 3DS display, for instance, uses a camera to present realtime images of physical space with overlaid virtual elements. However, some technologies, such as head-mounted displays, may be used to facilitate either augmented or virtual reality by presenting or not presenting physical space through the lenses.

Much of the work on virtual reality for wheelchair users involves a stationary session with the virtual reality application (where only virtual "movement" and perhaps some degree of bodily movement, takes place; no physical driving tasks or movement of the chair in physical space occur) and then possibly a trial in using the device in reality, e.g. [7, 18, 20, 22]. Bajcsy et al. [2] used coloured targets placed on the ground and a ceiling-mounted camera to track the movement of the wheelchair in physical space and respond accordingly in the virtual environment. Even so, this work was limited by the amount of physical space that could be traversed (i.e., how much floor space could be captured by the ceiling camera) and additionally by non-typical operating situations.

Rashid *et al.* [17] developed an augmented reality shopping system for people who have motor impairments and/or use wheelchairs using the Vuzix M100 Smart Glass. Their pilot results are promising, but a larger study that explores measures beyond accuracy of a particular task is needed to get fuller understanding of the efficacy of such a display. Like much of the work on virtual reality, this study did not require wheelchair movement. Further, it did not evaluate a dual attention task (for instance, operating the wheelchair while following on-screen instructions), which our study addresses.

A few research studies have investigated the efficacy of modern head-mounted displays (HMDs), especially Google Glass, which obviate the "wired" issue of the previous generation of HMDs. However, recent research [11, 13, 14] suggests that the touch and voice interface for such displays is difficult to use for older adults and people with varying abilities (many older powered chair users have difficulty with grip and hand and/or arm motor impairments), leading one group of researchers to design a separate touchpad interface to operate the Google Glass. This option is not ideal for powered chair users who already have to use a set of buttons and a joystick to operate their device. Additionally, there is a trade-off in line of sight and distraction with HMDs: while they do not require the user to glance away, they are fixed and potentially distracting for users who wish to attend to something other than the HUD.

## 2.2   HUDs for Motor Vehicles

The efficacy and usability of automotive HUDs, or HUDs for road motor vehicles, has been widely researched for many decades from a human factors standpoint. We draw from this literature because operating a powered chair is similar to driving a motor vehicle. Recent research has looked at HUDs versus head-down displays, or HDDs (such as the traditional dashboard setup), distraction and attention, display complexity, ageing, and cognitive load. In general, HUDs increase the amount of time the driver spends looking at the road and decreases the time it takes for the eye to accommodate to different focal depths [6]. However, contrast interference—when information on the HUD interferes with perception of information in the environment, or vice versa—and cognitive capture—when the processing of information presented on the HUD take priority over important information in the environment—remain issues of concern [6]. Indeed, concurrent use of a HUD while operating a motor vehicle appears to be a dual-attention task, with performance in at least one task suffering. This suggests that while a HUD may be a useful addition in certain contexts, its usefulness depends on its design and context of use. Therefore, we must carefully consider how the information is presented (will it distract the user from processing key information in the environment?) and the abilities (and limits) of human processing (especially for older people) within the intended context of use (is it necessary or can the operator do without it?).

Although there are similarities, we cannot be certain that what works for drivers of road motor vehicles will work for power chairs users. For instance, drivers of motor vehicles must attend to extra, relevant information on the dashboard that powered chair users do not, possibly increasing workload for drivers. Further, relying on general heuristics and usability techniques that have been designed for traditional interactive systems to develop and assess early-stage mixed reality prototypes is a known problem [16]. For these reasons, we have undertaken this study to assess the feasibility of a HUD and ensure that it is effective and safe for powered chair users during operation.

## 3    System Design

The main system setup is presented in Fig. 1. The design was guided by research findings on related technology for wheelchair users and human factors work on vehicle HUDs. As Fig. 1a shows, the HUD is a combination of a Microsoft Surface tablet and a Prompter Duo mirror that is attached to the powered chair using a mount arm and positioned to the right of the user's line of vision (people drive on the right side of the road in Japan). Each transparency mode is switched out during the trials as needed.

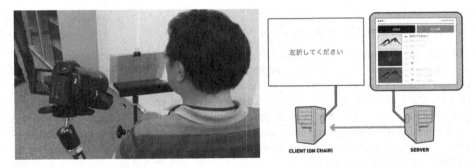

**Fig. 1.** Figures showing (a) view of system setup from behind where the opaque display mode is being used, and (b) network setup for server and client software and hardware.

Instructions are manually sent out by a human observer using a web-based application; the observer carefully assesses and responds to the user's actions based on their speed and how they have carried out previous instructions. The application was developed using JavaScript libraries (jQuery, Node.js, and Socket.io), PHP, and MySQL (which randomly selects from the counterbalanced table of possible trials). Instructions are sent to the tablet over an ad-hoc network hosted by the server computer; see Fig. 1b.

### 3.1    Head-up Display or Head-Down Display

Work on displays to provide extra, relevant information to drivers of motor vehicles has explored two configurations: head-up displays (HDDs) and head-down displays (HDDs). Research has consistently found that, all else considered, HDDs increase driver response time to hazards and other emergency information when compared to HUDs [9, 12]. In particular, HUDs seem to increase the amount of time users keep their eyes on the road [6]. This limits the need to re-focus (or re-accommodate) the eye, which can be challenging for everyone but particularly older drivers. This suggests that the safest and most efficient position of a display for powered chair users may be close to their line of vision rather than, say, a tablet held in their hand or placed on an armrest. Given the difficulty older drivers are known to have with divided attention tasks [5], such a setup may be especially appropriate. For these reasons, we decided to use a mount arm to position the device near the user's line of sight.

### 3.2   Display Transparency: Transparent, Semi-transparent, or Opaque

Despite the benefits found for vehicle HUDs, some research suggests that increased background complexity can reduce HUD legibility [6, 21]. To address this, we decided to compare three levels of transparency: completely transparent, semi-transparent (using translucent white plastic), and opaque (using white construction paper).

### 3.3   Presentation Mode: Icon, Text, or Icon + Text

The way that information is presented to the user—the sensory medium, or modality, of the information—is an essential consideration in interface design, especially in applications where a quick response might be necessary. Further, some research suggests that HUDs may be distracting because the information on the display must be processed at the same time the user is processing information in the environment [6]. Multimodality theory suggests that combining modalities that present the same information in a complementary or redundant way may be effective or ineffective depending on the context, task, and abilities of the user [19]. Therefore, we decided to explore the possible presentation modes afforded by a HUD—text, icon, or text + icon—to determine which most is most suitable for powered chair users during operation and navigation tasks.

## 4   Methods

We conducted a within-subjects pilot study to evaluate the usability of a HUD for powered chair users. Given the design considerations above, we hypothesized that there would be no differences among HUD styles in terms of ($H_01$) workload ratings, ($H_02$) usability ratings, ($H_03$) error rates, ($H_04$) delay, and ($H_05$) effect of presentation mode. The order of level for each variable was randomly assigned across participants to counterbalance the results and avoid learning effects.

## 4.1    Participants

Eight able-bodied males aged 25-54 who work at the National Institute of Advanced Industrial Science and Technology (AIST) in Tsukuba, Japan participated in the pilot study. All had received at least a university-level education and used a computer every day. Seven used tablets, four used smartphones, one used a basic cell phone, and one used an e-reader. Eight strongly agreed that they enjoyed learning about new technologies (one enjoyed learning about new technologies, but not strongly). Six agreed that they were generally comfortable with technology (one neither, one slightly disagreed). Seven considered themselves not technophobic, while one considered himself mildly technophobic and another considered himself moderately technophobic. Participants were recruited through word-of-mouth and convenience sampling. All were covered under company insurance; ethics was not required and no compensation was provided.

## 4.2    Location and Procedure

The pilot study was conducted in-lab at AIST. A large room was cleared of obstacles and clutter and secured for use in the study. First, participants filled out the pre-questionnaire and then were given 10 min in which to familiarize themselves with the powered chair, ask questions about its operation, and complete a pre-trial navigation task. Drawing from previous research on wheelchair training and HUDs for road motor vehicles, e.g. [7, 10], the main task was to attend and respond to 24 navigation instructions—comprised of move forward, stop, turn left, or turn right—provided through the HUD. Participants were asked to respond to these instructions as quickly, accurately, and safely as possible. They were also told that a camera would be recording the HUD and movement of the chair for data collection purposes only. Tasks were completed in the same order, but HUD style, transparency, and presentation mode were randomly attributed based on a counterbalanced table of variables and levels. After completing each trial, the participant filled out a post-trial questionnaire. Finally, participants were debriefed and given the opportunity to ask questions and provide feedback verbally.

## 4.3    Instruments and Data Analysis

Quantitative and qualitative data were collected through video recordings (camera positioned on the shoulder of the powered chair, capturing the HUD display and floor position) and pre-study and post-trial questionnaires. The video recordings were used to count the number of errors and response time per task based on the instructions displayed on the screen, HUD style, and presentation mode. The pre-study questionnaire captured basic demographics, and the post-trial questionnaire assessed usability through the Systems Usability Scale (SUS) [3] and workload through the NASA-TLX [8], as well as two additional subjective Likert scale questions ("I was distracted by the display" and "How satisfied were you with the display in general"). Descriptive and inferential statistics were used on all quantitative data.

# 5  Results

## 5.1  Workload (NASA-TLX, Distraction)

Workload (NASA-TLX) scores out of fifteen for each display transparency option are as follows: 5.15 for transparent ($SD = 3.27$), 4.72 for semi-transparent ($SD = 2.93$), and 5.07 for opaque ($SD = 2.7$). A repeated measures ANOVA found no difference among the three transparency styles, $p = .91$. However, a repeated measures ANOVA (Fig. 2a) found a significant effect of transparency on the subjective distraction measure, $F(2, 14) = 5.07$, $p = .022$, $\eta_p^2 = .42$. Within-subjects contrasts found a significant difference between the transparent and opaque styles, $F(1, 7) = 7.61$, $p = .028$, $\eta_p^2 = .52$.

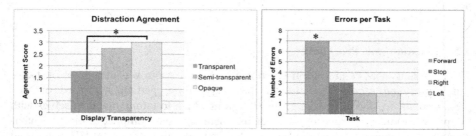

**Fig. 2.** Figures showing (a) subjective distraction agreement rating (lower scores better) and (b) errors per task. (Color figure online)

## 5.2  Usability (SUS, Satisfaction)

The mean SUS scores (out of 100) per display transparency option are as follows: 75 for transparent ($SD = 17.27$), 78.13 for semi-transparent ($SD = 12.3$), and 74.38 for opaque ($SD = 11.55$). No significant differences were found through one-way ANOVAs conducted to compare SUS scores ($p = .85$) and satisfaction scores ($p = .39$). Similarly, a repeated measures ANOVA conducted to compare SUS and satisfaction scores across participants and display transparency found no significant effect.

## 5.3  Errors

Participants made an average of 2.5 errors. In total, 14 partial incorrect actions (starting or end with the wrong action for the task) and 8 incorrect actions (wrong action for the task) were taken. One participant made 40 % of all errors and another made 25 % of all errors, with the remaining 35 % split between the other participants. Given that there were 36 tasks and hence 36 opportunities for error, participants made incorrect actions less than 7 % of the time. For the participants with the most errors, 22 % of all actions made for one and 14 % for the other were in error.

No statistically significant differences among display transparency styles ($p = .69$), presentation mode ($p = .52$), or their interaction ($p = .52$) were found. However, a one-way ANOVA comparing total errors per task (Fig. 2b) found a significant difference, $F(3, 44) = 10.30$, $p > .001$. A post hoc Tukey test showed that the "go forward" task differed significantly from all other tasks at $p > .001$.

### 5.4   Delay

The average time for participants to respond to navigation tasks (delay before action) was 0.99 s ($SD = 0.9$). A one-way ANOVA comparing delay across HUD styles found no significance ($p = .84$). However, a repeated measures ANOVA found a significant interaction between presentation mode and delay, $F(4, 20) = 4.04$, $p = .045$, $\eta_p^2 = .40$. Although contrasts were unable to pinpoint difference(s), the graph (Fig. 3) suggests that the text mode had the highest delay scores and the icon mode had the lowest.

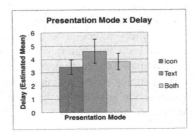

**Fig. 3.** Estimated marginal means for delay by presentation mode. Error bars are standard error (Color figure online)

## 6   Discussion

### 6.1   Hypotheses

**H01: There was no difference in workload ratings among HUDs.** We can reject this hypothesis in the case of the perception scores, which show that the opaque style was perceived to be more distracting than the transparent style. However, the NASA-TLX scores did not show a significant difference, so on the basis of these scores, we cannot reject this hypothesis. It is not clear why there was a difference between these related scores. The opaque condition may have been perceived as more distracting because, according to two participants, the clip used to hold the paper to the HUD was distracting, but this does not account for why the semi-transparent paper, which also used the same clip, was no significantly more distracting than the similar opaque style.

**H02: There was no difference in usability ratings among HUDs.** We found no difference in SUS or satisfaction scores among HUD styles, so we cannot reject this hypothesis. As far as subjective usability is concerned, no one style of HUD stood out.

**H03: There was no difference in error rates among HUDs.** We cannot reject this hypothesis, as there was no significant difference in error rates found. However, we did find a significant and unexpected difference based on task, which we discuss in 6.3.

**H04: There was no difference in delay among HUDs.** We cannot reject this hypothesis because we found no significant difference in delay among HUD styles.

**H05: Presentation mode did not have an effect on the above.** There was a significant difference found for delay based on presentation mode, so we can reject this hypothesis. The graph suggests that the icon presentation mode resulted in the shortest delays.

## 6.2  Usability in General

SUS scores across interface styles were above average, falling within the 70-85 % percentile ranking. In general, individual differences played a major role in the results across factors in two ways: (1) participants scoring equally on scores among HUD styles, but not similarly to each other; and (2) participants not scoring equally among HUD styles, regardless of how others scored. For instance, NASA-TLX workload scores were, on average, low for each transparency style (about 5 out of 15), and descriptive statistics for each participant suggest that, in general, higher scores were the result of one, rather than all, transparency styles. To take a specific example, Participant #2 workload for the transparent style was higher by about 6 points (or just over one-third of the possible score) than the other two.

## 6.3  Unexpected Finding: Errors and the "Go Forward" Task

We discovered that the "go forward" task yielded significantly more errors than the other three tasks. This is surprising because there is nothing in the literature to suggest that this is the case. Further, if we translate from road motor vehicle research, we should expect that right turning (in the case of Japan; left turning in North America) would yield more errors (e.g., [4]). Finally, since the default directionality of the vehicle controls is "forward," we would expect this to be the least error-prone task to undertake. Given this, we speculate that participants expected a more complicated task and so readied themselves for a switch of the default controls, leading to errors.

## 6.4  Limitations

This pilot test was limited by the number of participants and the lack of participants who regularly use powered chairs. However, we expect that those who already have experience with powered chairs will perform as well, or better, than participants who are not powered chair users, by virtue of having greater experience with the chair. This will be confirmed in the full study, which will involve powered chair users.

The method of delivery for the HUD instructions was limited to visual modalities: text and image. Future work could explore the addition of auditory cues and verbal instructions as an additional and/or complementary mode. Further, we did not capture workload and SUS data after each change of presentation mode, because this would have involved frequent disruptions that could have impacted the results (e.g. frustration with these procedure-based disruptions being recorded as performance-based frustration). Future work could prioritize exploring the impact of presentation mode rather than transparency.

Finally, we did not compare the head-up display to head-mounted displays, which could be explored in a form factor study.

# 7   Conclusion

Overall, the HUD was found to be usable across styles, participants, and measures. Individual differences played a major role in the results across factors, a common issue for small-n studies. It is therefore difficult to make a definitive conclusion about which style is best. However, significant differences among presentation styles on subjective distraction and delay indicate that a transparent display using icons to present navigation instructors may be the safest and most usable option during powered chair operation. Future work will evaluate the HUD within the context of a game-based mixed reality training platform with powered chair users.

**Acknowledgements.** We thank Dr. Peter Pennefather for his thorough feedback and advice on pico projectors and displays. We also thank our participants for generously volunteering their time. Finally, we thank AIST for providing the space in which to run the pilot study. This work was funded in part by the Japan Society for the Promotion of Science (JSPS) Summer Program and the Natural Sciences and Engineering Research Council of Canada (NSERC).

# References

1. Anstey, K.J., et al.: Cognitive, sensory and physical factors enabling driving safety in older adults. Clin. Psychol. Rev. **25**(1), 45–65 (2005)
2. Bajcsy, P. et al.: Immersive environments for rehabilitation activities. In: Proceedings of the 17th ACM International Conference on Multimedia, pp. 829–832. ACM, New York (2009)
3. Bangor, A., et al.: An empirical evaluation of the System Usability Scale. Int. J. Hum. Comput. Interact. **24**(6), 574–594 (2008)
4. Chovan, J.D., et al.: Examination of Intersection, Left Turn Across Path Crashes and Potential IVHS Countermeasures. National Highway Traffic Safety Administration, Washington (1994)
5. Flannagan, M.J., Harrison, A.K.: Effects of Automobile Head-up Display Location for Younger and Older Drivers. University of Michigan, Ann Arbor (1994)
6. Gish, K.W., Staplin, L.: Human factors aspects of using head up displays in automobiles: A review of the literature. U.S. Department of Transportation, National Highway Traffic Safety Administration, Ann Arbor, MI (1995)
7. Harrison, A., et al.: The role of virtual reality technology in the assessment and training of inexperienced powered wheelchair users. Disabil. Rehabil. **24**(11–12), 599–606 (2002)

8. Hart, S.G.: NASA-task load index (NASA-TLX); 20 years later. Proc. Hum. Factors Ergon. Soc. Annu. Meet. **50**(9), 904–908 (2006)
9. Horrey, W.J., Wickens, C.D.: Driving and side task performance: the effects of display clutter, separation, and modality. Hum. Factors J. Hum. Factors Ergon. Soc. **46**(4), 611–624 (2004)
10. Karvonen, H. et al.: In-car ubiquitous computing: driver tutoring messages presented on a head-up display. In: IEEE Intelligent Transportation Systems Conference, pp. 560–565. IEEE, Toronto (2006)
11. Kunze, K. et al.: Wearable computing for older adults: initial insights into head-mounted display usage. In: Proceedings of the 2014 ACM International Joint Conference on Pervasive and Ubiquitous Computing: Adjunct Publication, pp. 83–86 ACM, New York (2014)
12. Liu, Y.C., Wen, M.H.: Driving performance of commercial vehicle operators in Taiwan. Int. J. Hum Comput Stud. **61**(5), 679–697 (2004)
13. Malu, M., Findlater, L.: Personalized, wearable control of a head-mounted display for users with upper body motor impairments. In: Proceedings of the 33rd Annual ACM Conference on Human Factors in Computing Systems, pp. 221–230. ACM, New York (2015)
14. McNaney, R. et al.: Exploring the acceptability of google glass as an everyday assistive device for people with Parkinson's. In: Proceedings of the 32nd Annual ACM Conference on Human Factors in Computing Systems, pp. 2551–2554 ACM, New York (2014)
15. Milgram, P., Kishino, F.: A taxonomy of mixed reality visual displays. IEICE Trans. Inf. Syst. **77**(12), 1321–1329 (1994)
16. Nilsson, S., Johansson, B.: A cognitive systems engineering perspective on the design of mixed reality systems. In: Proceedings of the 13th Eurpoean Conference on Cognitive Ergonomics: Trust and Control in Complex Socio-technical Systems, pp. 154–161. ACM, New York (2006)
17. Rashid, Z. et al.: Cricking: Browsing physical space with smart glass. In: Proceedings of the 2014 ACM International Joint Conference on Pervasive and Ubiquitous Computing: Adjunct Publication, pp. 151–154. ACM, New York (2014)
18. Rossol, N. et al.: A framework for adaptive training and games in virtual reality rehabilitation environments. In: Proceedings of the 10th International Conference on Virtual Reality Continuum and Its Applications in Industry, pp. 343–346. ACM, New York (2011)
19. Sarter, N.B.: Multimodal information presentation: design guidance and research challenges. Int. J. Ind. Ergon. **36**(5), 439–445 (2006)
20. Takala, T.M.: RUIS: A toolkit for developing virtual reality applications with spatial interaction. In: Proceedings of the 2Nd ACM Symposium on Spatial User Interaction, pp. 94–103. ACM, New York (2014)
21. Ward, N.J., et al.: Effect of background scene complexity and field dependence on the legibility of head-up displays for automotive applications. Hum. Factors J. Hum. Factors Ergon. Soc. **37**(4), 735–745 (1995)
22. Yeh, S.-C. et al.: An integrated system: Virtual reality, haptics and modern sensing technique (VHS) for post-stroke rehabilitation. In: Proceedings of the ACM Symposium on Virtual Reality Software and Technology, pp. 59–62. ACM, New York (2005)

# Creating Inclusive Automotive Interfaces Using Situation Awareness as a Design Philosophy

Lee Skrypchuk[1(✉)], Patrick M. Langdon[2], P. John Clarkson[2],
and Alex Mouzakitis[1]

[1] Jaguar Land Rover, Research and Technology, Coventry, UK
{LSKRYPCH, AMOUZAK1}@jaguarlandrover.com,
LS578@cam.ac.uk,
[2] Engineering Design Centre, Engineering Department,
Cambridge University, Cambridge, UK
{PML24, PJC10}@cam.ac.uk

**Abstract.** This paper presents a methodology for designing automotive user interfaces using Situation Awareness (SA). The development of interfaces providing users with relevant, timely information is critical for optimal performance. This paper presents a variation on the original SA model allowing for a consideration of all situational factors in a modern motor car. "Dual Goal SA" provides environmental and cognitive considerations for developing interfaces used when multi-tasking. A pilot study was carried out to test the Dual Goal concept and identify appropriate measures. Subjective results proved inconclusive. Objective results showed good evidence supporting the hypothesis but most promising was a factor analysis involving all key objective measures. This produced factors that classified the experimental groups consistently with predictions, demonstrating evidence of variations in performance consistent with variations in SA for two competing goals.

**Keywords:** Automotive interfaces · Situation awareness · Driver distraction

## 1 Introduction

User interfaces in the car are required for an increasing number of features and functions [12]. Design approaches consider these features individually and not always as a function of the demands of the target environment. The vehicle environment can be divided into two groups of activities. Those directly related to the act of driving; Driving Related Activities (DRA) and those unrelated to the act of driving; Non-Driving Related Activities (NRA) [23].

The opportunity to engage in NRA in the vehicle is increasing, which directly conflict and oppose the goal of driving. Many existing methods for vehicle interface design are being ignored in favour of more agile methods [22]. Whilst the DRA has remained consistent, NRA's are constantly changing with inconsistencies existing between manufacturers. This causes difficulty for users moving between vehicles in understanding the UI logic if not managed correctly [17]. The challenge exists to

M. Antona and C. Stephanidis (Eds.): UAHCI 2016, Part III, LNCS 9739, pp. 639–649, 2016.
DOI: 10.1007/978-3-319-40238-3_61

develop interfaces for both DRA and NRA that can work in harmony and give optimal performance for the user during multi-task conditions.

## 2 Situation Awareness

### 2.1 A Definition

The most commonly used definition of Situation Awareness (SA) is *"the perception of the elements in the environment within a volume of time and space, the comprehension of their meaning, and the projection of their status in the near future"* [7]. Figure 1 shows Endsley's basic SA model. SA precedes decision making and action and is found within short term memory [5]. SA focuses on situational elements of an environment, how they develop over time and how knowledge of a situation forms [3].

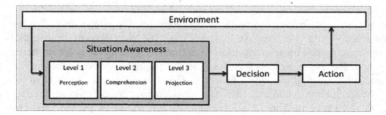

**Fig. 1.** A high level model of Situation Awareness, Endsley et al., 1995b

Endsley reports a three level process [6]. Level 1 (Perception) is goal directed [7]. Goals influence the selection of appropriate long term memory which direct attention and perception [4]. Level 2 (Comprehension) is a synthesis of perceived elements and formulates a Situation Model (SM) [16]. Level 2 requires domain knowledge otherwise inaccuracies developed in the SM may lead to operator error [4]. Level 3 (Projection) is where the SM is used to make predictions about how a situation may develop. In highly dynamic scenarios this is required for successful completion of an activity and is considered the mark of a skilled expert [5]. It is often the case that some people may not achieve L3 [4]. Level 3 is seen regularly in the driving when considering how drivers anticipate traffic situations and requires long term memory structures such as schema, scripts and mental models [9]. SA has been used to develop interfaces in domains such as aviation [1], military [15] and other professional environments [8].

### 2.2 Applying SA in the Automotive Domain

Driving was highlighted early on as an area of potential for SA [6, 7]. The main goal of driving is to travel from one place to another in a safe, timely manner, with the sub goals being; Control, Monitoring, Hazard Avoidance and Navigation [11].

Matthews et al., (2002) proposed a model of SA for driving using it to analyse how new interfaces affect driver performance [20]. A large number of publications have reported effects of mobile phone conversations on driving performance using SA [21, 24]. More recent SA research looked at interaction with other NRA's whilst driving to see whether drivers interact in a "situationally aware manner" [25].

Baumann, et al., (2007) decomposed SA for automotive using Construction Integration Theory [16] proposing a cognitive framework for driving SA [2]. A relationship similar to Endsley's is proposed using construction (Perception) and integration (LTM activations). These comparisons with LTM describe why experienced drivers perform better at hazard perception. For example, if the SM matches knowledge in LTM, the appropriate routine, or schema can be selected to complete the action faster and with more success. Whilst this model offers a cognitive approach to the DRA, it does not explicitly account for conditions when multi-tasking is present.

To date, driver behavior research has considered SA almost exclusively with respect to the DRA where SA is only built relative to the driving environment [10, 18, 19]. There is a general lack of consideration of how the NRA is an integral part of the SM.

## 2.3    A New Approach to SA in Automotive

In aviation, the goal is to safely control the aircraft. This "Single Goal SA" is an example of a professional operator domain where multitasking happens but is generally related to main goal. This is how the driving domain has been considered to date.

The vehicle exists in an environment where an operator can build SA to the DRA. This is where the similarities to aviation end because the car also has a number of potential competing activities to driving. This key characteristic is the difference between a professional environment, such as the pilot, and a private scenario. So far, SA research has focused on domains associated with those attempting to accomplish a professional role where performance regulation and continuous training is compulsory. This exposes difficulties in applying SA where multi-tasking across competing goals are an accepted part of the environment. There is need to adapt SA to include competing, unrelated goals for environments such as the vehicle.

A theoretical model is proposed (Fig. 2). The original SA model is expanded to include two goals, the DRA and NRA. The user must build up SM's specific to each goal by focusing on elements within each specific environment. Each SM will decay when out of focus and not part of situation assessment.

Goals can compete and so factors within the environment may be helpful for one goal, but unhelpful for another (e.g. sunlight, helpful for seeing outside of the car but makes in car displays difficult to read). By looking at SA through this lens it is hoped that identifying specific properties will lead to positive implications relating to UI design and also new ideas relating to attention and the cognitive properties of SA.

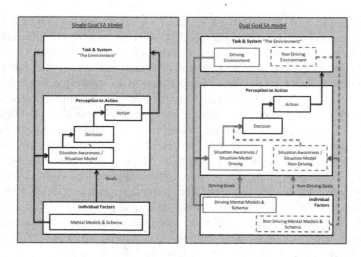

**Fig. 2.** The Dual Goal SA model compared to the original Single Goal SA model

## 3 Methodology

### 3.1 Experimental Design

A pilot study was proposed to identify a method of assessing two competing goals. The aim was to measure the effect SA has on task performance by varying SA across two competing activities. SA is difficult to measure but good task performance is indicative of good SA, thus good performance on both should be indicative of high SA in both.

The experimental design used was a between subjects, repeated measures design. 20 male participants all between the age of 20 and 40 were recruited. All had valid driver's licenses and all given a short cognitive test prior to running the experiment which showed no outliers. The independent variables used were DRA SA level (2 levels, High and Low) and NRA SA level (2 levels, High and Low). The $2 \times 2$ design meant 4 experimental conditions overall.

To generate the two DRA levels, Novices and Experienced drivers were used (10 per group). There is evidence to support that experience is a good measure of a ability to build awareness toward a situation [27]. The Experienced group were given 30–45 min of training prior to the trial. The Novice group were informed of the DRA pre-trial but were immediately exposed to the experimental condition without training.

The driving simulation used was Mario Kart Wii for the Nintendo Wii, with controls built into a traditional driving setup with steering wheel and pedals. This simulation was used to create a true novice grouping and due to it having a highly dynamic driving environment. The simulation was modified to remove any competitive elements (timing, position and threats) and participants were asked to complete three laps whilst keeping the vehicle between the centre line and the right hand side edge of the track. Participants were advised to avoid collisions with other road users and to carry out both activities. Each run lasted approximately 3 min.

To generate the two NRA levels, two interfaces were used which simulated high and low SA. All participants were exposed to both interfaces and the task used in the NRA was consistent, a simple Visual-Manual number entry task (Fig. 3).

The High SA condition used a telephone number pad with physical moving buttons to give people confidence on location and activation (Fixed Keypad). The Low SA condition used a touchscreen keypad to remove the physical properties. The keys were spread out across a region approximately 15 cm x 15 cm in size and moved randomly after each entry (Variable Keypad). This meant the user could not become familiar with the interface layout, a factor associated with an inability to build awareness.

The interfaces were located on the centre console of the rig, to the left of the participant. Each participant was given an instruction sheet explaining the tasks prior to the experiment but was not allowed to practice prior to the trial. The participants did attempt each in a single task condition before being exposed to dual task.

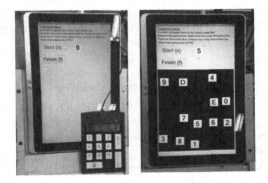

**Fig. 3.** NRA Interfaces, Fixed Keypad (left) and Variable Keypad (Right)

The main dependent variables were a combination of subjective and objective. For the subjective, self-reported workload using the NASA TLX [14] and Situation Awareness Rating Technique (SART) [26] were asked after each run. The question was asked for both tasks simultaneously which meant the user had to fill out two scores, one for each task. This was done to see whether the participant could distinguish the demand or SA requirement for the individual tasks when being attempted simultaneously.

The objective measures included both DRA and NRA based such as steering angle, driving time, lane exceedances, pedal activations, driving incidents, NRA completion rate, mean task time, errors and glances away from the road but to name a few. Despite the focus being on dual task, single task was also measured to confirm performance for the higher SA conditions in order to validate the approach.

## 3.2  Setup and Procedure

The experiment was run in a low fidelity driving simulator located at the Jaguar Land Rover HMI Research Lab. Participants were asked to complete a pre-test questionnaire and read instructions including a consent form. The Experienced group were then given their pre-exposure to the DRA (30-45 min) whereas the Novice group were taken straight into the experiment.

The run order varied per participant. The first 3 runs and the final run (run 6) were always the same with runs 4 and 5 counterbalanced to avoid learning effects on the DRA. The run order used was Driving Only, Fixed Keypad Only, Variable Keypad Only, Dual Task 1 (counter balanced), Dual Task 2 (counter balanced) and Driving Only. After each run the participant was asked to complete a post-test questionnaire for Workload and SART before moving on.

### 3.3  Hypothesis

This experiment focused on testing traditional performance measures and their ability to successfully classify SA corresponding to the experimental groups (Table 1). The hypothesis used was that significant differences would be found between conditions 4 and condition 1. A secondary hypothesis would be that performance for conditions 2 and 3 would fall in between conditions 1 and 4.

**Table 1.** Experimental Conditions

|  | Low SA DRA (Novice) | High SA DRA (Experienced) |
|---|---|---|
| Low SA NRA (Variable Keypad) | Condition 1 | Condition 2 |
| High SA NRA (Fixed Keypad) | Condition 3 | Condition 4 |

## 4  Results

All data passed normality tests and met the assumption of ANOVA and any significant outliers were removed. 3 factors were used in the test, Type (Fixed, Variable Keypad), Mode (Single, Dual Task) and Experience to the DRA (Novice, Experienced).

### 4.1  Subjective Results

An ANOVA of DRA Workload revealed significant effects between Type [DF $(3, 72)$, F-Value = 7.93, P-Value < 0.01]. No significant effect was found between the Dual-Task conditions. NRA Workload showed no significant results across all of the factors. There was however a trend for higher reported figures in the Dual-Task conditions.

An ANOVA for DRA SART demonstrated no significant effects for any condition. An ANOVA of NRA SART revealed significant effects of Type*Mode*Experience [DF $(2,108)$, F-Value = 3.42, P-Value = 0.036)], a Tukey Post hoc Pairwise comparison showed a differences between Fixed Keypad*Single*Novice and Variable Keypad*Dual*Experienced conditions ($P < 0.05$). All other differences were found to be insignificant and neither scale agreed with the primary or secondary hypothesis.

## 4.2   Objective Results

For DRA based objective data Driving Time, Steering Wheel Angle, Total off Track Time and Pedal Activations all showed support to the hypothesis to significant levels ($P < 0.05$). There was also general agreement of the secondary hypothesis.

ANOVA reported significant effects of Experience for all parameters ($P < 0.05$). For Driving, the Variable Keypad was significantly worse that the Fixed Keypad [$F(3, 75), = 7.76, p < 0.001$]. The same was true for Steering Wheel Angle for Type [$F(3, 72) = 6.30, p = 0.001$],, Pedal Up Time for Type [$F(3, 72) = 6.30, p = 0.001$].

ANOVA for NRA Completion Rate showed significant effects of Type [$F(2, 108) = 766.82, p < 0.001$], Mode [$F(1, 108) = 593.24, p < 0.001$], Experience [$F(1, 108) = 6.89, p = 0.010$) and Type*Mode [$F(2, 108) = 180.24, p < 0.001$]. A post hoc Tukey comparison proving the difference between the Variable and Fixed keypad conditions to be significant ($p < 0.05$). Mean Task Completion Time proved significant for Type [$F(2, 106) = 68.97, p < 0.001$], Mode [$F(1, 106) = 142.14, p < 0.001$], Type*Mode [$F(2, 106) = 44.82, p < 0.001$], Mode*Experience, [$F(1, 106) = 4.92, p = 0.029$], Type*Experience [$F(2, 106) = 9.70, p < 0.001$] and Type*Mode*Experience, [$F(2, 106) = 4.46, p = 0.014$].

## 4.3   Factor Analysis of Objective Measure

An un-rotated principle component factor analysis was carried out to correlate all of the measures into a smaller number of factors using Minitab (Table 2).

**Table 2.** Eigenvalues for Factor Analysis of Driving and Non-Driving based Measures

| Variable | Factor1 | Factor2 | Factor3 | Communality |
|---|---|---|---|---|
| **Driving Time** | 0.284 | −0.741 | 0.279 | 0.708 |
| **Steering Angle** | 0.126 | −0.82 | −0.382 | 0.834 |
| **Off Track** | 0.083 | −0.828 | −0.416 | 0.866 |
| **Average Pedal Up Time** | 0.148 | −0.521 | 0.608 | 0.663 |
| **Completion Rate** | −0.901 | −0.24 | 0.183 | 0.902 |
| **Task Time** | 0.915 | 0.233 | −0.184 | 0.925 |
| **Glance Time per Entry** | 0.941 | 0.07 | 0.01 | 0.89 |
| **Errors** | −0.415 | 0.085 | −0.57 | 0.504 |
| Variance | 2.8306 | 2.3032 | 1.1578 | 6.2917 |
| % Var | 0.354 | 0.288 | 0.145 | 0.786 |

The variables used were Driving Time, Steering Angle, Pedal Activations and Off Track time for driving and Completion Rate, Mean Completion Time, Errors and Mean Glance Time. The eigenvalues of the result can be seen in the Table 1.

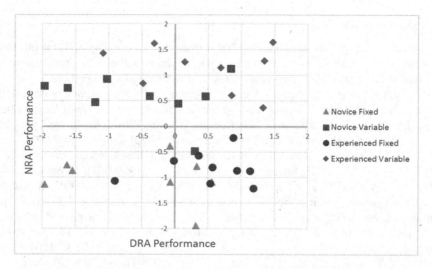

**Fig. 4.** Score Plot of Driving and Non Driving based Measures

Factor 1 is dominated by Completion Rate, Task Time, Glances and Errors and can therefore be known as **NRA Performance**. Factor 2 is dominated by Driving Time, Steering Angle, Off Track and Pedal Up Time and can therefore be known as **DRA Performance**. A third factor demonstrates correlation between Pedal Up Time and NRA Errors. This Factor appears to explain that errors are likely to happen when the user comes under some pressure in the DRA and can be known as **Incident Related Errors**. The data points for factors 1 and 2 can be seen in Fig. 4. The two main factors identified are able to classify the participants broadly into groups consistent with the original hypothesis.

## 5    Discussion

The factor analysis (FA) was successful in characterising the original experimental groups agreeing with the hypothesis. An FA is useful because the effects of performance in the NRA is seen in the DRA data and vice-versa. The separation between the two NRA is clear but the DRA shows more of an overlap between Novice and Experienced groups. The Novices learned quickly and in some cases became as good as some of the experienced group who were also affected by the environmental variability.

All DRA objective measures agreed with both the primary and secondary hypotheses. The NRA objective measures also agreed with the primary hypothesis but not entirely with the secondary hypothesis. The NRA values lay outside of those found in Cells 1 and 4 of Table 1 rather than inbetween. This can be explained by experience having an effect on the management of risk in a dual task scenario. Experienced users are more aware of what could happen and thus modulate their performance with the NRA.

The DRA measures covered a wide range of situational artefacts. It appears to be important to make use of complimentary and partially redundant measures. Driving Time complemented Pedal Activations; both appear to be useful in distinguishing between Low and High SA, although this seems to diminish with experience. Steering Angle and Off Track Events again are complimentary but seem to measure the same thing. Driving Time and Steering Angle have fine resolution but may fail to pick up short term events, which can be covered by the Pedal Activations and Off Track Events. Adding redundancy will ensure artefacts and significant SA events are accounted for.

For NRA, Mean Completion Time displays similar findings to that of Mean Completion Rate. Again root cause of poor response may be difficult to determine because of the demands of the driving environment. That said combining these with Errors and Glances away from the road will give equal level of redundancy. Mean Completion Time in combination with Task Errors may be a more appropriate match. Glances offer insight into how the user is managing attention but is inconsistent especially in the situation where an Auditory-Vocal interface with no visual information is used. During multi-tasking, performance may be counter intuitive, for example, if the driver is risk adverse performance may be more regulated. It is therefore important to use complimentary measures across the NRA and DRA. For example, Visual-Manual tasks are more likely to cause effects in the steering wheel trace than the pedal. If using an Auditory-Vocal task an equally complimentary measure needs to be found.

Driving Incidents was not considered in the factor analysis due to a lack of observable differences between the Low and High SA groups. Despite having awareness the High SA group still had numerous driving incidents. This demonstrates the load on the user by an NRA and the effect this has on the ability to balance both tasks. Incidents are not always caused by poor SA; this was especially true in the dynamic driving task used.

Neither subjective measures were able to classify the groups specified in the hypothesis. This could be due to methodological issue or individual perception of workload, especially in the Novice group. Workload could distinguish Single and Dual Task conditions but not the different types of Dual Task. This finding conflicts with previous work which found reported workload increases with task difficulty [13]. The approach in asking the question for each task shows promise from the scoring found as individuals were not just putting down the same score for each task.

# 6   Conclusion

The model proposed opens a new lens on how SA could be applied in the development of automotive user interfaces. The pilot study demonstrated that it is possible to use task performance to classify levels of SA especially when considering a Dual Goal scenario like automotive. A factor analysis proved able to classify groups according to the hypothesis and there is clear evidence that Experience can provide a useful proxy for high awareness. Knowledge built up over time could be considered a pre-cursor to being able to carry out tasks successfully in a demanding environment.

Subjective measures, which should have backed up the objective measures, require further development. There appears to be utility in separating out questions when multiple tasks are being assessed but modification of the questionnaire used and how it is applied is required. Future work would need to make use of a more realistic driving simulation and balance the gender of participants. It is also unlikely to get true novices in the DRA and thus focus here should switch to the NRA. The interface design aspect of this research will consider whether it is possible to design interfaces that enable SA for both DRA and NRA tasks, and whether this gives objective benefits in terms of performance in a modern automobile.

**Acknowledgement.** This work is funded by Jaguar Land Rover through the Centre for Advanced Photonics and Electronics (CAPE) at Cambridge University.

# References

1. Adams, M., Pew, R.: Situational Awareness in the Commercial Aircraft Cockpit: A Cognitive Perspective, pp. 519–524. IEEE (1990)
2. Baumann, M., Krems, J.: Situation awareness and driving: a cognitive model. In: Modelling Driver Behaviour in Automotive Environments, pp. 253–265 (2007)
3. Durso, F. et al.: Comprehension & situation awareness. In: Handbook of Applied Cognition, pp. 163– 193 (2007)
4. Endsley, M. et al.: What is situation awareness? In: Designing for Situation Awareness: An Approach to User-Centred Design, pp. 13–30 (2003)
5. Endsley, M., Garland, D.: Theoretical underpinnings of situation awareness: a critical review. In: Situation Awareness Analysis and Measurement. pp. 3–32 (2008)
6. Endsley, M.R.: Measurement of situation awareness in dynamic systems. Hum. Factors J. Hum. Factors Ergon. Soc. 37(1), 65–84 (1995)
7. Endsley, M.R.: Toward a theory of situation awareness in dynamic systems. Hum. Factors J. Hum. Factors Ergon. Soc. 37(1), 32–64 (1995)
8. Gaba, D.M., et al.: Situation awareness in anesthesiology. Hum. Factors J. Hum. Factors Ergon. Soc. 37(1), 20–31 (1995)
9. Gilson, R.D. et al.: Situation awareness for complex system operations. In: Proceedings of the Centre for Applied Human Factors in Aviation (CAHFA) Conference on Situation Awareness in Complex Systems (1993)
10. Gugerty, L.: Situation awareness during driving: explicit and implicit knowledge in dynamic spatial memory. J. Exp. Psychol. Appl. 3(1), 42–66 (1997)
11. Gugerty, L. et al.: Situation awareness in driving. In: Handbook for Driving Simulation, pp. 19-1–19-9 (2011)
12. Gunnarsson, D. et al.: Trends in automotive embedded systems. In: Proceedings of the tenth ACM international conference on Embedded software - EMSOFT 2012. p. 9 (2012)
13. Hancock, P., et al.: Influence of task demand characteristics on workload and performance. Int. J. Aviat. Psychol. 5(1), 87–106 (1995)

14. Hart, S., Staveland, L.: Development of NASA-TLX (Task Load Index): results of empirical and theoretical research. In: Human Mental Workload (1988)
15. Kim, Y.J., Hoffmann, C.M.: Enhanced battlefield visualization for situation awareness. Comput. Graph. **27**(6), 873–885 (2003)
16. Kintsch, W.: The role of knowledge in discourse comprehension: a construction-integration model. Psychol. Rev. **95**(2), 163–182 (1988)
17. Klauer, S.G. et al.: The impact of driver inattention on near crash/crash risk: an analysis using the 100-car naturalistic driving study data. Analysis, **226** (2006)
18. Krems, J.F., Baumann, M.: Driving and situation awareness: a cognitive model of memory-update processes. In: First International Conference on Human Centred Design, pp. 986–994 (2009)
19. Ma, R., Kaber, D.: Situation awareness and driving performance in a simulated navigation task. Proc. Hum. Factors Ergon. Soc. Annu. Meet **50**(3), 270–274 (2006)
20. Matthews, M.L.M., et al.: Model for situation awareness and driving: application to analysis and research for intelligent transportation systems. Transp. Res. Rec. **1779**, 26–32 (2002)
21. Parkes, A.M., Hooijmeijer, V.: The influence of the use of mobile phones on driver situation awareness. In: 1st Human-Centred Transportation Simulation Conference 2001, 1–8 June 2000 (2001)
22. Peacock, B., Karwowski, W.: Automotive Ergonomics. CRC Press, Boca Raton (1993)
23. Pfleging, B., Schmidt, A.: (Non-) Driving-related activities in the car: defining driver activities for manual and automated driving. In: CHI 2015, pp. 5–8 (2015)
24. Rakauskas, M.E., et al.: Effects of naturalistic cell phone conversations on driving performance. J. Safety Res. **35**(4), 453–464 (2004)
25. Schömig, N., et al.: Anticipatory and control processes in the interaction with secondary tasks while driving. Transp. Res. Part F Traffic Psychol. Behav. **14**(6), 525–538 (2011)
26. Selcon, S.J., Taylor, R.M.: Evaluation of the Situational Awareness Rating Technique (SART) as a tool for aircrew systems design. In: Situational Awareness in Aerospace Operations (1989)
27. Underwood, G., et al.: Visual search while driving: skill and awareness during inspection of the scene. Transp. Res. Part F Traffic Psychol. Behav. **5**(2), 87–97 (2002)

# Erratum to: Investigating the Use of Social Media Technologies by Adults with Autism Spectrum Disorder in Saudi Arabia

Alaa Mashat[✉], Mike Wald, and Sarah Parsons

University of Southampton, Southampton, UK
{a.mashat, mw, s.j.parsons}@soton.ac.uk

## Erratum to:
## Chapter 22: M. Antona and C. Stephanidis (Eds.)
## Universal Access in Human-Computer Interaction
## DOI: 10.1007/978-3-319-40238-3_22

In Table 1 on page 229 of the original version of the paper the last 5 rows were missing. The correct table is shown below.

**Table 1.** Participants' uses of social media

| Participant | Gender | Age | Devices | Used SN | Created SN for the study |
|---|---|---|---|---|---|
| P1 | Male | 30 | Ipad (shared with his sister) | None | Instagram |
| P2 | Male | 23 | Smartphone ipad PC Laptop | WhatsApp, (Facebook and Twitter, could not access it) | Instagram |
| P3 | Male | 22 | Smartphone Galaxy 5S laptop (broken) | WhatsApp, Snapchat | Instagram |
| P4 | Male | 19 | iphone 5S | WhatsApp, Snapchat, Instagram Facebook, Twitter, Keek, Path, BB messenger | None |
| Pb5 | Male | 23 | ipad 2 | WhatsApp | None |
| Pb6 | Male | 16 | ipod | None | None |

*(continued)*

The updated original online version for this chapter can be found at 10.1007/978-3-319-40238-3_22

© Springer International Publishing Switzerland 2016
M. Antona and C. Stephanidis (Eds.): UAHCI 2016, Part III, LNCS 9739, p. E1–E2, 2016.
DOI: 10.1007/978-3-319-40238-3_62

**Table 1.** (*continued*)

| Participant | Gender | Age | Devices | Used SN | Created SN for the study |
|---|---|---|---|---|---|
| Pb7 | Male | 25 | Galaxy smartphone and uses his sister's iphone 6 | None | None |
| Pb8 | Female | 19 | ipad 2 | None | None |
| Pb9 | Female | 15 | Does not have her own device | None | None |
| Pb10 | Female | 15 | xbox, playstation3, playstation4, ipod, iphone, wii, wii U, PC, laptop, Graphic drawing tablet | YouTube, Tumbler | None |
| Pb11 | Male | 28 | Samsung Galaxy smartphone, Toshiba Laptop | None | Instagram |
| Pb12 | Male | 15 | Does not have his own device | None | None |
| Pb13 | Male | 18 | Lenovo Smartphone, Tablet (being repaired) | WhatsApp, (Instagram and Facebook, could not access it) | None |

# Author Index

Printed in the United States
By Bookmasters